Kitāb ut-Tawḥeed

كتاب التوحيد

The Basis of Islam and the Reality of Monotheism

By

Professor Muḥammad ibn Abdullah al-Mas'ari

Volume 1

Cover design: N Uddin.

ISBN: 1986123596
ISBN-13: 978-1986123594

Volume 1:

The Foundations of *Deen* and its Fundamental Maxims

Contents

Acknowledgments v

Introduction 1

Part I

1 *Deen* and *Dunya* 12

2 Urbanisation, Civilisation and Culture 15

3 Distinguishing between '*Deen*' and '*Dunya*' 21

4 Islam is an intellectual creed 57

5 The Definition of Islam 68

6 The meaning of 'there is no deity except Allah' 74

7 The meaning of 'Muhammad is the Messenger of Allah' 79

8 The Grades of *Deen* 83

9 The Basis of Islam and its Essential Pillars 100

Part II

1 Revelation is both the Qur'ān and the *Sunnah* 138

2 'He doesn't speak of his own desire…' 143

3 'Whoever obeys the Prophet, indeed obeys Allah' 150

4 Types of Divine Revelation 157

5 'Whatever the Messenger gives you, take it…' 159

6 'I only follow what is revealed to me' 163

7 Prophet Muḥammad is the 'Excellent Exemplar' 166

8 'That Allah may forgive your previous and future sins' 170

9 Regarding the acts of the Prophet – can he forget? 179

10 Enjoining the good, forbidding all evil 184

11 The *Sunnah* as an independent source of law 193

12 The *Ḥikmah* and *Dhikr* are also revelation 204

13 The meaning of the word '*Dhikr*' 213

14 Testimony of the *Sunnah* to its proof 233

15 Some of what may or may not happen to the Prophets 272

16 Decepetion by false testimony? 281

17 Silence as a decisive proof? 311

18 The '*Dhikr*' also encompasses the *Sunnah* 318

19 The '*Dhikr*': Qur'ān & *Sunnah* are protected 337

20 A brief overview of the period of '*Sunnah* recordation' 347

Part III

1 The Seal of Prophethood 371

2 An excellence that exceeds all others 391

3 All previous Prophetic laws are abrogated 422

4 'If my companion Moses was alive, he would be following me' 440

5 Prohibition relating to excessive questioning 458

6 Permissibility is the original or default ruling 488

7 What is the original ruling concerning worship? 518

8 A '*Sunnah Tarkiyah*? 520

9 Actions are by intentions 554

10 Islam is the complete *Deen* 581

11 Prophet Muḥammad permits all the good, outlaws all the evil 602

12 Verily, Allah does not command indecency 628

About the author 637

Index 639

Acknowledgments

The work required to translate *Kitāb ut-Tawheed* has been considerable. In conjunction with the author, this first commenced several years ago. It could never have been produced but for our small team who undertook the difficult and time consuming task of translating this text. We are also indebted to I. A Choudhury and M. B. Awan for the manuscript review, comment and input on this project. Once again, N. Uddin provided not only the cover design but invaluable expert technical support. Lastly, special thanks is due to K. M. Hasan, for managing the project overall, from translation to publication.

Those conversant with the original text in Arabic will note that the English version is organised quite differently. The Arabic '*bāb's*' are presented as 'Parts' and each '*faṣl*' as a chapter. Chapter titles overall have been streamlined and abreviated. Quotations, including *aḥādith*, have been separated and indented from the main body of text. Footnotes are used, where appropriate, to facilitate ease of reading, for example instead of having copious references as part of the body-text. There are also some additional explanatory references that have been enclosed, where required. Moreover, some additional explanation has on occasion been written into the body-text to provide greater exemplification for the English reader. That has been done under the supervision and approval of the author.

A small number of paragraphs in Part 1 chapter 3 have been omitted altogether from the translated text. These relate to the use of rare Arabic words and isn't a necessary component to have translated in full. Chapter 20 in Part II (Events that occurred on the day of *Badr*), has been omitted altogether. Strictly speaking this doesn't form an essential component of the present volume relating to the foundational principles of *Deen,* but is rather an appendix to the study. None of the appendices that are referred to appear in this volume. It is intended to include these with the last volume in the series.

In tandem with our other publications, *aḥādith* are translated in full including the chains of transmission. On occasion the Arabic text has been omitted altogether where it is of considerable length, particularly in relation to large quotations made from works of exegesis. While some may dislike this method of presentation, it is our view that English translation should reflect the text in full and not be disconnected from the mode of transmission.

We ask Allah to accept our humble efforts, to forgive our mistakes and shortcomings. May the peace, blessings and greatest of salutations be upon Muḥammad, the best example and role-model sent forth to all of mankind.

Renascence Foundation

May 2019

بِسمِ اللهِ الرَّحمنِ الرَّحيمِ

Introduction

All praise and thanks are due to Allah; we praise him and ask him for help and forgiveness. We seek refuge with Allah from the evil within ourselves and our conduct. Whomsoever Allah guides, none can mislead and whomsoever he sends astray, none can guide. Whoever obeys Allah will be rightly guided and whoever disobeys Allah and his Messenger, will definitely stray afar. I bear witness that there are no multiple gods or deities, but there is only Allah alone; he has no partner, consort or offspring and I bear witness that Muḥammad is his servant and Messenger, the most beloved of all mankind.

يَا أَيُّهَا الَّذِينَ آمَنُوا اتَّقُوا اللَّهَ حَقَّ تُقَاتِهِ وَلَا تَمُوتُنَّ إِلَّا وَأَنتُم مُّسْلِمُونَ

O you who believe! Be mindful of (your duty to) *Allah with the care which is due to him, and do not die unless you are Muslims.* [1]

يَا أَيُّهَا النَّاسُ اتَّقُوا رَبَّكُمُ الَّذِي خَلَقَكُم مِّن نَّفْسٍ وَاحِدَةٍ وَخَلَقَ مِنْهَا زَوْجَهَا وَبَثَّ مِنْهُمَا رِجَالًا كَثِيرًا وَنِسَاءً وَاتَّقُوا اللَّهَ الَّذِي تَسَاءَلُونَ بِهِ وَالْأَرْحَامَ إِنَّ اللَّهَ كَانَ عَلَيْكُمْ رَقِيبًا

[1] *Qur'ān* 3: 102

O mankind! Be mindful of (your duty to) your Lord, who created you from a single being and created its mate of the same (kind) and spread from these two, many men and women; and be careful of (your duty to) *Allah, by whom you demand one of another* (your rights)*, and (to) the ties of relationship; surely Allah ever watches over you.* [2]

يَا أَيُّهَا الَّذِينَ آمَنُوا اتَّقُوا اللَّهَ وَقُولُوا قَوْلًا سَدِيدًا، يُصْلِحْ لَكُمْ أَعْمَالَكُمْ وَيَغْفِرْ لَكُمْ ذُنُوبَكُمْ وَمَن يُطِعِ اللَّهَ وَرَسُولَهُ فَقَدْ فَازَ فَوْزًا عَظِيمًا

O you who believe! Be mindful of (your duty to) Allah and speak the right word. He will put your deeds into a right state for you, and forgive you your faults; and whoever obeys Allah and His Messenger, he indeed achieves a mighty success. [3]

Truly the best of speech is the book of Allah and the best guidance is that from Muḥammad, peace and blessings be upon him. The worst of things are those that are newly invented without legal precedent; it is but an innovation (*bidāh'*) and all innovation results in misguidance. May the peace, blessings and greatest of salutations be upon Muḥammad, the best example and role-model sent forth to all of mankind. And may the blessings of Allah also be upon his noble family, his companions, their successors and all those who strive in the path of Allah.

To proceed - this treatise represents a study into the very root origins of Islam, the essential nature of *Tawḥeed* (monotheism), its proofs as found in the Qur'ān and that which has been established by the authentic *Sunnah*. Consequently the title that has been chosen for this work is: *Kitāb ut-Tawḥeed: 'Asās al-Islam wa Haqiqat-at-Tawḥeed* (the book of monotheism: the basis of Islam and the reality of monotheism). There are a number of reasons why this study was prepared, amongst them the following:

---

[2] *Qur'ān* 4: 1
[3] *Qur'ān* 33: 70/71

Firstly - the age-old problem concerning the precise nature of 'worship' (*ibādah*) and its exact relationship with the concept of a deity (*al-Ilāh*). Many have misunderstood this resulting in an extremely unsatisfactory answer which has led them to accuse the people of the *Qiblah* of polytheism (*Shirk*) which takes one outside the fold of the religion. Closely followed by this, was an unsound analysis and judgment by many of what actually constitutes *Shirk* (polytheism) resulting in one exiting the fold of Islam, which is a very serious matter indeed. Such line of reasoning has been extremely dangerous particularly when it has proceeded upon the basis of proofs that are neither decisive in nature and have more often than not been blatantly misapplied. Given the seriousness of the topic, there cannot be room for difference or interpretation; foundational principles must be based upon definitive evidences reaching the level of certitude.

Secondly – the confusion and ill-disciplined tripartite division of *Tawḥeed* which is espoused by the sect of Wahābi's, namely: *Tawḥeed ar-Rububiyyah* (monotheism of lordship), *Tawḥeed al-Uluhiyah* (monotheism of worship) and *Tawḥeed al-Asmā' wa'aṣ-Ṣifāt* (monotheism of names and attributes). Putting *Tawḥeed* into this classification originates with the Shaykh and Imām Ibn Taymiyyah. Indeed, the mistakes which underpinned his reasoning for placing *Tawḥeed* into this division are heinous, as are those made by Shaykh Muḥammad ibn Abdul-Wahāb who followed him in this regard, taking the division as being sacrosanct. The disorder in understanding ultimately lies with Imām Ibn Taymiyyah and his tripartite division which as we will show in this treatise is fundamentally flawed. In fact the decisive truth regarding the tripartite division is that it is seriously misleading and below-par for a division befitting in Islam. Several reasons can be advanced to demonstrate this:

1. The meaning of the words used to propound the 'conventional' Wahābi tripartite division is fallacious and invalid. These are not rooted in classical Arabic in which the Qur'ān was

revealed and they are neither found in legal custom which always furnishes the linguistic custom. Deep rooted flaws exist within the reasoning advanced with respect to '*Uluhiyah.*' None more so than the implied logic that the existence of a deity is somehow contingent upon those that undertake the performance of worship torwards it. Undoubtedly this is from the statements of disbelief (*kufr*), may Allah protect us from that. As will be demonstrated with decisive proofs and evidences the rejection of which would result in disbelief and ultimate exit from the fold of Islam.

2. Without accurately describing the reality of polytheism (*Shirk*) as it existed amongst the pre-Islamic Arabs it is false and misleading. However it goes further in that it stubbornly clings to this false understanding that the pre-Islamic Arabs did not have *Shirk* in the realm of lordship (*Rububiyyah*). In doing so it represents a denial of knowledge that is known by necessity from history which has reached us by way of recurrent transmission (*tawātur*) and the study of such reports. Taking such a line of argumentation, which is borne of obsession and often psychosis, to its natural conclusion ultimately would require one to claim that the Qur'ān is founded upon a lie, which is without question a statement of disbelief.

3. There is an inverted or upside-down logic to their claim that lordship (*Rububiyyah*) entails or requires worship (*Uluhiyah*) and not the opposite.

4. The analysis upon which the tripartite division is derived is ill conceived, in that it's various sub-divisions are not distinct and they overlap.

5. It is not succinct enough to withstand ideas being haphazardly inserted into each category that are not essentially based upon the principles of *Tawḥeed.* For example concerning the divine attributes (*Ṣifāt*) these are in actual fact a branch of *Tawḥeed* and not a stand-alone principle or an independent division by itself. Such points must be made in the face of the extremism resulting from the sect of Wahābism; whose adherents are experts in futility and superficiality, opposing thought and reason at every juncture. Through their rejection of the sound use of reason, thought and research, they revert to ignorance, basking in obtuseness while falsely clinging to a notion that they are the '*Salafiyah'*.

6. It is neither conclusive nor comprehensive in its divisions or constituents. Other important aspects of *Tawḥeed* are completely omitted. For example, issues relating to the divine entity (*Tawḥeed ath-Dhāt*) and its principle attributes are entirely absent as are matters relating to any points concerning the attribution of a consort, spouse or offspring. Monotheism of governance (*Tawḥeed Ḥākimiyah*) which is one of the pinnacles of *Tawḥeed,* an area of contention between many Prophets and their respective nations, is notably absent as well. Placing *Tawḥeed Ḥākimiyah* into the tripartite division cannot be done cleanly and in a way that it is not artificial.

As a result of the above, a great lie has ensued which has been used to wage a campaign of *Takfeer* upon the people of Islam and the major sin of striking them with the sword and justifying their blood to be spilt. This is besides many other difficulties and problems which have also arisen as a result.

Thirdly - several problems have emerged during the period of time which followed the end of the last Caliphate and the conversion of the whole world into *Dar-ul-Kufr* (domain of disbelief). These problems were about the reality of *Tawḥeed*, its sections and it how it corresponds to contemporary issues like ruling, governance and allegiance, *Tawḥeed Ḥākimiyah* and *Tawḥeed al-Muwāla wal-Mu'ādā*. Such problems resulted from weaknesses and faults of the aforementioned tripartite division. Further compounding this situation was the work of government scholars - rabbinical sycophants and soothsayers - descending from the tradition of Prophet killing. Openly standing at war with Allah, they have sought to amplify these problems as well as mislead the public. All the while acting in private service to their masters, the leaders of *kufr* and tyrannical oppression; they have brazenly changed the laws of the *Sharī'ah*, being the enemies of the '*Awliyā* of Allah. They have aligned themselves with the enemies of Allah, fighting the Muslims under the banner of disbelief, all for a pitiful transient monetary worldly gain. Thus, they have betrayed and breached the heavenly covenant:

وَإِذْ أَخَذَ اللَّهُ مِيثَاقَ الَّذِينَ أُوتُوا الْكِتَابَ لَتُبَيِّنُنَّهُ لِلنَّاسِ وَلَا تَكْتُمُونَهُ فَنَبَذُوهُ وَرَاءَ ظُهُورِهِمْ
وَاشْتَرَوْا بِهِ ثَمَنًا قَلِيلًا فَبِئْسَ مَا يَشْتَرُونَ

And when Allah made a covenant with those who were given the Book: You shall certainly make it known to men and you shall not hide it; but they cast it behind their backs and took a small price for it; evil is that which they buy. [4]

The tyrants of the Arabian Peninsula, the House of Saud, are at the forefront of this campaign, seeking to change the *Sharī'ah* laws at any opportunity. They align themselves with hostile disbelieving forces openly at war with Islam and actively supporting them against Muslims under their banner and chain of command. Such tyrannical rulers exceed all bounds and have surpassed all their fellow rulers in this regard, who are themselves rulers of darkness, yokes around the necks of Muslims. Is it any surprise therefore that the enemies of Islam have been able to base their forces in the Arabian Peninsula, the

---

[4] *Qur'ān* 3: 187

very heartlands of Islam? From these bases they laid siege to Iraq for many years, thereafter they occupied it wreaking untold carnage upon its people; humiliating them in the most brutal of ways.

All the while the House of Saud remains aloof, their 'scholars', modern day clergy, cling to their tails, being part and parcel of this grand deception. These 'scholars' who are the lackeys of the tyrannical rulers of the Arabian Peninsula are not a disparate group, rather they are a religious institution, an essential component in the oppressive state apparatus. In terms of their organisational structure, funding and indeed *modus operandi,* they differ very little from the Catholic Church of the Middle Ages. Hence, the 'Council of Senior Scholars' (*Kibār al-Ulemā'*) have deservedly earned their true title, that of the 'Church of Najd.' The Council being more reflective of the College of Cardinals expend great ink in support of their Pope, the 'Grand Mufti of Saudi Arabia', who is in effect a Minister of State by virtue of salary and rank through holding the position of chair of the 'Standing Committee for Scholarly Research, Issuance of Religious Edits, Propagation and Guidance'.

The ruling system upon which the House of Saud is built is a system built upon *kufr* and *Shirk,* a satanic system, rotten to its very core. Given the oddity of its political set-up it is more akin to a mafia-state founded upon criminality and the systematic looting of the wealth of Muslims. The state treasury is viewed as being nothing more than a family bank account, a mechanism for the self-enrichment of the mafia elite. Has history ever witnessed a similar gross and vulgar system? One built around the greed of the ruling family whose involvement in the drug trade, organised prostitution, alcohol, arms dealing and money-laundering is well known.

For that reason, their grand scholars are nothing more than hypocrites. They brazenly deceive the masses in order to protect the power-base of the House of Saud. *Tawḥeed* for them is a distorted idea, a *Tawḥeed* divorced from life, solely concerned and revolving around the dead, hence their obsessive preoccupation with graves, tombs and the like. This is even to the extent that they boastfully proclaim their destruction of all Islamic antiquities as objects of polytheism. In actuality, they are trying to destroy *Tawḥeed*, replacing it with a fixation of graves and the realm of the deceased. Writing in *Madārij as-Sālikeen*, Imām Ibn Qayyim succinctly summed up their pitiful condition:

> If the truth is in opposition to their route to power, they crush it and stain it with all their capacity. If they are unable to do that, they push it away aggressively. If they are unable to that, then they divert it away from their path and put it on another. Indeed they are prepared to push it away depending on the circumstance. So if they do not find a partner who would give them support and a platform, they distance it from being dispensed, ruled by, and implemented. If there is a supporter for them, they attack the truth, search for it and come to it in compliance with their supporters. They do not go to it because it is truth rather because it is in opposition with their goals and their desires: *And when they are called to Allah and His Messenger that he may judge between them, lo! A party of them turn aside. And if the truth be on their side, they come to him quickly, obedient. Is there in their hearts a disease, or are they in doubt, or do they fear that Allah and His Messenger will act wrongfully towards them? Nay! They themselves are the unjust.* [5]

These are the words of the esteemed scholar Ibn Qayyim, may Allah be pleased with him. Truly it is a beautiful characterisation of what they consider as vexatious. If one were in doubt concerning this, consider the announcements made by their treacherous priests and the groups of innovators that peddle their views; the self-appointed and proclaimed - '*people of Sunnah and ḥadith*', '*helpers of Muḥammad's*

---

[5] *Qur'ān* 24: 48/50

Sunnah' and '*troops of the Ṣaḥābah'*, let alone the publications which they freely distribute, entitled: '*Obedience to ar-Raḥman is obedience to the ruler'*, '*the heresy and fitna of al-Qutubiyyah*' in reference to Sayyid Qutb and '*Ḥākimiyyah and the fitna of takfeer*!'

وَمِنْهُم مَّن يَقُولُ ائْذَن لِّي وَلَا تَفْتِنِّي أَلَا فِي الْفِتْنَةِ سَقَطُوا وَإِنَّ جَهَنَّمَ لَمُحِيطَةٌ بِالْكَافِرِينَ

And among them there is he who says: Allow me and do not try me. Surely into trial have they already tumbled down, and most surely hell encompasses the disbelievers. [6]

Recent history is littered with horrible disasters and vile massacres that the people of Islam have endured at the hands of barbarous Wahābi groups, whether from the Armed Criminal Group (known as the GIA) in Algeria all the way to *Dā'esh* (State of Iraq and *Shām*) and the TTP (*Tarika* Taliban/Pakistan) of today. This also includes other organisations affiliated falsely to *al-Qā'eda* or the 'global *Jihād*', few of whom actually display any mercy. They have abandoned the fight against the warriors and aggressors from the people of idolatry, turning their swords instead against the people of Islam; brazenly slaughtering women, children and the ordinary peaceful citizens who themselves suffer immeasurably at the hands of tyranny. Know without doubt, nay with certain knowledge, that the Wahābi sect is a renegade sect that descends from the *Khawārij al-Azāriqa* who perished previously. They are, accordingly to scholarly consensus, upon manifest misguidance and were from the bloodiest people of Nahrawān. And indeed we are furnished also with the statement made by the Imām and established proof Abu Muḥammad Ali Ibn Ḥazm (may Allah be pleased with him) in his seminal work, *al-Fiṣal fi al-Milal wa al-Niḥal* (The Separator Concerning Religions, Heresies and Sects): 'But *al-Azāriqa* they were ignorant Arabs like cattle, they are on the path of misguidance.' The Wahābi sect is a sub-division from the *Khawārij* -

---

[6] *Qur'ān* 9: 49

al-Azāriqa – for indeed they are like cattle and are on a path of clear misguidance; may Allah protect us all from that.

We appeal to Allah, the exalted and majestic, to make this book useful and to guide us in order that all of our deeds be sincere, seeking Him alone. He has the power over all things. May the salutations, blessings and peace of Allah be upon His Messenger and servant Muḥammad and on his virtuous family and faithful companions until the day of judgement.

Praise be to Allah, Lord of all the worlds.

Professor Muḥammad ibn Abdullah al-Mas'ari

Part I.

Religion and Worldly Life

1 *Deen* and *Dunya*

Islam does not necessarily have a directly corresponding word for what is conveyed by the English term 'religion'. This is particularly the case when the word is set in the context of common parlance. The term employed, is '*Deen*', which means a comprehensive way of life; that is, a specific way of living based upon a comprehensive belief regarding the universe, man and life and its relationship with what precedes it (i.e. Allah, the almighty), and with what succeeds it (i.e. the day of judgement). *Deen* does not only regulate the relationship between man and Allah and identify some of the moral values and individual proprieties, but it is also a comprehensive regulation of man's life in its entirety. Thus, there is a clear distinction between this and the Western concept of religion, which is limited to very specific areas of life. In the West since the revolutions of the seventeenth and eighteenth centuries, as well as the 'age of Enlightenment', religion is viewed solely as being a collection of rituals through which man has a personal relationship with the supernatural. Yet for Muslims the term *Deen* is far wider, addressing the following:

1. Man's relationship with Allah regarding beliefs, rituals and designated acts of worship.

2. Man's relationship with himself concerning knowledge, intention, emotions (love, hate, loyalty, etc.), manners, food, clothing, and even extends to beautifying and adorning oneself.
3. Man's relationship with other human beings, including:
   i. Family relations such as marriage, kinship, inheritance.
   ii. Private or civil relations, that is, relations with other individuals concerning contracts, transactions, industry, agriculture, exchange of services in trade, institutions and corporations.
   iii. Public relations, such as between the ruler and the ruled; constitutional relations; relations with public authorities; the constitution of the state, the judicial system and the penal code (evidences, punishments), public funds, legislation concerning land tax, general taxation and excise duty, public ownership etc.
   iv. International relations like those concerning independent groups, nations and countries with regards to treaty provisions, *Jihād*, envoys and embassies
4. Man's relationship with other creatures, such as animals, plants, inanimate objects and the environment holistically.

Conversely, worldly life – *Dunya* - in this context means the empirical nature of the universe as it is, without any value judgments being formed. It is worth noting that the following are considered to be related to worldly matters:

1. Natural sciences such as physics, chemistry, botany and other sciences that are concerned with the laws of the physical world which involve the use of experimentation, observation, sense perception and reason.

2. The application of these sciences in the fields of engineering, agriculture and medicine and their related skills, handicrafts and arts: such as shipping, smith craft, architecture, etc.
3. Methods of making and increasing wealth by various means such as grazing, hunting, planting, manufacturing, and trading as well as sciences related to circulating money and funds and the nature of markets, that is, the science of economics.

All these sciences are considered related to 'worldly matters' or *Dunya.* All the permissible means of earning money, and channels through which it can be spent and all means of distributing wealth in society, referred to as the economic system or economic policy are not related to worldly matters but rather to religious matters, for they are certainly related to the perception of life, which is the comprehensive belief regarding the universe, man, life and its relationship with what precedes and what succeeds it. Allah, the exalted and ever majestic, revealed obligatory *Sharī'ah* legal judgments, that must be followed and for which man will be held accountable on the day of resurrection. This reckoning results in either eternal happiness which lies in the pleasure of Allah and enjoying the delights of paradise, or in permanent misery and damnation which is in the wrath of Allah the almighty and the severe torment of hell.

2 Urbanisation, Civilisation and Culture

Urbanisation (*madaniyyah*) is the total sum of the material manifestations of human activities that include the experimental and observatory sciences, the applied sciences and related skilled disciplines of the arts and crafts. Based upon this clear definition, it becomes apparent that urbanisation in origin, and in principle is universal, general, unbiased and has nothing to do with a specific perception or viewpoint of life. Urbanisation is also essentially similar in all nations regardless of their beliefs and culture. Therefore, it is possible for a Muslim to borrow it from any place and apply it in any manner he wishes to as long as it does not contradict any specific *Sharī'ah* legal text and that he is totally aware and permanently cautious of its possible cultural contamination with biased beliefs and doctrines. There is also a 'special' or 'specific urbanisation' that is related to and influenced by a perception of life. This type of urbanisation is uniquely related to a specific nation or people and Muslims should neither borrow nor copy it. This special urbanisation includes the arts of dancing, painting, sculpture, acting, theatrical performances and the like. It also includes some professions such as prostitution, Allah forbid, as well as certain physical sports, amusement and entertainment, like bull-fighting.

As for civilisation (*Ḥaḍārah*), it is commonly denoted as being a way of living, namely, the total set of beliefs, concepts, morals and criteria about life and its related 'culture' that is derived from this. Indeed, many times the use of these terms overlap so that the term civilisation is used when the actual term meant is urbanisation. Sometimes the two concepts are mixed up resulting in misconceptions. The clarity of the perception of belief is marred by such confusion and the process of taking a sound juristic attitude becomes difficult. Therefore, we should be accurate when dealing with these difficult concepts and take care that the meaning of a concept corresponds to the actual term itself, so that they do not overlap or become confused with one another. Otherwise the creedal, intellectual and practical consequences will be serious.

It is true that the term civilisation is close in its original meaning to that of urbanisation. However, civilisation is closer in meaning to denoting a particular way of living than urbanisation, in that it relates to stable living within an urban environment and utilises the practice of settled agriculture and industry. That is in marked contrast to a nomadic existence, which is characterised by a lack of settlement, hunting and movement according to seasonal shifts. These are two different types of living which are clearly distinct. Although there are differences between life in cities as opposed to villages, both of which relate to settled living; the utilisation of technology, crafts etc. only differ by degree in these settings.

In Arabic, the term '*Ḥaḍārah*' has been used to denote meanings related to thoughts. That is why it was much closer to expressing concepts. The Arabic dictionary has that "*/haḍura/* with a *dammah* is similar to */nadusa/,* that is, a man of eloquence and who is well-learned in jurisprudence. *Al-Lissan* also points out that '*rajulan haḍr*' with a *sukkun* on the /d/ denotes a man of eloquence. So, the term *Ḥaḍārah* (civilisation) is closer and more appropriate than urbanisation in denoting a set of concepts, moral and ideal values, i.e. how things ought to be, whereas urbanisation is more appropriate in denoting material forms, i.e. how things are. It is important to bear in mind the essential difference between the content of both concepts. As for these terms, they should not be incontestable. Nevertheless, being accurate in selecting a term that corresponds or is close to the intended meaning is still important and required.

The term 'culture' (*thaqāfa*) means all the sciences, knowledge and crafts which the belief of such a civilisation has instigated and out of which they emerged. It could also denote the knowledge that influences the mind and its moral judgment upon matters, like legislation, economics, history, language, and similar branches of knowledge. Thus civilisation, and culture which is a part of it, are necessarily biased and unique to each nation and people. It is related to the basic or fundamental beliefs that a nation holds. If such a civilisation emanated from a comprehensive belief regarding the universe, man and life – as in the case of the Islamic civilisation and the democratic-capitalist civilisation – it would be considered a religious or ideological civilisation. Civilisation is always connected to the unique features of people and the nation which emerged through historical development and the interaction with events happening with the passage of time. In this case, such a civilisation would be a man-made civilisation like the Greek, Babylonian, Assyrian, Chinese and European civilisation, that is, before the liberal-democratic-capitalist civilisation became victorious and dominated life in Europe, the United States and Western world. There is no doubt that the Greek, the Babylonians and the Assyrians in ancient times as well as the Americans and Europeans more recently had their own religions, be that paganism or Christianity. Yet these religions are just pure spiritual doctrines and moral codes. They do not include all the concepts, convictions, criteria, or legislation covering all aspects of life. Thus, no civilisation will emerge from these religions. The people agree on their own set of concepts and legislation pertaining to worldly affairs. These man-made concepts, convictions and criteria constitute their own civilisation though they are not specifically derived from their religion. This way the people have a non-religious-based civilisation, although they may believe in a certain religion, their civilisation is not derived from it, therefore it is a man-made civilisation.

Many modern people and nations, while embracing several different religions, follow the same civilisation, like the Japanese, the Indians, the Americans and the French, which is the Western democratic-capitalist civilisation. Islam has its own unique civilisation and culture. The culture included the sciences of the Arabic language and those of the *Deen* with its various branches. This civilisation filled the world with light, knowledge and guidance. Without doubt this is the most perfect civilisation in the whole world, which produced the largest number of books and references.

Western commentators often brag about what they call 'human civilization.' However, this is a false terminology as they marshal it to refer only to their own civilisation. Any serious objective study shows that this is a civilisation based essentially upon the edifice of Greco-Roman paganism with slight traces of the Christianity of Paul; not the genuine 'Christianity' of Jesus the son of Mary (peace be upon him and his mother), and a cursed racial Judaism, that of sinful scribes and rabbis who killed the Prophets; not the genuine 'Judaism' of the Torah and Moses (peace be upon him). Pauline Christianity diverged further several centuries after its emergence to become a spiteful and malicious Crusade. Western civilisation is a purely local phenomenon that has nothing to do with the beliefs, thoughts, concepts, convictions and customs of the rest of the world no matter how the proponents of globalisation brag and argue. The term was selected as it bears humanitarian and international connotations so as to deceive the other nations in the world, and Muslims in particular, to cunningly drive Muslims out of their own *Deen*. Embracing Western civilisation, falsely and erroneously known as 'humane' or 'humanitarian' and living according to it, inevitably entails Muslims' reverting to *kufr*, misguidance and to perpetual misery and a permanent curse ultimately ending in hellfire. The term is also strongly indicative of the racism and arrogance of the West and of its contempt for the rest of mankind. They claim that whatever is Western is 'humane' and 'international', while whatever is non-Western and belongs to other nations, is underdeveloped, backward, uncivilised and barbaric. In the best scenarios, it is limited, local and can never be universal.

From the previous discussion, this shows that *Deen* - in the eyes of the people of Islam - is not simply limited to pure ritualistic acts of worship, metaphysical beliefs or even beautiful manners and general morality as it is within the Western conception of religion. In fact, it relates to all voluntary human acts upon which a legal *Sharī'ah* judgment (*ḥukm sharī'*) is made, whether:

a. It is intended as being pure worship; drawing closer to Allah in order to achieve a particular spiritual, devotional or ascetic value, such as through the devotional acts of worship associated with prayer, remembrance and supplication.
b. Or intended to achieve a congenital ethical value, like being honest, generous and even considerate to animal welfare.
c. Intended as achieving a humanitarian value, such as helping others suffering from loss, like in war or in natural disasters; saving someone from drowning regardless of race, colour or religion etc.
d. People seek to gain a greater moral standing, by praise or glory.
e. Wanting to obtain a material benefit such as a monetary one obtained by payment or trade.

All of this division from optional human acts is considered within the domain of *ḥukm sharī'*. Adherence to the *ḥukm sharī'* is the spiritual side of worshipping in it. If a person wishes to realise worshipping Allah according to all its conditions, they must adhere to the *ḥukm sharī'* in all actions. That would result in being a spiritual worshipper.

Such an individual thus becomes worthy of praise and reward from Allah. 'Worship' here means acceptance of, contentment with, and obedience to the command of Allah, emerging from the utmost love and glorification of Allah, constructed upon firm belief to the level of certitude. It is also the absolute belief that Allah is the one true God, necessarily existing; *al-Ḥayy* (the ever-living) *al-Qayyum* (the self-existing by whom all subsist), the first who is uncreated and eternal, without beginning or end. He acts as he wills, creating whatsoever he wills or chooses. He cannot be questioned regarding what he does; nothing can reach his prerogative of command and he is swift in taking account.

In truth, this is 'spirituality' for it is a matter of consciousness and perception. There is nothing related to the matter of the spirit itself or whether the man is composed of material and spirit, regardless of whether that is a valid line of reasoning or not. As for what some of the scholars have said: 'Customs (or mores) become acts of worship if accompanied with a correct intention,' such wording is not strictly correct. Customs or to be more precise, the permissible, does not turn into that which is recommended (*mustaḥāb*) or obligated (*wājib*) on the basis of certain intentions or consciousness. Whilst the one undertaking this may be deserving of a particular reward or perhaps even punishment, it is fundamentally not the same act. All of this will be detailed in a later chapter.

3 Distinguishing between '*Deen*' and '*Dunya*'

The aforementioned arguments are easily recognisable with perception, reason and through the interpretation of the texts of revelation namely the Qur'ān and *Sunnah*. These are the only revealed legal texts. Allah, whose names and attributes are blessed and sanctified, has explicitly stated some of these points in the Qur'ān. He also revealed this to his infallible Prophet Abul-Qāsim Muḥammad ibn Abdullah ibn Abdul-Muṭṭalib, the Hashemite, Qurayshi, Adnāny, Arab, the unlettered Prophet and Messenger, the last of the Prophets, the leader of Messengers – directly and explicitly, so that no exegesis - even if all texts are brought together - would be needed to further prove it. In this regard, the following texts set out the scriptural basis of this argument.

As reported in the *Musnad* of Imām Aḥmad with the upmost acknowledged authentic channel of transmission upon the authority of 'Aisha, mother of the believers as well as Anas ibn Mālik:

حَدَّثَنَا عَفَّانُ قَالَ حَدَّثَنَا حَمَّادُ بْنُ سَلَمَةَ قَالَ أَخْبَرَنَا ثَابِتٌ عَنْ أَنَسٍ؛ وَهِشَامُ بْنُ عُرْوَةَ عَنْ عُرْوَةَ عَنْ عَائِشَةَ أَنَّ النَّبِيَّ، صلّى الله عليه وسلّم، سَمِعَ أَصْوَاتاً فَقَالَ: مَا هَذِهِ الأَصْوَاتُ؟؛ قَالُوا: النَّخْلُ يُؤَبِّرُونَهُ يَا رَسُولَ اللَّه، فَقَالَ لَوْ لَمْ

يَفْعَلُوا لَصَلُحَ. فَلَمْ يُوَبِّرُوا عَامَئِذٍ فَصَارَ شِيصاً فَذَكَرُوا ذَلِكَ لِلنَّبِيِّ، صلى الله عليه وسلم، فَقَالَ: إِذَا كَانَ شَيْئاً مِنْ أَمْرِ دُنْيَاكُمْ فَشَأْنُكُمْ بِهِ وَإِذَا كَانَ شَيْئاً مِنْ أَمْرِ دِينِكُمْ فَإِلَيَّ

'Affān narrated to us he said Ḥammād bin Salama narrated to us he said Thābit reported to us from Anas and Hishām bin 'Urwa from 'Urwa from 'Aisha that the Prophet (peace be upon him) heard some sounds. So, he asked - *What are these sounds?* It was said: It is the palm-tree being pollinated, O Messenger of Allah! He said: *If they had not done that, it would have been better.* So they did not do it that year and the date fruits did not ripen. They mentioned it to the Prophet (peace be upon him) and he said: *If it is something related to your worldly affairs, it is your affair and if it is something from the commands of your Deen it is unto me.*

Similar is reported in the *Sunan* of Ibn Mājah,[1] as well as in other collections, such as in the *Musnad* of Abu Ya'la[2] and by Ibn Ḥibbān in his *Ṣaḥīḥ*.[3] Commenting upon this narration, Shaykh Ḥussein Asad said that the channel of transmission was authentic (*isnād Ṣaḥīḥ*); whereas Shaykh Shu'ayb al-Arnā'uṭ said that it was authentic upon the conditions as set out by Imām Muslim. Additionally, on the same subject Imām Aḥmad cited the following narration in his *Musnad*:

حدثنا عبد الصّمد حدّثنا حمّاد عن ثابت عن أنس قال: سمع رسول الله، صلى الله عليه وسلم، أصواتا فقال: ما هذا؟ قالوا: يلقحون النخل، فقال: لو تركوه فلم يلقحوه لصلح، فتركوه فلم يلقحوه فخرج شيصا فقال النبي، صلى الله عليه وسلم: ما لكم؟!، قالوا: تركوه لما قلت!، فقال رسول الله، صلّى الله عليه وسلّم: إذا كانَ شيْءٌ مِن أمرِ دُنياكُمْ فَأنتُمْ أعلَمُ بِه، فإذا كَانَ مِنْ أَمْرِ دِينِكُمْ فَإِلَي

---

[1] *Sunan* Ibn Mājah Vol. 2 sec. 826, no. 2,471

[2] *Musnad* Abu Ya'la Vol. 6 sec. 199, no. 3,480 & Vol. 6 sec. 238, no. 3,531

[3] *Ṣaḥīḥ* Ibn Ḥibbān Vol. 1 sec. 202, no. 22

> Abdaṣ-Ṣammad narrated to us Ḥammād narrated to us from Thābit from Anas he said: The Prophet (peace be upon him) heard some sounds upon which he said: *What is this?* They replied pollinating date palms. So, he said: *If it is left it would be better.* They did not pollinate and less was yielded. Thus, the Prophet (peace be upon him) said: *What* (have) *you* (done)? They replied, we left it upon your statement. Upon this the Prophet (peace be upon him) said: *If it is related to your worldly affair, you* (are all) *more knowledgeable of it. If it is something related to your Deen, it is* (referred) *to me.*

Imām Muslim records a narration bearing the same meaning with an authentic chain of transmission in his *Ṣaḥīḥ*,[4] but with an insufficient summary. The narration contains the wording: *'You are more knowledgeable of your worldly affairs.'* It is an aborted version that people unfortunately use in most cases. Another version similar to that of Muslim was recorded by Dāraquṭni, as well as by Al-Bazzār in his *Musnad.* Imām Abu Muḥammad Ali Ibn Ḥazm cited this in his seminal work *al-Iḥkām fi Uṣul al-Aḥkām* (Judgement on the Principles of Law) via the channel as recorded by Al-Bazzār. The *ḥadith* related by Anas as found in Al-Bazzār states – '*You are more knowledgeable of what is good* (for you in) *worldly life. As for your hereafter, it is* (referred) *to me.'* This narration seems to be of similar meaning, for one of the narrators must have replaced the word '*your Deen'* with '*your hereafter.'*

As for what is said by Ḥammād ibn Salama, for example in *Fawā'id Tamām,*[5] – from Hishām bin Urwa from Urwa from 'Aisha, it is more likely than that to go against all of what has been reported from Khālid bin al-Hārith, Muhadir and Ḥafṣ bin Ghayāth and other than them, as it is reported as loose (*mursal*). This has been confirmed by Imām Dāraquṭni in his '*Illal* where it is stated:

---

[4] *Ṣaḥīḥ* Muslim Vol. 4 sec. 1,836, no. 2,363

[5] *Fawā'id Tamām* Vol. 3 sec. 83, no. 1082

And what is said from the *ḥadith* of ‘Urwa from ‘Aisha from the Prophet (peace be upon him) that he heard about the pollinating of date palms and said: (summary statements). He also said: as is reported from Ḥammād ibn Salama from Hishām from his father from ‘Aisha, is at odds with what has been reported from Khālid bin al-Harith, Muhadir and Ḥafṣ bin Ghayāth and other than them. The report from Hishām from his father is *mursal* and it is correct.

Imām Muslim records the next narration in his *Ṣaḥīḥ*:

حدّثنا عبد الله بن الرومي اليمامي وعبّاس بن عبد العظيم العنبري وأحمد بن جعفر المعقري قالوا: حدثنا النّضر بن محمّد، حدّثنا عكرمة وهو بن عمّار، حدّثنا أبو النّجاشي، حدثني رافع بن خديج قال: قدم نبيّ الله، صلّى الله عليه وسلّم، المدينة وهم يُؤَبرون النخل يقولون يلقحون النخل، فقال: ما تصنعون؟!، قالوا: كنا نصنعه، قال: لعلكم لو لم تفعلوا كان خيراً! ، فتركوه فنفضت أو فنقصت، قال فذكروا ذلك له فقال: (إنما أنا بشر إذا أمرتكم بشيء من دينكم فخذوا به وإذا أمرتكم بشيء من رأيي فإنّما أنا بشر، قال عكرمة: أو نحو هذا؛ قال المعقري: (فنفضت) ولم يشك

Abdullah bin ar-Roomi al-Yamāmi, ‘Abbās bin Abdal-‘Adtheem al-Anbari and Aḥmad bin Ja’far al-Ma’qiri narrated to us they said: an-Naḍr bin Muḥammad narrated to us ‘Ikrima narrated to us (and he is Ibn ‘Ammār) Abul-Najāshi narrated to us Rāfi’ bin Khadij narrated to me, he said the Prophet (peace be upon him) came to Medina and the people had been grafting the trees. He said: *What are you doing?* They said: We are grafting them, whereupon he said: *It may perhaps be good for you if you do not do that*, so they abandoned this practice (and the date-palms) began to yield less fruit. They made a mention of it (to the Prophet), whereupon he said: *I am a human being, so when I command you about a thing pertaining to religion, do accept it, and when I command you about a thing out of my personal opinion, keep it in mind that I am a human being.*

'Ikrima reported that he said something like this; al-Ma'qiri said (diminished) beyond any doubt.

Ibn Ḥibbān cites the same tradition in his *Ṣaḥīḥ*,[6] with the wording – '*I am only human, if I narrate something to you concerning matters in relation to Deen, take it; if I narrate something regarding your worldly affairs, I am but human.*' After which Ibn Ḥibbān says: 'Abul-Najāshi is the *mawla* of Rāfi', his name is 'Aṭā bin Ṣuhayb.' The narration is further reported in *Mu'jam al-Kabir* of Imām aṭ-Ṭabarāni,[7] with wording similar to that as reported by Ibn Ḥibbān. Concerning the narration, Shaykh Shu'ayb al-Arnā'uṭ said the *isnād* was *ḥasan*. Definitely the *ḥadith* is *Ṣaḥīḥ* and is established by way of definitive proofs. And what has been said about the semblance of disturbance (*iḍṭirāb*) in the *ḥadith* of 'Ikrima bin 'Ammār, he is *thiqa ma'moon* but only in his *ḥadith* from Yaḥya bin Abi Kathir and not other than it.

Following on from this, there is also the *ḥadith* of Jābir ibn Abdullah, which is related to the same subject matter and has an authentic channel of transmission as is its wording. Imām aṭ-Ṭabarāni reported this in the *Mu'jam al-Awsaṭ*:

حَدَّثَنَا أَحْمَدُ هو: أَبُو عَبْدِ اللهِ أَحْمَدُ بْنُ دَاوُدَ بْنِ مُوسَى الْمَكِّيُّ قَالَ: حَدَّثَنَا عَيَّاشُ بْنُ الْوَلِيدِ الرَّقَّامُ قَالَ: حَدَّثَنَا مُحَمَّدُ بْنُ فُضَيْلٍ قَالَ: حَدَّثَنَا مُجَالِدُ بْنُ سَعِيدٍ، عَنِ الشَّعْبِيِّ، عَنْ جَابِرٍ رَضِيَ اللَّهُ عَنْهُ قَالَ: أَبْصَرَ رَسُولُ اللهِ، صلى الله عليه وسلم، النَّاسَ يُلَقِّحُونَ النَّخْلَ، فَقَالَ: مَا لِلنَّاسِ؟ قَالَ: يُلَقِّحُونَ يَا رَسُولَ اللَّهِ قَالَ: لَا لِقَاحَ أَوْ مَا أَرَى اللِّقَاحَ بِشَيْءٍ قَالَ: فَتَرَكُوا اللِّقَاحَ، فَجَاءَ تَمْرُ النَّاسِ شِيصًا، فَقَالَ رَسُولُ اللهِ، صلى الله عليه وسلم: مَا أَنَا بِزَرَّاعٍ وَلَا صَاحِبِ نَخْلٍ، لَقِّحُوا!

Aḥmad narrated to us – he is Abu Abdullah Aḥmad bin Dāwud bin Musa al-Makki - he said 'Ayyāsh bin al-Waleed ar-Raqqām

[6] *Ṣaḥīḥ* Ibn Ḥibbān Vol. 1 sec. 202, no. 23

[7] *Mu'jam al-Kabir* aṭ-Ṭabarāni Vol. 4 sec. 281, no. 4,424

> narrated to us he said Muḥammad bin Fuḍeel narrated to us he said Mujālid bin Sa'eed narrated to us from ash-Sha'bi from Jābir may Allah be pleased with him), he said: The Prophet (peace be upon him) saw the people pollinating the date palms, so he said: *What are the people doing?* He said: Pollinating O Messenger of Allah. He said – *Don't pollinate* (or) *I don't see this pollination* (being) *anything*. He said: so, the people left the pollination of (their) dates. So, the Prophet said: *I am not an agriculturalist and not an owner of trees. You* (may) *pollinate*!

Ṭabarāni also reports the same in his *Mu'jam al-Kabir*.[8] It is also reported in *Sharḥ Mashkool al-Athār*[9] via essentially the same channel, after which Imām aṭ-Ṭaḥāwi elicits us with the following important comment:

> And this was not a report stemming from revelation that is from him (peace be upon him), but it was a speech concerning the apparent reality in which people are equal regarding to understand it, then they are going to disagree on this matter, and that will distinguish the people of knowledge and differ them from those who have no knowledge. And the Messenger (peace be upon him) wasn't among those who were experts of this (in other words, of planting, pollination), nor was his land one in which there were date-palms, because he (peace be upon him) was from Mecca. This is the contrary to that of Medina, where the Prophet (peace be upon him) had migrated to and he lent a hand and worked with its people in order to repair the planting of palm tree's, more so than the people of Mecca. The comment in this matter over the Prophet's speech is: it's possible that the Prophet said so, and his speech was according to what he thought to be impossible, and his speech was just from that doubt.

---

[8] *Mu'jam al-Kabir* aṭ-Ṭabarāni Vol. 1 sec. 6, no. 1034

[9] *Sharḥ Mashkool al-Athār* Vol. 4 sec. 425, no. 1723

There is also the narration which is in *Kashf al-Astār 'an Zawā'id al-Bazzār* with the alternate wording of:

حَدَّثَنَا مُحَمَّدُ بْنُ الْمُثَنَّى، حَدَّثَنَا عَيَّاشُ بْنُ أَبَانَ، حدثنا مُحَمَّدُ بْنُ فُضَيْلٍ، عَنْ مُجَالِدٍ، عَنِ الشَّعْبِيِّ، عَنْ جَابِرٍ، أَنَّ النَّبِيَّ، صلى الله عليه وسلم، مَرَّ بِقَوْمٍ يُلَقِّحُونَ النَّخْلَ، فَقَالَ: مَا أَرَى هَذَا يُغْنِي شَيْئًا، فَتَرَكُوهَا ذَلِكَ الْعَامَ، فَشَيَّصَتْ، فَأُخْبِرَ النَّبِيُّ، صلى الله عليه وسلم، فَقَالَ: أَنْتُمْ أَعْلَمُ بِمَا يُصْلِحُكُمْ فِي دُنْيَاكُمْ

Muḥammad ibn al-Muthanna narrated to us 'Ayyāsh bin Abbān narrated to us Muḥammad bin Fuḍeel narrated to us from Mujālid from ash-Sha'bi from Jābir that the Prophet (peace be upon him) once observed the people pollinating the date-palm and he said: (From) *what I see this won't do anything.* So the people left that the next year.

Al-Bazzār said: 'We don't know of it reported from Ibn Fuḍeel except by Muḥammad bin 'Amr at-Tanuri and 'Ayyāsh and they are both Basran.' As well as 'Ayyāsh bin Abbān and with this odd wording which is close to that from the single wording of the *aḥādith* by Imām Muslim, but it is from al-Bazzār, he was dictating this from his memory and there were many great errors. There is also what has been reported in *al-Kharrāj* of Yaḥya bin Adam:

أَخْبَرَنَا إِسْمَاعِيلُ قَالَ: حَدَّثَنَا الْحَسَنُ قَالَ: حَدَّثَنَا يَحْيَى قَالَ: حَدَّثَنَا أَبُو بَكْرِ بْنُ عَيَّاشٍ عَنْ سُلَيْمَانَ التَّيْمِيِّ عَنْ أَبِي مِجْلَزٍ، قَالَ: دَخَلَ رَسُولُ اللَّهِ، صلى الله عليه وسلم حَائِطًا لِلْأَنْصَارِ وَهُمْ يُلَقِّحُونَ نَخْلًا، فَقَالَ: وَيُغْنِي هَذَا شَيْئًا؟، فَتَرَكُوهُ، فَلَمْ تَحْمِلِ النَّخْلُ، فَقَالَ النَّبِيُّ، صلى الله عليه وسلم: عُودُوا، فَإِنَّمَا قُلْتُ لَكُمْ، وَلَا أَعْلَمُ

Ismā'il reported to us he said al-Ḥasan narrated to us he said Yaḥya narrated to us he said Abu Bakr bin 'Ayyāsh narrated to us from Sulaymān at-Taymi from Abu Mijlaz he said the Prophet (peace be upon him) went to a garden of the Anṣār and (there) they were pollinating date palms. So he (the Prophet) said: *this isn't of any use*. (Therefore) they left it and the date palms didn't bear dates. Thus, the Prophet (peace be upon him) said: *Come back, for what I said to you, I did not know.*

Imām Muslim also reports this in his *Ṣaḥīḥ*:

حدثنا قتيبة بن سعيد الثّقفي وأبو كامل الجحدري وتقاربا في اللفظ، وهذا حديث قتيبة قالا: حدثنا أبو عوانة عن سماك عن موسى بن طلحة عن أبيه قال: مررت مع رسول الله، صلّى الله عليه وسلّم، بقوم على رؤوس النّخل فقال: ما يصنع هؤلاء؟!، فقالوا: يلقحونه: يجعلون الذكر في الأنثى فيلقح، فقال رسول الله، صلّى الله عليه وسلّم: ما أظنّ يغني ذلك شيئا! ، قال: فأخبروا بذلك فتركوه فأخبر رسول الله، صلى الله عليه وسلم، بذلك فقال: إن كان ينفعهم ذلك فليصنعوه؛ فإني إنما ظننت ظنًّا فلا تؤاخذوني بالظّن، ولكن إذا حدّثتكم عن الله شيئا فخذوا به فإنّي لن اكذب على الله عزّ وجل

Qutayba bin Sa'eed ath-Thaqafi and Abu Kāmil al-Jaḥdari narrated to us and the wording converges and this is Qutayba's *ḥadith*; they said Abu 'Awāna narrated to us from Simmāk from Musa bin Ṭalḥa from his father he said: I and Allah's Messenger (peace be upon him) happened to pass by people near the date-palm trees. He (the Prophet) said: *What are these people doing*? They said: They are grafting, i.e. they combine the male with the female (tree) and thus they yield more fruit. Thereupon Allah's Messenger (peace be upon him) said: *I do not find it to be of any use*. The people were informed about it and they abandoned this practice. Allah's Messenger (peace be upon him) (was later) on informed (that the yield had dwindled), whereupon he said: *If there is any use of it, then they should do it, for it was just an assumption of mine, and do not go after my assumption; but when I say to you anything on behalf of Allah, then accept it, for I do not attribute a lie to Allah, the exalted and glorious.*

Imām Aḥmad bin Ḥanbal cites the report in his *Musnad* in two places.[10] The later, containing the wording: '*That was only my thought. If it will do any good, then do it. I am only mortal like you, and what I think may be right or wrong. But when I tell you: "Allah the exalted and majestic says", I will never tell lies about Allah, the exalted and majestic.*' The same narration is reported with authentic and good channels of narration in several collections.[11]

All of the above is reported via the channel of Simmāk bin Ḥarb from Musa bin Ṭalḥa from his father Ṭalḥa bin 'Ubaidallah may Allah be pleased with him. The *ḥadith* is connected and authentic and we know of no defect within it. Simmāk bin Ḥarb is trustworthy (*thiqa*) and truthful (*ṣadooq*). But there is a semblance of disturbance (*iḍṭirāb*) in some of the *ḥadith* from 'Ikrima.

The narration from Ṭalḥa bin 'Ubaidallah (may Allah be pleased with him) carries an important addition with significant implications. Contained with the narrative is the reported formulation of his words that he had expressed a thought made upon an assumption. As will be demonstrated later in exhaustive detail, the Prophet (peace be upon him) is rendered infallible in his delivery of the message by Allah. Hence the people had mistaken his assumption regarding a matter concerning human affairs, thinking that it was in some sense related to revelation. As shown in the text where he said: *That was only my thought. If it will do any good, then do it. I am only mortal like you, and what I think may be right or wrong. But when I tell you: "Allah the exalted and majestic said", I will never tell lies about Allah, the exalted and majestic.*'[12]

All narrations demonstrate this truth without any room for doubt.

---

[10] *Musnad* Aḥmad Vol. 1 sec. 162 no. 1395 and Vol. 1 sec. 163 no. 1399

[11] The listed references are: *Sunan* Ibn Mājah [Vol. 2 sec. 825, no. 2,470], *Musnad* aṭ-Ṭayālisi [Vol. 1 sec. 31, no. 230], *al-Kharrāj* of Yaḥya bin Adam [345], *Al-Aḥād wal-Mathāni* of Ibn Abi 'Aāṣim ash-Shaybāni [Vol. 1 sec. 166, no. 207], *Musnad* Abu Ya'la [Vol. 2 sec. 13, no. 639] and *Sharḥ Ma'āni al-Athār* of Imām aṭ-Ṭaḥāwi [Vol. 3 sec. 48].

[12] *Musnad* Aḥmad Vol. 1 sec. 162 no. 1395 and Vol. 1 sec. 163 no. 1399

Consequently, where he said: '*If they had not done that, it would have been better.*' In the case where its lettering was preserved and not from the narrators reporting it with the meaning, '*If they had left that pollination, it would have been better*;' the form being a meaning carrying an exclusion, a command to leave the pollination of palm trees. At the same time, he (peace be upon him) is an infallible Prophet, and rendering obedience to him is obliged. And his speech in that specific regard, was that of a thought, an assumption. If there was certainty in that matter, the manner of expression would have reflected that clearly, such as: if you do that, it will not produce the desired effect. And it became clearer when we said: 'maybe if you didn't so that would be better!'

Expressing the matter in the form of a wish or desire to, shows that there is an underlying assumption in the wording. That is clear from his speech, 'I don't think that pollination is going to benefit,' because when a person says, 'I think', it conveys that there is an assumption being made, which could be right or wrong in relation to the matter. When he (peace be upon him) said: '*I don't see this pollination* (being) *anything*,' which is more obvious, because: it was an opinion or thought, an assumption, which can be mistaken, without any doubt. The Prophet (peace be upon him) wasn't an individual who was an agriculturalist, he didn't cultivate or grow date-palms and would thus not have prior knowledge in relation to pollination and other similar processes. Hence, his statement of recall for what he had instructed: '*Come back, for what I said to you, I did not know.*' And that is expressly put, just like where he (peace be upon him) said: '*That was only my thought. If it will do any good, then do it,*' which is also explicit. The statements of the Prophet (peace be upon him) were perhaps not that of an express command, in other words saying: 'leave this pollination.' In reply, their reported wording was not that of 'you commanded us to obey and we thus complied.'

Understanding the distinction here is very important, given that the Prophet (peace be upon him) had also clarified this point. As revelation ultimately originates with Allah, it comes with certain knowledge and firm truth. Assumptions, even if made by the final messenger of Allah, cannot be construed as being truth, because in this area of opinion which does not ultimately emanate from revelation, he can make a mistake; such a mistake can never be regarded as correct.

And this also is entirely the case in what is conclusive evidence to support that he wasn't speaking from revelation, but that he was speaking from himself, similar to his acceptance or rejection of witness testimony by litigants in a judicial setting. Or even in relation to the reports which are brought before him. Greater detail concerning the subject will be detailed shortly, with the grace of Allah. Let us limit ourselves here with what we said, as has been reported in *Kashf al-Astār an Zawā'id al-Bazzār*:

حَدَّثَنَا إِسْمَاعِيلُ بْنُ عَبْدِ اللَّهِ الأَصْبَهَانِيُّ حدثنا حُسَيْنُ بْنُ حَفْصٍ حدثنا خَطَّابُ بْنُ جَعْفَرِ بْنِ أَبِي الْمُغِيرَةِ، عَنْ أَبِيهِ عَنْ سَعِيدِ بْنِ جُبَيْرٍ عَنِ ابْنِ عَبَّاسٍ قَالَ: كَانَ رَسُولُ اللَّهِ صلى الله عليه وسلم، يَطُوفُ فِي النَّخْلِ بِالْمَدِينَةِ، فَجَعَلَ النَّاسُ يَقُولُونَ فِيهَا وَسْقٌ، فَقَالَ النَّبِيُّ، صلى الله عليه وسلم: فِيهَا كَذَا وَكَذَا، فَقَالوا: صَدَقَ اللَّهُ وَرَسُولُهُ، فَقَالَ رَسُولُ اللَّهِ، صلى الله عليه وسلم: إِنَّمَا أَنَا بَشَرٌ فَمَا حَدَّثْتُكُمْ عَنِ اللَّهِ فَهُوَ حَقٌّ، وَمَا قُلْتُ فِيهِ مِنْ قِبَلِ نَفْسِي فَإِنَّمَا أَنَا بَشَرٌ أُصِيبُ وَأُخْطِئُ

Ismā'il ibn Abdullah al-Aṣbahāni narrated to us Ḥussein bin Ḥafṣ narrated to us Khaṭṭāb bin Ja'far bin Abul'Mughira narrated to us from his father from Sa'eed bin Jubayr from Ibn 'Abbās he said: The Messenger of Allah (peace be upon him) was passing in some date-palm (groves) in Medina. Thus, he made the people speak (concerning) a *wasq* (one camel load). The Prophet (peace be upon him) said: *This and that.* They replied: Allah and his Messenger have spoken the truth. The Prophet (peace be upon him) said: *Indeed, I am but mortal, so when I narrate to you from Allah, it is the truth. If what I say in it from myself, then indeed I am but mortal and suffer loss and am mistaken.*

After this, al-Bazzār commented by saying, 'We don't know of it being reported from Ibn 'Abbās by other than this (particular) *isnād*.' There is also another reported contained in *Kashf al-Astār an Zawā'id al-Bazzār*:

حَدَّثَنَا أَحْمَدُ بْنُ مَنْصُورٍ حدثنا عَبْدُ اللهِ بْنُ صَالِحٍ حدثنا اللَّيْثُ عَنِ ابْنِ عَجْلانَ عَنْ زَيْدٍ عَنْ أَبِي صَالِحٍ عَنْ أَبِي هُرَيْرَةَ عَنِ النَّبِيِّ صلى الله عليه وسلم، قَالَ: مَا أَخْبَرْتُكُمْ أَنَّهُ مِنْ عِنْدِ اللهِ فَهُوَ الَّذِي لا شَكَّ فِيهِ

Aḥmad bin Manṣur narrated to us Abdullah bin Ṣāliḥ narrated to us al-Layth narrated to us from Ibn 'Ajlān from Zayd from Abu Ṣāliḥ from Abu Hurayrah from the Prophet (peace be upon him), he said: *Whatever I reported to you that it was from Allah, it is beyond doubt.*

Again, after citing this, al-Bazzār comments by saying, 'We don't know of it being reported from Abu Hurayrah by other than this (particular) *isnād*.' Likewise, there is the report which is contained in the *Musnad* of Imām Aḥmad,[13] with an authentic channel of transmission and it is a particularly long narrative:

Yazeed bin Hārun narrated to us Ḥammād bin Salama reported to us from Thābit from Abdullah ibn Rabbāḥ from Abu Qatādah he said: We were with the Messenger of Allah (peace be upon him) on a journey. He said - *If you do not reach* (a place of) *water by tomorrow, you would become thirsty!* The people rushed seeking water, but I lingered behind with the Messenger of Allah (peace be upon him). Riding his camel, the Messenger of Allah (peace be upon him) leaned and he took a nap. So I tried to rest him on me and he rested on me. Then he

[13] *Musnad* Aḥmad Vol. 5 sec. 298, no. 22,599. Given the length of the *ḥadith* only the English is cited together with the translated *isnād*

leaned, and I tried to rest him on me and he rested. Then he lent again till he almost fell from his camel. Then I tried to rest him on me but he woke up and asked - *Who is the man*? I said Abu Qatādah. He asked: *How long have you been traveling*? I said, Since this night. He said: *May Allah safeguard you as you have safeguarded His Messenger!* He said, *What if we spent the night here*?

He lent towards the tree and climbed down the riding camel. Then he said - *Behold! Can you see anybody?"* I said - Here is one person on a camel. There is the other. The number came to a total of seven. He said: *Keep (try not to forget) the time of our prayer*! We slept over and were awakened only by the heat of the sun. We woke up and the Prophet (peace be upon him) rode his animal. He moved ahead and we moved slowly, then he got off asking - *Do you have water*? I said, Yes, I have a container with a little water. He said, *Bring it to me* and I did. He said - *Just take a dribble, just take a dribble*. The people performed ablution and there remained a small amount of water. He said, *Keep it Abu Qatādah, for it will be of use*. Then Bilāl called for the prayer and they performed two *rakat* before *Fajr* prayer and then performed *Fajr* prayer. Then he rode and we rode too.

People said to one another - We have not performed prayers properly (delaying its performance from due time). The Messenger of Allah (peace be upon him) said: *What is it that you are saying? If it is a worldly matter, it is up to you, but if it is a religious matter, it is* (referred) *to me*. We said, "O Messenger of Allah! We have not performed the due prayers properly. He said, *There is no negligence due to sleep, but it is while being awake. If it is so, then perform the same prayers tomorrow at its due time.* Then he said, *What do you think the people (say about us*)? They said - Yesterday, you said if you do not arrive to (a place of) water by tomorrow, you will become thirsty. People are at the place of water. The people woke up the next morning missing their Prophet (peace be upon him). They said to each other: The Messenger of Allah (peace

> be upon him) is at the place of water. Among the people were Abu Bakr and Umar. They said: O People! The Messenger of Allah (peace be upon him) can never precede you to the place of water and leave you behind!' If people were to obey Abu Bakr and Umar, they would have been guided.' (It was said three times).
>
> At noon, the Messenger of Allah (peace be upon him) rose to them. They said, O Messenger of Allah! We have almost died out of thirst. He said, *Allah forbids that you may perish.* Then he said, *'Abu Qatādah! Get your container.* I brought it to him. Then he said, *Untie my cup for me.* I did and brought it to him. He started to pour water in the cup, and provide the people with it. So people were crowded around him. He said, *O you people! Behave properly, for all will drink.* Everyone drank except myself and the Messenger of Allah (peace be upon him). He poured water for me saying, *Go ahead - drink Abu Qatādah.* I said, 'You drink first, O Messenger of Allah.' He said, *The person who gives water for the people is the last one to drink.* So I drank and he drank after me. The same amount of water that was in the container remained in it. That day, the people were about three hundred.

Abdullah ibn Aḥmad bin Ḥanbal said: 'Ibrāhim al-Ḥajjāj narrated to us Ḥammād bin Salama narrated to us from Thābit from Abdullah ibn Rabbāḥ from Abu Qatādah from the Prophet (peace be upon him) with a similar narration.' And Abdullah ibn Aḥmad bin Ḥanbal also said: 'Ibrāhim – who is Ibrāhim bin al-Ḥajjāj as-Salami – narrated to us Ḥammād narrated to us Ḥumayd narrated to us from Bakr bin Abdullah from Abdullah bin Rabbāḥ from Abu Qatādah from the Prophet (peace be upon him) similarly.' Concerning this Shaykh Shu'ayb al-Arnā'uṭ has said: 'The *isnād* is *Ṣaḥīḥ* upon the conditions of (Imām) Muslim and its men are trustworthy, (being) the men of the two Shaykh's (sic. Bukhāri and Muslim) bar Ḥammād bin Salama.' I would submit that Ḥammād bin Salama bin Dinār is resolutely trustworthy and from the scholars of the Muslims. Indeed, it is acknowledged that there was an objection raised from Bukhāri and he did not report from him. However many have accepted narrators considerably below his particular rank. Also Bukhāri did not report anything via Abdullah ibn Rabbāḥ and he is regarded as being trustworthy by scholarly consensus. Hence all of these channels are considered resolutely authentic and therefore taken as being decisive proof.[14]

Imām Muslim cites the next narration in his *Ṣaḥīḥ* via a channel other than that by way of Ḥammād ibn Salama. The *isnād* is resolutely authentic:

وَحَدَّثَنَا شَيْبَانُ بْنُ فَرُّوخَ حَدَّثَنَا سُلَيْمَانُ - يَعْنِى ابْنَ الْمُغِيرَةِ - حَدَّثَنَا ثَابِتٌ عَنْ عَبْدِ اللَّهِ بْنِ رَبَاحٍ عَنْ أَبِى قَتَادَةَ قَالَ: خَطَبَنَا رَسُولُ اللَّهِ، صلّى الله عليه وسلّم، فَقَالَ إِنَّكُمْ تَسِيرُونَ عَشِيَّتَكُمْ وَلَيْلَتَكُمْ وَتَأْتُونَ الْمَاءَ إِنْ شَاءَ اللَّهُ غَدًا. فَانْطَلَقَ النَّاسُ لاَ يَلْوِى أَحَدٌ عَلَى أَحَدٍ

And Shaybān bin Farrouk narrated to us Sulaymān – that is to say – ibn al-Mughira narrated to us Thābit narrated to us from Abudllah bin Rabbāḥ from Abu Qatādah he said: the Prophet (peace be upon him) addressed us and he said: *You would travel in the evening and the night till (God willing) you would come in the morning to a place of water.* So the people travelled (self-absorbed) without paying any heed to one another…[15]

The narration continues bearing the same meaning as those previously cited, however the crucial sentence - *If it is a worldly matter, it is up to you, but if it is a religious matter, it is* (referred*) to me* – is not reported, or its substitute wording. It also is reported in the *Musnad* of

[14] The Arabic text has a very short paragraph here at this juncture which details some of the meanings relating to some of the unusual words as they appear in the Arabic text of the *aḥādith*. This has been omitted for the English version.

[15] Only a short excerpt of the full *ḥadith* is cited

Ibn Ja'd. [16] The *ḥadith* – both in the long / shorter format – reach us through various channels, both *Ṣaḥīḥ* and *ḥasan*. It is noted that this is also reported in the *Ṣaḥīḥ* of Ibn Khuzayma in a shorter format;[17] the *Sunan* of Abu Dāwud;[18] *Sharḥ Ma'āni al-Athār* of Imām aṭ-Ṭaḥāwi,[19] and also in the *Sunan* of Imām Dāraquṭni.[20] Very briefly confined to the saying which the Messenger (peace be upon him) said: *'If it is one of the matters of your Deen, then it is referred to me.'* We say – Oh Messenger of Allah, we send our prayers upon you to excess. And he (peace be upon him) also said: '*There is no negligence in sleep. The negligence is in wakefulness. If any of you forget saying prayer, he should offer it when he remembers it and next day (he should say it) at its proper time.*' We have mentioned this beautiful and dignified *ḥadith* – indeed every *ḥadith* of the Prophet is beautiful and dignified – in relation to the judgement concerning the Prophetic signs which establish Muḥammad's (peace be upon him) Prophethood.

The authentic *aḥādith* previously mentioned rest upon the testimony of five of the Prophet's companions (may Allah be pleased with all of them). They are Anas bin Mālik, Rāfi' bin Khadij, Abu Qatādah, Imrān bin Ḥussein and Ṭalḥa bin 'Ubaidallah. These narratives are further supported by the *mursal* narratives which have reached us from 'Urwa bin az-Zubayr and he is from the older senior *Tābi'een* and perhaps it is taken from 'Aisha (may Allah be pleased with her) or from other senior *Ṣaḥābah*, which in turn are supported by the *mursal* narration of Abu Mijlaz. Abu Mijlaz is from the junior *Tābi'een*, having heard from Ibn 'Abbās as well as from Ibn Umar both of which are from the class of junior *Ṣaḥābah*. Indeed this has come upon the testimony of six authentic channels, each being independent from the other and being contrasted from the other. When looking at this objectively, it does not seem plausible that all the

---

[16] *Musnad* Ibn Ja'd Vol. 1 sec. 451, no. 3,075
[17] *Ṣaḥīḥ* Ibn Khuzayma Vol. 1 sec. 214, no. 410
[18] *Sunan* of Abu Dāwud Vol. 1 sec. 119, no. 437
[19] Imām aṭ-Ṭaḥāwi *Sharḥ Ma'āni al-Athār*, Vol. 1 sec. 401, no. 0
[20] *Sunan* Dāraquṭni Vol. 1 sec. 386, no. 13

narrators could have colluded in order to fabricate such an incident. Nor can it be said that the reported facts, given the independent channels are but a figment of the imagination borne of a mistaken narrator. One can thus be assured with decisive certainty that the Prophet (peace be upon him) has indeed said:

- *If it is something related to your worldly affairs, it is your affair and if it is something from the commands of your Deen it is unto me.*
- *You know* (better) *with what is related to your worldly affairs; that relating to your hereafter is* (referred) *to me.*
- *I am a human being, so when I command you about a thing pertaining to Deen, do accept it, and when I command you about a thing out of my personal opinion, keep it in mind that I am a human being.*
- *If it is related to your worldly affair, you* (are all) *more knowledgeable of it.*

It is like that to be the *riwayāt* with the meaning of the first *ḥadith* because of the more numerous reporting routes and the most powerful of the first *ḥadith* as it comes with the first wording. It is identical to the second *ḥadith* and not the third except in remote way, because he said: *'If I narrate to you something concerning your worldly affairs, I am but mortal.'* Consequently, the first part bears the condition, without the answer to this condition. It is discarded therefore by necessity – '*I am mortal like you all.*' Not having more knowledge than you, and not interfering in it; and I do not speak about it, it is your affair! Or close to that. Some narrators have given an exaggerated version of the meaning of the *ḥadith* or its shortened wording, as is the case of the version recorded by Imām Muslim. He only recorded, *'You are more knowledgeable of your worldly affairs.'* Thus, several significant points and judgments implied in the complete authentic version of the *ḥadith* were lost by this abridgement. This should be a lesson learned and a warning against narrating the meanings of *aḥādith* instead of the exact wording. It also emphasizes the necessity of strictly adhering to the infallible words uttered by the honorable and infallible Prophet (peace be upon him). Furthermore, this also necessitates tracing the chains of transmission and making sure of the different narrations.

When the Prophet (peace be upon him) said, *'If it is a worldly matter, it is up to you, but if it is a religious matter, it is (referred) to me'* he referred all worldly matters to the people and made it their own affair to study, discover, experience and apply them. In other words, the theoretical science acquired by the innate nature of people, their senses, experience and reason as well as the application, use of skill, specialisation of crafts, professions, industry, practices, methods and means, are all permissible and lawful for people. They are allowed to do what they want, whenever they want, and in whatever manner they wish. To further illustrate this point, let us examine critically once again the example of pollinating palm trees. When we examine the relationship between pollinating trees, both the ripeness of the fruit and the productivity of the crop and what is similar to that, it is considered a *worldly affair*. It is not a question of the legal judgment pertaining to pollination, whether or not it is obligatory, desirable, permissible, disliked or prohibited. Nor is it a moral judgment whether it was good or bad, for both aspects are purely 'religious.'

'Worldly life' (*Dunya*) is the perceptible world existing and bearing certain qualities and properties, whose constituents and concrete objects are related according to certain laws. In other words, the world as it is in itself. It covers all its concrete objects, qualities, powers, properties, the related sciences and knowledge, the related human skills, crafts, professions and industries and all the products and services resulting from all of these constituents. This is the exact definition of the phrase 'worldly life', as illustrated above by the detailed thorough examination of the reality of palm trees, their division into male and female; the need for the female tree to be pollinated by the male tree, of people undertaking the pollination process regularly to ensure its soundness and success, the quality of the product and its high productivity. Add to this, they do not depend on wind and bees, which originally and instinctively undertake the process to perform pollination.

Our *Deen* - al-Islam, is not merely just a collection of ritualistic acts of worship, belief in the unseen, or merely limited to morals and manners, as is the case in the Western concept of 'religion.' In fact, all the voluntary human deeds are subject to *Sharī'ah* legal judgment. In the Arabic language, the word '*ad-Deen'* is a considered a *maṣdar* or verbal noun. The act is *dāna, yadeen, deenan* and *diyāna*. It denotes anything that is worshipped beside Allah. The various denominations that the word can refer to is – customs, cults, reckoning or accounting, kingdom or dominion, ruling/judgement, reigning, and authority. The verb */dāna/* is to subdue, make others subservient and make others obedient. Whereas */dāna bi kadtha/* is to adopt something as a *Deen* and worship it. The term */dāna fulān fulānun/* is for one person to hold another accountable, to reward, punish him and control him. As it is reported in *an-Nihāya fi Ghareeb al-Athar:*[21]

> *Deen*: From the names of Allah, the most high, is *ad-Dayyān* and it is said that this is synonymous with his name, *al-Qahhār*, The Subduer. It is also stated that it is synonymous with The Ruler, The Judge. The word, *ad-Dayyān*, is an emphatic noun form from the phrase '*dānan-nas'* which means to subdue them to obey. It is said that when one says *'deen-tu-hum fa dānū'* that it means 'I have subdued them and so they obey'. Another evidence for this opinion is the poetry of al-'Amash al-Ḥirmāzī which addressed the Prophet, may Allah honour him and grant him peace, 'Master of people and *dayyān* of the Arabs'. There is also a *ḥadith*; *It is upon me to be the dayyān of this nation.*

[21] *an-Nihāya fi Ghareeb al-A'thar* Vol. 2 sec. 148, no. 1,216

> Also there is the *ḥadith* of 'Abi Ṭalib when the Prophet, may Allah honour him and grant him peace, said to him: *I want the Quraysh to say a word that, with it, they will tadīn the Arabs.* In other words *tadīn* means 'make them obey' and 'cause them to humbled.' Another *ḥadith* is, *The one who is of intellect and manners is the one who dāna over their soul and prepares for what is after death.* In other words, *dāna* here is 'to humble their soul and make a worshipper out of it.' It is also said that it means 'to account for their soul.'

In my opinion the most correct meaning is that *ad-Diyyān* is synonymous with the names of the ruler and the judge. Elsewhere in the same work, *an-Nihāya fi Ghareeb al-Athar*, the following is mentioned also:

> Al-Khaṭṭābi said: 'The scholars of the Muslims have unanimously agreed that the *Khawārij*, due to their misguidance, are a group from the deviant groups of the Muslims. Despite this, their marriages, slaughter of meat and testimonies are valid and accepted. When Ali bin 'Abi Ṭālib was questioned about them it was said to him, 'Are they non-believers?' He responded, 'What disbelief have they shown?' They said, 'Are they from the hypocrites?' He responded, 'Little do the hypocrites remember Allah and, as for them, they remember Allah in morning and evening.' It was then said, 'So what exactly are they?' Ali responded, 'A group of people who have been afflicted by a great calamity and have consequently become blind and deaf.'
>
> Al-Khaṭṭābi continues to say, 'Therefore the meaning of the Prophet's statement, may Allah honour him and grant him peace, 'they will pass through this *Deen*…' is that he intended by '*deen*', obedience. In other words, that they would exit from the obedience of the leader who it is obligatory to follow and that they would detach themselves from him; and Allah knows best.' And in the *ḥadith* of Salmān, 'Indeed Allah will *yadīn*

for the hornless livestock like he does with those that have horns', *yadīn* means 'to follow up and recompense' therefore *Deen* can also mean recompense.

The *Deen* of Islam therefore, is not just a spiritual belief on which a moral system is based and with which ritual acts of worship are associated. It is not just a 'religion' in the Western sense of the term. *Deen* denotes a certain way of living, how the world should be, i.e. how should we behave in this world. It is a holistic system and not just a set of beliefs regarding the unseen, ritual acts of worship, or proper morals and manners as is the case with the Western concept of the word 'religion'. As mentioned above, *Deen* is much wider in scope than that. It is a regulation of all relations and it is supported by an innumerable number of convincing evidences that are considered to be acknowledged facts. To further clarify the idea, some of the following examples may be outlined:

Post-Pollination

After the first incident of pollination in the early period at Medina, the Prophet (peace be upon him) stated that religious affairs should be referred only to him, while all worldly affairs were referred to the people. He reiterated this distinction at various junctures and through a number of authentic *ḥadith*. It has been established through recurrent incidents, historical facts, and through the acknowledgement of all believers and disbelievers that the Prophet (peace be upon him) had commanded, prohibited, informed and conducted innumerable transactions, punishments, governmental judgments, international affairs, war and peace and many other matters that definitely go beyond the unseen beliefs, acts of worship, and proper manners and morals. Consequently, this proves that all are considered matters of *Deen*.

Prescribing Punishment

Allah the exalted prescribed the penalty of lashing as a punishment for committing adultery. He also made it obligatory that a group of believers witness the execution of this penalty:

الزَّانِيَةُ وَالزَّانِي فَاجْلِدُوا كُلَّ وَاحِدٍ مِّنْهُمَا مِائَةَ جَلْدَةٍ وَلَا تَأْخُذْكُم بِهِمَا رَأْفَةٌ فِي دِينِ اللَّهِ إِن كُنتُمْ
تُؤْمِنُونَ بِاللَّهِ وَالْيَوْمِ الْآخِرِ وَلْيَشْهَدْ عَذَابَهُمَا طَائِفَةٌ مِّنَ الْمُؤْمِنِينَ

(As for) the fornicatress and the fornicator, flog each of them, (giving) a hundred stripes, and let not pity for them detain you in the matter of obedience to Allah, if you believe in Allah and the last day, and let a party of believers witness their chastisement.[22]

This is a conclusive *Sharī'ah* legal text, denoting the prohibition of adultery and the prescribed worldly penalty for it should neither be forgiven, nor tolerated out of tenderness or mercy towards those committing the crime. It also indicates that a number of believers witnessing adultery being committed and the number of believers witnessing the punishment are among the matters of the *Deen* of Allah.

The Prophet Yusuf

In the Qur'ān we are told of how Allah enabled Yusuf (peace be upon him) to detain his brother in Egypt. He executed the penalty of theft - prescribed in the jurisdiction of Ya'qub (peace be upon him) since it was enslaving thieves instead of the penalty prescribed in the jurisdiction of the king of Egypt. Allah says:

فَبَدَأَ بِأَوْعِيَتِهِمْ قَبْلَ وِعَاءِ أَخِيهِ ثُمَّ اسْتَخْرَجَهَا مِن وِعَاءِ أَخِيهِ كَذَٰلِكَ كِدْنَا لِيُوسُفَ مَا كَانَ لِيَأْخُذَ
أَخَاهُ فِي دِينِ الْمَلِكِ إِلَّا أَن يَشَاءَ اللَّهُ نَرْفَعُ دَرَجَاتٍ مَّن نَّشَاءُ وَفَوْقَ كُلِّ ذِي عِلْمٍ عَلِيمٌ

---

[22] *Qur'ān* 24: 2

[Joseph] began by searching their bags, then his brother's, and he pulled it out from his brother's bag. In this way, We devised a plan for Joseph— if Allah had not willed it so, he could not have detained his brother as a penalty under the king's law - We raise the rank of whoever We will. Above everyone who has knowledge there is the One who is all knowing. [23]

It is known by necessity that the discussion here does not deal with matters related to the unseen or ritual acts of worship, nor is it related to morals or even mannerisms. It deals with the crime of theft and whether its penalty is executed according to the jurisdiction of Ya'qub or that that of the king – which is the *Deen*, jurisdiction – as stated in the Qur'ān. His '*Deen*' means his laws and system and not his belief relating to the unseen, or rituals of worship. The discussion here does not deal with that and is not related to it at all. Limiting revelation to matters of 'religion' does not mean at all that revelation is not concerned with worldly matters. In fact, it might be concerned with some or many worldly matters.

In the *Musnad* of Imām Aḥmad the following *ḥadith* which is *Ṣaḥīḥ* is reported:

حَدَّثَنَا الْوَلِيدُ بْنُ مُسْلِمٍ حَدَّثَنِي عَبْدُ الْعَزِيزِ بْنُ إِسْمَاعِيلَ بْنِ عُبَيْدِ اللَّهِ أَنَّ سُلَيْمَانَ بْنَ حَبِيبٍ حَدَّثَهُمْ عَنْ أَبِي أُمَامَةَ الْبَاهِلِيِّ عَنْ رَسُولِ اللَّهِ، صلّى الله عليه وسلّم، قَالَ لَيُنْقَضَنَّ عُرَى الإِسْلَامِ عُرْوَةً عُرْوَةً، فَكُلَّمَا انْتَقَضَتْ عُرْوَةٌ تَشَبَّثَ النَّاسُ بِالَّتِي تَلِيهَا؛ وَأَوَّلُهُنَّ نَقْضاً الْحُكْمُ وَآخِرُهُنَّ الصَّلَاةُ

Al-Waleed bin Muslim narrated to us Abdul-Aziz bin Ismā'il bin 'Ubaidallah narrated to me that Sulaymān bin Ḥabeeb narrated to them from Abu Umāma al-Bāhili from the Prophet (peace be upon him), he said: *Verily, the knots of Islam will be undone one by one. Whenever one knot is lost then the people grab onto the one which came after it. The first of these knots will be the ruling (al-hukm) and the last will be the Ṣalāh*.

[23] *Qur'ān* 12: 76

It is also reported in a large number of *ḥadith* collections, such as:

- *Ṣaḥīḥ* Ibn Ḥibbān [Vol. 15 sec. 11, no. 6,715]. Shaykh Shu'ayb al-Arnā'uṭ said the *isnād* was strong (*qawi*). It is as he said, the *isnād* is strong, *Ṣaḥīḥ* and can be taken as a proof
- *Al-Mustadrak* of Al-Ḥākim [Vol. 4 sec. 104, no. 7,022] and following citation Al-Ḥākim said: 'And the *isnād*, all of it is *Ṣaḥīḥ*, but they did not record it.'
- In the works of Imām Ṭabarāni, *Mu'jam al-Kabir* [Vol. 8 sec. 98, no. 7,486] and *Musnad ash-Shāmiayn* [Vol. 2 sec. 411, no. 1,602]
- *Sha'b al-'Imān* by Imām Bayhaqy [Vol. 11 sec. 261, no. 5,045 & Vol. 16 sec. 72, no. 7,265]
- *Ma'rifa aṣ-Ṣaḥābah* by Abu Nu'aym al-Aṣbahāni [Vol. 11 sec. 47, no. 3,427]

The legal texts are explicit in relation to the fact that the ruling (*al-ḥukm*) of Islam is also used in the same sense as *the Deen* and *the Ṣalāh*. In this regard, they are completely alike. The term *'ḥa ka ma'* [ح ك م] or ruled, will be detailed further in relation to the word of *Ḥākimiyah*. From perusal of the Qur'ān it can be discerned that there are seven usages of the term:

1. *Ḥikmah* (wisdom): situating matters in their rightful position; whoever does so is *ḥakeem* (wise).

2. *Al-Iḥkām* (accuracy, perfection): relating to the perfection of crafts and achieving the ultimate aim of a deed, whoever does so is called *muḥkim*, namely the one who perfected.

3. Judging the deeds of mankind on the Day of Judgement and resolving their disputes finally and forever which is the exclusive right of Allah alone and the verses of the Glorious Qur'ān which prove demonstrate this are numerous.

4. Issuing judgement or *Fatwa*. This is not restricted to giving an opinion in a legal matter but can also relate to opinions in matters of perception, rational ideas, aesthetics or ethics. As an example, we rule, or judge - *naḥkum*, that reincarnation is a clear falsehood as is the Christian doctrine of the Trinity; telling lies is rationally unacceptable etc. Numerous examples abound to highlight this point, such as where Allah states:

أَفَنَجْعَلُ الْمُسْلِمِينَ كَالْمُجْرِمِينَ، مَا لَكُمْ كَيْفَ تَحْكُمُونَ

Should We treat those who submit to Us as We treat those who do evil? What is the matter with you? On what basis do you judge? [24]

5. Resolving disputes and issuing judgements that are legally binding. This specifically relates to the acts of judicial bodies and certain authorities that have this vested power. A judge is called a *ḥākim* and his legally binding verdict a *ḥukm*.

6. Management of public affairs. Under this comes the modern notion of public ruling and government, such as running the affairs of state, applying and executing laws etc. Whoever assumes this role is called a *ḥākim* – a ruler or can even be referred to as a *wali* or *wali ul-'amr*, *sultan* etc. Modern political usage has the term of *ḥūkumah* to mean the government and its executive branch.

7. Legislation. This relates to enacting and implementing laws, rules, regulations and delineating constitutional principles and boundaries.

Essentially the last four connotations of the word *ḥukm* concern this

[24] *Qur'ān* 68: 35/36

present research, namely: informed opinion and *fatwa*; judicial decisions; executive acts or actions, and legislation.

The word used – namely *Deen* - is narrower than that to mean only government and the judiciary. As has been reported from the dignified companion of the Prophet (peace be upon him), Abdullah ibn Mas'ud, cited in the *Muṣṣanaf* of Abdar-Razzāq with a good *isnād*:

أخبرنا عبد الرزّاق عن عاصم عن زرّ بن حبيش قال: قال ابن مسعود: السّحت: الرّشوة في الدّين؛ قال سفيان: يعني في الحكم

Abdar-Razzāq reported to us from 'Aāṣim from Zirr ibn Ḥubaysh he said Ibn Mas'ud said: *as-Suḥt* – (is) bribery in *Deen*. Sufyān said: that is to say, in the *ḥukm*.

It is also reported in *Akhbār al-Quḍā'*:

أَخْبَرَنِي إسحاق بْن حسن؛ قال: حَدَّثَنَا أَبُو حذيفة؛ قال: حَدَّثَنَا سُفْيَان، عَن عاصم، عَن زرّ، عَنْ عَبْدِ اللهِ: السُّحْت: الرشا في الدين

Isḥāq ibn Ḥasan reported to me he said Abu Ḥudhayfah narrated to us he said Sufyān narrated to us from 'Aāṣim from Zirr from Abdullah: *as-Suḥt* is bribery in *Deen*.

The word '*Deen*' may be used to denote *allegiance, affiliation,* and *carrying citizenship*. That is, either by way of utilising the name to signify all or a part of that for rhetorical purposes, which would also include referring to a part to signify the wider whole. Like what has been reported by Imām Bukhāri in his collection of *Ṣaḥīḥ*:

حَدَّثَنَا عَلِيُّ بْنُ عَبْدِ اللهِ حَدَّثَنَا سُفْيَانُ عَنْ أَيُّوبَ عَنْ عِكْرِمَةَ أَنَّ عَلِيًّا رَضِيَ اللَّهُ عَنْهُ حَرَّقَ قَوْمًا فَبَلَغَ ابْنَ عَبَّاسٍ فَقَالَ لَوْ كُنْتُ أَنَا لَمْ أُحَرِّقْهُمْ لِأَنَّ النَّبِيَّ، صلى

الله عليه وسلم، قَالَ لَا تُعَذِّبُوا بِعَذَابِ اللَّهِ، وَلَقَتَلْتُهُمْ كَمَا قَالَ النَّبِيُّ، صلى الله عليه وسلم: مَنْ بَدَّلَ دِينَهُ فَاقْتُلُوهُ

Ali ibn Abdullah narrated to us Sufyān narrated to us from Ayub from 'Ikrima that Ali may Allah be pleased with him, burnt some people and this matter reached Ibn 'Abbās who said: Had I been in his place, I would not have burnt them, as the Prophet peace be upon him said: *Don't punish with Allah's Punishment.* No doubt, I would have executed them, for the Prophet peace be upon him said: *Whoever changes his Deen, then he is to be executed.*[25]

Similar is also cited in the *Musnad* of Imām Aḥmad bin Ḥanbal, reported on the authority of Mu'ādth ibn Jabal:

حَدَّثَنَا عَبْدُ الرَّزَّاقِ أخبرَنا مَعْمَرٌ عَنْ أَيُّوبَ عَنْ حُمَيْدِ بْنِ هِلَالٍ الْعَدَوِيِّ عَنْ أَبِي بُرْدَةَ قَالَ قَدِمَ عَلَى أَبِي مُوسَى مُعَاذُ بْنُ جَبَلٍ بِالْيَمَنِ فَإِذَا رَجُلٌ عِنْدَهُ قَالَ مَا هَذَا قَالَ رَجُلٌ كَانَ يَهُودِيًّا فَأَسْلَمَ ثُمَّ تَهَوَّدَ وَنَحْنُ نُرِيدُهُ عَلَى الْإِسْلَامِ مُنْذُ قَالَ أَحْسَبُهُ شَهْرَيْنِ فَقَالَ وَاللَّهِ لَا أَقْعُدُ حَتَّى تَضْرِبُوا عُنُقَهُ فَضُرِبَتْ عُنُقُهُ فَقَالَ قَضَى اللَّهُ وَرَسُولُهُ أَنَّ (مَنْ رَجَعَ عَنْ دَيْنِهِ فَاقْتُلُوهُ) أَوْ قَالَ: مَنْ بَدَّلَ دَيْنَهُ فَاقْتُلُوهُ

Abdar-Razzāq narrated to us Ma'mar reported to us from Ayub from Ḥumayd ibn Hilāl al-Adawi from Abu Burda, he said: Abu Musa came upon Mu'ādth ibn Jabal in Yemen, when a man said: what is this? He said: There was a Jew who accepted (but) reverted from Islam two months (prior), and we wanted him to remain upon Islam. He said: By Allah, I shall not be seated until you strike his neck, so strike his neck since the Messenger of Allah said: *Whoever reverts from his Deen, he is to be executed.* Or he said: *Whoever changes his Deen, then he*

[25] *Ṣaḥīḥ* Bukhāri Vol. 3 sec. 1098, no. 2854 and Vol. 6 sec. 2537, no. 6524. A very large array of additional references is mentioned in the Arabic edition, as many scholars cited this tradition, appearing in the respective *Ṣaḥīḥ, Sunan*, *Musnad*, *Mu'jam* and *Muṣṣanaf* works.

> *is to be executed.*

That is also to be found in the *Muṣṣanaf* of Abdar-Razzāq with the addition carried by Abdar-Razzāq being: 'Ma'mar said: and I heard Qatādah saying, Mu'ādth said: by Allah, I shall not sit until they strike his back.'[26] Imām aṭ-Ṭabarāni reports in his *Mu'jam al-Kabir* from Mu'āwiya ibn Ḥayda:

> حدثنا داود بن محمد بن صالح المروزي حدثنا حوثرة بن أشرس حدثنا حماد بن سلمة عن بهز بن حكيم عن أبيه عن جده قال: قال رسول الله، صلى الله عليه وسلم: من بدل دينه فاقتلوه: لا يقبل الله توبة عبد كفر بعد إسلامه
>
> Dāwud ibn Muḥammad ibn Ṣāliḥ al-Marwazi narrated to us Ḥawtha ibn Ashras narrated to us Ḥammād ibn Salama narrated to us from Bahz ibn Ḥakeem from his father from his grandfather, he said: The Messenger of Allah peace be upon him said: *Whoever changes his Deen, execute him. No repentance of the slave is accepted by Allah, by Kufr after his Islam.*

It is also cited again by Ṭabarāni in *Mu'jam al-Awsaṭ*, upon the authority of Abu Hurayrah:

> حدثنا مسعود بن محمد الرملي حدثنا عمران بن هارون حدثنا بن لهيعة حدثني بكير بن عبد الله بن الأشج عن سليمان بن يسار عن أبي هريرة أن رسول الله، صلى الله عليه وسلم، قال: من بدل دينه فاقتلوه
>
> ثم قال الإمام الطبراني: لم يرو هذا الحديث عن بكير إلا بن لهيعة.
>
> Mas'ud ibn Muḥammad ar-Ramli narrated to us 'Imrān ibn Hārun narrated to us Ibn Lahiya narrated to us Bukeer ibn

[26] *Muṣṣanaf* Abdar-Razzālq [Vol. 10, sec. 168, no. 18705]

> Abdullah ibn al-Ashaj narrated to me from Sulaymān ibn Yassār from Abu Hurayrah, that the Messenger of Allah peace be upon him said: *Whoever changes his Deen, execute him*. Thereafter Imām aṭ-Ṭabarāni said: This *ḥadith* wasn't narrated from Bukeer except by way of Ibn Lahiya.

What is being expressed here it not merely one of switching from the *Deen*, namely what is construed as being apostasy from Islam in the classic sense of the term, or for that matter, conversion from one *Deen* to another in general, as has been construed by the majority of the *fuqahā* (jurists). Rather, it is the severance of affiliation; leaving the political community (*al-Jamā'ah*), and / or being accompanied by rebellion against the just lawfully constituted ruler. Leaving that obedience may be from amongst the following:

1. To renounce an ostensibly Islamic 'citizenship' and leave the domain of Islam (*dar al-Islam*) and move to a domain of war (*dar al-ḥarb*). By undertaking this act, the individual would be considered a 'waring apostate', aligning with hostile waring disbelieving forces.
2. To remain within the domain of Islam (*dar al-Islam*), but to engage in operations other than war, namely, to spy, engage in acts of sabotage or the like, on behalf of hostile waring disbelieving forces, an individual would be regarded as a 'waring apostate.'
3. To remain within the domain of Islam (*dar al-Islam*) and compel its people by armed force to disbelief and idolatry (*kufr* and *shirk*). Any individual undertaking that would be treated as waging war and fought accordingly, like the *Khawārij* and other types of insurrectionism.
4. Remaining within the domain of Islam (*dar al-Islam*) and engaging in brigandage.

5. Where a legitimate Imām has been justly appointed within the domain of Islam (*dar al-Islam*), but instead of being lawfully obeyed is opposed by force.

Such acts that relate to fighting are in relation to specific crimes, where the individual may at times be considered an apostate, at other times not. The proof for that, has been set out by the majestic, glorified be his names:

فَمَا لَكُمْ فِي الْمُنَافِقِينَ فِئَتَيْنِ وَاللَّهُ أَرْكَسَهُم بِمَا كَسَبُوا أَتُرِيدُونَ أَن تَهْدُوا مَنْ أَضَلَّ اللَّهُ وَمَن يُضْلِلِ اللَّهُ فَلَن تَجِدَ لَهُ سَبِيلًا

وَدُّوا لَوْ تَكْفُرُونَ كَمَا كَفَرُوا فَتَكُونُونَ سَوَاءً فَلَا تَتَّخِذُوا مِنْهُمْ أَوْلِيَاءَ حَتَّىٰ يُهَاجِرُوا فِي سَبِيلِ اللَّهِ فَإِن تَوَلَّوْا فَخُذُوهُمْ وَاقْتُلُوهُمْ حَيْثُ وَجَدتُّمُوهُمْ وَلَا تَتَّخِذُوا مِنْهُمْ وَلِيًّا وَلَا نَصِيرًا

إِلَّا الَّذِينَ يَصِلُونَ إِلَىٰ قَوْمٍ بَيْنَكُمْ وَبَيْنَهُم مِّيثَاقٌ أَوْ جَاءُوكُمْ حَصِرَتْ صُدُورُهُمْ أَن يُقَاتِلُوكُمْ أَوْ يُقَاتِلُوا قَوْمَهُمْ وَلَوْ شَاءَ اللَّهُ لَسَلَّطَهُمْ عَلَيْكُمْ فَلَقَاتَلُوكُمْ فَإِنِ اعْتَزَلُوكُمْ فَلَمْ يُقَاتِلُوكُمْ وَأَلْقَوْا إِلَيْكُمُ السَّلَمَ فَمَا جَعَلَ اللَّهُ لَكُمْ عَلَيْهِمْ سَبِيلًا

سَتَجِدُونَ آخَرِينَ يُرِيدُونَ أَن يَأْمَنُوكُمْ وَيَأْمَنُوا قَوْمَهُمْ كُلَّ مَا رُدُّوا إِلَى الْفِتْنَةِ أُرْكِسُوا فِيهَا فَإِن لَّمْ يَعْتَزِلُوكُمْ وَيُلْقُوا إِلَيْكُمُ السَّلَمَ وَيَكُفُّوا أَيْدِيَهُمْ فَخُذُوهُمْ وَاقْتُلُوهُمْ حَيْثُ ثَقِفْتُمُوهُمْ وَأُولَٰئِكُمْ جَعَلْنَا لَكُمْ عَلَيْهِمْ سُلْطَانًا مُّبِينًا

Why are you divided in two about the hypocrites, when Allah himself has rejected them because of what they have done? Do you want to guide those Allah has left to stray? If Allah leaves anyone to stray, you will never find the way for him.

They desire that you should disbelieve as they have disbelieved, to be like them. So do not take them as allies until they migrate for Allah's cause. If they turn [on you], *then seize and kill them wherever you encounter them. Take none of them as an ally or supporter.*

But as for those who seek refuge with people with whom you have a treaty, or who come over to you because their hearts shrink from fighting against you or against their own people, Allah could have given them power over you, and they would have fought you. So if they withdraw and do not fight you, and offer you peace, then Allah gives you no way against them.

You will find others who wish to be safe from you, and from their own people, but whenever they are back in a situation where they are tempted [to fight you], *they succumb to it. So if they neither withdraw, nor offer you peace, nor restrain themselves from fighting you, seize and kill them wherever you encounter them: We give you clear authority against such people.*[27]

Imām Muslim recorded the next narration in his collection of *Ṣaḥīḥ*:

حدثنا أحمد بن حنبل ومحمد بن المثنى واللفظ لأحمد قالا حدثنا عبد الرحمن بن مهدي عن سفيان عن الأعمش عن عبد الله بن مرة عن مسروق عن عبد الله قال قام فينا رسول الله، صلى الله عليه وسلم، فقال والذي لا إله غيره لا يحل دم رجل مسلم يشهد أن لا إله إلا الله وأني رسول الله إلا ثلاثة نفر: التارك الإسلام المفارق للجماعة (أو الجماعة شك فيه أحمد) والثيب الزاني والنفس بالنفس؛ قال الأعمش: (فحدثت به إبراهيم فحدثني عن الأسود عن عائشة بمثله

Aḥmad bin Ḥanbal and Muḥammad ibn al-Muthanna narrated to us, and (this is) the wording of Aḥmad, they said: Abdar-Raḥman ibn Mahdi narrated to us from Sufyān from al-'Amash from Abdullah ibn Murra from Masruq from Abdullah, he said: The Messenger of Allah peace be upon him stood up and said: *By Him besides whom there is no god but He, the blood of a Muslim who bears the testimony that there is no god but Allah, and I am His Messenger, may be lawfully shed only in the case of three persons: the one who abandons Islam, and deserts the community* [Aḥmad is doubtful whether the word used *li'l-jamā'ah* or *al-jamā'ah*), *and the married adulterer, and life for life*. Al-'Amash said: I narrated this tradition to Ibrāhim, he narrated to me similarly from al-Aswad from 'Aisha.

[27] *Qur'ān* 4: 88/91

Again, Imām Muslim records in his collection of *Ṣaḥīḥ* with the following wording:

حدثنا أبو بكر بن أبي شيبة حدثنا حفص بن غياث وأبو معاوية ووكيع عن الأعمش عن عبد الله بن مرة عن مسروق عن عبد الله قال: قال رسول الله، صلى الله عليه وسلم، لا يحل دم امرئ مسلم يشهد أن لا إله إلا الله وأني رسول الله إلا بإحدى ثلاث الثيب الزان والنفس بالنفس والتارك لدينه المفارق للجماعة

Abu Bakr ibn Abi Shayba narrated to us Ḥafṣ ibn Ghayāth, Mu'āwiya and Waki' narrated to us from al-'Amash from Abdullah ibn Murra from Masruq from Abdullah, he said: The Messenger of Allah peace be upon him said: *It is not permissible to take the life of a Muslim who testifies there is no god but Allah, and I am the Messenger of Allah, but in one of the three cases: the married adulterer, a life for life, and the deserter of his Deen, abandoning the community*.

Imām Bukhāri also has this in his collection of *Ṣaḥīḥ* with the following wording:

حدثنا عمر بن حفص حدثنا أبي حدثنا الأعمش عن عبد الله بن مرة عن مسروق عن عبد الله قال: قال رسول الله لا يحل دم امرئ مسلم يشهد أن لا إله إلا الله وأني رسول الله إلا بإحدى ثلاث النفس بالنفس والثيب الزاني والمفارق لدينه التارك للجماعة

Umar ibn Ḥafṣ narrated to us my father narrated to us al-'Amash narrated to us from Abdullah ibn Murra from Masruq from Abdullah, he said: The Messenger of Allah peace be upon him said: *The blood of a Muslim who testifies that there is no god Allah and that I am His Messenger, cannot be shed except in three cases: life for life, a married fornicator and the one who abandons his Deen and deserts the community*.

Reporting on the authority of 'Aisha, mother of the believers, Imām an-Nasā'i cites the next tradition in his *Sunan* with a *Ṣaḥīḥ isnād*:

> أخبرنا أحمد بن حفص بن عبد الله قال حدثني أبي قال حدثني إبراهيم عن عبد العزيز بن رفيع عن عبيد بن عمير عن عائشة أم المؤمنين عن رسول الله أنه قال لا يحل قتل مسلم إلا في إحدى ثلاث خصال: زان محصن فيرجم ورجل يقتل مسلما متعمدا، ورجل يخرج من الإسلام فيحارب الله ورسوله فيقتل أو يصلب أو ينفى من الأرض
>
> Aḥmad ibn Ḥafṣ ibn Abdullah reported to us he said my father narrated to me, he said Ibrāhim narrated to me from Abdal-Aziz ibn Rufeeh' from 'Ubayd ibn 'Umayr from 'Aisha, mother of the believers, from the Messenger of Allah peace be upon him that he said: *It is not permissible to kill a Muslim except in one of three cases: A adulterer who has been married, who is to be stoned; a man who kills a Muslim deliberately; and a man who exits Islam and wages war against Allah, the mighty and sublime and His Messenger, who is to be executed, crucified or banished from the land.*[28]

The wording reported '…*and a man who exits Islam and wages war against Allah, the mighty and sublime and His Messenger, who is to be killed, crucified or banished from the land,*' is confirmed as per the noble verses cited here:

إِنَّمَا جَزَاءُ الَّذِينَ يُحَارِبُونَ اللهَ وَرَسُولَهُ وَيَسْعَوْنَ فِي الْأَرْضِ فَسَادًا أَن يُقَتَّلُوا أَوْ يُصَلَّبُوا أَوْ تُقَطَّعَ أَيْدِيهِمْ وَأَرْجُلُهُم مِّنْ خِلَافٍ أَوْ يُنفَوْا مِنَ الْأَرْضِ ذَٰلِكَ لَهُمْ خِزْيٌ فِي الدُّنْيَا وَلَهُمْ فِي الْآخِرَةِ عَذَابٌ عَظِيمٌ. إِلَّا الَّذِينَ تَابُوا مِن قَبْلِ أَن تَقْدِرُوا عَلَيْهِمْ فَاعْلَمُوا أَنَّ اللهَ غَفُورٌ رَّحِيمٌ

[28] *Sunan* Nasā'i Vol. 8 sec 23, no. 4743. The majority of scholars cited this wording in their respective works. More often than not, the reported wording has '…*the one who forsakes his Deen and separates from the community.*' Again, the Arabic edition contains a very large array of additional references where this tradition is cited, appearing in the respective *Ṣaḥīḥ, Sunan, Musnad, Mu'jam* and *Muṣṣanaf* collections.

The punishment of those who wage war against Allah and His Messenger and strive to make mischief in the land is only this: that they should be executed or crucified, or their hands and their feet should be cut off on opposite sides or they should be imprisoned; this shall be as a disgrace for them in this world, and in the hereafter, they shall have a grievous chastisement. Except those who repent before you have them in your power; so know that Allah is forgiving, merciful.[29]

It would also apply to those involved in highway banditry from amongst the disobedient Muslims, that is from the essence of what we have said. But as a subject in itself, it is incredibly complex and requires a standalone in-depth study. That research, upon the invalidity of the *ḥadd* relating to apostasy, will by the grace of Allah be concluded soon.

What we have mentioned up till now is the first and the most significant *Sharī'ah* legal meaning of the term *Deen;* it is a certain way of living, a system of life. Islam is the true and only *Deen* that Allah accepts in the hereafter. Secularism or to be more accurate 'worldliness' is also a *Deen*. Yet it is a false *Deen*, as is the Western system of governance, modern representative democracy. Materialistic socialism is a third type of *Deen* characterised by disbelief and misguidance. As for the second *Sharī'ah* legal meaning of the term *'Deen'* it is punishment and reward, as indicated in the following verse where Allah says:

مَالِكِ يَوْمِ الدِّينِ

Master of the Day of Judgment. [30]

This means the day of reckoning and reward, in other words the day of

[29] *Qur'ān* 5: 33/34
[30] *Qur'ān* 1: 4

judgement. Further to this, Allah states of the disbelievers comments:

أَإِذَا مِتْنَا وَكُنَّا تُرَابًا وَعِظَامًا أَإِنَّا لَمَدِينُونَ

What! When we are dead and have become dust and bones, shall we then be certainly brought to judgment? [31]

When discussing matters of *Deen*, this is the prime specific concern of *Deen*. However, that that is not to say that revelation does not address matters relating to the present worldly affairs. Allah has said:

أَوَلَمْ يَرَوْا أَنَّا نَأْتِي الْأَرْضَ نَنقُصُهَا مِنْ أَطْرَافِهَا وَاللَّهُ يَحْكُمُ لَا مُعَقِّبَ لِحُكْمِهِ وَهُوَ سَرِيعُ الْحِسَابِ

Do they not see that We are bringing destruction upon the land by curtailing it of its sides? And Allah decides – none can reverse his decision, and He is swift to take account. [32]

وَرَبُّكَ يَخْلُقُ مَا يَشَاءُ وَيَخْتَارُ مَا كَانَ لَهُمُ الْخِيَرَةُ سُبْحَانَ اللَّهِ وَتَعَالَىٰ عَمَّا يُشْرِكُونَ

And your Lord creates and chooses whom He pleases; to choose is not theirs; glory be to Allah, and exalted be He above what they associate (with Him). [33]

خَالِدِينَ فِيهَا مَا دَامَتِ السَّمَاوَاتُ وَالْأَرْضُ إِلَّا مَا شَاءَ رَبُّكَ إِنَّ رَبَّكَ فَعَّالٌ لِّمَا يُرِيدُ

Abiding therein so long as the heavens and the earth endure, except as your Lord pleases; surely your Lord is the mighty doer of what He wills. [34]

---

[31] *Qur'ān* 37: 53
[32] *Qur'ān* 13: 41
[33] *Qur'ān* 28: 68
[34] *Qur'ān* 11: 107

فَعَّالٌ لِّمَا يُرِيدُ

Doer of what He wills.[35]

لَا يُسْأَلُ عَمَّا يَفْعَلُ وَهُمْ يُسْأَلُونَ

He cannot be questioned concerning what He does but they shall be questioned.[36]

The Prophet Nuḥ was given the knowledge of ship-building through *waḥy* (revelation) and it was a command concerning worldly affairs. The Prophet Dāwud was instructed through the medium of *waḥy* in relation to warfare and armour; the Prophet Sulaymān was given the understanding of the language of birds. To other Prophets, they were instructed in medicine and the treatment of illness. All of this, without doubt, is related to what is considered as being worldly affairs. Some of what was given to the Prophets was inculcated via mannerisms and grace, others by way of dignity and a blessing to their followers and heirs.

As for what has been reported from the almighty regarding the many facets in the universe, this is given as an education and guidance. It is also provided by way of Prophetic miracles, establishing compelling proof of their mission, their truth and to bolster delivery of the message. Notwithstanding this, the main purpose of *waḥy* is to inform us about 'religious' facts, such as the reporting of events from Allah, establishing the commands and prohibitions; relating information about the unseen and what is sacred as well as providing information concerning the day of judgement.

---

[35] *Qur'ān* 85: 16
[36] *Qur'ān* 21: 23

4 Islam is an intellectual creed

Islam is an intellectual creed from which emanates a complete system. The *Deen* of Islam therefore, is not just a spiritual belief on which a moral system is based and with which ritual acts of worship are associated. It is not just a 'religion' in the Western sense of the term. Rather it is a 'first principle'; a belief from which a system is derived; in English, it is called an ideology. Moreover, the Islamic ideology is a rational ideology because it is based on using reason and is built on the principle of sufficient reason. This principle necessitates the presence of an explanation or cause behind the existence of the whole universe. It answers the question: why does the universe exist in the first place? Such a *Deen* would not proceed except and until this fundamental issue is resolved. As will be seen throughout this present book, the Islamic ideology is a rational ideology and is the sole true ideology. The Islamic ideology is also a spiritual belief as it is based on having absolute faith and firm belief in the existence of Allah, the exalted. It is a belief that creation and the prerogative of command are matters that solely belong to Allah. In other words, He created the universe but neither did he step down, nor did He retire, high and exalted be Allah above such reprehensible opinions. He gives commands, makes prohibitions, sends messengers, reveals scripture, and enacts laws. This obviously contrasts and totally opposes all materialistic and atheistic creeds.

وَرَبُّكَ يَخْلُقُ مَا يَشَاءُ وَيَخْتَارُ مَا كَانَ لَهُمُ الْخِيَرَةُ سُبْحَانَ اللهِ وَتَعَالَى عَمَّا يُشْرِكُونَ

And your Lord creates and chooses whom He pleases; to choose is not theirs; glory be to Allah, and exalted be He above what they associate (with Him). [1]

Second, follows the necessity of recognising the connection between man and Allah, acknowledging it, submitting to Him who has made it an obligation, and rendering it the basis for all other relations, systems and legislation. In this respect, Islam is different and is in stark contrast to all secular, worldly and liberal sects. The Islamic ideology is also a political ideology, for its system encompasses all laws pertaining to life including subject-governor relationships, managing public affairs, and the relationship between nations.

By way of contrast, materialistic socialism is an ideology; it is an ideology from which a system is derived. According to the aforementioned definition, it is therefore, a *Deen*. The basic belief on which socialism is based is materialism, especially dialectical materialism, advanced by the so-called scientific socialists. With all its detailed sects, materialism is not a rational ideology, even if it so claims, for it is based on acknowledging the eternity of matter with its basic properties. That is to say, matter is 'necessarily existent', eternal and ancient, without the need to provide evidence thereto. The only aim of materialists is to attempt to sow the seeds of scepticism and to challenge the conclusive evidence that prove the existence of Allah. Such an ideology is, *a-priori*, a materialistic one, it can never be a spiritual one, for it denies the existence of anything other than matter, *a fortiori*, the existence of Allah. Concepts like spirituality, sacredness etc. have, evidently, no place in a materialist ideology.

---

[1] *Qur'ān* 28: 68

After a long period of gestation and development, liberal-democratic-capitalism became an ideology. This system is undoubtedly a '*Deen*.' Underpinning its core principles such as representative democracy, the rule of law, the separation of powers, the 'rights' of man (or human rights in modern parlance) etc., lies the core principle of secularism. Although there is variance in the application of this core tenet, it is held as being sacrosanct throughout the West. The ideological roots of this *Deen* developed over a long period time and were originally borne out of a schism within the Western Church. The Reformation in Europe and the subsequent wars of religion had the effect of fragmenting the religious uniformity of Christendom and ultimately gave rise to the concept of religious pluralism, toleration, and a view that religion should be kept apart from the practical aspects of governance and life. When it first emerged, secularism was merely a compromise, a set of incoherent procedures and agreements to solve the problem of this given conflict. But this was not the characteristic of an 'ideology' as it later became. This was followed by a sustained period where constitutional limits were placed upon monarchs. Man was no longer viewed as merely a subject of the monarch, or for that matter a pawn of the clergy, but as a citizen with rights that were based upon 'natural law' and reason. Against this backdrop, and subsequently very often through violent revolution, such as in the American colonies and France, philosophers, thinkers and men of capital, sought to redraw the political and economic framework.

The existence of God and revealed law lost centre stage as the philosophers and thinkers of this new era placed man at the centre of the universe. Man alone would decide for himself what system he would choose to live by. Providing the modern state did not encroach upon citizens cherished 'freedoms', man could pursue his own path to enlightenment and happiness. Even after this ideology developed, its central core remained irrational. Debate concerning the existence of God and His law became a matter only of personal conscience, not a burning issue that needed to be solved. Since such an ideology does not take the issue of Allah's existence into consideration, it is impossible for it to be a spiritual ideology.

Therefore to reiterate, it is imperative to distinguish between the following:

- What is and what is not a 'religious matter' i.e., the general law, and its related issues such as: civilisation, culture and special civilisation. A Muslim should not take any of these from a non-Muslim at all. It is impermissible to base them on anything other than the revealed texts.

- 'Worldly affairs' or affairs related to the perceptual world; its properties; laws; 'urbanisation' including science, crafts, professions etc. as well as the means and methods of regulating all permissible things, such as procedural systems and administrative regulations. All of these matters may be fearlessly and freely adopted and utilized from non-Muslims.

The ferocious attack on the Muslim world over the course of the last three-hundred years and the fact that most Muslim lands suffered from direct Western colonisation and imperialism, induce reactions of extreme anxiety. This reaction has prevented them from making use of general urbanisation elements, learning science, acquiring engineering or adopting administrative systems or procedures. Such reactions and agitation are mostly rooted in a spirit of defeatism that encourages people to assume defensive postures or to think negatively instead of being active and taking the initiative. The feeling of defeat coupled with an imprisoned ghetto frame of mind drives many Islamic activists and leaders to take defensive attitudes. They utter meaningless and terrible words that are more or less similar to those uttered by the crazy, deluded or insane. These two factors have also driven others to withdraw, retire from public life, despair of worldly life and invoke Allah for the quick advent of *'the awaited Mahdi.'*

To the discerning rational mind, looking into the lives of other nations, learning from their experiences, adopting their developed means and methods are not only logically correct, but a required facet of human progression. It is only logical that a person would make use of the available fruits and results, and then would focus efforts upon creativity in inventing countless matters anew, instead of mere mimicry, for this would only be re-inventing the wheel as the saying goes. However very often many minds completely overlook this point, coupled with the fact that it is in actuality, sanctioned by the legislative texts, as the following evidences will show. Imām Mālik recorded the following authentic tradition in his *Muwaṭṭā'*:

> عن محمّد بن عبد الرّحمن بن نوفل أنّه قال: أخبرني عروة ابن الزّبير عن عائشة أم المؤمنين عن جُدَامَة بنت وهب الأسديّة أنّها أخبرتها أنّها سمعت رسول الله، صلّى الله عليه وسلّم، يقول: لَقَدْ هَمَمْتُ أَنْ أَنْهَى عَنِ الْغِيلَةِ؛ حَتَّى ذَكَرْتُ أَنَّ الرُّومَ وَفَارِسَ يَصْنَعُونَ ذَلِكَ فَلاَ يَضُرُّ أَوْلاَدَهُمْ!، قال مالك: الْغِيلَةِ أن يمس الرجل امرأته وهي تُرضع
>
> From Muḥammad ibn Abdar-Raḥman ibn Nawfal that he said 'Urwa ibn az-Zubayr reported to me from 'Aisha, mother of the believers, that Judāma bint Wahb al-Asadiyya reported to her that she heard the Messenger of Allah (peace be upon him) say: *I intended to prohibit ghila but I remembered that the Greeks and Persians do that without it causing any injury to their children.* Mālik explained - *Ghila* is that a man has intercourse with his wife while she is breast-feeding.

Indeed, the *isnād* for this narration is *Ṣaḥīḥ* as is its textual content. Several other notable *ḥadith* collectors cited this in their respective works, such as Imām Muslim in his *Ṣaḥīḥ*, Tirmidhi, and Abu Dāwud.

At this juncture, it is important to stress that we are not about to delve into an extensive discussion of 'Prophetic intentions' i.e., whether these intentions are infallible and in accordance with the truth, or they are according to human nature. It could be an intention for doing something right or for doing something false; in which case Allah would prevent His Prophet (peace be upon him) from doing, saying or acknowledging something that arises from such a false intention. Rather than dwell upon the matter, the reader should refer to the research entitled *Hamm-ul-Anbiya'* (Intentions of the Prophets). That work conclusively sets out the evidences to show that the Prophet's concerns are not infallible, and thus, these intentions cannot be taken as the basis of making a legal argument. It could be an intention for doing something right or for doing something false; in which case, Allah would prevent His Prophet (peace be upon him) from doing, saying or acknowledging something that arises from such a false intention. Allah, the most glorified and most sublime, would prevent the Prophet (peace be upon him) in the manner He so wishes. He would either cause to dispel the intention so that the Prophet (peace be upon him) would no longer have the will or the determination to carry out the intended deed, He would send down a revelation preventing the Prophet (peace be upon him) from carrying it out, or inspire him with an alternate judgment. Allah, the almighty and all-wise may dissuade him in any other manner He wishes.

In the aforementioned incident, Allah the exalted prevented His Prophet (peace be upon him) from his *intended* act to prohibit men from having intercourse with their wives who are breast-feeding mothers for fear that it might do harm to their infants. He, most glorified and most sublime, diverted his attention inspiring him to look into the conditions of other peoples and learn from their experience, which situated this particular incident. He saw that whole nations practiced this over long periods of time without any harm being done to their infants. The Prophet (peace be upon him) had only intended by this prohibition to maintain the health of infants and avoid any harm that may be done to them, which is a matter that can be directly conceived by perception and reason. Therefore, it may be possible to look into the experience of other peoples, be they believers or unbelievers, pagans or people of the Scripture. Thus, it is even more possible to examine the confirmed and documented findings of scientific and medical research to solve the issue. That was what Allah inspired His Prophet (peace be upon him). All praises be to Allah, there is no God but Him, on whom we depend entirely and whose help we seek.

The Prophet (peace be upon him) did not only look into the experiences of other people, but he also guided others to do the same. In other words, he directed them to look into other nations' experiences and confirmed documented findings of scientific and medical results. Imām Muslim records the next tradition in his *Ṣaḥīḥ* which substantiates this point:

> حدثني محمد بن عبد الله بن نمير وزهير بن حرب واللفظ لابن نمير قالا حدثنا عبد الله بن يزيد المقبري حدثنا حيوة حدثني عياش بن عباس أن أبا النضر حدثه عن عامر بن سعد أن أسامة بن زيد أخبر والده سعد بن أبي وقاص أن رجلا جاء إلى رسول الله صلى الله عليه وسلم فقال إني أعزل عن امرأتي فقال له رسول الله صلى الله عليه وسلم لم تفعل ذلك فقال الرجل أشفق على ولدها أو على أولادها فقال رسول الله صلى الله عليه وسلم لو كان ذلك ضارا ضر فارس والروم و قال زهير في روايته إن كان لذلك فلا ما ضار ذلك فارس ولا الروم

> Muḥammad ibn Abdullah ibn Numayr and Zuhayr ibn Ḥarb narrated to me, and (this is) the wording of Ibn Numayr, they said Abdullah bin Yazeed al-Maqboori narrated to us Ḥaywat narrated to us 'Ayyāsh bin 'Abbās narrated to us that Abu Naḍr narrated to him from 'Aāmir bin Sa'eed that Usama bin Zayd reported to his father Sa'd ibn Abi Waqqās that a man came to the Messenger of Allah (peace be upon him) and said: I do '*coitus interuptus*' with my wife. Thereupon Allah's Messenger (peace be upon him) said: *Why do you do that?* The person said: I fear harm to her child or her children. Thereupon Allah's Messenger (peace be upon him) said: *If that were harmful it*

> *would (also) harm the Persians and the Greeks.* Zuhayr bin Ḥarb said in the same transmission - *If such was the case, this harmed neither the Persians nor the Romans.*

Similar *aḥādith* are also reported in other collections, such as in the *Musnad* of Aḥmad,[2] *Mu'jam al-Awsaṭ* of Imām aṭ-Ṭabarāni,[3] in the *Sunan al-Kubra* of Imām Bayhaqy,[4] as well as others. All of these transmissions are authentic and similar to the *ḥadith* of Zuhayr as reported in Muslim.

Given this, emphasis must be placed upon the reported statement of the Prophet (peace be upon him) in this authentic tradition – '*If that were harmful it would (also) harm the Persians and the Greeks.*' This implies what has been mentioned previously, yet in this situation, he was teaching the questioner. Thus the exhortation of looking into the lives of other people, learning from their experiences, adopting their developed means and methods is not only rationally correct, but it is also Islamically permissible; this has undoubtedly been established, all praises be to Allah, the Lord of the worlds. This was the same attitude adopted by the rightly guided Caliphs according to the consensus of all the Companions. For example, they adopted the different military tactics and stratagems of their respective age. They also used different methods of irrigation and drainage found in Iraq and benefited from administrative regulations and procedures pertaining to various methods and means. They even did not see any harm in leaving most *diwans* (official recorders) to use languages other than Arabic. In fact, all *diwans* were Arabized much later in the Umayyad reign. All this happened with nobody disputing or dissenting and without any discussion of any relevance.

At this juncture a reminder must be made, to advise ourselves and

---

[2] *Musnad* Aḥmad Vol. 5 sec. 203, no. 21,828
[3] *Mu'jam al-Awsaṭ* Vol. 1 sec. 65, no. 182
[4] *Sunan al-Kubra* Vol. 7 sec. 465, no. 15,463

all who call to Allah in this last age of ours to rise above such reactionary fervor as they try to lead man from one false attitude to another, and the latter could be even worse than the former. This was the disaster that befell the *Khawārij,* a reaction for remissness and negligence, most of which was minor and little of which was major. It then mushroomed into excessiveness and apostasy, which is an utterly devastating and damaging affair. It is much worse than any of the original remissness and negligence. An example of such an obsessive and extremist attitude can be found in what Shaykh Abdul Qādir ibn Abdul-Aziz mentioned in his book *al-Jāmi' fi Ṭalab al-'Ilm ash-Shareef* under the title of *'The Innovation of (the) man-made constitution.'*[5] The Shaykh wrote:

> As mentioned briefly before, man-made constitutions are derived from the bad fruits of evil secularism, which is considered the modern era of *Jāhiliyyah* (ignorance) after the pre-Islamic. The unbelievers have set down such constitutions because they have no sound religion or straight law to which they can refer. They were plagued by the perverted statutes which rabbis and monks altered as they wished and according to clerical synods. This made the unbelievers agree to set down books that fulfilled their interests as much as limited human reason can perceive. These books are the constitutions to which they refer as if they were divine scriptures…

Without question this is a deplorable statement and it becomes even more deplorable when made by a man like Shaykh Abdul Qādir ibn Abdul-Aziz, who is a good seeker of religious knowledge, whose good intentions, loyalty, and opposition toward tyrannical regimes, leaders of disbelief and misguidance, that currently dominate the Muslim world, is not doubted. It is even worse when seen in light of the *Ṣaḥeefa-tul-Madina* (the constitution or charter of the city of Medina).

---

[5] *al-Jāmi' fi Ṭalab al-'Ilm ash-Shareef* Vol. 2, p.778

The story of how it was written in its entirety has been proven and is authentic. It is in fact a '*constitution*' in the modern sense of the term. It may well in fact be the first constitution, as described thoroughly in our book entitled: *Obedience to the rulers – Limits and Restrictions*. If this well-known fact, together with the above set of proofs and discussion are taken into consideration, this will necessarily result in an important awareness that constitutional documents are good and desirable. They are not bad or evil innovations, contrary to Shaykh Abdul Qādir's flawed and obsessed opinion. His previous statement was a reaction to the ferocious secular attack on Islam. That is why the Sheikh reacted against an extreme with an extreme, but the true *Deen* of Allah is a middle-path between going to extremes and being misguided.

Rather than rubbish the matter as an evil innovation, everybody should consider very carefully all the Islamic draft resolutions and draft bills enacted during the past century, then adopt the strongest and the most accurately worded amongst them, complete the missing points and come out with a revised strengthened draft that can be taken as a constitution and a basis for an Islamic political entity, when established – Allah willing. In so doing, it will do no harm to benefit from the jurisprudential and legal formulae of wording used by other people especially that found in the West, as they have attained a high level of efficiency in this area.

By contrast, Islamic jurisprudence has stagnated and deteriorated after having been so vibrant for so long. Jurisprudential and legal formulae did not develop in Islamic law beyond giving judgments, some jurisprudential rules and studying similar and corresponding issues, and the like. On the other hand, Western jurisprudence took great steps toward formulating jurisprudential theories, such as tort. All these formulae form a bulk of means and methods. They have nothing to do with the legislation itself as a referential authority. They are not in any way related to questions like who is the sovereign or who can initiate legislation. Rather they are related to how a jurist formulates the judgments he deduces; what are the best methods of analysis, composition, and classification and arrangement etc. Therefore, there is no harm in adopting those methods regardless of their source as they can retain their fidelity to Allah's guidance.

5 The Definition of Islam

Al-Islam is the *Deen* that has been revealed and sent down from Allah, the one and only deity, the exalted and majestic, upon the final Prophet and Messenger, Muḥammad (peace and blessings be upon him). It is the last and final *Deen* which places a seal upon everything prior to it; all that was revealed prior to this is completely abrogated by the advent of this message. The present *Deen* is the sole determiner of what is considered right and wrong, nothing will therefore be accepted by Allah unless it is in accordance with its precepts and one cannot attain salvation in the afterlife by other than it. The foundation of Islam, its fundamental principles and its solid constituents are based upon the testimony that there is no god/deity except Allah and that Muḥammad is the Messenger of Allah.

Within the language, the word 'al-Islam' means complete and total submission. That is the very essence of al-Islam, namely: obedience to Allah in total and absolute submission and surrender, based upon the firm acknowledgement of his prerogative of command (*al-ḥākimiyyah*); to his final supreme sovereignty. In truth by his very essence, he has the ultimate and absolute right for ordering and forbidding, for declaring matters as being obliged or prohibited, unconditionally (albeit on the proviso against what he has obliged upon himself or forbidden himself from). That is because he is 'Allah' and there is without doubt no other god/deity; he is the one, the only; the ever-living, the self-subsisting; originator of the heavens and the earth, lord of all creation. He does as he wills, having mastery over everything; he creates as he wills and chooses and his knowledge encompasses all. And there has to be disbelief in all others considered as lords, rivals, oppressors and everything of that type. Allah the exalted and majestic has said:

وَمَن يَبْتَغِ غَيْرَ الْإِسْلَامِ دِينًا فَلَن يُقْبَلَ مِنْهُ وَهُوَ فِي الْآخِرَةِ مِنَ الْخَاسِرِينَ

And whoever desires a Deen other than Islam it shall not be accepted from him and in the hereafter he shall be one of the losers.[1]

إِنَّ الدِّينَ عِندَ اللَّهِ الْإِسْلَامُ وَمَا اخْتَلَفَ الَّذِينَ أُوتُوا الْكِتَابَ إِلَّا مِن بَعْدِ مَا جَاءَهُمُ الْعِلْمُ بَغْيًا بَيْنَهُمْ وَمَن يَكْفُرْ بِآيَاتِ اللَّهِ فَإِنَّ اللَّهَ سَرِيعُ الْحِسَابِ

Surely the (true) Deen with Allah is Islam, and those to whom the Book had been given did not show opposition but after knowledge had come to them, out of envy among themselves; and whoever disbelieves in the communications of Allah then surely Allah is quick in reckoning.[2]

وَوَصَّىٰ بِهَا إِبْرَاهِيمُ بَنِيهِ وَيَعْقُوبُ يَا بَنِيَّ إِنَّ اللَّهَ اصْطَفَىٰ لَكُمُ الدِّينَ فَلَا تَمُوتُنَّ إِلَّا وَأَنتُم مُّسْلِمُونَ

And the same did Ibrāhim enjoin on his sons and (so did) Ya'qub. O my sons! Surely Allah has chosen for you (this) faith, therefore die not unless you are Muslims.[3]

يَا أَيُّهَا الَّذِينَ آمَنُوا اتَّقُوا اللَّهَ حَقَّ تُقَاتِهِ وَلَا تَمُوتُنَّ إِلَّا وَأَنتُم مُّسْلِمُونَ

---

[1] *Qur'ān* 3: 85
[2] *Qur'ān* 3: 19
[3] *Qur'ān* 2: 132

O you who believe! Be mindful of (your duty to) Allah with the care which is due to Him, and do not die unless you are Muslims. [4]

فَإِنْ حَاجُّوكَ فَقُلْ أَسْلَمْتُ وَجْهِيَ لِلَّهِ وَمَنِ اتَّبَعَنِ وَقُل لِّلَّذِينَ أُوتُوا الْكِتَابَ وَالْأُمِّيِّينَ أَأَسْلَمْتُمْ فَإِنْ أَسْلَمُوا فَقَدِ اهْتَدَوا وَّإِن تَوَلَّوْا فَإِنَّمَا عَلَيْكَ الْبَلَاغُ وَاللَّهُ بَصِيرٌ بِالْعِبَادِ

But if they dispute with you, say: I have submitted myself entirely to Allah and everyone who follows me; and say to those who have been given the Book and the unlearned people: Do you submit yourselves? So if they submit then indeed they follow the right way; and if they turn back, then upon you is only the delivery of the message and Allah sees the servants. [5]

وَأَنِيبُوا إِلَىٰ رَبِّكُمْ وَأَسْلِمُوا لَهُ مِن قَبْلِ أَن يَأْتِيَكُمُ الْعَذَابُ ثُمَّ لَا تُنصَرُونَ

And return to your Lord time after time and submit to Him before there comes to you the punishment, then you shall not be helped. [6]

حُرِّمَتْ عَلَيْكُمُ الْمَيْتَةُ وَالدَّمُ وَلَحْمُ الْخِنزِيرِ وَمَا أُهِلَّ لِغَيْرِ اللَّهِ بِهِ وَالْمُنْخَنِقَةُ وَالْمَوْقُوذَةُ وَالْمُتَرَدِّيَةُ وَالنَّطِيحَةُ وَمَا أَكَلَ السَّبُعُ إِلَّا مَا ذَكَّيْتُمْ وَمَا ذُبِحَ عَلَى النُّصُبِ وَأَن تَسْتَقْسِمُوا بِالْأَزْلَامِ ذَٰلِكُمْ فِسْقٌ الْيَوْمَ يَئِسَ الَّذِينَ كَفَرُوا مِن دِينِكُمْ فَلَا تَخْشَوْهُمْ وَاخْشَوْنِ الْيَوْمَ أَكْمَلْتُ لَكُمْ دِينَكُمْ وَأَتْمَمْتُ عَلَيْكُمْ نِعْمَتِي وَرَضِيتُ لَكُمُ الْإِسْلَامَ دِينًا فَمَنِ اضْطُرَّ فِي مَخْمَصَةٍ غَيْرَ مُتَجَانِفٍ لِّإِثْمٍ فَإِنَّ اللَّهَ غَفُورٌ رَّحِيمٌ

Forbidden to you is that which dies of itself, and blood, and flesh of swine, and that on which any other name than that of Allah has been invoked, and the strangled (animal) and that beaten to death, and that killed by a fall and that killed by being smitten with the horn, and that which wild beasts have eaten, except what you slaughter, and what is sacrificed on stones set up (for idols) and that you divide by the arrows; that is a transgression. This day have those who disbelieve despaired of your Deen, so fear them not, and fear Me. This day have I perfected for you your Deen and completed My favour on

---

[4] *Qur'ān* 3: 102
[5] *Qur'ān* 3: 20
[6] *Qur'ān* 39: 54

you and chosen for you Islam as a religion; but whoever is compelled by hunger, not inclining wilfully to sin, then surely Allah is Forgiving, Merciful.[7]

The words 'Islam' and '*Muslimeen*' have been used in relation to the previous religions, an example of which can be found in the following verse in relation to the Torah, where the exalted has expressed the following:

إِنَّا أَنزَلْنَا التَّوْرَاةَ فِيهَا هُدًى وَنُورٌ يَحْكُمُ بِهَا النَّبِيُّونَ الَّذِينَ أَسْلَمُوا لِلَّذِينَ هَادُوا وَالرَّبَّانِيُّونَ وَالْأَحْبَارُ بِمَا اسْتُحْفِظُوا مِن كِتَابِ اللَّهِ وَكَانُوا عَلَيْهِ شُهَدَاءَ فَلَا تَخْشَوُا النَّاسَ وَاخْشَوْنِ وَلَا تَشْتَرُوا بِآيَاتِي ثَمَنًا قَلِيلًا وَمَن لَّمْ يَحْكُم بِمَا أَنزَلَ اللَّهُ فَأُولَٰئِكَ هُمُ الْكَافِرُونَ

Surely We revealed the Torah in which was guidance and light; with it the Prophets who submitted themselves (to Allah) judged (matters) for those who were Jews, and the masters of Divine knowledge and the doctors, because they were required to guard (part) of the Book of Allah, and they were witnesses thereof; therefore fear not the people and fear Me, and do not take a small price for My communications; and whoever did not judge by what Allah revealed, those are they that are the unbelievers.[8]

Similar is also found in the verse that mentions Ya'qub and his sons, peace be upon them:

وَوَصَّىٰ بِهَا إِبْرَاهِيمُ بَنِيهِ وَيَعْقُوبُ يَا بَنِيَّ إِنَّ اللَّهَ اصْطَفَىٰ لَكُمُ الدِّينَ فَلَا تَمُوتُنَّ إِلَّا وَأَنتُم مُّسْلِمُونَ

And the same did Ibrāhim enjoin on his sons and (so did) Ya'qub. O my sons! Surely Allah has chosen for you (this) faith, therefore die not unless you are Muslims.[9]

---

[7] *Qur'ān* 5: 3
[8] *Qur'ān* 5: 44
[9] *Qur'ān* 2: 132

Allah the exalted has also said the following:

أَفَغَيْرَ دِينِ اللَّهِ يَبْغُونَ وَلَهُ أَسْلَمَ مَن فِي السَّمَاوَاتِ وَالْأَرْضِ طَوْعًا وَكَرْهًا وَإِلَيْهِ يُرْجَعُونَ

Is it then other than Allah's religion that they seek (to follow), and to Him submits whoever is in the heavens and the earth, willingly or unwillingly, and to Him shall they be returned. [10]

From these verses it can reasonably be established that the intended sense of 'Islam' and 'Muslim' is the original linguistic one, which is submission and surrender. Moreover, it is the complete submission to Allah alone, total submissiveness, surrender and subjection towards him. It is based upon the acknowledgment of Allah's firmly established *ḥākimiyah*, the final supreme sovereign authority. Only he, in truth, is the ultimate determiner of what is to be commanded or prohibited; only he has the prerogative of command absolutely, without condition or qualification. That is, except where he has placed a restriction or condition upon himself not to enact or undertake something. He is Allah, there is no god or deity except him. He is the one and only, the ever living (*al-Ḥay*), the self-existing (*al-Qayyum*), originator of the heavens and the earth, lord of all creation. He acts as he wills and holds dominion over everything; he creates whatever he wishes according to his choice and his knowledge encompasses all. With regards to any tyrants, partners or rivals that are set up either beside or in tandem with him, there is total disbelief in all of them.

All the previous Prophets and those who believed in them and followed them were upon that which is good and guidance; therefore, they were upon 'Islam' in a general sense. But this isn't the 'Islam' in a specific sense; in other words, that as we specifically know it – the complete *Deen*; with its detailed *Shari'āh* and doctrines as has been

---

[10] *Qur'ān* 3: 83

revealed upon the seal of the Prophets, Muhammad ibn Abdullah (peace and blessings be upon him). Given that he is the final seal of Prophethood, there is no 'Islam' in its general sense anymore; rather there is only the Islam as set out and revealed to him and thereunto us.

6 The meaning of 'there is no deity except Allah'

The meaning of 'there is no deity except Allah' is that there is nothing whatsoever that has the attributes of divinity (*al-Uluhiyah*). It relates to him having the ability by his divine-self for action; acting independently in an absolute way, without need or recourse to others. In particular, this can be said of acts such as the initiation of creation from nothing, with its resultant follow-on of fashioning, imaging, configuring, managing, not least to say compelling this into existence through divine will. He alone has the prerogative of command, in origin to command and prohibit. Such action is by way of complete freedom, without any condition. There is nothing by necessity or by the necessity of reason compelling him to act, for in truth he is the only deity. He is the self-subsistent, or stated alternatively, the necessarily existent; acting by his express will and self, rich without any dependence. His knowledge is complete, all-encompassing; whatever he desires to be, that is what will be. Whatever he doesn't wish to be, will not therefore come to pass, for there is nothing that is characterized by such qualities except Allah. Even if anyone attributes any of these qualities to other than Allah, it will be a manifest lie, slander, false imagination, or an illusion that has nothing to do with the actual reality. Allah the exalted and majestic states:

ذَلِكَ بِأَنَّ اللَّهَ هُوَ الْحَقُّ وَأَنَّ مَا يَدْعُونَ مِن دُونِهِ هُوَ الْبَاطِلُ وَأَنَّ اللَّهَ هُوَ الْعَلِيُّ الْكَبِيرُ

That is because Allah is the truth and that what they call upon besides him, that is falsehood; because Allah is the high, the great.[1]

ذَلِكَ بِأَنَّ اللَّهَ هُوَ الْحَقُّ وَأَنَّ مَا يَدْعُونَ مِن دُونِهِ الْبَاطِلُ وَأَنَّ اللَّهَ هُوَ الْعَلِيُّ الْكَبِيرُ

This is because Allah is the truth, and that which they call upon besides him is the falsehood, and that Allah is the high, the great.[2]

فَاعْلَمْ أَنَّهُ لَا إِلَهَ إِلَّا اللَّهُ وَاسْتَغْفِرْ لِذَنبِكَ وَلِلْمُؤْمِنِينَ وَالْمُؤْمِنَاتِ وَاللَّهُ يَعْلَمُ مُتَقَلَّبَكُمْ وَمَثْوَاكُمْ

So know that there is no god but Allah and ask protection for your fault and for the believing men and women. Allah knows the place of your abiding.[3]

Moreover, the meaning behind 'there is no deity/god except Allah' is illustrated by his words where he states:

أَلَا لَهُ الْخَلْقُ وَالْأَمْرُ تَبَارَكَ اللَّهُ رَبُّ الْعَالَمِينَ

...surely his is the creation and the command; blessed is Allah, lord of all creation.[4]

There is also the statement which Allah informs us that in relation to the Prophet Yusuf (peace be upon him), conveying the meaning behind 'there is no deity/god except Allah' in the following verse:

---

[1] *Qur'ān* 22: 62
[2] *Qur'ān* 31: 30
[3] *Qur'ān* 47: 19
[4] *Qur'ān* 7: 54

مَا تَعْبُدُونَ مِن دُونِهِ إِلاَّ أَسْمَاء سَمَّيْتُمُوهَا أَنتُمْ وَآبَآؤُكُم مَّا أَنزَلَ اللّهُ بِهَا مِن سُلْطَانٍ إِنِ الْحُكْمُ إِلاَّ لِلّهِ أَمَرَ أَلاَّ تَعْبُدُواْ إِلاَّ إِيَّاهُ ذَلِكَ الدِّينُ الْقَيِّمُ وَلَـكِنَّ أَكْثَرَ النَّاسِ لاَ يَعْلَمُونَ

You do not worship besides him but names which you have named, you and your fathers; Allah has not sent down any authority for them; the ḥukm belongs to none but Allah. He has commanded that you shall not serve any but him; this is the right Deen but most people don't know.[5]

Pillars underpinning the testimony of faith (Shahāda)

Firstly, to completely reject the notion that any particle, substance, be that referred to as nature or the universe, holds any of the characteristics of divinity, except Allah the exalted. Specifically relating to the acts of creation, configuring, fashioning; apportioning the correct measure, benefit, harm and the like. Coupled together with the complete free will and ability of choice in determining these matters, as well as the knowledge of its proportionality. The proof of all these attributes, in totality, to the utmost beauty and perfection belongs to Allah the exalted. At the apex of this together with *ḥākimiyah*: the ultimate, final supreme sovereignty. In other words, only he – the exalted and magnificent, has prerogative of command, the ultimate choice in determining what is to be commanded or prohibited. He alone retains this by his very self or essence, with no partner.

Secondly, is the absolute, complete rejection and denial that anything from divinity can be given to other than Allah. That rejection is for all perceived gods/deities besides Allah, or for that matter, every lord (*rabb*) beside Allah. There must be complete disbelief in all that, because that disbelief here also encompasses disavowal and rejection. Allah the exalted and majestic has expressly stated:

[5] *Qur'ān* 12: 40

لاَ إِكْرَاهَ فِي الدِّينِ قَد تَّبَيَّنَ الرُّشْدُ مِنَ الْغَيِّ فَمَنْ يَكْفُرْ بِالطَّاغُوتِ وَيُؤْمِن بِاللهِ فَقَدِ اسْتَمْسَكَ بِالْعُرْوَةِ الْوُثْقَىَ لاَ انفِصَامَ لَهَا وَاللهُ سَمِيعٌ عَلِيمٌ

There is no compulsion in Deen; truth stands clear from error. Therefore whoever disbelieves in Ṭāghut and believes in Allah has grasped the firmest handle that doesn't break and Allah is hearing, knowing.[6]

And he has said of Ibrāhim (peace be upon him) while praising him specifically that:

وَإِذْ قَالَ إِبْرَاهِيمُ لِأَبِيهِ وَقَوْمِهِ إِنَّنِي بَرَاءٌ مِّمَّا تَعْبُدُونَ ، إِلَّا الَّذِي فَطَرَنِي فَإِنَّهُ سَيَهْدِينِ

And when Ibrāhim said to his father and his people, surely I am clear of what you worship. Save him who created me for surely he will guide me.[7]

There is also what has been authentically reported from the Messenger of Allah (peace and blessings be upon him), where he said:

من قال لا إله إلاّ الله، وكفر بما يُعبد من دون الله، حَرُمَ ماله وَدمُهُ، وحِسابه على الله عزّ وجلّ

Whoever testifies that there is no deity except Allah, and he disbelieves in whatever is worshipped besides Allah, his property and blood become inviolable, and it is for Allah the exalted and majestic to call him to account.

Consequently, the testimony of faith, *ash-Shahāda*, has two aspects: an affirmation that all qualities and characteristics which pertain to divinity belong solely to Allah, the almighty. The negation is to categorically deny that any of these divine qualities and characteristics

[6] *Qur'ān* 2: 256
[7] *Qur'ān* 43: 26/27

reside anywhere else. There is no being in existence other than Allah to whom these apply. Furthermore, it is to disbelieve in every *ṭawāgheet* – in every false deity, evil, and exorbitant tyranny. Without this specific affirmation and rejection, there is no Islam and no salvation in the hereafter.

7 The meaning of 'Muhammad is the Messenger of Allah'

The latter half of the proclamation relates to Muḥammad (peace and blessings be upon him) being the conveyer of Allah's truth and words, in a manner that is completely free of anything missing or added, as well as any form of error, lie or forgetfulness. The Prophet (peace be upon him) does not forget, but rather *he is made to forget*, so as to set for his nation Prophetic traditions pertaining to forgetfulness. As Allah the exalted has lucidly explained:

سَنُقْرِئُكَ فَلا تَنْسَى إِلَّا مَا شَاءَ اللَّهُ إِنَّهُ يَعْلَمُ الْجَهْرَ وَمَا يَخْفَى

We will make you recite so you shall not forget; except what Allah pleases, surely he knows the manifest and what is hidden.[1]

He is the best leader, the exemplar, the ideal to be followed. Neither does he speak of his own desire nor does he utter except that which is true. He never says anything except out of the knowledge that Allah

[1] *Qur'ān* 87: 6/7

has bestowed upon him or wishes to proceed ahead of his Lord. If he is asked about something new, he remains silent and waits until the divine ruling is revealed to him. He is simply a conveyer of Allah's truth and words, so he does not practice *ijtihād* (independent legal-juristic reasoning). He neither needs it nor did he practice it, for Allah has elevated him high above the need for that. But Allah gave honour and mercy to anyone of his nation who practices independent legal reasoning – whether or not the practice results in a sound or an erroneous judgement. He who reaches a sound judgment receives a double reward or more, whereas he who reaches an erroneous judgment receives a single reward for his effort.

To put the matter more expressly, we would say about him (peace be upon him), that he has no need or requirement to resort to *ijtihād* (independent legal juristic reasoning). There is no requirement for him to exercise substantive effort in undertaking the process that scholars from his nation are required to do to reach a legal judgement. He has no need or requirement to seek to deduce legal rulings from the detailed evidences. Therefore the meaning of '*Muḥammad is the Messenger of Allah'* is that none has the right to be followed except the Messenger of Allah (peace be upon him). Others beside the Messenger of Allah (peace be upon him) are not to be followed or obeyed *except by virtue of an established evidential command.* He who follows something without such evidence will be following falsehood. Even the following in permissible matters requires a proof, for permissibility is considered a 'legal ruling'. The following in permissible or 'optional rulings' is the same as the following in other legal rulings including the obligatory, the recommended, the undesirable, and the prohibited. This is similar to the following in so-called positive rulings including: cause, condition, allowance, easement, restriction, validity, invalidity and incorrectness. The legal ruling of such optional deeds performed by human beings cannot be identified except by means of a legal proof – no matter what the deed is. As for the deeds people perform by their own free will and determination during the pre-Islamic period and before the establishment of any legal proofs or authority, they are neither mandatory nor permissible. Permissibility is a legal ruling established by way of revelation.

Allah has set out some definitive parameters regarding obedience to the commissioned Prophets and Messengers, including the Prophet Muḥammad (peace be upon him) as per the following verses:

فَلاَ وَرَبِّكَ لاَ يُؤْمِنُونَ حَتَّىَ يُحَكِّمُوكَ فِيمَا شَجَرَ بَيْنَهُمْ ثُمَّ لاَ يَجِدُواْ فِي أَنفُسِهِمْ حَرَجاً مِّمَّا قَضَيْتَ وَيُسَلِّمُواْ تَسْلِيماً

But no! By your Lord! They do not believe until they make you a judge of that which has become a matter of disagreement among them, and then do not find any resistance in their hearts as to what you have decided and submit with complete submission.[2]

وَمَا كَانَ لِمُؤْمِنٍ وَلَا مُؤْمِنَةٍ إِذَا قَضَى اللَّهُ وَرَسُولُهُ أَمْراً أَن يَكُونَ لَهُمُ الْخِيَرَةُ مِنْ أَمْرِهِمْ وَمَن يَعْصِ اللَّهَ وَرَسُولَهُ فَقَدْ ضَلَّ ضَلَالاً مُّبِيناً

And it behoves not a believing man and a believing woman that they should have any choice in their matter when Allah and His Messenger have decided a matter; and whoever disobeys Allah and His Messenger, he surely strays off a manifest straying.[3]

مَّنْ يُطِعِ الرَّسُولَ فَقَدْ أَطَاعَ اللّهَ وَمَن تَوَلَّى فَمَا أَرْسَلْنَاكَ عَلَيْهِمْ حَفِيظاً

Whoever obeys the Messenger, he has indeed obeyed Allah and whoever turns back, so we haven't sent you as a keeper over them.[4]

وَمَا أَرْسَلْنَا مِن رَّسُولٍ إِلاَّ لِيُطَاعَ بِإِذْنِ اللّهِ وَلَوْ أَنَّهُمْ إِذ ظَّلَمُواْ أَنفُسَهُمْ جَآؤُوكَ فَاسْتَغْفَرُواْ اللّهَ

[2] *Qur'ān* 4: 65
[3] *Qur'ān* 33: 36
[4] *Qur'ān* 4: 80

وَاسْتَغْفَرَ لَهُمُ الرَّسُولُ لَوَجَدُواْ اللّهَ تَوَّاباً رَّحِيماً

And We did not send any Messenger except that he should be obeyed by Allah's permission; and had they, when they were unjust to themselves, come to you and asked forgiveness of Allah and the Messenger had (also) asked forgiveness for them, they would have found Allah oft-returning merciful. [5]

إِلَّا بَلَاغاً مِّنَ اللَّهِ وَرِسَالَاتِهِ: وَمَن يَعْصِ اللَّهَ وَرَسُولَهُ فَإِنَّ لَهُ نَارَ جَهَنَّمَ خَالِدِينَ فِيهَا أَبَداً

(It is) only a deliverance of the message from Allah and whoever disobeys Allah and his Messenger; surely, he shall have the fire of hell to abide therein for eons. [6]

تِلْكَ حُدُودُ اللَّهِ وَمَن يُطِعِ اللَّهَ وَرَسُولَهُ يُدْخِلْهُ جَنَّاتٍ تَجْرِي مِن تَحْتِهَا الْأَنْهَارُ خَالِدِينَ فِيهَا وَذَٰلِكَ الْفَوْزُ الْعَظِيمُ، وَمَن يَعْصِ اللَّهَ وَرَسُولَهُ وَيَتَعَدَّ حُدُودَهُ يُدْخِلْهُ نَارًا خَالِدًا فِيهَا وَلَهُ عَذَابٌ مُّهِينٌ

These are Allah's limits, and whoever obeys Allah and His Messenger, He will cause him to enter gardens beneath which rivers flow, to abide in them; and this is the great achievement. And whoever disobeys Allah and His Messenger and goes beyond His limits, He will cause him to enter fire to abide in it, and he shall have an abasing chastisement. [7]

---

[5] *Qur'ān* 4: 64
[6] *Qur'ān* 72: 23
[7] *Qur'ān* 4: 13/14

8 The Grades of *Deen*

The specific arrangement or ordering for the grades of *Deen* comes from the famous authentic *ḥadith* of Jibreel in which the Prophet (peace be upon him) was reported to have said: '*That was Jibreel* (Gabriel) *he came to teach you the affairs pertaining to your Deen*.' As for its transmission, this is available in all the major collections, the narrative being transmitted upon the authority of Abu Hurayrah and Umar bin al-Khaṭṭāb (may Allah be pleased with them) appear in *Ṣaḥīḥ* Bukhāri and Muslim, whereas that reported by Ibn 'Abbās (may Allah be pleased with him) appears with an authentic *isnād* in the *Musnad* of Imām Aḥmad.

To proceed, as has been reported in *Ṣaḥīḥ* Muslim upon the authority of Abu Hurayrah (may Allah be pleased with him):

حدثني زهير بن حرب حدثنا جرير عن عمارة وهو ابن القعقاع عن أبي زرعة عن أبي هريرة قال قال رسول الله صلى الله عليه وسلم سلوني فهابوه أن يسألوه فجاء رجل فجلس عند ركبتيه فقال يا رسول الله ما الإسلام قال لا تشرك بالله شيئا وتقيم الصلاة وتؤتي الزكاة وتصوم رمضان قال صدقت قال يا رسول الله ما الإيمان قال أن تؤمن بالله وملائكته وكتابه ولقائه ورسله وتؤمن بالبعث وتؤمن بالقدر كله قال صدقت قال يا رسول

الله ما الإحسان قال أن تخشى الله كأنك تراه فإنك إن لا تكن تراه فإنه يراك قال صدقت قال يا رسول الله متى تقوم الساعة قال ما المسئول عنها بأعلم من السائل وسأحدثك عن أشراطها إذا رأيت المرأة تلد ربها فذاك من أشراطها وإذا رأيت الحفاة العراة الصم البكم ملوك الأرض فذاك من أشراطها وإذا رأيت رعاء البهم يتطاولون في البنيان فذاك من أشراطها في خمس من الغيب لا يعلمهن إلا الله ثم قرأ إن الله عنده علم الساعة وينزل الغيث ويعلم ما في الأرحام وما تدري نفس ماذا تكسب غدا وما تدري نفس بأي أرض تموت إن الله عليم خبير قال ثم قام الرجل فقال رسول الله صلى الله عليه وسلم ردوه علي فالتمس فلم يجدوه فقال رسول الله صلى الله عليه وسلم هذا جبريل أراد أن تعلموا إذ لم تسألوا

Zuhayr ibn Ḥarb narrated to me Jarir narrated to us from Umāra – and he is Ibn al-Qa'qā'ah – from Zura' from Abu Hurayrah he said that the Messenger of Allah (peace be upon him) said: *Ask me*, but they (the Companions) were too much overawed out of profound respect to ask. In the meanwhile a man came and sat near his knees and said: Messenger of Allah, what is Islam? To which he (the Prophet) replied: *To not associate anything with Allah, and establish the prayer, to pay the Zakāt and to fast in Ramaḍān.* (The questioner) said: You have spoken the truth. He (again) asked: Messenger of Allah, what is *al-'Imān*? He (the Prophet) said: That you believe in Allah, his angels, his Books, his meeting, his messengers, and that you believe in resurrection and that you believe in *al-Qadr* in its entirety. (The questioner) said: You have spoken the truth. He (again) asked: Messenger of Allah, what is *al-Iḥsān*? Upon this he (the Prophet) said: that you fear Allah as if you are seeing him, although you do not, but verily he sees you.

(The questioner) said: You have spoken the truth. He (further) asked: Messenger of Allah, when is the hour? (The Prophet) said: *The one who is being asked about it is no better informed than the inquirer himself. However I will narrate to you some of its signs: when you see a slave (woman) giving birth to her master, that is one of the signs of; when you see barefooted, naked, deaf and dumb kings of the earth that is one of its portents. And when you see the shepherds of black*

> *camels exult in buildings, that is one of its portents. The (hour) is one of the five things (wrapped) in the unseen; no one knows them except Allah.* Then (the Prophet) recited: *Verily Allah is he with whom alone is the knowledge of the hour and he it is who sends down the rain and knows that which is in the wombs and no person knows whatsoever he shall earn on morrow and a person knows not in whatsoever land he shall die. Verily Allah is all knowing, aware.*[1] (Abu Hurayrah) said: Then the person stood up and went on his way. The Prophet (peace be upon him) said: *Bring him back to me*. He was searched for, but they (the Companions) could not find him. The Messenger of Allah (peace be upon him) thereupon said: *He was Jibreel* (Gabriel) *and he wanted to teach you (things pertaining to religion) when you did not ask* (them yourselves).

Imām Muslim reports the same tradition in other parts of his *Ṣaḥīḥ*.[2] As one would expect, the narration is widely reported, appearing in many notable collections of *ḥadith*.[3] Imām Muslim reports the next tradition in his *Ṣaḥīḥ* upon the authority of Abdullah ibn Umar:[4]

> Abu Khaythama Zuhayr ibn Ḥarb narrated to me Waki' narrated to us from Kahmas from Abdullah bin Burayda from Yaḥya bin Ya'mar (*ḥawala*) and Ubaidallah bin Mu'ādth al-Anbari narrated to us and this is his narrative; my father narrated to me Kahmas narrated to us from Ibn Buraydah from Yaḥya bin Ya'mar he said: the first man who discussed *Qadr* in

[1] *Qur'ān* 31: 34

[2] *Ṣaḥīḥ* Muslim Vol. 1 sec. 39, no. 9 & Vol. 1 sec. 40, no. 9

[3] A sizeable number of references are detailed, amongst them: *Ṣaḥīḥ* Bukhāri Vol. 1 sec. 28, no. 50 and Vol. 4 sec. 1793, no. 4499, *Ṣaḥīḥ* Ibn Ḥibbān Vol. 1 sec. 376 no. 159, *Ṣaḥīḥ* Ibn Khuzayma Vol. 4 sec. 6, no. 2244, *Sunan* Ibn Mājah Vol. 1 sec. 25, no. 64 and Vol. 2 sec. 1343, no. 4044, *Musnad* Aḥmad Vol. 1 sec. 28, no. 191 and Vol. 2 sec. 426, no. 9497, *Muṣṣanaf* Abu Bakr ibn Abi Shayba Vol. 6 sec. 157, no. 30,309 and Vol. 7 sec. 502, no. 37,557.

[4] Given the length of the narrative the Arabic text has been omitted. The original text can be found in *Ṣaḥīḥ* Muslim Vol. 1 sec. 36, no. 8

Baṣra was Ma'bad al-Juhani. I along with Humayd bin Abdar-Raḥman al Ḥimyari set out for pilgrimage or for *Umrah* and said: Should it so happen that we come into contact with one of the Companions of the Messenger of Allah (peace be upon him) we shall ask him about what is talked about *taqdir*. Accidentally we came across Abdullah ibn Umar ibn al-Khaṭṭāb, while he was entering the *masjid*. My companion and I surrounded him. One of us (stood) on his right and the other stood on his left. I expected that my companion would authorize me to speak. I therefore said: Abu Abdar-Raḥman!

There have appeared some people in our land who recite the Qur'ān and pursue knowledge. And then after talking about their affairs, added: They (such people) claim that there is no such thing as *Qadr*. He (Ibn Umar) said: When you happen to meet such people tell them that I have nothing to do with them and they have nothing to do with me. And verily they are in no way responsible for my (belief). Abdullah ibn Umar swore by Him (the Lord) (and said): If any one of them had with him gold equal to the bulk of (the mountain) *Uhud* and spent it (in the way of Allah), Allah would not accept it unless he affirmed his faith in *Qadr*. He further said: My father (Umar ibn al-Khaṭṭāb) narrated to me: One day we were sitting in the company of Allah's Messenger (peace be upon him) when there appeared before us a man dressed in pure white clothes, his hair extraordinarily black. There were no signs of travel on him. None amongst us recognized him.

At last he sat with the Prophet (peace be upon him); he knelt before him placed his palms on his thighs and said: Muḥammad, inform me about al-Islam. The Messenger of Allah (peace be upon him) said: *Al-Islam is that you testify that there is no deity but Allah and that Muḥammad is the Messenger of Allah, and you establish prayer, pay Zakāt, observe the fast of Ramaḍān, and perform pilgrimage to the house if you are solvent enough (to bear the expense of) the journey*. He (the inquirer) said: You have spoken the truth. He (Umar ibn al-Khaṭṭāb) said: It amazed us that he would put the question and then he would himself verify the truth. He (the inquirer) said: Inform me about *'Imān* (faith). He (the Prophet) replied: *That you believe in Allah, in his angels, in his Books, in his Messengers, in the day of judgment, and you believe in al-Qadr, (both) its good and bad.* He (the inquirer) said: You have spoken the truth. He (the inquirer) again said: Inform me about *al-Iḥsān*. He (the Prophet) said: *That you worship Allah as if you are seeing Him, for though you don't see him, verily he sees you.* He (the enquirer) again said: Inform me about the hour. He (the Prophet) remarked: *One who is asked knows no more than the one who is inquiring (about it).* He (the inquirer) said: Tell me some of its indications. He (the Prophet) said: *That the slave-girl will give birth to her mistress and master; that you will find barefooted, destitute goat-herders vying with one another in the construction of magnificent buildings.*

He (the narrator, Umar ibn al-Khaṭṭāb) said: Then he (the inquirer) went on his way but I stayed with him (the Prophet) for a long while. He then, said to me: Umar, do you know who this inquirer was? I replied: Allah and his Messenger know best. He (the Prophet) remarked: *He was Jibreel and he came to you in order to instruct you in matters of Deen.*

Similarly, this narration is widely reported, appearing in many notable collections of *ḥadith.*[5] But the following narration which appears in the *Musnad* of Imām Aḥmad contains the following additional wording:[6]

Abu Nu'aym narrated to us Sufyān narrated to us from

[5] The cited references are listed as: *Ṣaḥīḥ* Muslim Vol. 1 sec. 39, no. 8, *Sunan* Nasā'i Vol. 8 sec. 101, no. 4990, *Sunan al-Kubra* Nasā'i Vol. 6 sec. 528, no. 11,721, *Ṣaḥīḥ* Ibn Khuzayma Vol. 4 sec. 128, no. 2504, *Sunan* Ibn Mājah Vol. 1 sec. 25, no. 63, *Musnad* Aḥmad Vol. 1 sec. 52, no. 367191, *Sunan al-Kubra* Bayhaqy Vol. 4 sec. 325, no. 8393 and *Muṣṣanaf* Abu Bakr ibn Abi Shayba Vol. 7 sec. 502, no. 37,558.

[6] Again, given the length of the narrative the Arabic text has been omitted. The original text can be found in *Musnad* Aḥmad Vol. 1 sec. 53, no. 374.

'Alqama bin Marthad from Sulaymān bin Burayda from Ibn Ya'mar, he said: I said to Ibn Umar: we travel to different countries and we meet people who say there is no *Qadr*. Ibn Umar said: if you meet them report to them that Abdullah bin Umar has nothing to do with them and they have nothing to do with him - three times. Then he began to narrate: whilst we were with the Messenger of Allah (peace be upon him), there came a man - and he described his appearance. The Messenger of Allah (peace be upon him) said: *come closer*; so he came closer. He (again) said: *come closer,* so he came closer. (Then again) he said: *come closer,* so he came closer until his knees were nearly touching (the Prophet's knees). Then he said - O Messenger of Allah report to me what *'Imān* is - or about *'Imān*.

He (the Prophet) said: *To believe in Allah, his angels, his books, his Messengers, the last day and to believe in al qadr.* Sufyān said: I think he said: (both) *its good and its bad.* He said: So what is Islam? He (the Prophet) said: *To establish prayer, pay zakāt, perform pilgrimage to the house, to fast Ramaḍān and to perform ghusl in the case of janābah* (major ritual impurity) – *all of that.* For all of that he (the stranger) said: You have spoken the truth, you have spoken the truth. The people said - we never saw any man show more respect to the Messenger of Allah (peace be upon him) than this man did. It was as if he was teaching the Messenger of Allah (peace be upon him). Then he said: O Messenger of Allah report to me about *al-Iḥsān*. He (the Prophet) said: *It is to worship Allah as if you see him - for even if you do not see him, verily he sees you.*

For all of that we said - we never saw any man show more respect to the Messenger of Allah (peace be upon him) than this man did; he said you are right, you are right. He said: report to me about the hour. He (the Prophet) said: *The one who is asked about it does not know more about it than the one who is asking.* He said: you have spoken the truth, which he said several times and we never saw any man show more respect to

> the Messenger of Allah (peace be upon him) than this man did. Then he left. Sufyān said: I heard that the Messenger of Allah (peace be upon him) said: *look for him*, but they did not find him. He said: *That was Jibreel who came to you to teach you your Deen. He never came to me in any form but I recognised him, except for this form.*

A similar narration in terms of wording to that of Imām Aḥmad appears in the *Muṣṣanaf* of Abu Bakr ibn Abi Shayba, albeit via a different channel.

> حَدَّثَنَا ابْنُ فُضَيْلٍ عَنْ عَطَاءِ بْنِ السَّائِبِ عَنْ مُحَارِبِ بْنِ دِثَارٍ عَنِ ابْنِ بُرَيْدَةَ قَالَ: وَرَدْنَا الْمَدِينَةَ، فَأَتَيْنَا عَبْدَ اللهِ بْنَ عُمَرَ، فَقُلْنَا: يَا أَبَا عَبْدِ الرَّحْمَنِ، إِنَّا نُمْعِنُ فِي الأَرْضِ فَنَلْقَى قَوْمًا يَزْعُمُونَ أَنْ لاَ قَدَرَ، فَقَالَ: مِنَ الْمُسْلِمِينَ مِمَّنْ يُصَلِّي إِلَى الْقِبْلَةِ، قُلْنَا نَعَمْ مِمَّنْ يُصَلِّي إِلَى الْقِبْلَةِ، قَالَ: فَغَضِبَ حَتَّى وَدِدْت أَنِّي لَمْ أَكُنْ سَأَلْتُهُ، ثُمَّ قَالَ: إِذَا لَقِيت أُولَئِكَ فَأَخْبِرْهُمْ، أَنَّ عَبْدَ اللهِ بْنَ عُمَرَ مِنْهُمْ بَرِيءٌ وَأَنَّهُمْ مِنْهُ بُرَآءُ، ثُمَّ قَالَ: إِنْ شِئْتَ حَدَّثْتُك، عَنْ رَسُولِ اللهِ، صلى الله عليه وسلم، فقلت: أَجَلْ فَقَالَ: كُنَّا عِنْدَ رَسُولِ اللهِ، صلى الله عليه وسلم، فَأَتَاهُ رَجُلٌ جَيِّدُ الثِّيَابِ طَيِّبُ الرِّيحِ حَسَنُ الْوَجْهِ، فَقَالَ: يَا رَسُولَ اللهِ، مَا الإِسْلاَمُ، قَالَ رَسُولُ اللهِ، صلى الله عليه وسلم: تُقِيمُ الصَّلاَةَ وَتُؤْتِي الزَّكَاةَ وَتَصُومُ رَمَضَانَ وَتَحُجُّ الْبَيْتَ؛ وَتَغْتَسِلُ مِنَ الْجَنَابَةِ، قَالَ: صَدَقْت، فَمَا الإِيمَانُ، قَالَ رَسُولُ اللهِ، صلى الله عليه وسلم: تُؤْمِنُ بِاللهِ وَالْيَوْمِ الآخِرِ وَالْمَلاَئِكَةِ وَالْكِتَابِ وَالنَّبِيِّينَ وَبِالْقَدَرِ كُلِّهِ خَيْرِهِ وَشَرِّهِ وَحُلْوِهِ وَمُرِّهِ، قَالَ: صَدَقْت، ثُمَّ انْصَرَفَ، فَقَالَ رَسُولُ اللهِ، صلى الله عليه وسلم: عَلَيَّ بِالرَّجُلِ، قَالَ: فَقُمْنَا بِأَجْمَعِنَا فَلَمْ نَقْدِرْ عَلَيْهِ، فَقَالَ النَّبِيُّ، صلى الله عليه وسلم: هَذَا جِبْرِيلُ أَتَاكُمْ يُعَلِّمُكُمْ أَمْرُ دِينَكُمْ

> Ibn Fuḍeel narrated to us from ‘Aṭā bin as-Sā’ib from Muḥārib bin Dithār from Ibn Burayda he said we alighted back at Medina and came upon Abdullah ibn Umar, so we said to him - O Abu Abdar-Raḥman, indeed we meet people in the land and peoples who claim that there is no *Qadr*. He (Ibn Umar) said: from amongst the Muslims who pray towards the *Qibla*. We said: Yes, from those who pray towards the *Qibla*. He (the

> narrator) said: he was angered by this until (the point) I wish that I didn't ask him this. Thereafter he said: If you come across such people inform them that Abdullah ibn Umar has nothing to do with them and they have nothing to do with him. Then he said: If you would like, I (will) narrate to you from the Prophet (peace be upon him), so he said: We were with the Messenger of Allah when a man came very well dressed with a handsome face. He said - O Messenger of Allah, what is al-Islam? He (the Prophet) said: to establish the *Ṣalāh, to pay the Zakāt, to fast in Ramaḍān, to undertake pilgrimage to the house, and to perform ghusl from Janābah*. He (the questioner) said: You have spoken the truth. So what of *al-'Imān*? *The Prophet (peace be upon him) said: to believe in Allah and the final day; (to believe in) his angels, the book and the Prophets and al-Qadr, all of its good and bad, (and in) its sweetness and its bitterness.* He (the questioner) said: You have spoken the truth. He then departed. Upon which the Prophet (peace be upon him) said: *Recall this man* (to me). We looked but could not see him. Thus the Prophet (peace be upon him) said: *this (is) Jibreel, he came to you to teach you all the affairs of your Deen.*

Concerning this narrative there is no fear in relation to the 'mixing up' (*ikhtilāṭ*) resulting from 'Aṭā ibn as-Sā'ib, since Muḥammad bin Fuḍeel heard from him both before and after his *ikhtilāṭ*. Additionally there is no fear here either particularly given that it has also come via the channel of Shareek bin Abdullah al-Qāḍi and he is old in hearing from 'Aṭā. Imām an-Nasā'i also cites similarly in his *Sunan al-Kubra*, albeit again with some additional wording:

> Abu Dāwud reports, he said: Yazeed bin Hārun narrated to us he said Shareek reports from ar-Rakeen bin ar-Rabih' from Yaḥya bin Ya'mar and from 'Aṭā bin as-Sā'ib (from Muḥārib bin Dithār) from Ibn Burayda he said: we performed *Ḥajj* and *Umrah* and then came to Medina and came upon Ibn Umar. So

we asked him and said to him O Abu Abdar-Raḥman, indeed (during our) expeditions in this land we encounter people who say to our faces (there is) no *Qadr*. Then (Ibn Umar) said: if you meet with such people then note that Abdullah bin Umar has nothing to do with them or them with him. Thereafter he said: We were in the midst of the Messenger of Allah when a man came with a handsome face, well kept and a good fragrance. We wondered at such a man approaching upon the Messenger of Allah. Then he approached closer and said: Shall I come closer O Messenger of Allah? (The Prophet) said: Yes. (Ibn Umar) said: so we came closer (as well). Then he came closer. We were amazed by the veneration that he gave to the Prophet (peace be upon him). Then he said Shall I come closer O Messenger of Allah? (Ibn Umar) said: so we came closer (as well, as did he) until he put his thigh next to that of the Messenger of Allah (peace be upon him) and his leg was beside his.

He then said, O Messenger of Allah what is *al-'Imān*? He (the Prophet) said: *That you believe in Allah, his angels, books, Messengers and the final day; the resurrection after death and its accounting, and al-Qadr, (be it) its good, its bad and its sweetness and bitterness.* He (the questioner) said: You have spoken the truth; we wondered at his speech to the Prophet (peace be upon him), (as he said) you have spoken the truth. Then he said: O Messenger of Allah what is Islam? He (the Prophet) said: *You testify that there is no deity except Allah and that I and the Messenger of Allah; to establish the Ṣalāh, to pay the Zakāt, to fast in Ramaḍān and pilgrimage to the house; and to make ghusl from janābah.* He (the questioner) said: You have spoken the truth. We (were) amazed by his attestation of the truth before the Messenger of Allah (peace be upon him). Then he said: O Messenger of Allah what is *al-Iḥsān*? (The Prophet) said: *To fear Allah like you see him, though you don't see him, he sees you.* He (the questioner) said: You have spoken the truth. We (were) amazed by his attestation of the truth before the Messenger of Allah (peace be upon him). Thereafter he slipped away so the Messenger of Allah (peace be upon him) said bring this man to me. So we called for him but couldn't find him. The Messenger of Allah (peace be upon him) said: *This (was) Jibreel, he came to teach you all the affairs of your Deen.* And what never came to me except that I recognise him, but this image of him.

In *as-Sunan al-Kubra* Imām al-Bayhaqy reports the following narration with more complete wording:

أخبرنا علي بن محمد بن عبد الله بن بشران العدل ببغداد أنبأ أبو جعفر محمد بن عمرو بن البختري الرزاز حدثنا محمد بن عبيد الله بن يزيد حدثنا يونس بن محمد حدثنا معتمر هو بن سليمان عن أبيه عن يحيى بن يعمر قال قلت لابن عمر يا أبا عبد الرحمن إن قوما يزعمون أن ليس قدر قال فهل عندنا منهم أحد قال قلت لا قال فأبلغهم عني إذا لقيتهم أن بن عمر بريء إلى الله منكم وأنتم برئاء منه سمعت عمر بن الخطاب رضي الله عنه يقول بينما نحن جلوس عند رسول الله، صلى الله عليه وسلم، إذ جاء رجل عليه سحناء سفر وليس من أهل البلد يتخطى حتى ورك بين يدي رسول الله، صلى الله عليه وسلم، كما يجلس أحدنا في الصلاة ثم وضع يده على ركبتي رسول الله، صلى الله عليه وسلم، فقال يا محمد ما الإسلام قال أن تشهد أن لا إله إلا الله وأن محمدا رسول الله؛ وأن تقيم الصلاة؛ وتؤتي الزكاة؛ وتحج البيت وتعتمر؛ وتغتسل من الجنابة وتتم الوضوء؛ وتصوم رمضان قال فإن قلت هذا فأنا مسلم قال نعم قال صدقت؛... وذكر الحديث

Ali Muḥammad ibn Abdullah ibn Bishrān al-'Adl reported to us in Baghdad, Abu Ja'far ibn Muḥammad ibn 'Amr ibn al-Bukhtari ar-Razāz reports, Muḥammad bin 'Ubaidallah ibn Yazeed narrated to us Yunus bin Muḥammad narrated to us Mu'tamir, he is Ibn Sulaymān narrated to us from his father from Yaḥya bin Ya'mar he said: I said to Ibn Umar, O Abdar-Raḥman there are some people who conceive that there isn't *Qadr*, so are we one from among them? He (Ibn Umar) said: No. So, convey to them when you meet them that Ibn Umar, by Allah, has nothing to do with them and they nothing to do with him. I heard Umar bin al-Khaṭṭāb (may Allah be pleased

> with him) saying: while we were sitting with the Messenger of Allah (peace be upon him) a man came along without signs of travel and not from the people of the country, until he sat at the Prophet (peace be upon him), his thigh between his hands and he said: O Muḥammad, what is Islam? He (the Prophet) said: *That you testify that there is no deity but Allah and that Muḥammad is the Messenger of Allah; and that the Ṣalāh is established; the Zakāt is paid, pilgrimage to the house and Umrah, and performing ghusl from Janābah and completing the wuḍu'; and the fast of Ramaḍān.* He (the questioner) said: If I say this will I be Muslim? He (the Prophet) said: *Yes*. He (the questioner) said: You have spoken the truth, (then mentioned the *ḥadith*).

Thereafter Imām Bayhaqy said: 'It is reported by Muslim in the *Ṣaḥīḥ* from Ḥajjāj bin ash-Shā'ir from Yunus bin Muḥammad except that he did not take its (reported) wording.' It is also reported by Imām Dāraquṭni in his *Sunan*;[7] in *Ṣaḥīḥ* Ibn Khuzayma with the following channel – Abu Ya'qub Yusuf bin Wāḍih al-Hāshami narrated to us al-Mu'tamir bin Sulaymān narrated to us (etc).[8] Ibn Ḥibbān also cites this in his *Ṣaḥīḥ* from the channel of Ibn Khuzayma.[9]

Given the above, I would submit that performing *ghusl* from *Janābah* is proven from the aforementioned channels without any doubt, although this was not reported via the channels as set out by Imām Muslim. The full wording from the text thus resolutely confirms the pillar which is purification, *aṭ-Ṭahāra*, or at the very minimum, performing *ghusl* from *Janābah* and completing the *wuḍu'*, because it is a necessary condition to establish a legitimate *Ṣalāh*, thus establishing this inevitably as a stand-alone pillar by itself. In origin that has been established with certitude in the book of Allah:

---

[7] *Sunan* Dāraquṭni Vol. 2 sec. 283, no. 207

[8] *Ṣaḥīḥ* Ibn Khuzayma Vol. 1 sec. 4, no. 1

[9] *Ṣaḥīḥ* Ibn Ḥibbān Vol. 1 sec. 399, no. 173

يَا أَيُّهَا الَّذِينَ آمَنُوا إِذَا قُمْتُمْ إِلَى الصَّلَاةِ فَاغْسِلُوا وُجُوهَكُمْ وَأَيْدِيَكُمْ إِلَى الْمَرَافِقِ وَامْسَحُوا بِرُءُوسِكُمْ وَأَرْجُلَكُمْ إِلَى الْكَعْبَيْنِ وَإِنْ كُنْتُمْ جُنُبًا فَاطَّهَّرُوا وَإِنْ كُنْتُمْ مَرْضَى أَوْ عَلَى سَفَرٍ أَوْ جَاءَ أَحَدٌ مِنْكُمْ مِنَ الْغَائِطِ أَوْ لَامَسْتُمُ النِّسَاءَ فَلَمْ تَجِدُوا مَاءً فَتَيَمَّمُوا صَعِيدًا طَيِّبًا فَامْسَحُوا بِوُجُوهِكُمْ وَأَيْدِيكُمْ مِنْهُ مَا يُرِيدُ اللَّهُ لِيَجْعَلَ عَلَيْكُمْ مِنْ حَرَجٍ وَلَكِنْ يُرِيدُ لِيُطَهِّرَكُمْ وَلِيُتِمَّ نِعْمَتَهُ عَلَيْكُمْ لَعَلَّكُمْ تَشْكُرُونَ

O you who believe! When you stand for prayer, wash your faces and your hands as far as the elbows, and wipe your heads and your feet to the ankles; and if you are under an obligation to perform a total ablution, then wash (yourselves) and if you are sick or on a journey, or one of you come from the privy, or you have touched the women, and you cannot find water, betake yourselves to pure earth and wipe your faces and your hands therewith, Allah does not desire to put on you any difficulty, but He wishes to purify you and that He may complete his favour on you, so that you may be grateful.[10]

Also, there is what has been reported in the *Mu'jam* (*Mashkul*) of Ṭabarāni:

> Ḥussein bin Bihān al-'Askari narrated to us Sahl bin Uthmān narrated to us (*ḥawala*) and Muḥammad bin Ḥussein bin Mukram narrated to us al-Ḥasan bin Ḥammād Sajjādah narrated to us, they said: al-Muṭṭalib bin Ziyād ath-Thaqafi narrated to us from Manṣur bin al-Mu'tamir from 'Aṭā from Ibn Umar he said: A man came to Ibn Umar and said: O Abu Abdar-Raḥman, indeed we travel and meet people who say there is no *Qadr*. He said: If you meet with them inform them that Ibn Umar has nothing to do with them. We were with the Messenger of Allah when a handsome man with a handsome face came along, with a good fragrance and immaculate clothing. He said: peace to you O Messenger of Allah (peace be upon him), may I come closer to you? He (the Prophet): (you may) come closer. He came closer and we came closer as well, (saying) that a number of times until his knees were

[10] *Qur'ān* 5: 6

touching the Prophet's knees (peace be upon him).

He said: O Messenger of Allah, what is Islam? He (the Prophet) said: *Testifying that there is no deity except Allah and that Muḥammad is the Messenger of Allah. And to establish the Ṣalāh, pay the Zakāt, pilgrimage to the house and fasting in Ramaḍān and performing ghusl from Janābah.* He (the questioner) said: If I do that will I be Muslim. He (the Prophet) said: *Yes.* He (the questioner) said: You have spoken the truth (and continued to say), what of *al-'Imān*? He (the Prophet) said: *Al-'Imān is to believe in Allah, his angels, his books and Messengers and heaven and the fire (hell); the (the day of) judgement and al-Qadr – its good, bad, its sweetness and bitterness is from Allah.* He (the questioner) said: If I do that, will I be a believer (*mu'min*)? He (the Prophet) said: *Yes.* He (the questioner) said: You have spoken the truth, and what of *al-Iḥsān*? He (the Prophet) said: *To worship Allah as if you see him, although you cannot see him he sees you.* He (the questioner) said: If I do that, will I be *Muḥsin*? He (the Prophet) said: *Yes.* He (the questioner) said: You have spoken the truth.

We said – we have seen a man with a handsome face and a good fragrance (displaying) great courtesy to the Prophet (peace be upon him) and saying to the Prophet (peace be upon him), you have spoken the truth. So the Messenger of Allah (peace be upon him) said: *Bring this man to me.* So we searched and searched upon street after street in Medina but could not find him anywhere. Thus the Messenger of Allah (peace be upon him) said: *Do you know of this (man)?* We replied, Allah and his Messenger know. He said: *This (was) Jibreel peace be upon him, he teaches you all the rituals of your Deen.* What came to me is the image (of him), but I never knew him, but this image.

It is also reported in the collection of forty traditions by Ibn al-Muqra':

> Muḥammad bin Muḥammad bin Badr bin Abdullah al-Bāhili al-Baghdādi narrated to us in Egypt al-Ḥasan bin Ḥammād Sajjādah narrated to us al-Muṭalib bin Ziyād ath-Thaqafi narrated to us from Manṣur from 'Aṭā from Ibn Umar, he said: A man came and said O Abu Abdar-Raḥman indeed we travel and we pass by people who say (there is) no *Qadr* (then as previously narrated).

Moreover, it is also reported in the *Musnad* of Imām Aḥmad with an authentic channel of transmission upon the authority of Ibn 'Abbās:

> Abu Naḍr narrated to us Abdul-Ḥameed narrated to us Shahr narrated to us Abdullah bin 'Abbās narrated to me he said: The Messenger of Allah (peace be upon him) sat in a gathering of his and Jibreel came to him and sat in front of the Messenger of Allah (peace be upon him), placing his hands on the knees of the Messenger of Allah (peace be upon him). He said: O Messenger of Allah, tell me about Islam. The Messenger of Allah (peace be upon him) said: *Islam is to turn your face towards Allah; to bear witness that there is no deity except Allah alone, with no partner or associate and to bear witness that Muḥammad is his slave and Messenger*. He (Jibreel) said: If I do that, will I have become Muslim? He said: *If you do that, you will have become Muslim*. He said: O Messenger of Allah, tell me about *al-'Imān*. He said: *al-'Imān means to believe in Allah, the last day, the angels, the book and the Prophets; to believe in death and in life after death and to believe in paradise, hell, the reckoning (al-Ḥisāb) and the balance (al-Mizān); and to believe in al-Qadr – all of it both good and bad*. He said: And if I do that, will I have believed? He said: *If you do that, you will have believed*.
>
> He said: O Messenger of Allah, tell me about *al-Iḥsān*. He said: *Al-Iḥsān means to strive for the sake of Allah as if you can see him; although you cannot see him, he sees you*. He said: O Messenger of Allah, tell me about the hour. He said:

Subḥānallah! There are five matters of the unseen which no one knows except him – 'Verily Allah is he with whom is the knowledge of the hour; He sends down the rain and he knows what is in the wombs and o one knows what he shall earn on the morrow and no one knows in what land he shall die, surely Allah is knowing, aware.'[11] *But if you wish, I will tell you some of the signs of its approach.* He said: Yes O Messenger of Allah tell me. The Messenger of Allah (peace be upon him) said*: When you see the slave woman give birth to her mistress or master and you see the shepherds competing in the construction of lofty buildings and you see the barefoot, hungry dependents become prominent figures among the people – those are signs and portents of the hour.* He said: O Messenger of Allah, who are the shepherds and the barefoot, hungry dependents? He said: The Arabs.

And it is also to be found in *Itaḥāf al-Khayra al-Mahra*:

وَقَالَ الْحَارِثُ بْنُ مُحَمَّدِ بْنِ أَبِي أُسَامَةَ: حَدَّثَنَا أَبُو الْحُسَيْنِ عَاصِمُ بْنُ عَلِيٍّ حَدَّثَنَا الْحَكَمُ بْنُ فَصِيلٍ حَدَّثَنَا سَيَّارٌ أَبُو الْحَكَمِ، عَنْ شَهْرِ بْنِ حَوْشَبٍ عَنِ ابْنِ عَبَّاسٍ قَالَ: بَيْنَا رَسُولُ الله صلى الله عليه وسلم، قَاعِدٌ فِي النَّاسِ، إِذْ دَخَلَ رَجُلٌ يَتَخَطَّى النَّاسَ، حَتَّى وَضَعَ يَدَيْهِ عَلَى رُكْبَتَيِ النَّبِيِّ، صلى الله عليه وسلم،... فساقه بنحو ما سلف؛ ثم قَالَ: فَانْطَلَقَ الرَّجُلُ حَتَّى تَوَارَى، قَالَ: عَلَيَّ الرَّجُلُ، فَطُلِبَ فَلَمْ يُوجَدْ، فَقَالَ رَسُولُ الله، صلى الله عليه وسلم: هَذَا جِبْرِيلُ أَتَاكُمْ لِيُعَلِّمَكُمْ دِينَكُمْ، وَمَا أَتَانِي فِي صُورَةٍ إِلاَّ عَرَفْتُهُ فِيهَا غَيْرَ مَرَّتِهِ هَذِهِ

Al-Ḥārith ibn Muḥammad ibn Abi Usāma said: Abul' Ḥussein 'Aāṣim ibn Ali narrated to us al-Ḥakam bin Fuṣeel narrated to us Sayyār Abul' Ḥakam narrated to us from Shahr bin Ḥawshab from Ibn 'Abbās, he said: While the Messenger of Allah (peace be upon him) was sitting with the people, a man entered upon them until he put his hands upon the knees of the Prophet

[11] *Qur'ān* 31: 34

> (peace be upon him)...he mentioned what (was said) previously. Then he said: thereafter the man set off and disappeared. He (the Prophet) said: bring the man to me. So I looked but didn't find him. Then the Prophet (peace be upon him) said: *This (was) Jibreel, he came to teach you your Deen.* What came to me in this image, except that I knew of it, other than this time.

It is also cited in the works of Ibn Bishrān, via the following channel:

> أخبرنا أبو محمد عبد الخالق بن الحسن المعدل، حدثنا أبو سعيد عبد الله بن الحسن الحراني، حدثنا عاصم بن علي، به
>
> Abu Muḥammad Abdal-Khāliq bin al-Ḥasan al-Mu'dal reported to us Abu Sa'eed Abdullah bin al-Ḥasan al-Ḥirāni narrated to us 'Aāṣim bin Ali narrated to us, with it.

The *ḥadith* of Jibreel is in reality but an explanation of the components of Islam and its composition, as well as that pertaining to the subject of *al-'Imān* and *al-Iḥsān* and an explanation of its foundations, clarifying what this is and mentioning some of its pillars. It is not in reality a specific arrangement or order of specified grades or degrees. The arrangement can be discerned from other legal texts that are continuously recurrent (*mutawātir*) from the book and the *Sunnah.* According to the people, that will establish what a 'Muslim' will be, although that will not inevitably be the root of *al-'Imān* and the root of *al-Iḥsān.* Islam is operationalised via '*Imān* and *Iḥsān.* It is the laying out of its pillars and boundaries. They do not in fact intend to demonstrate any grading or arrangement. However, this order can be deduced from other legal recurrent texts of the glorious Qur'ān. The *Sunnah* shows that a person is considered a Muslim who has the basis or root of 'faith' as well as the basis or root 'perfection'. He cannot however be regarded as a 'Muslim' or someone with 'faith' or with 'perfection' arbitrarily without fulfilling certain conditions. Thereafter the person becomes more knowledgeable as his faith grows deeper and even more conscious of Allah, the exalted and majestic. This makes him undertake all prescribed duties and abandon all prohibitions. Such a person becomes worthy of being called a *'mu'min'* (faithful).

Following on from this, the individual adopts several recommended matters and avoids the dislikable ones, even giving up on some permissible matters as a sign of deep faith and of being extremely conscious of Allah, the exalted and majestic, for he worships his Lord as if he can see him, as noted in the *ḥadith*. If any person reaches this level he becomes worthy of being called a *'muḥsin'*, i.e., someone with a 'perfection'. Each *'muḥsin'* is a *'mu'min'* and each *'mu'min'* is a Muslim but not vice versa, except under certain conditions and restrictions.

Understanding the reality of *'al-'Imān'* is a difficult and thorny topic, particularly when seeking to flesh out all its unique boundaries, including the precise interplay with what are considered its nullifiers that would lead someone into disbelief. Expounding this in exhaustive detail, by the help and grace of Allah, will be presented in a separate forthcoming treatise that has been devoted solely to this topic and is entitled: *The Reality of al-'Imān and the Categorisation of Kufr*.

9 The Basis of Islam and its Essential Pillars

In tandem with the nature of our present book, it carries this intended meaning, to be an exposition upon the basis of Islam and the reality of *Tawḥeed.* In other words, with the meaning of what the testimony of faith is – that there is no god/deity but Allah and that Muḥammad is the Messenger of Allah. The abridgement of what is commonly referred to by many people as being the 'Five Pillars of Islam' is good parlance. Yet it is necessary to correct some of the errors that have arisen therein, as well as dispelling some of the confusions that have become quite commonplace. In particular, the word 'Pillar' (*rukn,* pl. *Arkān*) is notably absent from the *Sharī'ah* texts, although it has been used extensively by previous scholars. It has largely been taken from the famous *ḥadith* of Abdullah ibn Umar al-Khaṭṭāb (may Allah be pleased with him), as has been reported in the *Ṣaḥīḥ* of Imām Bukhāri:

حَدَّثَنَا عُبَيْدُ اللَّهِ بْنُ مُوسَى قَالَ أَخْبَرَنَا حَنْظَلَةُ بْنُ أَبِي سُفْيَانَ عَنْ عِكْرِمَةَ بْنِ
خَالِدٍ عَنْ ابْنِ عُمَرَ رَضِيَ اللَّهُ عَنْهُمَا قال: قال رَسُولُ اللَّهِ، صلى الله عليه
وسلم، بُنِيَ الْإِسْلَامُ عَلَى خَمْسٍ شَهَادَةِ أَنْ لَا إِلَهَ إِلَّا اللَّهُ وَأَنَّ مُحَمَّدًا رَسُولُ اللَّهِ
وَإِقَامِ الصَّلَاةِ وَإِيتَاءِ الزَّكَاةِ وَالْحَجِّ وَصَوْمِ رَمَضَانَ

'Ubaidallah bin Musa narrated to us he said Ḥandthala bin Abi

> Sufyān reported to us from 'Ikrima bin Khālid from Ibn Umar (may Allah be pleased with him) he said: the Prophet (peace be upon him) said: *Islam is built upon five – to testify that there is no deity but Allah and that Muḥammad is the messenger of Allah; to establish Ṣalāh, to pay Zakāt, Ḥajj and the fast of Ramaḍān.*

The *ḥadith* is widely reported such as in *Ṣaḥīḥ* Muslim,[1] in the *Sunan* of Nasā'i,[2] as well in *Ṣaḥīḥ* Ibn Ḥibbān.[3] Following this citation, the Imām Abu Ḥātim Ibn Ḥibbān furnishes us with a very important and lucid comment,[4] he writes:

> These two reports have both come to address (matters) according to (or based upon) the given situation, because he (peace be upon him) mentioned *al-'Imān* then enumerated four qualities, then he mentioned al-Islam and enumerated five qualities. And this is what we say in our book, because when the Arabs mention something known in their language which has such enumeration, it doesn't mean that the listed number of matters is to the exclusion of all others. With his speech, he (peace be upon him) did not say that *al-'Imān* is only what was stated in the report of Ibn 'Abbās because he (peace be upon him) mentioned in other reports a great number of things regarding *al-'Imān* which are not mentioned in either of the reports which both Ibn 'Abbās and Ibn Umar have conveyed.

A considerable number of scholars of *ḥadith* have cited this tradition in their respective works.[5] Elsewhere in his *Ṣaḥīḥ*, Imām Bukhāri has a

---

[1] *Ṣaḥīḥ* Muslim Vol. 1 sec. 45 & 46, no. 16
[2] *Sunan* Nasā'i Vol. 8 sec. 108, no. 5001
[3] *Ṣaḥīḥ* Ibn Ḥibbān Vol. 1 sec. 375, no. 158 and Vol. 4 sec. 295, no. 1446
[4] Appearing after citing the *ḥadith* of Ibn Umar at Vol. 1 sec. 375, no. 158 in the *Ṣaḥīḥ*
[5] The listed references are: *Ṣaḥīḥ* Ibn Khuzayma Vol. 1 sec. 159, no. 308; Vol. 1 sec. 160, no. 309, Vol. 3 sec. 187, no. 1880 and Vol. 4 sec. 128, no. 2505, *Musnad* Imām

fuller explanation of the narrative, albeit in *mawquf* (halted) form:

حَدَّثَنَا مُحَمَّدُ بْنُ بَشَّارٍ حَدَّثَنَا عَبْدُ الْوَهَّابِ حَدَّثَنَا عُبَيْدُ اللَّهِ عَنْ نَافِعٍ عَنْ ابْنِ عُمَرَ رَضِيَ اللَّهُ عَنْهُمَا أَتَاهُ رَجُلَانِ فِي فِتْنَةِ ابْنِ الزُّبَيْرِ فَقَالَا إِنَّ النَّاسَ صَنَعُوا وَأَنْتَ ابْنُ عُمَرَ وَصَاحِبُ النَّبِيِّ، صلى الله عليه وسلم، فَمَا يَمْنَعُكَ أَنْ تَخْرُجَ فَقَالَ يَمْنَعُنِي أَنَّ اللَّهَ حَرَّمَ دَمَ أَخِي فَقَالَا أَلَمْ يَقُلْ اللَّهُ ﴿وَقَاتِلُوهُمْ حَتَّى لَا تَكُونَ فِتْنَةٌ﴾ فَقَالَ قَاتَلْنَا حَتَّى لَمْ تَكُنْ فِتْنَةٌ وَكَانَ الدِّينُ لِلَّهِ وَأَنْتُمْ تُرِيدُونَ أَنْ تُقَاتِلُوا حَتَّى تَكُونَ فِتْنَةٌ وَيَكُونَ الدِّينُ لِغَيْرِ اللَّهِ وَزَادَ عُثْمَانُ بْنُ صَالِحٍ عَنْ ابْنِ وَهْبٍ قَالَ أَخْبَرَنِي فُلَانٌ وَحَيْوَةُ بْنُ شُرَيْحٍ عَنْ بَكْرِ بْنِ عَمْرٍو الْمَعَافِرِيِّ أَنَّ بُكَيْرَ بْنَ عَبْدِ اللَّهِ حَدَّثَهُ عَنْ نَافِعٍ أَنَّ رَجُلًا أَتَى ابْنَ عُمَرَ فَقَالَ يَا أَبَا عَبْدِ الرَّحْمَنِ مَا حَمَلَكَ عَلَى أَنْ تَحُجَّ عَامًا وَتَعْتَمِرَ عَامًا وَتَتْرُكَ الْجِهَادَ فِي سَبِيلِ اللَّهِ عَزَّ وَجَلَّ وَقَدْ عَلِمْتَ مَا رَغَّبَ اللَّهُ فِيهِ قَالَ يَا ابْنَ أَخِي بُنِيَ الْإِسْلَامُ عَلَى خَمْسٍ إِيمَانٍ بِاللَّهِ وَرَسُولِهِ وَالصَّلَاةِ الْخَمْسِ وَصِيَامِ رَمَضَانَ وَأَدَاءِ الزَّكَاةِ وَحَجِّ الْبَيْتِ قَالَ يَا أَبَا عَبْدِ الرَّحْمَنِ أَلَا تَسْمَعُ مَا ذَكَرَ اللَّهُ فِي كِتَابِهِ: ﴿وَإِنْ طَائِفَتَانِ مِنْ الْمُؤْمِنِينَ اقْتَتَلُوا فَأَصْلِحُوا بَيْنَهُمَا فَإِنْ بَغَتْ إِحْدَاهُمَا عَلَى الْأُخْرَى فَقَاتِلُوا الَّتِي تَبْغِي حَتَّى تَفِيءَ إِلَى أَمْرِ اللَّهِ﴾، ﴿قَاتِلُوهُمْ حَتَّى لَا تَكُونَ فِتْنَةٌ﴾، قَالَ: فَعَلْنَا عَلَى عَهْدِ رَسُولِ اللَّهِ، صلى الله عليه وسلم، وَكَانَ الْإِسْلَامُ قَلِيلًا فَكَانَ الرَّجُلُ يُفْتَنُ فِي دِينِهِ إِمَّا قَتَلُوهُ وَإِمَّا يُعَذِّبُونَهُ حَتَّى كَثُرَ الْإِسْلَامُ فَلَمْ تَكُنْ فِتْنَةٌ قَالَ فَمَا قَوْلُكَ فِي عَلِيٍّ وَعُثْمَانَ قَالَ أَمَّا عُثْمَانُ فَكَأَنَّ اللَّهَ عَفَا عَنْهُ وَأَمَّا أَنْتُمْ فَكَرِهْتُمْ أَنْ تَعْفُوا عَنْهُ وَأَمَّا عَلِيٌّ فَابْنُ عَمِّ رَسُولِ اللَّهِ، صلى الله عليه وسلم، وَخَتَنُهُ وَأَشَارَ بِيَدِهِ فَقَالَ هَذَا بَيْتُهُ حَيْثُ تَرَوْنَ

Muḥammad ibn Bashār narrated to us Abdul-Wahāb narrated to us 'Ubaidallah narrated to us from Nāfi' from Ibn Umar, may Allah be pleased with him: During the affliction of Ibn az-Zubayr, two men came to Ibn Umar and said: 'The people are lost, and you are the son of Umar, and the companion of the Prophet, so what forbids you from coming out?' He said: 'What

---

Aḥmad bin Ḥanbal Vol. 2 sec. 120, no. 6015 and Vol. 2 sec. 143, no. 6301, *Musnad* Ḥumaydi Vol. 2 sec. 308, no. 703, *Musnad* Abu Ya'la Vol. 10 sec. 166, no. 5788, Ṭabarāni *Mu'jam Kabir* Vol. 12 sec. 309, no. 13,203 and Vol. 12 sec. 412, no. 13,518, Ṭabarāni *Mu'jam al-Awsaṭ* Vol. 6 sec. 230, no. 0; Vol. 6 sec. 230, no. 6264 and Vol. 7 sec. 34, no. 6770, Imām Nasā'i *Sunan al-Kubra* Vol. 6 sec. 531, no. 11,732, *Sunan* Nasā'i Vol. 6 sec. 531, no. 11,732, *Sunan* Tirmidhi Vol. 5 sec. 6, no. 2609 and Bayhaqy *Sunan al-Kubra* Vol. 1 sec. 358, no. 1561; Vol. 4 sec. 81, no. 7013 and Vol. 4 sec. 199, no. 7680.

forbids me is that Allah has prohibited the shedding of my brother's blood.' They both said: 'Didn't Allah say: *And fight then until there is no more affliction*?' He said: 'We fought until there was no more affliction and the *Deen* is for Allah, while you want to fight until there is affliction and until the *Deen* becomes for other than Allah.'

And (from) Uthmān bin Ṣāliḥ from Ibn Wahb he said, Ḥaywa bin Shurayḥ and so and so reported to me from Bakr bin Amr al-Ma'āfiry that Bukeer bin Abdullah narrated to him from Nāfi' (the following) is added: that a man came to Ibn Umar and said: 'O Abu Abdar-Raḥman! What made you perform *Ḥajj* in one year and *Umra* in another and leave the *Jihād* in the path of Allah, though you know how much Allah recommends it?' Ibn Umar replied: 'O son of my brother! Islam is founded upon five: '*Imān* in Allah and his messenger; the five-prayers, the fasting of *Ramaḍān*; rendering of *Zakāt* and pilgrimage (*Hajj*) to the house.

The man said: 'O Abu Abdar-Raḥman! Won't you listen to why Allah has mentioned in his book: *If two groups of believers fight each other, then make peace between them, but if one of then transgresses beyond bounds against the other, then you all fight against the one that transgresses*; and *fight them till there is no more affliction*.' Ibn Umar said: We did it, during the lifetime of Allah's Messenger (peace be upon him) when Islam had only a few followers. A man would be put to trial because of his *Deen*; he would either be killed or tortured. But when the Muslims increased, there was no more affliction or oppression.' The man said: 'What is your opinion about Uthmān and `Ali?' Ibn Umar said: 'As for Uthmān, it seems that Allah has forgiven him, but you people dislike that he should be forgiven. And as for Ali, he is the cousin of Allah's Messenger (peace be upon him) and his son-in-law.' Then he pointed with his hand and said, 'That is his house which you see.'

Imām Aḥmad also cites similarly in his *Musnad* again in *mawquf* (halted) form:

حَدَّثَنَا وَكِيعٌ عَنْ سُفْيَانَ عَنْ مَنْصُورٍ عَنْ سَالِمِ بْنِ أَبِي الْجَعْدِ عَنْ يَزِيدَ بْنِ بِشْرٍ عَنِ ابْنِ عُمَرَ قَالَ بُنِيَ الْإِسْلَامُ عَلَى خَمْسٍ شَهَادَةِ أَنْ لَا إِلَهَ إِلَّا اللَّهُ وَإِقَامِ الصَّلَاةِ وَإِيتَاءِ الزَّكَاةِ وَحَجِّ الْبَيْتِ وَصَوْمِ رَمَضَانَ قَالَ فَقَالَ لَهُ رَجُلٌ وَالْجِهَادُ فِي سَبِيلِ اللَّهِ قَالَ ابْنُ عُمَرَ الْجِهَادُ حَسَنٌ هَكَذَا حَدَّثَنَا رَسُولُ اللَّهِ، صلى الله عليه وسلم

> Waki' narrated to us from Sufyān from Manṣur from Sālim bin Abi al-Ja'd from Yazeed bin Bishr from Ibn Umar, he said: Islam is built upon five: testifying that there is no deity but Allah; establishing the prayer, paying the *Zakat*; pilgrimage to the house and the fast of *Ramaḍān*. A man said to him: And *Jihād* in the way of Allah? Ibn Umar said – *Jihād* is good, thus as the Prophet (peace be upon him) narrated to us.

I would submit that there is great difference in the narrative as set out on multiple occasions and shown by these various *aḥādith* that have been reported. Yet in none of the narratives presented thus far, is there an explicit mention of hearing this directly from the Prophet (peace be upon him) by Ibn Umar. What he does mention is – 'he said, the Prophet said;' 'from the Prophet, he said,' or 'the Prophet narrated to us.' It is something which strengthens the contention that it would appear to be a deduction (*istinbāṭ*) that has been made by Abdullah ibn Umar bin al-Khaṭṭāb from the famous *ḥadith* of Jibreel, which he took from his father Umar; more pertinently, he was not a direct eyewitness to that event. In any case, it is a continuously recurrent tradition (*mutawātir*) from Ibn Umar, as it has been reported by the majority of trustworthy narrators from the *Tābi'een*.

Within the *Musnad* of Imām Aḥmad the following is reported upon the authority of Jarir ibn Abdullah:

حَدَّثَنَا هَاشِمٌ حَدَّثَنَا إِسْرَائِيلُ عَنْ جَابِرٍ عَنْ عَامِرٍ عَنْ جَرِيرٍ قَالَ: قَالَ رَسُولُ اللَّهِ، صلى الله عليه وسلم: بُنِيَ الإِسْلامُ عَلَى خَمْسٍ، شَهَادَةِ أَنْ لا إِلَهَ إِلاَّ اللَّهُ، وَإِقَامِ الصَّلاةِ، وَإِيتَاءِ الزَّكَاةِ، وَحَجِّ الْبَيْتِ، وَصَوْمِ رَمَضَانَ

Hāshim narrated to us Isrā'il narrated to us from Jābir from 'Aāmir from Jarir he said the Messenger of Allah (peace be upon him) said: *Islam is built upon five; testifying that there is no deity but Allah, establishing the Ṣalāh, paying the Zakāt, pilgrimage to the house and the fast of Ramaḍān.*

Ṭabarāni also reports this in *Mu'jam al-Kabir,*[6] as does Abu Ya'la in his *Musnad,*[7] as well as other than them. Next, Imām Aḥmad has recorded the following, again in his *Musnad:*

حَدَّثَنَا مَكِّيٌّ حَدَّثَنَا دَاوُدُ بْنُ يَزِيدَ الأَوْدِيُّ عَنْ عَامِرٍ عَنْ جَرِيرِ بْنِ عَبْدِ اللَّهِ قَالَ سَمِعْتُ رَسُولَ اللَّهِ، صلى الله عليه وسلم، يَقُولُ بُنِيَ الإِسْلاَمُ عَلَى خَمْسٍ شَهَادَةِ أَنْ لاَ إِلَهَ إِلاَّ اللَّهُ وَإِقَامِ الصَّلاَةِ وَإِيتَاءِ الزَّكَاةِ وَحَجِّ الْبَيْتِ وَصِيَامِ رَمَضَانَ

Makki narrated to us Dāwud bin Yazeed al-Awdi narrated to us from 'Aāmir from Jarir ibn Abdullah he said I heard the Prophet (peace be upon him) saying: *Islam is built upon five; testifying that there is no deity but Allah, establishing the Ṣalāh, paying the Zakāt, pilgrimage to the house and the fast of Ramaḍān.*

As with the above, Ṭabarāni also reports this in *Mu'jam al-Kabir*[8] as does Abu Ya'la in his *Musnad,*[9] amongst others. The following narration has been cited by Ṭabarāni in his *Mu'jam al-Kabir*:

---

[6] Ṭabarāni *Mu'jam al-Kabir*, Vol. 2 sec. 326, no. 2363
[7] *Musnad* Abu Ya'la Vol. 13 sec. 490, no. 7502
[8] Ṭabarāni *Mu'jam al-Kabir*, Vol. 2 sec. 326, no. 2364
[9] *Musnad* Abu Ya'la Vol. 13 sec. 497, no. 7507

حدثنا الحسن بن عليل الغزي حدثنا أبو كريب حدثنا معاوية بن هشام حدثنا شيبان عن جابر عن الشعبي عن جرير قال بني الإسلام على خمس شهادة أن لا إله إلا الله وإقام الصلاة وإيتاء الزكاة وحج البيت وصيام رمضان

Al-Ḥasan bin 'Aleel al-Ghazi narrated to us Abu Kareeb narrated to us Mu'āwiya bin Hishām narrated to us Shaybān narrated to us from Jābir from ash-Sha'bi from Jarir he said: Islam is built upon five; testifying that there is no deity but Allah, establishing the *Ṣalāh*, paying the *Zakāt*, pilgrimage to the house and the fast of *Ramaḍān*.

Again, Ṭabarāni has the next narration, albeit recorded in his *Mu'jam Ṣaghir*:

حَدَّثَنَا مُحَمَّدُ بْنُ أَحْمَدَ بْنِ حَمَّادٍ أَبُو بِشْرٍ الدُّولَابِيُّ، بِمِصْرَ، حَدَّثَنَا أَبِي، حَدَّثَنَا أَشْعَثُ، عَنْ عَطَّافٍ، عَنْ عَبْدِ اللهِ بْنِ حَبِيبِ بْنِ أَبِي ثَابِتٍ، عَنِ الشَّعْبِيِّ، عَنْ جَرِيرِ بْنِ عَبْدِ اللهِ الْبَجَلِيِّ: عَنِ النَّبِيِّ صَلَّى اللهُ عَلَيْهِ وَآلِهِ وَسَلَّمَ قَالَ: بُنِيَ الْإِسْلَامُ عَلَى خَمْسٍ: شَهَادَةُ أَنْ لَا إِلَهَ إِلَّا اللهُ، وَإِقَامُ الصَّلَاةِ، وَإِيتَاءُ الزَّكَاةِ، وَحَجُّ الْبَيْتِ، وَصَوْمُ رَمَضَانَ

Muḥammad bin Aḥmad bin Ḥammād Abu Bishr al-Dawlābi narrated to us in Egypt my father narrated to us Ash'ath narrated to us from 'Aṭāf from Abdullah bin Ḥabeeb bin Abi Thābit from ash-Sha'bi from Jarir bin Abdullah al-Bajili from the Prophet (peace be upon him) he said: *Islam is built upon five; testifying that there is no deity but Allah, establishing the Ṣalāh, paying the Zakāt, pilgrimage to the house and the fast of Ramaḍān.*

Following each of these narrations, I would submit that there is some divergence in the reporting routes concerning this from Jarir bin Abdullah and its *mawquf* and '*an-an*' formats. Also, there is a distinct lack of explicit mention of hearing this directly from the Prophet (peace be upon him), in a similar manner to the aforementioned narratives from Ibn Umar. Perhaps it is also an *ijtihād* that is being transmitted from Jarir bin Abdullah al-Bajili may Allah be pleased with him.

Ṭabarāni has the next narration, this time in *Mu'jam al-Kabir*:

> حدثنا أبو يزيد القراطيسي حدثنا أسد بن موسى حدثنا مؤمل بن إسماعيل عن حماد بن زيد عن عمرو بن مالك عن أبي الجوزاء عن بن عباس رضي الله عنهما ولا أعلمه إلا رفعه إلى النبي، صلى الله عليه وسلم، قال بني الإسلام على خمس شهادة أن لا إله إلا الله والصلاة وصيام رمضان فمن ترك واحدة منهن كان كافرا حلال الدم
>
> Abu Yazeed al-Qarāṭisi narrated to us Asad bin Musa narrated to us Muwamil bin Ismā'il narrated to us from Ḥammād bin Zayd from Amr bin Mālik from Abul'Jawza' from Ibn 'Abbās may Allah be pleased with them and I don't know of it except that it is raised to the Prophet (peace be upon him) he said: Islam is built upon five; testifying that there is no deity but Allah, the *Ṣalāh* and the fast of *Ramaḍān* and whoever leaves one from amongst them he is a *kāfir* whose blood is lawful.

Consequently, this narration with its slanderous addition is rejected both in terms of its transmission and reported text. Moreover, it is from the vagaries of Muwamil bin Ismā'il and he is not *thiqa*.

All the narratives considered thus far represent what al-Islam is being built and constructed upon; to reiterate again, it is noteworthy that the word 'pillar' is not used originally in any reports. The word doesn't appear in any of the reported texts. Such an inaccuracy begins with the first listed, as the testimony, *al-Shahāda*, being a pillar from amongst the pillars upon which Islam is built. Nay, it is more important than that and it is of the upmost importance. It is the solid base of Islam; it is the basis and foundation of Islam itself upon which all pillars and columns are built from. But the texts that have been outlined thus far make 'al-Islam' to be '*al-Shahāda*' by itself; other texts make 'al-Islam' to be *al-'Imān*, of which this will be cited shortly. One will therefore discern that without any doubt whatsoever, that the 'Pillars of Islam' are in fact more numerous than the famous five. And with that the unusual observation which was made by Imām Abu Ḥātim Muḥammad ibn Ḥibbān as cited previously where he said:

> These two reports have both come to address (matters) according to (or based upon) the given situation, because he (peace be upon him) mentioned *al-'Imān* then enumerated four qualities, then he mentioned al-Islam and enumerated five qualities. And this is what we say in our book, because when the Arabs mention something known in their language which has such enumeration, it doesn't mean that the listed number of matters is to the exclusion of all others. With his speech, he (peace be upon him) did not say that *al-'Imān* is only what was stated in the report of Ibn 'Abbās because he (peace be upon him) mentioned in other reports a great number of things regarding *al-'Imān* which are not mentioned in either of the reports which both Ibn 'Abbās and Ibn Umar have conveyed.

It has not been received upon the qualities of Islam not from Imām Ibn Ḥibbān by himself and not from other than him, with that at present we have here that it is not greatly different from the qualities of *al-'Imān*. As has been reported in the *Sunan* of Imām Tirmidhi:[10]

> Muḥammad ibn Ismā'il narrated to us Musa ibn Ismā'il narrated to us 'Abbān bin Yazeed narrated to us Yaḥya bin Abi Kathir narrated to us from Yazeed bin Salām that Abu Salām narrated to him that al-Ḥārith al-Ash'ari narrated to him that the

[10] The Arabic text of the narration has been omitted given its considerable size.

Prophet (peace be upon him) said: *Indeed, Allah commanded Yaḥya bin Zakariyya with five commandments to abide by, and to command the Children of Israel to abide by them. But he was slow in doing so. So Esa said: Indeed, Allah commanded you with five commandments to abide by and to command the Children of Israel to abide by. Either you command them, or I shall command them. So Yaḥya said: 'I fear that if you precede me in this, then the earth may swallow me, or I shall be punished.' So he gathered the people in Jerusalem, and they filled* (the *masjid*) *and sat upon its balconies. So he said: Indeed Allah has commanded me with five commandments to abide by, and to command you to abide by. The first of them is that you worship Allah and not associate anything with him. The parable of the one who associates others with Allah is that of a man who buys a servant with his own gold or silver, then he says to him: 'This is my home and this is my business so take care of it and give me the profits.' So he takes care of it and gives the profits to someone other than his master. Which of you would live to have a servant like that?*

And Allah commands you to perform Ṣalāh, and when you perform Ṣalāh then do not turn away, for Allah is facing the face of His worshipers as long as he does not turn away. And He commands you with fasting. For indeed the parable of fasting, is that of a man in a group with a sachet containing musk. All of them enjoy its fragrance. Indeed the breath of the fasting person is more pleasant to Allah than the scent of musk. And He commands you to give charity. The parable of that, is a man captured by his enemies, tying his hands to his neck, and they come to him to beat his neck. Then he said: *I can ransom myself from you with a little or a lot so he ransoms himself from them. And He commands you to remember Allah. For indeed the parable of that, is a man whose enemy quickly tracks him until he reaches an impermeable fortress in which he protects himself from them. This is how the worshiper is; he does not protect himself from the Shayṭān except by the remembrance of Allah.* The Prophet (peace be upon him) said: *And I command you with five that Allah commanded me:*

> *Listening and obeying, Jihād, Hijrah, and the Jamā'ah. For indeed whoever parts from the Jamā'ah the measure of a hand-span, then he has cast off the yoke of Islam from his neck, unless he returns. And whoever calls with the call of Jāhiliyyah then he is from the coals of hell.* A man said: O Messenger of Allah! Even if he performs *Ṣalāh* and fasts? So he (peace be upon him) said: *Even if he performs Ṣalāh and fasts. So call with the call that Allah named you with: Muslims, believers, worshipers of Allah.*

After citing this tradition, Abu Esa at-Tirmidhi makes the following comment:

> This *ḥadith* is *ḥasan Ṣaḥīḥ, ghareeb* (strange). Muḥammad ibn Ismā'il has said: 'al-Ḥārith al-Ash'ari was a companion and he has *ḥadith* other than this.' Muḥammad ibn Bashār narrated to us Abu Dāwud aṭ-Ṭayālisi narrated to us 'Abbān bin Yazeed narrated to us from Yaḥya bin Abi Kathir from Yazeed bin Salām from Abi Salām from al-Ḥārith al-Ash'ari from the Prophet peace be upon him - the remainder with a similar meaning. Abu Esa said: This *ḥadith* is *ḥasan Ṣaḥīḥ ghareeb.* And (of) Abu Salām al-Ḥabashi, his name is Mamṭur and he reports from Ali bin al-Mubārak from Yaḥya bin Abi Kathir.

Muḥammad ibn Ismā'il is none other than Abu Abdullah al-Bukhāri, the famed Imām of the *dunya* and the companion of what is termed as authentic, *Ṣaḥīḥ*. The *ḥadith* is reported widely, cited in many notble collections.[11]

---

[11] The listed references are: *Ṣaḥīḥ* Ibn Ḥibbān Vol. 14 sec. 128, no. 6233, *Ṣaḥīḥ* Ibn Khuzayma Vol. 1 sec. 244 no. 483; Vol. 2 sec. 65, no. 930 and Vol. 3 sec. 196, no. 1895, *Musnad* Aḥmad Vol. 4 sec. 130, no. 17,209; Vol. 4 sec. 202, no. 17,833, *Mustadrak* of al-Ḥākim Vol. 1 sec. 204, no. 405; Vol. 1 sec. 205, no. 406; Vol. 1 sec. 362, no. 863 and Vol. 1 sec. 583, no. 1534, *Musnad* Ṭayālisi Vol. 1 sec. 159, no. 1161, Ṭabarāni *Mu'jam al-Kabir* Vol. 3 sec. 287, no. 3427; Vol. 3 sec. 287, no. 3428; Vol. 3

It is also reported by Imām an-Nasā'i in his *Sunan al-Kubra*, albeit, only the last paragraph:

أخبرنا هشام بن عمار قال حدثنا محمد بن شعيب قال أخبرني معاوية بن سلام أن أخاه زيد بن سلام أخبره عن جده أبي سلام أنه أخبره قال أخبرني الحارث الأشعري عن رسول الله، صلى الله عليه وسلم، قال: من دعا بدعوى جاهلية فإنه من جثى جهنم! ، فقال رجل: يا رسول الله وإن صام وصلى؟! قال: نعم وإن صام وصلى - فادعوا بدعوة الله التي سماكم الله بها: المسلمين، المؤمنين، عباد الله

Hishām ibn 'Ammār reported to us he said Muḥammad bin Shu'ayb narrated to us he said Mu'āwiya bin Salām reported to me that his brother Yazeed bin Salām reported to him from his grandfather Abu Salām that he reported to him, he said al-Ḥārith al-Ash'ari reported to me from the Prophet (peace be upon him): *And whoever calls with the call of Jāhiliyyah then he is from the coals of hell!* A man said: O Messenger of Allah, (even if) he prays and fasts? He (the Prophet) said: *Yes,* (even if) *he prays and fasts. So call with the call that Allah named you with: Muslims, believers, worshipers of Allah*.

I would submit, there is no mention in this of the pilgrimage - *Ḥajj*. Instead there comes that of the 'remembrance of Allah.' There is also the addition in relation to the five also, here being: listening and obeying, *Jihād*, *Hijrah* and al-*Jamā'ah* (the community). Also, it appears in the *Muṣṣanaf* of Abu Bakr ibn Abi Shayba with a very authentic channel of transmission:

حَدَّثَنَا غُنْدَرٌ عَنْ شُعْبَةَ عَنْ أَبِي جَمْرَةَ عَنِ ابْنِ عَبَّاسٍ أَنَّ وَفْدَ عَبْدِ الْقَيْسِ أَتَوْا النَّبِيَّ صلى الله عليه وسلم، فَقَالَ رَسُولُ اللهِ صلى الله عليه وسلم: مَنِ الْوَفْدُ،

sec. 289, no. 3430, Ṭabarāni *Mu'jam ash-Shāmiayn* Vol. 4 sec. 112, no. 2870, Bayhaqy *Sunan al-Kubra* Vol. 2 sec. 282, no. 3348, and *Musnad* Abu Ya'la Vol. 3 sec. 143, no. 1571.

أَوْ مَنِ الْقَوْمُ، قَالُوا: رَبِيعَةُ، قَالَ: مَرْحَبًا بِالْقَوْمِ، أَوْ بِالْوَفْدِ غَيْرَ خَزَايَا، وَلا نَدَامَى، فَقَالُوا: يَا رَسُولَ اللهِ، إِنَّا نَأْتِيك مِنْ شُقَّةٍ بَعِيدَةٍ، وَإِنَّ بَيْنَنَا وَبَيْنَكَ هَذَا الْحَيَّ مِنْ كُفَّارِ مُضَرَ، وَإِنَّا لاَ نَسْتَطِيعُ أَنْ نَأْتِيَك إِلاَّ فِي الشَّهْرِ الْحَرَامِ، فَمُرْنَا بِأَمْرٍ فَصْلٍ نُخْبِرُ بِهِ مَنْ وَرَاءَنَا نَدْخُلُ بِهِ الْجَنَّةَ، قَالَ: فَأَمَرَهُمْ بِأَرْبَعٍ وَنَهَاهُمْ عَنْ أَرْبَعٍ: أَمَرَهُمْ بِالإِيمَانِ بِاللهِ وَحْدَهُ، وَقَالَ: هَلْ تَدْرُونَ مَا الإِيمَانُ بِاللهِ، قَالُوا: اللهُ وَرَسُولُهُ أَعْلَمُ، قَالَ: شَهَادَةُ أَنْ لاَ إِلَهَ إِلاَّ اللهُ، وَأَنَّ مُحَمَّدًا رَسُولُ اللهِ وَإِقَامُ الصَّلاَةِ وَإِيتَاءُ الزَّكَاةِ وَصَوْمُ رَمَضَانَ، وَأَنْ تُعْطُوا الْخُمُسَ مِنَ الْمَغْنَمِ، فَقَالَ: احْفَظُوهُ وَأَخْبِرُوا بِهِ مَنْ وَرَاءَكُمْ

Ghundar narrated to us from Shu'ba from Abu Jamrah from Ibn 'Abbās: that a delegation from Abd'il Qays came to the Prophet (peace be upon him). So the Prophet (peace be upon him) said: Who are the people? (or) who are the delegates? They replied: We are from the tribe of Rabi'ah. He (the Prophet) said: *Welcome O delegation - or delegates - neither you will have disgrace, nor you will regret.* They said: O Messenger of Allah We have come to you from a distant place and there is the tribe of the *kuffar* of Muḍar intervening between you and us and we cannot come to you except in the sacred month, so please order us to do something good and that we may also inform our people whom we have left behind (at home) and that we may enter paradise. He (the Prophet) said: *I command you with four and prohibit you from four: I command you all to believe in Allah alone.* And he (the Prophet) said: *Do you know what is meant by believing in Allah alone?* They replied - Allah and His Messenger know best. He (the Prophet) said: *To testify that there is no deity except Allah and that Muḥammad is the Messenger of Allah; to establish the ṣalāh, to render the zakāt, to fast in Ramaḍān and that you give the fifth from the booty.* He (the Prophet also further) said: *Memorise them and tell them to the people whom you have left behind.*

I would submit that here again there is no mention of *Ḥajj* within the narrative. It is likely that this may have been before the obligation of *Ḥajj* because Abd'il Qays are from the older period of Islam; although, the narration does contain the addition of giving a fifth from the booty.

Abu Bakr ibn Abi Shayba also cites the following in his *Muṣṣanaf*:

حَدَّثَنَا ابْنُ فُضَيْلٍ عَنْ عَطَاءِ بْنِ السَّائِبِ عَنْ سَالِمِ بْنِ أَبِي الْجَعْدِ عَنِ ابْنِ عَبَّاسٍ قَالَ: جَاءَ أَعْرَابِيٌّ إِلَى النَّبِيِّ صلى الله عليه وسلم، فَقَالَ: السَّلامُ عَلَيْكَ يَا غُلامَ بَنِي عَبْدِ الْمُطَّلِبِ، فَقَالَ: وَعَلَيْك، فقَالَ: إِنِّي رَجُلٌ مِنْ أَخْوَالِكَ مِنْ بَنِي سَعْدِ بْنِ بَكْرٍ وَأَنَا رَسُولُ قَوْمِي إِلَيْك وَوَافِدُهُمْ وَأَنَا سَائِلُك فَمُشْتَدَّةٌ مَسْأَلَتِي إياك، وَمُنَاشِدُك فَمُشْتَدَّةٌ مُنَاشَدَتِي إِيَّاكَ، قَالَ: خُذْ يَا أَخَا بَنِي سَعْدٍ، قَالَ: مَنْ خَلَقَك وَهُوَ خَالِقُ مَنْ قَبْلَك وَهُوَ خَالِقُ مَنْ بَعْدَكَ؟ قَالَ: اللَّهُ، قَالَ: نَشَدْتُك بِذَلِكَ أَهُوَ أَرْسَلَك؟ قَالَ: نَعَمْ، قَالَ: مَنْ خَلَقَ السَّمَاوَاتِ السَّبْعَ وَالأَرْضِينَ السَّبْعَ وَأَجْرَى بَيْنَهُنَّ الرِّزْقَ؟ قَالَ: اللَّهُ، قَالَ: نَشَدْتُك بِذَلِكَ أَهُوَ أَرْسَلَكَ؟ قَالَ: نَعَمْ، قَالَ: فَإِنَّا وَجَدْنَا فِي كِتَابِكَ وَأَمَرَتْنَا رُسُلُك أَنْ نُصَلِّيَ فِي الْيَوْمِ وَاللَّيْلَةِ خَمْسَ صَلَوَاتٍ لِمَوَاقِيتِهَا فَنَشَدْتُك بِذَلِكَ أَهُوَ أَمَرَك بِهِ؟ قَالَ: نَعَمْ، قَالَ: فَإِنَّا وَجَدْنَا فِي كِتَابِكَ وَأَمَرَتْنَا رُسُلُك أَنْ نَأْخُذَ مِنْ حَوَاشِي أَمْوَالِنَا فَنَرُدَّهَا عَلَى فُقَرَائِنَا فَنَشَدْتُك بِذَلِكَ أَهُوَ أَمَرَك بِذَلِكَ؟ قَالَ: نَعَمْ، ثُمَّ قَالَ: أَمَّا الْخَامِسَةُ فَلَسْت سَائلك عنها، وَلا أَرَبَ لِي فِيهَا، قَالَ: ثُمَّ قَالَ: أَمَا وَالَّذِي بَعَثَك بِالْحَقِّ لأَعْمَلَنَّ بِهَا وَمَنْ أَطَاعَنِي مِنْ قَوْمِي، ثُمَّ رَجَعَ فَضَحِكَ رَسُولُ اللهِ، صلى الله عليه وسلم، حَتَّى بَدَتْ نَوَاجِذُهُ، ثُمَّ قَالَ: وَالَّذِي نَفْسِي بِيَدِهِ لَئِنْ صَدَقَ لَيَدْخُلَنَّ الْجَنَّةَ

Ibn Fuḍeel narrated to us from ‘Aṭā ibn as-Sā’ib from Sālim bin Abi al-Ja’d from Ibn ‘Abbās he said: an Arab came to the Prophet (peace be upon him) and he said – Peace be upon you oh boy from Bani Abdal-Muṭṭalib. Then he said: *and upon you*. Then he replied: I am a man from the maternal uncles of Bani Sa’d bin Bakr and I am the Messenger of this people sent unto you, and delegated unto you. I am going to ask you questions about issues, being harsh in enquiry. And implore you strongly that you (respond) to my appeal. He said: *O my brother of Bani Sa’d, take*. He said: Who created you and who is the creator; it is the creator of you after you. He said: *Allah*. I implore you with that, is it he that sent you? He replied: *yes*. He said: who has created the seven heavens and the worlds, providing therein provision? He said: *Allah*. He said: I adjure you, did he send you with that? He said: *Yes*. He said: and indeed, we find in your book that, that your Prophet ordered us with five-prayers in a day and a night at its fixed times. I adjure you, has he ordered you with that? He replied: *yes*. He said: And we find in your book that, that your Prophet ordered us that we take from the source of our margins of our wealth so that a tribute of that may be passed on to our poor, I adjure you, has he ordered you with that? He replied: *yes*. Then he said: As for the fifth, you are not asked from it and no Arab to have from it. Then he said: By him who has sent you with the truth whoever acts upon that and whomsoever obeys me from my nation. Then the Prophet reverted laughing until his teeth were visible, thereafter he said: *By him in whose hand my soul he has spoken the truth and will enter heaven.*

Again, as has been collected in the *Mușșanaf* of Abu Bakr ibn Abi Shayba:

حَدَّثَنَا غُنْدَرٌ عَنْ شُعْبَةَ عَنِ الْحَكَمِ قَالَ: سَمِعْتُ عُرْوَةَ بْنَ النَّزَّالِ يُحَدِّثُ عَنْ مُعَاذِ بْنِ جَبَلٍ قَالَ: أَقْبَلْنَا مَعَ رَسُولِ اللهِ صلى الله عليه وسلم، مِنْ غَزْوَةِ تَبُوكَ، فَلَمَّا رَأَيْته خَالِيًا قُلْتُ: يَا رَسُولَ اللهِ، أَخْبِرْنِي بِعَمَلٍ يُدْخِلُنِي الْجَنَّةَ، فقَالَ: بَخٍ، لَقَدْ سَأَلْت عَنْ عَظِيمٍ، وَهُوَ يَسِيرٌ عَلَى مَنْ يَسَّرَهُ اللَّهُ عَلَيْهِ: تُقِيمُ الصَّلاَةَ الْمَكْتُوبَةَ وَتُؤَدِّي الزَّكَاةَ الْمَفْرُوضَةَ وَتَلْقَى اللَّهَ لاَ تُشْرِكُ بِهِ شَيْئًا، أَوَلا أَدُلُّك عَلَى رَأْسِ الأَمْرِ وَعَمُودِهِ وَذِرْوَةِ سَنَامِهِ؟ أَمَّا رَأْسُ الأَمْرِ فَالإِسْلام مَنْ أَسْلَمَ سَلِمَ، وَأَمَّا عَمُوده فَالصَّلاة، وَأَمَّا ذِرْوَته وَسَنَامه فَالْجِهَادُ فِي سَبِيلِ اللهِ

Ghundar narrated to us from Shu'ba from al-Ḥakam he said I heard 'Urwa ibn an-Nazzāl narrate from Mu'ādth ibn Jabal he said: We came back with the Messenger of Allah (peace be upon him) from the expedition (*ghazwa*) of Tabuk. When I saw him free I said: O Messenger of Allah, direct me to a deed which will admit me to paradise. *Bravo, verily you have asked me about a matter of great importance, but it is easy for one for whom Allah makes it easy; to offer the obligatory prayer, to render the obligatory zakāt and to meet Allah without associating anything with him whatsoever. Shall I not guide you upon the head of the matter, its column and its apex? As for the head of the matter, it is Islam, whoever accepts and submits. And as for its column, it's the Ṣalāh, as for its apex it is Jihād in the path of Allah.*

Once more, there is another narration from the *Muṣṣanaf* of Abu Bakr ibn Abi Shayba:

حَدَّثَنَا عَبِيدَةُ بْنُ حُمَيْدٍ عَنِ الْحَكَمِ عَنِ الأَعْمَشِ عَنْ مَيْمُونِ بْنِ أَبِي شبيب عَنْ مُعَاذِ بْنِ جَبَلٍ قَالَ: خَرَجْنَا مَعَ رَسُولِ اللهِ، صلى الله عليه وسلم، غَزْوَةَ تَبُوكَ... ثُمَّ ذَكَرَ نَحْوَهُ

'Abeeda bin Ḥumayd narrated to us from al-Ḥakam from al-'Amash from Maymoon bin Abu Shabeeb from Mu'ādth bin Jabal he said: We set out with the Messenger of Allah (peace be upon him) to the *Ghazwa* of Tabuk (then mentioned the remainder).

Here I would submit, that this was at the end of the ninth year, after which the obligations of pilgrimage and fasting have already taken effect, and neither are mentioned. There is mention though of *Jihād* in the path of Allah as being the apex and pinnacle. Imām Ṭayālisi has the next tradition recorded in his *Musnad* from the wording reported by Ḥudhayfah. The *isnād* is exceptionally authentic and is upon the conditions of Bukhāri and Muslim:

حدثنا شعبة عن أبي إسحاق قال سمعت صلة بن زفر يحدث عن حذيفة قال: الإِسْلاَمُ ثَمَانِيَةُ أَسْهُمٍ: الإِسْلاَمُ سَهْمٌ، وَالصَّلاَةُ سَهْمٌ، وَالزَّكَاةُ سَهْمٌ، وَالْحَجُّ سَهْمٌ، وَالْجِهَادُ فِي سَبِيلِ اللهِ سَهْمٌ، وَصَوْمُ رَمَضَانَ سَهْمٌ، وَالأَمْرُ بِالْمَعْرُوفِ سَهْمٌ، وَالنَّهِيُ عَنِ الْمُنْكَرِ سَهْمٌ، وَقَد خَابَ مَنْ لاَ سَهْمَ لَهُ

Shu'ba narrated to us from Abu Isḥāq he said I heard Ṣilah bin Zufar narrate from Ḥudhayfah, he said: al-Islam is made of eight-shares: al-Islam is a share; *ṣalāh* is a share, *zakāt* is a

> share, *Ḥajj* is a share; *Jihād* in the way of Allah is a share, fasting in *Ramaḍān* is a share and commanding the good and forbidding the evil is a share. And indeed, one who has no share therein has lost.

I would submit, that that he has given the description of 'Islam being a share,' that is to say, the testimonial that there is no god/deity except Allah and that Muḥammad is the Messenger of Allah. That is shown in the next narration which was collected by the Imām Abdar-Razzāq in his *Muṣṣanaf*:

> عن معمر والثوري عن أبي إسحاق عن صلة بن زفر عن حذيفة قال: (بني الاسلام على ثمانية أسهم شهادة أن لا إله الا الله وأن محمدا رسول الله وإقام الصلاة وإيتاء الزكاة وحج البيت وصوم شهر رمضان والجهاد والأمر بالمعروف والنهي عن المنكر وقد خاب من لا سهم له
>
> From Ma'mar and ath-Thawri from Abu Isḥāq from Ṣilah bin Zufah from Ḥudhayfah, he said: Islam is build upon eight-shares: testifying that there is no deity except Allah and that Muḥammad is the Messenger of Allah; establishing the *ṣalāh*, rendering the *zakāt*, pilgrimage to the house, fasting the month of *Ramaḍān*, *Jihād*, commanding the good and forbidding the evil. And indeed, one who has no share therein has lost.

Similar is also found in *mawdu* form in his *Muṣṣanaf*,[12] but the wording of *Jihād* being a share is omitted from the text. Imām Abu Bakr ibn Abi Shayba has also cited the narration in two places in his *Muṣṣanaf*.[13] Imām Abu Ya'la cites the next narration in his *Musnad*:

---

[12] *Muṣṣanaf* Abdar-Razzāq Vol. 5 sec. 173, no. 9280

[13] *Muṣṣanaf* Ibn Abi Shayba Vol. 4 sec. 230, no. 19,561 and Vol. 6 sec. 158, no. 30,313

حَدَّثَنَا سُوَيْدُ بْنُ سَعِيدٍ حَدَّثَنَا حَبِيبُ بْنُ حَبِيبٍ - أَخُو حَمْزَةَ الزَّيَّاتِ - عَنْ أَبِي إِسْحَاقَ عَنِ الْحَارِثِ عَنْ عَلِيٍّ - رَضِيَ الله عَنْهُ - عَنِ النَّبِيِّ صلى الله عليه وسلم، قَالَ: الإِسْلاَمُ ثَمَانِيةُ أَسْهُمٍ: الإِسْلاَمُ سَهْمٌ، وَالصَّلاَةُ سَهْمٌ، وَالزَّكَاةُ سَهْمٌ، وَالْحَجُّ سَهْمٌ، وَالْجِهَادُ سَهْمٌ، وَصَوْمُ رَمَضَانَ سَهْمٌ، وَالأَمْرُ بِالْمَعْرُوفِ سَهْمٌ، وَالنَّهِيُ عَنِ الْمُنْكَرِ سَهْمٌ، وَخَابَ مَنْ لاَ سَهْمَ لَهُ

Suwayd ibn Sa'eed narrated to us Ḥabeeb ibn Ḥabeeb – brother of Ḥamza az-Zayyāt – narrated to us from Abu Isḥāq from al-Ḥārith from Ali (may Allah be pleased with him) from the Prophet (peace be upon him) he said: *al-Islam is eight-shares – Islam is a share; ṣalāh is a share, zakāt is a share, Ḥajj is a share; Jihād is a share, fasting in Ramaḍān is a share and commanding the good is a share and forbidding the evil is a share. And indeed, one who has no share therein has lost.*

Essentially the *ḥadith* is the same as the former, albeit here with Ḥabeeb ibn Ḥabeeb az-Zayyāt and it is a weak tradition in grading (*ḍaef*); in its *isnād* it is attributed to being from al-Ḥārith from Ali as *marfu'*. Perhaps it is a defect from Suwayd ibn Sa'eed given that he is much greater in age and his uncle and consequently had defects. It is also in the *Sunnah* of Abu Bakr bin Khilāl (as per the *Shāmila*):

حدثنا أبو عبد الله قال: حدثنا وكيع قال: حدثنا أبي وإسرائيل وعلي بن صالح عن أبي إسحاق عن صلة بن زفر العبسي عن حذيفة، قال: الإسلام ثمانية أسهم: الإسلام سهم، والصلاة سهم، والزكاة سهم، والحج سهم، ورمضان سهم، والجهاد سهم، والأمر بالمعروف سهم، والنهي عن المنكر سهم، وقد خاب من لا سهم له

Abu Abdullah narrated to us he said Waki' narrated to us he said my father, Isrā'il and Ali bin Ṣāliḥ narrated to us from Abu Isḥāq from Ṣillah bin Zufar al-'Absi (who) narrated to us from Ḥudhayfah he said: Al-Islam is eight-shares; Islam is a share and *ṣalāh* is a share; *zakāt* is a share, *Ḥajj* is a share; *Ramaḍān* is a share and commanding the good is a share and forbidding the evil is a share. And indeed, one who has no share therein has lost.

Furthermore, as has been reported by al-Bazzār in his *Musnad*:

> حَدَّثَنَا مُحَمَّدُ بْنُ سَعِيدِ بْنِ يَزِيدَ بْنِ إِبْرَاهِيمَ التُّسْتَرِيُّ، قَالَ: أَخْبَرَنَا يَعْقُوبُ بْنُ إِسْحَاقَ الْحَضْرَمِيُّ قَالَ: أَخْبَرَنَا يَزِيدُ بْنُ عَطَاءٍ قَالَ: أَخْبَرَنَا أَبُو إِسْحَاقَ عَنْ صِلَةَ عَنْ حُذَيْفَةَ رَضِيَ اللَّهُ عَنْهُ عَنِ النَّبِيِّ صلى الله عليه وسلم، قَالَ: الإِسْلامُ ثَمَانِيَةُ أَسْهُمٍ الإِسْلامُ سَهْمٌ، وَالصَّلاةُ سَهْمٌ، وَالزَّكَاةُ سَهْمٌ، وَحَجُّ الْبَيْتِ سَهْمٌ، وَالصِّيَامُ سَهْمٌ، وَالأَمْرُ بِالْمَعْرُوفِ سَهْمٌ، وَالنَّهْيُ عَنِ الْمُنْكَرِ سَهْمٌ، وَالْجِهَادُ فِي سَبِيلِ اللهِ سَهْمٌ، وَقَدْ خَابَ مَنْ لاَ سَهْمَ لَهُ؛ وَأَخْبَرَنَاهُ مُحَمَّدُ بْنُ الْمُثَنَّى، قَالَ: أَخْبَرَنَا مُحَمَّدُ بْنُ جَعْفَرٍ، قَالَ: أَخْبَرَنَا شُعْبَةُ، عَنْ أَبِي إِسْحَاقَ، عَنْ صِلَةَ بْنِ زُفَرَ، عَنْ حُذَيْفَةَ رَضِيَ اللَّهُ عَنْهُ أَنَّهُ قَالَ: الإِسْلامُ ثَمَانِيَةُ أَسْهُمٍ ثُمَّ ذَكَرَ مِثْلَهُ وَلَمْ يُسْنِدْهُ
>
> Muḥammad ibn Sa'eed bin Yazeed bin Ibrāhim at-Tastari narrated to us he said Ya'qub bin Isḥāq al-Haḍrami reported to us he said Yazeed bin 'Aṭā reported to us he said Abu Isḥāq reported to us from Ṣilla from Ḥudhayfah may Allah be pleased with him from the Prophet (peace be upon him) he said: *Islam is made from eight-shares. The first share, is believing in Islam, performing Ṣalāh is one share; paying zakāt is a share; pilgrimage to the house is a share, fasting is a share, commanding the good is a share, forbidding the evil is a share as is Jihād in the path of Allah. Verily (there is) failure for one who has no share in it.* And Muḥammad bin al-Muthanna reported it he said Muḥammad bin Ja'far reported to us he said Shu'ba reported to us from Abu Isḥāq from Ṣilla bin Zufar from Ḥudhayfah may Allah be pleased with him, that he said: al-Islam is eight-shares, then mentioned the remainder without its channel.

Thereafter al-Bazzār commented: 'And this *ḥadith* we do not know of it by this *isnād*, that is to say, it is raised, except by way of Yazeed bin 'Aṭā from Abu Isḥāq.' Imām aṭ-Ṭabarāni has the next narration in both *Mu'jam al-Kabir* and *Mu'jam al-Awsaṭ:*

حَدَّثَنَا مَحْمُودُ بْنُ مُحَمَّدٍ الْمَرْوَزِيُّ حدثنا حَامِدُ بْنُ آدَمَ حدثنا عَلِيُّ بْنُ عَاصِمٍ حدثنا خَالِدٌ الْحَذَّاءُ عَنْ عِكْرِمَةَ عَنِ ابْنِ عَبَّاسٍ قال: قال رَسُولُ اللَّهِ صلى الله عليه وسلم: <u>الْإِسْلَامُ عَشْرَةُ أَسْهُمٍ، وَقَدْ خَابَ مَنْ لَا سَهْمَ لَهُ</u>: شَهَادَةُ أَنْ لَا إِلَهَ إِلَّا اللَّهُ، وَهِيَ الْمِلَّةُ، وَالثَّانِيَةُ الصَّلَاةُ وَهِيَ الْفِطْرَةُ، وَالثَّالِثَةُ الزَّكَاةُ وَهِيَ الطَّهُورُ، وَالرَّابِعَةُ الصَّوْمُ وَهِيَ الْجُنَّةُ، وَالْخَامِسَةُ الْحَجُّ وَهِيَ الشَّرِيعَةُ، وَالسَّادِسَةُ الْجِهَادُ وَهِيَ الْعُرْوَةُ، وَالسَّابِعَةُ الْأَمْرُ بِالْمَعْرُوفِ وَهُوَ الْوَفَاءُ، وَالثَّامِنَةُ النَّهْيُ عَنِ الْمُنْكَرِ وَهِيَ الْحُجَّةُ، وَالتَّاسِعَةُ الْجَمَاعَةُ وَهِيَ الْأُلْفَةُ، وَالْعَاشِرَةُ الطَّاعَةُ وَهِيَ الْعِصْمَةُ

> Muḥammad ibn Muḥammad al-Marwazi narrated to us Ḥāmid ibn Adam narrated to us Ali ibn 'Aāṣim narrated to us Khālid ibn al-Ḥadth'a narrated to us from 'Ikrima from Ibn 'Abbās he said that the Messenger of Allah (peace be upon him) said: <u>*Al-Islam is ten-shares and indeed one who has no share therein has lost*</u>. *Testifying that there is no deity except Allah, and it is the millah; secondly, the prayer, it is the fiṭra, thirdly the zakāt and it is the Ṭahur (purity). Fourth, the fast and it is the shield. Fifth, al-Ḥajj and it is the Shari'āh. Sixth, al-Jihād and it is adherence. Seventh, commanding the good and it is a debt. Eight, forbidding the evil and it is the proof. Ninth, the community (al-Jamā'ah) and it is the affinity. And tenth, obedience and it is the listening.*

In *al-Awsaṭ*, he then writes: 'This *ḥadith* isn't recited from Khālid bin al-Ḥadth'a except by way of Ali bin 'Aāṣim and Ḥāmid bin Adam individually.' I would submit that Ḥāmid bin Adam bin Muslim al-Azdi al-Tiliyāni al-Marwazi is different in it. Ibn 'Adi has said: 'I didn't see in his *ḥadith* if he narrated from a trustworthy narrator anything that is *munkar*, but if that happened then his narration is considered weak.' He mentioned the comment of Ibn Ḥibbān in *ath-Thiqāt*, 'Maybe (he has) mistakes,' and al-Khalili said in *al-Irshād*, 'Ḥāmid bin Adam al-Marwazi is *thiqa*, he narrates from several scholars and Muḥammad bin Ḥamdawe Abu Rajā' and other than him; he heard from Abu Ghānim Yunus bin Nāfi and other than him.' But some of them have accused him of lying, which would seem to suggest that this charge has been unfairly put, as it has been mentioned elsewhere, in explaining the sentences like the saying from these two testimonials: 'it is the *milla*' except where its saying from 'Aṭā; 'and it is infallible', something from the strangers. Perhaps subsumed from the words of Ibn 'Abbās or those without narrators. As for the texts, they are words of truth from Ḥudhayfah with the additions of 'the community' *(al-Jamā'ah)* 'and obedience' *(aṭ-Ṭā'a)* and this is stemming from the *ḥadith* of al-Ḥārith al-Ash'ari and all of it is established from the truth of the Qur'ān as well as the continuously recurrent *aḥādith*.

Imām aṭ-Ṭabarāni furnishes us with the next narration that is in the *Musnad Shāmiayn*:

حدثنا محمد بن عمرو بن خالد الحراني حدثنا أبي عن عيسى بن يونس عن ثور بن يزيد عن خالد بن معدان عن أبي هريرة أن رسول الله، صلى الله عليه وسلم، قال: إن للإسلام صوى ومنارا كمنار الطريق من ذلك: أن يعبد الله لا يشرك به شيئا، وتقام الصلاة، وتؤتى الزكاة، ويحج البيت، ويصام رمضان، والأمر بالمعروف، والنهي عن المنكر، وتسليمك على أهل بيتك إذا دخلت عليهم، وتسليمك على بني آدم إذا لقيتهم فإن ردوا عليك ردت عليهم الملائكة وإن لم يردوا عليك ردت عليك الملائكة ولعنتهم أو سكتت عنهم؛ ومن انتقص منهن شيئا فهو سهم من الإسلام تركه؛ ومن نبذهن فقد ولى الإسلام ظهره

Muḥammad bin 'Amr bin Khālid al-Ḥarāni narrated to us my father narrated to us from Esa bin Yunus from Thawr bin Yazeed from Khālid bin Ma'dān from Abu Hurayrah that the Messenger of Allah (peace be upon him) said: *Verily like roads, Islam has a guidepost and a lighthouse. From that, that you worship Allah and do not associate anything with him; to establish the Ṣalāh, render the zakāt, to make pilgrimage to the house and to fast in Ramaḍān. To enjoin the good and forbid the evil, to give your salam* (the greeting of) *to the people of your house when you enter upon them and to give your salam upon Bani Adam whence you encounter them. If the respondents don't reply, the angels will receive the salam and respond in kind despite their silence. And whosoever leaves anything from these shares of Islam it would be incomplete, and whomsoever would have their Islam* (in that manner) *would be ostracized by this.*

Similar is also found in the *Ta'dtheem Qadra al-Ṣalāt* of Muḥammad bin Naṣr al-Marwazi, the *isnād* of which contains men who are authentic narrators:

حَدَّثَنَا مُحَمَّدُ بْنُ بَشَّارٍ حدثنا رَوْحُ بْنُ عُبَادَةَ حدثنا ثَوْرُ بْنُ يَزِيدَ عَنْ خَالِدِ بْنِ مَعْدَانَ عَنْ أَبِي هُرَيْرَةَ قَالَ: قَالَ رَسُولُ اللَّهِ صلى الله عليه وسلم: إِنَّ لِلْإِسْلَامِ صُوًى وَمَنَارًا كَمَنَارِ الطَّرِيقِ، مِنْ ذَلِكَ أَنْ تَعْبُدَ اللَّهَ وَلَا تُشْرِكَ بِهِ شَيْئًا، وَأَنْ تُقِيمَ الصَّلَاةَ، وَتُؤْتِيَ الزَّكَاةَ، وَتَصُومَ رَمَضَانَ، وَالْأَمْرُ بِالْمَعْرُوفِ، وَالنَّهْيُ عَنِ الْمُنْكَرِ، وَتَسْلِيمُكَ عَلَى بَنِي آدَمَ إِذَا لَقِيتَهُمْ، فَإِنْ رَدُّوا عَلَيْكَ رَدَّتْ عَلَيْكَ وَعَلَيْهِمُ الْمَلَائِكَةُ، وَإِنْ لَمْ يَرُدُّوا عَلَيْكَ رَدَّتْ عَلَيْكَ الْمَلَائِكَةُ، وَلَعَنَتْهُمْ أَوْ سَكَتَتْ عَنْهُمْ، وَتَسْلِيمُكَ عَلَى أَهْلِ بَيْتِكَ إِذَا دَخَلْتَ عَلَيْهِمْ، فَمَنِ انْتَقَصَ مِنْهُنَّ شَيْئًا فَهُوَ سَهْمٌ مِنَ الْإِسْلَامِ تَرَكَهُ، وَمَنْ تَرَكَهُنَّ فَقَدْ نَبَذَ الْإِسْلَامَ وَرَاءَ ظَهْرِهِ

Muḥammad ibn Bashār narrated to us Ruḥ bin 'Ubāda narrated to us Thawr bin Yazeed narrated to us from Khālid bin Ma'dān from Abu Hurayrah he said the Messenger of Allah (peace be upon him) said: *Verily like roads, Islam has a guidepost and a lighthouse. From that, that you worship Allah and do not associate anything with him. And that you establish the Ṣalāh, render the zakāt, fast in Ramaḍān; enjoin the good and forbid the evil. To send your salam upon mankind when you encounter them and if they do not respond the angels will do so and either curse them or remain silent upon them. To send your salam upon the people of your household when you enter upon them. Whoever leaves anything from them will be incomplete as these are the shares of Islam; leaving them will be leaving Islam behind ones back.*

In the *Mustadrak* al-Ḥākim collected the following narration:

حدثنا أبو بكر بن إسحاق حدثنا عبيد بن عبد الواحد حدثنا محمد بن أبي السري حدثنا الوليد بن مسلم عن ثور بن يزيد عن خالد بن معدان عن أبي هريرة، رضي الله عنه، عن النبي، صلى الله عليه وسلم، قال: الإسلام أن تعبد الله لا تشرك به شيئا وتقيم الصلاة وتؤتي الزكاة وتصوم رمضان وتحج البيت والأمر بالمعروف والنهي عن المنكر وتسليمك على أهلك؛ فمن انتقص شيئا منهن فهو سهم من الإسلام يدعه ومن تركهن كلهن فقد ولى الإسلام ظهره

Abu Bakr ibn Isḥāq narrated to us 'Ubaid ibn Abdal-Wāhid narrated to us Muḥammad bin Abul'as-Sarri narrated to us al-Waleed bin Muslim narrated to us from Thawr bin Yazeed from Khālid bin Ma'dān from Abu Hurayrah may Allah be pleased with him from the Prophet (peace be upon him), he said: *Al-Islam is that you worship Allah and do not associate anything (whatsoever) with him; to establish the prayer to render the zakāt, to fast in Ramaḍān; to make pilgrimage to the house and commanding the good and forbidding the evil; to send your greetings upon your family. Whoever leaves anything from them will be incomplete as these are the shares of Islam; leaving them in totality would be to leave Islam altogether.*

Thereafter al-Ḥākim writes: 'This *ḥadith* is like the first in uprightness (*al-Istiqāmah*).' I would submit here that there is no fear from *tadlees* occurring in relation to the narrator al-Waleed bin Muslim as it testified by the channel that appears in the *Musnad ash-Shāmiayn,*[14] given the omission of the sentence that relates to '*To send your salam upon mankind when you encounter them and if they do not respond the*

[14] *Musnad ash-Shāmiayn* Vol. 1 sec. 243, no. 429

angels will do so and either curse them or remain silent upon them.' It may have been cut short due to the ignorance of one of the narrators regarding this, despite its great reward that has been attested to.

The narration also appears in the work of *Commanding the Good* (*'Amr bil-Ma'rouf*) by Abdal-Ghani al-Maqdisi:

أخبرنا أبو طاهر أحمد بن محمد بن أحمد بن محمد بن إبراهيم السلفي الأصبهاني بالإسكندرية وأبو الفتح محمد بن عبد الباقي بن أحمد بن سلمان ببغداد قالا: أخبرنا أبو بكر أحمد بن علي بن الحسين بن زكريا الطريثيثي أخبرنا أبو القاسم هبة الله بن الحسن بن منصور الطبري الحافظ أخبرنا محمد بن عبد الرحمن بن العباس إجازة أخبرنا سعيد بن محمد بن الراحبان حدثنا نصر بن داود بن طوق قال: قال أبو عبيد حدثنيه يحيى بن سعيد القطان عن ثور بن يزيد عن خالد بن معدان عن رجل عن أبي هريرة، عن النبي، صلى الله عليه وسلم، أنه قال: إن للإسلام صوى ومنارا كمنار الطريق منها أن تؤمنوا بالله ولا تشرك به شيئا وإقام الصلاة وإيتاء الزكاة وصوم رمضان وحج البيت وأن تسلم على أهلك إذا دخلت عليهم وأن تسلم على القوم إذا مررت بهم فمن ترك شيئا من ذلك فقد ترك سهما من الإسلام ومن نبذ ذلك فقد ولى الإسلام ظهره

Abu Ṭāhir Aḥmad bin Muḥammad bin Aḥmad bin Muḥammad bin Ibrāhim al-Salfi al-Aṣbahāni in Alexandria and Abu al-Fatḥ Muḥammad bin Abdal-Bāqi bin Aḥmad bin Salmān in Baghdad reported to us, they both said: Abu Bakr Aḥmad bin Ali bin al-Ḥussein bin Zakariyā aṭ-Ṭareeshshee reported to us Abul' Qāsim Habat-Allah bin al-Ḥasan bin Manṣur aṭ-Ṭabari al-Ḥāfiz reported to us Muḥammad bin Abdur-Raḥman bin al-Abbās Ijāza reported to us Sa'eed bin Muḥammad bin ar-Raḥbān reported to us Naṣr bin Dāwud bin Ṭawq narrated to us he said that Abu Ubaid said Yaḥya bin Sa'eed al-Qahṭān narrated it to me from Thawr bin Yazeed from Khālid bin Ma'dān from a man from Abu Hurayrah from the Prophet (peace be upon him) that he said: *Verily like roads, Islam has a guidepost and a lighthouse from that; that you believe in Allah and do not associate anything with him. To establish the Ṣalāh, render the zakāt, fast in Ramaḍān; make pilgrimage to the house and that*

> *you send your salam about your people when you enter upon them and that you give salam upon your people when you encounter them. Whoever leaves anything from that has left a share of Islam and that is a rejection of Islam.*

Following this citation Abdal-Ghani writes: 'It is reported by al-Ḥāfiz Ṭabari in the book of *Sunnah* like that.' Additionally, the narration is found in *al-'Imān* of al-Qāsim bin Sallām:

> وَمِنَ التِّسْعِ حَدِيثُ أَبِي هُرَيْرَةَ عَنِ النَّبِيِّ صلى الله عليه وسلم أَنَّهُ قَالَ: إِنَّ لِلْإِسْلَامِ صُوًى وَمَنَارًا كَمَنَارِ الطَّرِيقِ» - قَالَ أَبُو عُبَيْدٍ: صُوًى: هِيَ مَا غَلُظَ وَارْتَفَعَ مِنَ الْأَرْضِ، وَاحِدَتُهَا صُوَّةٌ - «مِنْهَا: أَنْ تُؤْمِنَ بِاللَّهِ، وَلَا تُشْرِكَ بِهِ شَيْئًا، وَإِقَامَةُ الصَّلَاةِ، وَإِيتَاءُ الزَّكَاةِ، وَصَوْمُ رَمَضَانَ، وَحَجُّ الْبَيْتِ، وَالْأَمْرُ بِالْمَعْرُوفِ، وَالنَّهْيُ عَنِ الْمُنْكَرِ، وَأَنْ تُسَلِّمَ عَلَى أَهْلِكَ إِذَا دَخَلْتَ عَلَيْهِمْ، وَأَنْ تُسَلِّمَ عَلَى الْقَوْمِ إِذَا مَرَرْتَ بِهِمْ، فَمَنْ تَرَكَ مِنْ ذَلِكَ شَيْئًا فَقَدْ تَرَكَ سَهْمًا مِنَ الْإِسْلَامِ، وَمَنْ تَرَكَهُنَّ فَقَدْ وَلَّى الْإِسْلَامَ ظَهْرَهُ
>
> And from the ninth *ḥadith* of Abu Hurayrah from the Prophet (peace be upon him) that he said: '*Verily like roads, Islam has a guidepost and a lighthouse.'* Abu 'Ubaid said: the guideposts are what has been thickened and arisen from the earth. What is thickened and rose from the ground '*From it that you worship Allah and do not associate anything with him. And that you establish the Ṣalāh, render the zakāt, fast in Ramaḍān; make pilgrimage to the house and enjoin the good and forbid the evil. And that you send your salam upon your family when you enter upon them and that you send your salam upon the people when you encounter them. Whoever leaves anything from that has left a share of Islam and that is a rejection of Islam.'*

Abu 'Ubaid then says:

> Yaḥya ibn Sa'eed al-Attar narrated it to him from Thawr bin

> Yazeed from Khālid bin Ma'dān from a man from Abu Hurayrah from the Prophet (peace be upon him). That is how it is originally 'al-Aṭṭār' but it is (in actuality) al-Qahtān, Yaḥya bin Sa'eed al-Qahṭān, the reputable Imām; al-Ḥāfiz, firmly established as a proof may Allah be pleased with him. And he commented and said: some from the ignorant thought that these *aḥādith* contradict each other and they traced it back to the differences in its (reported) number. But, praise be to Allah, it is far and away from being in contradiction to each other. The matter of its variance is because, as you know, the principle obligations of faith (*al-'Imān*) were revealed separately. So, whenever a new matter would arise, the Prophet (peace be upon him) added it to the previous commandments. Then, as Allah sent a new one, he (peace be upon him) added it at once. That is why the *aḥādith* that are mentioned exceed that of over seventy.

And lastly from the words of Khālid bin Ma'dān in the works of Ibn Bishrān we have the following:

> وَأَخْبَرَنَا جَعْفَرٌ أنبا جَعْفَرٌ حدثنا أَبُو عُبَيْدٍ حدثنا يَحْيَى بْنُ سَعِيدٍ عَنْ نُورِ بْنِ يَزِيدَ عَنْ خَالِدِ بْنِ مَعْدَانَ، قَالَ: إِنَّ لِلْإِسْلَامِ صُوًى وَمَنَارًا كَمَنَارِ الطَّرِيقِ، فَمِنْهَا أَنْ تُؤْمِنَ بِاللَّهِ عَزَّ وَجَلَّ لَا تُشْرِكْ بِهِ شَيْئًا، وَإِقَامَ الصَّلَاةِ، وَإِيتَاءُ الزَّكَاةِ، وَصَوْمُ رَمَضَانَ، وَحَجُّ الْبَيْتِ، وَالْأَمْرُ بِالْمَعْرُوفِ، وَالنَّهْيُ عَنِ الْمُنْكَرِ، وَأَنْ تُسَلِّمَ عَلَى أَهْلِكَ إِذَا دَخَلْتَ عَلَيْهِمْ، وَأَنْ تُسَلِّمَ عَلَى قَوْمٍ إِذَا مَرَرْتَ بِهِمْ، فَمَنْ تَرَكَ مِنْ ذَلِكَ شَيْئًا فَقَدْ تَرَكَ سَهْمًا مِنَ الْإِسْلَامِ، وَمَنْ تَرَكَهُنَّ فَقَدْ وَلَّى لِلْإِسْلَامِ ظَهْرَهُ
>
> Ja'far reported to us Ja'far reports: Abu 'Ubaid narrated to us Yaḥya bin Sa'eed narrated to us from Thawr bin Yazeed from Khālid bin Ma'dān he said: Verily like roads, Islam has a guidepost and a lighthouse. That you worship Allah the exalted and do not associate anything with him. And that you establish the *Ṣalāh,* render the *zakāt*, fast in *Ramaḍān*; make pilgrimage to the house and enjoin the good and forbid the evil.

> And that you send your *salam* upon your people when you enter upon them and that you send your *salam* upon people when you encounter them. Whoever leaves anything from that has left a share of Islam and that is a rejection of Islam.

Firstly, it would appear apparent from the narrations of Abu 'Ubaid and Abdal-Ghani al-Maqdisi that concerning Khālid bin Ma'dān, he has taken the narrative from an unknown man from Abu Hurayrah. If this man was truthful and recorded the *ḥadith* in an appropriate way, then the channel of transmission would be considered authentic (*isnād Ṣaḥīḥ*). As for the *matn* (text) of the report, it is one of uprightness, because he just mentioned these adjectives as a beacon, exactly like the lighthouse which distinguishes it, or the lighthouse which sailors use to navigate away from the danger of rocks. The word *Ṣuwa* are stones that are erected amidst a wasteland of an empty desert, evidenced by the signs on the road. The singular form is '*Ṣwa*', in the same rhyme of this word as '*Quwa*', also its called '*Al-Rajoom*' or '*al-Rijām'* and its singular form is '*rijm'*. The narrator has conveyed that Islam has a special appearance and signs, in which proves its existence; some of these signs are like pillars or markers, others not, by necessity.

Secondly, that the commentary of Imām Ibn Ḥibbān has been given greater precedence over that asserted by Imām Abu Ubaid. What this shows is that there is several different viewpoints when it comes to discussing these matters in relation to the pillars, guideposts and shares of Islam. When it comes to talking about the different aspects of faith (*al-'Imān*), the numerous accolades that the Prophet (peace be upon him) has over the previous prophets; the nature of the major sins (*kabā'ir*) and the like, items are mentioned according to the relevant situation and the circumstances of the recipients. It is not necessary that all aspects are detailed and mentioned in one sitting, but rather mentioning a short number to facilitate easy understanding and memorisation.

In *Musnad Shāmiayn* Imām Ṭabarāni cites the following:

حَدَّثَنَا بَكْرُ بْنُ سَهْلٍ حَدَّثَنَا عَبْدُ اللَّهِ بْنُ صَالِحٍ حَدَّثَنِي مُعَاوِيَةُ بْنُ صَالِحٍ عَنْ أَبِي الزَّاهِرِيَّةِ عَنْ أَبِي الدَّرْدَاءِ عَنِ النَّبِيِّ صلى الله عليه وسلم، قَالَ: إِنَّ لِلْإِسْلَامِ صُوًى وَعَلَامَاتٍ كَمَنَارِ الطَّرِيقِ، فَرَأْسُهَا وَجِمَالُهَا شَهَادَةُ أَنْ لَا إِلَهَ إِلَّا اللَّهُ، وَأَنَّ مُحَمَّدًا عَبْدُهُ وَرَسُولُهُ، وَإِقَامُ الصَّلَاةِ، وَإِيتَاءُ الزَّكَاةِ، وَتَمَامُ الْوضُوءِ، وَالْحُكْمُ بِكِتَابِ اللَّهِ، وَسُنَّةِ نَبِيِّهِ، صلى الله عليه وسلم، وَطَاعَةُ وِلَاةِ الْأَمْرِ، وَتَسْلِيمُكُمْ عَلَى أَنْفُسِكُمْ، وَتَسْلِيمُكُمْ إِذَا دَخَلْتُمْ بُيُوتَكُمْ، وَتَسْلِيمُكُمْ عَلَى بَنِي آدَمَ إِذَا لَقِيتُمُوهُمْ

Bakr bin Sahl narrated to us Abdullah bin Ṣāliḥ narrated to us Mu'āwiyah bin Ṣāliḥ narrated to me from Abu az-Zāhiriyah from Abu Darda' from the Prophet (peace be upon him) that *Verily like roads, Islam has a signpost and a lighthouse. Its pinnacle and beauty is the testimony that there is no god/deity except Allah and that Muḥammad is his slave and messenger. To establish the Ṣalāh, render the zakāt, and complete the wuḍu and the ḥukm of the book of Allah and the Sunnah of his Prophet (peace be upon him) and to obey the rulers and to send your salam upon all and your salam upon the people of your house when you enter and to send your salam upon all of mankind.*

Following this, Ḥamdi bin Abdal-Majeed as-Salafi has a comment regarding this in his *Tahqeeq* (*Nashr Ma'soosa ar-Risāla*) saying: 'And Ibn Daust narrated it in al-Amāli from the channel of Abdullah ibn Ṣāliḥ from Mu'āwiyah with him and it is observed here that these two channels are together considered good (*ḥasan*).' Here it has been narrated with the wording '*its beauty*' perhaps because additional sources have it saying: '*and its group*.' Regarding this I would submit that improvement of Ḥamdi bin Abdal-Majeed as-Salafi with his collection of channels is not *ḥasan*. This is because there is a break in the channel between Abu az-Zāhiriyah Ḥadeer bin Kureeb and Abu Darda' that is still listed. But it may be the case that it would provide an improvement of the *ḥadith* of Abu Hurayrah in this regard, as both being a testimony to one another. There is some disagreement concerning the wording '*has a signpost and a lighthouse*' but also because of the unknown narrator between Abu az-Zāhiriyah and Abu Darda' and that is not the unknown narrator in relation to the *ḥadith* of Abu Hurayrah.

There is also the report that is in the *Muṣṣanaf* of Abu Bakr ibn Abi Shayba:

حَدَّثَنَا مُحَمَّدُ بْنُ فُضَيْلٍ عَنْ عُمَارَةَ عَنْ أَبِي زُرْعَةَ قَالَ عُمَرُ: عُرَى الإِيمَانِ أَرْبَعٌ: الصَّلاةُ وَالزَّكَاةُ وَالْجِهَادُ وَالأَمَانَةُ

Muḥammad bin Fuḍeel narrated to us from Umāra from Abu Zur'a he said Umar mentioned four (things regarding) *al-'Imān*: the *Ṣalāh, the zakāt*, the *Jihād* and trusts (*amānah*).

Imām Ṭabarāni has the next narration in his *Mu'jam*:

حدثنا عَبْدُ اللَّهِ بن مُحَمَّدِ بن عَبْدِ الْعَزِيزِ الْبَغَوِيُّ حَدَّثَنَا صَالِحُ بن مَالِكٍ الْخَوَارِزْمِيُّ حَدَّثَنَا عَبْدُ الأَعْلَى بن أَبِي الْمُسَاوِرِ حَدَّثَنِي عَامِرٌ الشَّعْبِيُّ قَالَ: قَدِمَ عَدِيُّ بن حَاتِمٍ الطَّائِيُّ الْكُوفَةَ، فَأَتَيْتُهُ فِي أُنَاسٍ مِنْ أَهْلِ الْكُوفَةِ، فَقُلْنَا لَهُ حَدِّثْنَا بِحَدِيثٍ سَمِعْتَهُ مِنْ رَسُولِ اللَّهِ، صلى الله عليه وسلم، فَقَالَ: بُعِثَ رَسُولُ اللَّهِ، صلى الله عليه وسلم، بِالنُّبُوَّةِ، وَلا أَعْلَمُ أَحَدًا مِنَ الْعَرَبِ كَانَ أَشَدَّ لَهُ بُغْضًا، وَلا أَشَدَّ لَهُ كَرَاهِيَةً مِنِّي، حَتَّى لَحِقْتُ بِالرُّومِ، فَتَنَصَّرْتُ فِيهِمْ، فَلَمَّا بَلَغَنِي مَا يَدْعُو إِلَيْهِ مِنَ الأَخْلاقِ الْحَسَنَةِ، وَمَا قَدِ اجْتَمَعَ إِلَيْهِ مِنَ النَّاسِ ارْتَحَلْتُ حَتَّى أَتَيْتُهُ، فَوَقَفْتُ عَلَيْهِ، وَعِنْدَهُ صُهَيْبٌ وَبِلالٌ وَسَلْمَانُ، فَقَالَ: يَا عَدِيُّ بن حَاتِمٍ، أَسْلِمْ تَسْلَمْ، فَقُلْتُ: أَخْ أَخْ، فَأَنَخْتُ، وَجَلَسْتُ، وَأَلْزَقْتُ رُكْبَتِي بِرُكْبَتِهِ، فَقُلْتُ: يَا رَسُولَ اللَّهِ، مَا الإِسْلامُ؟ قَالَ: تُؤْمِنُ بِاللَّهِ، وَمَلائِكَتِهِ، وَكُتُبِهِ، وَرُسُلِهِ، وَتُؤْمِنُ بِالْقَدَرِ خَيْرِهِ وَشَرِّهِ، وَحُلْوِهِ وَمُرِّهِ؛ يَا عَدِيُّ بن حَاتِمٍ: لا تَقُومُ السَّاعَةُ حَتَّى تُفْتَحَ خَزَائِنُ كِسْرَى وَقَيْصَرَ؛ يَا عَدِيُّ بن حَاتِمٍ: لا تَقُومُ السَّاعَةُ حَتَّى تَأْتِيَ الظَّعِينَةُ مِنَ الْحِيرَةِ، وَلَمْ يَكُنْ يَوْمِئِذٍ كُوفَةُ، حَتَّى تَطُوفَ بِهَذِهِ الْكَعْبَةِ بِغَيْرِ خَفِيرٍ، يَا عَدِيُّ بن حَاتِمٍ، لا تَقُومُ السَّاعَةُ حَتَّى تَطُوفَ جِرَابُ الْمَالِ،

فَتَطُوفَ بِهِ وَلا تَجِدُ لَهُ أَحَدًا يَقْبَلُهُ، فَتَضْرِبَ بِهِ الأَرْضَ، فَتَقُولَ: لَيْتَكَ لَمْ تَكُنْ، لَيْتَكَ كُنْتَ تُرَابًا

Abdullah bin Muḥammad bin Abdul-Aziz al-Baghawi narrated to us Ṣāliḥ bin Mālik al-Khawārizmi narrated to us Abdal-'Ala bin Abul'Musāwir narrated to us 'Aāmir ash-Sha'bi narrated to me he said 'Adi bin Ḥātim aṭ-Ṭā'ie came to Kufa and came upon the people of Kufa. We said narrate to us some *ḥadith* that you heard from the Messenger of Allah (peace be upon him). He replied the messenger of Allah (peace be upon him) was sent with Prophethood and none from among the Arabs disliked it more so than I, until my encounter with Rome. When I had heard that the call was to mannerisms and the good. And I came upon a group from amongst the people until I arrived upon them. I stood before them and they were Ṣuhayb, Bilāl and Salmān. He said: *O 'Adi bin Ḥātim, enter Islam and you will be safe*. So, I said: brother, brother. I thus purified myself and I sat down on the ground, my knees next to his knees. Thereafter I said O Messenger of Allah, what is Islam? He replied: *To believe in Allah, his angels, his books, his messengers and to believe in al-Qadr, the good or bad, its sweetness or bitterness. O 'Adi bin Ḥātim the hour will not be established until the treasures of Kisra and Qayṣar are opened.*[15] *O 'Adi bin Ḥātim the hour will not be established until the lady from al-Ḥira comes, and not that day from Kufa, to perform circumambulation of the Ka'ba and fears none. O 'Adi bin Ḥātim, the hour will not be established until circumambulation is undertaken for money, and in that it won't be acceptable to anyone and the striking of the earth, until it's said: I wish it wasn't; I wish you were dust.*

Here there isn't a great deal in general, the pathway saying '*testifying that there is no god/deity except Allah and that Muḥammad is the messenger of Allah.*' Some have abbreviated this only to '*testifying that there is no god/deity except Allah*'. Others have expressed this as

[15] The titles that were given to the rulers of Persia and Rome – Khosrau and Caesar

'*the oneness of Allah,*' or '*that you worship Allah and disbelieve in anything besides him.*' Alternatively, there is also '*al-'Imān* in Allah and his Messenger,' which is surmised or detailed as being '*to believe in Allah, his angels, his books, his messengers and to believe in al-Qadr, its good, bad, its sweetness and its bitterness.*'

Imām Muslim cites the following two narrations in his collection:

حدثنا محمد بن عبد الله بن نمير الهمداني حدثنا أبو خالد يعني سليمان بن حيان الأحمر عن أبي مالك الأشجعي عن سعد بن عبيدة عن بن عمر عن النبي، صلى الله عليه وسلم، قال بني الإسلام على خمسة على أن يوحد الله وإقام الصلاة وإيتاء الزكاة وصيام رمضان والحج فقال رجل الحج وصيام رمضان قال لا صيام رمضان والحج هكذا سمعته من رسول الله، صلى الله عليه وسلم

Muḥammad bin Numayr al-Hamdāni narrated to us Abu Khālid, that is to say, Sulaymān bin Ḥayyān al-Aḥmar narrated to us from Abu Mālik al-Ashja'ee from Sa'd bin 'Ubadah from Ibn Umar from the Prophet (peace be upon him), he said: *Al-Islam is raised upon five: upon the oneness of Allah, the establishment of prayer, payment of Zakāt, the fast of Ramaḍān and Ḥajj.* A person said: Which of the two precedes the other - *Ḥajj* or the fast of *Ramaḍān*? He (Ibn Umar) replied: No - the fast of *Ramaḍān* and (then) *Ḥajj* as it has been heard from the Messenger of Allah (peace be upon him).

وحدثنا سهل بن عثمان العسكري حدثنا يحيى بن زكريا حدثنا سعد بن طارق قال حدثني سعد بن عبيدة السلمي عن بن عمر عن النبي، صلى الله عليه وسلم، قال بني الإسلام على خمس على أن يعبد الله ويكفر بما دونه وإقام الصلاة وإيتاء الزكاة وحج البيت وصوم رمضان

And Sahl bin Uthmān al-'Askari narrated to us Yaḥya bin Zakariyā narrated to us Sa'd bin Ṭāriq narrated to us he said Sa'd bin 'Ubayda as-Salami narrated to me from Ibn Umar from the Prophet (peace be upon him), he said: *Al-Islam is built*

> *upon five: that Allah alone should be worshipped and to disbelieve all others besides him; the establishment of prayer, the payment of Zakāt, Ḥajj to the house, and the fast of Ramaḍān.*

Regarding the nature of this important topic, a study relating to the pillars of Islam, the starting point should necessarily should be the Qur'ān. Then for consistency, the authentic established *Sunnah* which by necessity explains and expounds upon the entire Qur'ān. Perhaps there are other points that can be marshalled which would provide further restriction upon the absolute statements and further specify the general. Regrettably such efforts diminished after the period of the rightly guided *Khulafā'* (caliphs), after which began the onset of the 'era of interpretation,' *(aṣr at-Tā'weel)* inaugurated by the usurpation of the *Khilafah* by Mu'āwiya bin Abu Sufyān. The situation worsened immensely at the hands of the hypocritical scholars associated with the rulers with a small distortion becoming much bigger. Divine texts were disregarded in favour of accumulated interpretation, ushering in an era of what can be considered outright change, in order at times, to suit the whims of rulers. While such methods were often very subtle during that era, they have become magnified in the present era where such distortion is brazen and explicit. Documenting such matters would in fact require an entire separate detailed study. Returning to the original question in relation to the pillars of Islam, it is necessary to consider the words of Allah the exalted at this juncture where he has stated the following:

فَمَا أُوتِيتُم مِّن شَيْءٍ فَمَتَاعُ الْحَيَاةِ الدُّنْيَا وَمَا عِندَ اللَّهِ خَيْرٌ وَأَبْقَىٰ لِلَّذِينَ آمَنُوا وَعَلَىٰ رَبِّهِمْ
يَتَوَكَّلُونَ

So, whatever thing you are given, that is only a provision of this world's life, and what is with Allah is better and more lasting for those who believe and rely on their Lord.

وَالَّذِينَ يَجْتَنِبُونَ كَبَائِرَ الْإِثْمِ وَالْفَوَاحِشَ وَإِذَا مَا غَضِبُوا هُمْ يَغْفِرُونَ

And those who shun the great sins and indecencies, and whenever they are angry they forgive.

وَالَّذِينَ اسْتَجَابُوا لِرَبِّهِمْ وَأَقَامُوا الصَّلَاةَ وَأَمْرُهُمْ شُورَىٰ بَيْنَهُمْ وَمِمَّا رَزَقْنَاهُمْ يُنفِقُونَ

And those who respond to their Lord and keep up prayer, and their rule is to make consultation among themselves, and who spend out of what We have given them.

وَالَّذِينَ إِذَا أَصَابَهُمُ الْبَغْيُ هُمْ يَنتَصِرُونَ

And those who, when great wrong afflicts them, defend themselves.

وَجَزَاءُ سَيِّئَةٍ سَيِّئَةٌ مِّثْلُهَا فَمَنْ عَفَا وَأَصْلَحَ فَأَجْرُهُ عَلَى اللَّهِ إِنَّهُ لَا يُحِبُّ الظَّالِمِينَ

And the recompense of evil is punishment like it, but whoever forgives and amends, he shall have his reward from Allah; surely, He does not love the unjust

وَلَمَنِ انتَصَرَ بَعْدَ ظُلْمِهِ فَأُولَٰئِكَ مَا عَلَيْهِم مِّن سَبِيلٍ

And whoever defends himself after his being oppressed, these it is against whom there is no way (to blame)

إِنَّمَا السَّبِيلُ عَلَى الَّذِينَ يَظْلِمُونَ النَّاسَ وَيَبْغُونَ فِي الْأَرْضِ بِغَيْرِ الْحَقِّ أُولَٰئِكَ لَهُمْ عَذَابٌ أَلِيمٌ

The way (to blame) is only against those who oppress men and revolt in the earth unjustly; these shall have a painful punishment.

وَلَمَن صَبَرَ وَغَفَرَ إِنَّ ذَٰلِكَ لَمِنْ عَزْمِ الْأُمُورِ

And whoever is patient and forgiving, these most surely are actions due to courage.[16]

Here the verses cited from the Qur'ān are Meccan. Coupled with this are the words of the exalted in the verse revealed to his Prophet in Medina:

فَبِمَا رَحْمَةٍ مِنَ اللهِ لِنْتَ لَهُمْ وَلَوْ كُنْتَ فَظًّا غَلِيظَ الْقَلْبِ لَانْفَضُّوا مِنْ حَوْلِكَ فَاعْفُ عَنْهُمْ وَاسْتَغْفِرْ لَهُمْ وَشَاوِرْهُمْ فِي الْأَمْرِ فَإِذَا عَزَمْتَ فَتَوَكَّلْ عَلَى اللهِ إِنَّ اللهَ يُحِبُّ الْمُتَوَكِّلِينَ

Thus, it is due to mercy from Allah that you deal with them gently and had you been rough, hard hearted, they would certainly have dispersed from being around you; pardon them therefore and ask pardon for them and consult with them in the affair so when you have decided, then place your trust in Allah – surely Allah loves those who trust.[17]

From the aforementioned verse, Allah has mentioned '*ash-Shu'ra*' after establishing the *ṣalāh* and before the obligatory spending - which includes payment of the *zakāt*, giving a fifth from the booty – all of which is deemed as an obligation. Consultation, '*ash-Shura*' necessarily is from the pillars of Islam, similar to *ṣalāh* and *zakāt* without any difference or distinction. Yet these we do not find enumerated as being from amongst the essential pillars of Islam?! Nay, they are not even mentioned as being from amongst the essential obligations like you would find it in the pages of debates being devalued, where it is asked: Is '*ash-Shura*' a binding requisite or merely something suggested – glory be to Allah!

---

[16] *Qur'ān*, 42: 36/43
[17] *Qur'ān*, 3: 159

Therefore, to sum up: that the basis of Islam is:

- *To testify that there is no god/deity except Allah and that Muḥammad is the Messenger of Allah*

Or to say in an abridged and concise form only:

- *Testifying that there is no god/deity except Allah*

Or alternatively saying:

- *That you worship Allah and disbelieve in all else beside him*

And perhaps with the intended meaning that it relates to the oneness of Allah –

- That it is to worship Allah and to disbelieve in whatever is worshipped besides him and has the expression from which *al-'Imān* stems, namely '*Imān* in Allah and his Messenger, which is the *mujmal*.

- Or as *mufaṣṣil*: '*Imān* in Allah, his angels, books and his Messengers and '*Imān* in al-Qadr, the good and bad of it as well as its sweetness and bitterness.

Indeed, this is the solid basis and solid foundation upon which everything is to be based upon. Concerning the pillars (*arkān*) they are greater than the five-pillars which are the most well-known, for indeed they are in total, greater than ten:

1. The *ṣalāh* with its accompanying conditions and the importance of the prerequisite of complete *ṭahāra*
2. The *zakāt*
3. Payment of a fifth from the booty
4. Performance of *Ḥajj* (and also the *Umrah*)
5. Fasting during the month of *Ramaḍān*
6. *Jihād* in the path of Allah (and it is the pinnacle or apex of Islam)
7. Enjoining the good and forbidding the evil (and its most important aspect of accounting the oppressive rulers and forbidding their evil of their rule. Indeed, it is from amongst the divisions of *Jihād* and indeed it is from its pinnacle and apex of both *Jihād* and Islam)
8. *Hijrah* (migration)
9. *Shu'ra* (consultation)
10. *al-Jamā'ah* (the community)
11. To listen and obey the lawfully instituted rulers and governors
12. To send *salam* upon your family when entering upon them
13. To send *salam* upon mankind (Bani Adam) when passing them by

Regarding no. 13, sending *salam* upon mankind (Bani Adam) when passing them by, this doesn't only relate to the utterance of words. But rather it also extends to safety and security; providing reassurance to establish long-term relationships as well as disseminating cordial relations, affection and harmony amongst mankind.

By no means is this now the complete picture in totality. It would not be correct to say that until the remaining nullifiers (*nawāqiḍ*) of Islam have been detailed. They further provide important elucidation particularly in relation to what actually constitutes disbelief (*kufr*) and polytheism (*shirk*), which the remainder of this present work is intended to set out. Some of the serious sins (*mubiqāt*) involve leaving a pillar from amongst the main pillars, such as leaving the prayer, not paying the *zakāt*, consuming the *khums* etc. Also within this rubric comes a significant number of matters, such as taking a life that Allah has prohibited without due process of law; consuming the wealth of an orphan, consuming interest (*ribā*), inappropriately taking public wealth, fleeing from the battlefield and casting malicious unsolicited accusations against chaste believing women. There is also repudiating one's effort after making migration in Allah's cause, thus making a renunciation of one's Islamic citizenship after securing it; disobeying one's parents, providing false witness/testimony and / or perjury. To despair of the hope of Allah or his mercy; to commit adultery, incest or fornication; to repudiate one's pledge of allegiance by raising arms unjustly against the community of Muslims, and to partake in brigandage. There are other sins which fall within the rubric or category of being major sins (*kabā'ir*); we ask Allah and beseech him for refuge from all of them, including any action that would bring his wrath and result us being considered from amongst the inmates of hell.

Part II.

The Nature of Revelation and the Revealed ‘*Dhikr*’

1 Revelation is <u>both</u> the Qur'ān and the *Sunnah*

Some people might think that the revelation consists *only* of the glorious Qur'ān. Limiting revelation to only Qur'ān is a fatal mistake. It is so serious that it has the propensity to land one into serious deviation, ultimately leading to *kufr* (disbelief), taking a believer out of the fold of Islam. Essentially the truth of this matter is that revelation is of two types.

<u>Revelation Type (1)</u>

The first type of revelation is that which is inspired, orally reported and recited. The glorious Qur'ān, the final revelation from Allah sent down to the Prophet Muḥammad (peace be upon him) epitomises this. In a similar manner, the revelation which Allah wrote for Musa (peace be upon him) in the Tablets also comes under this essential type, as do other books and previous scriptures. Although less voluminous, its standing and substance is paramount. Furthermore, the Qur'ān may be recited as a means of worshipping Allah, while other revelations are not. Some of these revelations, in particular the Qur'ān, Allah has chosen to preserve, others not; they were memorised by Prophets, priests and the devout, like the scriptures of Musa (peace be upon him). The Qur'ān remains with us intact unlike other previous revelations which are lost, such as the scriptures of Ibrāhim (peace be upon him).

Revelation Type (2)

The second type of revelation is broader and more voluminous than the first; although inspired it need not be reported verbally by necessity. In the final revelation, it is the noble Prophetic *Sunnah,* consisting of the Prophet's (peace be upon him) statements, *ḥadith qudsi*, gestures, acts and approvals. Most of the previous scriptures that we have (such as the Old and the New Testament) are essentially of this kind, containing the sayings of the previous Prophets, their acts, what they tacitly approved, biographies and the general condition of their nations at that time. In this sense, the Old and the New Testament are more akin to the books of *Seerah* (biography) that exist for the Muslims, including that of *ḥadith qudsi*; in that sense, it is unlike the glorious Qur'ān, except for a few limited paragraphs.

The glorious Qur'ān consists of the words of Allah, revealed to Prophet Muḥammad (peace be upon him) and recorded, as it is written in the pages, as well as being carried by memorisation and recitation from the heart. In the modern age it is carried even further via many different technological platforms. The glorious Qur'ān is miraculous in wording, inimitable in its literary style and reciting it is a means of worship. It was transmitted from the Prophet (peace be upon him) both written and orally by *tawātur* - continuous recurrent transmission from a large number of narrators whose collusion to fabricate a lie is considered impossible. This transmission is in a manner providing productive and definitive knowledge, which is necessary for all mankind, be they Muslim or not. Its transmission was done completely, letter by letter; word by word, as it came to Muḥammad ibn Abdullah bin Abd'al-Muṭalib ash-Shāmi al-Qurayshi al-Adnāni al-'Arabi, may the peace and blessings of Allah be upon him and his family.

As for the Prophetic *Sunnah*, it is the sayings, the verbal pronouncements, including gestures; actions and approvals of the Prophet (peace be upon him). All of which is inspired by Allah and expressed by his Messenger (peace be upon him). It also encompasses articulating meaning, for example, that of a revelation that is sent down from Allah of which the Prophet (peace be upon him) expressed in his own words (or gestures that could be used instead of words) and also expressed in his acts. For Allah protected him from committing, approving or keeping silent in the face of anything reprehensible, whether he saw it directly or was informed thereof, since it would constitute a tacit approval or acquiescence. Should we wish to provide a more precise and accurate formulation, it would be obligatory to state that the Prophets *Sunnah* is not merely a particular revelation from Allah, rather it is a formulated expression of an infallible Prophetic revelation that has come from Allah. It is not the designated revelation of Allah, like the glorious Qur'ān. A more limited expression would be simply to state, as earlier, that the Prophetic *Sunnah* is also a revelation from Allah. Yet this stricter definition as outlined here, is more precise.

As for the Prophetic sayings relating to conveying the message from Allah, it is unambiguous and forthright as it relates to the message being conveyed from Allah; its manner is that of being declaratory and binding. It is not likely for it to be based upon interpretation (*tā'weel*) and it is impossible for it to be immediately based upon a mistake or a lie by the necessity of reason, given our dictum: the infallibility of the Prophets as it specifically relates to the reporting from Allah in a manner that is declaratory and binding. If it is not set out in this manner, in essence, Prophethood would lose its meaning. Moreover, it would be impossible to rectify the situation if a Prophet were to state he had erred or made a mistake in delivering the message and reporting from Allah. Thus, it would not be able to conclusively establish the necessary proof that we have been commanded to worship Allah alone. Such line of reasoning would be impossible because the message emanating from Allah must be presented in an unequivocal manner, with respondents not being able to marshal such a charge. No one can therefore seek refuge in such argumentation, given that Allah does not render punishment, whether in this life or the hereafter, unless and until a decisive argument has been presented, leaving no one with any excuse whatsoever. If it was not the case, then the line of argumentation, namely that the message delivered by the Prophet was not declaratory and binding; that it was inconclusive or replete with error and did not purport to what it claimed, would have ground, thereby seeking to render Allah as being manifestly unjust – and he blessed be his names is far above any form of injustice. Allah the exalted has forbidden injustice for himself, he would never be unjust. It would render the very meaning of Prophethood into an absurdity, depriving it of its essential meaning and would bring the notion of Prophetic infallibility in this regard into question, Allah forbid!

Examples of this conveyance of the message that is declaratory and binding, is where he (peace be upon him) says: this is the Qur'ānic wording as send down from Allah, to believe in and practice; these are his orders and prohibitions and this is not my wording. Similarly as it would apply to Musa (peace be upon him): this is the tablets that Allah has ordained, outlining his commandments and prohibitions. Or as it would apply to any Prophet from amongst the Prophets which have been sent for them to unequivocally outline, 'Allah ordains this and prohibits that'; 'Allah warns of the punishment of hell for this act', or 'Verily Allah has revealed / inspired to me to inform you regarding x or y.' Hence for that reason it must be that Prophetic statements, conveying the message, which have expressly been authorised and formulated as being a communication from Allah are set forth as such; statements which are of significance and definitive in character. Thus a Prophet presents unequivocal truthful and honest statements relating to reports from Allah, such as saying 'Allah has said' or 'Your lord has obligated this' and containing no mistakes therein. Moreover, a

Prophet cannot retort with 'I forgot to mention this from Allah.' These points must all be established by absolute rational necessity.

Regarding conveyance of the message, this relates to conveying information accurately and doesn't by the necessity of reason require the individual to be infallible (*ma'ṣoom*) per se in all facets. As a principle what is required is that the person is truthful and trustworthy, because it doesn't entail account or punishment. As an example, one may consider the reports of Yusuf (peace be upon him) as they related to the interpretation of the strange dream that the King of Egypt had.[1] This is of course only if one first accepts that Yusuf (peace be upon him) was specifically delegated as a Prophet prior to this and not sent with a message after this. Secondly, that the interpretation of the Kings dream was inspired by revelation and not as a result of his own endeavour at interpretation (*ijtihād*).

[1] See: *Qur'ān* 10: 43/51

2 'He doesn't speak of his own desire...'

At this juncture one may ask, what about the sayings of the Prophet (peace be upon him) in which it is not explicitly indicated that it is a revelation emanating from Allah, such as where he is reported to have said: '*Money paid to a prostitute is khabeeth*' or '*Ḥajj is (attendance) at 'Arafah*' as well as other innumerable sayings, gestures, acts and that which he tacitly approved? Is it an expression indicative of an infallible revelation from Allah? Or is it limited to an expression being made from the viewpoint of the Prophet, indicating his own view or inclination? The truth is that all this concerning our Prophet (peace be upon him), at least, perhaps also of former Prophets, is that it all constitutes an infallible revelation from Allah that contains no lie, mistake or forgetfulness which is proved by the following definite evidence where Allah himself declares:

وَالنَّجْمِ إِذَا هَوَىٰ ، مَا ضَلَّ صَاحِبُكُمْ وَمَا غَوَىٰ ، وَمَا يَنطِقُ عَنِ الْهَوَىٰ ، إِنْ هُوَ إِلَّا وَحْيٌ يُوحَىٰ ، عَلَّمَهُ شَدِيدُ الْقُوَىٰ

I swear by the star when it goes down. Your companion does not err, nor does he go astray; nor does he speak out of his own desire. It is but revelation that is revealed to him, the Lord of mighty power has taught him.[1]

We know as an acknowledged fact that the Prophet (peace be upon him) spoke about many matters concerning religion other than that which is detailed in the glorious Qur'ān. If such matters are not a revelation from Allah, then what is detailed here in this Qur'ānic verse would be a lie. It follows that it would necessarily be revealed by other than Allah. A matter that is against the established proofs of Prophethood, as we will soon detail, as well as the definite evidence that proves this matter. It is an acknowledged fact that the Qur'ān is revealed from Allah, otherwise, Allah would either be lying or in error in this verse which is impossible and Allah is far above any such claim.

Someone may claim that the word to 'speak' or 'utter' in the aforementioned verse relates only to the Qur'ān and not to other sayings from the Prophet (peace be upon him). In reply we would say that such an assertion is a lie and a misinterpretation of the Arabic language. The glorious Qur'ān is to be 'recited'; the Arabs say 'Muḥammad recited the Qur'ān', 'Muḥammad came with the Qur'ān.' It has never been claimed that 'Muḥammad spoke or uttered the Qur'ān.' The speech mentioned is relating to an absolute form, as is said by the philosophers in their definition of a mankind, man is an animal that speaks; the ability to speak, talk and converse being a characteristic feature. The certainty of this point is developed by the Qur'ān itself and the best explainer of the Qur'ān is the Qur'ān, it is enough in itself to testify to this. Allah blessed be his names says:

قَالَ بَلْ فَعَلَهُ كَبِيرُهُمْ هَٰذَا فَاسْأَلُوهُمْ إِن كَانُوا يَنطِقُونَ

He said: 'No, it was done by the biggest of them– this one. Ask them, if they

---

[1] *Qur'ān* 53: 1/5

can talk.'[2]

This is indicative of any manner of speech and not related to this speech as set out in the Qur'ān or the word of Allah; not recited, not read and not learned. Allah has said:

فَوَرَبِّ السَّمَاءِ وَالْأَرْضِ إِنَّهُ لَحَقٌّ مِّثْلَ مَا أَنَّكُمْ تَنطِقُونَ

And by the Lord of the heavens and the earth! It is most surely the truth, just as you do speak. [3]

Again, this indicates any manner of speech or appreciation of words that is well known by direct sensory perception and reflection, with the verse directly addressing the obstinate and stubborn. Allah the exalted also says, narrating the words of Sulaymān (peace be upon him):

وَوَرِثَ سُلَيْمَانُ دَاوُودَ وَقَالَ يَا أَيُّهَا النَّاسُ عُلِّمْنَا مَنطِقَ الطَّيْرِ وَأُوتِينَا مِن كُلِّ شَيْءٍ إِنَّ هَٰذَا لَهُوَ الْفَضْلُ الْمُبِينُ

And Sulaymān was Dāwud's heir, and he said: O men! We have been taught the language of birds, and we have been given all things; most surely this is manifest grace. [4]

Once again the wording is general, indicating the language of any birds and how they express themselves and this is not of the genus (logic) of humans originally. It is nothing to do with the Qur'ān as such or the word of Allah absolutely. He blessed and exalted be his names says:

---

[2] *Qur'ān* 21: 63
[3] *Qur'ān* 51: 23
[4] *Qur'ān* 27: 16

وَقَالُوا لِجُلُودِهِمْ لِمَ شَهِدتُّمْ عَلَيْنَا قَالُوا أَنطَقَنَا اللَّهُ الَّذِي أَنطَقَ كُلَّ شَيْءٍ وَهُوَ خَلَقَكُمْ أَوَّلَ مَرَّةٍ وَإِلَيْهِ تُرْجَعُونَ

And they shall say to their skins: Why have you borne witness against us? They shall say: Allah who makes everything speak has made us speak, and He created you at first, and to Him you shall be brought back. [5]

The aforesaid point is exemplified in a many other Qur'ānic verses as well; it relates to one sense only, that of speech and speaking, generally. That point would invalidate anyone to claim that the verses cited above from *Surah Najm* only relate to the Qur'ān and not to other sayings from the Prophet (peace be upon him). If it was only intended to relate to the Qur'ān and nothing else it would be more correct and appropriate to say 'The lord of mighty power read to him or recited to him' or words similar to this. Yet the Qur'ānic text as verbally recited and taught is otherwise, as we find:

عَلَّمَهُ شَدِيدُ الْقُوَىٰ

The Lord of mighty power has taught him.[6]

Without doubt that is the Prophet (peace be upon him), he was taught the Qur'ān definitely by the lord of power. There is no doubt concerning this and it relates to more than just being in receipt of the Qur'ānic letters and sounds only. The word used in the verse [علمه] taught him is not generally specific to his knowledge of the Qur'ān, but rather of this and many other things.

Moreover, how does one judge that the word 'Qur'ān' itself is not just limited to a particular chapter such as *al-Baqarah* or *al-'Imrān* or

---

[5] *Qur'ān* 41: 21
[6] *Qur'ān* 53: 5

indeed any other verse and not concerned with the complete contents contained between its two covers? If it is possible that the word 'speak' is only concerned with the act of 'reciting the Qur'ān' and it is not to be understood in its full generality. To utter all other matters, in absolute generality and full comprehensive meaning, as it is an acknowledged fact known by necessity from the Arabic language, to argue otherwise would be merely to assert without evidence. So it is logical and correct to also let the word 'Qur'ān' be understood in its completeness and not limited to what is between the covers of the well-known book. Otherwise, we would be contradicting ourselves and acting according to desires and choosing that which is false. In a different verse we find Allah stating:

قُلْ إِنَّمَا أُنذِرُكُم بِالْوَحْيِ وَلَا يَسْمَعُ الصُّمُّ الدُّعَاءَ إِذَا مَا يُنذَرُونَ

Say: I warn you only by revelation; and the deaf do not hear the call whenever they are warned.[7]

The verse has a linguistic form of restriction (*ṣeeghat-ḥaṣr*) with its opening wording. That is to say, I do not warn *except* by way of revelation; the warning which is brought forth is a revelation from Allah, the almighty. The Prophet (peace be upon him) used to warn people using a variety of language and not only by way of verses from the Qur'ān. He used to warn people with the hellfire for different sins and to warn of the consequences resulting from the abandonment of duties. He used to enact different laws as well as deliver various warnings and proclamations. If all of that is not considered from among revelation that is ultimately being revealed from Allah, then the aforementioned Qur'ānic verse would be manifestly wrong – Allah the exalted, blessed be his names is far above any erroneous charge. Furthermore, it would also be in direct conflict with the proofs of

---

[7] *Qur'ān* 21: 45

Prophecy and those relating to the established proofs that the Qur'ān is the final revelation from Allah, as will be detailed in due course.

For anyone to claim that the word 'revelation' mentioned in the previous verse only pertains to the Qur'ān, would be asserting a lie. In fact it would be violation of what is true and is at odds with what is proved as an acknowledged fact through history and biographical evidence. Any such claim would be a denial of the Qur'ān itself, given that it is the same Qur'ān that named what Allah had revealed to Musa and his mother (peace be upon him) as revelation at the same time that we know that this revelation was not considered as the Qur'ān or even similar to it in either kind or language. In fact such claims are far worse, for it would mean that Allah is not able to use appropriate and complete expression – yet he is far elevated above all such imperfection. There is nothing in the world that can be easier than saying, 'I warn you solely according to the glorious Qur'ān', or 'I warn you solely according to the scripture.' But this verse was not revealed in that manner, so we know for sure that anyone who claims that the word 'revelation' is limited only to the 'Qur'ān' is in manifest error. This becomes more evident given that Allah says:

قُلْ أَيُّ شَيْءٍ أَكْبَرُ شَهَادَةً قُلِ اللهُ شَهِيدٌ بَيْنِي وَبَيْنَكُمْ وَأُوحِيَ إِلَيَّ هَٰذَا الْقُرْآنُ لِأُنذِرَكُم بِهِ وَمَن
بَلَغَ أَئِنَّكُمْ لَتَشْهَدُونَ أَنَّ مَعَ اللهِ آلِهَةً أُخْرَىٰ قُل لَّا أَشْهَدُ قُلْ إِنَّمَا هُوَ إِلَٰهٌ وَاحِدٌ وَإِنَّنِي بَرِيءٌ مِّمَّا
تُشْرِكُونَ

Say: What thing is the weightiest in testimony? Say: Allah is witness between you and me; this Qur'ān has been revealed to me that with it I may warn you and whomsoever it reaches. Do you really bear witness that there are other gods with Allah? Say: I do not bear witness. Say: He is only one Allah and surely I am clear of that which you set up (with Him). [8]

This verse explicitly mentioned the Qur'ān and mentioned that among

[8] *Qur'ān* 6: 19

the purposes for revealing it is to warn people in a method that was not restricted. The Qur'ān has other purposes beside giving warnings such as providing glad tidings, reminding people, encouraging / challenging people to think and ponder, etc. Giving warnings may be done through the glorious Qur'ān or through means other than it. For instance Imām's warn and threaten the congregation during sermons at Friday prayer; poets do the same using their poetry. Such warnings are according to the discretion of scholars and poetry of the poets but they are not revelation. It may be derived from revelation and may be this derivation is right or wrong. Yet the verse under consideration here in this section relates to the final Messenger of Allah, Muḥammad (peace be upon him) and Allah elucidated clearly for him and us:

قُلْ إِنَّمَا أُنذِرُكُم بِالْوَحْيِ وَلَا يَسْمَعُ الصُّمُّ الدُّعَاءَ إِذَا مَا يُنذَرُونَ

Say: I warn you only by revelation; and the deaf do not hear the call whenever they are warned. [9]

[9] *Qur'ān* 21: 45

3 'Whoever obeys the Prophet, indeed obeys Allah'

Allah, glorified and blessed be his names says:

مَّنْ يُطِعِ الرَّسُولَ فَقَدْ أَطَاعَ اللَّهَ وَمَن تَوَلَّىٰ فَمَا أَرْسَلْنَاكَ عَلَيْهِمْ حَفِيظًا

Whoever obeys the Prophet he indeed obeys Allah, and whoever turns back, We have not sent you as a keeper over them. [1]

وَمَا أَرْسَلْنَا مِن رَّسُولٍ إِلَّا لِيُطَاعَ بِإِذْنِ اللَّهِ وَلَوْ أَنَّهُمْ إِذ ظَّلَمُوا أَنفُسَهُمْ جَاءُوكَ فَاسْتَغْفَرُوا اللَّهَ
وَاسْتَغْفَرَ لَهُمُ الرَّسُولُ لَوَجَدُوا اللَّهَ تَوَّابًا رَّحِيمًا

And We did not send any Messenger but that he should be obeyed by Allah's permission; and had they, when they were unjust to themselves, come to you and asked forgiveness of Allah and the Messenger had (also) asked forgiveness for them, they would have found Allah oft-returning, merciful. [2]

Notwithstanding the aforementioned verses, there are in fact many others also in which Allah has ordered us to obey the Prophet (peace

---

[1] *Qur'ān* 4: 80
[2] *Qur'ān* 4: 64

be upon him) unconditionally. He declares that obeying His Messenger is a condition for guidance and disobeying him will lead to us going astray. There are also other verses in which Allah threatens whoever disobeys Him or disobeys His Messengers in general, with eternal punishment in the fire of hell. For example, Allah blessed be his names says:

وَمَن يَعْصِ اللَّهَ وَرَسُولَهُ وَيَتَعَدَّ حُدُودَهُ يُدْخِلْهُ نَارًا خَالِدًا فِيهَا وَلَهُ عَذَابٌ مُّهِينٌ

And whoever disobeys Allah and His Messenger and goes beyond His limits, He will cause him to enter fire to abide therein, and he shall have an abasing chastisement. [3]

إِلَّا بَلَاغًا مِّنَ اللَّهِ وَرِسَالَاتِهِ وَمَن يَعْصِ اللَّهَ وَرَسُولَهُ فَإِنَّ لَهُ نَارَ جَهَنَّمَ خَالِدِينَ فِيهَا أَبَدًا

I only deliver [what I receive] from Allah– only His messages.' Whoever disobeys God and His Messenger will have Hell's Fire as his permanent home. [4]

لَيْسَ عَلَى الْأَعْمَى حَرَجٌ وَلَا عَلَى الْأَعْرَجِ حَرَجٌ وَلَا عَلَى الْمَرِيضِ حَرَجٌ وَمَن يُطِعِ اللَّهَ وَرَسُولَهُ يُدْخِلْهُ جَنَّاتٍ تَجْرِي مِن تَحْتِهَا الْأَنْهَارُ وَمَن يَتَوَلَّ يُعَذِّبْهُ عَذَابًا أَلِيمًا

There is no harm in the blind, nor is there any harm in the lame, nor is there any harm in the sick (if they do not go forth); and whoever obeys Allah and His Messenger, He will cause him to enter gardens beneath which rivers flow, and whoever turns back, He will punish him with a painful punishment. [5]

وَمَا كَانَ لِمُؤْمِنٍ وَلَا مُؤْمِنَةٍ إِذَا قَضَى اللَّهُ وَرَسُولُهُ أَمْرًا أَن يَكُونَ لَهُمُ الْخِيَرَةُ مِنْ أَمْرِهِمْ وَمَن يَعْصِ اللَّهَ وَرَسُولَهُ فَقَدْ ضَلَّ ضَلَالًا مُّبِينًا

---

[3] *Qur'ān* 4: 14
[4] *Qur'ān* 72: 23
[5] *Qur'ān* 48: 17

And it behoves not a believing man and a believing woman that they should have any choice in their matter when Allah and His Messenger have decided a matter; and whoever disobeys Allah and His Messenger, he surely strays off a manifest straying. [6]

يُصْلِحْ لَكُمْ أَعْمَالَكُمْ وَيَغْفِرْ لَكُمْ ذُنُوبَكُمْ وَمَن يُطِعِ اللَّهَ وَرَسُولَهُ فَقَدْ فَازَ فَوْزًا عَظِيمًا

He will put your deeds into a right state for you, and forgive you your faults; and whoever obeys Allah and His Messenger, he indeed achieves a mighty success. [7]

قُلْ أَطِيعُوا اللَّهَ وَأَطِيعُوا الرَّسُولَ فَإِن تَوَلَّوْا فَإِنَّمَا عَلَيْهِ مَا حُمِّلَ وَعَلَيْكُم مَّا حُمِّلْتُمْ وَإِن تُطِيعُوهُ تَهْتَدُوا وَمَا عَلَى الرَّسُولِ إِلَّا الْبَلَاغُ الْمُبِينُ

Say: Obey Allah and obey the Messenger; but if you turn back, then on him rests that which is imposed on him and on you rests that which is imposed on you; and if you obey him, you are on the right way; and nothing rests on the Messenger but clear delivery (of the message). [8]

وَأَطِيعُوا اللَّهَ وَأَطِيعُوا الرَّسُولَ وَاحْذَرُوا فَإِن تَوَلَّيْتُمْ فَاعْلَمُوا أَنَّمَا عَلَىٰ رَسُولِنَا الْبَلَاغُ الْمُبِينُ

And obey Allah and obey the Messenger and be cautious; but if you turn back, then know that only a clear deliverance of the message is (incumbent) on Our Messenger. [9]

وَأَطِيعُوا اللَّهَ وَأَطِيعُوا الرَّسُولَ فَإِن تَوَلَّيْتُمْ فَإِنَّمَا عَلَىٰ رَسُولِنَا الْبَلَاغُ الْمُبِينُ

And obey Allah and obey the Messenger, but if you turn back, then upon Our

---

[6] *Qur'ān* 33: 36
[7] *Qur'ān* 33: 71
[8] *Qur'ān* 24: 54
[9] *Qur'ān* 5: 92

Messenger devolves only the clear delivery (of the message). [10]

يَا أَيُّهَا الَّذِينَ آمَنُوا أَطِيعُوا اللَّهَ وَأَطِيعُوا الرَّسُولَ وَلَا تُبْطِلُوا أَعْمَالَكُمْ

O you who believe! Obey Allah and obey the Messenger, and do not make your deeds of no effect. [11]

The verse shows that Allah appointed his majestic self as well as his Messenger as the only and absolute point of reference in matters where disputes arise. While Allah and his Messenger are to be obeyed in absolute terms, this is not the case for temporal rulers, as is well established in the famous verse:

يَا أَيُّهَا الَّذِينَ آمَنُوا أَطِيعُوا اللَّهَ وَأَطِيعُوا الرَّسُولَ وَأُولِي الْأَمْرِ مِنكُمْ فَإِن تَنَازَعْتُمْ فِي شَيْءٍ فَرُدُّوهُ إِلَى اللَّهِ وَالرَّسُولِ إِن كُنتُمْ تُؤْمِنُونَ بِاللَّهِ وَالْيَوْمِ الْآخِرِ ذَٰلِكَ خَيْرٌ وَأَحْسَنُ تَأْوِيلًا

O you who believe! Obey Allah and obey the Messenger and those in authority from among you; then if you differ about anything, refer it to Allah and the Messenger, if you believe in Allah and the last day; this is better and very good in the end. [12]

In the next verse, Allah distinguished his Messenger by ordering us to obey him without mentioning himself and made this obedience to him a condition in order to gain his divine mercy:

وَأَقِيمُوا الصَّلَاةَ وَآتُوا الزَّكَاةَ وَأَطِيعُوا الرَّسُولَ لَعَلَّكُمْ تُرْحَمُونَ

And keep up prayer and pay zakāt and obey the Messenger so that mercy may

[10] *Qur'ān* 64: 12
[11] *Qur'ān* 47: 33
[12] *Qur'ān* 4: 59

be shown to you. [13]

Furthermore, Allah has emphasised that obeying his Prophet is a condition for gaining his love, which is without doubt one of the greatest accolades, whilst disobeying him is from amongst the types of disbelief which would earn the removal of his pleasure. Allah says:

قُلْ إِن كُنتُمْ تُحِبُّونَ اللَّهَ فَاتَّبِعُونِي يُحْبِبْكُمُ اللَّهُ وَيَغْفِرْ لَكُمْ ذُنُوبَكُمْ وَاللَّهُ غَفُورٌ رَّحِيمٌ ، قُلْ أَطِيعُوا اللَّهَ وَالرَّسُولَ فَإِن تَوَلَّوْا فَإِنَّ اللَّهَ لَا يُحِبُّ الْكَافِرِينَ

Say: If you love Allah, then follow me, Allah will love you and forgive you your faults and Allah is forgiving, merciful. Say: Obey Allah and the Messenger; but if they turn back, then surely Allah does not love the kāfireen. [14]

Allah provides further illustration of this point in the next verse where he says:

وَمَن يُطِعِ اللَّهَ وَرَسُولَهُ وَيَخْشَ اللَّهَ وَيَتَّقْهِ فَأُولَٰئِكَ هُمُ الْفَائِزُونَ

And he who obeys Allah and His Messenger, fears Allah and is careful of (his duty to) Him, they are the achievers [15]

The verse indicates that fear and being watchful are not complete without obedience to Allah the exalted and his Messenger (peace be upon him). The word 'Messenger' has been co-joined to the word 'Allah' in a way that indicates that both are equally worthy of being obeyed, although there is a striking infinite difference between Allah,

---

[13] *Qur'ān* 24: 56
[14] *Qur'ān* 3: 31/32
[15] *Qur'ān* 24: 52

the ever-living; the self-subsisting; the necessarily-existent and his Messenger (peace be upon him) who is the created, contingent, mortal and finite. Allah the exalted has taken issue with anyone seeking to place a wedge between himself and his Messenger or seek to make differentiation. Worse than this would be for anyone to seek to manoeuvre between them, claiming to believe in some parts while rejecting others. Allah has shut down all avenues towards this by categorically stating:

إِنَّ الَّذِينَ يَكْفُرُونَ بِاللَّهِ وَرُسُلِهِ وَيُرِيدُونَ أَن يُفَرِّقُوا بَيْنَ اللَّهِ وَرُسُلِهِ وَيَقُولُونَ نُؤْمِنُ بِبَعْضٍ وَنَكْفُرُ بِبَعْضٍ وَيُرِيدُونَ أَن يَتَّخِذُوا بَيْنَ ذَٰلِكَ سَبِيلًا ، أُولَٰئِكَ هُمُ الْكَافِرُونَ حَقًّا وَأَعْتَدْنَا لِلْكَافِرِينَ عَذَابًا مُّهِينًا

Surely those who disbelieve in Allah and His Messengers and desire to make a distinction between Allah and His Messengers by saying: We believe in some and disbelieve in others, and desire to take a course between (this and) that. These it is that are truly disbelievers, and We have prepared for the disbelievers a disgraceful chastisement. [16]

Allah showed that Prophets are obeyed by His express divine command and that they are obeyed for His cause. Obedience to the Prophets directly corresponds to obedience to Allah; it constitutes the same level of authoritative command. To reiterate, Allah has refused to accept anyone trying to make a distinction between Him and His Messengers (peace be upon them all). Any attempts of making a distinction or to be crude, driving a wedge between Allah and His Messengers will end in total failure. Evidence has been established from the divine verse to show that any such attempt is truly a manifest and open *kufr*, which will ultimately result in eternal damnation. Without doubt, based upon the necessity of reason and irrefutable evidence established from the *Sharī'ah* there is a clear distinction between the Prophet (peace be upon him) as a mortal contingent being

---

[16] *Qur'ān* 4: 150/151

and Allah, the creator of all existence. The two are separate entities on completely different plains of existence. He (peace be upon him) is not the same as Allah in nature or essence; his will is different from that of the will of Allah

Messengers have been chosen to convey the *waḥy* and to bolster delivery of this Allah has rendered them infallible – *ma'ṣoom* - in this aspect. Consequently it is an absolute necessity that the Prophetic *Sunnah* is an infallible proclamation from Allah. The Prophetic expression and formulation is an infallible revelation which has come from Allah. If it were possible that any such proclamation was based upon the sole desire of the Prophet (peace be upon him) without being based on infallible revelation from Allah, his mission would have lost its significance; it would cease to be considered an authority. If such a proposition were correct, how would Allah establish the proof against those rejecting His law and very existence on the day of judgement? The need for the *Sharī'ah* would be obviated. Making any such claim would be in clear conflict with the mutually supporting Qur'ānic verses. As such the glorious Qur'ān would be self-contradictory and it should not be considered as having been sent down from Allah - Allah forbid and protect us from such vain and baseless claims.

4 Types of Divine Revelation

A critic may argue that it is feasible that the Prophet (peace be upon him) might have been led to do that certain actions or prohibited matters according to his nature or bodily composure resultant from hereditary qualities. In response, we would submit that this is of no avail. It could not have been possible for the Prophet (peace be upon him) to be of this 'nature' in such a manner that his taste does not accept, and that his mind does not settle except with Allah's will, as it is known in reality with certitude only to Allah himself, except with a prior knowledge, a determined destiny, or a creation, by the will of Allah, and according to his determination. It was the creative will and determination of Allah that resolved that the Prophet (peace be upon him) be created in a certain destined manner. His unique condition conforms to Allah's legislative will, for the mission of this very specific Prophet (peace be upon him), in such a way that the Prophet (peace be upon him) be created ideally prepared for the infallible conveyance of the last message for mankind. Nobody, whether that be a scholar, a critic or even a heretic should say that neither this nor anything like it can be described as revelation. Moreover as stated earlier, the Prophetic expression and formulation is an infallible revelation which has come from Allah. Allah has said:

وَأَوْحَىٰ رَبُّكَ إِلَى النَّحْلِ أَنِ اتَّخِذِي مِنَ الْجِبَالِ بُيُوتًا وَمِنَ الشَّجَرِ وَمِمَّا يَعْرِشُونَ

And your Lord revealed to the bee saying: make hives in the mountains and in the trees and in what they build.[1]

It is well known that that the *waḥy* was granted to the bees by Allah, it is planted in their hereditary stock (chromosomes and genes) and in a particular way that made them use mountains, trees and what they build up in a certain way. Definitely this *waḥy* is not a holy Qur'ān that can be recited, nor did it happen by the descent of an angel or by a vision during sleep or the like. From the aforementioned verse we note that *waḥy* can be of several types, ranging from that which is implanted in the genes in the origin of innate character to the glorious Qur'ān, which is the divine word, revealed literally and verbally, in its words and letters, miraculous in its composition, whose recitation is a type of worship. In between there are other types, which are expectoration in fear, or an inspiration to a soul without prior knowledge of it, or having a true vision, the appearance of an angelic messenger to the human messenger orally addressing him; the sending down of ready written scriptures and tablets from heaven, etc. All of these are called *waḥy*; all these types of *waḥy* are infallible. Regarding the Prophets they are without any lie, error or forgetfulness in reporting from Allah; otherwise there would be no significance in Prophethood altogether.

---

[1] *Qur'ān* 16: 68

5 'Whatever the Messenger gives you, take it…'

Allah the almighty blessed be his names has said:

مَّا أَفَاءَ اللَّهُ عَلَىٰ رَسُولِهِ مِنْ أَهْلِ الْقُرَىٰ فَلِلَّهِ وَلِلرَّسُولِ وَلِذِي الْقُرْبَىٰ وَالْيَتَامَىٰ وَالْمَسَاكِينِ وَابْنِ السَّبِيلِ كَيْ لَا يَكُونَ دُولَةً بَيْنَ الْأَغْنِيَاءِ مِنكُمْ وَمَا آتَاكُمُ الرَّسُولُ فَخُذُوهُ وَمَا نَهَاكُمْ عَنْهُ فَانتَهُوا وَاتَّقُوا اللَّهَ إِنَّ اللَّهَ شَدِيدُ الْعِقَابِ

Whatever Allah has restored to His Messenger from the people of the towns, it is for Allah and for the Messenger and for the near of kin, the orphans, the needy and the wayfarer, so that it may not be a thing taken by turns among the rich of you, and whatever the Messenger gives you, take it and from whatever he forbids you abstain; be careful of (your duty to) Allah; surely Allah is severe in retribution. [1]

This is a firm command, followed by a confirmed warning that strictly obligates people to accept *all* the commands of the Prophet (peace be upon him) without any exception. The wording used in the verse, 'and whatever' is a general formulation, without limitation or qualification, thus it cannot be construed as being conditional or restrictive. History

[1] *Qur'ān* 59: 7

attests to the fact that the Prophet (peace be upon him) did not come bearing gold or silver. Nor was he a merchant providing markets with goods or a despotic tyrannical king doling out gifts, grants, positions and lands through the bestowal of patronage. Yet by Allah, he brought something of great value - innumerable reports concerning Allah, his angels, books, messengers and the last day. He explained the conditions of the hour of resurrection and its signs; provided news of the previous Prophets and nations. He brought forth lessons to be learnt in different forms, sometimes in the form of speeches, stories and parables, in addition to other forms of lessons. He also brought forth several commands, prohibitions, instructions, advice and guidance. He uttered marvellous wise sayings. All these have been brought forward by the Prophet of Allah (peace be upon him); he accepted them as a necessary religious duty, which is not to be disputed according to the verse of the Qur'ān. By virtue of every type, we may list the following:

- To take his reports and believe in them decisively; acknowledging them inwardly and outwardly. Submitting to them thereby fostering 'religiosity,' in other words to draw closer to Allah seeking his pleasure via this submission and belief.
- To take the command and being obedient to it; demonstrating compliance within the limits of what can be done.
- To take what has been prohibited, in other words recognising it as such and abstaining from it, except where the conditions of necessity and duress apply.
- And taking other matters also according to their type. For example, if the Prophet (peace be upon him) granted you a plot of land it is to be taken as a legitimate good possession. If it is given to another, then you would be happy for the lucky person and wish yourself the same but not show envy or rancour at the other, Allah forbid.

All these are truly sent down from Allah. For it is impossible that Allah commands us to believe a false report, or obey a command that he never ordered or prohibit something he did not render impermissible, or accept a gift which we are not entitled to, Allah forbid. As expressed in the verse, Allah blessed be his names says – '*and from whatever he forbids you, abstain*' by necessity it includes all that he outlines as forbidden or prohibited. He also says: '*and whatever the Messenger gives you, take it*'. It is from the utmost kindness that the particular has been annexed to the general, the part to the whole. Such use of rhetoric has been provided to confirm the legislation with an eloquence of the highest magnitude. Thus it can be established from this verse:

- ✓ The importance of abstaining and being deterred from things the Messenger of Allah, (peace be upon him) prohibited without a stipulation of ability and capability. For abstaining from prohibited things are a negative attitude; i.e. it is a not-to-do action, which is within the remit of all people.
- ✓ Invalidating any possibly confusing matter about the beginning of the verse '*...and whatever the Messenger gives you, take it...*' that it might refer to things other than reports, commands and prohibitions, or it might refer to glorious Qur'ān only. Since prohibitions have been mentioned separately and explicitly, it is necessary that the sentence be inclusive of all prohibitions and that which is similar to it, things that can be described as being brought by a Prophetic deed or saying; i.e., inclusive of all reports and commands, etc.

The sentence '*and whatever the Messenger gives you, take it*' is *a priori* a verse signifying all Qur'ānic texts. So if the Messenger (peace be upon him) says, this is Qur'ān, then our response should be: we hear and we obey and accept it as the glorious Qur'ān and record it in the scripture. If he says this verse that was of the glorious Qur'ān has been lifted, abrogated and removed from the scripture and we must not recite it again, our reply should be: at your command. We will do as commanded; such should be our attitude forever. Whatever the Messenger (peace be upon him) brings to us, we should accept, and what he prohibits us, should be abandoned.

6 ‘I only follow what is revealed to me’

Allah the exalted and majestic states in the following verses:

قُلْ لَا أَقُولُ لَكُمْ عِنْدِي خَزَائِنُ اللَّهِ وَلَا أَعْلَمُ الْغَيْبَ وَلَا أَقُولُ لَكُمْ إِنِّي مَلَكٌ إِنْ أَتَّبِعُ إِلَّا مَا يُوحَىٰ إِلَيَّ قُلْ هَلْ يَسْتَوِي الْأَعْمَىٰ وَالْبَصِيرُ أَفَلَا تَتَفَكَّرُونَ

Say: I do not say to you, I have with me the treasures of Allah, nor do I know the unseen, nor do I say to you that I am an angel; I do not follow anything save that which is revealed to me. Say: Are the blind and the seeing one alike? Do you not then reflect? [1]

وَإِذَا تُتْلَىٰ عَلَيْهِمْ آيَاتُنَا بَيِّنَاتٍ قَالَ الَّذِينَ لَا يَرْجُونَ لِقَاءَنَا ائْتِ بِقُرْآنٍ غَيْرِ هَٰذَا أَوْ بَدِّلْهُ قُلْ مَا يَكُونُ لِي أَنْ أُبَدِّلَهُ مِنْ تِلْقَاءِ نَفْسِي إِنْ أَتَّبِعُ إِلَّا مَا يُوحَىٰ إِلَيَّ إِنِّي أَخَافُ إِنْ عَصَيْتُ رَبِّي عَذَابَ يَوْمٍ عَظِيمٍ

And when Our clear communications are recited to them, those who hope not for Our meeting say: Bring a Qur’ān other than this or change it. Say: It does not beseem me that I should change it of myself; I follow naught but what is revealed to me; surely I fear, if I disobey my Lord, the punishment of a mighty

[1] *Qur’ān* 6: 50

day. [2]

قُلْ مَا كُنتُ بِدْعًا مِّنَ الرُّسُلِ وَمَا أَدْرِي مَا يُفْعَلُ بِي وَلَا بِكُمْ إِنْ أَتَّبِعُ إِلَّا مَا يُوحَىٰ إِلَيَّ وَمَا أَنَا إِلَّا نَذِيرٌ مُّبِينٌ

Say: I am not the first of the Prophets and I do not know what will be done with me or with you: I do not follow anything but that which is revealed to me and I am nothing but a plain warner. [3]

The verse has a linguistic form of restriction (*ṣeeghat-ḥaṣr*), that is to say, he (peace be upon him) does not follow anything *but the revelation*, whether that be in the form of acts or speech, with the notion of acts being the obvious immediate meaning. One must also note that the Prophet (peace be upon him) used to perform several deeds that were not explicitly mentioned within the corpus of Qur'ānic text. For example, he would kiss his wives and consummate marriages; he (peace be upon him) was intimate with his wives during fasting and their menstruation, stopping short of actual intercourse. Regarding his speech, he (peace be upon him) would formulate things in his own manner, quite distinctive from the Qur'ānic style. If all these were not considered to be revelation, then the Qur'ānic verse would be rendered void. Accordingly, the Qur'ān would not be necessarily sent down from Allah. This is in contradistinction to the Prophethood which we know is established beyond doubt by irrefutable striking evidence. Such evidence establishes that the Qur'ān is necessarily sent down from Allah. Otherwise, Allah would be lying in this verse which is the height of absurdity as Allah is above all imperfections.

Previously we mentioned that the word *waḥy* (revelation) is not synonymous with the word Qur'ān; every revelation is not Qur'ān,

---

[2] *Qur'ān* 10: 15
[3] *Qur'ān* 46: 9

though the Qur'ān is undoubtedly revelation from Allah. What is further noteworthy is that the phrase used in the verse *was not* formulated as 'I only follow the Qur'ān,' (إن أتّبع إلا القرآن) although that would have been easy to express and eloquent in formulation. Thus we know with certainty that his following of revelation as indicated in the Qur'ānic sentence is not limited to that of the Qur'ān only. Consequently the verse in correct formulation outlines striking evidence of revelation that is not limited to that of the Qur'ān which the Prophet (peace be upon him) is having revealed to him and which he is acting in accordance with.

7 Prophet Muḥammad is the 'Excellent Exemplar'

In chapter thirty-three of the glorious Qur'ān, Allah the exalted furnishes us with the following indisputable statement. He says:

لَّقَدْ كَانَ لَكُمْ فِي رَسُولِ اللَّهِ أُسْوَةٌ حَسَنَةٌ لِّمَن كَانَ يَرْجُو اللَّهَ وَالْيَوْمَ الْآخِرَ وَذَكَرَ اللَّهَ كَثِيرًا

Certainly, you have in the Messenger of Allah an excellent exemplar for him who hopes in Allah and the latter day and remembers Allah much. [1]

As demonstrated unequivocally in the verse, the Prophet (peace be upon him) has been described as the *'ustwatun ḥasana'*, the most perfect and complete exemplar. This absolute general statement has been made without any limitation or qualification. However, in relation to the leader of all pious people, Ibrāhim the friend of Allah (peace and blessings be upon him), Allah has said:

قَدْ كَانَتْ لَكُمْ أُسْوَةٌ حَسَنَةٌ فِي إِبْرَاهِيمَ وَالَّذِينَ مَعَهُ إِذْ قَالُوا لِقَوْمِهِمْ إِنَّا بُرَآءُ مِنكُمْ وَمِمَّا تَعْبُدُونَ مِن دُونِ اللَّهِ كَفَرْنَا بِكُمْ وَبَدَا بَيْنَنَا وَبَيْنَكُمُ الْعَدَاوَةُ وَالْبَغْضَاءُ أَبَدًا حَتَّىٰ تُؤْمِنُوا بِاللَّهِ وَحْدَهُ إِلَّا

[1] *Qur'ān* 33: 21

قَوْلَ إِبْرَاهِيمَ لِأَبِيهِ لَأَسْتَغْفِرَنَّ لَكَ وَمَا أَمْلِكُ لَكَ مِنَ اللَّهِ مِن شَيْءٍ رَّبَّنَا عَلَيْكَ تَوَكَّلْنَا وَإِلَيْكَ أَنَبْنَا وَإِلَيْكَ الْمَصِيرُ

Indeed, there is for you a good example in Ibrāhim and those with him when they said to their people: Surely, we are clear of you and of what you serve besides Allah; we declare ourselves to be clear of you and enmity and hatred have appeared between us and you forever until you believe in Allah alone-- but not in what Ibrāhim said to his father: I would certainly ask forgiveness for you, and I do not control for you aught from Allah - our Lord! Upon you do we rely and to you do we turn, and to you is the eventual coming. [2]

Allah made him a '*uswatun ḥasana*' only in the matter of allegiance since he was free and disassociated from his people who insisted on disbelief and were outspoken in their hostility towards him as demonstrated by them attempting to murder him (peace be upon him). Though, Allah mentioned an acceptable excuse for him for asking forgiveness for his father. He also praised him for ceasing to ask forgiveness – after the excuse ceased to exist. Allah, whose names are blessed, says:

وَمَا كَانَ اسْتِغْفَارُ إِبْرَاهِيمَ لِأَبِيهِ إِلَّا عَن مَّوْعِدَةٍ وَعَدَهَا إِيَّاهُ فَلَمَّا تَبَيَّنَ لَهُ أَنَّهُ عَدُوٌّ لِّلَّهِ تَبَرَّأَ مِنْهُ إِنَّ إِبْرَاهِيمَ لَأَوَّاهٌ حَلِيمٌ

And Ibrāhim asking forgiveness for his father was only owing to a promise which he had made to him; but when it became clear to him that he was an enemy of Allah, he declared himself to be clear of him; most surely Ibrāhim was very tender-hearted, forbearing. [3]

Yet Allah made an exception from the good example and leadership of Ibrāhim (peace be upon him), which is his asking forgiveness for his father, though he was intending only the good and was excused in

---

[2] *Qur'ān* 60: 4
[3] *Qur'ān* 9: 114

doing that. By Allah, Ibrāhim (peace be upon him) did not commit an impermissible deed or a sin. He just did only the less desirable with a good intention and while being dutiful to his father. He asked forgiveness because it was originally permitted and allowed to be done. At that time, he was not ordered otherwise but he abandoned it when Allah prohibited it explicitly.

In contradistinction to the matter of Ibrāhim (peace be upon him), it was never mentioned in the Qur'ān that the leader of Prophets and the master of all sent messengers, the nearest one to the Lord of the worlds, Muḥammad ibn Abdullah (peace be upon him) was excluded from being taken as an example to be necessarily guided. This fact when considered with evidences that following his example is Allah's command, necessarily proves that he is the good and infallible example in all his words and deeds with no exception whatsoever. The verses mentioned above provide compelling evidential basis: as outlined by: '*I do not follow anything but that which is revealed to me*' (*Surah al-An'ām* verse 50, *Surah Yunus* verse 10 and *Surah al-Aḥqāf* verse 9); then with the verse '*Certainly you have in the Messenger of Allah an excellent exemplar for him who hopes in Allah and the latter day and remembers Allah much.*' (*Surah al-Aḥ'zāb* verse 21) and with the verses: '*Say: If you love Allah, then follow me, Allah will love you and forgive you your faults and Allah is forgiving, merciful. Say: Obey Allah and the Messenger; but if they turn back, then surely Allah does not love the kāfireen*' (*Surah al-'Imrān* verses 32/33). Considering these evidences together we can necessarily conclude that the Prophet's (peace be upon him) deeds are an infallible revelation that can be considered an excellent example without any qualification or limitation.

Another key principle that can be outlined from what has been presented thus far: whatever the Prophet (peace be upon him) did after revelation began can never be prohibited for the rest of his *Ummah,* unless it has been categorically proven that it relates only to what is specifically legislated for him. Hence his acts can be emulated and followed without fear or hardship. Yet performing mere acts does not make them obligatory or even desirable, except by virtue of clear evidence to that effect. It is inconceivable that the Prophet (peace be upon him) could have performed an undesirable act unless there was a material evidence to show that he performed it only to prove that no one who performs it would be committing something unlawful outright. Though abstaining from performing such a deed would be better. This is partly one of the requirements of being designated as *ustwatun ḥasana.* Likewise, abstinence from a certain act would provide striking proof that this deed is not obligatory on the *Ummah.* Besides, there should be evidence to support the prohibition, the undesirability, or just the permissibility of a deed. It is inconceivable that the Prophet (peace be upon him) would cease to perform a desirable deed, unless he had an evidence showing that he just ceased to perform it to prove that it is not a questionable matter, so as not to burden his *Ummah*, or for any other reasons that will be discussed in due course.

Again, these are some of the requirements of being designated as *ustwatun ḥasana.* It is impossible for the Prophet (peace be upon him) to perform a deed which is prohibited for his *Ummah* or to leave what is obligatory for his *Ummah.* Although it is possible that he may perform something that is of a different category than the former, such as abandoning a desirable deed or performing a disliked deed. This would be a 'sin' for want of a better word between himself and Allah, though it is most definitely not a sin when performed by a member of his *Ummah*.

8 'That Allah may forgive your previous and future sins'

Given the foregoing discussion, this is the only meaning which is contextually compatible with the previous verses, or with other verses definitely stating that the Prophet's words and deeds are infallible. The meaning is also relevant to other texts that appeared as ambiguous to some people. At the forefront of these are the following where Allah has said:

لِّيَغْفِرَ لَكَ اللَّهُ مَا تَقَدَّمَ مِن ذَنبِكَ وَمَا تَأَخَّرَ وَيُتِمَّ نِعْمَتَهُ عَلَيْكَ وَيَهْدِيَكَ صِرَاطًا مُّسْتَقِيمًا

That Allah may forgive your previous and future sins and complete His favour to you and keep you on a right way. [1]

As well as the verse where the Prophet (peace be upon him) was chided by Allah for turning away:

عَبَسَ وَتَوَلَّىٰ ، أَن جَاءَهُ الْأَعْمَىٰ

[1] *Qur'ān* 48: 2

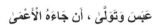

He frowned and turned (his) back, because there came to him a blind man. [2]

عَفَا اللَّهُ عَنكَ لِمَ أَذِنتَ لَهُمْ حَتَّىٰ يَتَبَيَّنَ لَكَ الَّذِينَ صَدَقُوا وَتَعْلَمَ الْكَاذِبِينَ

Allah pardon you! Why did you give them leave until those who spoke the truth had become manifest to you and you had known the liars? [3]

In order to place these verses within the context of what has transpired thus far, it is necessary to consider the various *aḥādith* which are related to these verses. By doing so it will enable clarity to be brought to the notion of what is considered the 'sins' of the Prophet (peace be upon him), which are in fact not related to him committing that which is prohibited for his *Ummah*. Firstly, Imām Muslim recorded the following *ḥadith* in his *Ṣaḥīḥ*:

حدثنا يحيى بن يحيى وقتيبة بن سعيد وأبو الربيع العتكي جميعا عن حماد قال يحيى أخبرنا حمّاد بن زيد عن ثابت عن أبي بردة عن الأغر المزني، وكانت له صحبة، أنّ رسول الله، صلّى الله عليه وسلّم، قال: إنّه ليغان على قلبي وإني لأستغفر الله في اليوم مائة مرة

Yaḥya ibn Yaḥya, Qutayba ibn Sa'eed and Abu Rabih' al-'Ataki narrated to us, all of them from Ḥammād, Yaḥya said Ḥammād ibn Zayd reported to us from Thābit from Abu Burda from Al-Agharr al-Muzani, who was one amongst the Companions, he reported that Allah's Messenger (peace be upon him) said: *There is* (at times) *some sort of shade upon my heart and I seek forgiveness from Allah a hundred times a day.*

The same narration is reported with authentic and good channels of

[2] *Qur'ān* 80: 1/2
[3] *Qur'ān* 9: 43

narration in a large number of *ḥadith* collections.[4] It is also reported in the *Ṣaḥīḥ* of Ibn Ḥibbān in two places.[5] Regarding this Shaykh Shu'ayb al-Arnā'uṭ said the *isnād* of the *ḥadith* is *Ṣaḥīḥ*. Imām Abu Ḥātim ibn Ḥibbān also commented on this by saying:

> The statement of the Prophet (peace be upon him) '*Innahu la-yughānu ala' qalbi'* refers to the anxious thoughts straining his heart when he is concerned, thinking about some acts of worship or a ruling not known to him before its revelation. As in the case when the Prophet (peace be upon him) was in Mecca. Having no knowledge of the rulings revealed in the chapter of *al-Baqarah* in Medina, he considered it a sin on him that strained his heart. That is why he used to ask Allah for forgiveness a hundred times each day. It was not that his heart was burdened by a sin which he commits akin to that felt by members of his *Ummah* when they sin.

In the *Mu'jam al-Kabir* of Imām aṭ-Ṭabarāni he has recorded the following narration:

> حدّثنا محمّد بن محمّد الجذوعي القاضي قال: سمعت العبّاس بن الوليد النّرسي يقول: سألت أبا عبيدة معمر بن المثنّى عن تفسير قوله: إنّه ليغان على قلبي، فلم يفسّره لي، وسألت الأصمعي عنه فلم يفسّره
>
> Muḥammad bin Muḥammad al-Juzoo'ee the judge narrated to

---

4 Amongst these, are the following: *Al-Adab al-Mufrad*, Bukhāri [Vol. 1 sec. 218, no. 621], *Sunan* Abu Dāwud [Vol. 2 sec. 85, no. 1,515], *Musnad* Aḥmad bin Ḥanbal [Vol. 4 sec. 211, no. 17,880 / 17,883; Vol. 4 sec. 260, no. 18,317 / 18,320; Vol. 5 sec. 411, no. 23,535], *Musnad* aṭ-Ṭayālisi [Vol. 1 sec. 167, no. 1,202], *Mu'jam al-Kabir* aṭ-Ṭabarāni [Vol. 1 sec. 301, no. 882 / 889], *Sunan al-Kubra,* an-Nasā'i [Vol. 6 sec. 116, no. 10,276 / 10,281], *Al-Aḥād wal-Mathāni* of Ibn Abi 'Aāṣim ash-Shaybāni [Vol. 2 sec. 357, no. 1,127], *Sunan al-Kubra,* Bayhaqy [Vol. 7 sec. 52, no. 13,119], *Musnad* 'Abd ibn Ḥumayd [Vol. 1 sec. 142, no. 363 / 364], and *Muṣṣanaf* of Abu Bakr ibn Abi Shayba [Vol. 6 sec. 57, no. 29,444 & 29,448].

5 *Ṣaḥīḥ* Ibn Ḥibbān Vol. 3 sec. 210, no. 931, 929

> us, he said I heard al-Abbāb bin al-Waleed an-Narsee he said I asked Abu 'Ubaida Ma'mar bin al-Muthanna about the *Tafsir* of the statement – *'Innahu la-yughānu ala' qalbi'* and he gave no *Tafsir*. I asked Al-Aṣma'i about it but he did not give me an explanation either.

I would submit that the word *'ghayn'* is the light cloud which shields the figure of the sun without shielding much of its light, in contradistinction to the work *'ghaym'*, which is the thick dark cloud. So the Messenger of Allah (peace be upon him) used to ask forgiveness from even the slightest clouding of the heart and it is well known that this is not considered as being a sin in the traditional sense for his *Ummah*.

As well as this there is an additional narration that is reported in *Sunan* Abu Dāwud with an authentic chain of transmission from Abdullah ibn Umar.

> حدّثنا الحسن بن علي حدّثنا أبو أسامة عن مالك بن مِغْوَل عن محمد بن سوقة عن نافع عن بن عمر قال: إن كنا لنعُدّ لرسول الله، صلى الله عليه وسلم، في المجلس الواحد مائة مرة: رب اغفر لي، وتب علي إنك أنت التّواب الرّحيم
>
> al-Ḥasan bin Ali narrated to us Abu Usāma narrated to us from Mālik bin Mighwal from Muḥammad bin Sooqa from Nāfi from Ibn Umar who said: We counted that the Messenger of Allah (peace be upon him) would say a hundred times during a meeting - *My Lord, forgive me and pardon me; thou art the pardoning and forgiving one.*

Albāni said of this that it was *Ṣaḥīḥ*. It is well known and reported by several Imām's in their respective collections of *ḥadith*. Most of them have reported this *ḥadith* from the channel of Nāfi from Ibn Umar and others from the channel of Mujāhid or Abu Faḍl from Ibn Umar. Imām Aḥmad records similar in his *Musnad* but on the authority of Abu Hurayrah:

حدّثنا عبد الرزّاق قال معمرعن الزهري عن أبي سلمة عن أبي هريرة عن النّبي، صلّى الله عليه وسلّم، قال: إني لأستغفر الله في اليوم أكثر من سبعين مرّة وأتوب إليه

Abdar-Razzāq narrated to us, Ma'mar said from az-Zuhri from Abu Salama from Abu Hurayrah from the Messenger (peace be upon him) who said: *I ask forgiveness from Allah more than seventy times in a day and repent to him.*

Imām Aḥmad also records similarly elsewhere in his *Musnad.* Albāni said of this that it was *ḥasan Ṣaḥīḥ*. The *ḥadith* has also been recorded by Ibn Ḥibbān in his *Ṣaḥīḥ;*[6] in the *Sunan* of Ibn Mājah;[7] in *Sunan al-Kubra* of Nasā'i[8] as well as in other noted collections. In *Mu'jam aṣ-Ṣagheer* Imām Ṭabarāni records the following:

حدثنا إبراهيم بن محمد الغزالي البصري المعدّل حدثنا خلاّد بن أسلم المروزي حدّثنا النّضر بن شميل أنبأنا حمّاد بن سلمة عن عاصم بن بهدلة عن أبي صالح عن أبي هريرة قال: قال رسول الله، صلّى الله عليه وسلّم: إنّي لأستغفر الله في اليوم وأتوب إليه في كل يوم مائة مرّة

Ibrāhim bin Muḥammad al-Ghazli al-Baṣri al-Mu'addal narrated to us Khalad bin Aslam al-Marwazi narrated to us an-Naḍr bin Shumayl narrated to us Ḥammād bin Salama reports from 'Aāṣim bin Bahdala from Abu Ṣāliḥ from Abu Hurayrah he said that Messenger of Allah (peace be upon him) said: *I seek the forgiveness of Allah and repent to Him one hundred*

---

[6] *Ṣaḥīḥ* Ibn Hibbān Vol. 3 sec. 205, no. 925
[7] *Sunan* Ibn Mājah Vol. 2 sec. 1,254, no. 3,815
[8] *Sunan al-Kubra* Nasā'i Vol. 6 sec. 114, no. 10,265; 10,268 & 10,273 & Vol. 6 sec. 460, no. 11,495

times each day.

Imām Ṭabarāni writes concerning this: 'Nobody related this version on the authority of 'Aāṣim except Ḥammād bin Salama and an-Naḍr was a sole narrator.' I would say in reply that it is of no consequence, given that both are considered trustworthy honest narrators and respected Imām's. It is also found in *Sharḥ Ma'āni al-Athār* via the following channel:

حدّثنا بن أبي داود قال حدّثنا خطّاب بن عثمان وحيوة بن شريح قالا حدّثنا بقيّة بن الوليد عن الزّبيدي عن الزّهري عن عبد الملك بن أبي بكر بن الحارث بن هشام عن أبي هريرة أنه كان يقول: سمعت رسول الله، صلى الله عليه وسلم: إني لأتوب في اليوم مائة مرّة، وقال أنس إنّما قال: سبعين مرّة

Ibn Abi Dāwud narrated to us he said Khaṭṭāb bin Uthmān and Ḥaywa bin Shurayḥ narrated to us, they said Baqia bin al-Waleed narrated to us from az-Zubaydi from az-Zuhri from Abdal-Malik bin Abi Bakr bin al-Ḥārith bin Hāshim from Abu Hurayrah that he was saying: I heard the Messenger of Allah (say): *I repent one-hundred times a day.* And he said Anas said that it was seventy-times.

Ibn Ḥibbān records the narration from Anas bin Mālik may Allah be pleased with him via an authentic channel in his *Ṣaḥīḥ*:

أخبرنا الحسن بن سفيان قال حدّثنا هريم بن عبد الأعلى قال حدّثنا معتمر بن سليمان قال سمعت أبي يقول حدّثنا قتادة عن أنس قال: قال رسول الله، صلى الله عليه وسلم: إني لأتوب في اليوم سبعين مرّة

Al-Ḥasan bin Sufyān reported to us he said Huraym bin Abdal-'Alā narrated to us he said Mu'tamir bin Sulaymān narrated to us he said I heard my father say Qatādah narrated to us from Anas he said the Messenger of Allah (peace be upon him) said:

I repent seventy-times a day.

This *isnād* is authentic according to the conditions of Imām Muslim; it has also been recorded by Imām an-Nasā'i in his *Sunan al-Kubra,*[9] in the *Musnad* of Abu Ya'la[10] as well as in other collections. The next narration is in the *Sunan* of Ibn Mājah reported on the authority of Abu Musa al-Ash'ari may Allah be pleased with him:

حدّثنا علي بن محمّد حدّثنا وكيع عن مغيرة بن أبي الحرّ عن سعيد بن أبي بردة بن أبي موسى عن أبيه عن جده قال: قال رسول الله، صلّى الله عليه وسلّم: إنّي لأستغفر الله وأتوب إليه في اليوم سبعين مرّة

Ali bin Muḥammad narrated to us Waki' narrated to us from Mughira bin Abul'Ḥurr from Sa'eed bin Abi Burda bin Abi Musa from his father from his grandfather who said: The Messenger of Allah (peace be upon him) said: *I seek the forgiveness of Allah and repent to Him seventy times each day.*

Imām Aḥmad also cites this *ḥadith* in his *Musnad.*[11] I would argue that the *isnād* is *ḥasan* because Mughira bin Abul'Ḥurri al-Kindi is truthful (*ṣadooq*) however when taken with the supporting narrative as found in the *Sunan al-Kubra* of an-Nasā'i it can be regarded as *Ṣaḥīḥ.*[12] Elsewhere in the *Sunan al-Kubra* Imām an-Nasā'i reported the following narratives on the authority of Ḥudhayfah may Allah be pleased with him:

أخبرنا عبد الحميد بن محمّد حدّثنا مخلد حدّثنا سفيان عن أبي إسحاق عن أبي المغيرة عن حذيفة قال أتيت النّبي، صلّى الله عليه وسلّم، فقلت: أحرقني

[9] Nasā'i *Sunan al-Kubra* Vol. 6 sec. 114, no. 10,266 / 10,267
[10] *Musnad* Abu Ya'la Vol. 5 sec. 311, no. 2,934
[11] *Musnad* Aḥmad Vol. 4 sec. 410, no. 19,687
[12] Nasā'i *Sunan al-Kubra* Vol. 6 sec. 115, no. 10,274

لساني؛ وذكر من ذرابته على أهله؛ قال: أين أنت من الاستغفار؟! إنّي لأستغفر الله في اليوم وأتوب إليه مائة مرّة

Abd'al-Ḥumayd bin Muḥammad reported to us Makhlad narrated to us Sufyān narrated to us from Abi Isḥāq from Abu'l Mughira from Ḥudhayfah he said the Prophet (peace be upon him) came and I said to him that I mentioned that I was harsh in the way I spoke to my family, but not to others. He said: *What about asking Allah for forgiveness? Verily, I ask Allah for forgiveness a hundred times a day.*

أخبرنا قتيبة بن سعيد حدّثنا أبو الأحوص عن أبي إسحاق عن أبي المغيرة قال: قال حذيفة شكوت إلى رسول الله، صلى الله عليه وسلم، ذرب لساني فقال: أين أنت من الاستغفار؟! إنّي لأستغفر الله كلّ يوم مائة مرّة

Qutayba ibn Sa'eed reported to us Abul' Aḥwaṣ narrated to us from Abi Isḥāq from Abu'l Mughira he said Ḥudhayfah said: I complained to the Prophet (peace be upon him) about the sharpness of my tongue, so he said: *Why don't you ask for forgiveness? Verily, every day I ask Allah for forgiveness a hundred times.*

The narration is also reported in the *Muṣṣanaf* of Abu Bakr ibn Abi Shayba in a number of places as well as in other collections.[13] The next narration is reported via 'a man from the Anṣār' again as found in the *Sunan al-Kubra* of Imām an-Nasā'i:

أخبرني إبراهيم بن يعقوب قال حدّثني عبد الله بن الرّبيع قال: حدّثنا عبّاد بن العوّام عن حصين عن هلال بن يساف عن زاذان عن رجل من الأنصار نسي اسمه انّه رأى النّبي، صلّى الله عليه وسلّم، صلّى ركعتي الضّحى فلمّا جلس سمعته يقول: رب اعفر لي وتب عليّ إنّك أنت التّواب الرّحيم، حتّى بلغ مائة مرّة

[13] *Muṣṣanaf* Ibn Abi Shayba Vol. 7 sec. 173, no. 35,078 & Vol. 6 sec. 56, no. 29,441

> Ibrāhim bin Ya'qub reported to me he said Abdullah bin Rabih' narrated to me he said 'Abbād bin al-'Awwām reported from Huṣayn from Hilāl bin Yasāf from Zādhān from a man from the Anṣār whose name he forgot; that he saw the Prophet (peace be upon him) perform two *rak'ahs* of the forenoon prayer then sat and he heard him say: *My Lord, forgive me and pardon me; thou art the pardoning and forgiving one*, until he said it a hundred-times.

Imām an-Nasā'i mentions this same narration in another place also in the *Sunan al-Kubra.* I would submit that Abdullah bin ar-Rabih' al-Khurāsāni is Abu Abdar-Raḥman Abdullah bin Muḥammad bin ar-Rabih' al-'Aāizi al-Kirmāni al-Khurāsāni, he was stationed in *maṣeeṣa* in the path of Allah. He is considered *thiqa* and from the tenth of the senior followers.

From all of this we would say that the reports reach the level of *tawātur,* thus we can affirm beyond any doubt that this demonstrates that the 'sins' of the Prophet (peace be upon him) are not related to him committing that which is prohibited for his *Ummah.* Yet it could still be considered as a point of contention that he leaves a matter which is considered desirable or recommended for his *Ummah*; perhaps such a matter would be considered as obliged upon him personally. Or he has committed that which considered as being disliked for his *Ummah*; perhaps the matter is considered prohibited for him personally. However it is not conceivable that the Prophet (peace be upon him) could have abandoned a deed that was made obligatory on his *Ummah* or performed a deed prohibited for his *Ummah.* Hence the notion of his 'sins' are essentially of the former type and not the latter.

9 Regarding the acts of the Prophet – can he forget?

One issue remains, that he (peace be upon him) can perhaps forbid a matter (such as the issue of facing the *Qibla* while urinating or defecating) then after that, he undertakes the act in question (urinating facing the *Qibla* with his back to *Bayt al-Maqdis*, Jerusalem). It has been said by some scholars and specialists in the fundamentals of jurisprudence that the way to explain this can be to interpret the matter as showing that the Prophet (peace be upon him) forgot while doing the act; that it wasn't done deliberately or intentionally in that regard. Although being *ma'ṣoom* he is not excluded altogether from forgetfulness as people are. Given such circumstances where his act appears to go against a previous verbal prohibition, it is the verbal statement outlining the prohibition which would take precedence.

In reply, I would argue that this line of reasoning contains a number of fundamental errors. To begin, it is not necessary to proceed with that line of reasoning. Where there is a statement and act, it could very well be argued that the subsequent act operates to serve or explain that the previous prohibition that it is not one of being *ḥarām* per se but rather being a disliked matter. Or it could be considered as being a matter of abrogation (*naskh*), if it can be established with certainty the latter act clarifies that its not one related to prohibition. This is right ordering, from which we can further state - firstly, that he (peace be upon him) had gumption and was established with fervour of mind and a powerful memory, as is known from the necessity of history, a matter recognised by believer and disbeliever alike. To argue that it may be the case that there is a small percentage chance of him being forgetful in a particular incident or situation would need a proof to establish that conclusively. Just as is the case with narrators that are trustworthy (*thiqa*); error or forgetfulness shouldn't be attributed to them in their reporting and channels of narration except with a specific proof. As for the objection that it is merely a rational possibility, that isn't permissible since it would disrupt the balance of reporting as the witness of history attests. Secondly, as the glorified and exalted has said:

سَنُقْرِئُكَ فَلَا تَنسَىٰ ، إِلَّا مَا شَاءَ اللَّهُ إِنَّهُ يَعْلَمُ الْجَهْرَ وَمَا يَخْفَىٰ

We will make you recite so you shall not forget, except what Allah pleases surely He knows the manifest and what is hidden. [1]

He states – *except what Allah pleases* – thereby the speech shows we will make you recite so you will not forget anything from the Qur'ān in an absolute sense, unless that which Allah causes you to forget, that will be abrogation, whereby some words are lifted or raised from the Qur'ān. By necessity the abrogation will operate for every wording related to various legal injunctions (*aḥkām*) as well unless otherwise stated with proof. This authenticity is further put into proportion by the statement of Allah where he says:

مَا نَنسَخْ مِنْ آيَةٍ أَوْ نُنسِهَا نَأْتِ بِخَيْرٍ مِّنْهَا أَوْ مِثْلِهَا أَلَمْ تَعْلَمْ أَنَّ اللَّهَ عَلَىٰ كُلِّ شَيْءٍ قَدِيرٌ

Whatever communications we abrogate or cause to be forgotten, we bring one

[1] *Qur'ān* 87: 6/7

(forth) *better than it or like it. Do you not know that Allah has power over all things?* [2]

If the wording here was only for the text of the Qur'ān, then it is also a further exemplification of the word [سنقرئك] '*we will make you recite*' for it is a blessing from Allah if he causes his Prophet to forget a text from the texts of the glorious Qur'ān. He reveals the words, the devout recite it, it is miraculous in its style and meaning. Abrogation of the text for that reason has with it all its related rules or legal provisions (*aḥkām*). Given the elevated rank of the Qur'ān and its sacredness, by greater reasoning, the thing forgotten would also apply to the *Sunnah*. *Thus the prohibition regarding facing the Qibla while urinating or defecating after that the future change of the Qibla from Jerusalem was abrogated by prohibition and likewise*. If the word [سنقرئك] '*we will make you recite*' was meant for teaching and instruction then it shall be inclusive of all revelation – both the Qur'ān and *Sunnah*. As is like the saying of the exalted:

ذَلِكَ نَتْلُوهُ عَلَيْكَ مِنَ الْآيَاتِ وَالذِّكْرِ الْحَكِيمِ

This we recite to you of the communications and the wise reminder (dhikr). [3]

As will be detailed in this volume, the 'wise reminder' - *dhikr* includes both the glorious Qur'ān and the *Sunnah*. However the word used in the aforementioned verse is to 'recite' giving priority to the Qur'ān as a result of its high standing. Or because the meaning of the language in *uṣul* is 'sequence something after something' and 'allegiance to something after the thing'; the argument being self-evident obviating the need to invoke the notion of greater reasoning.

---

[2] *Qur'ān* 2: 106
[3] *Qur'ān* 3: 58

Thirdly, that he (peace be upon him) is but human and like all other human beings prone to forget, except that it is the Prophet that is commissioned to deliver the message. Yet the responsibility for the collection and explanation rests upon Allah, for he exalted be his names has said:

إِنَّ عَلَيْنَا جَمْعَهُ وَقُرْآنَهُ ، فَإِذَا قَرَأْنَاهُ فَاتَّبِعْ قُرْآنَهُ ، ثُمَّ إِنَّ عَلَيْنَا بَيَانَهُ

Surely on us (devolves) the collection and its recitation; therefore when we have recited it, follow its recitation. Again upon us (devolves) *the explanation of it.* [4]

Allah the exalted and majestic has also said:

وَيَوْمَ نَبْعَثُ فِي كُلِّ أُمَّةٍ شَهِيدًا عَلَيْهِم مِّنْ أَنفُسِهِمْ وَجِئْنَا بِكَ شَهِيدًا عَلَىٰ هَٰؤُلَاءِ وَنَزَّلْنَا عَلَيْكَ
الْكِتَابَ تِبْيَانًا لِّكُلِّ شَيْءٍ وَهُدًى وَرَحْمَةً وَبُشْرَىٰ لِلْمُسْلِمِينَ

And on the day when We will raise up in every people a witness against them from among themselves and bring you as a witness against these-- and We have revealed the Book to you explaining clearly everything and a guidance and mercy and good news for those who submit. [5]

هَٰذَا بَيَانٌ لِّلنَّاسِ وَهُدًى وَمَوْعِظَةٌ لِّلْمُتَّقِينَ

This is a clear statement for men, guidance and an admonition to those who are God-conscious. [6]

Necessity dictates that Allah communicates revelation directly to the Prophet. That extends even to what one might consider a small issue,

---

[4] *Qur'ān* 75: 17/19
[5] *Qur'ān* 16: 89
[6] *Qur'ān* 3: 138

such as when *Jibreel* conveyed to him that when one prays and takes off his sandals, he should not harm anyone in that.[7] Given that he was not informed of this previously, it is Allah who provides this to establish a new ruling. Or the medium can be to inspire an issue in the minds of some of his Companions (or the other issue related to the prayer at noon where he prayed two units of prayer instead of four, thereby enabling the demonstration of how to correct an omission made during the prayer, as well as the matter of where he forgot to pronounce a verse in the prayer and the companions raised the point after it finished). There is also the point of the Prophet (peace be upon him) alerting his Companions to a matter beforehand in a given situation in order to demonstrate a particular ruling, like explaining to them how to correct the Imām in prayer, that the men should exclaim and the women should clap to signify for example where a verse was misread.

Interestingly, there is a relevant statement regarding this point that has been reported from Imām Mālik in the *Muwaṭṭā'* that the Prophet said: '*I forget or I am made to forget so that I may establish the Sunnah.*'[8] This is one of the few narrations in the *Muwaṭṭā'*, (four in total), where it has not been able to provide a fully connected channel to the Prophet (peace be upon him) despite intensive research and investigation. It is also plagued by misreading, where most people thought the Prophetic comment relates to a pure error, placing it in the same context as the concurrent well known reports concerning the prostration of forgetfulness.

---

[7] See the tradition as reported in the *Sunan* of Abu Dāwud, book of prayer

[8] See: Mālik, *Muwaṭṭā'* book 4 'forgetfulness in prayer'

10 Enjoining the good, forbidding all evil

The following verses are where Allah answered Musa (peace be upon him) when he apologised for his people and asked for forgiveness and tolerance after being afflicted with the deadly shock upon the mountain. Allah blessed be his names states:

وَاكْتُبْ لَنَا فِي هَٰذِهِ الدُّنْيَا حَسَنَةً وَفِي الْآخِرَةِ إِنَّا هُدْنَا إِلَيْكَ قَالَ عَذَابِي أُصِيبُ بِهِ مَنْ أَشَاءُ
وَرَحْمَتِي وَسِعَتْ كُلَّ شَيْءٍ فَسَأَكْتُبُهَا لِلَّذِينَ يَتَّقُونَ وَيُؤْتُونَ الزَّكَاةَ وَالَّذِينَ هُم بِآيَاتِنَا يُؤْمِنُونَ

الَّذِينَ يَتَّبِعُونَ الرَّسُولَ النَّبِيَّ الْأُمِّيَّ الَّذِي يَجِدُونَهُ مَكْتُوبًا عِندَهُمْ فِي التَّوْرَاةِ وَالْإِنجِيلِ يَأْمُرُهُم
بِالْمَعْرُوفِ وَيَنْهَاهُمْ عَنِ الْمُنكَرِ وَيُحِلُّ لَهُمُ الطَّيِّبَاتِ وَيُحَرِّمُ عَلَيْهِمُ الْخَبَائِثَ وَيَضَعُ عَنْهُمْ
إِصْرَهُمْ وَالْأَغْلَالَ الَّتِي كَانَتْ عَلَيْهِمْ فَالَّذِينَ آمَنُوا بِهِ وَعَزَّرُوهُ وَنَصَرُوهُ وَاتَّبَعُوا النُّورَ الَّذِي
أُنزِلَ مَعَهُ أُولَٰئِكَ هُمُ الْمُفْلِحُونَ

قُلْ يَا أَيُّهَا النَّاسُ إِنِّي رَسُولُ اللَّهِ إِلَيْكُمْ جَمِيعًا الَّذِي لَهُ مُلْكُ السَّمَاوَاتِ وَالْأَرْضِ لَا إِلَٰهَ إِلَّا هُوَ
يُحْيِي وَيُمِيتُ فَآمِنُوا بِاللَّهِ وَرَسُولِهِ النَّبِيِّ الْأُمِّيِّ الَّذِي يُؤْمِنُ بِاللَّهِ وَكَلِمَاتِهِ وَاتَّبِعُوهُ لَعَلَّكُمْ
تَهْتَدُونَ

And ordain for us good in this world's life and in the hereafter, for surely we turn to Thee. He said: (As for) My chastisement, I will afflict with it whom I please, and My mercy encompasses all things; so I will ordain it (specially) for those who guard (against evil) and pay the poor-rate, and those who believe in Our communications.

Those who follow the Messenger-Prophet, the unlettered, whom they find written down with them in the Torah and the Injeel (who) enjoins upon them good and forbids them evil, and makes lawful to them the good things and makes unlawful to them impure things, and removes from them their burden and the shackles which were upon them; so (as for) those who believe in him and honour him and help him, and follow the light which has been sent down with him, these it is that are the successful.

Say: O people! surely I am the Messenger of Allah to you all, of Him Whose is the kingdom of the heavens and the earth there is no god but He; He brings to life and causes to die therefore believe in Allah and His Messenger, the unlettered Prophet who believes in Allah and His words, and follow him so that you may walk in the right way. [1]

The verses are considered as a glad tiding regarding of the advent of the unlettered Prophet Muḥammad (peace be upon him) who is equal in rank to Musa (if not higher), whom Allah will send to the people of Israel (and others) from among their brethren (i.e. the descendent of Ismā'il the brother of Isḥāq who is the grandfather of the people of Israel) which is still preserved in the Book of Deuteronomy (book 18), one of the books of the Torah. It has been as preserved by divine power from distortion, perversion and forgery to which most former divine books were subject. Verses 15 to 21 are here presented in full:

15. *The Lord thy God will raise up unto thee a Prophet from the midst of thee, of thy brethren, like unto me; unto him ye shall hearken;*

16. *According to all that thou desires of the Lord thy God in Horeb in the day of the assembly, saying, Let me not hear again the voice of the Lord my God, neither let me see this great fire any more, that I die not.*

---

[1] *Qur'ān* 7: 156/158

> 17. *And the Lord said unto me, They have well spoken that which they have spoken.*
>
> 18. *I will raise them up a Prophet from among their brethren, like unto thee, and will put my words in his mouth; and he shall speak unto them all that I shall command him.*
>
> 19. *And it shall come to pass, that whosoever will not hearken unto my words which he shall speak in my name, I will require it of him.*
>
> 20. *But the Prophet, who shall presume to speak a word in my name, which I have not commanded him to speak, or that shall speak in the name of other gods, even that Prophet shall die.*
>
> 21. *And if thou say in your heart, How shall we know the word which the Lord has not spoken?*
>
> 22. *When a Prophet speaks in the name of the Lord, if the thing follows not, nor come to pass, that is the thing which the Lord has not spoken, but the prophet has spoken it presumptuously: thou shalt not be afraid of him.*

One should note how Musa (peace be upon him) hoped that Allah bestowed upon Israel a Prophet like him from amongst themselves, as in verse 15 above where he says: '*The Lord thy God will raise up unto thee a Prophet from the midst of thee, of thy brethren, like unto me; unto him ye shall hearken.*' But the text further goes on to say, as in verse 18 where Allah said: '*I will raise them up a Prophet from among their brethren, like unto thee, and will put my words in his mouth; and he shall speak unto them all that I shall command him,*' emphasis being placed upon the Prophet being from among their brethren and not from among themselves!

Returning to the prophecy outlined in Deuteronomy, we have in this great final sealed revelation an explicit verse where Allah has given his final unlettered Prophet (peace be upon him) a distinctive quality in that he '*...enjoins upon them good and forbids them evil.*' That is, the Prophet (peace be upon him) prohibits *all evil* regardless of its genus or type. It is therefore necessary that the Prophet (peace be upon him) prohibits decisively any evil that he sees or that he is informed about whether by means of words or through clear gestures. He may prohibit an evil by virtue of a clearly obvious action denoting prohibition. If the Prophet (peace be upon him) approves of a deed, this means that it is not evil nor prohibited. He may then identify the deed as disliked, or purely permissible, desirable or an obligation. This identification is an additional classification of what is already approved of. The deed would therefore definitely not be designated as prohibited. Thus we know for sure that the Prophet (peace be upon him) does not approve of an evil or approve of prohibited deeds and that he acknowledges nothing but true good deeds. Otherwise, the statement of Allah would be false and his promise would be fake – exalted is he above all of that. Allah blessed and exalted further informs us in another verse:

يَا أَيُّهَا الرَّسُولُ بَلِّغْ مَا أُنزِلَ إِلَيْكَ مِن رَّبِّكَ وَإِن لَّمْ تَفْعَلْ فَمَا بَلَّغْتَ رِسَالَتَهُ وَاللَّهُ يَعْصِمُكَ مِنَ النَّاسِ إِنَّ اللَّهَ لَا يَهْدِي الْقَوْمَ الْكَافِرِينَ

O Messenger! Deliver what has been revealed to you from your Lord; and if you do it not, then you have not delivered His message and Allah will protect you from the people; surely Allah will not guide the unbelieving people.[2]

It has been proven that he (peace be upon him) dismissed all centurions and was not guarded after this verse was revealed. He had no porters till he died and met His Lord. Allah protected him from being harmed by anyone. Hence there cannot be a charge that he (peace be upon him) could not speak against all evil for fear of being harmed. Further elaboration upon this point is provided in a number of *aḥādith* and accompanying narratives, which we will consider in turn.

---

[2] *Qur'ān* 5: 67

As is reported in *al-Mustadrak a'la Ṣaḥīḥayn* of Al-Ḥākim upon the authority of 'Aisha mother of the believers, may Allah be pleased with her:

> حدثنا عبد الصمد بن علي البزاز ببغداد أنبأ أحمد بن محمد بن عيسى القاضي حدثنا مسلم بن إبراهيم حدثنا الحارث بن عبيد حدثنا معبد الجريري عن عبد الله بن شقيق عن عائشة رضي الله تعالى عنها، قالت: كان النبي، صلى الله عليه وسلم، يحرس حتى نزلت هذه الآية: {وَاللَّهُ يَعْصِمُكَ مِنَ النَّاسِ}، فأخرج النبي، صلى الله عليه وسلم، رأسه من القبة فقال لهم: أيها الناس انصرفوا فقد عصمني الله
>
> Abduṣ-Ṣammad bin Ali al-Bazzāz narrated to us in Baghdad, Aḥmad bin Muḥammad bin Esa al-Qāḍi reports, Muslim bin Ibrāhim narrated to us al-Ḥārith bin 'Ubaid narrated to us Ma'bad al-Jariri narrated to us from Abdullah bin Shaqiq from 'Aisha may Allah be pleased with her, she said: the Prophet (peace be upon him) was being guarded until this verse was revealed: *Allah will protect you from mankind.* So the Messenger of Allah (peace be upon him) came out from the room and said: *O you people! Go, for Allah shall protect me.*

Al-Ḥākim has said: 'This *ḥadith* has an authentic chain of transmission but they (Bukhāri and Muslim) did not record it.' In *at-Talkeeṣ* adh-Dhahaby said it is *Ṣaḥīḥ*; it is as they said, particularly given the various channels from which it comes. It is also reported by at-Tirmidhi in his *Sunan*.[3] Albāni said of it that it was *ḥasan*. Imām Bayhaqy has this in both *as-Sunan al-Kubra* and *Dalā'il an-Naboowa* (signs of Prophethood);[4] Ibn Abi Ḥātim collected this in his *Tafsir*,[5] and it is also in *aṭ-Ṭabaqāt al-Kubra* as well as in other collections. In the *Tafsir* of the grand Imām aṭ-Ṭabari he has the following narration

---

[3] *Sunan* Tirmidhi Vol. 5 sec. 252, no. 3,046

[4] *Sunan al-Kubra* Vol. 9 sec. 8, no. 17,508; *Dalā'il an-Naboowa* Vol. 2 sec. 57, no. 489

[5] *Tafsir* Ibn Abi Ḥātim Vol. 5 sec. 34, no. 6,650

which has an authentic channel, though it is *mursal*, only reaching to Abdullah ibn Shaqeeq:

> حدثني يعقوب بن إبراهيم وابن وكيع قالا حدثنا ابن علية، عن الجُريريّ، عن عبد الله بن شقيق، أن رسول الله، صلى الله عليه وسلم، كان يعتقِبه ناسٌ من أصحابه، فلما نزلت: {والله يعصمك من الناس}، خرج فقال: يا أيها الناس، الحقوا بملاحِقِكم، فإنّ الله قد عصمني من الناس
>
> Ya'qub bin Ibrāhim and Ibn Waki' narrated to me, they said Ibn 'Aliyah narrated to us from al-Jurreeri from Abdullah ibn Shaqeeq that the Messenger of Allah (peace be upon him) was protected from people by his Companions. Then the verse was revealed - *Allah will protect you from mankind.* He came out and said: '*O people! Leave, for Allah has protected me from the people.*

I would submit that the words given by Abdullah bin Shaqeeq in this narration of the incident are the wording as has been reported from 'Aisha (may Allah be pleased with her). Her narration as outlined previously gives the exact wording and context. The narrative coming via Sa'eed bin Iyās provide two independent versions of the event. That perturbed some scholars, as they thought it troublesome in the *isnād;* for that reason Imām Tirmidhi was astonished that the *ḥadith* was *marfu'* and *mutaṣṣil* (raised and connected), he said: 'This *ḥadith* is strange and reported by some this *ḥadith* from al-Jarirri from ibn Shaqeeq who said the Prophet (peace be upon him) did not mention about the guard as did 'Aisha.' It is not so but this report is an additional report and it is found in the *Tārikh Madina - History of Medina* in *mursal* form with an authentic *isnād* up to that point - Ḥabbān bin Hilāl narrated to us he said Abdal-'Ala (ibn Abdal-'Ala) as-Sāmi narrated to us he said Sa'eed al-Jariri narrated to us / till the end.

It has also been reported in the *Tafsir* of Imām aṭ-Ṭabari in *mursal* form, *ḥasan Ṣaḥīḥ* by *isnād* to Sa'eed ibn Jubayr:

حدثنا هناد وابن وكيع قالا: حدثنا جرير عن ثعلبة عن جعفر عن سعيد بن جبير قال: لما نزلت: {يا أيها الرسول بلغ ما أنزل إليك من ربك وإن لم تفعل فما بلغت رسالته والله يعصمك من الناس}، قال رسول الله، صلى الله عليه وسلم: لا تحرسوني، إنّ ربّي قد عَصَمَني

Hannād and Ibn Waki' narrated to us, they said Jarir narrated to us from Thalabah from Ja'far from Sa'eed bin Jubayr he said when the verse was revealed: *O Messenger! Deliver what has been revealed to you from your Lord; and if you do it not, then you have not delivered His message and Allah will protect you from the people* the Prophet (peace be upon him) said: *Don't safeguard me, verily Allah will protect me.*

There is also another *mursal* narration with an authentic *isnād* to Muḥammad bin Ka'b al-Qurazhi found in *Tārikh Medina:*

حدثنا عثمان بن عبد الوهاب قال: حدثنا مروان بن معاوية، عن عاصم بن محمد بن زيد، عن محمد بن كعب القرظي قال: أمر رسول الله، صلى الله عليه وسلم، بالحرس، فنزلت: {والله يعصمك من الناس}، فترك الحرس

Uthmān bin Abdal-Wahhāb narrated to us he said Marwān bin Mu'āwiya narrated to us from 'Aāṣim bin Muḥammad bin Zayd from Muḥammad bin Ka'b al-Qurazhi he said: The Prophet (peace be upon him) ordered the (release) of the guard when the verse was revealed: *Allah will protect you from the people*, (thereafter) the guard left.

Another narration can also be found in Ṭabarāni's *al-Mu'jam al-Kabir*:

حَدَّثَنَا يَعْقُوبُ بن غَيْلانَ، حَدَّثَنَا أَبُو كُرَيْبٍ، حَدَّثَنَا عَبْدُ الْحَمِيدِ الْحِمَّانِيُّ، عَنِ

> النَّضْرِ أَبِي عُمَرَ، عَنْ عِكْرِمَةَ، عَنِ ابْنِ عَبَّاسٍ، قَالَ: كَانَ رَسُولُ اللهِ، صلى الله عليه وسلم، يُحْرَسُ، فَكَانَ يُرْسِلُ مَعَهُ عَمُّهُ (أَبُو طَالِب) كُلَّ يَوْمٍ رِجَالا مِنْ بَنِي هَاشِمٍ يَحْرُسُونَهُ، حَتَّى نَزَلَتْ هَذِهِ الآيَةُ {يَا أَيُّهَا الرَّسُولُ بَلِّغْ مَا أُنْزِلَ إِلَيْكَ مِنْ رَبِّكَ}، إِلَى قَوْلِهِ: وَاللَّهُ يَعْصِمُكَ مِنَ النَّاسِ}، فَأَرَادَ عَمُّهُ أَنْ يُرْسِلَ مَعَهُ مَنْ يَحْرُسُهُ، فَقَالَ: يَا عَمِّ إِنَّ اللَّهَ عَزَّ وَجَلَّ قَدْ عَصَمَنِي مِنَ الْجِنِّ وَالإِنْسِ
>
> Ya'qub bin Ghaylān narrated to us Abu Kureeb narrated to us Abdul-Ḥameed al-Ḥimānni narrated to us from an-Naḍr Abi Umar from 'Ikrimah from Ibn 'Abbās he said: the Prophet (peace be upon him) was guarded by his uncle (Abu Ṭālib) who would send men everyday to safeguard him; until that is the verse was revealed: *O Messenger! Deliver what has been revealed to you from your Lord* to when he said - *Allah will protect you from the people* so he wanted his uncle to send him his guard thereafter he said: *O my uncle, verily Allah the exalted will protect me from men and jinn.*

Here Abu Ṭālib has been mentioned in the narration however that could be as a result of a slip by the narrator, perhaps an-Naḍr Abu Umar given that he is *ḍaef* (weak), it is likely that the origin of the story rests with al-'Abbās or that he has fallen from the channel and sentence 'Then he was also guarded in the city until it was revealed' or even the origin of the order as evidenced by the following narrative that is found in Ṭabarāni's *Mu'jam al-Awsaṭ* as well as in *Mu'jam aṣ-Ṣagheer*:

> حدثنا حمد بن محمد بن حمد أبو نصر الكاتب قال حدثنا كردوس بن محمد الواسطي قال حدثنا معلى بن عبد الرحمن عن فضيل بن مرزوق عن عطية العوفي عن أبي سعيد الخدري قال كان العباس عمّ رسول الله، صلى الله عليه وسلم، فيمن يحرسه فلما نزلت هذه الآية يا أيها الرسول بلغ ما أنزل اليك من ربك وإن لم تفعل فما بلغت رسالته والله يعصمك من الناس ترك رسول الله، صلى الله عليه وسلم، الحرس
>
> Ḥamd bin Muḥammad bin Ḥamd Abu Naṣr the scribe narrated

> to us and said Kurdoos bin Muḥammad al-Wāsiṭi narrated to us he said Mu'ala bin Abdar-Raḥman narrated to us from Fuḍeel bin Marzooq from 'Aṭiya al-Awfi from Abu Sa'eed al-Khudari he said al-'Abbās said the uncle of the Messenger of Allah (peace be upon him), was the one who guarded him when this verse was revealed: *Allah will protect you from the people*, (thereafter) the guard left.

Of this Imām Ṭabarāni said 'It's not reported from Fuḍeel except by al-Mu'ala and not from Abu Sa'eed al-Khudari except by this *isnād*.' If we accept and bear witness that Muḥammad is the Messenger of Allah established upon truth and honesty then it is necessary that he is not silent in the face of any act or matter that is prohibited, nor does he leave that which is obligatory. There is no denying these matters. What would make him cease to object to an evil deed or approve of a prohibited one, knowing that Allah has made him infallible and has protected him from all creatures, so that none can hurt him? Most people are prevented from obeying what is true, only if they are afraid of being hurt? For that reason, our knowledge and faith increased thereby with certainty that he is not silent in the face of a prohibited act, nor does he leave an obligation.

It is necessary to hasten to clarify that it is only silence upon the 'acts' namely any declaratory voluntary acts which may be designated as prohibited. This is nothing to do with his silence in relation to sayings or utterances that it is impossible to sense and reason be described presently prohibited, but can be described only as a truth, sincerity or lies and falsehood. It is not in a similar manner to silence related to approvals and may not be described as honesty or lies as will be established in its proper place.

11 The *Sunnah* as an independent source of law

There are many rulings that have been established solely by the Prophetic *Sunnah*. They are referred to in the glorious Qur'ān in other contexts in which they are stated as being part of Allah's law and that they are as binding as the rulings stipulated in the Qur'ān. The following are only a few examples of such rulings:

Establishment of the first *Qibla*

It is known by necessity and historical fact that the first *Qibla* which was faced towards was that at Jerusalem, *Bayt-ul-Maqdis*. Significantly though, there is not a single verse in the Qur'ān which details this original command. *Bayt-ul-Maqdis* was a *Qibla* for all Muslims established solely by virtue of the command rendered from the Prophet (peace be upon him). As it was obligatory to face it in prayer Allah mentioned it within the context of its abrogation, where he ordained facing *Masjid al-Ḥaram* instead. The verse makes explicit that the first *Qibla* was being made by Allah. Allah tells us:

وَكَذَٰلِكَ جَعَلْنَاكُمْ أُمَّةً وَسَطًا لِّتَكُونُوا شُهَدَاءَ عَلَى النَّاسِ وَيَكُونَ الرَّسُولُ عَلَيْكُمْ شَهِيدًا وَمَا

جَعَلْنَا الْقِبْلَةَ الَّتِي كُنتَ عَلَيْهَا إِلَّا لِنَعْلَمَ مَن يَتَّبِعُ الرَّسُولَ مِمَّن يَنقَلِبُ عَلَىٰ عَقِبَيْهِ وَإِن كَانَتْ لَكَبِيرَةً إِلَّا عَلَى الَّذِينَ هَدَى اللَّهُ وَمَا كَانَ اللَّهُ لِيُضِيعَ إِيمَانَكُمْ إِنَّ اللَّهَ بِالنَّاسِ لَرَءُوفٌ رَّحِيمٌ

And thus We have made you a well-balanced just nation that you may be the bearers of witness to the people and (that) the Messenger may be a bearer of witness to you; and We did not make that which you would have to be the Qibla but that We might distinguish him who follows the Messenger from him who turns back upon his heels, and this was surely hard except for those whom Allah has guided aright; and Allah was not going to make your faith to be fruitless; most surely Allah is affectionate, merciful to the people. [1]

The Rebuke of Allah

Allah rebuked the believers for not paying heed to the Prophet (peace be upon him) when he was about to stand to deliver the Friday sermon. This strong reprimand indicated that the believers actions were not permissible, for if it were allowed, they would not have been reprimanded. This means that they must have committed something prohibited. As Allah had not mentioned in the Qur'ān anything about the Friday sermon before that, rendering it obligatory or desirable was by virtue of Prophetic tradition not by virtue of a Qur'ānic text. It is true that the Qur'ān did mention it as an obligatory deed in the same context of reprimanding the believers, but the former definitely came prior to the revelation of the latter.

It is also known that the *Adthān* was used to call people for Friday prayers as well as other congregational prayers prior to the revelation of such verses. Those verses refer to the *Adthān* as the established legal way of calling people to prayer. So whenever the call to Friday prayer is heard, it is obligatory on people to rally to perform it and leave any other business as expressed in the following verse:

يَا أَيُّهَا الَّذِينَ آمَنُوا إِذَا نُودِيَ لِلصَّلَاةِ مِن يَوْمِ الْجُمُعَةِ فَاسْعَوْا إِلَىٰ ذِكْرِ اللَّهِ وَذَرُوا الْبَيْعَ ذَٰلِكُمْ

---

[1] *Qur'ān* 2: 143

خَيْرٌ لَّكُمْ إِن كُنتُمْ تَعْلَمُونَ ، فَإِذَا قُضِيَتِ الصَّلَاةُ فَانتَشِرُوا فِي الْأَرْضِ وَابْتَغُوا مِن فَضْلِ اللَّهِ وَاذْكُرُوا اللَّهَ كَثِيرًا لَّعَلَّكُمْ تُفْلِحُونَ ، وَإِذَا رَأَوْا تِجَارَةً أَوْ لَهْوًا انفَضُّوا إِلَيْهَا وَتَرَكُوكَ قَائِمًا قُلْ مَا عِندَ اللَّهِ خَيْرٌ مِّنَ اللَّهْوِ وَمِنَ التِّجَارَةِ وَاللَّهُ خَيْرُ الرَّازِقِينَ

O you who believe! When the call is made for prayer on Friday, then hasten to the remembrance of Allah and leave off trading; that is better for you, if you know. But when the prayer is ended then disperse about in the land and seek of Allah's grace and remember Allah much, that you may be successful. And when they see merchandise or sport they break up for It and leave you standing. Say: What is with Allah is better than sport and merchandise and Allah is the best of sustainers. [2]

Battle of Uḥud

After the crisis that befell the Muslim army at the battle of *Uḥud* and the withdrawal of the Qurayshi army, Abu Sufyān, the leader of Quraysh, regretted that he withdrew before completely vanquishing the army against him. So he pondered upon attacking them again to root them out. After this crisis the Prophet (peace be upon him) called out all Muslims and despite their injuries and losses, they managed to chase and fight the Qurayshi army covering a considerable distance. The news about their advancement reached Abu Sufyān, whose heart was immediately filled with terror that he preferred to flee back to Mecca. Consequently, the Muslims returned safe without fighting or suffering any new injuries. Allah commended those who responded to the Prophetic summons despite the injuries they suffered. Concerning this incident he said:

يَسْتَبْشِرُونَ بِنِعْمَةٍ مِّنَ اللَّهِ وَفَضْلٍ وَأَنَّ اللَّهَ لَا يُضِيعُ أَجْرَ الْمُؤْمِنِينَ ، الَّذِينَ اسْتَجَابُوا لِلَّهِ وَالرَّسُولِ مِن بَعْدِ مَا أَصَابَهُمُ الْقَرْحُ لِلَّذِينَ أَحْسَنُوا مِنْهُمْ وَاتَّقَوْا أَجْرٌ عَظِيمٌ

They rejoice on account of favour from Allah and (His) grace, and that Allah will not waste the reward of the believers. (As for) those who responded (at

---

[2] *Qur'ān* 62: 9/11

Uḥud) to the call of Allah and the Prophet after the wound had befallen them, those among them who do good (to others) and guard (against evil) shall have a great reward.[3]

Thus, some were deemed responsive to Allah and to the Messenger (peace be upon him), although summoning them was made by virtue of the Prophet's decision without a single letter of Qur'ānic text being revealed to him.

<u>*Distribution of Zakāt*</u>

When some of the hypocrites resented the way the Prophet (peace be upon him) distributed the *Zakāt* they slandered, backbit and censured the Prophet (peace be upon him). Whereupon, Allah disclosed what they did and informs us in the Book of the following:

وَمِنْهُم مَّن يَلْمِزُكَ فِي الصَّدَقَاتِ فَإِنْ أُعْطُوا مِنْهَا رَضُوا وَإِن لَّمْ يُعْطَوْا مِنْهَا إِذَا هُمْ يَسْخَطُونَ، وَلَوْ أَنَّهُمْ رَضُوا مَا آتَاهُمُ اللَّهُ وَرَسُولُهُ وَقَالُوا حَسْبُنَا اللَّهُ سَيُؤْتِينَا اللَّهُ مِن فَضْلِهِ وَرَسُولُهُ إِنَّا إِلَى اللَّهِ رَاغِبُونَ

And of them there are those who blame you with respect to the alms; so if they are given from it they are pleased and if they are not given from it, lo! They are full of rage. And if they were content with what Allah and His Apostle gave them and had said: Allah is sufficient for us; Allah will soon give us (more) out of His grace and His Messenger too; surely to Allah do we make our petition.[4]

The verse explicitly states that what the Prophet (peace be upon him) distributed to them, whether they received anything or not, was their legitimate right, just as it was the will of Allah the exalted and his gift

---

[3] *Qur'ān* 3: 171/172
[4] *Qur'ān* 9: 58/59

to them. That is why he said: '*what Allah and his Messenger gave them.*' A distribution given by the Prophet is also a distribution of Allah, although we know by necessity that no Qur'ānic verse had been previously revealed in this regard. Therefore this gift was based on a revelation other than that of the Qur'ān.

The 'Secret Talk'

Allah the exalted has said:

وَإِذْ أَسَرَّ النَّبِيُّ إِلَىٰ بَعْضِ أَزْوَاجِهِ حَدِيثًا فَلَمَّا نَبَّأَتْ بِهِ وَأَظْهَرَهُ اللَّهُ عَلَيْهِ عَرَّفَ بَعْضَهُ وَأَعْرَضَ عَن بَعْضٍ فَلَمَّا نَبَّأَهَا بِهِ قَالَتْ مَنْ أَنبَأَكَ هَٰذَا قَالَ نَبَّأَنِيَ الْعَلِيمُ الْخَبِيرُ

And when the Prophet secretly communicated a piece of information to one of his wives - but when she informed (others) of it, and Allah made him to know it, he made known part of it and avoided part; so when he informed her of it, she said: Who informed you of this? He said: The knowing, the aware, informed me. [5]

The Qur'ān though does not contain a single letter of this secret private talk, about which Allah informed his Prophet (peace be upon him). Therefore, this provides a conclusive proof that he (peace be upon him) had received a revelation from Allah other than that of the Qur'ān even in this private situation.

Early Prayers

Allah blessed and sanctified are his names tells us:

أَرَأَيْتَ الَّذِي يَنْهَىٰ ، عَبْدًا إِذَا صَلَّىٰ، أَرَأَيْتَ إِن كَانَ عَلَى الْهُدَىٰ

[5] *Qur'ān* 66: 3

Have you seen him who forbids a servant when he prays? Have you considered if he were on the right way? [6]

These are some of the earliest verses revealed in Mecca. Therein it contains conclusive evidence that the Prophet (peace be upon him) was praying in a manner of which a disbelieving leader of the Quraysh disapproved of. By necessity this shows that prayer, the *Ṣalāh* was already legislated, whether as an obligatory or a recommend act. It was performed in a manner similar to that of the prayers we perform today, or rather in an abrogated manner prior to the revelation above of these verses, which were among the earliest verses revealed. None of the verses prior to this include any reference to prayers. Therefore, *Ṣalāh* the pillar of the *Deen* was initially legislated by virtue of the Prophetic command, i.e. a revelation other than that of an explicit verse in the Qur'ān. After that, Qur'ānic verses and *ḥadith* recurred stressing that prayers are mandatory and highly glorified, describing its prerequisites and completing its rites.

Pre-Badr Skirmishes

Before the major battle of Badr, Allah commanded his Messenger (peace be upon him) to send out troops to encounter the enemy, though some believers strongly resented the idea and feared the consequences of fighting the powerful tribe of Quraysh, the leaders and 'bankers' of Arabia. It was considered the strongest polity in the Arabian Peninsula at that time. Muslims feared fighting them especially after hearing the news about the marching of their army. Then Allah granted them a promise of either seizing the caravans of the Quraysh or vanquishing their army. This came through a revelation other than the Qur'ān, which does not contain a single word of it. Nevertheless, Allah recorded it in the Qur'ān *after* the end of the battle, as Allah whose

[6] *Qur'ān* 96: 9/11

attributes are sanctified says:

كَمَا أَخْرَجَكَ رَبُّكَ مِن بَيْتِكَ بِالْحَقِّ وَإِنَّ فَرِيقًا مِّنَ الْمُؤْمِنِينَ لَكَارِهُونَ ، يُجَادِلُونَكَ فِي الْحَقِّ
بَعْدَمَا تَبَيَّنَ كَأَنَّمَا يُسَاقُونَ إِلَى الْمَوْتِ وَهُمْ يَنظُرُونَ ، وَإِذْ يَعِدُكُمُ اللَّهُ إِحْدَى الطَّائِفَتَيْنِ أَنَّهَا لَكُمْ
وَتَوَدُّونَ أَنَّ غَيْرَ ذَاتِ الشَّوْكَةِ تَكُونُ لَكُمْ وَيُرِيدُ اللَّهُ أَن يُحِقَّ الْحَقَّ بِكَلِمَاتِهِ وَيَقْطَعَ دَابِرَ
الْكَافِرِينَ

Even as your Lord caused you to go forth from your house with the truth, though a party of the believers were surely averse; they disputed with you about the truth after it had become clear, (and they went forth) as if they were being driven to death while they saw (it).

And when Allah promised you one of the two parties that it shall be yours and you loved that the one not armed should be yours and Allah desired to manifest the truth of what was true by His words and to cut off the root of the unbelievers. [7]

<u>*The Command to Fight*</u>

The explicit command not to fight was authorised by the Prophet (peace be upon him) to his Companions while still in Mecca. After migration to Medina, this order was rescinded, with the authorisation being explicitly given to fight. As is chronicled in the following verse:

أَلَمْ تَرَ إِلَى الَّذِينَ قِيلَ لَهُمْ كُفُّوا أَيْدِيَكُمْ وَأَقِيمُوا الصَّلَاةَ وَآتُوا الزَّكَاةَ فَلَمَّا كُتِبَ عَلَيْهِمُ الْقِتَالُ إِذَا
فَرِيقٌ مِّنْهُمْ يَخْشَوْنَ النَّاسَ كَخَشْيَةِ اللَّهِ أَوْ أَشَدَّ خَشْيَةً وَقَالُوا رَبَّنَا لِمَ كَتَبْتَ عَلَيْنَا الْقِتَالَ لَوْلَا
أَخَّرْتَنَا إِلَىٰ أَجَلٍ قَرِيبٍ قُلْ مَتَاعُ الدُّنْيَا قَلِيلٌ وَالْآخِرَةُ خَيْرٌ لِّمَنِ اتَّقَىٰ وَلَا تُظْلَمُونَ فَتِيلًا

Have you not seen those to whom it was said: withhold your hands, and keep up prayer and zakāt; but when fighting is prescribed for them, lo! a party of them fear men as they ought to have feared Allah, or (even) with a greater fear, and say: Our Lord! Why have you ordained fighting for us? Wherefore didst Thou not grant us a delay to a near end? Say: the provision of this world

[7] *Qur'ān* 8: 5/7

is short, and the hereafter is better for him who guards (against evil); and you shall not be wronged the husk of a date stone.[8]

One can clearly discern by the necessity of reason and perception from the aforementioned Qur'ānic proofs that have been cited, without recourse to any text from the *Sunnah*, that they prove decisively that the Prophet (peace be upon him) is *ma'ṣoom* (infallible) in his conveyance of the divine message from Allah. All his sayings, acts and approvals are considered as being an infallible revelation from Allah. Therefore, it is all an infallible revelation emanating from Allah. Revelation should not therefore only be limited to that of the Qur'ān; it also includes that which was revealed to Muḥammad (peace be upon him), namely the Prophetic *Sunnah*, consisting of the total sum of his words, deeds and acknowledgements or approvals. Taken holistically, the *waḥy* which is the Qur'ān and the Prophetic *Sunnah* is authoritative and binding. Or expressed in another way, the Prophetic *Sunnah* is not merely a particular revelation from Allah; rather it is a formulated expression of an infallible Prophetic revelation that has come from Allah.

The Qur'ānic text itself is an explicit categorical revelation sent down from Allah upon Muḥammad (peace be upon him); whose recitation is considered as worship and its style inimitable. Greater detail upon this will be outlined in a separate section. Suffice is to say that the Qur'ān is self-contained, nothing being subtracted or entering into it. Alongside it though is the noble Prophetic *Sunnah*, revelation other than the Qur'ān. All of this is affirmed categorically thus to dispute it would render an individual to exit the fold of Islam completely. That the revelation which descended upon Muḥammad (peace be upon him) is not only limited to text of the glorious Qur'ān as found between its pages but also includes the Prophetic *Sunnah* of Muḥammad (peace be upon him) consisting of the total sum of his

[8] *Qur'ān* 4: 77

words, deeds and acknowledgements or approvals.

In terms of what constitutes or is considered as being 'revelation', *al-waḥy*, there is no essential difference between the Qur'ān and the *Sunnah*. Furthermore both are similarly binding and authoritative, as an example Allah the blessed and exalted says: *'There is no blame on you in seeking bounty from your Lord...'*[9] relating to the authorisation of trading during the *Ḥajj* season and where he says: '*And you shall have half of what your wives leave if they have no child...*'[10] both verses stipulating decisive rulings valid until the day of judgement. Similarly, the Prophet's (peace be upon him) statements of '*No bequest must be made to an heir*'[11] and '*One-third, yet even one third is too much*'[12] outlining the maximum limit to bequeath, are equally binding and authoritative until the day of judgement. Even if the first examples are borne of the Qur'ān, a revelation by wording which can be recited in prayer; the speech from the necessarily-existent ever-living eternal creator, while the latter examples are the reported Prophetic words from Muḥammad (peace be upon him) who is mortal and finite, both are deemed as revelation being equally binding and authoritative.

Indeed without the slightest doubt the words of the Qur'ān are far above the speech of the creation, it is protection from every form of misguidance, a shield from every *fitna*, for it is the book of Allah the majestic:

لَّا يَأْتِيهِ الْبَاطِلُ مِن بَيْنِ يَدَيْهِ وَلَا مِنْ خَلْفِهِ تَنزِيلٌ مِّنْ حَكِيمٍ حَمِيدٍ

Falsehood shall not come to it from before nor from behind it; a revelation

[9] Excerpt from *Qur'ān* 2: 198

[10] Excerpt from *Qur'ān* 4: 12

[11] Reported in the *Sunan* collections such as Abu Dāwud, Nasā'i, Ibn Mājah, Tirmidhi as well as others.

[12] A short excerpt from the *ḥadith* relating to bequeathing one-third for example in a will. It is widely reported and appears in the collections of Bukhāri, Muslim, Nasā'i and others.

from the wise, the praised one. [13]

Contained within it is news of what came before us, what will come to pass and the rulings between us all for the present. It contains matters of serious import which are not for jest, providing guidance and other innumerable bounties. We cling to the Qur'ān because it is rope of Allah, the *Dhikr* (reminder) and the *Ḥakeem* (wisdom); it has manifest light and lays out the steps on the straight path. All of creation has marvelled at it, as Allah details the remarks of the *Jinn* for us:

... إِنَّا سَمِعْنَا قُرْآنًا عَجَبًا، يَهْدِي إِلَى الرُّشْدِ فَآمَنَّا بِهِ وَلَن نُّشْرِكَ بِرَبِّنَا أَحَدًا

....Surely we have heard a wonderful Qur'ān! Guiding to the right way, so we believe in it, and we will not set up any partner with our Lord. [14]

Whoever speaks from it assuredly speaks the truth; by acting upon its rulings, justice will prevail. It is a healing and an intercession; those who stick to it shall not fail, nor shall they be swayed or corrupted. Those who recite the Qur'ān are rewarded abundantly given that reward has been promised for each letter read as opposed to each word. It is true indeed that the ever-glorious Qur'ān is of the greatest worth, the most unique sanctity and is of a rank that the *Sunnah* does not reach, particularly given that it is the literal revealed speech of Allah, whose recitation is worship and whose style is inimitable, miraculous in nature. Yet it is an independent issue of whether or not the two types of revelation - the Qur'ān and the *Sunnah* - are qualitatively of the same rank in being authoritative and binding. These two issues are independent of whether or not the Qur'ān can be abrogated by the *Sunnah*. All these different contrasting issues are rationally independent. They should not be confused, otherwise the

[13] *Qur'ān* 41: 42
[14] *Qur'ān* 72: 1/2

consequences would be extremely serious, in fact it would involve being misled away from the straight path, which is disbelief – Allah, the exalted and glorious, forbid!

To argue that the Qur'ān is the *only* sent-down revelation from Allah is a grave misnomer. Just as it is to say that the *Sunnah* is not revelation at all, or to be more precise - that the Prophetic expression is not borne of an infallible revelation from Allah and that it is not considered as a binding authority. Such a view and other similar statements are outright disbelief (*kufr*). Holding such views as doctrinal beliefs would result in a believer exiting the fold of Islam completely, unless that is, it was borne of complete ignorance, under compulsion or with any of the other impediments to the pronouncement of disbelief (*takfeer*).

12 The *Ḥikmah* and *Dhikr* are also revelation

Textually, Allah revealed to his Prophet (peace be upon him) the wisdom - '*ḥikmah.*' He says:

وَلَوْلَا فَضْلُ اللَّهِ عَلَيْكَ وَرَحْمَتُهُ لَهَمَّت طَّائِفَةٌ مِّنْهُمْ أَن يُضِلُّوكَ وَمَا يُضِلُّونَ إِلَّا أَنفُسَهُمْ وَمَا
يَضُرُّونَكَ مِن شَيْءٍ <u>وَأَنزَلَ اللَّهُ عَلَيْكَ الْكِتَابَ وَالْحِكْمَةَ</u> وَعَلَّمَكَ مَا لَمْ تَكُن تَعْلَمُ وَكَانَ فَضْلُ اللَّهِ
عَلَيْكَ عَظِيمًا

And were it not for Allah's grace upon you and His mercy a party of them had certainly designed to bring you to perdition and they do not bring (aught) to perdition but their own souls, and they shall not harm you in any way, and <u>Allah has revealed to you the Book and the hikmah</u> and He has taught you what you did not know and Allah's grace on you is very great. [1]

From this, three matters arise. Allah revealed the book to his Prophet; contained within it is wisdom (*ḥikmah*) and abundant knowledge, all of which he learned. Here the meaning intended is that of the text of the Qur'ān at the very least. And he has also revealed to him the '*ḥikmah'*, which is something far broader than the Qur'ānic texts. It

---

[1] *Qur'ān* 4: 113

glitters the concepts that were penned for the Prophetic statements, actions and approvals or acknowledgements, which he was well versed in. Inflection and '*ḥikmah*' upon the book from each pathway on all parts, be it general or specific. It is not the case that the '*ḥikmah*' is the book because to inflect upon the thing is to designate its essence and place and it is not that according to reason, sense or language. Knowledge given by the Lord above regarding a great many things which no one had known, the most important is the book (Qur'ān), the *ḥikmah* as well as other matters like some tribal dialects, the logic of some of the animals, such as when the camel complained of its owner and many other things which no one knows except Allah the exalted. The *ḥikmah* mentioned in the verse definitely relates to the revealed revelation and it is not the Qur'ān. By necessity it relates to the noble Prophetic *Sunnah* as eloquently evidenced by the next following verses which appear in *Surah aṭ-Ṭalāq*:

أَعَدَّ اللَّهُ لَهُمْ عَذَابًا شَدِيدًا فَاتَّقُوا اللَّهَ يَا أُولِي الْأَلْبَابِ الَّذِينَ آمَنُوا قَدْ أَنزَلَ اللَّهُ إِلَيْكُمْ ذِكْرًا رَّسُولًا يَتْلُو عَلَيْكُمْ آيَاتِ اللَّهِ مُبَيِّنَاتٍ لِّيُخْرِجَ الَّذِينَ آمَنُوا وَعَمِلُوا الصَّالِحَاتِ مِنَ الظُّلُمَاتِ إِلَى النُّورِ وَمَن يُؤْمِن بِاللَّهِ وَيَعْمَلْ صَالِحًا يُدْخِلْهُ جَنَّاتٍ تَجْرِي مِن تَحْتِهَا الْأَنْهَارُ خَالِدِينَ فِيهَا أَبَدًا قَدْ أَحْسَنَ اللَّهُ لَهُ رِزْقًا

Allah has prepared for them a severe chastisement, therefore be careful of (your duty to) *Allah, O men of understanding who believe! Allah has indeed revealed to you a dhikr, a Messenger who recites to you the clear communications of Allah so that he may bring forth those who believe and do good deeds from darkness into light; and whoever believes in Allah and does good deeds, He will cause him to enter gardens beneath which rivers now, to abide therein forever, Allah has indeed given him a goodly sustenance.*[2]

More will be said about this blessed verse, by the grace and will of Allah, when the subject turns to that of the *Dhikr*. Allah the exalted also says:

---

[2] *Qur'ān* 65: 10/11

ذَٰلِكَ مِمَّا أَوْحَىٰ إِلَيْكَ رَبُّكَ مِنَ الْحِكْمَةِ وَلَا تَجْعَلْ مَعَ اللهِ إِلَٰهًا آخَرَ فَتُلْقَىٰ فِي جَهَنَّمَ مَلُومًا مَّدْحُورًا

This is of what your Lord has revealed to you of hikmah and do not associate any other god with Allah lest you should be thrown into hell, blamed, cast away. [3]

The text conclusively supports that of the etiquette and comprehensive rulings mentioned before this verse, some of the *ḥikmah* as revealed and sent down by Allah through inspiration to Abul'Qāsim Muḥammad ibn Abdullah seal of all the Prophets (peace and blessings be upon him). It is from the *ḥikmah* and it is as of any book. It is a conclusive indication that some of the book is from *al-ḥikmah*, but the whole of the book is considered as being *ḥikmah* / wisdom by the legitimate necessity of perception and reason. In another verse Allah says:

الر تِلْكَ آيَاتُ الْكِتَابِ الْحَكِيمِ

Alif Lam Ra; these are the verses of the wise Book. [4]

Allah stresses in the next verse:

يس ، وَالْقُرْآنِ الْحَكِيمِ

Ya Seen; I swear by the Qur'ān full of wisdom. [5]

---

[3] *Qur'ān* 17: 39
[4] *Qur'ān* 10: 1
[5] *Qur'ān* 36: 1/2

And that the original / mother of the protected book being full of wisdom:

وَإِنَّهُ فِي أُمِّ الْكِتَابِ لَدَيْنَا لَعَلِيٌّ حَكِيمٌ

And surely it is in the original of the Book with Us, truly elevated, full of wisdom.[6]

If the totality of the book is considered being from the revealed *ḥikmah* then the necessity of perception and reason show that will be the revealed *ḥikmah* upon Muḥammad is only the text of the glorious Qur'ān. As for what we mentioned previously above, the glorious Qur'ān in totality is from the revealed wisdom sent to Muḥammad and it is some of the revealed *ḥikmah* with certainty. Not all the *ḥikmah* is revealed upon Muḥammad; here other things from *al-ḥikmah* have been revealed other than the text of the Qur'ān. Allah blessed be his names says:

وَإِذَا طَلَّقْتُمُ النِّسَاءَ فَبَلَغْنَ أَجَلَهُنَّ فَأَمْسِكُوهُنَّ بِمَعْرُوفٍ أَوْ سَرِّحُوهُنَّ بِمَعْرُوفٍ وَلَا تُمْسِكُوهُنَّ ضِرَارًا لِّتَعْتَدُوا وَمَن يَفْعَلْ ذَٰلِكَ فَقَدْ ظَلَمَ نَفْسَهُ وَلَا تَتَّخِذُوا آيَاتِ اللَّهِ هُزُوًا وَاذْكُرُوا نِعْمَتَ اللَّهِ عَلَيْكُمْ وَمَا أَنزَلَ عَلَيْكُم مِّنَ الْكِتَابِ وَالْحِكْمَةِ يَعِظُكُم بِهِ وَاتَّقُوا اللَّهَ وَاعْلَمُوا أَنَّ اللَّهَ بِكُلِّ شَيْءٍ عَلِيمٌ

And when you divorce women and they reach their prescribed time, then either retain them in good fellowship or set them free with liberality, and do not retain them for injury, so that you exceed the limits, and whoever does this, he indeed is unjust to his own soul; and do not take Allah's communications for a mockery, and remember the favour of Allah upon you, and that which He has revealed to you of the book and the hikmah, admonishing you thereby; and be careful (of your duty to) *Allah, and know*

[6] *Qur'ān* 43: 4

that Allah is the knower of all things. [7]

The revelation did not decend randomly upon all with immediacy. Rather, it was revealed to Muḥammad (peace be upon him) firstly, then we took it from him, as if it were sent upon us directly. It is all totally binding in nature, the book, the *ḥikmah*, namely: the Qur'ān and the *Sunnah*.

The command of Allah to the mothers of the believers was to remain within their homes; to partake in the *ḥijāb* and to attend to the study, memorisation and understanding of the verses of Allah. This is in addition to attending to the memorisation of the *ḥikmah* which they had learned from the Prophet (peace be upon him), as Allah says in the verse:

وَاذْكُرْنَ مَا يُتْلَىٰ فِي بُيُوتِكُنَّ مِنْ آيَاتِ اللَّهِ وَالْحِكْمَةِ إِنَّ اللَّهَ كَانَ لَطِيفًا خَبِيرًا

And keep in mind what is recited in your houses of the communications of Allah and the hikmah; surely Allah is knower of subtleties, aware. [8]

Allah has indeed blessed the believers as he outlines in next three verses and says:

لَقَدْ مَنَّ اللَّهُ عَلَى الْمُؤْمِنِينَ إِذْ بَعَثَ فِيهِمْ رَسُولًا مِّنْ أَنفُسِهِمْ يَتْلُو عَلَيْهِمْ آيَاتِهِ وَيُزَكِّيهِمْ وَيُعَلِّمُهُمُ الْكِتَابَ وَالْحِكْمَةَ وَإِن كَانُوا مِن قَبْلُ لَفِي ضَلَالٍ مُّبِينٍ

Certainly Allah conferred a benefit upon the believers when He raised among them a Prophet from among themselves, reciting to them His communications and purifying them and teaching them the Book and the hikmah although

[7] *Qur'ān* 2: 231
[8] *Qur'ān* 33: 34

before that they were surely in manifest error. [9]

كَمَا أَرْسَلْنَا فِيكُمْ رَسُولًا مِّنكُمْ يَتْلُو عَلَيْكُمْ آيَاتِنَا وَيُزَكِّيكُمْ وَيُعَلِّمُكُمُ الْكِتَابَ وَالْحِكْمَةَ وَيُعَلِّمُكُم مَّا لَمْ تَكُونُوا تَعْلَمُونَ

Even as We have sent among you a Prophet from among you who recites to you Our communications and purifies you and teaches you the Book and the hikmah and teaches you that which you did not know. [10]

هُوَ الَّذِي بَعَثَ فِي الْأُمِّيِّينَ رَسُولًا مِّنْهُمْ يَتْلُو عَلَيْهِمْ آيَاتِهِ وَيُزَكِّيهِمْ وَيُعَلِّمُهُمُ الْكِتَابَ وَالْحِكْمَةَ وَإِن كَانُوا مِن قَبْلُ لَفِي ضَلَالٍ مُّبِينٍ

He it is who raised a Messenger from among themselves, who recites to them his signs and purifies them, and teaches them the Book and the hikmah, although they were before certainly in clear error. [11]

Furthermore, he also said the following in relation to the response given, following the call of Ibrāhim and Ismā'il:

رَبَّنَا وَابْعَثْ فِيهِمْ رَسُولًا مِّنْهُمْ يَتْلُو عَلَيْهِمْ آيَاتِكَ وَيُعَلِّمُهُمُ الْكِتَابَ وَالْحِكْمَةَ وَيُزَكِّيهِمْ إِنَّكَ أَنتَ الْعَزِيزُ الْحَكِيمُ

Our Lord! And raise up in them a Prophet from among them who shall recite to them Thy communications and teach them the Book and the hikmah, and purify them; surely Thou art the mighty, the wise. [12]

It would be wrong to think of the Prophet (peace be upon him) as being as a mere tape recorder or a robotic message carrier,

[9] *Qur'ān* 3: 164
[10] *Qur'ān* 2: 151
[11] *Qur'ān* 62: 2
[12] *Qur'ān* 2: 129

mechanically delivering the signs of Allah. Far greater was his role and mission, for he was a wise sublime educator. He was that teacher for his *Ummah* of the book and the *ḥikmah*. The intended book here is the glorious Qur'ān. Perhaps it was also intended to make his *Ummah* a literary nation; a nation of astute study, science and advanced research. Given that they were previously in dire ignorance and are now being led by truth. Indeed he (peace be upon him) did accomplish that lofty task. The Prophet (peace be upon him) was not a new novelty in relation to the Prophets that preceded him, but he is like the previous Prophets in this regard – Allah provided them with books and *ḥikmah*, for he says:

وَإِذْ أَخَذَ اللَّهُ مِيثَاقَ النَّبِيِّينَ لَمَا آتَيْتُكُم مِّن كِتَابٍ وَحِكْمَةٍ ثُمَّ جَاءَكُمْ رَسُولٌ مُّصَدِّقٌ لِّمَا مَعَكُمْ لَتُؤْمِنُنَّ بِهِ وَلَتَنصُرُنَّهُ قَالَ أَأَقْرَرْتُمْ وَأَخَذْتُمْ عَلَىٰ ذَٰلِكُمْ إِصْرِي قَالُوا أَقْرَرْنَا قَالَ فَاشْهَدُوا وَأَنَا مَعَكُم مِّنَ الشَّاهِدِينَ

And when Allah made a covenant through the Prophets: Certainly what I have given you of Book and ḥikmah-- then a Messenger comes to you verifying that which is with you, you must believe in him and you must aid him. He said: Do you affirm and accept My compact in this (matter)? *They said: We do affirm. He said: Then bear witness, and I am of the bearers of witness with you.* [13]

In particular the glorious Qur'ān provides further illustration with the example of Esa ibn Maryam (peace be upon him and his mother), mentioning similarly of him in several places:

وَاتَّقُوا يَوْمًا لَّا تَجْزِي نَفْسٌ عَن نَّفْسٍ شَيْئًا وَلَا يُقْبَلُ مِنْهَا شَفَاعَةٌ وَلَا يُؤْخَذُ مِنْهَا عَدْلٌ وَلَا هُمْ يُنصَرُونَ

And be on your guard against a day when one soul shall not avail another in

[13] *Qur'ān* 3: 81

the least, neither shall intercession on its behalf be accepted, nor shall any compensation be taken from it, nor shall they be helped. [14]

إِذْ قَالَ اللَّهُ يَا عِيسَى ابْنَ مَرْيَمَ اذْكُرْ نِعْمَتِي عَلَيْكَ وَعَلَىٰ وَالِدَتِكَ إِذْ أَيَّدتُّكَ بِرُوحِ الْقُدُسِ تُكَلِّمُ النَّاسَ فِي الْمَهْدِ وَكَهْلًا وَإِذْ عَلَّمْتُكَ الْكِتَابَ وَالْحِكْمَةَ وَالتَّوْرَاةَ وَالْإِنجِيلَ وَإِذْ تَخْلُقُ مِنَ الطِّينِ كَهَيْئَةِ الطَّيْرِ بِإِذْنِي فَتَنفُخُ فِيهَا فَتَكُونُ طَيْرًا بِإِذْنِي وَتُبْرِئُ الْأَكْمَهَ وَالْأَبْرَصَ بِإِذْنِي وَإِذْ تُخْرِجُ الْمَوْتَىٰ بِإِذْنِي وَإِذْ كَفَفْتُ بَنِي إِسْرَائِيلَ عَنكَ إِذْ جِئْتَهُم بِالْبَيِّنَاتِ فَقَالَ الَّذِينَ كَفَرُوا مِنْهُمْ إِنْ هَٰذَا إِلَّا سِحْرٌ مُّبِينٌ

When Allah will say: O Jesus son of Mary! Remember My favour on you and on your mother, when I strengthened you I with the holy Spirit, you spoke to the people in the cradle and I when of old age and when I taught you the Book and the ḥikmah and the Torah and the Injeel; and when you determined out of clay a thing like the form of a bird by My permission, then you breathed into it and it became a bird by My permission, and you healed the blind and the leprous by My permission; and when you brought forth the dead by My permission and when I withheld the Israel from you when you came to them with clear arguments, but those who disbelieved among them said: This is nothing but clear enchantment. [15]

Moreover, the example of Ibrāhim is also illustrative of this:

أَمْ يَحْسُدُونَ النَّاسَ عَلَىٰ مَا آتَاهُمُ اللَّهُ مِن فَضْلِهِ <u>فَقَدْ آتَيْنَا آلَ إِبْرَاهِيمَ الْكِتَابَ وَالْحِكْمَةَ</u> وَآتَيْنَاهُم مُّلْكًا عَظِيمًا

Or do they envy the people for what Allah has given them of His grace? But indeed we have <u>given to Ibrāhim's children the Book and the hikmah</u> and We have given them a grand kingdom. [16]

To conclude we may affirm with certainty without suspicion or doubt

[14] *Qur'ān* 3: 48
[15] *Qur'ān* 5: 110
[16] *Qur'ān* 4: 54

that that there is a revealed revelation other than the text of the glorious Qur'ān. It is the *ḥikmah* and in particular it is the noble Prophetic *Sunnah*, without any addition or subtraction. That the *ḥikmah* is also a binding revelation has been set forth with decisive certain proofs, just like the glorious Qur'ān.

13 The meaning of the word '*Dhikr*'

The word formulation '*dh/ka/ra*' (ذَكَرَ) appears in the glorious Qur'ān in quite a large number of places and can bear several intended meanings. The first of which is related to 'the speech about something;' to talk about something and refer or mention something, that being opposed to neglect and reluctance in that context. Its root is '*Dhikr*' (ذِكْر) and within it is the saying: 'You mentioned so-and-so is fine.' Various Qur'ānic verses are demonstrative of this:

وَقَالَ لِلَّذِي ظَنَّ أَنَّهُ نَاجٍ مِّنْهُمَا اذْكُرْنِي عِندَ رَبِّكَ فَأَنسَاهُ الشَّيْطَانُ ذِكْرَ رَبِّهِ فَلَبِثَ فِي السِّجْنِ بِضْعَ سِنِينَ

And he [Yusuf] said to whom he knew would be delivered of the two [prisoners]: Remember me with your lord; but the Shayṭān caused him to forget mentioning (it) to his lord, so he remained in the prison a few years. [1]

وَجَعَلْنَا عَلَىٰ قُلُوبِهِمْ أَكِنَّةً أَن يَفْقَهُوهُ وَفِي آذَانِهِمْ وَقْرًا وَإِذَا ذَكَرْتَ رَبَّكَ فِي الْقُرْآنِ وَحْدَهُ وَلَّوْا عَلَىٰ أَدْبَارِهِمْ نُفُورًا

[1] *Qur'ān* 12: 42

And We have placed coverings on their hearts and a heaviness in their ears lest they understand it and when you mention your Lord alone in the Qur'ān they turn their backs in aversion. [2]

قَالُوا تَاللَّهِ تَفْتَأُ تَذْكُرُ يُوسُفَ حَتَّىٰ تَكُونَ حَرَضًا أَوْ تَكُونَ مِنَ الْهَالِكِينَ

They said: By Allah! You will not cease to remember Yusuf until you are a prey to constant disease or (until) you are of those who perish. [3]

قَالُوا سَمِعْنَا فَتًى يَذْكُرُهُمْ يُقَالُ لَهُ إِبْرَاهِيمُ

They said: We heard a youth called Ibrāhim speak of them. [4]

وَاذْكُرْ فِي الْكِتَابِ مَرْيَمَ إِذِ انتَبَذَتْ مِنْ أَهْلِهَا مَكَانًا شَرْقِيًّا

And mention Maryam in the Book when she drew aside from her family to an eastern place. [5]

قَالَ فَإِنِ اتَّبَعْتَنِي فَلَا تَسْأَلْنِي عَن شَيْءٍ حَتَّىٰ أُحْدِثَ لَكَ مِنْهُ ذِكْرًا

He said: If you would follow me, then do not question me about anything until I mention it to you. [6]

وَيَسْأَلُونَكَ عَن ذِي الْقَرْنَيْنِ قُلْ سَأَتْلُو عَلَيْكُم مِّنْهُ ذِكْرًا

And they ask you about Zulqarnayn. Say: I will recite to you an account of him. [7]

---

[2] *Qur'ān* 17: 46
[3] *Qur'ān* 12: 85
[4] *Qur'ān* 21: 60
[5] *Qur'ān* 19: 16
[6] *Qur'ān* 18: 70
[7] *Qur'ān* 18: 83

وَيَقُولُ الَّذِينَ آمَنُوا لَوْلَا نُزِّلَتْ سُورَةٌ فَإِذَا أُنزِلَتْ سُورَةٌ مُّحْكَمَةٌ وَذُكِرَ فِيهَا الْقِتَالُ رَأَيْتَ الَّذِينَ فِي قُلُوبِهِم مَّرَضٌ يَنظُرُونَ إِلَيْكَ نَظَرَ الْمَغْشِيِّ عَلَيْهِ مِنَ الْمَوْتِ فَأَوْلَىٰ لَهُمْ

Those who believe ask why no chapter (about fighting) *has been sent down. Yet when a decisive chapter* (that mentions fighting) *is sent down, you can see the sick at heart looking at you* (Prophet) *and visibly fainting at the prospect of death. Woe to them.*[8]

From this is the first type, that is mentioning Allah ['*Dhikr* Allah' (ذِكْر اللهِ)], has a specific meaning namely of glorifying his name and praising him, such as via *tasbeeḥ, takbeer* and '*taleel* and through supplication, *duā'*. These are the varieties of *dhikr* or remembrance. Again the root is '*dhikr,*' and this appears a great many times in the Qur'ān, such as in the following verses:

فَاذْكُرُونِي أَذْكُرْكُمْ وَاشْكُرُوا لِي وَلَا تَكْفُرُونِ

So remember me, I will remember you be thankful to me and do not be ungrateful.[9]

قَالَ رَبِّ اجْعَل لِّي آيَةً قَالَ آيَتُكَ أَلَّا تُكَلِّمَ النَّاسَ ثَلَاثَةَ أَيَّامٍ إِلَّا رَمْزًا وَاذْكُر رَّبَّكَ كَثِيرًا وَسَبِّحْ بِالْعَشِيِّ وَالْإِبْكَارِ

He said: My Lord! Appoint a sign for me. He said: Your sign is that you should not speak to men for three days except by signs; and remember your Lord much and glorify Him in the evening and the morning.[10]

الَّذِينَ أُخْرِجُوا مِن دِيَارِهِم بِغَيْرِ حَقٍّ إِلَّا أَن يَقُولُوا رَبُّنَا اللَّهُ وَلَوْلَا دَفْعُ اللَّهِ النَّاسَ بَعْضَهُم بِبَعْضٍ لَّهُدِّمَتْ صَوَامِعُ وَبِيَعٌ وَصَلَوَاتٌ وَمَسَاجِدُ يُذْكَرُ فِيهَا اسْمُ اللَّهِ كَثِيرًا وَلَيَنصُرَنَّ اللَّهُ مَن يَنصُرُهُ إِنَّ اللَّهَ لَقَوِيٌّ عَزِيزٌ

[8] *Qur'ān* 47: 20
[9] *Qur'ān* 2: 152
[10] *Qur'ān* 3: 41

Those who have been driven unjustly from their homes only for saying, 'Our Lord is Allah.' If Allah did not repel some people by means of others, many monasteries, churches, synagogues, <u>and mosques, where Allah's name is much invoked</u>, would have been destroyed. Allah is sure to help those who help His cause– Allah is strong and mighty.[11]

<u>وَاذْكُرُوا اللَّهَ فِي أَيَّامٍ مَّعْدُودَاتٍ</u> فَمَن تَعَجَّلَ فِي يَوْمَيْنِ فَلَا إِثْمَ عَلَيْهِ وَمَن تَأَخَّرَ فَلَا إِثْمَ عَلَيْهِ لِمَنِ اتَّقَىٰ وَاتَّقُوا اللَّهَ وَاعْلَمُوا أَنَّكُمْ إِلَيْهِ تُحْشَرُونَ

<u>Remember Allah on the appointed days</u>. If anyone is in a hurry to leave after two days, there is no blame on him, nor is there any blame on anyone who stays on, so long as they are mindful of Allah. Be mindful of Allah, and remember that you will be gathered to Him.[12]

يَسْأَلُونَكَ مَاذَا أُحِلَّ لَهُمْ قُلْ أُحِلَّ لَكُمُ الطَّيِّبَاتُ وَمَا عَلَّمْتُم مِّنَ الْجَوَارِحِ مُكَلِّبِينَ تُعَلِّمُونَهُنَّ مِمَّا عَلَّمَكُمُ اللَّهُ فَكُلُوا مِمَّا أَمْسَكْنَ عَلَيْكُمْ <u>وَاذْكُرُوا اسْمَ اللَّهِ عَلَيْهِ</u> وَاتَّقُوا اللَّهَ إِنَّ اللَّهَ سَرِيعُ الْحِسَابِ

They ask you as to what is lawful for them. Say: The good things are lawful for you and what you have taught the beasts and birds of prey, training them to hunt-- you teach them of what Allah has taught you-- so eat of that which they catch for you <u>and mention the name of Allah over it</u>; and be careful of (your duty to) Allah; surely Allah is swift in reckoning.[13]

فَقَالَ إِنِّي أَحْبَبْتُ حُبَّ الْخَيْرِ <u>عَن ذِكْرِ رَبِّي</u> حَتَّىٰ تَوَارَتْ بِالْحِجَابِ

He kept saying, 'My love of fine things is part of my <u>remembering my Lord</u>!' until [the horses] disappeared from sight.[14]

إِنَّ الْمُسْلِمِينَ وَالْمُسْلِمَاتِ وَالْمُؤْمِنِينَ وَالْمُؤْمِنَاتِ وَالْقَانِتِينَ وَالْقَانِتَاتِ وَالصَّادِقِينَ وَالصَّادِقَاتِ وَالصَّابِرِينَ وَالصَّابِرَاتِ وَالْخَاشِعِينَ وَالْخَاشِعَاتِ وَالْمُتَصَدِّقِينَ وَالْمُتَصَدِّقَاتِ وَالصَّائِمِينَ

---

[11] *Qur'ān* 22: 40
[12] *Qur'ān* 2: 203
[13] *Qur'ān* 5: 4
[14] *Qur'ān* 38: 32

وَالصَّائِمَاتِ وَالْحَافِظِينَ فُرُوجَهُمْ وَالْحَافِظَاتِ وَالذَّاكِرِينَ اللَّهَ كَثِيرًا وَالذَّاكِرَاتِ أَعَدَّ اللَّهُ لَهُم مَّغْفِرَةً وَأَجْرًا عَظِيمًا

Surely the men who submit and the women who submit, and the believing men and the believing women, and the obeying men and the obeying women, and the truthful men and the truthful women, and the patient men and the patient women and the humble men and the humble women, and the almsgiving men and the almsgiving women, and the fasting men and the fasting women, and the men who guard their private parts and the women who guard, and the men who remember Allah much and the women who remember-- Allah has prepared for them forgiveness and a mighty reward. [15]

يَا أَيُّهَا الَّذِينَ آمَنُوا إِذَا نُودِيَ لِلصَّلَاةِ مِن يَوْمِ الْجُمُعَةِ فَاسْعَوْا إِلَىٰ ذِكْرِ اللَّهِ وَذَرُوا الْبَيْعَ ذَٰلِكُمْ خَيْرٌ لَّكُمْ إِن كُنتُمْ تَعْلَمُونَ

O you who believe! When the call is made for prayer on Friday, then hasten to the remembrance of Allah and leave off trading; that is better for you, if you know. [16]

The second meaning is 'against forgetfulness'; it is the presence of something in the mind. The root is remind/remember [*dhikr*' (ذِكْر)] or the reminder/remembrance [*al-dhikra'* (الذِّكْرَى)] or it can be reflection/recall [*tadhakkar'* (تَذَكُّر)]. In this regard, it appears as so in the following verses where Allah says:

قَالَ أَرَأَيْتَ إِذْ أَوَيْنَا إِلَى الصَّخْرَةِ فَإِنِّي نَسِيتُ الْحُوتَ وَمَا أَنسَانِيهُ إِلَّا الشَّيْطَانُ أَنْ أَذْكُرَهُ وَاتَّخَذَ سَبِيلَهُ فِي الْبَحْرِ عَجَبًا

He said: Did you see when we took refuge on the rock then I forgot the fish, and nothing made me forget to speak of it but the Shaytān and it took its way

[15] *Qur'ān* 33: 35
[16] *Qur'ān* 62: 9

into the river; what a wonder! [17]

فَسَتَذْكُرُونَ مَا أَقُولُ لَكُمْ وَأُفَوِّضُ أَمْرِي إِلَى اللَّهِ إِنَّ اللَّهَ بَصِيرٌ بِالْعِبَادِ

So you shall remember what I say to you, and I entrust my affair to Allah, surely Allah sees the servants. [18]

أَوَلَا يَذْكُرُ الْإِنسَانُ أَنَّا خَلَقْنَاهُ مِن قَبْلُ وَلَمْ يَكُ شَيْئًا

Doen't man remember that We created him before, when he was nothing? [19]

وَجِيءَ يَوْمَئِذٍ بِجَهَنَّمَ يَوْمَئِذٍ يَتَذَكَّرُ الْإِنسَانُ وَأَنَّىٰ لَهُ الذِّكْرَىٰ

And hell is made to appear on that day. On that day shall man be mindful and what shall being mindful (then) avail him? [20]

Thirdly, there is the meaning of memorisation and diligent study, to keep in mind and understand the future implication of something which is in contrast to negligence and the lack of study. Another derived form of *dhikr* is the word 'memorisation' [*madhākara* (المذاكرة)] which means to review what has been studied, understand it and retain it in long-term memory. In this sense, it is meant in plural form. Allah mentions as such in the following verses in plural not singular form:

وَاذْكُرْنَ مَا يُتْلَىٰ فِي بُيُوتِكُنَّ مِنْ آيَاتِ اللَّهِ وَالْحِكْمَةِ إِنَّ اللَّهَ كَانَ لَطِيفًا خَبِيرًا

And keep in mind what is recited in your houses of the verses of Allah and the

---

[17] *Qur'ān* 18: 63
[18] *Qur'ān* 40: 44
[19] *Qur'ān* 18: 67
[20] *Qur'ān* 89: 23

wisdom; surely Allah is knower of subtleties, aware. [21]

Meaning, study, understand and memorise. What is recited in houses from the verses of Allah and the wisdom [*ḥikmah* (الحكمة)] and from the Qur'ān and *Sunnah*, oh wives of the Prophet, may the peace and blessings of Allah be upon them all, then propagate and convey this thereafter to the *Ummah* so they may understand it.

وَإِذْ أَخَذْنَا مِيثَاقَكُمْ وَرَفَعْنَا فَوْقَكُمُ الطُّورَ خُذُوا مَا آتَيْنَاكُم بِقُوَّةٍ وَاذْكُرُوا مَا فِيهِ لَعَلَّكُمْ تَتَّقُونَ

And when We took a promise from you and lifted the mountain over you: Take hold of the law We have given you with firmness and bear in mind what is in it, so that you may guard against evil. [22]

وَإِذْ نَتَقْنَا الْجَبَلَ فَوْقَهُمْ كَأَنَّهُ ظُلَّةٌ وَظَنُّوا أَنَّهُ وَاقِعٌ بِهِمْ خُذُوا مَا آتَيْنَاكُم بِقُوَّةٍ وَاذْكُرُوا مَا فِيهِ لَعَلَّكُمْ تَتَّقُونَ

And when We shook the mountain over them as if it were a covering overhead, and they thought that it was going to fall down upon them: Take hold of what We have given you with firmness, and be mindful of what is in it, so that you may guard (against evil). [23]

Meaning collectively study; understand and memorise what has come to you, to take heed and put it into practice.

وَلَقَدْ يَسَّرْنَا الْقُرْآنَ لِلذِّكْرِ فَهَلْ مِن مُّدَّكِرٍ

And certainly We have made the Qur'ān easy for remembrance, but is there

[21] *Qur'ān* 33: 34
[22] *Qur'ān* 2: 63
[23] *Qur'ān* 7: 171

anyone who will mind? [24]

Namely, we have made the Qur'ān easy for studying, to understand and memorise, will you not therefore partake in this endeavour?

Fourthly, there is the meaning of reputation, goodness, honour and eminence, for the well-known have their names repeated upon the tongues of people and are closer to the minds of others in that regard. The root form here is mention (*dhikr* (ذِكْر)], concerning this meaning Allah says in the following verses:

وَرَفَعْنَا لَكَ ذِكْرَكَ

And exalted for you your esteem? [25]

وَإِنَّهُ لَذِكْرٌ لَّكَ وَلِقَوْمِكَ وَسَوْفَ تُسْأَلُونَ

And most surely it is a reminder for you and your people, and you shall soon be questioned. [26]

When interpreted in such a way, this religion elevated the eminence that was considered benign to you and your nation, after that they were sluggish given that other nations did not care for them.

ص وَالْقُرْآنِ ذِي الذِّكْرِ

Ṣaad, I swear by the Qur'ān, full of admonition. [27]

---

[24] *Qur'ān* 54: 17, 22, 32 & 40
[25] *Qur'ān* 94: 4
[26] *Qur'ān* 43: 44
[27] *Qur'ān* 38: 1

Some interpret the verse as meaning, the Qur'ān is well known, with a lofty and praiseworthy status, and this is the most fitting of what is said. Others mention that the verse means: I swear by the the well recognised and known Qur'ān that it has a right to be memorised, studied, and understood. This also an acceptable interpretation.

Fifthly, there is the meaning of the 'revealed reminder' or the 'sent-down reminder', [*al-Dhikr al-Munazil* (الذّكر المنزَّل)]. It is a type of revelation that has been sent-down by Allah and specifically has the wording *dhikr* contained within it, because it deserves that specific mention, that which is memorised and studied as well as being held in presence of mind. Moreover, it reminds the people of their relationship with Allah, the reason behind their existence; the afterlife which awaits all of us with its day of reckoning, reward and punishment as well as being filled with the remembrance and praise of Allah contained therein. The root is '*dhikr*' (ذِكْر). Above all this is the meaning which is paramount and it has been elucidated in the following Qur'ānic verses:

وَمَا أَرْسَلْنَا مِن قَبْلِكَ إِلَّا رِجَالًا نُّوحِي إِلَيْهِمْ فَاسْأَلُوا أَهْلَ الذِّكْرِ إِن كُنتُمْ لَا تَعْلَمُونَ بِالْبَيِّنَاتِ
وَالزُّبُرِ وَأَنزَلْنَا إِلَيْكَ الذِّكْرَ لِتُبَيِّنَ لِلنَّاسِ مَا نُزِّلَ إِلَيْهِمْ وَلَعَلَّهُمْ يَتَفَكَّرُونَ

And We did not send before you any but men to whom We sent revelation-- so ask the followers of the dhikr if you do not know. With clear arguments and scriptures and We have revealed to you the dhikr that you may make clear to men what has been revealed to them and that haply they may reflect. [28]

وَمَا أَرْسَلْنَا قَبْلَكَ إِلَّا رِجَالًا نُّوحِي إِلَيْهِمْ فَاسْأَلُوا أَهْلَ الذِّكْرِ إِن كُنتُمْ لَا تَعْلَمُونَ

And We did not send before you any but men to whom We sent revelation, so ask the followers of the dhikr if you do not know. [29]

---

[28] *Qur'ān* 16: 43/44
[29] *Qur'ān* 21: 7

Which is to ask the *Ulemā'*, those intimately acquainted with the sent-down revelation as it is found in the previous books. Originally the people of the book were challenging the veracity of the Prophethood of Muḥammad (peace be upon him) on the basis that he was only mortal. So the people of Islam or the people of the Qur'ān are ordered by these verses to ask the people of the earlier books about the former Prophets – were they from the angels or were they mortal as well? The second part of the verse which says: '*We have revealed to you the Reminder that you may make clear to men what has been revealed to them and that haply they may reflect*' will be discussed in greater detail below, together with the verse where Allah the almighty says:

إِنَّا نَحْنُ نَزَّلْنَا الذِّكْرَ وَإِنَّا لَهُ لَحَافِظُونَ

Surely We have revealed the dhikr and We will most surely be its guardian.[30]

قَالُوا سُبْحَانَكَ مَا كَانَ يَنبَغِي لَنَا أَن نَّتَّخِذَ مِن دُونِكَ مِنْ أَوْلِيَاءَ وَلَٰكِن مَّتَّعْتَهُمْ وَآبَاءَهُمْ حَتَّىٰ نَسُوا الذِّكْرَ وَكَانُوا قَوْمًا بُورًا

They shall say: Glory be to you; it was not befitting for us that we should take any guardians besides you, but you didn't make them and their fathers to enjoy until they forsook the dhikr, and they were a people in perdition.[31]

The verse relates to them forgetting the sent-down revelation, they neglected it and turned away from it. The sent-down revelation here is every type which Allah revealed throughout the ages, as dictated by the context and not only what was revealed to Muḥammad (peace be upon him) and therefore by greater reasoning not only the text of the Qur'ān.

---

30 *Qur'ān* 15: 9
31 *Qur'ān* 25: 18

لَقَدْ أَضَلَّنِي عَنِ الذِّكْرِ بَعْدَ إِذْ جَاءَنِي وَكَانَ الشَّيْطَانُ لِلْإِنسَانِ خَذُولًا

Certainly he led me astray from the dhikr after it had come to me; and the Shayṭān fails to aid man. [32]

Like its predecessor, *dhikr* here means the sent-down revelation upon the Messenger, which was not followed by the wayward deceased individual set out in the verse. In this verse, the individual is described as biting his hand with regret. This is similar to the case of every tyrant who sets himself against the path laid out by the Messenger, not only as it relates to the Prophet Muḥammad (peace be upon him) and his specific way.

إِنَّمَا تُنذِرُ مَنِ اتَّبَعَ الذِّكْرَ وَخَشِيَ الرَّحْمَٰنَ بِالْغَيْبِ فَبَشِّرْهُ بِمَغْفِرَةٍ وَأَجْرٍ كَرِيمٍ

You can only warn him who follows the dhikr and fears the beneficent Allah in secret; announce to him forgiveness and an honourable reward. [33]

This also means those who follow its predecessors, the sent-down revelation, but is specific to Muḥammad (peace be upon him) as is shown by the context.

وَلَقَدْ كَتَبْنَا فِي الزَّبُورِ مِن بَعْدِ الذِّكْرِ أَنَّ الْأَرْضَ يَرِثُهَا عِبَادِيَ الصَّالِحُونَ

And certainly We wrote in the Zaboor after the dhikr that (as for) the land, my righteous servants shall inherit it. [34]

Hence this *al-dhikr* referred to relates to something earlier than the Psalms (*Zuboor*). Most of the *mufasireen* have interpreted this to

---

[32] *Qur'ān* 25: 29
[33] *Qur'ān* 36: 11
[34] *Qur'ān* 21: 105

mean the preserved tablet (*al-Lawḥ al-Maḥfouz*), which is a euphemism regarding the knowledge of Allah or his original judgement. It is most possible here that the verse means: *'that (as for) the land, my righteous servants shall inherit it'*, before we write it in the Psalms or it is possible that the *dhikr* is a term used for revealed books in general, or the book of Dāwud (peace be upon him) specifically. Some of the *mufasireen* said that '*al-dhikr*' is intended to relate to the Torah, whatever the case, the '*dhikr*' here is definitely something else other than the text of the Qur'ān:

وَهَٰذَا ذِكْرٌ مُّبَارَكٌ أَنزَلْنَاهُ أَفَأَنتُمْ لَهُ مُنكِرُونَ

And this is a blessed dhikr which We have revealed; will you then deny it? [35]

It is likely that '*And this is a blessed dhikr*', means the Qur'ān, because the Qur'ān is a blessed reminder. This understanding is further verified because it comes in relation to the revelation upon Musa and Hārun – the criterion, illumination and reminder to the pious God-fearing. Thus, it is appropriate 'the reminder' means the overall *waḥy* which is sent-down and revealed to Muḥammad (peace be upon him), all of which is truth containing no doubt therein.

ذَٰلِكَ نَتْلُوهُ عَلَيْكَ مِنَ الْآيَاتِ وَالذِّكْرِ الْحَكِيمِ

This, We do recite to you of the communications and the wise reminder. [36]

Recognising the words here, *dhikr* probably refers to those previous verses which relate the chosen al-'Imrān, offspring from Yaḥya bin Zakariyā peace and blessings be upon them both and the whole story

---

[35] *Qur'ān* 21: 50
[36] *Qur'ān* 3: 58

of Esa ibn Maryam peace and blessings be upon him and his mother, is some of what is recited upon you from these signs and some of what these signs are detailed from the wise reminder. It would be adjoined to the recited verses upon *al-Dhikr al-Ḥakeem* from the some to the all, adjoining the specific to the general out of respect to those specific verses, raising to its extent for reasons of explanation and rhetoric as well as others, rather than only to say '*that which is recited upon you from the glorious reminder'*. The term *al-Dhikr al-Ḥakeem* - the glorious reminder - is from amongst the names of the Qur'ān with the connotation given by the wording 'recited'. Here the wording will be about the Qur'ān only however with that it does not entail that this absolutely necessitates that in each context the mention of the *dhikr* will refer to the Qur'ān only.

The verses could also mean: some of what is recited upon you from these verses and some of it which we have revealed is *al-Dhikr al-Ḥakeem.* Consequently *al-Dhikr al-Ḥakeem* overall is the revelation, recited or not recited. Often the presumption is that where the word *Dhikr* is used it is for the Qur'ān, whereas it is used to express the notion of revelation generally. Also, the connotation related to the revelation of these verses was about the debate with the Christians of Najrān and the invitation to them for invokocation of the curse of Allah upon the liar (*mubāhala)*. It is known by necessity that the Prophet (peace be upon him) debated them with his words and speech. No one argues that the revelation referred to here was only that which was used during the debate. Even if this verse was not peremptory in actuality that the *al-Dhikr al-Ḥakeem* is the Qur'ān, if this was the preponderant meaning. Yet there is no doubt that the Qur'ān is the *Dhikr* and no doubt that it is *Ḥakeem* and that it deserves to be entitled – *al-Dhikr al-Ḥakeem*. The salient question therefore being – is *al-Dhikr al-Ḥakeem* the Qur'ān exclusively, so that other than it may not be called *al-Dhikr al-Ḥakeem*?

إِنَّ الَّذِينَ كَفَرُوا بِالذِّكْرِ لَمَّا جَاءَهُمْ وَإِنَّهُ لَكِتَابٌ عَزِيزٌ

Surely those who disbelieve in the reminder when it comes to them, most surely it is a mighty book. [37]

Contained within this verse the '*dhikr*' here is either to be considered from amongst the names of the Qur'ān which is also referred to as the 'mighty book' (*kitābun 'aziz*), but it may be the '*dhikr*' is the name for all the sent-down revelation. All of this sent-down revelation in truth is preserved, for indeed it is a 'mighty book'; no falsehood approaches it between its covers or from behind it. It is revealed from the praised lord. By necessity it is not this book that is the Qur'ān and it is not by necessity that only held within its lofty pages. Allah declares:

أَوَعَجِبْتُمْ أَن جَاءَكُمْ ذِكْرٌ مِّن رَّبِّكُمْ عَلَىٰ رَجُلٍ مِّنكُمْ لِيُنذِرَكُمْ وَلِتَتَّقُوا وَلَعَلَّكُمْ تُرْحَمُونَ

What! Do you wonder that a dhikr has come to you from your Lord through a man from among you, that he might warn you and that you might guard (against evil) and so that mercy may be shown to you? [38]

أَوَعَجِبْتُمْ أَن جَاءَكُمْ ذِكْرٌ مِّن رَّبِّكُمْ عَلَىٰ رَجُلٍ مِّنكُمْ لِيُنذِرَكُمْ وَاذْكُرُوا إِذْ جَعَلَكُمْ خُلَفَاءَ مِن بَعْدِ قَوْمِ نُوحٍ وَزَادَكُمْ فِي الْخَلْقِ بَسْطَةً فَاذْكُرُوا آلَاءَ اللَّهِ لَعَلَّكُمْ تُفْلِحُونَ

What, do you wonder that a dhikr from your Lord should come to you by the lips of a man from among you? That he may warn you; and remember when He appointed you as successors after the people of Noah, and increased you in stature broadly; remember Allah's bounties; haply you will prosper. [39]

Without doubt as shown by this prudent sentence contained within the verse– '*dhikr from your lord*' which here means the revelation from your lord, or a message from your lord. It doesn't make the

[37] *Qur'ān* 41: 41
[38] *Qur'ān* 7: 63
[39] *Qur'ān* 7: 69

connection to the text of the Qur'ān originally because the wording here is about the nations of Nuḥ and Hud (peace be upon them both). Allah the exalted also says:

مَا يَأْتِيهِم مِّن ذِكْرٍ مِّن رَّبِّهِم مُّحْدَثٍ إِلَّا اسْتَمَعُوهُ وَهُمْ يَلْعَبُونَ

There comes not to them a new dhikr from their Lord but they hear it while they sport. [40]

وَمَا يَأْتِيهِم مِّن ذِكْرٍ مِّنَ الرَّحْمَٰنِ مُحْدَثٍ إِلَّا كَانُوا عَنْهُ مُعْرِضِينَ

And there does not come to them a new dhikr from Allah, ar-Raḥman but they turn aside from it. [41]

By necessity, it is not specifically addressed to the disbelievers of Quraysh and not to the previous nations, the denouncement is upon all of them turning away from the new revelation. This proclamation or revelation may be considered a portion from the Qur'ān, it may be in this manner and all of that '*a new reminder from the Allah, ar-Raḥman*'. For example, the Prophet (peace be upon him) asked after ascending to mount Ṣafā – '*If I were to inform you that an army are proceeding up the side of this mountain, would you believe me*?' or as he also then said: '*I am a plain warner to all of you of a coming severe punishment.*' Some of the attendees retorted with: 'May you perish this day! You called us to this?' turning away and disbelieving. The *Seerah* is replete with such instances. Allah the majestic says:

إِنْ هُوَ إِلَّا ذِكْرٌ لِّلْعَالَمِينَ

[40] *Qur'ān* 21: 2
[41] *Qur'ān* 26: 5

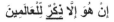

It is nothing but a reminder to all creation;[42]

It is likely that *dhikr* refers to the Qur'ān here, due to the fact that the Prophet is being referred to in the previous two verses.

وَإِن يَكَادُ الَّذِينَ كَفَرُوا لَيُزْلِقُونَكَ بِأَبْصَارِهِمْ لَمَّا سَمِعُوا الذِّكْرَ وَيَقُولُونَ إِنَّهُ لَمَجْنُونٌ ، وَمَا هُوَ إِلَّا ذِكْرٌ لِّلْعَالَمِينَ

And those who disbelieve would almost smite you with their eyes when they hear the reminder, and they say: Most surely, he is mad. And it is nothing but a reminder to all creation.[43]

The reason why the Prophet is accused of being mad here is because he was not only reciting the Qur'ān like a tape recorder.

إِنْ هُوَ إِلَّا ذِكْرٌ لِّلْعَالَمِينَ

It is but a reminder for all creation.[44]

Here the context seems to confirm that the reference being made is to the Qur'ān only, since the preceding verses which state:

إِنَّهُ لَقَوْلُ رَسُولٍ كَرِيمٍ ، ذِي قُوَّةٍ عِندَ ذِي الْعَرْشِ مَكِينٍ ... وَمَا هُوَ بِقَوْلِ شَيْطَانٍ رَّجِيمٍ

Most surely it is the word of an honoured messenger, the posessor of strength, having an honourable place with the lord of the dominion....nor is it the word

[42] *Qur'ān* 38: 87
[43] *Qur'ān* 68: 51/52
[44] *Qur'ān* 81: 27

of the cursed Shayṭān.[45]

Without doubt the Qur'ān is a reminder to all of creation. Moreover, there can be no doubt that that the Qur'ān is not singularly *al-Dhikr* (the reminder) or *Dhikr* to all creation. The next three verses when taken together say:

وَقَالُوا يَا أَيُّهَا الَّذِي نُزِّلَ عَلَيْهِ الذِّكْرُ إِنَّكَ لَمَجْنُونٌ

And they say: O you to whom the Reminder has been revealed! You are most surely insane[46]

أَأُنزِلَ عَلَيْهِ الذِّكْرُ مِن بَيْنِنَا بَلْ هُمْ فِي شَكٍّ مِّن ذِكْرِي بَل لَّمَّا يَذُوقُوا عَذَابِ

Has the reminder been revealed to him from among us? Nay! They are in doubt as to My reminder. Nay! they have not yet tasted My chastisement![47]

أَأُلْقِيَ الذِّكْرُ عَلَيْهِ مِن بَيْنِنَا بَلْ هُوَ كَذَّابٌ أَشِرٌ

Has the reminder been made to light upon him from among us? Nay! He is an insolent liar![48]

So potentially, when these verses are read together, one may gather the impression that it will carry the meaning of referring to the Qur'ān only. The verses are better understood to mean the revelation sent down to the Messenger in its entirety. Yet to purport to the former view would not be an outright falsity only because the Qur'ān is from Allah. Indeed they believe the Prophet (peace be upon him) in

---

[45] *Qur'ān* 81: 19/20, 25
[46] *Qur'ān* 15: 6
[47] *Qur'ān* 38: 8
[48] *Qur'ān* 54: 25

everything else, but limiting the verses only to the Qur'ān, whereas it should be for all the revelation, would indeed be a lie. Elsewhere Allah the exalted says:

وَمَا عَلَّمْنَاهُ الشِّعْرَ وَمَا يَنبَغِي لَهُ إِنْ هُوَ إِلَّا ذِكْرٌ وَقُرْآنٌ مُّبِينٌ

And We have not taught him poetry, nor is it befitting for him; it is nothing but a dhikr and a plain Qur'ān. [49]

The verse requires some cause for reflection and detailed consideration, given that the wording expresses: '*it is nothing but a dhikr and a plain Qur'ān.*' A casual observer may think that the Qur'ān in linguistic style is from the genus of poetry. Yet it is not so because Muḥammad (peace be upon him) was no poet, nor is it befitting for it to be considered poetry. His lord did not teach him poetry originally. But the *dhikr* is the revelation in its actual content. The Qur'ān as pronounced is eloquent in its formulation. Here the eloquence is about the Qur'ān, from the essence of its means and formulation. Potentially that will also be co-joining or adjoining the Qur'ān with the *dhikr*, the specific upon the general in meaning. It wouldn't make sense for the *dhikr* here as referred to in the verse to also mean the Qur'ān, in other words for the two to be the same thing in this specific verse. Muḥammad was not a poet nor versed in poetry. But what came to him was revelation as sent from Allah. Some of this revelation that came is this '*Qur'ān mubeen*', which as the verse says is the miraculous revelation sent-down with its wording. Some people have confused this point thinking that its system being poetic it was a form of poetry. Allah blessed be his names also says:

أَعَدَّ اللَّهُ لَهُمْ عَذَابًا شَدِيدًا فَاتَّقُوا اللَّهَ يَا أُولِي الْأَلْبَابِ الَّذِينَ آمَنُوا قَدْ أَنزَلَ اللَّهُ إِلَيْكُمْ ذِكْرًا رَّسُولًا يَتْلُو عَلَيْكُمْ آيَاتِ اللَّهِ مُبَيِّنَاتٍ لِّيُخْرِجَ الَّذِينَ آمَنُوا وَعَمِلُوا الصَّالِحَاتِ مِنَ الظُّلُمَاتِ إِلَى النُّورِ

---

[49] *Qur'ān* 36: 69

وَمَن يُؤْمِن بِاللَّهِ وَيَعْمَلْ صَالِحًا يُدْخِلْهُ جَنَّاتٍ تَجْرِي مِن تَحْتِهَا الْأَنْهَارُ خَالِدِينَ فِيهَا أَبَدًا قَدْ أَحْسَنَ اللَّهُ لَهُ رِزْقًا

Allah has prepared for them severe chastisement, therefore be careful of (your duty to) Allah, O men of understanding who believe! Allah has indeed revealed to you a reminder, a Prophet who recites to you the clear communications of Allah so that he may bring forth those who believe and do good deeds from darkness into light; whoever believes in Allah and does good deeds, He will cause him to enter gardens beneath which rivers now, to abide therein forever, Allah has indeed given him a goodly sustenance.[50]

Thus, it is significant that the Qur'ān explains that the revealed *Dhikr* is not only the Qur'ān. But it is wider, for it is this Prophet who recites the clear signs of Allah. We know by necessity of perception and reason that the Prophet is a creation from earth, in other words, he did not descend from heaven, but is borne of the earth, being made of flesh and blood. Consequently, by necessity it is not the Prophet as an entity that has been 'sent down' given that he is mortal, but it is mentioned in relation to the entity of the Prophet in the form of linguistic expression. That the *waḥy* is not only the recited verses, but it is all of that which descends upon the Prophet, encompassing his very being and expressed via his sayings, actions and what he approves. Hence it necessitates anything from the Prophet that deserves to be properly termed as revealed to, as already mentioned previously in this section in the form of numerous proofs established from the Qur'ān itself as well as the sayings, acts and approvals of the Prophet. When understood in a general manner, this categorically affirms without doubt that the word '*dhikr*', '*the revealed sent-down dhikr*' (each prefixed with the definite article 'al') or *'dhikr sent from Allah'* means revelation in general. It is not simply synonymous with the glorious Qur'ān only or only a euphemism for the Qur'ān, although both *al-Dhikr* and *al-Ḥakeem* are without doubt from amongst the names and attributes of the Qur'ān.

---

[50] *Qur'ān* 65: 10/11

For all the aforementioned reasons the false assertions and sophisms of those who call themselves 'Qur'ānists', crumble to dust. The assertion that the sent-down revealed and protected *dhikr* is only the Qur'ān does not withstand any anxious scrutiny. Neither does their conception that the *Sunnah* is not revelation or not a binding authority as the Qur'ān is. For the sane rational mind their views and judgements concerning revelation are based upon manifest error. Their views seek to forge outright lies against the manifest text of the Qur'ān; they have utter disregard for it, yet they claim they uphold true belief in it. The truth is that 'Qur'ānists' are people of whims and desires; some of them are outright people of *nifāq* (hypocrisy), others outright *zandeeq* (heretics). They are ignorant of the book of Allah and violate its principles, seeking to try and demolish Islam itself throughout their sophistic calls.

14 Testimony of the *Sunnah* to its proof

As has been demonstrated previously with decisive evidences, the Prophetic *Sunnah* is an infallible revelation. To be more precise, the Prophetic *Sunnah* is not merely a particular revelation from Allah rather it is a formulated expression of an infallible Prophetic revelation that has come from Allah. Moreover, as has been proved, the Prophetic *Sunnah* is of the same class as the Qur'ān, carrying the same level of proof that it has. By the necessity of perception and reason as well as the proofs from the Qur'ān only utilising its texts, the *Sunnah* is of the same level of authority as it. In order not to fall into contradictions and circulatory what has been detailed from the texts of the *Sunnah* were not used as primary proof, they were only used by way of further illustration. As demonstrated previously, the *Sunnah* is an infallible revelation hence generally it should not involve any discrepancies, internal inconsistencies or contradictions. It is a stand-alone proof, being permissible to invoke on its own as an authority. Given its status as being an infallible revelation, it is not permissible for it to be contradictory, it must remain consistent generally, precisely because it is an infallible revelation. Foremost again this rests in particular upon the condition that what is being invoked from the Prophet (peace be upon him) has in fact been ascertained categorically beyond reasonable doubt that it is prophetic.

To consider the specific evidences which have reached us from the Prophetic *aḥādith*, we begin by citing the following narration reported on the authority of 'Uqba bin 'Aāmr al-Juhany (may Allah be pleased with him) as it appears in the *Mustadrak* of al-Ḥākim:

> أخبرني أبو بكر إسماعيل بن محمّد الفقيه بالري حدثنا أبو حاتم الرازي حدثني أبو أيوب سليمان بن عبد الرحمن الدمشقي حدثني عبد الله بن وهب حدثنا مالك بن خير الزيادي عن أبي قبيل عن عقبة بن عامر رضي الله عنه قال: سمعت رسول الله، صلى الله عليه وسلم، يقول: سيهلك من أمتي أهل الكتاب وأهل اللبن! ؛ قال عقبة: ما أهل الكتاب يا رسول الله؟!؛ قال: قوم يتعلّمون كتاب الله يجادلون به الذين آمنوا! ؛ قال: فقلت: ما أهل اللبن يا رسول الله؟!؛ قال: قوم يتّبعون الشهوات ويضيّعون الصلوات!
>
> Abu Bakr Ismā'il bin Muḥammad al-Faqeehi reported to me in Rai[1] Abu Ḥātim ar-Rāzi narrated to us Abu Ayub Sulaymān bin Abdar-Raḥman ad-Dimishqi narrated to me Abdullah bin Wahb narrated to me Mālik bin Khayr az-Ziyādi narrated to us from Abi Qabeel from 'Uqba bin 'Aāmr who said I heard the Messenger of Allah (peace be upon him) say: *The perishing of my Ummah lies in the people of the book and people of milk.* 'Uqba said: What are the people of the book oh Messenger of Allah? He replied: *People who learn the book of Allah and use it to argue with the believers*. I ('Uqba) said: And what of the people of milk oh Messenger of Allah? He replied: *People who follow desires and waste (away) prayers!*

After this citing this *ḥadith* al-Ḥākim said: 'This *ḥadith* has an authentic channel and they did not record it.' I would submit it is as he said and it has come more in relation to the 'people of milk'; people like milk hence they would depart from adherence to the *Jamā'ah* (congregation) and leave congregational prayers. Similar was reported

[1] Located outside of modern day Tehran, Iran

by Imām Aḥmad in his *Musnad* with slightly different wording which has: '*they would love milk to the extent that they would abandon praying in congregation and Friday Prayers and go out to the desert* (for milk).'[2] Imām Ṭabarāni also records the same with similar wording in his *Mu'jam al-Kabir,*[3] and Imām Abu Ya'la also records this in his *Musnad.*[4]

The *ḥadith* which is authentic and establishes that whoever misinterprets the glorious Qur'ān, using it to argue with the believers will end up in ruin. A correct and sound interpretation of the Qur'ān can only be known with certitude through the Prophet (peace be upon him), conveying that infallible conveyance from Allah, who guaranteed to give a convincing, plausible and binding proclamation. For he whose names are blessed made a true promise when he said:

فَإِذَا قَرَأْنَاهُ فَاتَّبِعْ قُرْآنَهُ، ثُمَّ إِنَّ عَلَيْنَا بَيَانَهُ

Therefore when We have recited it, follow its recitation. Again upon Us is its explanation.[5]

.... وَمَنْ أَوْفَىٰ بِعَهْدِهِ مِنَ اللَّهِ

....and who is more faithful to his covenant than Allah?[6]

Next, Imām Tirmidhi recorded this *ḥadith* in his *Sunan* on the authority of Ibn 'Abbās (may Allah be pleased with him):

حدثنا محمود بن غيلان حدثنا بشر بن السري حدثنا سفيان عن عبد الأعلى

---

[2] *Musnad* Aḥmad Vol. 4 sec 146, no. 17,356 and sec. 155, no. 17,451

[3] *Mu'jam al-Kabir,* Ṭabarāni Vol. 17 sec. 296, no. 815 / 817

[4] *Musnad* Abu Ya'la Vol. 3 sec. 286, no. 1,746

[5] *Qur'ān* 75: 18/19

[6] *Qur'ān* 9: 111

عن سعيد بن جبير عن بن عباس رضي الله عنهما قال: قال رسول الله، صلى الله عليه وسلم: من قال في القرآن بغير علم فليتبوأ مقعده من النار

> Maḥmud bin Ghaylān narrated to us Bishr bin as-Sirri narrated to us Sufyān narrated to us from Abdal-'Ala from Sa'eed bin Jubayr from Ibn 'Abbās who said the Messenger of Allah (peace be upon him) said: *Whoever says* (something) *about the Qur'ān without knowledge, then let him take his seat in the fire.*

Concerning this Abu Esa said that the *ḥadith* was *ḥasan Ṣaḥīḥ*. Other notable Imām's included this tradition in their respective collections, amongst them Aḥmad in his *Musnad* in more than one place,[7] Nasā'i in his *Sunan al-Kubra,*[8] and other than them. Knowledge attained with certainty regarding the Qur'ān is acquired by way of the Prophet (peace be upon him) as mentioned previously.

Further to this, Imām an-Nasā'i recorded the next tradition by way of an authentic channel of transmission in his *Sunan*:

أخبرنا عتبة بن عبد الله قال: أنبأنا بن المبارك عن سفيان عن جعفر بن محمد عن أبيه عن جابر بن عبد الله قال: كان رسول الله، صلى الله عليه وسلم، يقول في خطبته: يحمد الله ويثني عليه بما هو أهله، ثم يقول: من يهده الله فلا مضل له، ومن يضلله فلا هادي له. إن أصدق الحديث كتاب الله، وأحسن الهدي هدي محمد، وشر الأمور محدثاتها، وكل محدثة بدعة، وكل بدعة ضلالة، وكل ضلالة في النار! ، ثم يقول: بعثت أنا والساعة كهاتين، وكان إذا ذكر الساعة احمرت وجنتاه، وعلا صوته، واشتد غضبه، كأنه نذير جيش يقول: صبّحكم مسّاكم، ثم قال: من ترك مالا فلأهله، ومن ترك دينا أو ضياعا فإلي أو علي وأنا أولى بالمؤمنين

> 'Utbah bin Abdullah reported to us he said ibn Mubārak informed from Sufyān from Ja'far bin Muḥammad from his father from Jābir bin Abdullah who said: In his *Khuṭbah* the

---

[7] *Musnad* Aḥmad Vol. 1 sec. 233, no. 2,069 and sec. 269, no. 2,429

[8] *Sunan al-Kubra* Vol. 5 sec. 31, no. 8,084 / 8,085

Messenger of Allah (peace be upon him) used to praise Allah as He deserves to be praised, then he would say: *Whomsoever Allah guides, none can lead him astray, and whomsoever Allah sends astray, none can guide. The truest of word is the book of Allah and best of guidance is the guidance of Muḥammad. The worst of things are those that are newly invented; every newly-invented thing is an innovation and every innovation is misguidance and every misguidance is in the fire.* Then he said: *The hour and I have been sent like these two*. Whenever he mentioned the hour, his cheeks would turn red and he would raise his voice and become angry, as if he were warning of an approaching army and saying: *An army is coming to attack you in the morning, or in the evening*!' (Then he said): *Whoever leaves behind wealth, it is for his family and whoever leaves behind a debt or dependents, then these are my responsibility and I am the most entitled to take care of the believers.*

Similar narrations have been reported by Imām Aḥmad[9] and Nasā'i[10] in more than one place. Ibn Khuzayma has this in his *Ṣaḥīḥ*[11] and it is found in other collections as well. It has also been reported from the wording of authentic channels back to Abdullah ibn Ma'sud. Also it has been reported from Ṭalḥa ibn Naḍeela (may Allah be pleased with him) who reported:

سعِّر لنا، يا رسول الله! ، فقال: لا يسألني الله عن سنّة أحدثتها فيكم، لم يأمرني بها؛ ولكن اسألوا الله من فضله!

It was said to the Messenger of Allah (peace be upon him) - O Messenger of Allah! Fix prices for us. He said: *Allah will ask me about whatever Sunnah I told you about that He did not order me with. Ask Allah from His favour* (instead).

[9] *Musnad* Aḥmad Vol. 3 sec. 311, no. 14,373 and sec. 319, 14,471
[10] *Sunan al-Kubra* Vol. 1 sec. 550, no. 1,786 and Vol. 3 sec. 450, no. 5,892
[11] *Ṣaḥīḥ* Ibn Khuzayma Vol. 3, sec. 144, no. 1,785

The narration is an authentic *ḥadith* that proves what we had mentioned previously, that the Prophet (peace be upon him) did not order or forbid anything from his own self, rather he informs us of what Allah had revealed to him in every matter. This *ḥadith* was recorded by Ibn Abi 'Aāṣim in *Al-Aḥād wal-Mathāni*, by Bayhaqy in *al-Madkhal* as well as by Ṭabarāni through several channels, Ibn as-Sakan and many others.

'Aisha, mother of the believers (may Allah be pleased with her) reported from the Prophet (peace be upon him):

> ستة لعنتهم، لعنهم الله، وكل نبي مجاب: المكذب بقدر الله؛ والزائد في كتاب الله؛ والمتسلّط بالجبروت يذل من أعز الله، ويعز من أذل الله؛ والمستحل لحُرَم الله؛ والمستحل من عترتي ما حرّم الله؛ والتارك لسنّتي
>
> (There are) *six persons that I cursed and Allah cursed them and every Prophet cursed them.* (They are): *who denies the Qadr of Allah, who adds to the book of Allah, who owns power and authority using them in humiliating whomever Allah had honoured, who transgresses against my sanctuary, who transgresses against my kinship and who abandons my Sunnah.*

The *ḥadith* is *Ṣaḥīḥ* and it is recorded by al-Ḥākim.[12] Regarding this he said: 'This *ḥadith* is *Ṣaḥīḥ* and I don't know of it (being) problematic and they did not record it.' Adh-Dhahaby wavered over it agreeing with al-Ḥākim upon its authenticity from one angle, keeping silent about it in another way and objecting to it thirdly. He recorded in his work entitled *al-Kabā'ir* after he had completed his study of knowledge and his thought and personality had matured, may Allah be merciful to him. He said of it that the *isnād* was *Ṣaḥīḥ* and he was correct in this.[13] It has also been reported from Ḥasān from Imām

---

[12] *Mustadrak* Vol. 1 sec. 91, no. 102

[13] The Arabic version has an extended study of this *ḥadith* contained separately in an appendix

Zayn al-'Aābideen from his father from his grandfather (peace be upon him). Al-Ḥākim reports it in several other places[14] as does Tirmidhi in his *Sunan;*[15] it also appears in *Ṣaḥīḥ* Ibn Ḥibbān[16] and Ṭabarāni has this in *Mu'jam al-Kabir* as well as *Mu'jam al-Awsaṭ.*[17] In one of the narratives found in *Mu'jam al-Kabir* from 'Amr bin Sa'wā a seventh person is added namely one who absorbs the *Fay'.*[18] The *ḥadith* is a decisive proof which establishes that abandoning the *Sunnah* of the Prophet (peace be upon him) is amongst the most grievous of sins. It is on par with adding to the book of Allah and declaring lawful what Allah has prohibited (*istiḥlāl*). Such matters are in opposition to Islam, '*Imān* and *Tawḥeed.*

Abdullah ibn 'Amr ibn al-'Aāṣ used to write what the Messenger of Allah (peace be upon him) was saying in his gatherings. Some men from among the Quraysh scolded him by saying, 'You are writing what the Messenger of Allah (peace be upon him) is saying, he is just a human and becomes angry as human become sometimes angry.' Abdullah replied, 'I went to the Messenger of Allah (peace be upon him) and informed him regarding that. He pointed to his lips and said, '*By him in whose soul my hand rests, all what is coming out from these is true. Write (everything)!*' The report is *Ṣaḥīḥ* and can be found in the *Mustadrak* of al-Ḥākim.[19] Adh-Dhahaby agreed with al-Ḥākim in relation to the traditions authenticity. Its wording also comes via another channel from Abdal-Wāḥid bin Qays from Abdullah bin 'Amr. There is also a further report via another authentic channel which is reported by Yusuf bin Māhik. There are other authentic and good channels where this is reported from other than these two *Tābi'een.* Hence its conveyance can be regarded as being *tawātur* (continuously

---

[14] *Mustadrak* Vol. 2 sec. 572, 3,940; Vol. 2 sec. 572, no. 3,941 and Vol. 4 sec. 101, 7,011

[15] *Sunan* Tirmidhi Vol. 4 sec. 457, no. 2,154

[16] *Ṣaḥīḥ* Ibn Ḥibbān Vol. 13 sec. 61, no. 5,749

[17] *Mu'jam al-Kabir* Vol. 3 sec. 127, no. 2,883, *Mu'jam al-Awsaṭ* Vol. 2 sec. 186, no. 1,667

[18] *Mu'jam al-Kabir* Vol. 17 sec. 43, no. 89

[19] *Mustadrak* Vol. 1 sec. 186, no. 357

recurrent) from Abdullah ibn ‘Amr ibn al-‘Aāṣ from the Prophet (peace be upon him). The second way is the same authentic chain which was recorded by Aḥmad in his *Musnad.* The Prophet (peace be upon him) is infallible. He says the truth during cases of anger and dissatisfaction as well as cases in of seriousness as will now be detailed.

Abu Hurayrah (may Allah be pleased with him) is reported to have narrated that the Messenger of Allah (peace be upon him) said: ‘*Indeed I do not speak except that which is truth.*’ Some of the *Ṣaḥābah* said: O Messenger of Allah! You (sometimes) joke with us? He (peace be upon him) replied with: ‘*Indeed I do not speak except that which is truth.*’ The *ḥadith* is *Ṣaḥīḥ* and it appears in a number of collections, such as in *Musnad* Aḥmad;[20] Bukhāri’s *Adab al Mufrad,*[21] the *Sunan al-Kubra* of Bayhaqy[22] and the *Sunan* of Tirmidhi.[23] Concerning this, Tirmidhi said it was *ḥasan Ṣaḥīḥ* and in actuality it is.[24]

Next, Imām Abu Dāwud records in his *Sunan* the following tradition upon the authority of ‘Irbāḍ bin Sāriya as-Salami (may Allah be pleased with him), which has a good and strong chain of transmission. It is evidence in itself, and was regarded as authentic by the grand Imām Ali Ibn Ḥazm; Albāni considered it good also. Truly it is *Ṣaḥīḥ* when considered with all its additions. ‘Irbāḍ bin Sāriya narrates as follows:

نزلنا مع النبي صلى الله عليه وعلى آله وسلم، خيبر، ومعه من معه من أصحابه، وكان صاحب خيبر رجلاً مارداً منكراً، فأقبل إلى النبي، صلى الله عليه وعلى آله وسلم، فقال: يا محمّد! ألكم أن تذبحوا حُمُرنا، وتأكلوا ثمرنا، وتضربوا نساءنا؟!! فغضب النبي، صلى الله عليه وعلى آله وسلم، وقال:

---

[20] *Musnad* Aḥmad Vol. 2 sec. 340, no. 8,462 and sec. 360, no. 8,708
[21] *Adab al-Mufrad* Vol. 1 sec. 102, no. 265
[22] *Sunan al-Kubra* Vol. 10 sec. 248, no. 20,962 / 3
[23] *Sunan* Tirmidhi Vol. 4 sec. 357, no. 1,990
[24] The Arabic version has an extended study of this *ḥadith* in its annex

«يا ابن عوف! اركب فرسك ثم نادي: إن الجنة لا تحل إلا لمؤمن، وأن اجتمعوا للصلاة! ، قال: فاجتمعوا للصلاة، فصلى بهم رسول الله، صلى الله عليه وعلى آله وسلم، ثم قام خطيباً فقال: أيحسب أحدكم (وفي رواية: لا أجد أحدكم) متكئاً على أريكته قد يظن أن الله لم يحرم شيئاً إلا ما في القرآن؟!! ألا وإني، والله، قد أمرت، ووعظت، ونهيت عن أشياء: إنها مثل هذا القرآن، أو أكثر! وإن الله، عز وجل، لم يحل لكم أن تدخلوا بيوت أهل الكتاب، إلا بإذن، ولا ضرب نسائهم، ولا أكل ثمارهم، إذا أعطوكم الذي عليهم

> We alighted with the Prophet (peace be upon him) at Khaybar, and he had his companions with him. The chief of Khaybar was a defiant and abominable man. He came to the Prophet (peace be upon him) and said: Is it proper for you, Muḥammad, that you slaughter our donkeys, eat our fruit, and beat our women? The Prophet (peace be upon him) became angry and said: *Ibn 'Awf, ride your horse, and call loudly: Beware, Paradise is lawful only for a believer, and that they (the people) should gather for prayer.* They gathered and the Prophet (peace be upon him) led them in prayer, stood up and said: *Does any of you, while reclining on his couch, imagine that Allah has prohibited only that which is to be found in this Qur'ān? By Allah I have preached, commanded and prohibited various matters as numerous as that which is found in the Qur'ān, or more so. Allah has not permitted you to enter the houses of the people of the book without permission, or beat their women, or eat their fruits when they give you that which is imposed on them.*

Other *ḥadith* collectors cited this tradition in their respective works. To name but a few, Ṭabarāni cites this in all three of his major works – *Mu'jam al-Kabir*[25], *Musnad ash-Shāmiayn*[26] and *Mu'jam al-Awsaṭ;*[27] it is in *Al-Aḥād wal-Mathāni*[28] of Ibn Abi 'Aāṣim ash-Shaybāni and the

[25] *Mu'jam al-Kabir* Vol. 18 sec. 258, no. 645
[26] *Musnad ash-Shāmiayn* Vol. 1 sec. 401, no. 695
[27] *Mu'jam al-Awsaṭ* Vol. 7 sec. 184, no. 7,226
[28] *Al-Aḥād wal-Mathāni* Vol. 3 sec. 46, no. 1,336

Sunan al-Kubra of Bayhaqy.[29]

If we consider carefully this honourable *ḥadith* which is from amongst the evidences of the Prophethood of Muḥammad (peace be upon him), some key points emerge. Firstly, the Prophet (peace be upon him) started with the saying that paradise is prohibited for the *kuffār* (disbelievers) and that only believers will enter it, so everyone must beware for himself and check the truth and sincerity of his own faith. Secondly, he called them to perform prayer and when he preached to them, he pointed out that Allah the exalted made some matters lawful or unlawful, warned and forbade matters, through his Prophet (peace be upon him). These matters are not included in the Qur'ān and were not mentioned in it. Thus it is definite evidence that the order of command is of the same level as that of the Qur'ān as well as the fact that the Prophetic orders are also more numerous. Thirdly, another ruling was detailed, that concerning the *Dhimma* – non-Muslim citizens under the protection of Islamic rule. As long as the *Dhimma* submit to the sovereign Islamic authority, paying what is required of them and the like, then the authority must guarantee protection for their wealth, dignity, honour and property. In this regard, they have the same rights as any Muslim. Moreover, the tradition provides an exemplification for the Qur'ānic verse where Allah says:

•

أُوتُوا الْكِتَابَ حَتَّىٰ يُعْطُوا الْجِزْيَةَ عَن يَدٍ وَهُمْ صَاغِرُونَ

....out of those who have been given the book, until they pay the tax in acknowledgment of superiority and they are in a state of subjection.[30]

The verse uses the Arabic word '*Ṣāghiroon*' which means to be under subjection. It doesn't mean in this context - humiliation, degradation

[29] *Sunan al-Kubra* Vol. 9 sec. 204, no. 18,508
[30] *Qur'ān* 9: 29

or the violation of honour and dignity, although the word can encompass this, such as in the following verse:

قَالَ فَاهْبِطْ مِنْهَا فَمَا يَكُونُ لَكَ أَن تَتَكَبَّرَ فِيهَا فَاخْرُجْ إِنَّكَ مِنَ الصَّاغِرِينَ

He said: Then get forth from this (state), for it does not befit you to behave proudly therein. Go forth, therefore, surely you are of the abject ones.[31]

Some of the major scholars of jurisprudence held this view, notably, Imām Abu Ḥanifah. Here it relates to submission, in other words, as long as they have submitted to the rule of Islam and pay what is thereby obligated upon them. If it is not for this infallible and definite explanation, we would had been obliged to understand 'under subjection' according to all its possible meanings in Arabic language or to remain in state of confusion about deciding the right meaning - which would no doubt constitute a major problem, one that I do not know how the Qur'ānists and rejecters of the Prophetic *Sunnah* would be able to solve. Furthermore, Abu Dāwud collected in his *Sunan* the next narration from Abdullah bin Rāfih from his father from the Prophet (peace be upon him):

عن عبيد الله بن أبي رافع عن أبيه عن النبي، صلى الله عليه وعلى آله وسلم، قال: لا ألفين أحدَكم متكئاً على أريكته، يأتيه الأمر من أمري، مما أمرت به أو نهيت عنه، فيقول: لا ندري! ما وجدنا في كتاب الله اتّبعناه

The Prophet (peace be upon him) said: *Let me not find any one of you reclining on his couch when he hears something regarding me which I have commanded or forbidden and saying: We do not know. What we found in Allah's book we have followed.*

[31] *Qur'ān* 7: 13

Again, the *ḥadith* is *Ṣaḥīḥ* and several notable collectors cited this in their respective works.[32] The *ḥadith* is also *Ṣaḥīḥ* from the channel of Sufyān bin 'Uyayna, as well as from the channel of Mālik and thirdly via al-Layth ibn Sa'd. All of these channels are strong and reinforce one-another. Regarding this al-Ḥākim said: 'It is *Ṣaḥīḥ* according to the conditions of the two Shaykh's (Bukhāri and Muslim) although they did not record it.' Indeed it is, particularly when considered in tandem with the text of the previous and following narrations. Imām Ṭabarāni cites the next *ḥadith* in his *Mu'jam al-Kabir*:

حدثنا أبو زرعة عبد الرحمن بن عمرو الدمشقي حدثنا علي بن عياش الحمصي (ح) وحدثنا أبو زيد أحمد بن عبد الرحيم بن زيد الحوطي حدثنا أبو اليمان الحكم بن نافع قالا: حدثنا حريز بن عثمان (ح) وحدثنا الحسين بن إسحاق التستري حدثنا علي بن بحر حدثنا الوليد بن مسلم حدثنا حريز بن عثمان عن عبد الرحمن بن أبي عوف عن المقدام بن معدي كرب قال: قال رسول الله، صلى الله عليه وسلم: أوتيت الكتاب ومثله؛ ألا يوشك شبعان على أريكته يقول عليكم بالقرآن فما وجدتم فيه من حلال فأحلّوه، وما وجدتم فيه من حرام فحرّموه: ألا لا يحل لكم الحمار الأهلي؛ ولا كل ذي ناب من السباع؛ ولا لقطة معاهد إلا أن يستغني عنها صاحبها؛ ومن نزل بقوم فعليهم أن يقروه

Abu Zur'a Abdar-Raḥman bin 'Amr ad-Dimishqi narrated to us Ali bin 'Ayāsh al-Ḥimṣi narrated to us (*ḥawala*) and Abu Zayd Aḥmad bin Abdar-Raḥeem bin Zayd al-Ḥuṭi narrated to us Abu'l Yammān al-Ḥakm bin Nāfi narrated to us, they said: Ḥareez bin Uthmān narrated to us (*ḥawala*) and al-Ḥussain bin Isḥāq at-Tartusi narrated to us Ali bin Baḥr narrated to us al-Waleed bin Muslim narrated to us Ḥareez bin Uthmān narrated to us from Abdar-Raḥman bin Abi 'Auf from al-Miqdām bin

---

32 The listed citations are: *Musnad* Ḥumaydi [Vol. 1 sec. 252, no. 551], *Sunan* Ibn Mājah [Vol. 1 sec. 7, no. 13], *Mu'jam al-Kabir* of aṭ-Ṭabarāni [Vol. 1 sec. 316, no. 934 and sec. 327, no. 975] as well as in *Mu'jam al-Awsaṭ* [Vol. 8 sec. 292, no. 8,671], *Sharḥ Ma'āni al-Athār* of Imām aṭ-Ṭaḥāwi [Vol. 4 sec. 209, no. 0], *Sunan al-Kubra* Bayhaqy [Vol. 7 sec. 76, no. 13,219], *Sunan* Tirmidhi [Vol. 5 sec. 38, no. 2,663] of which he said the narration was *ḥasan Ṣaḥīḥ*, and *Mustadrak* al-Ḥākim [Vol. 1 sec. 191, no. 368].

Mahdi Karib he said the Messenger of Allah (peace be upon him) said: *Beware! I have been given the book and something like it, yet the time is coming when a man replete on his couch will say: Keep to the Qur'ān; what you find in it to be permissible treat as permissible, and what you find in it to be prohibited treat as prohibited. Beware! The domestic ass, beasts of prey with fangs, a find belonging to a confederate, unless its owner does not want it, are not permissible to you. If anyone comes to some people, they must entertain him, but if they do not, he has a right to mulct them to an amount equivalent to his entertainment.*

The same tradition is also reported in the *Sunan* of Abu Dāwud,[33] the *Musnad* of Imām Aḥmad,[34] *Musnad ash-Shāmiayn* of Ṭabarāni,[35] as well as in other collections. Also in the *Mu'jam al-Kabir* Ṭabarāni has the following *ḥadith*, which is good by itself (*ḥasan li'dhātihi*), and considered *Ṣaḥīḥ* when read together with the previously cited narrations.

حدثنا أحمد بن المعلى الدمشقي والحسين بن إسحاق التستري قالا: حدثنا هشام بن عمار حدثنا يحيى بن حمزة حدثني محمّد بن الوليد الزبيدي عن مروان بن رؤبة عن عبد الرحمن بن أبي عوف الجرشي عن المقدام بن معدي كرب أن رسول الله، صلى الله عليه وسلم، قال: أوتيت الكتاب وما يعدله؛ يوشك شبعان على أريكته يقول بيننا وبينكم هذا الكتاب فما كان فيه من حلال أحللناه، وما كان فيه من حرام حرّمناه؛ ألا وإنه ليس كذلك: لا يحلّ ذو ناب من السّباع، ولا الحمار الأهلي، ولا اللقطة من المعاهد إلا أن يستغني عنها، وأيما رجل ضاف قوما ولم يقروه فعليهم أن يغصبهم بمثل قراه

Aḥmad bin al-Mu'la ad-Dimishqi and al-Ḥussain bin Isḥāq at-Tartusi narrated to us, they said Hishām bin 'Ammār narrated

[33] *Sunan* Abu Dāwud Vol. 4 sec. 200, no. 4,604

[34] *Musnad* Aḥmad Vol. 4 sec. 131, no. 17,213

[35] *Musnad ash-Shāmiayn* Vol. 2 sec. 137, no. 1,061

to us Yaḥya bin Ḥamza narrated to us Muḥammad bin al-Waleed az-Zubaydi narrated to me from Marwān bin Ru'ba from Abdar-Raḥman bin Abi 'Auf al-Jarshi from al-Miqdām bin Mahdi Karib that the Messenger of Allah (peace be upon him) said: *I have been given the book and its justice;* (a man) *will recline on his couch saying what is found between this book to be lawful, treat it as lawful and what is prohibited, treat as prohibited. It should not be like this. The fanged beast of prey is not lawful, nor the domestic asses, nor the find from the property of a man with whom a treaty has been concluded, except that he did not need it. If anyone is a guest of people who provide no hospitality for him, he is entitled to take from them the equivalent of the hospitality due to him.*

Again, quite a few notable Imām's cited this in their respective collections of *ḥadith*.[36] In the *Mustadrak*, al-Ḥākim cites the next narration:

فأخبرناه أبو الحسن أحمد بن محمد بن عبدوس حدثنا عثمان بن سعيد الدارمي حدثنا عبد الله بن صالح أن معاوية بن صالح أخبره وأخبرنا أحمد بن جعفر القطيعي حدثنا عبد الله بن أحمد بن حنبل حدثني أبي حدثنا عبد الرحمن وهو بن مهدي حدثنا معاوية بن صالح حدثني الحسن بن جابر أنه سمع المقدام بن معد يكرب الكندي صاحب النبي، صلى الله عليه وسلم، يقول: حرَّم النبي، صلى الله عليه وعلى آله وسلم، أشياء يوم خيبر، منها الحمار الأهلي، وغيره، فقال رسول الله، صلى الله عليه وعلى آله وسلم: «يوشك أن يقعد الرجل منكم على أريكته يحدِّث بحديثي فيقول: (بيني وبينكم كتاب الله: فما وجدنا فيه حلالاً استحللناه، وما وجدنا فيه حراماً حرّمناه. وإن ما حرّم رسول الله، صلى الله عليه وعلى آله وسلم، كما حرّم الله!

Al-Ḥasan Aḥmad bin Muḥammad bin 'Abdous reported to us

[36] Amongst them are the following references: *Ṣaḥīḥ* Ibn Ḥibbān [Vol. 1 sec. 190 & 212, no. 12], *Sunan* Abu Dāwud [Vol. 3 sec. 355, no. 3,804], *Sharḥ Ma'āni al-Athār* of Imām aṭ-Ṭaḥāwi [Vol. 1 sec. 209, no. 0], *Sunan al-Kubra* Bayhaqy [Vol. 9 sec. 332, no. 1,925], *Sunan* Dāraquṭni [Vol. 4 sec. 287, no. 59], and *Mu'jam al-Kabir* of aṭ-Ṭabarāni [Vol. 20 sec. 282, no. 667].

> Uthmān bin Sa'eed ad-Dārimi narrated to us Abdullah ibn Ṣāliḥ narrated to us that Mu'āwiya bin Ṣāliḥ ireported to him and Aḥmad bin Ja'far al-Qaṭee'ee reported to us Abdullah bin Aḥmad bin Ḥanbal narrated to us (he said) my father narrated to me Abdar-Raḥman (and he is) bin Mahdi narrated to us Mu'āwiya bin Ṣāliḥ narrated to us al-Ḥasan bin Jābir narrated to me that he heard al-Miqdām Ma'd Yakrib al-Kindi companion of the Prophet (peace be upon him) said: *Lo! Soon a ḥadith from me will be conveyed to a man, while he is reclining on his couch, and he says: Between us and you is Allah's Book. So whatever we find in it that is lawful, we consider lawful, and whatever we find in it that is unlawful, we consider it unlawful.* Indeed, whatever the Messenger of Allah (peace be upon him) made unlawful, it is the same as what Allah made unlawful!

The *ḥadith* is authentic upon the conditions as set out by Imām Muslim. Several collectors cited this tradition in their respective collections.[37] Al-Albāni regarded it as an authentic *ḥadith* and mentioned in its chain of transmission via 'Abbās at-Taraqufy, listing many good and authentic ways through which it was narrated. Further to this, Abu Hurayrah reported that the Prophet (peace be upon him) said:

> لا أعرفن أحداً منكم أتاه عني حديث، وهو متكئ في أريكته، فيقول: اتل عليّ به قرآناً!
>
> *No one from among you would be a true believer if he was informed with my ḥadith while he is reclining on his couch and says - bring me a proof from the Qur'ān!*

---

37 As found in: *Musnad* Aḥmad [Vol. 4 sec. 132, no. 17,233], *Sunan* Tirmidhi [Vol. 5 sec. 38, no. 2,664], *Sunan* Ibn Mājah [Vol. 1 sec. 6, no. 12], *Mu'jam al-Kabir* Ṭabarāni [Vol. 20 sec. 275, no. 649 / 650], *Sunan al-Kubra* Bayhaqy [Vol. 7 sec. 76, no. 13,220 and Vol. 9 sec. 332, no. 19,252], and *Muṣṣanaf* Abu Bakr ibn Abi Shayba [Vol. 1 sec. 153, no. 586].

The *ḥadith* is found in the *Musnad* of Imām Aḥmad with a chain of transmission that contains Imām al-Maghāzi Abu Ma'shar as-Sindi who is considered trustworthy (*ṣadooq*) but has weakness. Ibn Mājah also recorded it in his *Sunan* through other different and independent channels, but weaker overall as the transmission has some rejected additions. The origin of this *ḥadith* may be the one that was narrated by Abu Hurayrah - including this part above - which is a good *ḥadith* according to previous evidences, neglecting all other parts that were only recorded by weak channels.

There are also a number of *marāseel* which have reached us from Abu Dāwud that are worthy of consideration given the preceding discussion:

حدثنا عبد السلام بن عتيق الدمشقي حدثنا أبو مسهر حدثني خالد بن زيد حدثني هشام بن الغاز عن مكحول قال: قال رسول الله، صلى الله عليه وسلم: آتاني الله القرآن ومن الحكمة مثليه

Abdas-Salām bin 'Ateeq ad-Dimishqi narrated to us Abu Mushir narrated to us Khālid bin Zayd narrated to me Hishām bin al-Ghāz narrated to me from Makḥul he said the Prophet (peace be upon him) said: *Allah has inspired to me the Qur'ān and the Ḥikmah which is similar to it*.

حدثنا عدي بن حماد أخبرنا الليث عن ابن عجلان عن أبي سعيد مولى ابن كريز عن الحسن البصري أن النبي، صلى الله عليه وسلم، قال: من أحدث حدثا أو آوى محدثا فعليه لعنة الله والملائكة والناس أجمعين لا يقبل منه صرف ولا عدل؛ قالوا: وما الحدث يا رسول الله؟؛ قال: بدعة بغير سنّة؛ مثلة بغير حد؛ نهبة بغير حق

'Adi bin Ḥammād narrated to us al-Layth reported to us from ibn Ijlān from Abu Sa'eed *mawla* of ibn Kareez from al-Ḥasan al- Baṣri that the Prophet (peace be upon him) said: *Whoever makes innovation or gives protection to an innovator, there is*

> *upon him the curse of Allah the angels and all mankind; it is without justice and not accepted.* They said and what is this O Messenger of Allah? He said: *Innovation without Sunnah; examples without end taken unjustly without right.*

> حدثنا محمد بن المثنى حدثنا روح بن عبادة حدثنا الأوزاعي عن حسان بن عطية قال: (كان جبريل عليه السلام ينزل على رسول الله، صلى الله عليه وسلم، بالسنّة كما ينزل عليه بالقرآن ويعلّمه إياها كما يعلّمه القرآن

> Muḥammad bin al-Muthanna narrated to us Rawḥ bin 'Ubāda narrated to us al-Awzā'i narrated to us from Ḥassān bin 'Aṭiya he said: Jibreel (peace be upon him) sent-down upon the Prophet (peace upon him) the *Sunnah* just as he brought down the Qur'ān and he taught him in this just as he taught him the Qur'ān.

Ad-Dārimi also records this tradition from Muḥammad bin Kathir from al-Awzā'i. Thus in the round, we would say that the reports considered altogether can be considered as *tawātur* (continuously recurrent) as narrated by 'Irbāḍ bin Sāriya as-Salami, Abu Rāfi', al-Miqdām bin Mahdi Kareeb al-Kindi and Abu Hurayrah – may Allah be pleased with all of them. All these are demonstrative of the fact that the Prophet (peace be upon him) was given the Qur'ān and something other like it. As for some of the wording which comes via various *ḥadith* channels further exemplify the point, namely, that *'I have preached, commanded and prohibited various matters as numerous as that which is found in the Qur'ān, or more so'*; 'Indeed whatever the Messenger of Allah (peace be upon him) made unlawful, is the same as what Allah made unlawful'. All of these recurrently reported meanings overlap and match.

In the same context, there is a useful comment which has reached us from al-Ḥasan al-Baṣri:

بينما عمران بن حصين، رضي الله عنه، يحدث عن سنّة نبينا، صلى الله عليه وعلى آله وسلم، إذ قال رجل: يا أبا نجيد حدثنا بالقرآن، فقال له عمران: أنت وأصحابك يقرؤون القرآن، أكنت محدّثي عن الصلاة، وما فيها، وحدودها؟! أكنت محدثي عن الزكاة في الذّهب، والإبل، والبقر، وأصناف المال؟! ولكن قد شهدتُ وغبتَ! ثم قال: فرض علينا رسول الله، صلى الله عليه وعلى آله وسلم، في الزكاة كذا، وكذا! وقال الرجل: أحييتني أحياك الله!] وقال الحسن البصري، رحمه الله: [فما مات ذلك الرجل حتى صار من فقهاء المسلمين

While 'Imrān bin Ḥuṣṣain (may Allah be pleased with him) was talking about *ḥadith's* of the Prophet (peace be upon him), a man came and said: O Abu Najid! Talk to us by the Qur'ān (by mentioning evidences from the Qur'ān). 'Imrān replied - You and your companions are reciting the Qur'ān; can you tell me about prayer, what is included and its limits? Can you tell me about *Zakāt* that is imposed in gold, camels, cows and other types of wealth? You were reciting and did not know. Then he said - The Messenger of Allah (peace be upon him) imposed so and so in *Zakāt*. The man said, You have revived me, may Allah revive you. Al-Ḥasan al-Baṣri - This man died while he was among jurists of Muslims.

The narrative report (*athar*) is *Ṣaḥīḥ* and al-Ḥākim graded it as such in terms of its *isnād* in his *Mustadrak*;[38] Ṭabarāni also cites this in his *Mu'jam al-Kabir*.[39] Imām Abu Dāwud reports a similar tradition in his *Sunan* from an alternate channel, which contains an amusing anecdote:

حدثنا محمد بن بشار حدثني محمد بن عبد الله الأنصاري حدثنا صرد بن أبي المنازل قال: سمعت حبيبا المالكي قال: قال رجل لعمران بن حصين: يا أبا نجيد إنكم لتحدّثوننا بأحاديث ما نجد لها أصلا في القرآن! فغضب عمران وقال للرجل: أوجدتم في كل أربعين درهما درهم ومن كل كذا وكذا شاة شاة ومن كل كذا وكذا بعيرا كذا وكذا؟ أوجدتم هذا في القرآن؟ قال: لا، قال: فعن

[38] *Mustadrak* Vol. 1 sec. 192, no. 372
[39] *Mu'jam al-Kabir* Vol. 18 sec. 166, no. 369

من أخذتم هذا؟ أخذتموه عنا وأخذناه عن نبي الله، صلى الله عليه وسلم، وذكر أشياء نحو هذا

Muḥammad ibn Bashār narrated to us Muḥammad bin Abdullah al-Anṣāri narrated to me Ṣurad bin Abul-Munāzil he said I heard Ḥabib al-Māliki say: A man said to 'Imrān bin Ḥuṣṣain: Abu Najid you narrate to us traditions whose basis we do not find in the Qur'ān. Thereupon, 'Imrān got angry and said to the man: Do you find in the Qur'ān that one *dirham* is due on forty *dirhams* (as *Zakāt*), and one goat is due on such-and-such number of goats, and one camel will be due on such-and-such number of camels? He replied: No. He said: From whom did you take it? You took it from us, from the Messenger of Allah (peace be upon him). He mentioned many similar things.

Imām aṭ-Ṭabarāni has the next narration in his *Mu'jam al-Kabir* with good wording:

حدثنا يحيى بن زكريا الساجي وأحمد بن زهير التستري قالا: حدثنا محمد بن بشار حدثنا محمد بن عبد الله الأنصاري حدثنا صرد بن أبي المبارك قال: سمعت حبيب بن أبي فضالة المكي قال: لمّا بني هذا المسجد، مسجد الجامع، كان عمران بن حصين جالساً فذكروا عنده الشفاعة فقال رجل من القوم: يا أبا نجيد: إنكم لتحدّثونا بأحاديث ما نجد لها أصلا في القرآن! ؛ فغضب عمران بن حصين وقال للرجل: قرأت القرآن؟ قال: نعم، قال: وجدت فيه صلاة المغرب ثلاثا وصلاة العشاء أربعا وصلاة الغداة ركعتين والأولى أربعا والعصر أربعا؟ قال: لا، قال: فعمّن أخذتم هذا الشأن؟ ألستم أخذتموه عنا وأخذناه عن رسول الله، صلى الله عليه وسلم؟ أوجدتم في كل أربعين درهما درهم وفي كل كذا وكذا شاة وفي كل كذا وكذا بعير كذا أوجدتم في القرآن؟ قال: لا، قال: فعمّن أخذتم هذا؟ أخذناه عن رسول الله، صلى الله عليه وسلم، وأخذتموه عنا؟ قال: فهل وجدتم في القرآن وليطوفوا بالبيت العتيق؟ وجدتم هذا: طوفوا سبعا واركعوا ركعتين خلف المقام؟ أوجدتم هذا في القرآن عمن أخذتموه؟ ألستم أخذتموه عنا وأخذناه عن نبي الله، صلى الله عليه وسلم؟ أوجدتم في القرآن: لا جلب ولا جنب ولا شغار

> في الإسلام؟ قال: لا، قال: إني سمعت رسول الله، صلى الله عليه وسلم، يقول: (لا جلب ولا جنب ولا شغار في الإسلام)، أسمعتم الله يقول لأقوام في كتابه: ما سلككم في سقر، قالوا لم نك من المصلين ولم نك نطعم المسكين حتى بلغ فما تنفعهم شفاعة الشافعين

> Yaḥya bin Zakariyā as-Sāji and Aḥmad bin Zuhayr at-Tastari narrated to us, they said Muḥammad bin Bashār narrated to us Muḥammad bin Abdullah al-Anṣāri narrated to us Ṣurad bin Abi Mubārak narrated to us, he said I heard Ḥabib bin Abi Faḍāla al-Makki he said: When this *masjid*, this congregational *masjid* was built ‘Imrān bin Ḥuṣṣain was sitting and I brought up the topic of intercession and a man from the people said: Oh Abu Najeed! <u>You narrate statements for which we find no basis in the Qur’ān!</u> ‘Imrān bin Ḥuṣṣain became angry and said to the man: Have you read the Qur'ān? Did you find in that the *Maghrib* prayer was three-*rak'ahs* and that the *Esha* prayer was four? To which he responded: No. So how did you get to know about this matter? Didn't you take it from us and we took it from the Messenger of Allah peace and blessings of Allah be upon him? (regarding the matter of *zakāt*) Did you find in the Qur'ān that for every four silver coins, one should be given in charity, and like thereof regarding cattle and such? Didn't you take it from us and we took it from the Messenger of Allah? Did you find it in the Qur'ān, to which the man said: No. ‘Imrān said: I heard the Messenger of Allah, peace and blessings of Allah be upon him say: *There is no 'bringing', no 'avoidance' and no Shighār in Islam.* Did you not hear that Allah addressed the following in his book – (regarding the *mujrimeen*) *What has brought you into hell? They shall say – we were not of those who prayed; and we didn’t feed the poor*, until it was mentioned – *so the intercession of intercessors shall not avail them.*

I would submit that this is a good comment from Imām al-Ḥasan al-Baṣri. Can anyone imagine *fiqh* (jurisprudence) without the *Sunnah* of the Prophet (peace be upon him) and his guidance? Whoever has any doubt in that let him consider carefully the '*fiqh*' of the *Khawārij* who are renowned for their neglect of the *Sunnah*. As a sect, they are characterised by severe strictness and spiteful deviation. Whoever wants to know more about that should read opinions of the 'Qur'ānists' - those who hold the Qur'ān as the sole reference for Islam denying the authority of *Sunnah*. Such defiance of the Prophetic *Sunnah* has led them to support ridiculous sayings going above-and-beyond triviality, leaving reason and logic and ending in a *cul-de-sac* of thought. Sayings which emanate from this group seek to defy the revelation and are more akin to the ramblings of the insane.

In his *Mu'jam al-Kabir* Imām aṭ-Ṭabarāni cites the following tradition:

حدثنا أحمد بن النضر العسكري حدثنا أحمد بن النعمان الفراء المصيصي حدثنا عبد الرحمن بن عثمان الحاطبي عن أبيه عن عبد الله بن محمد الجهني عن عبد الله بن الحسن بن علي عن أبيه قال: صعد رسول الله، صلى الله عليه وسلم، المنبر يوم غزوة تبوك فحمد الله وأثنى عليه ثم قال: أيها الناس إني والله ما أمركم إلا بما أمركم الله به، ولا أنهاكم إلا عمّا نهاكم الله عنه، فأجملوا في الطلب! فوالذي نفس أبي القاسم بيده إن أحدكم ليطلبه رزقه كما يطلبه أجله فإن تعسر عليكم شيء منه فاطلبوه بطاعة الله عز وجل

Aḥmad bin an-Naḍr al-Askari narrated to us Aḥmad bin an-Nu'mān al-Firā'a al-Maṣeeṣee narrated to us Abdar-Raḥman bin 'Uthmān al-Ḥāṭabi narrated to us from his father from Abdullah bin Muḥammad al-Juhany from Abdullah bin al-Ḥasan bin Ali from his father he said: The Prophet (peace be upon him) ascended on the pulpit on the day of the *Ghazwa* of Tabuk. He glorified Allah, praising him and then said: *O people! Verily by Allah whatever I commanded you to is that commanded by Allah. And what I have prohibited you is by the prohibition from Allah. Behave correctly in your endeavours! By him whose hand lies the soul of Abul' Qāsim! If one of you seeks his rizq like he seeks his ajl [lifespan] and it then becomes hard upon him then let him seek it via obedience to*

Allah, Lord of Majesty and Honour with obedience to Allah the exalted.

In the *Sunan al-Kubra* of Bayhaqy, he collected the following:

أخبرنا أبو زكريا بن أبي إسحاق وأبو بكر بن الحسن قالا: حدثنا أبو العباس محمد بن يعقوب أنبأ الربيع بن سليمان أنبأ الشافعي أنبأ عبد الوهاب الثقفي قال: سمعت يحيى بن سعيد يقول حدثني بن أبي مليكة أن عبيد بن عمير الليثي حدثه أن رسول الله، صلى الله عليه وسلم، أمر أبا بكر رضي الله عنه أن يصلي بالناس فذكر الحديث إلى أن قال فمكث رسول الله، صلى الله عليه وسلم، مكانه وجلس إلى جنب الحجر يحذر الفتن وقال: إني والله لا يمسك الناس علي بشيء: إلا أني لا أُحلّ إلا ما أحلّ الله في كتابه ولا أُحرّم إلا ما حرّم الله في كتابه

Abu Zakariyā bin Abi Isḥāq and Abu Bakr bin al-Ḥasan reported to us, they said Abul''Abbās Muḥammad bin Ya'qub narrated to us ar-Rabih' bin Sulaymān reported (from) ash-Shāfi'i reported (from) Abdal-Wahhāb ath-Thaqafi he said: I heard Yaḥya bin Sa'eed say – Ibn Abi Maleeka narrated to me that Ubaid bin Umayr al-Laythi narrated to him that the Prophet (peace be upon him) commanded Abu Bakr (may Allah be pleased with him) to pray with the people, mentioning the *ḥadith* except that he said he remained with Allah's messenger (peace be upon him) and sat in the place beside his apartment where he warned of tribulation and said: *Verily by Allah I have not withheld anything from the people; I have made lawful save what is made lawful in the book of Allah and prohibited only what is prohibited in the book of Allah.*

Also what has been reported in *aṭ-Ṭabaqāt al-Kubra* of Muḥammad ibn Sa'd, he records:

أخبرنا محمد بن عمر حدثني سليمان بن بلال وعاصم بن عمر عن يحيى بن

سعيد عن بن أبي مليكة عن عبيد بن عمير قال: قال رسول الله، صلى الله عليه وسلم، في مرضه الذي توفي فيه: «أيها الناس والله لا تمسكون علي بشيء: إني لا أُحلّ إلا ما أحلّ الله، ولا أحرّم إلا ما حرّم الله. يا فاطمة بنت رسول الله، يا صفية عمة رسول الله: اعملا لما عند الله: إني لا أغني عنكما من الله شيئا

Muḥammad ibn Umar reported to us Sulaymān bin Bilāl and 'Aāṣim bin Umar narrated to me from Yaḥya bin Sa'eed from Ibn Abi Maleeka from Ubaid bin Umayr he said the Messenger of Allah (peace be upon him) said in his illness which he died from: *O people, by Allah I haven't kept anything from you. Verily I haven't made lawful except what Allah made lawful and I haven't prohibited except what Allah prohibited. O Fāṭima daughter of the Prophet, O Ṣafiya aunt of the Prophet. I undertake that set forth by Allah, but verily I cannot avail you at all against Allah.*

Also found in *aṭ-Ṭabaqāt al-Kubra* is the following narration:

أخبرنا محمد بن عمر حدثني سليمان بن بلال عن يحيى بن سعيد عن القاسم بن محمّد عن عائشة أن رسول الله، صلى الله عليه وسلم، قال في مرضه الذي توفي فيه: أيها الناس لا تعلّقوا علي بواحدة: ما أحللت إلا ما أحلّ الله، وما حرّمت إلا ما حرّم الله

Muḥammad bin Umar reported to us Sulaymān bin Bilāl narrated to me from Yaḥya bin Sa'eed from al-Qāsim bin Muḥammad from Aisha that the Messenger of Allah (peace be upon him) said during his illness which he died from: *O people! Do not cling to me in isolation, I have not permitted for you except that which Allah permitted, and I have not forbidden anything for you except that which Allah has prohibited.*

Next in the *Mustadrak a'la Ṣaḥīḥayn* of Al-Ḥākim records the following:

أَخْبَرَنَا أَبُو بَكْرِ بْنُ إِسْحَاقَ، أَنْبَأَ أَحْمَدُ بْنُ إِبْرَاهِيمَ بْنِ مِلْحَانَ، حَدَّثَنَا ابْنُ أَبِي بُكَيْرٍ، حَدَّثَنِي اللَّيْثُ بْنُ سَعْدٍ، عَنْ خَالِدِ بْنِ يَزِيدَ، عَنْ سَعِيدِ بْنِ أَبِي هِلَالٍ، عَنْ سَعِيدِ بْنِ أَبِي أُمَيَّةَ الثَّقَفِيِّ، عَنْ يُونُسَ بْنِ بُكَيْرٍ، عَنِ ابْنِ مَسْعُودٍ، أَنَّ رَسُولَ اللَّهِ صَلَّى اللهُ عَلَيْهِ وَسَلَّمَ قَالَ: لَيْسَ مِنْ عَمَلٍ يُقَرِّبُ إِلَى الْجَنَّةِ، إِلَّا قَدْ أَمَرْتُكُمْ بِهِ، وَلَا عَمَلٌ يُقَرِّبُ إِلَى النَّارِ، إِلَّا قَدْ نَهَيْتُكُمْ عَنْهُ؛ لَا يَسْتَبْطِئَنَّ أَحَدٌ مِنْكُمْ رِزْقَهُ أَنَّ جِبْرِيلَ عَلَيْهِ السَّلَامُ أَلْقَى فِي رُوعِيَ أَنَّ أَحَدًا مِنْكُمْ لَنْ يَخْرُجَ مِنَ الدُّنْيَا حَتَّى يَسْتَكْمِلَ رِزْقَهُ، فَاتَّقُوا اللَّهَ أَيُّهَا النَّاسُ، وَأَجْمِلُوا فِي الطَّلَبِ، فَإِنِ اسْتَبْطَأَ أَحَدٌ مِنْكُمْ رِزْقَهُ، فَلَا يَطْلُبْهُ بِمَعْصِيَةِ اللَّهِ، فَإِنَّ اللَّهَ لَا يُنَالُ فَضْلُهُ بِمَعْصِيَةِ

Abu Bakr bin Isḥāq reported to us Aḥmad bin Ibrāhim bin Milḥān reports: Ibn Abi Bukeer narrated to us al-Layth bin Sa'd narrated to me from Khālid bin Yazeed from Sa'eed bin Abi Hilāl from Sa'eed bin Abi Amiya ath-Thaqafi from Yunus bin Bukeer from Ibn Mas'ud that the Prophet (peace be upon him) said: *There isn't* (any) *act that will take you closer to paradise, but that I have commanded you all with. And there is no act that will take you closer to the fire except that I have prohibited you from undertaking it. Do not be impatient to receive your livelihood because certainly Jibreel revealed to me: None of you shall go out of the life of this world before completing their (receipt of) livelihood. Fear Allah O you people, and be moderate in your requests. If any of you are looking forward to receive sustenance that does not demand by disobeying Allah for surely we do not get the favours of Allah by disobeying him.*

In the *Mușșanaf* of Imām Abu Bakr ibn Abi Shayba he cites the following tradition from another alternate channel:

حدثنا محمد بن بشر قال: حدثنا إسماعيل بن أبي خالد عن عبد الملك بن عمير قال: أُخبرت أن ابن مسعود قال: قال رسول الله، صلى الله عليه وسلم: أيها الناس إنه ليس من شيء يقرّبكم إلى الجنّة ويبعدكم من النار إلا قد أمرتكم به وليس شيء يقرّبكم من النار ويبعدكم من الجنّة إلا قد نهيتكم عنه؛ وإن الروح الأمين نفث في روعي أنه ليس من نفس تموت حتى تستوفي

رزقها، فاتقوا الله وأجملوا في الطلب ولا يحملكم استبطاء الرزق على أن تطلبوه بمعاصي الله، فانه لا ينال ما عنده إلا بطاعته

Muḥammad ibn Bishr narrated to us he said Ismā'il bin Abi Khālid narrated to us from Abdal-Malik bin Umayr he said I was informed that Ibn Mas'ud said that the Prophet (peace be upon him) said: *O people!* *Verily, there is not a thing which would bring you closer to paradise and protect you from the fire except that I have commanded you with and there is not a thing which would bring you closer to the fire and shield you from paradise that I have not forbidden to you. The trustworthy spirit has inspired me [with the thought] that no soul will ever die until it will receive its full provision. So fear Allah and be moderate in seeking your livelihood and do not let having to wait for sustenance carry you to seeking what is with Allah by acts of disobedience, for what is with Allah is obtained only through obedience.*

Imām al-Baghawi also reports similarly in his *Tafsir* as well as in *Sharḥ as-Sunnah*:

أَخْبَرَنَا أَبُو مَنْصُورٍ مُحَمَّدُ بْنُ عَبْدِ الْمَلِكِ الْمُظَفَّرِيُّ أَخْبَرَنَا أَبُو سَعِيدٍ أَحْمَدُ بْنُ مُحَمَّدِ بْنِ الْفَضْلِ الْفَقِيهُ أَخْبَرَنَا أَبُو نَصْرِ بْنُ حَمْدُوَيْهِ الْمُطَّوِّعِيُّ أَخْبَرَنَا أَبُو الْمُوَجِّهِ مُحَمَّدُ بْنُ عمرو أَخْبَرَنَا عَبْدَانُ عَنْ أَبِي حَمْزَةَ عَنْ إِسْمَاعِيلَ هُوَ ابْنُ أَبِي خَالِدٍ عَنْ رَجُلَيْنِ أَحَدُهُمَا زُبَيْدُ الْيَامِيُّ عَنْ عَبْدِ اللَّهِ بْنِ مَسْعُودٍ عَنِ النَّبِيِّ، صلى الله عليه وسلم، أَنَّهُ قَالَ: أَيُّهَا النَّاسُ لَيسَ مِنْ شَيْءٍ يُقَرِّبُكُمْ إِلَى الْجَنَّةِ وَيُبَاعِدُكُمْ مِنَ النَّارِ إِلَّا وَقَدْ أَمَرْتُكُمْ بِهِ، وَلَيْسَ شَيْءٌ يُقَرِّبُكُمْ إِلَى النَّارِ وَيُبَاعِدُكُمْ مِنَ الْجَنَّةِ إِلَّا وَقَدْ نَهَيْتُكُمْ عَنْهُ؛ وَإِنَّ الرُّوحَ الْأَمِينَ قَدْ نَفَثَ فِي رُوعِي أَنَّهُ لَيْسَ مِنْ نَفْسٍ تَمُوتُ حَتَّى تَسْتَوْفِيَ رِزْقَهَا، فَاتَّقُوا اللَّهَ وَأَجْمِلُوا فِي الطَّلَبِ وَلَا يَحْمِلَنَّكُمُ اسْتِبْطَاءُ الرِّزْقِ أَنْ تَطْلُبُوهُ بِمَعَاصِي اللَّهِ فَإِنَّهُ لَا يُدْرَكُ مَا عِنْدَ اللَّهِ إِلَّا بِطَاعَتِهِ. وَقَالَ هُشَيْمٌ عَنْ إِسْمَاعِيلَ عن زبيد اليامي عَمَّنْ أَخْبَرَهُ عَنِ ابْنِ مَسْعُودٍ

Abu Manṣur Muḥammad bin Abdal-Malik al-Mudthafari reported to us Abu Sa'eed Aḥmad bin Muḥammad bin al-Faḍl

> al-Faqih reported to us Abu Naṣr bin Ḥamduwi al-Muṭawi'ee reported to us Abul'Muwajjhi Muḥammad bin Amr reported to us 'Abdān reported to us from Abu Ḥamza from Ismā'il – who is ibn Abi Khālid from two men one of which (is) Zubayd al-Yāmi from Abdullah ibn Mas'ud from the Prophet (peace be upon him) that he said: *O people! There is not a thing which would bring you closer to paradise and protect you from the fire except that I have commanded you with and there is not a thing which would bring you closer to the fire and shield you from paradise that I have not forbidden to you. The trustworthy spirit has inspired me [with the thought] that no soul will ever die until it will receive its full provision. So fear Allah and do not let the provision coming to you slowly let you take it in a way that is disobedient to Allah, for verily Allah does not give what He has except through obedience to Him.* And Hushaym said: from Ismā'il from Zayd al-Yāmi who reported it from Ibn Mas'ud.

Finally, we have the following which is reported both in the *Musnad* of Imām Shāfi'i as well as in what is arguably one of his most famous works, *ar-Risāla*:

> أَخْبَرَنَا الشَّافِعِيُّ رَضِيَ اللَّهُ عَنْهُ، قَالَ: أَخْبَرَنَا عَبْدُ الْعَزِيزِ بْنُ مُحَمَّدٍ (هو: الدراوردي)، عَنْ عَمْرِو بْنِ أَبِي عَمْرٍو مَوْلَى الْمُطَّلِبِ بْنِ حَنْطَبٍ، عَنِ الْمُطَّلِبِ بْنِ حَنْطَبٍ، رَضِيَ اللَّهُ عَنْهُ: أَنَّ النَّبِيَّ، صلى الله عليه وسلم، قَالَ: مَا تَرَكْتُ شَيْئًا مِمَّا أَمَرَكُمُ اللَّهُ بِهِ إِلا وَقَدْ أَمَرْتُكُمْ بِهِ، وَلا تَرَكْتُ شَيْئًا مِمَّا نَهَاكُمُ اللَّهُ عَنْهُ إِلا وَقَدْ نَهَيْتُكُمْ عَنْهُ؛ وَإِنَّ الرُّوحَ الأَمِينَ قَدْ نَفَثَ فِي رُوعِي أَنَّهُ لَيْسَ تَمُوتُ نَفْسٌ حَتَّى تَسْتَوْفِيَ رِزْقَهَا فَأَجْمِلُوا فِي الطَّلَبِ
>
> Ash-Shāfi'i may Allah be pleased with him reported to us he said Abdal-Aziz bin Muḥammad (he is: ad-Darārwardi) reported to us from Amr bin Abi Amr *mawla* al-Muṭṭalib bin Ḥanṭab from al-Muṭṭalib bin Ḥanṭab may Allah be pleased with him that the Prophet (peace be upon him) said: *I have left nothing concerning which Allah has given you an order without*

giving you that order; nor have I neglected anything concerning which He has given you a prohibition without giving you that prohibition. The trustworthy spirit has inspired me [with the thought] that no soul will ever die until it will receive its full provision. Be therefore moderate in your request.

The *isnād* that Imām Shāfi'i provides us with is *mursal.* Yet when taken together with the other connected traditions cited above, it can also be considered as authentic; it does not substantively conflict with the connected *aḥādith* already cited. In the round, all of these traditions provide further clarification that all that the Prophet (peace be upon him) only commanded and prohibited that which was emanating from Allah and no other. Within this it is evident that he conveyed the message in its entirety, which is what Allah required. What remains is the good from the *wājib* or *mustaḥab* that he ordered or commanded and the iniquity from the *ḥarām* that he prohibited us from.

In his *Sunan* Imām Ibn Mājah recorded what has become quite a well-known *ḥadith* which is reported on the authority of 'Irbāḍ bin Sāriya:

حَدَّثَنَا عَبْدُ اللَّهِ بْنُ أَحْمَدَ بْنِ بَشِيرِ بْنِ ذَكْوَانَ الدِّمَشْقِيُّ حَدَّثَنَا الْوَلِيدُ بْنُ مُسْلِمٍ قَالَ: حَدَّثَنَا عَبْدُ اللَّهِ بْنُ الْعَلَاءِ (يَعْنِي ابْنَ زَبْرٍ) قَالَ: حَدَّثَنِي يَحْيَى بْنُ أَبِي الْمُطَاعِ، قَالَ: سَمِعْتُ الْعِرْبَاضَ بْنَ سَارِيَةَ، يَقُولُ: قَامَ فِينَا رَسُولُ اللَّهِ صَلَّى اللهُ عَلَيْهِ وَسَلَّمَ ذَاتَ يَوْمٍ، فَوَعَظَنَا مَوْعِظَةً بَلِيغَةً، وَجِلَتْ مِنْهَا الْقُلُوبُ، وَذَرَفَتْ مِنْهَا الْعُيُونُ، فَقِيلَ يَا رَسُولَ اللَّهِ: وَعَظْتَنَا مَوْعِظَةَ مُوَدِّعٍ، فَاعْهَدْ إِلَيْنَا بِعَهْدٍ، فَقَالَ: عَلَيْكُمْ بِتَقْوَى اللَّهِ، وَالسَّمْعِ وَالطَّاعَةِ، وَإِنْ عَبْدًا حَبَشِيًّا، وَسَتَرَوْنَ مِنْ بَعْدِي اخْتِلَافًا شَدِيدًا، فَعَلَيْكُمْ بِسُنَّتِي، وَسُنَّةِ الْخُلَفَاءِ الرَّاشِدِينَ الْمَهْدِيِّينَ، عَضُّوا عَلَيْهَا بِالنَّوَاجِذِ، وَإِيَّاكُمْ وَالْأُمُورَ الْمُحْدَثَاتِ، فَإِنَّ كُلَّ بِدْعَةٍ ضَلَالَةٌ

Abdullah ibn Aḥmad ibn Basheer ibn Dhakwān ad-Dimishqi narrated to us al-Waleed bin Muslim narrated to us he said

> Abdullah bin al-'Ala (that is to say ibn Zabr) narrated to us he said Yaḥya bin Abul'Muṭā' he said I heard 'Irbāḍ bin Sāriya say: One day, the Messenger of Allah stood up among us and delivered a deeply moving speech to us that melted our hearts and caused our eyes to overflow with tears. It was said to him: O Messenger of Allah, you have delivered a speech of farewell, so enjoin something upon us. He said: *I urge you to fear Allah, and to listen and obey, even if (your leader) is an Abyssinian slave. After I am gone, you will see great conflict. I urge you to adhere to my Sunnah and the path of the Rightly-Guided Caliphs and cling stubbornly to it. And beware of newly-invented matters, for every innovation is misguidance.*

Elsewhere the narration appears in quite a number of *ḥadith* collections, although it is noticeably absent from the respective *Ṣaḥīḥ* collections of Imām Bukhāri and Muslim.[40] After citing this in the *Mustadrak,* al-Ḥākim writes:

> Indeed, the survey relating to whether this *ḥadith* is authentic has been investigated. As for what has been written by the Imām of the scholars of *ḥadith* - Shu'ba, in the *ḥadith* of Abdullah ibn 'Aṭā from 'Uqba bin 'Aāmir as addressed in Baṣra, Kufa, Medina and Mecca. Then he returned the *ḥadith* to Shahr ibn Ḥawshab so he left it. Then Shu'ba said because this is like the authentic (report) unto me from the Prophet (peace be upon him). It was dearer to me than my parents and all people together. Indeed, this is an authentic *ḥadith,* praise be to Allah

[40] The listed references are: *Sunan* Tirmidhi [Vol. 5 sec. 45, no. 2,676] of which he said it was *ḥasan Ṣaḥīḥ*, *Musnad* Aḥmad [Vol. 4 sec. 126, no. 17,182; 17,184 and Vol. 4 sec. 127, no. 17,186 / 17,187], *Mustadrak* al-Ḥākim [Vol. 1 sec. 175, no. 329; 331 and Vol. 1 sec. 177, no. 333], *Sunan* ad-Dārimi [Vol. 1 sec. 58, no. 95], *Sunan al-Kubra* Bayhaqy [Vol. 10 sec. 114, no. 20,125], *Mu'jam al-Kabir* aṭ-Ṭabarāni [Vol. 18 sec. 246, no. 617 / 618; vol. 18 sec. 248, no. 622 / 644 and vol. 18 sec. 257, no. 642], *Musnad Shāmiayn* aṭ-Ṭabarāni [Vol. 1 sec. 254, no. 437; vol. 1 sec. 402, no. 697; Vol. 1 sec. 446, no. 786; vol. 2 sec. 198, no. 1,180 and vol. 2 sec. 299, no. 1,379], and *Mu'jam al-Awsaṭ* aṭ-Ṭabarāni [Vol. 1 sec. 28, no. 66].

and peace and blessings upon Muḥammad and all his companions.

Yes indeed - all praise belongs to Allah and blessings are due upon our Prophet Muḥammad his family and noble companions. Without doubt the command to uphold and cling unwaveringly to his *Sunnah* is established. There is the stern warning upon introducing innovations without legal precedent into this *Deen*, because that stems from the path of misguidance, landing the innovator into the fire of hell. His *Sunnah* (peace be upon him) is his reported speech, actions and approvals all of which constitute legal proof and not other than that.

As for what is mentioned concerning the *Sunnah* of the rightly guided *Khulafā*, it refers to the *general* guidance in everything which they established and built upon according to the Qur'ān and the Prophetic *Sunnah*; their overriding commitment to the law of Allah in every matter, be that concerning war and peace; whether in hardship or ease, or whether in wealth or poverty. They were equitable and just as Islam demands; distributing wealth according to its due right; upholding the *ḥudud* of Allah both with immediacy and over the duration of their tenure in office, whether towards friend or foe.

Given this, several important points must be noted. Firstly, that of the complete submission that Islam requires of all its adherents and the recognition of the absolute sovereignty of the *Sharī'ah*; sovereignty does not reside within man or the institutions of men. Secondly, authority was legitimated via the mechanism of the *bay'ah* (pledge of allegiance) from the Muslims by way of their own free choice and to their satisfaction. It was not by way of *coup d'état*, usurpation, nor for that matter by way of 'divine right', such as is claimed by a hereditary monarchy or even a dictatorship. Thirdly, there was an explicit recognition that the authority rests with the *Ummah*. The Islamic leadership undertook the management of public affairs only by way of being the representative of the *Ummah*.

Authority entailed both responsibility and obligation. Indeed it wasn't viewed flippantly, but rather as being a weighty burden which by the help and grace of Allah they would endure. They did not exercise political authority in the same manner as individuals exercise authority over a personal possession, believing that they alone must reap its benefits, treating those subject to their authority as mere chattel. Neither did they cling to power through all manner of Machiavellian machinations together with the most unspeakable levels of violence. Any impartial observer would readily note the stark contrast between the ruling of the rightly guided *Khulafā* and that of the contemporary rulers found within the lands of Islam - the hereditary monarchs and dictators. Therefore, this is the underlying meaning of adhering to the *Sunnah* of the rightly guided *Khulafā*. It is not the *Sunnah* in the same sense as that of the *Sunnah* of the Prophet (peace be upon him), as denoted by his reported speech, actions and approvals all of which constitute legal proof. The reason being, is that the Prophet (peace be upon him) is infallible (*ma'ṣoom*) whereas the rightly guided *Khulafā* were not. They were human and made mistakes, were liable to forget; they were not immune from sin and they differed in various legal judgements the sum of which cannot all be correct.

As has been reported from some of the *Ṣaḥābah* as well as the major successors (*kibār at-Tā'bieen*) which will now be considered, they employed the term – *the revealed/sent-down book of Allah* (*Kitāb Allah al-Munazil*). We know categorically with certainty that this term was not employed in relation to the specific text of the Qur'ān, nor did it specifically relate to the previously revealed books. Rather, what was being referred to, was the Prophetic *Sunnah*. Imām Abu Bakr ibn Abi Shayba recorded the following narration in his *Muṣṣanaf* with an authentic *isnād*:

حدثنا عبيد الله عن شيبان عن الأعمش عن سالم بن أبي الجعد عن عبد الله بن عمرو قال: (إنا لنجد في كتاب الله المنزّل صنفين في النار: قوم يكونون في آخر الزمان معهم سياط كأنها أذناب البقر يضربون بها الناس على غير

جرم: لا يدخلون بطونهم إلا خبيثا؛ ونساء كاسيات عاريات مائلات مميلات لا يدخلن الجنة ولا يجدن ريحها

'Ubaidallah narrated to us from Shaybān from al-'Amash from Sālim bin Abi Ja'd from Abdullah bin 'Amr he said: Indeed, we find in the revealed/sent-down book of Allah two types (of people) in the fire: People who will appear towards the end of time who are beating people with whips that are like the tails of the cow; nothing enters their stomachs except that which is *khabeeth*, and women that are dressed but naked. They will not enter *jannah* nor even experience its aroma.

Additionally, this has also been reported by Imām Muslim in his *Ṣaḥīḥ* in two places but with a connected channel to the Messenger of Allah (peace be upon him):

حدثني زهير بن حرب حدثنا جرير عن سهيل عن أبيه عن أبي هريرة قال: قال رسول الله، صلى الله عليه وسلم: صنفان من أهل النار لم أرهما قوم معهم سياط كأذناب البقر يضربون بها الناس، ونساء كاسيات عاريات مميلات مائلات رؤوسهن كأسنمة البخت المائلة لا يدخلن الجنة ولا يجدن ريحها، وإن ريحها ليوجد من مسيرة كذا وكذا

Zuhayr bin Ḥarb narrated to me Jarir narrated to us from Suhayl from his father from Abu Hurayrah he said the Messenger of Allah (peace be upon him) said: *Two are the types of the denizens of Hell whom I did not see: people having whips like the tails of the ox with them and they would be beating people, and the women who would be dressed but appear to be naked, who would be inclined (to evil) and make their husbands incline towards it. Their heads would be like the humps of the bukht camel inclined to one side. They will not enter Paradise and they would not smell its odour whereas its odour would be smelt from such and such distance.*

In *Mu'jam al-Awsaṭ* aṭ-Ṭabarāni cites the following:

حدثنا محمد بن يعقوب بن سورة البغدادي حدثنا أبو الوليد الطيالسي (ح) وحدثنا أحمد بن علي الأبار البغدادي حدثنا علي بن عثمان اللاحقي قالا: حدثنا عبد الله بن بجير القيسي عن سيار الشامي عن أبي أمامة أن رسول الله، صلى الله عليه وسلم، قال: يخرج من هذه الأمة قوم معهم سياط كأنها أذناب البقر يغدون في سخط الله ويروحون في غضبه

Muḥammad bin Ya'qub bin Soorah al-Baghdādi Abul' Waleed aṭ-Ṭayālisi narrated to us (*ḥawala*) Aḥmad bin Ali al-Abār al-Baghdādi narrated to us Ali bin Uthmān al-Lāḥaqi narrated to us, they said Abdullah bin Jubayr al-Qaysi narrated to us from Sayyār ash-Shāmi from Abu Umāma that the Prophet (peace be upon him) said: *There will come out of this Ummah a people having with them whips like the tails of cows incurring the anger of Allah.*

Aṭ-Ṭabarāni also has a similar narration as found in his *Mu'jam al-Kabir*:

حدثنا محمد بن الحسين بن مكرم حدثنا إبراهيم بن المستمر العروقي حدثنا عمرو بن عاصم حدثنا حماد بن زيد المنقري حدثنا مخلد بن عقبة بن شرحبيل عن أبي شقرة قال: قال رسول الله، صلى الله عليه وسلم: إذا رأيتم اللاتي ألقين على رؤوسهن مثل أسنمة البقر فأعلموهن أنه لا يقبل لهن صلاة

Muḥammad bin al-Ḥussein bin Makram narrated to us Ibrāhim bin al-Mustamir al-'Arooqi narrated to us 'Amr bin 'Aāṣim narrated to us Ḥammād bin Zayd al-Munqari narrated to us Makhlad bin 'Uqba bin Shuraḥbil narrated to us from Abu Shaqra he said the Messenger of Allah (peace be upon him) said: *If you see those who are thrown on their heads like the humps of cows, you know that their prayers are not accepted.*

In addition to the above, there is also the very long narrative that has been reported in the *Mustadrak* of al-Ḥākim: [41]

> Aḥmad bin Uthmān al-Muqri and Bakr bin Muḥammad al-Marwazi narrated to us they said Abu Qilāba narrated to us Abduṣ-Ṣammad bin Abdal-Wārith narrated to us my father narrated to us Ḥussain bin Dhakwān the teacher narrated to us Ubaidallah bin Buraida al-Aslami narrated to us that Sulāyman bin Rabia' al-'Anzi narrated to him in *Ḥajj* during the reign of Mu'āwiya and with him al-Muntaṣir bin al-Ḥārith aḍ-Ḍabbi in a group of the readers from the people of Baṣra. (The narrator said): when they finished their rituals, they said: by Allah, we won't go back to Baṣra till we meet the men from the companions of Muḥammad peace be upon him, to inform us of numerous *ḥadith*, that we may relay these to our companions when we return to them. He said we kept asking till we were told that Abdullah ibn 'Amr ibn al-'Aāṣ (may Allah be pleased with him) had been accosted by the borders of Mecca. We then approached him and suddenly we found ourselves by a great caravan consisting of three hundred camels. And they were divided into two groups: with a hundred leaving and two hundred remaining. We then wondered for whom did this caravan belong to.
>
> We were told that it belonged to Abdullah ibn 'Amr. Then we asked whether it all belonged to him and we were told that he was the most humble person of that time. Then we were asked: Where are we from? Then we told them that we are from Iraq, then they responded to us saying you are a people of fault oh Iraqi people, as you asked about this caravan, there's one hundred of them that are used to carry brothers on its back, and the other two hundred camels are to be ridden by guests who come to visit him. Then the narrator said: we asked to be guided to where Abdullah ibn 'Amr was. The people told us

---

[41] Given the length of the narration, only the English text, together with the translated *isnād* is presented here.

that he was in the *masjid.* So we went to seek him out until we found him at the back of the *Ka'ba* sitting down. He was a short, bald man wearing two garments and a turban, without a shirt, holding his shoes in his left hand.

We said: Oh Abdullah! Indeed, you are a man from the companions of Muḥammad (peace be upon him) so narrate to us a useful report, that Allah the exalted may bless us with it after today. So he said to us: and who are you all? So we said to him, don't ask who we are, narrate to us and may Allah forgive you! But I (cannot) narrate anything to you all until you tell me who you are. We said: And we wished if you just told us about the *ḥadith* without asking about our identities. He answered: by Allah I'll never tell you until you tell me from which region you are from. The narrator said: and when we saw him about to leave us we said - we are from Iraq. He said: oh dear! You people of Iraq have been accused of lying and mockery. (The narrator said) when he mentioned this word of mockery we felt an extreme shame and we said: Heaven forbid that we should make fun of one like you, as you said that we are lying - oh Allah, the lies spread among us as well as it spread among others. But we just suspect in case when we listen to a *ḥadith* that we didn't listen to it from a trusted narrator previously, and when it comes to your word, no one of the Muslims is able to take the risk of mocking of you; by Allah you are (from among) the Muslims, a master, as we know. You are one of the early migrants and we have been told that you recited the Qur'an in the presence of Muḥammad (peace be upon him), and you were the most curious *Qurayshi* for his parents, and you had the pretiest eyes among the people.

Then eyes watered because of crying out of the fear of Allah, and that you read all books after the death of the Messenger of Allah (peace be upon him). According to us there is no one better than you regarding this aspect of knowledge and we knew that you are the only remnant Arab who seeks knowledge from the other regional scholars instead of seeking it from the scholars of your own region. So, tell us may Allah forgive you, then he said: I'm not going to talk to you until you give me your oath that you won't accuse me of lies or lie to me, and neither mock me. The narrator said we said: we accept all your conditions and oath. Then he said: Allah's covenant and covenants be upon you not to accuse me of lies or lie to me nor mock (anything) of what I'm going to tell you about. Then we said we will do so, then he said: verily Allah is Sponsor and agent upon you. We said: yes, then he stated: O Allah be witness upon them, thereupon he said: I swear by the lord of the sacred house, and the sacred precincts, and the sacred month, and your sacred sworn oath. Then we said: yes you did your best.

He then continued: That *Banu Qanturā bin Kar-Karri* who are snub-nosed, with small eyes and their faces look like the hammered shields as what's been mentioned in Allah's revealed book are going to devastate you, coming out across Khurasān and Sijistān, and they are undertaking great violence; wearing sandals that are made of hair, and they are hanging swords over their waists till they reach "*Ayalah*". He asked what is the area of "*Ayalah*" to the distance of Baṣra? Then we said four *farāsiq*, then he said they will tie up a horse in every single palm tree from the palm-trees of the Tigris. Then they'll send a warning to the people of Baṣra to leave it before coming to you, then a group of people will go forward to Jerusalem and some others will go forward to Medina and some others will go forward Mecca and some others will go to live with the Bedouins.

They will stay for a year in Baṣra, then they will send to the people of Kufa that they leave it before coming after you, then the people of Kufa will move in to many places, some of them will go forward to Jerusalem, and some others to Medina, and some others to Mecca and some others are going to live with the Bedouins. Then they will kill and capture anyone among those who perform prayers and they will bring him to trial to judge in his blood in the way they desire. The narrator said: then we left him after feeling upset of what he told us about.

After we left and by a near distance of him, Al-Muntaṣir bin al-Ḥārith aḍ-Ḍabbi went back to him and said: O Abdullah ibn ‘Amr! Your speech has terrified us, and we don't know whom will be going to witness these horrible events. Tell us, is there any sign regarding this? He replied: Don’t hesitate, yes there's a mark for it. Muntaṣir said: So what is it? Abdullah said: The mark is a sign. Muntaṣir asked: What is this mark? Abdullah said: It is the government of boys. When (immature) boys become kings, so if you attend one of these boy’s coronation, then recognise that it’s the time for this matter to take place. And, for your information, it has already happened.

Muntaṣir left him for a short distance but went back for Abdullah to ask him more about the coming event, then we asked Muntaṣir (the narrator said): why does he keep bothering that old man of the Prophet (peace be upon him)? He responded by saying: I swear, I won’t stop doing that till he explains everything to me, and when he went back to Abdullah he explained everything he needed to understand.

This also is reported by Imām Abu Bakr ibn Abi Shayba in his *Muṣṣanaf* with an authentic *isnād*:

حَدَّثَنَا مُحَمَّدُ بْنُ فُضَيْلٍ، عَنْ حُصَيْنٍ، عَنْ حَسَّانَ بْنِ أَبِي الْمُخَارِقِ، عَنْ أَبِي عَبْدِ اللَّهِ الْجَدَلِيِّ، قَالَ: أَتَيْتُ بَيْتَ الْمَقْدِسِ فَإِذَا عُبَادَةُ بْنُ الصَّامِتِ وَعَبْدُ اللَّهِ بْنُ عَمْرٍو وَكَعْبُ الْأَحْبَارِ يَتَحَدَّثُونَ فِي بَيْتِ الْمَقْدِسِ، قَالَ فَقَالَ عُبَادَةُ: إِذَا كَانَ يَوْمُ الْقِيَامَةِ جُمِعَ النَّاسُ فِي صَعِيدٍ وَاحِدٍ فَيَنْفُذُهُمُ الْبَصَرُ وَيَسْمَعُهُمُ الدَّاعِي وَيَقُولُ اللَّهُ: {هَذَا يَوْمُ الْفَصْلِ جَمَعْنَاكُمْ وَالْأَوَّلِينَ فَإِنْ كَانَ لَكُمْ كَيْدٌ فَكِيدُونِ} [المرسلات: 39] الْيَوْمَ لَا يَنْجُو مِنِّي جَبَّارٌ عَنِيدٌ وَلَا شَيْطَانٌ مَرِيدٌ، قَالَ: فَقَالَ عَبْدُ اللَّهِ بْنُ عَمْرٍو: (إِنَّا نَجِدُ فِي الْكِتَابِ): أَنَّهُ يَخْرُجُ يَوْمَئِذٍ عُنُقٌ مِنَ النَّارِ فَيَنْطَلِقُ مُعَنَّقًا حَتَّى إِذَا كَانَ بَيْنَ ظَهْرَانِي النَّاسِ قَالَ: يَا أَيُّهَا النَّاسُ، إِنِّي بُعِثْتُ إِلَى ثَلَاثَةٍ، أَنَا أَعْرَفُ بِهِمْ مِنَ الْوَالِدِ بِوَلَدِهِ وَمِنَ الْأَخِ بِأَخِيهِ، لَا يُغْنِيهِمْ مِنِّي وِرْدٌ وَلَا تُخْفِيهِمْ مِنِّي خَافِيَةٌ: الَّذِي جَعَلَ مَعَ اللَّهِ إِلَهًا آخَرَ، وَكُلُّ جَبَّارٍ عَنِيدٍ، وَكُلُّ شَيْطَانٍ مَرِيدٍ، قَالَ: فَيَنْطَوِي عَلَيْهِمْ فَيَقْذِفُهُمْ فِي النَّارِ قَبْلَ الْحِسَابِ بِأَرْبَعِينَ (قَالَ حُصَيْنٌ: إِمَّا أَرْبَعِينَ عَامًا أَوْ أَرْبَعِينَ يَوْمًا)، قَالَ: وَيَهْرَعُ قَوْمٌ

إِلَى الْجَنَّةِ فَتَقُولُ لَهُمُ الْمَلَائِكَةُ: قِفُوا لِلْحِسَابِ، قَالَ: فَيَقُولُونَ: وَاللهِ مَا كَانَتْ لَنَا أَمْوَالٌ وَمَا كُنَّا بِعُمَّالٍ، قَالَ: فَيَقُولُ اللهُ: صَدَقَ عِبَادِي أَنَا أَحَقُّ مَنْ أَوْفَى بِعَهْدِهِ، ادْخُلُوا الْجَنَّةَ، قَالَ: فَيَدْخُلُونَ الْجَنَّةَ قَبْلَ الْحِسَابِ بِأَرْبَعِينَ إِمَّا قَالَ عَامًا وَإِمَّا يَوْمًا

Muḥammad bin Fuḍeel narrated to us from Ḥuṣayn from Ḥassān bin Abul'Mukhāriq from Abu Abdullah al-Jandali he said: I came to *bayt-al-Maqdis* (Jerusalem) then 'Ubāda bin aṣ-Ṣāmit, Abdullah bin 'Amr and Ka'b al-Aḥbār conversed therein. 'Ubāda said if mankind is gathered on the day of judgement in a plateau and they won't able to see the most far point of their sight, and their voice will be heard from a distance hearing the call of the statement of Allah when he says: *This is the day of decision: We have gathered you and those of yore; so if you have a plan, plan against Me.*[42] He (also) said – this day there is no survival for the arrogant, stubborn and neither the sick devil before me. Abdullah bin 'Amr said: Indeed, we find in the book, that which comes from the neck of the fire starting quickly in the presence of people. It will say – Oh people! I have been appointed in relation to three; I know them completely, more so than a father has knowledge of his son, and the brother of his own brother. None can prevent or hide them from me, and they are as follows: whoever made another god with Allah and every powerful stubborn one and every serpent supporter of *Shayṭān*. He said: this neck will hold them and throw them into the hellfire before the day of judgment by forty (Ḥuṣayn said: either for forty days or forty years). A group of people will hurry on to paradise then the angels will say to them to go and stand for judgment. Then those people will say: oh Allah we had no money and we weren't of wealth. Allah will say: My slaves said the truth and I'm the worthiest one to execute my promise, go to paradise. Abdullah said: they will enter into paradise before the account by way of forty years or days.

[42] *Qur'ān* 77: 39

It is also to be found in *Dar al-Manshoor* in the *Tafsir bil'Māthur*, as reported by Sa'eed bin Manṣur, Ibn Abi Shayba and Ibn al-Mundthir from Abu Abdullah al-Jadli. It is also found in the *Tafsir* of Ibn Abi Ḥātim with the channel – Ali bin al-Mundthir aṭ-Ṭareefi al-Awdi narrated to us Muḥammad bin Fuḍeel narrated to us Ḥuṣayn narrated to us about it except that he said, 'in the fire before accounting by (a period) of forty years.'

The phrase used in the narrations – '*neck from the fire*' (*unq min an-nār*) is undoubtedly not from the text of the Qur'ān nor for that matter amongst any other books of revelation which were prior to that in the hands of the people. This phrase however appears in the noble Prophetic *ḥadith* only. Similar is reported in the *Musnad* of Imām Aḥmad, albeit through a channel that contains 'Aṭiya bin Sa'd al-Kufi, who is not strong. The channel in full and text is reported as follows:

> حدثنا معاوية بن هشام حدثنا شيبان عن فراس عن عطية عن أبي سعيد عن أبي سعيد الخدري عن نبي الله، صلى الله عليه وسلم، انه قال يخرج عنق من النار يتكلم يقول: وكلت اليوم بثلاثة: بكل جبار؛ وبمن جعل مع الله الها آخر؛ وبمن قتل نفسا بغير نفس فينطوي عليهم فيقذفهم في غمرات جهنم
>
> Mu'āwiya bin Hishām narrated to us Shaybān narrated to us from Firās from 'Aṭiya bin Sa'd al-Kufi from Abu Sa'eed al-Khudri from the Prophet (peace be upon him) that he said: *A neck from the fire will come out on the day of judgement and speak, saying: This day I am charged with three: for every arrogant one and whoever makes another god with Allah also, and whoever is involved in killing a soul. All of them are to be thrown into the throngs of hell.*

The totality of established and corroborating evidences thus far mentioned in this regard provides proof to the level of certainty that the noble Prophetic *Sunnah* is a revelation from Allah and distinguished from the revealed text of the Qur'ān. Denial of this leads one into disbelief and ultimately to exit the fold of Islam completely. Thus, the noble Prophetic *Sunnah* is an established proof and underpins the essence of the latter half of the testimony of faith – that Muḥammad is the Messenger of Allah, a weighty testimony indeed for the day of judgement. Only the disbeliever, the one cursed would seek to object to this, like the so-called 'Qur'ānists' who have no share in Islam and are but stuck in profound ignorance with their absurd claims.

15 Some of what may or may not happen to the Prophets

Based upon the arguments thus far presented, it is perhaps pertinent at this juncture to outline some points in relation to what may or indeed may not happen to the Prophets, and in particular, the Prophet Muḥammad (peace be upon him). It is important to note that such matters may not be within the purview of natural human limitation. Firstly, like all his previous brethren Prophets and other humans, he (peace be upon him) may have enemies; he may be subjected to harm, humiliation, torture, or even be imprisoned, driven out of his home country, or be at risk of death. Some of these afflictions actually took place, a famous example being the murder of the Prophet Yaḥya bin Zakariyyā (peace be upon him) who was killed at the behest of a prostitute. Other Prophets were protected from such an afflictions from the outset, such as Musa and his brother Hārun (peace be upon them both). The Prophet Muḥammad (peace be upon him) was divinely protected from the actions of others only towards the end of the Medinan period, after which he ordered his guards to disperse. Before that, he was harmed - he was stoned by the mean people of Thaqif until they caused him to bleed, while the fools from among the tribe of Quraysh threw dirt on his honourable back. He sustained a head injury and his teeth were damaged during the battle of Uḥud and subjected to other kinds of injury until he was divinely protected.

Secondly, like all his previous brethren Prophets and other humans, he (peace be upon him) may suffer physical illness in all its variety, whether major or not, repulsive or not, except for the one whom Allah grants the protection of not being afflicted with such things. For example, Muḥammad (peace be upon him) was safe from being afflicted with pleurisy. In fact, perhaps the purpose of afflicting the Prophets with deadly afflictions and resultant pain is for them to be an example of how to endure this with patience. Nevertheless, in general, Prophets may not suffer from mental or psychological illness, for this type of illness requires being rendered incapacitated, thus the 'pen would be lifted'; yet Prophethood necessitates the soundness of mind and reporting of speech.

Thirdly, like his previous brethren Prophets, the Prophet (peace be upon him), may be subjected to other universal ordeals like loss of loved ones; financial loss, having to endure the difficulties of lack of sustenance or support and even being let down by people, such as their own family and tribe. It could be argued that such setbacks are more difficult when compared to others, thereby providing a good model of behaviour to emulate.

Fourthly, the Prophet (peace be upon him), like all his former brethren Prophets, may perceive at certain times the perceptible world in a different manner to the reality of the situation, or in terms of how reports are presented; this is distinct from truth in itself. A multiplicity of reasons could exist for this, just as it does for most of mankind, such as:

- Deception of senses, which can occur as a result of magic. Like in the verse where Allah recounts the story of Musa (peace be upon him) and the challenge before the magicians at the Pharonic court:

قَالَ بَلْ أَلْقُوا فَإِذَا حِبَالُهُمْ وَعِصِيُّهُمْ يُخَيَّلُ إِلَيْهِ مِن سِحْرِهِمْ أَنَّهَا تَسْعَىٰ

He said: Nay cast down! Then lo! Their cords and their rods-- it was imaged to him on account of their magic as if they were running. [1]

or by a physical illness that spoils the taste of food, or the feeling of heat and cold.

- Mistakes made in reporting, either unintentional or deliberate, particularly concerning judicial witnesses appearing before court, lying under oath, forging documentation and the like. The reason may also be a lack of sufficient evidence necessary to prove the truth, though it is established as being the truth before Allah's knowledge.

This is the best of the Prophets of Allah, the seal of all Prophethood who has been protected by Allah, peace and blessings be upon him and his family. He was not protected from being deceived by people lying in court. He would have to issue judgement based upon the given facts and testimony. However, he (peace be upon him) has clarified this matter in the following *ḥadith*, where he was reported to have said:

I am only mortal and you people (litigants) come to me with your cases; and it may be that one of you can present his case eloquently in a more convincing way than the other, and I give my verdict according to what I hear. So, if ever I judge and give the right of a brother to another, then he (the latter)

---

[1] *Qur'ān* 20: 66

should not take it, for I am giving him only a piece of fire.[2]

Without question the *ḥadith* is authentic and has been recorded by many such as Bukhāri, Mālik, Aḥmad, and Abu Dāwud in their respective works. Collectively these chains of transmission provide conclusive evidence. Based upon this, a number of important points can be discerned. Falsehood might be very well presented and substantiated to such an extent, that it can deceive even those that are infallible in revelation, like the Prophet (peace be upon him). If such an eventuality can happen to the Prophet (peace be upon him), then it may also happen more often than not, to others well below his rank. Given the importance of this point, a separate section in this work will explore its consequences.

For that reason, the Prophetic reports about 'worldly affairs', in other words, pertaining to the reality in and of itself as well as the general properties and events are indeed similar to reports of other human beings, in that they may be accurate or inaccurate, especially when they are expressed as opinion. Examples of this are reported in the *ḥadith* as cited earlier in part one where the Prophet (peace be upon him) passed comment about the pollination of palm trees. Much of what many people nowadays falsely call 'Prophetic medicine' often falls within this category. Such matters need to be subjected to very careful scrutiny and reservation, so as not attribute a matter to revelation in error since that would be a grave crime.

Fifthly, like his other previous brethren Prophets, the Prophet Muḥammad (peace be upon him) may leave the most appropriate among permissible matters (*mubāḥāt*) for something else, which is likewise also permissible. Amongst the various examples of this are

---

[2] The wording of the narration is taken from Bukhāri as reported in the book of *aḥkām* under the chapter '*The advice of the Imām to litigants*.' The *isnād* is authentic and Bukhāri reports it as follows: Abdullah ibn Maslama narrated to us from Mālik from Hishām from his father from Zaynab daughter of Abu Salama from Umm Salama (may Allah be pleased with her) that the Prophet (peace be upon him) said.

selecting a specific field for battle; choosing a specific method of administration, or using certain equipment instead of others. Experts may be more efficient than others in selecting the most appropriate thing to do, in which case, the Prophet (peace be upon him) would consider their opinion instead. An example of this was the opinion of al-Ḥubāb bin al-Mundthir to change the position of the army during the great battle of Badr. Undoubtedly, the Prophet (peace be upon him), like other people of sound mind, exerts his utmost effort and does his best, even more than anyone else to reach the best possible opinion. Some might argue that this 'opinion' of the Prophet (peace be upon him) would constitute an *ijtihād*. It might well be, if taken literally, but it is not of the same concept as that of legal independent reasoning in the terminology of *uṣul*. For it does not befit the Prophet (peace be upon him) to say that he exercised independent legal reasoning, as will be outlined in due course.

Sixthly, like his other previous brethren Prophets, the Prophet Muḥammad (peace be upon him) may perform what is legally deemed to be undesirable (*makruh*) and he may leave a recommended act (*mustaḥab*) with a number of considerations in mind:

a. To illustrate the legislative ruling after a prohibition (*nahy*) has been revealed, to clarify that it is in actuality, undesirable (*makruh*). To abstain from performing it is rewarded, but undertaking it is not sinful. The same would also apply to the recommended deeds (*mustaḥabāt*), all of which being established via the infallible revelation emanating from Allah. Although ultimately only Allah knows best, it may be that this was established in this manner in order to provide concrete practical examples to those who have the tendency for excessiveness in religion (*ghuluw fi-deen*). Such people may not readily accept such points solely by virtue of verbal pronouncements, except when accompanied by practical example. Moreover, there are certain rulings which have to be fully illustrated in practice and not merely by words.

b. To give priority to mercy (*raḥma*). Such as what the Prophet (peace be upon him) did with the prisoners of the battle of Badr.

c. To give priority to the call of Islam (*dawah*) in order that it reaches people of significance, as mentioned in the Qurānic narrative in *Surah 'Abasa.*

d. Or to give predominance to kindness and gentleness as demonstrated with the companions in the verse of *Surah Tawba.*[3]

Together with the aforementioned points b), c) and d), we may also add that He (peace be upon him) might have thought or had the intention of doing something and then not acted upon that. Also, the Prophet (peace be upon him) may raise his hands and invoke Allah against people unintentionally, by mentioning customary Arab phrases like 'may you be made barren' or 'may your mother be bereft of you' or the like. These are some of the types of deeds for which Allah chided the Prophet (peace be upon him), and which He described as 'sins' on the part of his Prophet. Then, Allah granted him a general pardon for all his past and future errors after the treaty of Ḥudaybiyah, he said:

إِنَّا فَتَحْنَا لَكَ فَتْحًا مُّبِينًا ، لِّيَغْفِرَ لَكَ اللَّهُ مَا تَقَدَّمَ مِن ذَنبِكَ وَمَا تَأَخَّرَ وَيُتِمَّ نِعْمَتَهُ عَلَيْكَ وَيَهْدِيَكَ صِرَاطًا مُّسْتَقِيمًا، وَيَنصُرَكَ اللَّهُ نَصْرًا عَزِيزًا

Surely We have given to you a clear victory; that Allah may forgive your community their past faults and those to follow and complete His favour to you and keep you on a right way, and that Allah might help you with a mighty

[3] See *Qur'ān* 9: 43

help. [4]

Many fools, in particular those from the *Khawārij*, typified by the likes of Dhul-Khuwayṣirah at-Tamimi, held the view that the Prophet (peace be upon him) could commit both major and minor sins. Nothing could be further from the truth in this regard. What the *Khawārij* and others who followed them failed to acknowledge was the precise nature of the 'sins' that were mentioned in the context of the Prophet's acts (peace be upon him). It is not the same as what constitutes 'sin' as it is for the rest of his *Ummah*. Rather, his (peace be upon him) 'sin' related to what he expressed as being lapses of God-consciousness. Furthermore, it would also encompass performing a deed that is undesirable (*makruh*) and the non-performance of a recommended deed – both of which are not 'sins' in the strict sense as it applies to the *Ummah* generally, given that both do not lead to punishment. Those who argued that the Prophet (peace be upon him) could commit major and minor sins in truth have lesser intellect than donkeys; at least donkeys and other beasts of burden have more consciousness of Allah than to advance such a claim.

Seventh, it is not befitting that the Prophet Muḥammad (peace be upon him) may commit a prohibited act (*ḥarām*) be that major or minor. In the same regard, it is also not befitting that he (peace be upon him) would cease to perform any matter that was deemed an obligation (*wājib*), except where that would be considered to reside within his own specialisation and there is conclusive evidence relating to it as such. In fact, the Prophet (peace be upon him) undertaking the act would be conclusive evidence that it is permissible for his *Ummah*. Nevertheless, we would need additional evidence in order to determine whether such a deed was undesirable (*makruh*), recommended (*mustaḥab*) or obligatory (*wājib*). Conversely, if the Prophet (peace be upon him) abandoned a deed this would be clear evidence that it is not

---

[4] *Qur'ān* 48: 1/3

an obligation. Again there would need to be an additional evidence to demonstrate that falls into another classification, be that undesirable (*makruh*), permissible (*mubāḥ*), recommended (*mustaḥab*) or prohibited (*ḥarām*). The same line of argument cannot be said however with regards to the earlier Prophets. There is no compelling logical or legal evidence to apply the aforesaid reasoning to them, peace be upon them all. In fact, there is a textual example of the opposite – namely, in the case of the Prophet Yunus (peace be upon him). Thus the case of the final seal of the Prophets, Muḥammad (peace be upon him) is different in this respect to his predecessors. Hence those who would dismiss everything that is found in the old books of revelation regarding the Prophets as a complete lie or fabrication, on the basis that it is contrary to the general infallibility of the Prophets do not have a substantive argument. Whilst we can establish with certainty based upon conclusive proof for the Prophet Muḥammad (peace be upon him) similar cannot be applied to earlier Prophets in the absence of such evidence.

Eighth, whatever the Prophet (peace be upon him) reports on affairs other than 'worldly affairs' is true and correct. His reports pertaining to previous nations and past facts are certainly true revelation sent from Allah, the almighty. The same applies to the Prophet's reporting on future events whose knowledge is only the preserve of Allah and cannot be known except by his leave. Such reporting cannot be subject to error or mistake lest it would lose its overall significance and not be part of Allah's establishment of proof to his servants.

Ninth, when the Prophet (peace be upon him) elicits reports which relate to commands and prohibitions, these are from revelation and nothing else. He (peace be upon him) did not speak of his own desire nor did he warn except by way of revelation. If it were possible for him to issue any command or warn against anything from his own desire without being based upon revelation from Allah, then it would be possible that *all* such commands and warnings were from desire.

Hence, the Prophetic mission would be devoid of significance and it would bring the notion of revelation as a whole into question.

Tenth, it is not befitting for the Prophet (peace be upon him) to remain silent in relation to a *munkar* (evil, the reprehensible), generally. He is duty-bound to convey the message of Islam and to enjoin all the good and forbid all the evil. For that reason, his silence about any act or specific approval of it, by necessity, denotes that it is not prohibited (*ḥarām*). Then as mentioned previously, further evidence will be needed to establish whether the matter is undesirable, permissible, recommended or obligatory. Again as noted above, conclusive evidence from revelation or from the necessity and dictates of reason does not enable us to apply this principle to the rest of the Prophets that preceded him (peace be upon him). Although many have argued for this very point, it has not been established with conclusive proofs, thus it cannot be taken further.

Finally, the notion of *ijtihād* in its specific technical sense – devising a legal provision from the detailed evidences – does not apply to the Prophet (peace be upon him). It cannot apply given that he is the owner of the text, in other words, he is the commissioned Prophet through which revelation is communicated. His speech constitutes text (*naṣṣ*) as does his actions and approvals, for it is the legislation. Through this medium the law is conveyed as it is revealed to him by Allah. He doesn't extrapolate or deduce the law from its sources, for he (peace be upon him) is conveying it by way of revelation. In modern legal parlance, he is a lawgiver, protected by infallibility which Allah conferred upon him in order to convey the revelation. May the mercy and blessings of Allah be conferred upon him, his family and all his noble companions.

16 Deception by false testimony?

Previously we detailed what may or may not happen to the last Messenger, the seal of all the Prophets, Muḥammad (peace be upon him) as well as his former brethren Prophets which preceded him. He (peace be upon him) recognises the reality before him as perceived through the senses or as reported and brought before him, unlike the reality in itself which is in relation to the reporting of a liar and their mistake. Likewise, this can be said to occur within a judicial setting in relation to witness testimony, the falsification of documents; in relation to oaths which are false, and how a litigant presents his case, which may appear to be the truth. It can also extend to a lack of evidence in a case to establish who is right (or not being able to establish the requisite proof itself), that remains within the knowledge of Allah, and other examples like this.

The decisive proof upon this matter which can be upheld with certainty is as follows: that the last final messenger, the seal of the Prophet's (peace be upon him) is rendered infallible (*ma'ṣoom*) and protected by the directive of Allah. Yet this protection does not extend to being duped by the hypocrisy (*nifāq*) of the hypocrite (*munāfiq*), the lie of the liar, or having to make judgment upon the apparent when faced with an unscrupulous witness, or those having a good ability to skilfully argue and present their case. Allah the exalted, blessed be his names has said:

وَلَوْلَا فَضْلُ اللَّهِ عَلَيْكَ وَرَحْمَتُهُ لَهَمَّت طَّائِفَةٌ مِّنْهُمْ أَن يُضِلُّوكَ وَمَا يُضِلُّونَ إِلَّا أَنفُسَهُمْ وَمَا يَضُرُّونَكَ مِن شَيْءٍ وَأَنزَلَ اللَّهُ عَلَيْكَ الْكِتَابَ وَالْحِكْمَةَ وَعَلَّمَكَ مَا لَمْ تَكُن تَعْلَمُ وَكَانَ فَضْلُ اللَّهِ عَلَيْكَ عَظِيمًا

And were it not for Allah's grace upon you and His mercy a party of them had certainly designed to bring you to perdition and they do not bring to perdition but their own souls, and they shall not harm you in any way, and Allah has revealed to you the Book and the wisdom, and He has taught you what you did not know and Allah's grace on you is very great. [1]

The background to this verse is the famous story relating to Ṭa'mah bin Ubayriq who was a *munāfiq* from amongst the men of the Anṣār. He was a thief who had stolen some goods; he denied the charges against him and had planted the stolen items with a Jew, whom he subsequently tried to frame with the crime. Allah the majestic exposed the truth of this and the story has thereafter been preserved for posterity. Writing in his *Tafsir*, the grand Imām aṭ-Ṭabari provides a comprehensive account of these events:[2]

> …that is to say, the exalted explains with his statement: '*Surely We have revealed the Book to you with the truth that you may judge between people by means of that which Allah has taught you; and be not an advocate on behalf of the treacherous.*' [3] Surely we have revealed to you oh Muḥammad, the book, that

[1] *Qur'ān* 4: 113

[2] Given the considerable length of the cited narrative from the *Tafsir*, only the translated English text is presented

[3] *Qur'ān* 4: 105

is to say the Qur'ān, '...*that you may judge between people*;' to make decrees between people and determine judgements, disputes between them '...*by means of that which Allah has taught you*.' That is to say, with what Allah has revealed unto you from his book, '...*and be not an advocate on behalf of the treacherous*.' And do not betray a Muslim or a *Mu'āhid* (an ally, a person who is granted the pledge of protection by the Muslims) in their person or in their wealth; contending in argumentation and quarrels about it, and not to press such demands or requests except by way of right and not betrayal.

'*And seek forgiveness from Allah*,'[4] Muḥammad to forgive your sins (and rescind) punishment concerning those who are antagonistic to you, (and) about the treacherous or traitor or other than that; '...*surely Allah is forgiving, merciful*.'[5] And he said: Verily Allah forgives the sins of his believing servants by leaving the punishment upon them if they seek forgiveness from him, (he is) merciful (towards) them. So act accordingly, oh Muḥammad; Allah will forgive you regarding this precedent from your opponents about this traitor. It has been said that the Prophet (peace be upon him) was not at odds with the traitor, but it was so. Hence Allah ordered him to seek forgiveness and they to do so similarly. And reminded that the treacherous, those whom Allah admonished and exalted his Prophet in the matter of Banu Ubayriq. And (there is) disagreement amongst the people of interpretation in the matter of treachery, which it was described by Allah. It's been said by some (concerning) the matter of stealing. Those who said as such:

Muḥammad bin 'Amr narrated to me he said Abu 'Aāṣim narrated to us from 'Esa from Ibn Najiḥ from Mujāhid in relation to the statement of Allah, '*Surely We have revealed the Book to you with the truth that you may judge between people by means of that which Allah has taught you*' to where he says

---

[4] *Qur'ān* 4: 106
[5] *Qur'ān* 4: 23

'*...whoever does this seeking Allah's pleasure...*' [6]

Al-Muthanna narrated to me he said Abu Ḥudhayfah narrated to us he said Shibl narrated to us from Ibn Abi Najiḥ from Mujāhid about it.

Al-Ḥasan bin Aḥmad bin Abi Shu'ayb Abu Muslim al-Ḥarāni narrated to us he said Muḥammad bin Salama narrated to us he said Muḥammad bin Isḥāq narrated to us from 'Aāṣim bin Umar bin Qatādah from his father from his grandfather Qatādah bin an-Nu'mān he said: There was a household among us called Banu Ubayriq, among whom was a Bishr, a Bushayr, and a Mubashar. Bushayr was a hypocrite who would recite poetry reviling the Companions of the Prophet (peace be upon him) then he would attribute it to some of the Arabs. Then he would say: 'So-and-so said this and that.' So when the Companions of the Prophet (peace be upon) would hear that poetry, they would say: By Allah! No one but this filthy person said this poetry - or as the man said - and they would say: Ibn Al-Ubayriq said it.

He said: They were a poor and needy household during *Jāhiliyyah* and Islam. The only food the people of Medina had was dates and barely. When a man was able to, he would import flour from the Levant which he bought and kept for himself. As for his dependants, their only food was dates and barely. So an import arrived from Syria, and my uncle Rifā'ah bin Zayd bought a load of it, which he put in a storage area he had, where he kept his weapons - his shield and his sword. But it was taken from him from under the house. The storage was broken into and the food and weapons were taken. In the morning, my uncle Rifā'ah came to me and said: O my nephew! We were robbed during the night, our storage was broken into, and our food and weapons are gone! He said: They overheard us in the house, and questioned us, and someone said to us, we saw Banu Ubayriq cooking during the night, and it looked like they had some of your food.

---

[6] *Qur'ān* 4: 114

He said: Banu Ubayriq was saying while we were questioning them amidst their dwellings – 'By Allah! We do not think the one you are looking for is other than Labeed bin Sahl, a man among us who is righteous and accepted Islam.' When Labeed heard that, he brandished his sword and said: I stole? By Allah! Either you prove this theft, or I will take to you with this sword! They said: 'Leave us O men! You are not the one who has it.' So we continued questioning in the dwellings until we had no doubt that they had taken it. My uncle said to me: O my nephew! You should go to the Messenger of Allah (peace be upon him) and tell him about that. Qatādah said: So I went to the Messenger of Allah (peace be upon him) and said: 'A family among us are ill-mannered, and they conspired against my uncle Rifā'ah bin Zayd. They broke into his storage and took his weapons and his food. We want them to return our weapons, but we have no need for the food.' So, the Prophet (peace be upon him) said: *I will decide about that.* When Banu Ubayriq heard about this, they brought a man from among them named Usayr bin Urwa to talk to him about that, and some people from their houses gathered and said: 'O Messenger of Allah! Qatādah bin an-Nu'mān and his uncle came to a family among us who are a people of Islam and righteousness, accusing them of stealing without proof or (any) confirmation.'

Qatādah said: I went to the Messenger of Allah (peace be upon him) and spoke to him, and he said: You went to a family among them known for their Islam and righteousness, and accused them of stealing without confirmation or proof? He said: So I returned wishing that I had lost some of my wealth, and that the Messenger of Allah (peace be upon him) had not spoken to me about that. My uncle Rifā'ah came to me and said: 'O my nephew! What did you do?' So I told him what the Messenger of Allah (peace be upon him) said to me, so he said: 'It is from Allah whom we seek help!' It was not long before the Qur'ān was revealed: *'Surely We have revealed the Book to you with the truth that you may judge between people by means of that which Allah has taught you; and be not an advocate on behalf of the treacherous.'*[7] That is to say, Banu Ubayriq; '*And seek forgiveness from Allah,'*[8] (that is to say) from what you said to Qatādah. *And do not plead on behalf of those who act unfaithfully to their souls;*[9] which is Banu Ubayriq. *....Surely Allah does not love him who is treacherous, sinful;*[10] until his statement *....then asks forgiveness of Allah, he shall find Allah forgiving, merciful,*[11] which is, that they make repentance to Allah and Allah forgave them. *And whoever commits a sin, he only commits it against his own soul; and Allah is knowing, wise,*[12] a manifest sin, their saying about Labeed. *And were it not for Allah's grace upon you and His mercy a party of them had certainly designed to bring you to perdition,*[13] Usayr and his companions, *...and they do not bring to perdition but their own souls, and they shall not harm you in any way, and Allah has revealed to you the Book and the ḥikmah...*[14] to where he says ... *We shall grant him a mighty reward.*[15]

So when the Qur'ān was revealed, the Messenger of Allah (peace be upon him) brought the weapon and returned it to Rifā'ah. Qatādah said: 'When the weapon was brought to my uncle - and he was a weak elderly man in *Jāhiliyyah*, and I thought that he merely had entered into Islam (without real sincerity) but when I brought it to him, he said: 'O my nephew! It is for Allah's cause.' So I knew that his Islam was genuine. When the Qur'ān was revealed, Bushayr went with the idolaters; staying with Sulāfah bint Sa'd bin Sahl. So Allah revealed: *And whoever acts in hostility to the Prophet after that guidance has become manifest to him, and follows other than the way of the believers,*[16] until where he says *...and whoever*

---

[7] *Qur'ān* 4: 105
[8] *Qur'ān* 4: 106
[9] *Qur'ān* 4: 107
[10] *Qur'ān* 4: 107
[11] *Qur'ān* 4: 110
[12] *Qur'ān* 4: 111
[13] *Qur'ān* 4: 113
[14] *Qur'ān* 4: 113
[15] *Qur'ān* 4: 74
[16] *Qur'ān* 4: 115

associates anything with Allah, he indeed strays off into manifest error. [17] When he went to stay with Sulāfah, Ḥassān bin Thābit lampooned her with verses of poetry. So she took his saddle, put it on her head; then she left with it to cast into the valley. Then she said: 'You gave me the poetry of Ḥassān - you did not bring me any good.'

Bishr bin Mu'ādth narrated to us he said Yazeed narrated to us he said Sa'eed narrated to us from Qatādah: *'Surely We have revealed the Book to you with the truth that you may judge between people by means of that which Allah has taught you...'* [18] what Allah has revealed to you and between you, '*...and be not an advocate on behalf of the treacherous'* when read until he says: *....Surely Allah does not love him who is treacherous, sinful*; [19] mentioned to us that these verses were revealed concerning the dishonour of Ṭa'mah bin Ubayriq in what troubled the Prophet of Allah (peace be upon him). Allah demonstrated his excuse was dishonour; he had pleaded with the Prophet (peace be upon him) and warned him not to advocate on behalf of the treacherous. Ṭa'mah bin Ubayriq was a man from the Anṣār then a Bani Dthafr. He stole a shield for his uncle and tried to conceal it by throwing it to a Jew, claiming it to be with him. (The Jew) he was Zayd bin as-Sameen so the Jews came to the Prophet (peace be upon him). He cheered when he saw that his people, Banu Dthafr came to the Prophet (peace be upon him) to seek for their companion to be excused. The Prophet (peace be upon him) was troubled by his alibi, until Allah revealed regarding his dishonour, thus he said: *And do not plead on behalf of those who act unfaithfully to their souls;*[20] to where he said: *Behold! You are they who (may) plead for them in the life of this world, but who will plead for them with Allah on the day of judgement?* [21] That is to say, with that his people - *And whoever commits a fault or a*

[17] *Qur'ān* 4: 116
[18] *Qur'ān* 4: 105
[19] *Qur'ān* 4: 107
[20] *Qur'ān* 4: 107
[21] *Qur'ān* 4: 109

sin, then accuses of it one innocent, he indeed takes upon himself the burden of a calumny and a manifest sin. [22] Ṭa'mah's innocence dissipated. When the matter of Allah exposing the dishonour of Ṭa'mah came to pass and his hypocrisy with the *mushrikeen* of Mecca, Allah revealed regarding this dishonour, in (the verse): *And whoever acts in hostility to the Prophet after that guidance has become manifest to him, and follows other than the way of the believers, we will turn him to that to which he has turned, and make him enter hell, and it is an evil destination.*[23]

Muḥammad bin Sa'd narrated to me he said my father narrated to me he said my uncle narrated to me he said my father narrated to me from his father from Ibn 'Abbās, regarding the statement: *Surely We have revealed the Book to you with the truth that you may judge between people by means of that which Allah has taught you; and be not an advocate on behalf of the treacherous.*[24]

Yunus narrated to me he said Ibn Wahb reported to us he said Ibn Zayd said in relation to the statement: *Surely, We have revealed the Book to you with the truth that you may judge between people by means of that which Allah has taught you.* The verse he said was (about) a man who was a thief who stole an iron shield in the time of the Prophet (peace be upon him). He placed the stolen item upon a Jew and said of the Jew, by Allah he has stolen it oh Abul-Qāsim! And they said – Oh Messenger of Allah, verily this evil Jew (who) disbelieves in Allah and I came across it (i.e. the stolen item). He said until the wealth came upon the Prophet (peace be upon him) and with some of that speech. Thus, Allah the exalted reproached him in that and thereafter said: *'Surely We have revealed the Book to you with the truth that you may judge between people by means of that which Allah has taught you; and be not an advocate on behalf of the treacherous. And seek forgiveness*

---

[22] *Qur'ān* 4: 112
[23] *Qur'ān* 4: 115
[24] *Qur'ān* 4: 105

from Allah,'[25] as you said to the Jew – '*....verily Allah is forgiving, merciful.*' Then turning to his neighbours he said: '*Behold! You are they who (may) plead for them in the life of this world,*' read until the pronouncement '*....but who will plead for them with Allah on the day of judgement?* '[26] Thereafter he said – then show repentance and (continued by saying): '*And whoever does evil or acts unjustly to his soul, then asks forgiveness of Allah, he shall find Allah forgiving, merciful.*' [27] '*And Allah is knowing, wise. And whoever commits a fault or a sin, then accuses of it one innocent,*' [28] What all of you entered oh people upon this transgression speaking about it? '*....he indeed takes upon himself the burden of a calumny and a manifest sin.*' [29] Thus read until he makes the pronouncement – '*And whoever acts in hostility to the Prophet after that guidance has become manifest to him...*'[30] He said – (Ṭa'mah) refused to accept the repentance that Allah showed to him and fled to the *mushrikeen* of Mecca. So he ransacked the house with this theft, thus Allah mentioned his destruction and killing, so for that reason he said: – '*And whoever acts in hostility to the Prophet after that guidance has become manifest to him...*'[31] and read until the pronouncement '*....and it is an evil resort.*' [32] And it is said – he is Ṭa'mah bin Ubayriq and he was a descendent of Bani Dthafr.

And others have said, that the treachery, which is the characterisation that Allah used in the verse is in relation to his saying '*....and be not an advocate on behalf of the treacherous....*' His denial and (breach of) trust was the (main item) which was mentioned. Those who said as such are as follows:

---

[25] *Qur'ān* 4: 105/106
[26] *Qur'ān* 4: 109
[27] *Qur'ān* 4: 110
[28] *Qur'ān* 4: 111/112
[29] *Qur'ān* 4: 112
[30] *Qur'ān* 4: 115
[31] *Qur'ān* 4: 115
[32] *Qur'ān* 4: 97

Muḥammad bin al-Ḥussain narrated to us he said Aḥmad bin Mufaḍḍal narrated to us he said Asbāṭ narrated to us from as-Suddi – '*Surely We have revealed the Book to you with the truth that you may judge between people by means of that which Allah has taught you...*' He said: As for – '*that which Allah has taught you*' what Allah revealed unto you. He said: (the verse) descended in relation to Ṭa'mah bin Ubayriq and to deliver the shield to a man from the Jews. So he went out to his home, and then buried it with a Jew. There was disagreement regarding where Ṭa'mah had hidden the shield. So he took it. The Jew came to request the shield that he had concealed. So he went to the people of the Jews of his clan and he thus said: they released (it to) me, for indeed I know where the shield has been put. When he knew it was with them, Ṭa'mah took the shield and threw it in the house of Abu Muleel al-Anṣāri. When the Jew came to ask for the shield its presence was there. Ṭa'mah has put the item with him and the people from his people reviled him. And he said: do you wish to betray me? They demanded that it be obtained from his house. Then they proceeded towards the house of Abu Muleel.

Ṭa'mah said Abu Muleel took the shield and the Anṣār joined in on behalf of Ṭa'mah, and he said to them – go forth with me to the Messenger (peace be upon him) and you tell him that I have proof that the Jewish argument is a lie; if I prove (this) lie of the Jew to the people of Medina. People from the Anṣār said: Oh Messenger of Allah, we would urge you to support Ṭa'mah, since the Jew is lying. The Prophet (peace be upon him) considered doing this, thereafter Allah revealed upon this matter: '*...and be not an advocate on behalf of the treacherous. And ask forgiveness of Allah.*' Out of what you wanted; '*...Surely Allah is forgiving, merciful. And do not plead on behalf of those who act unfaithfully to their souls, verily Allah does not love him who is treacherous, sinful.*' Then He mentioned the Anṣār and the trouble they caused about it, so saying: '*They hide themselves from men and do not hide themselves from Allah, and He is with them when they meditate by night words which do not please him...*' Saying, what they say is not pleasing of speech. *'Behold! You are they who (may) plead for them in the life of this world, but who will plead for them with Allah on the day of judgement?'* Then he called (them) to repentance and so said: *'And whoever does evil or acts unjustly to his soul, then asks forgiveness of Allah, he shall find Allah forgiving, merciful.'*

Then it was mentioned where he said, take it Abu Muleel, saying: *'And whoever commits a sin, he only commits it against his own soul. And whoever commits a fault or a sin, then accuses someone innocent of it, he indeed takes upon himself the burden of a calumny and a manifest sin.'* The great manifest sin. Then he mentioned the Anṣār and their arrival and that they were trying to exude on behalf of their companion, arguing for him, thus he says: *'...a party of them had certainly designed to bring you to perdition and they do not bring to perdition but their own souls, and they shall not harm you in any way, and Allah has revealed to you the Book and the ḥikmah...'* Saying the Prophecy; then he mentioned the trouble they gave about it, they wanted the lie (perpetuated) about Ṭa'mah, so he said: *'There is no good in most of their secret counsels...'* except whoever ordered with charity or good or *islāḥ* (reform) between the people. When Allah exposed Ṭa'mah in Medina by way of the Qur'ān, he fled until he came to Mecca. Thus he disbelieved after his Islam and stayed with al-Ḥajjāj bin 'Ilāt as-Sulami.

Thereafter, he rummaged in the house of al- Ḥajjāj and wanted to steal from him. Al- Ḥajjāj heard the rustling in his house and the clutter and skins were with him. So he looked if it was Ṭa'mah and thus said - my guest and my cousin that wants to steal from me? So he took him and he died by Bani Sulaym a *kāfir* (disbeliever). And Allah revealed in relation to this *'...and whoever acts in hostility to the Messenger after guidance has become manifest to him and follows other than the way of the believers; we will turn him to that which he turned himself....and it is an evil resort.'*[33]

Al-Qāsim narrated to us he said al-Ḥussain narrated to us he said Ḥajjāj narrated to me from Ibn Jurayj from 'Ikrima he said - A man entrusted from the Anṣār, Ṭa'mah bin Ubayriq, he had commandeered the shield and thereafter went absent. A man from the Anṣār then came and opened his apartment and didn't find his shield. He asked Ṭa'mah bin Ubayriq regarding it, so he threw it to a man from the Jews and said to him that Zayd bin as-Sameen has it attached to his shield and armour. When he saw that his people came to the Prophet (peace be upon him) they told him to stave off the matter. Thereafter Allah blessed and majestic revealed – '*Surely We have revealed the Book to you with the truth that you may judge between people by means of that which Allah has taught you; and be not an advocate on behalf of the treacherous. And ask forgiveness of Allah; surely Allah is forgiving, merciful. And do not plead on behalf of those who act unfaithfully to their own selves;'* that is to say, Ṭa'mah bin Ubayriq and his people. '*Behold, you are they who (may) plead for them in this world, but who will plead for them with Allah on the day of judgement, or who shall be their protector?'* Muḥammad (peace be upon him) and the people of Ṭa'mah. '*And whoever does evil or acts unjustly to his soul, then asks forgiveness of Allah, he shall find Allah forgiving, merciful.*' Muḥammad, Ṭa'mah and his people; he said – '*and whoever commits a sin he only commits it against his own soul.'*

The verse about Ṭa'mah – '*And whoever commits a fault or a sin, then accuses of it one innocent,'* that is to say, Zayd bin as-Sameen, '*he indeed takes upon himself the burden of a calumny and a manifest sin,*' (i.e.) Ṭa'mah bin Ubayriq. '*And were it not for Allah's grace upon you and his mercy,'* Oh Muḥammad, *'a party of them had certainly designed to bring you to perdition and they do not bring to perdition but their own souls, and they shall not harm you in any way,'* the people

[33] *Qur'ān* 4: 115

of Ṭa'mah bin Ubayriq. *'And Allah has revealed to you the Book and the ḥikmah, and He has taught you what you did not know, and Allah's grace on you is very great,'* Muḥammad (peace be upon him). *'There is no good in most of their secret counsels except (in his) who enjoins charity or goodness,'* until (it was) completed (with) the verse to the general people, *'And whoever acts in hostility to the Prophet after that guidance has become manifest to him, and follows other than the way of the believers.'* (In relation to the verse) he said what is revealed of the Qur'ān concerning Ṭa'mah bin Ubayriq (that he) ran to the Quryash and turned upon his religion. Then except upon the compartment of Ḥajjāj bin 'Ilāṭ al-Bahzi, an ally at peace with the Prophet, Abd' ad-Dār. Ibn Jurayj said: Thus this is the verse, all of it in it, revealed to where he said: *'Surely Allah does not forgive that anything should be associated with him, and (he) forgives what is beside that.'* It was revealed (concerning) Ṭa'mah bin Ubayriq and it is said that he threw the shield in the house of Muleel bin Abdullah al-Khazraji. Therefore the Qur'ān descended as he ran to the Quraysh, so it was, what was ordered.

It was narrated from al-Ḥussain bin al-Faraj he said I heard Abu Mu'ādth, 'Ubaid bin Salmān narrated to us he said I heard aḍ-Ḍaḥḥāk said in relation to the verse - *that you may judge between people by means of that which Allah has taught you* – he said: what was revealed upon you and taught to you in his book, and revealed this verse in relation to a man from the Anṣār who commandeered the shield from its owner. So the treacherous man from amongst the companions of the Prophet (peace be upon him) (would be) angry with his people. And they came (to the) Prophet (peace be upon him) and they said: our treacherous companion? And (yet) he is a truthful Muslim, oh Prophet excuse him as he has been slandered. So, he stood (before) the Prophet of Allah and lied to him, knowing he was innocent and falsely attributing (the theft) to him. Thus Allah explained (this) and revealed accordingly: *Surely We have revealed the Book to you with the truth that you may judge between people by means of that which Allah has taught you,*

> until where he said: *or who shall be their protector?* So following his betrayal of Allah, he went with the *mushrikeen* from the people of Mecca and left Islam. So (the following was) revealed – *And whoever acts in hostility to the Prophet after that guidance has become manifest to him* – unto where he says: *and it is (hell) an evil resort.*
>
> Abu Ja'far said: and firstly in relation to the interpretation in that with what is indicated by the apparent meaning of the verse, those who said it was treachery which Allah described in this verse, rejection with what's been entrusted; because that is recognised from the meaning of treachery in the language of the Arabs. And this steers the interpretation of the Qur'ān gathered from the meaning of the speech of the Arabs, what is found in it primarily.

Despite its considerable length, the extract from the *Tafsir* of the grand Imām Abu Ja'far Muḥammad ibn Jarir aṭ-Ṭabari, provides us with considerable insight and knowledge concerning the ruling on the present topic at hand.

In relation to the above, I would submit firstly that the incident as recorded by Imām aṭ-Ṭabari depends upon whether it is supported and uninterrupted concerning the channel from 'Aāṣim bin 'Amr bin Qatādah from his father from his grandfather, Qatādah bin an-Nu'mān, instead of being from amongst the *marāseel* and *munqaṭi'āt*, and which shows that in reality the crime of theft was committed. That Allah named those people as the treacherous, not because they were solely charged with denial or rejection (*jaḥd*), but rather it was because they lied to the Prophet (peace be upon him). For indeed, 'truth is a trust and the lie a betrayal,' just as Abu Bakr aṣ-Ṣadeeq (may Allah be pleased with him) said. Lying to the Prophet (peace be upon him) is no doubt from amongst the major destructive sins, the *mubiqāt*, and is vile and repudiated. The lie was done with intent and was thus a specific repudiation of the compact made with Allah when they bore witness that 'Muḥammad is the Messenger of Allah,' therefore breaking the compact through this disloyalty and treachery. Regardless of any difference in the specific details of the incident itself, the outcome – with regard to the present theme, that he (peace be upon him) acted according to what he perceived before him and was misled by the allegations made by a hypocrite and had initially defended his position until Allah the majestic intervened and exposed the true nature of events. Thereafter the traitors were exposed and the truth of the matter was fully demonstrated. This wasn't because of the requirements of Prophetic infallibility or related to the requirements of Prophethood and delivery of the message, but outlining what originally occurred in the sequence of events.

To conclude this matter, we make a small commentary footnote to the *isnād* as relayed by Imām Ṭabari - Al-Ḥasan bin Aḥmad bin Abu Shu'ayb Abu Muslim al-Ḥirāni narrated to us he said Muḥammad bin Salama narrated to us he said Muḥammad ibn Isḥāq narrated to us from 'Aāṣim bin Amar bin Qatādah from his father from his grandfather, Qatādah bin an-Numān. Contained within it is Muḥammad ibn Isḥāq as reporting 'from'. In reality though, this channel is connected and authentic, because Muḥammad ibn Isḥāq did indeed explicitly hear this from the next individual in the chain of transmission, as is the ruling demonstrated from other related channels.

Al-Ḥākim cited the following narrative in his *Mustadrak a'la Ṣaḥīḥayn*:[34]

> Abul'-'Abbās Muḥammad bin Ya'qub narrated to us Aḥmad bin Abdal-Jabbār narrated to us Yunus bin Bukeer narrated to us Muḥammad bin Isḥāq narrated to me 'Aāṣim 'Amr bin Qatādah from his father from his grandfather Qatādah bin an-Nu'mān may Allah be pleased with him, he said: The sons of

[34] Along with the other citations from *Tafsir*, the present narration is too long to cite the Arabic text in full. The full text is from the *Mustadrak* Vol. 4 sec. 426, no. 8164

Ubayriq were a group from the tribe of Dthafr and they were three men, Basheer, Bashr and Mubashar. Basheer was the agnomen of Ṭa'mah's father. He was a poet and a hypocrite. He used to satirize the companions of the Messenger of Allah peace be upon him. Then he used to claim that someone else was expressing satirical poetry against them, but whenever the companions heard it, they would say that it was a lie by an enemy of Allah. He said –

Or whenever the men said a poem * they (companions) say that Ubayriq said it**

They sneezed as if I were afraid of them * I wish (that) if Allah blocked their noses.**

They were poor and needy in *Jāhiliyah* and after Islam. My uncle, Rifā'ah bin Zayd was a well-known man who attained Islam. And by Allah, never saw any benefit in his Islam. If he had some money and whenever a caravan passed by him carrying the white flour, he would have bought it for himself, while he would feed his children the barley. Once the caravan of the Nabataeans passed by, carrying flour on the camel's back from both sides. He then bought the camel load from them in the upper part of the house and he had two shields in addition to what suited them in this room. After midnight, Bashir went to the top of the house and took the food and then he took the armour. When my uncle Rifā'ah awoke, he sent for me, then I went to him. He said we have been robbed last night and our food and weaponry are gone. Bashir and his brothers said to him, 'By Allah no one but Labeed bin Sahl stole your possessions.' Labeed was an honourable man. When he heard of these words spoken he went to them and said: 'O sons of the Ubayriq! You claim that I'm the thief? O Allah I will make you taste the blade of my sword or show to you the actual thief.'

In reply, they said: 'Go away, you are innocent of this robbery,' and he said: 'No, and you have claimed (this).' Then we inquired in order to discover the stolen items, until we were told Banu Ubayriq made a fancy dinner that night, what we see only on your goods, we are to remain investigating until we were about to be certain and believe that they are the culprits. I went to the Messenger of Allah pace be upon him and told him about this. They had a cousin whose name was Aseer bin 'Urwa and he gathered his tribesmen and then came to the Messenger of Allah peace be upon him. He said that Rifā'ah bin Zayd and his nephew Qatādah bin an-Nu'mān have deliberately insulted one of our household known for their honour and the goodness of their morals and they have accused them of theft without any substantive proof or actual witnesses, putting this before the Messenger of Allah peace be upon him, then leaving. Once I came to the Messenger of Allah peace be upon him and he said harshly: '*What you did is fully wrong; shame on these deeds. You went to a house of honourable people accusing them of theft, without having any proof or clear evidence?*'

I heard from the Messenger of Allah peace be upon him, what I never liked to hear from him and I turned away from him. I said, 'By Allah, I wished if I had lost all my money and it would be better than hearing this from him peace be upon him in this matter and I will never go back to him.' Thus, he said by Allah whose help is sought; the Qur'ān was revealed: *Indeed, we have revealed the book to you with the truth, that you may judge between people by means of that which Allah has taught you; and be not an advocate on behalf of the treacherous,*[35] about Ṭa'mah bin Ubayriq. He thus read until he came to: '*then accuses of it one innocent,*'[36] and this verse referred to Labeed bin Sahl.

Following the revelation of Qur'ānic verses, Ibn Ubayriq fled to Mecca. Then the Messenger of Allah peace be upon him sent for him to get the two shields and their coats of armour back; after which he gave them back to Rifā'ah. Qatādah said, when I brought the shields back to Rifā'ah he

---

[35] *Qur'ān,* 4: 105
[36] *Qur'ān*, 4: 112

said: 'oh my nephew! They are alms for the sake of Allah.' Then I wondered if my uncle's Islam had got better. But I was wrong, he wasn't as I had thought. Ibn Ubayriq went out until he encountered Salāmah, the daughter of Sa'd bin Sahl, the sister of Bani 'Amr ibn Auf being with Ṭalḥa bin Abi Ṭalḥa in Mecca. And all of a sudden, he met with the Messenger of Allah peace be upon him and his companions and he insulted them. Then Hasān bin Thābit mentioned their fathers and said:

Oh he who steals the shields, if you want to speak * don't mention the honour of men by your tongue**

And the daughter of Sa'd hosted him and became * with the skin of his estrangement and conflict**

So your family came to you willingly * unto him and did not want to please him**

You thought that you would hide what you have done * and among you a Prophet has revelation and has placed it**

Thus if it were not men insulting of your tribe * I would have been overwhelmed**

If you remember a heel to what you attributed to * like the rain when it destroys the flour.**

When Hasān's poem reached her, she departed taking with the luggage and put it on her head, until I threw it down. Then she shaved her hair and made a hole in her ears and she gave an oath that he had to leave the house. I was guided by the poetry that Hasān bin Thābit made, what had been good to descend upon me. When she got him out of the house, he went towards Ṭā'if. He entered an abandoned house where there was no one. And this house fell upon him (caved in) and it killed him. After this, the Quraysh kept saying: 'Oh Allah, Muḥammad would never leave any one of his good companions away from him.'

Similar has been reported in several collections, such as the following:

- *Sunan* Tirmidhi [Vol. 5 sec. 247, no. 3036] with the wording and channel of transmission like that of Imām Ṭabari: Al-Ḥasan bin Aḥmad bin Abi Shu'ayb Abu Muslim al-Ḥarāni narrated to us Muḥammad bin Salama al-Ḥarāni narrated to us Muḥammad ibn Isḥāq narrated to us from 'Aāṣim bin Umar bin Qatādah from his father from his grandfather Qatādah bin an-Nu'mān he said: There was a household among us called Banu Ubayriq (et. al).
- And similar is found in the *Mu'jam al-Kabir* of Imām Ṭabarāni [Vol. 19 sec. 12, no. 15]: Abu Shu'ayb Abdullah bin al-Ḥasan bin Aḥmad bin Abu Shu'ayb narrated to us – my father narrated to me, Muḥammad bin Salama narrated to us from Muḥammad bin Isḥāq from 'Aāṣim bin Umar bin Qatādah from his father from his grandfather Qatādah bin an-Nu'mān he said.
- *Tārikh Madina* (History of Medina) by Ibn Shaba [Vol. 2 sec. 408]: al-Ḥasan bin Aḥmad bin Abu Shu'ayb as-Samarqandi narrated to us he said Muḥammad bin Salama al-Ḥarāni narrated to us Muḥammad bin Isḥāq narrated to us from A'āṣim bin Umar bin Qatādah from his father from his grandfather Qatādah bin an-Nu'mān he said.
- In *al-Jalis aṣ-Ṣāliḥ wal'Anees an-Nāṣiḥ* [sec. 226, as per the numbering in the *Shāmila*]: Yaḥya bin Muḥammad bin Ṣā'id narrated to us (in the) year 318, he said: Abu Muslim al-Ḥasan bin Aḥmad al-Ḥarāni narrated to us in Baghdad (in the) year 248, he said Muḥammad bin Salama al-Ḥarāni narrated to us he said Muḥammad bin Isḥāq narrated to us from 'Aāṣim bin Umar bin Qatādah from his father from his grandfather Qatādah bin an-Nu'mān, he said.
- In *an-Sāb al-Ashrāf* [sec. 1/120, as per the numbering in the *Shāmila*]: and reported from Muḥammad bin Isḥāq from A'āṣim bin Umar bin Qatādah adth-Dthafari from his father from his grandfather Qatādah bin an-Nu'mān bin Zayd 'Aāmir bin Sawād bin Dhafr, he said.
- *Tārikh Dimishq* (History of Damascus) by Ibn Asākir [Vol. 49 sec. 270]: Abu Ghālib Aḥmad and Abu Abdullah Yaḥya reported to us al-Ḥasan reported to us, they said: Sa'd ibn Muḥammad ibn al-Ḥussain bin Aḥmad al-Faqihi reported to us Abu Ṭāhir Muḥammad bin Abdar-Raḥman bin al-'Abbās al-Mukhliṣ reported to us Yaḥya

bin Muḥammad bin Ṣā'id narrated to us Abu Muslim al-Ḥasan bin Aḥmad al-Ḥarāni narrated to us Muḥammad ibn Salama al-Ḥarāni narrated to us Muḥammad bin Isḥāq narrated to us from 'Aāṣim bin Umar bin Qatādah from his father from his grandfather Qatādah bin an-Nu'mān, he said.

Allah the exalted, blessed be his names has said:

وَمِمَّنْ حَوْلَكُم مِّنَ الْأَعْرَابِ مُنَافِقُونَ وَمِنْ أَهْلِ الْمَدِينَةِ مَرَدُوا عَلَى النِّفَاقِ لَا تَعْلَمُهُمْ نَحْنُ نَعْلَمُهُمْ سَنُعَذِّبُهُم مَّرَّتَيْنِ ثُمَّ يُرَدُّونَ إِلَىٰ عَذَابٍ عَظِيمٍ

Some of the desert Arabs around you are hypocrites, as are some of the people of Medina– they are obstinate in their hypocrisy. You [Prophet] do not know them, but We know them well: We shall punish them twice and then they will be returned to [face] a painful punishment.[37]

From this verse, we see Allah attesting to the fact that contained within the blessed city of Medina, there were *munāfiqeen* (hypocrites), indeed, stubborn in hypocrisy. Moreover, the Prophet (peace be upon him) as shown by this verse did not know them. By necessity this requires that he judges all inhabitants – the believers, the truthful and all others – on the basis of the apparent and on their oaths and testimonies, be they ultimately true or false. Allah says:

إِذَا جَاءَكَ الْمُنَافِقُونَ قَالُوا نَشْهَدُ إِنَّكَ لَرَسُولُ اللَّهِ وَاللَّهُ يَعْلَمُ إِنَّكَ لَرَسُولُهُ وَاللَّهُ يَشْهَدُ إِنَّ الْمُنَافِقِينَ لَكَاذِبُونَ

When the hypocrites come to you, they say: We bear witness that you are most surely Allah's Messenger; and Allah knows that you are most surely His

[37] *Qur'ān* 9: 101

Messenger, and Allah bears witness that the hypocrites are surely liars. [38]

We would hasten to add that this does not mean that he did not need to know or that he wasn't informed by revelation in specific instances that certain people were indeed hypocrites, as has also been mentioned by Imām Abu Muḥammad Ali Ibn Ḥazm. Moreover, Allah the exalted has explained:

يَا أَيُّهَا الَّذِينَ آمَنُوا إِن جَاءَكُمْ فَاسِقٌ بِنَبَإٍ فَتَبَيَّنُوا أَن تُصِيبُوا قَوْمًا بِجَهَالَةٍ فَتُصْبِحُوا عَلَىٰ مَا فَعَلْتُمْ نَادِمِينَ

O you who believe! If an evil-doer comes to you with a report, look carefully into it, lest you harm a people in ignorance, then be sorry for what you have done. [39]

The reason behind the revelation of this verse are *mutawātir* and famous. There are several channels of transmission which outline the specific details. Amongst them, Imām Ṭabarāni records the following long narration in *Mu'jam al-Kabir:*[40]

> Abdullah ibn Aḥmad bin Ḥanbal narrated to us Muḥammad bin Abu 'Utāb Abu Bakr al-'Ayn narrated to me (*ḥawala*) and Muḥammad bin Abdullah al-Ḥaḍrami narrated to us Abdullah bin al-Ḥakam bin Abu Ziyād al-Qaṭawāni narrated to us (*ḥawala*) and Muḥammad bin Aḥmad al-Ḥimāl al-Aṣbahāni narrated to us Muḥammad bin Esa az-Zujāj narrated to us; they said Muḥammad bin Sābiq reported to us Esa bin Dinār al-Muwazan narrated to us – my father narrated to me that he heard al-Ḥārith bin Ḍirār al-Khuzā'y say: I arrived upon the

[38] *Qur'ān* 63: 1
[39] *Qur'ān* 49: 6
[40] Given the length of the narration, only the English text is presented together with the translated *isnād*.

Prophet (peace be upon him) the Prophet invited me to Islam and I entered into it and I accepted it. And he invited me to the *Zakāt* and I accepted that, thereafter I said: O Prophet! I am going back to my people. There, I will call them to Islam and upon their response I will collect the *Zakāt* from them. O Prophet, please send someone at such and such time so that I will hand over the (collected) *Zakāt* money to him. (His people) responded to him and al-Ḥārith collected the *Zakāt* in a timely manner and wanted to send that to the Prophet (peace be upon him). He retained it with him for the Prophet to collect. Al-Ḥārith thought (given that no one came to collect) that he had in some way, earned the displeasure of Allah and his messenger (peace be upon him). So he summoned his people and said to them: It is time for me to send a messenger to the Prophet (peace be upon him) in relation to the *Zakāt* which has been collected.

Meanwhile, the Prophet (peace be upon him) had sent Waleed bin ‘Uqba to al-Ḥārith to collect the *Zakāt*. However, when Waleed had travelled half-way there, he returned to the Prophet (peace be upon him). Al-Waleed bin ‘Uqba said: Oh messenger of Allah, indeed al-Ḥārith prevented me to collect the *Zakāt* and wanted to kill me, messenger of Allah - despatch a force to al-Ḥārith to strike at him. So a force of companions was despatched to go to al-Ḥārith. On route they came across al-Ḥārith and he asked, to whom have you been sent? They said: to you! He said, but why? They said: Indeed the Prophet (peace be upon him) despatched al-Waleed bin ‘Uqba and he came back and claimed that you prevented the collection of *Zakāt* and wanted to kill him. Al-Ḥārith said: I swear by the one who raised Muḥammad (peace be upon him) with the truth! I did not see him (Waleed) and he did not come to me, nor did I seek to retain it (*Zakāt*). Thereafter *al-Ḥujjarāt* was revealed - *O you who believe! If a fāsiq comes to you with a report, look carefully into it, lest you harm a people in ignorance, then be sorry for what you have done* (49: 6) until where it is said - *by grace from Allah and as a favour; and Allah is Knowing, Wise* (49: 8).

Similar is reported in the *Musnad* of Imām Aḥmad where he records, 'Muḥammad bin Sābiq narrated to us with its full channel and text.' I would submit that here also is where the Prophet (peace be upon him) did not have foreknowledge of the liar in his midst, namely al-Waleed bin 'Uqba. He had sent a military expeditionary force which almost resulted in disaster, but for the divine intervention by the blessing of Allah. Next, Bukhāri cited the following narration in his *Ṣaḥīḥ*, which is exceptionality authentic:

> حدثنا أبو اليمان أخبرنا شعيب عن الزهري أخبرني عروة بن الزبير أن زينب بنت أبي سلمة أخبرته عن أمها أم سلمة قالت: سمع النبي، صلى الله عليه وسلم، جلبة خصام عند بابه فخرج عليهم فقال: إنما أنا بشر، وإنه يأتيني الخصم، فلعل بعضاً أن يكون أبلغ من بعض، أقضي له بذلك، وأحسب أنه صادق! فمن قضيت له بحق مسلم فإنما هي قطعة من النار فليأخذها أو ليدعها
>
> Abul'Yamān narrated to us Shu'ayb reported to us from az-Zuhri, Urwa bin az-Zubayr reported to me that Zaynab the daughter of Abu Salama reported to her from her aunt Umm Salama, she said – the Prophet (peace be upon him) heard the voices of some people quarrelling near his gate, so he went to them and said: *I am only mortal and litigants with cases involving disputes come to me, and maybe one of them presents his case eloquently in a more convincing and impressive way than the other, and I give my verdict in his favour thinking he is truthful. If I give a Muslim's right to another then that is a piece of fire, which is up to him to take it or leave it.*

Imām Bukhāri has recorded similarly elsewhere within his *Ṣaḥīḥ*. It is a tradition which is reported by almost all scholars of note in their respective collections. It appears in several places in *Ṣaḥīḥ* Muslim, as well as in the *Sunan* collections of Bayhaqy, Dāraquṭni, Nasā'i, Tirmidhi, Ibn Majāh and Abu Dāwud. It is also in the *Musnad* collections such as that of Aḥmad, Abu Ya'la, and Ṭabarāni, in the *Muwaṭṭā'* of Mālik, as well as in the various *Muṣṣanaf* collections like that of Abu Bakr ibn Abi Shayba. Without any shred of doubt, this narrative that has reached us from the Prophet (peace be upon him) is a decisive proof established with certainty.

Moreover, this *ḥadith* confirms several key facts which are of the utmost importance. It provides a dire warning to litigants who may be well-versed in presenting an eloquent case in court, yet behind this their claim is invalid. Such eloquent counsel by itself can even mislead the infallible Prophet (peace be upon him) to the extent that he could rule or judge in their favour, whether the litigation related to wealth, honour or blood. By greater reasoning, it is entirely plausible for the likes of famous companions such as Ibn 'Abbās or indeed other companions, may Allah be please with them all, to fall prey to crafty litigants in court. The noble companions, and indeed every other Islamic scholar or judge, does not receive revelation as the Prophet (peace be upon him) did in the aforementioned examples to expose the true nature of events. All must judge on the apparent and on the basis of evidence which is brought before them, and in this, like the Prophet (peace be upon him), they are not immune from error.

A portion of this chapter was relayed on the internet in response to a debate with an unfortunate idiotic *Wahābi* donkey from amongst the more 'learned' of the propagandists in the '*Salafi*' movement. Despite such efforts, these fell on deaf ears. Indeed, how should one respond when faced with his constructive criticism after perusing this section, he retorts: 'You are (from) the heretics (*zanādiqa*)!' He continued:

> That as long as your (argument stands that the) Prophet is misled by the lie of a liar, why not exclude the stories in relation to the previous nations as they appear in the Qur'ān given that all of it can be a deception made by the lie of a liar? As long as he can be misled by the lies of the liars, and that

> which is falsehood presented before him, why isn't many of the good things that he perceives also be considered a deception?

We would say, what is mentioned by this conceited individual is from the remarks of the heretics (*zanādiqa*) – and we hope to Allah that we are never from amongst them. Yet it is not new altogether. For indeed, the Quraysh said as such, arguing that they knew human nature and that before his pronouncement (peace be upon him), with that discourse. Similar outrageous comments have been uttered by the Orientalists.

The Prophethood of Muḥammad (peace be upon him) is established by proven decisive evidences, including this miraculous Qur'ān in our present possession. It is unlike the miracles of the previous Prophets which were temporary and demonstrated before a specific people. Many of the Prophetic miracles of Muḥammad (peace be upon him) are established through *tawātur*, continuously recurrent reports. He split the moon; he fed a large number of people from a very small quantity of food, through to predicting the attacks of the Mongols which occurred hundreds of years into the future. He (peace be upon him) used to deliver sermons while standing beside, or leaning against, the trunk of a date palm tree. When he (peace be upon him) used his pulpit instead, the tree began to cry and wail. The entire course of history was changed during the lifetime of the Prophet; he changed the entire Arabian Peninsula in one generation, this was despite losing his uncle and original protector through to the hostility of fifth-columnists which he faced in Medina. All of this and many other decisive evidences pertaining to the fact will be outlined later in the present work.

Muḥammad (peace be upon him) is the Prophet of Allah, a conveyer of the pronouncement made from Allah and in that, he is infallible, even before he uttered from the glorious Qur'ān. Therefore as established with decisive certain evidences by the necessities of perception and reason, as well as by the text of the Qur'ān, that he (peace be upon him) is infallible in his speech, without lie or error. Concerning his acts, he does not commit anything prohibited. It is also further established that the *Dhikr* was revealed to him – the *Dhikr* being both the Qur'ān and the *Sunnah*, both of which is protected by Allah. Consequently, it is an attested and established proof when he (peace be upon him) said:

> *I am only mortal and litigants with cases involving disputes come to me, and maybe one of them presents his case eloquently in a more convincing and impressive way than the other, and I give my verdict in his favour thinking he is truthful. If I give a Muslim's right to another then that is a piece of fire, which is up to him to take it or leave it.*

In reply, we say Allah and His Messenger spoke the truth and that speech in no manner undermines their truthfulness; the Prophet sitting in court before litigants is one of the best displays of this proof, or the fact that a liar may conceal his real motives in testimony. None of that is in conflict with the notion of infallibility in reporting from Allah.

Oh Allah and oh Muslims – when was a person's report as a litigant in a court of judgement concerning the ownership of agricultural land or even a camel or a donkey, a report or pronouncement from Allah via such a person? Moreover, what precisely has a litigant in court presenting *his evidence* before the Prophet (peace be upon him) got to do with the Prophet's receipt of revelation and conveyance from Allah? Oh Allah and oh Muslims – when was Abul-Qāsim, seal of the Prophets, whose infallibility was preserved by Allah, taking reporting about Allah from one amongst the people? Even as originally presented by our questioner when he said: *and that which is falsehood presented before him, why isn't many of the good things that he perceives also be considered a deception?*

After this the conceited questioner said:

> Know that the *ḥadith* that you mentioned to prove that the Prophet (peace be upon him) can be deceived by the lies of liars does not mean what you have understood. Nay, this is a special case specific *ḥadith* mentioned in the area of judicial ruling and is clearly known. There are clear differences between judicial ruling and informing about Allah regarding legislation or interpretation of the Qur'ān. The statement of Ibn 'Abbās is from this second type. The judge only rules with what results from proof and upon testimony, even if it were contrary to reality, for he is required to act upon what is indicated by proof and testimony. Most of the scholars assert that the judge has to rule according to the proof and testimony even if he knew by himself that the truth is contrary to what he has ruled. For more in this regard, see: *Badā'i aṣ-Ṣanā'i* Vol. 7, p. 7; *at-Tamheed* Vol. 22, p. 219, *Rawḍa aṭ-Ṭālibeen* Vol. 11, p. 156 and *al-Mughny* Vol. 9, p. 53.

In reply, I submit – *mā'shā'Allah;* whatever Allah wills, will undoubtedly be. What specific relationship does this originally have to the chapter of judgment or the wider topic at hand? Fundamentally, the issue is whether it is possible that the Prophet can be misled by a litigant persuasively arguing *his case* in a legal setting, or deliberately being misled by a litigant lying outright to pursue his case; can this happen before an infallible Prophet? Alternatively, is it impossible for this to happen to him because he is an infallible Prophet? The *ḥadith* which relate to this area of judicial ruling, makes the matter even worse, being deceived by lies or ornamented false proofs in court is much worse, given that potentially, money, reputation, and lives can be at stake.

The Prophet (peace be upon him) rendered all trusts, conveyed the message, and warned that none after him will be protected or rendered infallible against believing a deceitful litigant, one who can conceal his dishonesty and successfully present his case in court. That also would not be limited to a particular type of litigation, but rather involving all, be that in relation to money, reputation, blood or otherwise. By greater reasoning, others may be misled by litigants in court, but also by other forms of sworn testimony. A notable example which perhaps befell the great trusted Imām, Ibn 'Abbās concerning the mythical story of al-Lāt, formerly a pious man who served *Saweeq* for pilgrims. If Ibn 'Abbās were to enquire of the Arabs of his time to testify to the correctness of this myth, they may have well done so, arguing that it was heard from their forefathers. Yet what can be proven from hearing such testimony of even sworn oath or even other forms of hearsay?

As for the words of the obstinate questioner regarding what majority of scholars, as he would claim, believed in concerning the judge ruling according to proof and testimony, even if he knew that the truth was contrary to what he ruled, this has nothing to do with this subject and there is no gain out of it, notwithstanding its historical controversy. It is more likely that this opinion is wrong, notwithstanding that it would require an exhaustive study. Cases falling under the penal code generally, and especially those of adultery and reputation, are not like a dispute about the ownership of camel or a lot of land. Evidence and proof is not of the same kind or even degree. But to those who are small minded and shallow thinking, like the questioner, they would think it likely to be the case. Such discourse is typical from those who go to extremes in religion, typified by the *Wahābi / Salafist* sect. Instead of pursuing such line of discourse, it would have benefitted the questioner to seek detailed knowledge and ask a more meaningful question.

The ruling of a judge with his knowledge has no relationship with our subject except if that questioner claimed that the Prophet (peace be upon him) knew that the witnesses lie; if they lied and discovered their falsification but he only ruled with what is apparent and lied and deceived us by saying:

> *I am only mortal and litigants with cases involving disputes come to me, and maybe one of them presents his case eloquently in a more convincing and impressive way than the other, and I give my verdict in his favour thinking he is truthful. If I give a Muslim's right to another then that is a piece of fire, which is up to him to take it or leave it.*

The Prophet (peace be upon him) did not say something like – 'I was protected by Allah against believing your lies or eloquent speech but there will come after me people who will be deceived and misguided. If any of you ruled with anything but the truth, it is really a portion of Hellfire, so do not take it.' Thus, the false premise upon which the questioner posed his question, would ultimately lead to the conclusion that the Prophet (peace be upon him) was lying – and this is a serious problem. Forming such conclusion is evidently *kufr* (disbelief) and *Shirk* (polytheism). The questioner should have thought twice before opening his mouth, and before uttering such a major lie.

Although, there is a way out of *kufr* and heresy by rejecting this *ḥadith*; for this to be done in a systematic and consistent way, one would have to repudiate all single-narrator reports and join the ranks of the extreme Mu'tazilites. Undoubtedly this would also mean rejecting all the unconnected broken-channel mythical narrations and stories regarding al-Lāt, one of the cornerstones of the *Wahābi / Salafist* doctrine. Yet this is the same story which the questioner expended great effort in trying to defend, seeking to argue that it is historically sound, all the while because it agrees with the lie perpetuated by the *Wahābi / Salafist* sect.

That is not a reasonable or persuasive course of action to take in order to try and stick by a series of lies and arguments with flimsy premises. Naturally adopting this approach would lead to abandonment of the texts of the *Sunnah* which are not *mutawātir*. How then would we work with the Qur'ān, only on the basis of *tawātur*? How is the Qur'ān operationalised without the *Sunnah* and how would we determine the precise rulings of many chapters?

Alas, the obstinate questioner finds himself openly contradicting the *Ṣaḥiḥ aḥādith*, while rejecting others, with neither fear of sin or even reason to reign him in; a hallmark of his very *madthab* (school of thought). That *madthab* being like that from the *Wahābi*'s, those that would claim they are calling to and followers of the '*Salafiyah.*' If they deny that, they have denied far worse, since they are the most obstinate of innovators. They are characterised by being extremely unprincipled and dishonest; their followers mere hooligans. Agreeing only where the *Ṣaḥiḥ aḥādith* are in conforming to their desires, and readings from that which are *mutwātir*, when they are in mood, in a manner like a hit and run. Infamous in their use of a martyrdom of words – '*all the scholars*' and '*the schools of thought from the majority.*' And their saying, 'the righteous predecessors' (*as-Salaf aṣ-Ṣāliḥ*), suddenly morphs into 'the statement of a companion is a (legal) proof'; not to mention also 'blocking the means,' 'consideration of the greatest benefit/interest,' as well as other forms of gibberish and nonsense.

17 Silence as a decisive proof?

As previously detailed with decisive evidences, the Prophet's (peace be upon him) infallibility (*ma'ṣoom*) does not extend to the matter of being covered against a witness presenting a false testimony, or outright lying, within a court or judicial setting. Litigants who present their case in an eloquent and convincing manner before the Prophet (peace be upon him) were forewarned by him that if he rules in their favour, and they are not ultimately in the right, they will be obtaining a piece of hell-fire. Taking this matter one step further, by greater reasoning the Prophet's silence is also not covered by this infallibility, neither is the situation where he does not comment upon a matter. If he (peace be upon him) does not comment in relation to where someone attests to the truth or falsity of something, this is not a proof in itself originally and in principle.

Indeed, if someone utters words or an argument in his presence in opposition to what Allah has commanded and his reporting of the message to people, then without doubt he would be angered and deny that. He would speak against such a matter which in reality is *kufr* in itself, or maybe it would be excused if it was said in ignorance, or out of forgetfulness or from amongst the other impediments to *takfeer*; and not only because it is erroneous by its nature, but because blessings and peace be upon him, his mission was as a teacher, calling to the correct faith (*al-'Imān*). He (peace be upon him) though was not a teacher of philosophy, history, or the unseen wonders of the present world, if he had come in relation to all of that. Several examples can be presented to fully detail this point, so that it may become clear as crystal to the discerning mind.

In his *Ṣaḥīḥ*, Imām Muslim records the following *ḥadith* which has a particularly strong channel of transmission:

> حدثنا عبيد الله بن معاذ العنبري حدثنا أبي حدثنا شعبة عن سعد بن إبراهيم عن محمد بن المنكدر قال: رأيت جابر بن عبد الله يحلف بالله أن بن صائد الدجال فقلت: أتحلف بالله؟ قال: إني سمعت عمر يحلف على ذلك عند النبي، صلى الله عليه وسلم، فلم ينكره النبي، صلى الله عليه وسلم
>
> 'Ubaidallah ibn Mu'ādth al-Anbari narrated to us my father narrated to us Shu'ba narrated to us from Sa'd ibn Ibrāhim from Muḥammad bin Munkadir he said: I saw Jābir ibn Abdullah taking an oath in the name of Allah that it was Ibn Ṣā'id was the *Dajjāl*. I said: Do you take an oath in the name of Allah? Thereupon he said: I heard 'Umar taking an oath in the presence of the Messenger of Allah to this effect and he did not disapprove of it.

Similar is reported in the *Sunan* of Abu Dāwud;[1] Bukhāri records the same in his *Ṣaḥīḥ*, albeit via the following route, Ḥammād bin Ḥumayd narrated to us 'Ubaidallah bin Mu'ādth al-Anbari etc,'[2] and others have reported the same tradition in their collections.

From this *ḥadith* we learn that Jābir bin Abdullah heard Umar swear in the presence of the Prophet (peace be upon him) that Abdullah bin Ṣā'id was the *Dajjāl*. The Prophet (peace be upon him)

---

[1] *Sunan* Abu Dāwud Vol. 4 sec. 121, no. 4,331

[2] *Ṣaḥīḥ* Bukhāri Vol. 6 sec. 2,677, no. 6,922

did not disapprove of the statement which Umar made. So Jābir thought that this is from the genus of approvals, by the fact that it was an 'act' done in the presence of the Prophet. Similar is reported from Abdullah ibn Mas'ud, Abu Sa'eed al-Khudri as well as from others from amongst the *Ṣaḥāba* (may Allah be pleased with them all). It is unfortunate that this error in understanding was bequeathed from some of the *Ṣaḥābah* to the *Tābi'een* and so on and so forth, to the extent that it continues to bedevil scholars to this day. As a result, such an understanding can in turn lead to other problems in understanding textual evidences and this specific mistake can lead to fundamental contradictions.

Indeed, one may make the following deduction given the report at hand: it is permissible for one to make a verbal oath based upon what one is convinced of or believes to be correct; there is no sin as such in itself, even if the actual content of what is being attested to turns out to be demonstrably false. Some scholars have stated as such previously. Applying this to the aforementioned *ḥadith* shows this point quite eloquently, given that the incident took place in front of the Prophet (peace be upon him). The Prophet (peace be upon him) forbade the killing of this individual – named as Ibn Ṣā'id or Abdullah bin Ṣayyād, saying: *'If he should be him (i.e. Dajjāl) then you cannot overpower him, and should he not be him, then you are not going to benefit by murdering him.'*[3] It is certainly likely or after this, but even this way the point previously raised - it is permissible for one to make a verbal oath based upon what one convinced of or believes to be correct; there is no sin as such in itself, even if the actual content of what is being attested to turns out to be demonstrably false – can be upheld by other textual evidences. By the necessity of reason and common sense, as well as being upheld by other textual evidences, the prohibition of deliberate lying is a clear matter. Deliberately providing a false oath or testimony is from amongst the major sins (*kabā'ir*). It was also seen from amongst the hypocrites in Medina and the Bedouin Arabs at

---

[3] As reported by Bukhāri

the time of the Prophet (peace be upon him), despite the false excuses that they sought to marshal. They asked him to pray for forgiveness for this while some of them knowingly lied and some had even doubted the truth of his message. What the Prophet (peace be upon him) said to one from amongst them to his face, that he had lied.

He was not ordered to dwell into the underlying motivations of people, or to try and open their chests to explore the state of their hearts, nor was he authorised to spy on them; because he (peace be upon him) was a created mortal. He did not have knowledge of matters unseen, bar that which Allah showed to him. Even in that, it was related to the requirement of conveying the message or as a blessing from Allah for him and his *Ummah*. This, by the praise of Allah is clearly demonstrated as follows from the *ḥadith* that has reached us from Abu Namla (may Allah be pleased with him), recorded in the *Ṣaḥīḥ* of Ibn Ḥibbān:

أخبرنا بن قتيبة قال: حدثنا حرملة قال حدثنا بن وهب قال: أخبرنا يونس عن بن شهاب أن نملة بن أبي نملة الأنصاري حدثه أن أبا نملة أخبره أنه بينما هو جالس عند رسول الله، صلى الله عليه وسلم، جاء رجل من اليهود فقال: هل تكلم هذه الجنازة؟!، فقال رسول الله، صلى الله عليه وسلم: الله أعلم، فقال اليهودي: أنا أشهد أنها تتكلم! ، فقال رسول الله، صلى الله عليه وسلم: ما حدّثكم أهل الكتاب فلا تصدقوهم ولا تكذبوهم وقولوا آمنا بالله وملائكته وكتبه ورسله: فإن كان حقا لم تكذبوهم، وإن كان باطلا لم تصدقوهم، وقال: قاتل الله اليهود: لقد أوتوا علماً

Ibn Qutayba reported to us he said Ḥarmala narrated to us he said Ibn Wahb narrated to us he said Yunus reported to us from Ibn Shihāb that Namla bin Abi Namla al-Anṣāri narrated to him that Abu Namla reported to him that while he sat in the presence of the Messenger of Allah (peace be upon him) a Jew was also with him, a funeral passed by him. He (the Jew) asked (Him): Muḥammad, does this funeral speak? The Prophet (peace be upon him) said: *Allah has more knowledge*. The Jew said: I witness that it speaks. The Messenger of Allah (peace be upon him) said: *Whatever the people of the Book tell you, do not verify it, nor claim it to be false, but say - we believe in Allah and His Messenger. If it is false, do not confirm it, and if it is right, do not falsify it.* And he said: *Allah destroy the Jews; indeed, they were given knowledge.*

Shaykh Shu'ayb al-Arnā'uṭ said the *isnād* is strong; the tradition is authentic, *Ṣaḥīḥ*, particularly when considering the number of routes from which it has been reported, which is quite wide and appears in several collections.[4] Furthermore, in relation to this story, it has also been reported from 'Aāmir bin Rabi'ah (may Allah be pleased with him). Al-Ḥākim has this in the *Mustadrak*:

أخبرناه أبو الفضل الفقيه حدثنا عثمان بن سعيد الدارمي أخبرنا عبد الله بن عبد الجبار بحمص حدثنا الحارث بن عبيدة حدثنا الزهري عن سالم عن أبيه عن عامر بن ربيعة قال: كنا مع رسول الله، صلى الله عليه وسلم، فمر بجنازة فقال رجل من اليهود: يا محمد تكلم هذه الجنازة؟!، فسكت رسول الله، صلى الله عليه وسلم، فقال اليهودي: أنا أشهد أنها تكلم!، فقال رسول الله، صلى الله عليه وسلم: إذا حدثكم أهل الكتاب حديثا فقولوا آمنا بالله وملائكته وكتبه ورسله

Abu'l Faḍal al-Faqihi reported it to us Uthmān bin Sa'eed ad-Dārimi narrated to us Abdullah bin Abdal-Jabbār reported to us in Ḥimṣ al-Ḥārith bin Ubaida narrated to us az-Zuhri narrated to us from Sālim from his father from 'Aāmir bin Rabi'ah he said – was with the Prophet (peace be upon him) – We were with the Prophet (peace be upon him) and a funeral was passing by. A man from amongst the Jews said – O Muḥammad! This funeral (bier) speaks? The Prophet (peace be upon him) remained silent. The Jew further said: I testify that it speaks!

[4] For example, as found in: *Sunan* Abu Dāwud (Vol. 3 sec. 318, no. 3,644], *Musnad* Aḥmad (Vol. 4 sec. 136, no. 17,264, *Al-Aḥād wal-Mathāni* of Ibn Abi 'Aāṣim ash-Shaybāni [Vol. 4 sec. 142, no. 2,121], *Muṣṣanaf* Abdar-Razzāq [Vol. 6 sec. 111, no. 10,160], *Mu'jam al-Kabir* of Ṭabarāni [Vol. 22 sec. 350, no. 874/879], and *Sunan al-Kubra* of Imām Bayhaqy [Vol. 2 sec. 10, no. 2,071].

> So, the Prophet (peace be upon him) said: *If the people of the book narrate to you information then you should say, we believe in Allah, his angels, books and messengers.*

After recording this tradition Al-Ḥākim said:

> This *ḥadith* is known with al-Ḥārith bin ‘Ubaid ar-Rahāwy from az-Zuhri and we wrote it in other copies from Yunus bin Yazeed from az-Zuhri – Abul’Qāsim Abdullah ibn Muḥammad narrated to us in Nisapur, al-Qāsim bin Abdullah bin Mahdi narrated to us my uncle narrated to us a man narrated to us (his name is al-Qāsim bin Mabrur) Zayd bin Yunus narrated to us from Yazeed from az-Zuhri he said Sālim said indeed Abdullah bin Umar said – when I put the *Janāzah*, Rāfi’ bin Khadeej mentioned the *ḥadith*.

I would submit that al-Ḥārith bin ‘Ubaid ar-Rahāwy is not strong as a narrator and in the *isnād* it is regarded as having a lacuna (*saqṭ*), because the *isnād* which we have from Ṭabarāni in *Musnad Shāmiayn* has the following text:

> حدثنا عثمان بن خالد بن عمرو السلفي حدثنا عبد الجبار الخبائري حدثنا الحارث بن عبيدة حدثنا بقية بن الوليد عن الزبيدي عن الزهري عن سالم بن عمر عن عامر بن ربيعة، بنحوه
>
> Uthmān bin Khālid bin ‘Amr as-Salafi narrated to us Abdal-Jabbār al-Khabā’iri narrated to us al-Ḥārith bin Ubaida narrated to us Baqiya bin al-Waleed narrated to us from az-Zubaydi from az-Zuhri from Sālim bin ‘Amr from ‘Aāmir bin Rabi’ah and mentioned it.

And also, the *isnād* which is contained in *Ma’rifa aṣ-Ṣaḥābah* by Abu

Nu'aym al-Aṣbahāni:

> Abu Isḥāq bin Ḥamza narrated to us Aḥmad bin Khālid bin 'Amr as-Salafi narrated to us his father narrated to us al-Ḥārith bin U'baid narrated to us az-Zubaydi narrated to me from az-Zuhri from Sālim bin Abdullah from his father from 'Aāmir bin Rabi'a.

So here from these narrations we have the final Prophet of Allah refraining from commenting upon that which was spoken by a Jew in relation to the funeral bier. He did not affirm what was said as truth or claim that it was a lie, stating only that Allah knows best. This was also a guideline provided for the correct approach to be taken, which no Muslim with intellect or any others can ignore – '*do not verify it, nor claim it to be false, but say in reply, we believe in Allah, his angels, his books and his messengers; if it is false, do not confirm it, and if it is right, do not falsify it';* with a confirmation that they had been given knowledge and an affirmation as such with the exclamation made – '*Allah destroy the Jews, indeed they were given knowledge.*'

18 The '*Dhikr*' also encompasses the *Sunnah*

Earlier we detailed the proofs relating to the word the '*al-Dhikr al-Munazil'*, the 'revealed reminder' or the 'sent-down reminder', that it relates to the totality of the sent-down revelation. The totality of this revelation covers both the glorious Qur'ān as well as the Prophetic *Sunnah*. Furthermore, the claim that the *Dhikr* only relates to the glorious Qur'ān is an erroneous claim for it is a mere assertion without either a substantive basis or a sound reading of the texts of revelation. Hence it does not lend itself to being an established proof. Yet the real proof establishes other than this, particularly since 'the wisdom', *al-Ḥikmah* is another revealed or sent-down book of revelation, as detailed previously with evidences based upon certainty. All of this is summed up in the verse where the exalted and glorious says:

....وَأَنزَلْنَا إِلَيْكَ الذِّكْرَ لِتُبَيِّنَ لِلنَّاسِ مَا نُزِّلَ إِلَيْهِمْ وَلَعَلَّهُمْ يَتَفَكَّرُونَ

....and We have revealed to you the Dhikr that you may make clear to men what has been revealed to them, and that haply they may reflect.[1]

---

[1] *Qur'ān* 16: 44

The meaning becomes even clearer when this verse is read in tandem with the following:

إِنَّ عَلَيْنَا جَمْعَهُ وَقُرْآنَهُ، فَإِذَا قَرَأْنَاهُ فَاتَّبِعْ قُرْآنَهُ، ثُمَّ إِنَّ عَلَيْنَا بَيَانَهُ

Surely on Us (devolves) the collecting of it and the reciting of it. Therefore, when We have recited it, follow its recitation. Thereafter upon Us (devolves) the explaining of it.[2]

It is important to identify the exact meaning of '*al-Dhikr al-Munazil*' in order to accurately determine its nature and precise import. The first verse is definitive proof that there are two distinct 'sent-down' revelations.

- The first revelation relates to an earlier period; what has already been sent-down to the general people. It is in the hands of the people, regardless of how they obtained it.

- The second revelation relates to a later time and is so named, *al-Dhikr*. This is the sent-down or revealed reminder (*al-Dhikr al-Munazil*). Moreover, it is that which is specifically revealed to the final Messenger of Allah from the beginning and not to the general public; It doesn't appear before the people except by way of the conduit, i.e. the Prophet (peace be upon him). It is performed or taken up by the general public thereafter. Based upon this, the *Dhikr* is protected and infallible (*ma'ṣoom*). The Prophet (peace be upon him) undertakes the function of illustrating and explaining the *Dhikr* which has been revealed and sent-down. By itself, the *Dhikr* is not a *bayān* (proclamation), rather it is the 'raw

[2] *Qur'ān* 75: 17/19

material' which the Messenger uses to undertake the function of illustration and explanation.

But what is meant by the *Tanzeel* that was formerly sent, described as *'that which was previously revealed to people generally'*? What is its precise reality? Indeed, the phrase *'that which was previously revealed to people generally'* can be sub-divided or categorised as follows:

- As an infallible, protected revelation from Allah.
- Clarification and illustration is required, either for some, or all of it.
- One of the important functions of this revealed sent-down *Dhikr* is that it is the second subsequent revelation. It is the 'raw material' which is based upon the Prophet (peace be upon him) in which the clarification is provided. Therefore the first revelation, *'that which was previously revealed to people generally'*, this may be the *Dhikr al-Munazil*, having other functions also. In speech it is not regarded as a form of restriction (*ṣeeghat-ḥaṣr*) or what can be construed as such.

The minimum which can be said to explain the phrase which appears in the verse *'make clear to men what has been revealed to them,'* is that it seems relates to the glorious Qur'ān. By necessity this is what one would assume. Upon first sight, this would appear to be the apparent or literal meaning of the verse. Also because it is primarily intended, it is usually association with the word *Tanzeel* (revealed) and its associated derivatives. It is also the revealed word and its characteristic. People received this revelation directly from the lips of the Prophet (peace be upon him) by his recitation and expressed in his precise delivery. It is as if he revealed it to them directly and without an intermediary. Or that it is as if it was revealed as written on parchment or engraved in tablets. Therefore there is merit that he said '*revealed to them'* as in the verse, unlike the *Dhikr* which was specifically revealed unto the Prophet Muḥammad (peace be upon him). Hence the Prophet elicits the *bayān* or explanation for this, which is making it clear to the people. Had the Prophet not undertaken the explanation of the *Dhikr Munazil* raw material, when people know the existence of this *Dhikr Munzail* originally and have witnessed all of it. If so and based upon this minimum approach, there is no doubt then that the great book, or with its precise wording some of which is the glorious Qur'ān is required for explanation or elucidation (*bayān*). This is a constant, not only in this verse, but also by necessity with the statement of the almighty where he has mentioned:

إِنَّ عَلَيْنَا جَمْعَهُ وَقُرْآنَهُ، فَإِذَا قَرَأْنَاهُ فَاتَّبِعْ قُرْآنَهُ ، ثُمَّ إِنَّ عَلَيْنَا بَيَانَهُ

Surely on Us (devolves) the collecting of it and the reciting of it. Therefore when We have recited it, follow its recitation. Thereafter upon Us (devolves) the explaining of it. [3]

The blessed verse is talking exclusively about the glorious Qur'ān and nothing but the Qur'ān as the usage of the word recital (*qur'ānah*) beyond doubt proves. The verse is a testimony that Allah has taken it upon himself to conduct the *bayān* of the Qur'ān as and where required or needed. However the explanation is usually after a period of time, as is signified by the word '*thereafter*' in the verse: '*Thereafter upon Us (devolves) the explaining of it*'. But this explanation is not delayed for the time when it is needed. Otherwise the meaning here would be lost and the promise that Allah has taken upon himself to provided the explanation would be void, and Allah does not state a promise he doesn't keep.

[3] *Qur'ān* 75: 17/19

وَالَّذِينَ فِي أَمْوَالِهِمْ حَقٌّ مَّعْلُومٌ، لِّلسَّائِلِ وَالْمَحْرُومِ

And those in whose wealth there is a fixed portion. For him who begs and for him who is denied.[4]

There is an obligation to spend from fixed earned wealth, and Allah has also said:

وَهُوَ الَّذِي أَنشَأَ جَنَّاتٍ مَّعْرُوشَاتٍ وَغَيْرَ مَعْرُوشَاتٍ وَالنَّخْلَ وَالزَّرْعَ مُخْتَلِفًا أُكُلُهُ وَالزَّيْتُونَ وَالرُّمَّانَ مُتَشَابِهًا وَغَيْرَ مُتَشَابِهٍ كُلُوا مِن ثَمَرِهِ إِذَا أَثْمَرَ وَآتُوا حَقَّهُ يَوْمَ حَصَادِهِ وَلَا تُسْرِفُوا إِنَّهُ لَا يُحِبُّ الْمُسْرِفِينَ

And He it is who produces gardens (of vine), trellised and untrellised, and palms and seed-produce of which the fruits are of various sorts, and olives and pomegranates, like and unlike; eat of its fruit when it bears fruit, and pay the due of it on the day of its reaping, and do not act extravagantly; surely He does not love the extravagant.[5]

Whilst we can see from the verse that a due must be paid on such produce, the verse doesn't specify exactly when this is to be taken; is it immediately at harvest or is the harvest referred to a daily matter? By greater reasoning, we don't know of the timing and amount which must be levied in relation to funds mentioned for *zakāt* - all of which is not specified in this particular verse, but requires other explanations and clarification to be given. Allah has also said:

إِنَّمَا الصَّدَقَاتُ لِلْفُقَرَاءِ وَالْمَسَاكِينِ وَالْعَامِلِينَ عَلَيْهَا وَالْمُؤَلَّفَةِ قُلُوبُهُمْ وَفِي الرِّقَابِ وَالْغَارِمِينَ وَفِي سَبِيلِ اللهِ وَابْنِ السَّبِيلِ فَرِيضَةً مِّنَ اللهِ وَاللهُ عَلِيمٌ حَكِيمٌ

---

[4] *Qur'ān* 70: 24/25
[5] *Qur'ān* 6: 141

Alms are only for the poor and the needy, and the officials (appointed) over them, and those whose hearts are made to incline (to truth) and the (ransoming of) captives and those in debts and in the way of Allah and the wayfarer; an ordinance from Allah; and Allah is knowing, wise. [6]

We know the classification given by the verse of the categories upon which charity is to be given to from this verse. But we do not know how to distribute them, nor do we know who precisely is to execute this, is it only individuals who are tasked with this? Or is to be done by the state? There is no further verse providing explanation in relation to this contained within the Qur'ānic text. Thus by necessity the explanation must come by way of the Prophetic *Sunnah*. Otherwise, the report where Allah says: '*and We have revealed to you the Dhikr that you may make clear to men what has been revealed to them, and that haply they may reflect,*' would in effect be false and his promise - *'Thereafter upon Us (devolves) the explaining of it,'* would be void. Yet Allah is far above anything related to lying or providing a false promise.

Allah has ensured that an explanation and clarification is sent-down for the Qur'ān after its collection and recitation, when there is a need for such. The word 'thereafter' or 'then' is used in the arrangement of the verse to show this, that the explanation is devolved upon Allah. Moreover, it is necessarily known from history that the Qur'ān was sent-down incrementally and followed by the Prophet (peace be upon him). This enabled for it to be memorised, committed to writing and for it to be established with decisive certitude. But it also enables greater clarification of processes that are detailed and need time to set out properly, an obvious example, being that of the ritual observance of prayer (*ṣalāh*). All these characteristics which exist for the text of the Qur'ān is in essence contrasted to the characteristics which accompanied the revealed sent-down *Dhikr*

[6] *Qur'ān* 9: 60

which was revealed to Muḥammad, which was to be the 'raw material' that was utilised in relation to the *bayān*. The two are radically different in that given respect.

1. The majestic Qur'ān requires explanation and clarification, which is usually done where required, as previously stated. But *al-Dhikr al-Munazil*, it is the raw material sent down upon the Prophet to provide explanation and clarification accompanying that of the Qur'ānic text where necessary and required.
2. The text of the Qur'ān is general revelation direct to mankind so to speak. Indeed it firstly descended upon the Prophet. Thereafter, he expounds that to the people. However the role of the Prophet in the first instance is to pronounce and expound this recitation only. It is then recorded and written down by the people. Yet the *al-Dhikr al-Munazil* is essentially different in respect of the fact that this is the 'raw material' which underpins and informs the Prophetic *bayān* or explanation via his actions, speech and approvals.

Consequently this is the fundamental difference which distinguishes *al-Dhikr al-Munazil* to be a raw material that underpins the Prophetic explanation and exposition. Indeed, it is qualitatively different from the text of the glorious Qur'ān and distinguished from it in these very respects.

But *al-Dhikr al-Munazil* is also another type, from the sent-down revelation emanating from Allah and nothing originally that is rightly to be placed as revelation to be sent down specifically upon the Prophet. Then the people take the explanation regarding it from him, by his statements, acts and approvals, that is the noble Prophetic *Sunnah*, or to be more precise with wording, the Prophetic *Sunnah* is a type or kind of explanation (*bayān*) which comes from the texts of the

Qur'ān, which is needed to explain or exemplify it. But the truth is that all of the Prophetic *Sunnah* is but a *bayān* with the text of the Qur'ān, because the explanation is not only to specify the general, as well as the absolute and restricted, as well as seeking to provide detailed ruling upon certain areas. No doubt this totally escapes the dysfunctional minds from amongst the Qur'ānists. Yet it is much broader than this, encompassing the *Tafsir* of it altogether as well; its explanation (*bayān*) and interpretation. Every *Sunnah* is but the *Tafsir* which is being made by Allah, blessed be his names, like where he says in the following Qur'ānic verses:

يَا أَيُّهَا الَّذِينَ آمَنُوا أَطِيعُوا اللَّهَ وَأَطِيعُوا الرَّسُولَ وَأُولِي الْأَمْرِ مِنكُمْ فَإِن تَنَازَعْتُمْ فِي شَيْءٍ فَرُدُّوهُ إِلَى اللَّهِ وَالرَّسُولِ إِن كُنتُمْ تُؤْمِنُونَ بِاللَّهِ وَالْيَوْمِ الْآخِرِ ذَٰلِكَ خَيْرٌ وَأَحْسَنُ تَأْوِيلًا

O you who believe! Obey Allah and obey the Messenger and those in authority among you; if you differ on anything, refer it to Allah and the Messenger, if you believe in Allah and the last day; this is better and very good in the end.[7]

مَّا أَفَاءَ اللَّهُ عَلَىٰ رَسُولِهِ مِنْ أَهْلِ الْقُرَىٰ فَلِلَّهِ وَلِلرَّسُولِ وَلِذِي الْقُرْبَىٰ وَالْيَتَامَىٰ وَالْمَسَاكِينِ وَابْنِ السَّبِيلِ كَيْ لَا يَكُونَ دُولَةً بَيْنَ الْأَغْنِيَاءِ مِنكُمْ وَمَا آتَاكُمُ الرَّسُولُ فَخُذُوهُ وَمَا نَهَاكُمْ عَنْهُ فَانتَهُوا وَاتَّقُوا اللَّهَ إِنَّ اللَّهَ شَدِيدُ الْعِقَابِ

Whatever Allah has restored to His Messenger from the people of the towns, it is for Allah and for the Messenger, and for the near of kin and the orphans and the needy and the wayfarer, so that it may not be a thing taken by turns among the rich of you, and whatever the Messenger gives you, accept it, and from whatever he forbids you, keep back, and be careful of (your duty to) Allah; surely Allah is severe in retributing (evil). [8]

وَاكْتُبْ لَنَا فِي هَٰذِهِ الدُّنْيَا حَسَنَةً وَفِي الْآخِرَةِ إِنَّا هُدْنَا إِلَيْكَ قَالَ عَذَابِي أُصِيبُ بِهِ مَنْ أَشَاءُ

---

[7] *Qur'ān* 4: 59
[8] *Qur'ān* 59: 7

وَرَحْمَتِي وَسِعَتْ كُلَّ شَيْءٍ فَسَأَكْتُبُهَا لِلَّذِينَ يَتَّقُونَ وَيُؤْتُونَ الزَّكَاةَ وَالَّذِينَ هُم بِآيَاتِنَا يُؤْمِنُونَ

الَّذِينَ يَتَّبِعُونَ الرَّسُولَ النَّبِيَّ الْأُمِّيَّ الَّذِي يَجِدُونَهُ مَكْتُوبًا عِندَهُمْ فِي التَّوْرَاةِ وَالْإِنجِيلِ يَأْمُرُهُم بِالْمَعْرُوفِ وَيَنْهَاهُمْ عَنِ الْمُنكَرِ وَيُحِلُّ لَهُمُ الطَّيِّبَاتِ وَيُحَرِّمُ عَلَيْهِمُ الْخَبَائِثَ وَيَضَعُ عَنْهُمْ إِصْرَهُمْ وَالْأَغْلَالَ الَّتِي كَانَتْ عَلَيْهِمْ فَالَّذِينَ آمَنُوا بِهِ وَعَزَّرُوهُ وَنَصَرُوهُ وَاتَّبَعُوا النُّورَ الَّذِي أُنزِلَ مَعَهُ أُولَٰئِكَ هُمُ الْمُفْلِحُونَ

قُلْ يَا أَيُّهَا النَّاسُ إِنِّي رَسُولُ اللَّهِ إِلَيْكُمْ جَمِيعًا الَّذِي لَهُ مُلْكُ السَّمَاوَاتِ وَالْأَرْضِ لَا إِلَٰهَ إِلَّا هُوَ يُحْيِي وَيُمِيتُ فَآمِنُوا بِاللَّهِ وَرَسُولِهِ النَّبِيِّ الْأُمِّيِّ الَّذِي يُؤْمِنُ بِاللَّهِ وَكَلِمَاتِهِ وَاتَّبِعُوهُ لَعَلَّكُمْ تَهْتَدُونَ

And ordain for us good in this world's life and in the hereafter, for surely we turn to Thee. He said: (As for) My chastisement, I will afflict with it whom I please, and My mercy encompasses all things; so I will ordain it (specially) for those who guard (against evil) and pay the poor-rate, and those who believe in Our communications.

Those who follow the Messenger-Prophet, the Ummi, whom they find written down with them in the Torah and the Bible (who) enjoins them good and forbids them evil, and makes lawful to them the good things and makes unlawful to them impure things, and removes from them their burden and the shackles which were upon them; so those who believe in him and honour him and help him, and follow the light which has been sent down with him, these it is that are the successful.

Say: O people! Surely I am the Messenger of Allah to you all, of Him Whose is the kingdom of the heavens and the earth there is no god but He; He brings to life and causes to die therefore believe in Allah and His apostle, the Ummi Prophet who believes in Allah and His words, and follow him so that you may walk in the right way.[9]

But the text of the Qur'ān upon that great Qur'ān is mentioned as well and it is called '*al-Dhikr al-Ḥakeem.*' Other types of revelation are also described as *Dhikr*. For that reason the wording must be *al-Dhikr al-Munazil* or *al-Dhikr*, in place of the wording about the general

---

[9] *Qur'ān* 7: 156/158

revelation without specifying the explanation or other than it. A comprehensive or compendium of revelation, and more specifically, the Qur'ān and *Sunnah*; it is not possible that the *Dhikr* can only be the Qur'ān; it must also include revelation other than the Qur'ān, as we have previously demonstrated. If it is decisively proved that the *Dhikr* which is sent-down and revealed is not solely the Qur'ān, but it is the Qur'ān and *Sunnah* or to be more accurate with wording: the Qur'ān and some *Sunnah*. But if it was some of the *Sunnah* that is mentioned therefore all of it is from the *Dhikr* necessarily, because all of it is an infallible revelation. It is one class, having a single rank in terms of its authenticity and binding status.

But to say the minimum that can be imagined for this - *'that which was previously revealed to people generally,'* as already mentioned, because the phrase with '*what was revealed to them*,' already holds the meaning of all the revelation that was sent down until that particular moment or juncture. It is with that which the explanation is lacking. This original revelation if it is by necessity either of the following:

1. Anything from the glorious Qur'ān to get its explanation and has certainly come for a time and to expound upon it, as already outlined.
2. A previous *ḥikmah* and *Sunan*, although still lacking explanation or further explanation. It came for its time and it is with that, the people received it. Thus it is preserved, studied and remembered. Reconciled that said about it, that it is from *what is revealed to them*, because it has reached them and it is in reality held by them.

It must therefore be a Prophetic explanation for which this relates to, i.e. *'that which was previously revealed to people generally,'* in other words, a new revelation to join that which was already revealed previously. There is no essential difference between the Qur'ān or the *Sunnah*, all of it is a complete self-contained revelation. So, it becomes a complete explanation or exposition. It does not need a new revelation to provide explanation for any part of it. It was completed in full prior to the death of the seal of the Prophets of Allah (peace be upon him), and indeed, all thanks and praise are due to Allah for this.

The Prophetic explanation (*bayān*) is by necessity comprised of the following:

1. The statements of the Prophet (peace be upon him) and arising from them, his gestures
2. His acts
3. What he approves

All of that comprises the Prophetic *Sunnah* and nothing less or even above and beyond that. The Prophetic *Sunnah* is from the revealed *Dhikr* by necessity. Therefore by any detailed account or hypotheses the revealed sent-down *Dhikr* (*al-Dhikr al-Munazil*) is indeed inclusive of the entire Qur'ān and the *Sunnah* by necessity. It is not possible that it is anything less or even more than that, because the sent-down revelation is only but these two. It must therefore be *al-Dhikr al-Munazil* and it is precisely the entire revelation, which is the Qur'ān and the *Sunnah* only and nothing other than it.

Hence the wording *al-Dhikr al-Munazil*, is what has been elucidated and should be understood and known as such when referring to what has been revealed or revelation. Inevitably such revelation is inclusive of the *Sunnah*, thus the truth of our manifest statement regarding our statement that the *Sunnah* is the expounder of the Qur'ān. And we also say that the Qur'ān and *Sunnah* complement and provide clarification upon each other. We would also submit that *al-Dhikr al-Munazil* which is the Qur'ān and *Sunnah* provide that complementary clarification upon each other's contents. It is a sufficient explanation and proclamation which establishes the proof of Allah upon his servants, all the way to the day of judgement. That is the truth of the matter; one entails the other by necessity.

Indeed some of the claims which are made from those who are called the 'Qur'ānists' are that the explanation would only be a new Qur'ān and not with other than the present Qur'ān. In reply, we would undoubtedly submit that these are baseless points and lies for the following reasons:

1. What is revealed from the Qur'ān lacking with regard to explanation. And this explanation by the necessity of perception and reason is not by another portion of the Qur'ān, because Allah ensured and proved with it and there isn't laxity in relation to any portion that has been revealed.
2. If the explanation of the Qur'ān is to be restricted exclusively by the Qur'ān itself, then it would be necessary for another Qur'ān to be sent forth after its revelation and completion. For the present Qur'ān as it exists now, does not provide explanation or exposition on all parts by itself. Seeking to cling to such a line of reason is nothing by stubbornness and a flight from sense and reason as the evidences presented earlier in this regard are compelling. One need only acknowledge if this line of reasoning were correct, how one would perform and establish the prescribed prayer?
3. The word 'its explanation', as mentioned in the verse '*Thereafter upon Us* (devolves) *the explaining of it*'[10] is known with the *iḍāfa* (possessive construction) and the word is known by its type or genus. Here, by necessity, its definition is related to the genus or type. Because we don't know that we have the verse by itself revealed yet. What is the usual agreed explanation upon it, there may be a definition of type here.

---

[10] *Qur'ān* 75: 17/19

So Allah the exalted may ensure if the genus of explanation is comprehensive for each of its components that can be imagined from it:

a. From the text other than the Qur'ān, this can be expounded at a later date. This explanation is a necessary duty for *Deen* would be incomplete without it.
b. Or from other revelation, its translation by the Prophet to flesh out this explanation by his actions, statements (and from that his gestures), and his approvals. What this is, is none other than the noble Prophetic *Sunnah*, which are the actions, statements, gestures and approvals and of the Prophet. By necessity this is a necessary explanation which *Deen* cannot be considered complete without.
c. Or even what may emerge in the future, be that from scientific or engineering discoveries, or even from discoveries in archaeology. From all of that, a new explanation may indeed be made to that existing from some of the Qur'ān. By way of a brief example of this can be seen from the statement of Allah where he said: *He created mankind from a clot ('alaq).*[11] As is understood from classical Arabic which the Qur'ān was revealed in, this denotes that mankind was created from nothing or from something which 'clings'. The extent of which the earlier commentators of the Qur'ān could present was that this is similar in some manner to a leech like substance that clings. Yet with the advent of modern scientific techniques, it has provided a further exemplification of the verse, showing that this clinging substance relates to the initial stage of the embryo which clings inside the womb. Without doubt given the advances in the medical sciences,

[11] *Qur'ān*, 96: 2

these have provided a verification and fuller explanation of precisely what the verse in question was saying.

The third type of explanation is indeed a *bayān*, except that it is not considered to be from revelation in itself or the sent-down revealed *Dhikr*. It is one of thus additional desirable explanations, which not only can provide some additional details of clarification, but also acts as additional proof establishing that the revelation is ultimately from Allah in origin. It is no doubt a blessing which Allah has bestowed upon his servants. By necessity it cannot be considered as being '*Deen*', because that was completed via the final Prophet who acted as both a seal on Prophethood and sent-down revelation. As already noted, such additional explanations do provide further proofs and on occasion, have clarified matters that many predecessors could not provide fully comprehend or outline in their commentaries. This added explanation, *bayān,* is from the grace of Allah, and an additional blessing, as he the exalted has said:

سَنُرِيهِمْ آيَاتِنَا فِي الْآفَاقِ وَفِي أَنفُسِهِمْ حَتَّىٰ يَتَبَيَّنَ لَهُمْ أَنَّهُ الْحَقُّ أَوَلَمْ يَكْفِ بِرَبِّكَ أَنَّهُ عَلَىٰ كُلِّ شَيْءٍ شَهِيدٌ

We will soon show them Our signs in the universe and in their own souls, until it will become quite clear to them that it is the truth. Is it not sufficient as regards your Lord that He is a witness over all things? [12]

To allege that the explanation (*bayān*) only will be by a new Qur'ān, nothing else, is but simply a claim and an invalid judgement, borne of obstinacy by necessity; a resistance to perceptible reasoning and a denial of the Qur'ān, and a specification with what came generally not from the Qur'ān. And this is cannot be with the text of the Qur'ān:

[12] *Qur'ān* 41: 53

'Say: bring your proof if you are truthful.'[13] So the sent-down revealed *Dhikr* is by necessity of perception and reason and by the witnessing of the Qur'ān itself, to include both the Qur'ān and the *Sunnah* with no other addition or subtraction. And we have seen as mentioned earlier that:

1. The infallible revelation is not only the Qur'ān; the *Sunnah* is an infallible revelation also. Alternatively, with a more precise and accurate wording: that the Prophetic *Sunnah* is not with its specific wording revelation from Allah but that it is a formulation and expression of an infallible Prophetic revelation which came from Allah.
2. And that the sent-down revealed *Dhikr* is not only the Qur'ān, but rather it is the Qur'ān and the *Sunnah*, with the *Sunnah* being the explainer or expounder of the Qur'ān. That is borne out and confirmed by a great number of texts which also establish the proof of the Prophetic *Sunnah* itself.

What we have mentioned regarding this established proof is not new, except that we have sought to delineate it more precisely, separating out each of the individual points which make up the subject and absorbing what the earlier scholars said regarding this. They had touched upon this, realising it instinctively and witnessed that there was a consensus upon this matter. As it has been presented in the seminal work of the grand Imām and pillar of knowledge, Abu Muḥammad Ali Ibn Ḥazm, *al-Iḥkām fi Uṣul al-Aḥkām* (Judgement on the Principles of Law):

> Ali said: and this is where we take *inshā'Allah* in the import of proofs upon that relating to *khabar al-wāhid,* it's rightness and

[13] *Qur'ān* 27: 64

(that it is) uninterrupted to the Messenger (peace be upon him) in *Aḥkām Sharī'ah.* It engenders knowledge and there shall be no illusion or lie in it. Hence we say, and with Allah the majestic is all success, Allah exalted and majestic said about his Prophet (peace be upon him) *'....nor does he speak out of his own desire. It is but revelation that is revealed to him.'*[14] And the almighty commanded to His Prophet (peace be upon him) to say: *'Say: I am not the first of the messengers, and I do not know what will be done with me or with you; I do not follow anything but that which is revealed to me, and I am nothing but a plain warner.'* [15] And he the almighty said: '*Surely We have revealed the Dhikr and We will most surely be its guardian.*' [16] And he (also) said: *'With clear arguments and scriptures and we have revealed to you the Dhikr that you may make clear to men what has been revealed to them and that haply they may reflect.'* [17] Thus it is true that the speech of the Messenger of Allah (peace be upon him), all of it in relation to *Deen* is revelation emanating from Allah the exalted. No doubt exists in relation to that and no disagreement raised by anyone from the people of language and *Sharī'ah*, that all of it is revealed that has been revealed from Allah the exalted and it is the revealed sent-down *Dhikr*. The entire revelation, all of it is protected (*maḥfouz*) by Allah; he has protected this with certainty.

Allah ensures the preservation of its contents. Nothing has been neglected from it, nor has anything been ever distorted from it and neither is the accompanying explanation of it invalid. It is not possible that the speech of Allah can be a falsity and it is a specific guarantee to the discerning mind, that which came to us by Muḥammad (peace be upon him) is protected; Allah has undertaken to preserve it and its conveyance, all of it that he has ensured until the end of the world. And the exalted said: *'Say: What thing is the weightiest in testimony? Say: Allah is witness between you and me; and*

[14] *Qur'ān* 53: 3/4
[15] *Qur'ān* 46: 9
[16] *Qur'ān* 15: 9
[17] *Qur'ān* 16: 44

this Qur'ān has been revealed to me that with it I may warn you and whomsoever it reaches. Do you really bear witness that there are other gods with Allah? Say: I do not bear witness. Say: He is only one Allah, and surely I am clear of that which you set up (with Him).' [18] Therefore, since it also by necessity that we know that there is no issue concerning the loss of something that the Messenger (peace be upon him) said in *Deen*. There is no way at all that it is mixed up with that which is *bāṭil* or fabricated, this is not put forth by anyone amongst the people, with certainty.

And if it were possible that the *Dhikr* was not protected, then the statement of Allah where he says - '*Surely We have revealed the Dhikr and We will most surely be its guardian,*'[19] would be an untruth and this cannot be said by a Muslim. He who would utter a saying, (is alleging) that the almighty alone preserved the Qur'ān but not other revelation which is not the Qur'ān. We say he has, and with Allah is all success, made a false assertion without proof to seek to specify the *Dhikr* without requisite evidence; thus it is *bāṭil* and devoid of meaning and the almighty says: *And they say: 'None shall enter the garden (or paradise) except he who is a Jew or a Christian. These are their vain desires. Say: Bring your proof if you are truthful.'* [20] Indeed the truth that he has no proof upon such a call, and there is no truth in it. The *Dhikr*, its name in reality is upon all what Allah revealed unto his Prophet (peace be upon him), from the Qur'ān or from the *Sunnah*, as it is shown by the Qur'ān. Also as Allah says: *'With clear arguments and scriptures and we have revealed to you the Dhikr that you may make clear to men what has been revealed to them and that haply they may reflect.'* [21] The truth that he (peace be upon him) was one who was put in charge with the explanation of the Qur'ān to the people. And the ambivalent (*mujmal*) in the Qur'ān are many, like the *ṣalāh, zakāt*, the *ḥajj* and other than it. We don't know what Allah

[18] *Qur'ān* 6: 19
[19] *Qur'ān* 15: 9
[20] *Qur'ān* 2: 111
[21] *Qur'ān* 16: 44

prescribed in it with wording, except with the explanation as given by the Prophet (peace be upon him).

So, when was his explanation (peace be upon him) altogether for that reason, not *maḥfouz* and not guaranteed? There is nothing from him, nor is there anything beneficial which has been lost from the text of the Qur'ān, so it invalidates the view that many of the laws that are supposed to be incumbent upon us within it are absent. So if no wonder Allah intended from it to be authentic, what mistake is found therein or a lie or even deliberate falsehood; and Allah forbid this. Thus, if we did not know that which was intended by Allah the almighty from it to be *Ṣaḥīḥ* (authentic), what mistake is found therein or the intentional lie of the liar - and Allah is distant from this. Also, we would say to whoever said that the *khabar al-wāḥid* (single-narrator report) of the just upright (*'adl)* narrator conveying from its like unto the Prophet (peace be upon him), does not obligate knowledge, given that its content may not have been accurately memorised and may contain within it a lie or an illusion; inform us then: is it possible that a *Sharī'ah* obligation (*farḍ*) or prohibition (*taḥreem*) brought by the Messenger of Allah peace be upon him (and he died and these rules still remain necessary by the Muslims; they were never abrogated and after all that) became unknown with certain knowledge to any Muslim from the people of Islam globally ever?

Moreover, according to your imagination, is it possible that a lie, fabrication or an illusion may have been overlooked and has been mixed up with the *Aḥkām Sharī'ah* and this mixture is so perfect that not one of the Muslims in the whole world can recognise it? Or you don't have any of these faces (outlooks) to (lay) claim (to)? If they say, the two claims can never be aligned, but we already believe in that, then they have arrived at what we have said and been cut-off; namely, that every *khabr* (report) narrated by the trustworthy narrator (*thiqa*) from another of its like and connected (*musnad*) to the Messenger of Allah, peace be upon him in the matter of religion, indeed it is

> truth. He peace be upon him said it as it is and that it is obliged to (accept) knowledge that we extract by way of that which is authentic. And it is not permissible to mix up with it the fabricated report (*khabr mawḍu'*) or that which is illusory, because the Messenger peace be upon him did not say that, such that the truth cannot be properly distinguished from falsehood ever.
>
> Indeed, if they say all of this is quite possible, they would have judged that the *Deen*, all of the *Deen* of Islam, to have been corrupted and invalidated. The orders of Allah the almighty would be mixed, that which he ordered and that which he didn't, not ever distinguishing anything of it. They would never know what is the difference between the matters that Allah ordered them with and that which he didn't order them to do. Moreover, they wouldn't know the difference between what was brought by the Messenger peace be upon him and that which was interpolated by imposters and liars, except by way of doubt, guesswork of those who would lie in the *ḥadith*, and no harmony from the truth ever. This is secession from Islam, questioning of its laws and destruction of the *Deen*.

One can clearly discern from the many words as cited here from Imām Abu Muḥammad Ali ibn Ḥazm, may Allah have mercy upon him, it is only in regard to the proven established *Sunnah* which is from amongst the proofs upon which that of the single narrator report – *al-khabar al-aḥad* is built. The *Sunnah* is by itself revelation and all of the revelation constitutes the revealed *Dhikr*; it is from the axioms which all the people of language and *Sharī'ah* concur upon. Let us now turn to the issue concerning the protection of the *Dhikr*, by the blessing of Allah.

19 The '*Dhikr*': Qur'ān & *Sunnah* are protected

Previously we had mentioned that the Qur'ān is the revealed word of Allah; sent-down upon Muḥammad (peace be upon him) word-by-word, as it is written in the *maṣāḥif* and preserved in the breasts of mankind; orally recited, recorded upon tapes and by other means of preservation which are now presently available by the advances made in modern technology. It was conveyed to the people by the Prophet, both verbally and in writing by continuous recurrent transmission (*tawātur*) as it was revealed incrementally. Contained within it is necessary knowledge for all of mankind, both Muslim and non-Muslim alike. All of this has become settled and established, much to the resentment and annoyance of the heretics and disbelievers of old and their newer vicious modern counterparts, such as the Orientalists and others advocating Westernisation. Over the centuries their efforts at seeking to challenge the veracity of the Qur'ān has amounted to nothing, leading to bitter disappointment amongst them and their apostate adulators. Thus, it has been settled and acknowledged amongst all people, both Muslim and non-Muslim alike, that the Qur'ān was brought forth by the Prophet (peace be upon him), all that is contained between its two covers. All praise and thanks is to Allah.

Yet while it has now been acknowledged that Muḥammad (peace

be upon him) brought forth the Qur'ān, those who disbelieve in Islam still remain in doubt over whether it ultimately originated with Allah as a whole and what is contained between its covers. It seems they have not seriously pondered over this aspect, considering the knowledge contained therein and that it is free of contradiction, originating from Allah, as he says:

أَفَلَا يَتَدَبَّرُونَ الْقُرْآنَ وَلَوْ كَانَ مِنْ عِندِ غَيْرِ اللَّهِ لَوَجَدُوا فِيهِ اخْتِلَافًا كَثِيرًا

Do they not then ponder on the Qur'ān? And if it were from any other than Allah, they would have found in it many a discrepancy. [1]

Moreover, if detractors were serious about seeking to mount a challenge to the veracity of the Qur'ān, they would have readily taken on its open challenge:

فَلْيَأْتُوا بِحَدِيثٍ مِّثْلِهِ إِن كَانُوا صَادِقِينَ

Then let them bring an announcement like it if they are truthful! [2]

وَإِن كُنتُمْ فِي رَيْبٍ مِّمَّا نَزَّلْنَا عَلَىٰ عَبْدِنَا فَأْتُوا بِسُورَةٍ مِّن مِّثْلِهِ وَادْعُوا شُهَدَاءَكُم مِّن دُونِ اللَّهِ إِن كُنتُمْ صَادِقِينَ

And if you are in doubt as to that which We have revealed to Our servant, then produce a chapter like it and call on your witnesses besides Allah if you are truthful. [3]

Given that all have failed to take up this serious challenge, notwithstanding the warning contained from Allah in these verses, we

[1] *Qur'ān* 4: 82
[2] *Qur'ān* 52: 34
[3] *Qur'ān* 2: 23

know with certitude that those seeking to challenge the Qur'ān's veracity are stubborn, obstinate liars. They have lost objective insight, being blinded by tribalism, partisanship, racism, nationalism, the following of their forbearers; besotted with the love of the world, as well as other desires and interests. Or is it borne of laziness, trading the hereafter for the life of the present? Contained within the present work we have sought to document many of the Prophetic signs and proofs, which are indeed full of guidance and light for mankind. These prophecies establish the truth as brought by Muḥammad ibn Abdullah al-Hāshimi the unlettered Arab, may the blessings of Allah be showered upon him. A separate chapter has been prepared within this book to detail such proofs establishing that the Muḥammad is the messenger of Allah.

The truth is that the entirety of the Qur'ān, all that which is contained therein between its two covers, is with certitude the word of Allah. It is also an established truth that Allah has guaranteed to preserve the entire great book, the *Dhikr*. He has said, blessed be his names:

إِنَّا نَحْنُ نَزَّلْنَا الذِّكْرَ وَإِنَّا لَهُ لَحَافِظُونَ

Indeed, We have revealed the dhikr and We will surely be its guardian.[4]

Within the Arabic language this is the highest form of confirmation. As for the text of the Qur'ān, namely that which we presently possess in our hands and all its contents, and in addition to the aforementioned verse which mentions the word *ḥifz* (to preserve, protect, guard) it is decisively proven rationally with substantive evidence that it has reached us by continuous recurrent transmission (*tawātur*) in its entirety. That is to say, word by word, letter by letter, consonant by consonant. This phenomenon is a matter of decisive certain

[4] *Qur'ān* 15: 9

knowledge, by necessity, that the transmission of the Qur'ān was directly from Muḥammad (peace be upon him) historically, regardless of whether one believes it to ultimately originate with Allah or not. This, the verse of *al-Ḥifz*, as previously mentioned, which not only encapsulates the speech of Muḥammad it is also from Allah and we believe and bear witness that it originates from Allah. Given that there is unequivocal decisive evidence which substantiates the Prophethood of Muḥammad (peace be upon him), the final seal of all Prophets and Messengers. More upon that very point will be detail later in this present work when considering the proofs of *Tawḥeed.*

All but a glimpse of this has been outlined thus far, for it will be spelled out in exhaustive detail later in the present work. Suffice is to say here that by necessity we affirm that the entire Qur'ānic text is preserved and protected (*maḥfouz*); not merely some of the text but the text in its entirety. There is no missing section, nor are there any missing verses, words, characters or consonants. Allah has declared by his express statement that he promises to preserve it. For anyone to claim that Allah does not keep his promise or that he has lied in this instance is making a statement of great magnitude which ultimately crumbles to dust.

Yet the matter doesn't end here with the verse of *al-Ḥifz*, because Allah has said that he has guaranteed to protect '*al-Dhikr*', namely *the Dhikr* in its entirety. The present work has exhaustively set out the decisive proofs which underpin that, namely that it is the entirety of the Qur'ān by itself and that the noble Prophetic *Sunnah* is in fact a division from amongst the divisions of the *Dhikr*. The *Sunnah* is revelation and a proof just as the Qur'ān is. Indeed, the *Sunnah* is more voluminous than the Qur'ān, carrying greater clarification and explanation, being a testimony in itself, as we have previously outlined. Foremost the Qur'ān is the established proof of the *Dhikr* and it is an undeniable proof; a testimony to itself. However, it does require detailed explanation and clarification (*bayān*), again, as we have detailed previously.

By necessity and induction, we know that the noble Prophetic *Sunnah* is testified to by the Qur'ān itself and it provides a greater detailed exposition of many rulings as well as providing specification upon matters which are general, absolute and qualified. If all of this is in fact the case, and with certitude it is, one may legitimately inquire, what is the point of only having the idea of preservation applying solely to the Qur'ān? Should it not also apply in principle to the *Sunnah*? For the *Sunnah* is the *ḥikmah* and as a whole, is considered from the protected *Dhikr* as well. One of the key essential points to reiterate is that the *Sunnah* is itself revelation (*waḥy*) just as the Qur'ān is. Given that they are emanating from Allah and carry the designation of *waḥy*, why would one be preserved and not the other? Allah has provided this protection and preservation to both, not only as a blessing and from his grace, but also to serve as a proof upon his servants.

There is a portion of the noble Prophetic *Sunnah* which is *mutawātir* thereby establishing itself with certitude. Although the vast majority of it is textually conveyed by the single-narrator report or transmission (*khabar al-wāhid*), which by itself doesn't reach the level of certitude in terms of transmission. As for the books of *Seerah* (biography) they contain many reports which are attributed to the Prophet (peace be upon him) and may not always be to the highest exacting standards that one would expect in terms of transmission, yet no sane person could reasonably claim that all of that in its entirety is fabricated.

One may reasonably ask therefore upon what basis or in what precise sense is the *Sunnah* protected and preserved (*maḥfouz*)? Is it a rationally tenable position? There is no doubt that the *Sunnah*, has matters transmitted by continuous recurrent transmission (*tawātur*), including a portion of *Seerah*, although it is not transmitted or preserved in exactly the same manner as the Qur'ān. Hence it would be a mistake to confuse it with the preservation of the Qur'ān arguing that exactly the same method applies to that of the *Sunnah*. The truth of the matter is that each has been preserved and protected according to its own specific nature.

If it is a necessity to establish that the noble Prophetic *Sunnah* has been preserved and protected to the level which can be demonstrated with proofs reaching the level of certitude, given that it is part of the *Dhikr* and preserved in a manner different from that of the Qur'ān, then no doubt it will be incumbent to specifically identify this manner and provide a detailed characterisation and description. By necessity it is established through history that the bulk of reporting concerning the *Sunnah*, excluding the not insignificant portion which is transmitted by *tawātur*, has been via the single-narrator report. Scholarship in the field of *ḥadith* and its sciences has subjected this to the most rigorous scrutiny, even up to the present day. Each and every report is known and nothing has been lost in relation to the entire corpus. Therefore, when mention is made that the noble Prophetic *Sunnah* is protected and preserved, it is done through this manner by the grace and blessing of Allah, given that it is part of the *Dhikr* and therefore protected and preserved.

Allah the exalted himself has undertaken the pledge to protect and preserve the *Dhikr*, the *Sunnah* being an essential part of that very *Dhikr*. Given the need for this component of the *Dhikr,* Allah has ensured nothing from it is lost and as a corpus it is preserved through its transmission. Indeed, Allah has guaranteed to expose all who forge a lie against the Prophet (peace be upon him), even if it is only a single occasion. Various indicators (*qarā'in*) expose those who may be lying, the unknown or even the untoward within a given channel of transmission, notwithstanding those who are prone to making mistakes and are not from the high level of exactitude required for trustworthy narrators. And it doesn't end there. The anomalous (*shadth*) is singled out, as is that which contains hidden or less obvious and apparent defects. Rather than simply a process, this is termed the science of '*illal*', subjecting each and every report to meticulous scrutiny. All of which has been made possible by the blessing and grace which Allah has bestowed upon the nation of Muḥammad (peace be upon him).

In tandem with this, there is also the scrutiny given to the actual subject matter or substance which a report carries. Textual criticism uncovers and exposes weak or fabricated reports, such as by way of inspecting such reports against the established Qur'ān and *Sunnah* reported by recurrent transmission (*tawātur*) as well as the necessities of sense and reason. Scholars of the Muslim *Ummah* continually partake within this endeavour and it is never a closed door, being always ajar for further study, revision and scrutiny. The reader will no doubt come across some of this methodology even in the present work, where studies are detailed upon various *isnād's* as well as the individuals contained therein. To the casual reader this may seem at times be hair-splitting, particularly in relation to the criticism of narrators, but it demonstrates the lengths which are required for this field of knowledge.

Through keeping everything protected and preserved commensurate with its given nature, the noble Prophetic *Sunnah* is no doubt *maḥfouz*, but it is *maḥfouz* in terms of its totality as a corpus until the day of judgement and there are five-aspects to this:

1. Nothing has been lost from the corpus as a whole. If one is not able to find a particular channel (*riwayāt*) in a particular *Musnad* or *Muṣṣanaf*, then it can be found or sought out elsewhere in other books, works and collections.
2. Nothing may enter into the corpus that has never been seen, characterised or identified. More explicitly, if an individual scholar of *ḥadith* is taken in by a specific story or channel of transmission which is ultimately void, everyone else will not be. It will ultimately be discovered, highlighted and signposted as a warning by other more diligent and studious scholars.

3. It may not be that all which has been abrogated / repealed (*mansukh*) has been preserved; or that the ambivalent (*mujmal*), the general (*aā'mm*) and the absolute (*muṭlaq*) is lost, or that the abrogating (*nāsikh*), clarified (*muffasir*), specified (*mukhaṣiṣ*) or the qualified (*muqqayad*) is altogether neglected.
4. The *Sunnah* is not confined to the books of *Sunan*, *Musnad* or other collections. It is greater than that.
5. The books of *Sunnah* and *Seerah* also include the statements made by the scholars (*ulemā'*) and wordings which have fallen upon narrators, and maybe also *aḥādith* which are *mawḍu* (fabricated). Whomsoever were to claim that each and every character found in such-and-such book other than the Qur'ān is ultimately from Allah, would find themselves as a liar or even worse, an accursed *kāfir*.

Then none should say when the following is said: a trustworthy (*thiqa*) narrator is not considered to be from the infallible (*ma'ṣoom*) or protected from the liar, errors and mistakes, therefore, according to the dictates of reason and perception, it can only be that the continuously recurrent narration (*mutawātir*) that transmission is established and proven. Nobody should utter as such, because Allah has indeed undertaken to protect and preserve the *Dhikr* by his express command even before a solitary transmission by trustworthy narrators. And this requires by necessity that Allah will guarantee to expose whomsoever lies upon the Prophet (peace be upon him), even in a single instance. Thereby Allah has facilitated the authorities in this field to uncover these lacunas and errors by way of various indicators contained within a channel of narration, as well as those who have made mistakes in *ḥadith* itself, either by way of text or transmission, as we have mentioned previously.

The established proofs of the Qur'ān and the *mutawātir Sunnah* are decisive and unequivocal upon the existence of reports by a trustworthy individual in pronouncements, oaths, witness testimony and *bayān* (explanation). Also, this has demonstrated that this is the manner in which testimony and knowledge is received, and it is so by the narration of *Sunnah* until the day of judgement. The same viewpoint was certainly held by the consensus of the companions (*ijmā' aṣ-Ṣaḥābah*). Furthermore, it was also held by the scholars of *uṣul* in the books of knowledge and *Tawḥeed* as well as the scholars of *uṣul al-fiqh* and sciences of *ḥadith*. For with that guarantee Allah the majestic has preserved and protected the *Sunnah* ensuring that by its universal measure those expounders is routed by way of singular channel transmission.

For that reason, it is an obligatory condition to accept what has been reported or narrated by a trustworthy reliable singular narration. From amongst them there are some which are uninterrupted (*mutaṣṣil*) as well as those which are free from inherent problems or hidden defects (*illal*), or from the anomalous (*shadth*), the rejected (*munkar*) in the *isnād* or text (*matn*). These are the reasons behind the detailed principles which underpin this noble branch of knowledge. Thus, one cannot openly challenge an authentic single narrator report (*Ṣaḥīḥ khabar al-aḥad*), except with compelling proof. Whosoever would seek to rebut or challenge a *Ṣaḥīḥ khabar al-aḥad* without a substantive argument and proof then the individual has transgressed into disobedience because of following desires. Taken at its highest, it may even lead to *kufr* and disavowal from Islam, may Allah forbid that. Consequently, as has been detailed thus far, the Prophetic *Sunnah* as a corpus is *maḥfouz* without doubt, expounding upon the *bayān*. Indeed, the weight of evidence to substantiate this reaches the level of certitude. Other scholars have elaborated at length upon this subject. And it is in the well-established *aḥādith* that are *Ṣaḥīḥ* and *Ḥasan,* and it is an established decisive proof like the Qur'ān and *mutawātir Sunnah* and so on and so forth.

Similarly, the Arabic language is *maḥfouz* and can be considered an important component or necessary adjunct to the *Dhikr* itself.

Although not *waḥy* (revelation) in itself, in the technical sense or for that matter, the sent-down revealed *Dhikr*. It is revealed or sent-down in the same sense that the Qur'ān and *Sunnah* has, except that it is a necessary condition for understanding and even accessing the *Dhikr* itself. Thus the revelatory texts, the Qur'ān and *Sunnah* cannot be understood or truly valued without the medium of the language in which it is conveyed. Given that it is the medium through which the *Dhikr* is conveyed, it can be stated with certainty that Allah has also preserved and protected the Arabic language as well, both in totality and in terms of its grammar, conjugation, exposition and its beautiful eloquence. History has demonstrated already how it occurred and it is a subject upon which a consensus exists amongst Muslims and other than them. Even the ultra-Orientalists and missionaries such as Goldzeir and Schacht, despite their ridiculous claims that the Prophetic *Sunnah* was built upon a series of falsehoods, particularly with regards to its detailed laws, even though they gave acceptance to the *Seerah* and the battle campaigns (*maghāzi*), they did not say that the Arabic language is not the one spoken by the Arabs at the time of the advent of Islam. Neither did they take up the challenge of Islam to produce the like thereof, even though they were well versed in the language. Instead of recognising the truth as it is, they turned on their heels, making ridiculous sweeping statements alleging that it is all a fabrication.

20 A brief overview of the period of '*Sunnah* recordation'

At this juncture, it is necessary to provide an overview of how the Prophetic *Sunnah* was recorded and documented. A great many people, including amongst 'intellectual' elites are surprisingly unaware of this. What has not helped this situation has been the pseudo-intellectualism of the Orientalists as well as their imitators, such as the 'Qur'ānists' – those who would reject the *Sunnah* in its entirety as a matter of course, arguing that it is completely fabricated. Many of these groups have misconstrued and misunderstood the words and indeed the terminology which appear in the corpus of *aḥādith* as utilised by the *muḥadditheen* (scholars / collectors of *ḥadith*). Commonly, the terms 'narrated to us' and 'narrated to me' (حدّثنا ، حدّثني) have been misunderstood to construe that the Prophetic *Sunnah* was *only* reported orally, with no accompanying written record, *until* the time when Imām Mālik composed the *Muwaṭṭā'*, thereby ushering in the era which has been termed - 'documenting the *Sunnah*.' In tandem with this, the narrative also notes that this was the time when the two Ḥammād's; the two Sufyān's, Sa'eed ibn Abi 'Aruba, Ma'mar bin Rāshid and other than them, put their respective *Sunan* collections into public circulation. All of this was against the backdrop of the insistence from the then 'Abbāsi *Khaleefah*, Abu Ja'far al-Manṣur. Most who cite this narrative rely upon the events as detailed in the work of history composed by Imām aṭ-Ṭabari.

Yet the difficulty with this narrative and the claims of the Orientalists, is that it is baseless and without substantive foundation. Preservation of the Prophetic *Sunnah*, in writing specifically, began *during the era of the Prophet* (peace be upon him). The detailed writings of the Prophet's companions will be considered shortly. Suffice is to say that it is an acknowledged fact that almost all companions had their own manuscripts during the era of the Prophet (peace be upon him). Not only were these in relation to the Qur'ān, which was being revealed, but also covered the Prophetic *aḥādith*, which was preserved by writing. These manuscripts were reviewed, updated and revised as a matter of course during the period of revelation.

As has been reported by al-Rāmhurmuzi in *al-Muḥadith al-Fāṣil bayn ar-Rāwi wal'Wā'ee*, with an *isnād* that is *ḥasan*:

حَدَّثَنَا مُحَمَّدُ بْنُ يَحْيَى الْمَرْوَزِيُّ، حدثنا عَاصِمُ بْنُ عَلِيٍّ، حدثنا إِسْحَاقُ بْنُ يَحْيَى بْنِ طَلْحَةَ بْنِ عُبَيْدِ اللَّهِ، عَنْ مُجَاهِدٍ، عَنْ عَبْدِ اللهِ بْنِ عَمْرٍو قَالَ: كَانَ عِنْدَ رَسُولِ اللَّهِ، صلى الله عليه وسلم، نَاسٌ مِنْ أَصْحَابِهِ وَأَنَا مَعَهُمْ وَأَنَا أَصْغَرُ الْقَوْمِ، فَقَالَ النَّبِيُّ، صلى الله عليه وسلم: مَنْ كَذَبَ عَلَيَّ مُتَعَمِّدًا فَلْيَتَبَوَّأْ مَقْعَدَهُ مِنَ النَّارِ؛ فَلَمَّا خَرَجَ الْقَوْمُ قُلْتُ لَهُمْ: كَيْفَ تُحَدِّثُونَ عَنْ رَسُولِ اللَّهِ، صلى الله عليه وسلم، وَقَدْ سَمِعْتُمْ مَا قَالَ، وَأَنْتُمْ تَنْهَمِكُونَ فِي الْحَدِيثِ عَنْ رَسُولِ اللَّهِ، صلى الله عليه وسلم،؟ قَالَ: فَضَحِكُوا، وَقَالُوا: يَا ابْنَ أَخِينَا، إِنَّ كُلَّ مَا سَمِعْنَا مِنْهُ فَهُوَ عِنْدَنَا فِي كِتَابٍ

Muḥammad bin Yaḥya al-Marwazi narrated to us 'Aāṣim bin Ali narrated to us Isḥāq bin Yaḥya bin Ṭalḥa bin 'Ubaidallah narrated to us from Mujāhid from Abdullah bin 'Amr he said: When the Messenger of Allah (peace be upon him), people from his companions and I (were) with them and I, less among the people. So the Prophet (peace be upon him) said: *Whoever*

> *tells lies about me deliberately, let him take his place in hell.* When the people came out I told them – how do you narrate from the Messenger (peace be upon him)? Have you heard what he said and you are all insatiable in *ḥadith* from the Prophet (peace be upon him)? In reply – they laughed and they said oh son of our brother! All that we have heard from him, it is (taken from) the book.

I would submit - Muḥammad bin Yaḥya al-Marwazi is most probably Muḥammad bin Yaḥya bin Sulaymān al-Marwazi, Abu Bakr al-Warrāq. He resided in Baghdad, being a companion of Abu 'Ubaid. He is trustworthy and studied from scholars of Imām an-Nasā'i. He died in the year 298 AH. Similar is reported in *Taqreeb at-Tahzeeb* of Ibn Ḥajar.[1]

It may also be that Muḥammad bin Yaḥya bin Khālid al-Marwazi, Abu Yaḥya al-Masha'rāni is also *thiqa* – as per what is in *Taqreeb at-Tahzeeb.*[2] But according to the majority, (he is) weak upon the (view of) Isḥāq bin Yaḥya bin Ṭalḥā bin 'Ubaidallah at-Taymi. But Imām Bukhāri said: '(he is) a mountain of memorisation; Imām of the world and leader of moderation,' in the book of *ḍua'fā';*[3] 'speaks (from his) memorisation; write his *ḥadith.*' And he also says to reiterate – '(There is) concern (about) some things, however he is trustworthy.' And Ya'qub ibn Shayba said: 'There is nothing untoward with him *(la ba'sa bihi*) and his *ḥadith* are very vexatious (*muḍṭarib*).' Al-Ḥāfiz Muḥammad bin Abdullah bin 'Aāmar al-Mawṣili (Abu Ya'la) said: 'Righteous, valid (*Ṣāliḥ*).' All of this is from *Tahzeeb at-Tahzeeb.*[4] Writing in his famous work *ath-Thiqāt,*[5] Ibn Ḥibbān said: 'Mistaken in (some) matters. We may have introduced Isḥāq bin Yaḥya, this in the weak ones (*aḍ-ḍua'fā*). What was in it or giving the impression that

[1] *Taqreeb at-Tahzeeb* Vol. 1 sec. 512, n. 6,385
[2] Ibid. no. 6,383
[3] *Kitāb aḍ- ḍua'fā'* Vol. 1 sec. 17, n. 21
[4] *Tahzeeb at-Tahzeeb* Vol. 1 sec. 222, n. 479
[5] *ath-Thiqāt* Vol. 6 sec. 45, n. 6,652

(he) reported it. If the *ijtihād* led to leaving him what didn't pursue from him, he is worthy of inclusion in the *thiqāt* (trustworthy narrators) after that…'

The aforementioned report, appears to have been the motivation behind Abdullah ibn 'Amr ibn al-'Aāṣ (may Allah be pleased with him) composition of his famous pamphlet which was entitled '*aṣ-Ṣādiqa*.' This pamphlet included about a thousand *aḥādith* that he heard directly from the Prophet (peace be upon him). So guarded was this work of Abdullah ibn 'Amr, he kept it in a closed box which only he accessed. It was only brought forth in order to make revisions and / or to dictate to his students. Indeed, Abdullah ibn 'Amr utilised the written work during study-circles where he would dictate to his students. Use of the pamphlet was regular, since Abdullah ibn 'Amr (may Allah be pleased with him) held many scholarly circles. In fact one of his renowned students, Ḥussein bin Shafi bin Māti' al-Aṣbaḥi in Egypt, copied this work into two books or volumes, one of which was dedicated to the rulings given by the Prophet (peace be upon him). The work was formatted in the manner of 'Judgements – concerning this and that; and he said this in relation to this matter' and 'What events will occur up to the day of judgement.' His children and grandsons inherited that pamphlet. The Quraysh had previously objected to his writing and his consultation with the Prophet (peace be upon him) over the issue. However, the Prophet approved to him that he can write and record what he hears. A number of proofs exist to substantiate these points. For example, the following has been reported by al-Rāmhurmuzi in *al-Muḥadith al-Fāṣil*:

حَدَّثَنَا عَبْدُ اللَّهِ بْنُ غَنَّامٍ، حَدَّثَنَا عَلِيُّ بْنُ حَكِيمٍ، حَدَّثَنَا شَرِيكٌ، عَنْ لَيْثٍ، عَنْ مُجَاهِدٍ عَنْ عَبْدِ اللَّهِ بْنِ عَمْرٍو قَالَ: مَا يُرَغِّبُنِي فِي الْحَيَاةِ إِلَّا خَصْلَتَانِ؛ الْوَهْطُ، وَالصَّادِقَةُ: صَحِيفَةٌ كُنْتُ اسْتَأْذَنْتُ رَسُولَ اللَّهِ، صلى الله عليه وسلم، أَنْ أَكْتُبَهَا عَنْهُ فَكَتَبْتُهَا وَهِيَ الصَّادِقَةُ

Abdullah ibn Ghanām narrated to us Ali bin Ḥakeem narrated

to us Shareek narrated to us from Layth from Mujāhid from Abdullah bin 'Amr he said: What do you wish in this life except these two qualities – *al-Waht* (a land near Ṭā'if) and *as-Sādiqa*? I asked the permission of the Prophet (peace be upon him) regarding the *Ṣaḥifa*, that I could write it and have it as a book and it is *as-Sādiqa*.

Also cited in the same work there are another three channels of note:

حَدَّثَنِي عُمَرُ بْنُ الْحَسَنِ بْنِ جُبَيْرٍ الْوَاسِطِيُّ، حدثنا مُحَمَّدُ بْنُ عِيسَى الْعَطَّارُ، حدثنا عَاصِمُ بْنُ عَلِيٍّ، حدثنا إِسْحَاقُ بْنُ يَحْيَى بْنِ طَلْحَةَ، عَنْ مُجَاهِدٍ قَالَ: رَأَيْتُ عِنْدَ عَبْدِ اللَّهِ بْنِ عَمْرٍو صَحِيفَةً، فَذَهَبْتُ أَتَنَاوَلُهَا فَقَالَ: (مَهْ يَا غُلَامَ بَنِي مَخْزُومٍ قُلْتُ: مَا كُنْتَ تَمْنَعُنِي شَيْئًا قَالَ: (هَذِهِ الصَّادِقَةُ، فِيهَا مَا سَمِعْتُهُ مِنْ رَسُولِ اللَّهِ، صلى الله عليه وسلم، لَيْسَ بَيْنِي وَبَيْنَهُ فِيهَا أَحَدٌ

Umar bin al-Ḥasan bin Jubayr al-Wāsiṭi narrated to me Muḥammad bin Esa al-'Aṭār narrated to us 'Aāsim bin Ali narrated to us Isḥāq bin Yaḥya bin Ṭalḥa narrated to us from Mujāhid he said: I saw Abdullah bin 'Amr with *Ṣaḥifa*. So I went to obtain it. He replied – Stop oh you (young) lad from Bani Maḥzoom. I said what (is the reason) you are preventing me from something? He said: This is *as-Sādiqa*, in it is what I heard from the Messenger of Allah (peace be upon him); there isn't anyone in it between me and between him.

حَدَّثَنَا الْحَضْرَمِيُّ، حدثنا عَبْدُ اللَّهِ بْنُ عُمَرَ، حدثنا سُفْيَانُ بْنُ عُيَيْنَةَ، عَنْ عَمْرٍو، عَنْ وَهْبِ بْنِ مُنَبِّهٍ، عَنْ أَخِيهِ قَالَ: سَمِعْتُ أَبَا هُرَيْرَةَ يَقُولُ: مَا أَحَدٌ مِنْ أَصْحَابِ مُحَمَّدٍ، صلى الله عليه وسلم، أَكْثَرُ حَدِيثًا مِنِّي، عَنْ رَسُولِ اللَّهِ، صلى الله عليه وسلم، إِلَّا عَبْدُ اللَّهِ بْنُ عَمْرٍو، فَإِنَّهُ كَانَ يَكْتُبُ، وَأَنَا لَا أَكْتُبُ

Al-Ḥaḍrami narrated to us Abdullah bin Umar narrated to us Sufyān bin 'Uyayna narrated to us from 'Amr from Wahb bin Munabbih from his brother he said: I heard Abu Hurayrah say – Indeed, is there one of the companions of Muḥammad (peace be upon him) (who) has more *ḥadith* from the Prophet (peace be upon him) except Abdullah bin ‘Amr? Indeed he was writing while I didn’t write.

حَدَّثَنَا مُحَمَّدُ بْنُ يَعْقُوب، حدثنا أَبُو الْخَطَّابِ، حدثنا عَبْدُ الأَعْلَى، حدثنا مُحَمَّدُ بْنُ إِسْحَاقَ، عَنْ عَمْرِو بْنِ شُعَيْبٍ، عَنِ الْمُغِيرَةِ بْنِ حَكِيمٍ، عَنْ أَبِي هُرَيْرَةَ قَالَ: كُنْتُ أَعِي بِقَلْبِي، وَكَانَ هُوَ يَعِي بِقَلْبِهِ، وَيَكْتُبُ بِيَدِهِ يَعْنِي: عَبْدَ اللَّهِ بْنَ عَمْرٍو

Muḥammad bin Ya’qub narrated to us Abul-Khaṭṭāb narrated to us Abdul ‘Alā narrated to us Muḥammad bin Isḥāq narrated to us from ‘Amr bin Shu’ayb from al-Mughira bin Ḥakeem from Abu Hurayrah he said: I was aware of my heart and he is aware of his heart, and he writes with his hand, that is to say – Abdullah ibn ‘Amr.

The famous *litterateur* Ibn ‘Abbās (may Allah be pleased with him) was diligent in the recordation of knowledge and its preservation by writing. After the death of the Prophet (peace be upon him) Ibn ‘Abbās made extensive enquires to the companions and wrote a considerable amount of material, to the extent that he had them carried by camel. His books were preserved and it is reliably trustworthy. Confirmation of this written material which Ibn ‘Abbās had, has reached us via several reports. One of which, with an authentic *isnād*, is contained in *aṭ-Ṭabaqāt al-Kubra* of Ibn Sa’d:

أَخْبَرَنَا أَحْمَدُ بْنُ عَبْدِ اللَّهِ بْنِ يُونُسَ قَالَ: حَدَّثَنَا زُهَيْرٌ قَالَ: حَدَّثَنَا مُوسَى بْنُ عُقْبَةَ قَالَ: وَضَعَ عِنْدَنَا كُرَيْبٌ حِمْلَ بَعِيرٍ أَوْ عِدْلَ بَعِيرٍ مِنْ كُتُبِ ابْنِ عَبَّاسٍ. قَالَ: فَكَانَ عَلِيُّ بْنُ عَبْدِ اللَّهِ بْنِ عَبَّاسٍ إِذَا أَرَادَ الْكِتَابَ كَتَبَ إِلَيْهِ: ابْعَثْ إِلَيَّ بِصَحِيفَةِ كَذَا وَكَذَا. قَالَ: فَيَنْسَخُهَا، فَيَبْعَثُ إِلَيْهِ بِإِحْدَاهُمَا

Aḥmad bin Abdullah bin Yunus reported to us he said Zuhayr narrated to us he said Musa bin ‘Uqba narrated to us he said,

> Kurayb (ibn Muslim) deposited with us a camel's loan of the books of Ibn 'Abbās. When his own son Ali ibn Abdullah ibn 'Abbās wanted a book, he wrote to Kurayb saying – search amongst the *Ṣaḥifa* (for) this and this. He said: copy / transcribe it and send to him one of the two copies (i.e. the original or copy).

Similar has also been reported in *Tārikh al-Kabir* of Ibn Abu Khaythama and *Taqayyad al-'Ilm* of Khaṭeeb Baghdadi, with the following transmission channel – 'Abul'Ḥasan Muḥammad bin Aḥmad bin Razqwehi reported to us 'Uthmān bin Aḥmad ad-Daqqāq reported to us Ḥanbal bin Isḥāq narrated to us Aḥmad bin Yunus narrated to us.' Imām Bayhaqy also reports this in *Sunan al-Kubra* via the channel of – 'Abul'Ḥussein reported to us Abu 'Amr reported to us Ḥanbal narrated to us Aḥmad bin Yunus narrated to us.'

It is also noteworthy that the book of Abdullah ibn 'Abbās was well known, copied, put into public circulation and read during his lifetime, as mentioned in the weak tradition recorded in the *Sunan* of Imām Tirmidhi:

> حدثنا سويد بن نصر حدثنا علي بن الحسين بن واقد عن أبي عصمة عن يزيد النحوي عن عكرمة: أن نفرا قدموا على ابن عباس من أهل الطائف، بكتب من كتبه، فجعل يقرأ عليهم، فيقدم، ويؤخر، فقال: إني بليت بهذه المصيبة، فاقرؤوا علي، فإن إقراري به كقراءتي عليكم

> Suwayd bin Naṣr narrated to us Ali bin al-Ḥussein bin Wāqid narrated to us from Abu Uṣama from Yazeed an-Naḥwe from 'Ikrima: some people from Ṭā'if came to Ibn 'Abbās with books (taken / copied) from his books. When he began to read the books in front of them he would lose his place. So he said – 'I have been tested with this calamity (short-sightedness or blindness), so read in front of me and my agreeing to what you read is just like my reading it out to you.'

From the above it can be discerned that the books of Abdullah ibn 'Abbās were many. It would be incredulous to claim that these books would be devoid of Prophetic *aḥādith*. Rather, these must have been the substantive core of the books. Moreover, Abdullah ibn Ma'sud bequeathed written material to his children and students, as reported from Mis'ar from Ma'n who said: 'Go out to Abdar-Raḥman bin Abdullah bin Mas'ud, I swear that the book is composed by his father's hand.'

Furthermore, there are several pamphlets, which the Prophet (peace be upon him) dictated to more that one of his administrative officials, when appointing them as governors, judges or tax collectors in the remote outer regions of Islamic lands. Usually this included important rulings related to *zakāt*, as well as matters concerning general behaviour or mannerisms; rulings in relation to blood-money as well as general commands and directives. Some of these include the following:

- The *Ṣaḥifa* of 'Amr bin Ḥazm al-Anṣāry (may Allah be pleased with him), who was appointed as governor over the people of Najrān
- The book of al-'Alā bin al-Ḥaḍrami when he was sent to al-Mundhur bin Sāwi. 'Alā said: 'Write for me oh Messenger of Allah a book, I can take with me.' The Prophet (peace be upon him) wrote to him detailing obligations, what can be levied on livestock as well as rulings on gold and silver.
- The book of Wā'el bin Ḥujr bin Sa'eed bin Masrooq, Abu Haneeda al-Ḥaḍrami al-Kindi. He was one of the kings of Yemen. The Prophet (peace be upon him) wrote to him for 'the people of Wā'el bin Ḥujr in Ḥaḍramawt.' Contained within this major work, were the parameters of Islam and the details of *zakāt*; the lawful punishment for *zinā*, the prohibition of alcohol and that every intoxicant is prohibited.

- The *Ṣaḥifa* of Anas ibn Mālik (may Allah be pleased with him) when he was utilised to collect the *zakāt* from the people of Baḥrain by the Messenger of Allah (peace be upon him). This same document was also utilised under the *Khilafah* of Abu Bakr.
- A copy of the *Ṣaḥifa* was commissioned by Abu Bakr from the Prophet (peace be upon him) and contained the stamp of the noble Prophetic seal. Many letters and correspondence were also made during this time. There were other books held by Anas ibn Mālik (may Allah be pleased with him), within them *aḥādith* which he directly wrote from the Prophet (peace be upon him) and confirmed with him. This 'presentation' to the Shaykh is reading, in other words, reading back what he had recorded from these *ḥadith* and confirming them to the Shaykh himself. This was done to ensure the validity and accuracy of what had been dictated.

Next, the following has been reported in *Tārikh al-Wāsiṭ* with a good *isnād*:

حدثنا الْعَبَّاسُ بْنُ الْوَلِيدِ بْنِ مَزْيَدٍ، قَالَ: حدثنا أَبُو شُعَيْبٍ (وَهُوَ مُحَمَّدُ بْنُ شُعَيْبِ بْنِ شَابُورَ الدِّمَشْقِيُّ)، قَالَ: حدثنا عُتْبَةُ بْنُ أَبِي الْحَكِيمِ عَنْ هُبَيْرَةَ بْنِ عَبْدِ الرَّحْمَنِ (وَهُوَ أَبُو عُمَرَ بْنُ هُبَيْرَةَ) قَالَ: كَانَ أَنَسُ بْنُ مَالِكٍ إِذَا حَدَّثَ وَكَثُرَ عليه الناس جاء يكتب فَأَلْقَاهَا، ثُمَّ قَالَ: (هَذِهِ أَحَادِيثُ <u>سَمِعْتُهَا</u> مِنْ رَسُولِ اللَّهِ، صلى الله عليه وسلم، <u>وَكَتَبْتُهَا</u> عَنْ رَسُولِ اللَّهِ، صلى الله عليه وسلم، <u>وعرضتها</u> عليه

Al-'Abbās bin al-Waleed bin Mazeed narrated to us he said Abu Shu'ayb (and he is Muḥammad bin Shu'ayb bin Shābur ad-Dimishqi) narrated to us he said 'Utba bin Abu al-Ḥakim narrated to us from Hubayra bin Abdar-Raḥman (and he is Abu Umar bin Hubayra) he said (once it) occurred that Anas bin Mālik was taking audience and many people came to write from him. Then he said: <u>This is the *aḥādith* I heard them</u> from

> the Prophet (peace be upon him) and I wrote them from the Prophet (peace be upon him) and <u>presented them before him</u>.

A shorter version of the aforementioned narration is contained within *al-Muḥadith al-Fāṣl* of al-Rāmhurmuzi:

> حَدَّثَنَا الْحَضْرَمِيُّ، حدثنا مُحَمَّدُ بْنُ حَنَانٍ الْحِمْصِيُّ، حدثنا بَقِيَّةُ بْنُ الْوَلِيدِ، عَنْ عُتْبَةَ بْنِ أَبِي حَكِيمٍ، عَنْ هُبَيْرَةَ بْنِ عَبْدِ الرَّحْمَنِ قَالَ: كُنَّا إِذَا أَكْثَرْنَا عَلَى أَنَسِ بْنِ مَالِكٍ أَلْقَى إِلَيْنَا مِخْلَاةً فَقَالَ: هَذِهِ أَحَادِيثٌ <u>كَتَبْتُهَا</u> عَنْ رَسُولِ اللَّهِ، صلى الله عليه وسلم
>
> Al-Ḥaḍrami narrated to us Muḥammad bin Ḥanān al-Ḥimṣi narrated to us Baqiya bin al-Waleed narrated to us from 'Uqba bin Abi Ḥakeem from Hubayra bin Abdar-Raḥman he said – When we used to press much, Anas would take out note-books and say – These are the *aḥādith* <u>I wrote</u> from the Prophet (peace be upon him).

Imām Bukhāri has substantiated this narration by way of comment on the narrator Hubayra bin Abdar-Raḥman in his *al-Tārikh al-Kabir*. He writes: 'Hubayra bin Abdar-Raḥman said - When we attended upon Anas bin Mālik he delivered to us from a record and said - This is the *aḥādith* which I wrote from the Messenger (peace be upon him) then I presented them to him.' Moreover, this is also reported in the *Mustadrak* of al-Ḥākim:

> حَدَّثَنَا أَبُو الْعَبَّاسِ مُحَمَّدُ بْنُ يَعْقُوبَ، أَنْبَأَ الْعَبَّاسُ بْنُ الْوَلِيدِ بْنِ مَزِيدٍ الْبَيْرُوتِيُّ، حَدَّثَنَا مُحَمَّدُ بْنُ شُعَيْبِ بْنِ شَابُورٍ، حَدَّثَنِي عُتْبَةُ بْنُ أَبِي حَكِيمٍ، عَنْ مَعْبَدِ بْنِ هِلَالٍ، قَالَ: كُنَّا إِذَا أَكْثَرْنَا عَلَى أَنَسِ بْنِ مَالِكٍ رَضِيَ اللَّهُ عَنْهُ أَخْرَجَ إِلَيْنَا مَجَالَّ عِنْدَهُ، فَقَالَ: هَذِهِ <u>سَمِعْتُهَا</u> مِنَ النَّبِيِّ، صلى الله عليه وسلم، <u>فَكَتَبْتُهَا وَعَرَضْتُهَا عَلَيْهِ</u>

> Abul'-'Abbās Muḥammad bin Ya'qub narrated to us al-'Abbās bin al-Waleed bin Mazeed al-Bayrooti reports: Muḥammad bin Shu'ayb bin Shāboor narrated to us 'Utba bin Abi Ḥakeem narrated to me from Ma'bad bin Hilāl he said: When we used to press much (during attendance) upon Anas bin Mālik (may Allah be pleased with him), he came out to us from an area and he said – this is what I heard from the Prophet (peace be upon him) and I wrote it and presented it to him.

The aforementioned channel comes via Ma'bad bin Hilāl. It may have been that 'Utba bin Abi Ḥakeem heard from both Hubayra bin Abdar-Raḥman and Ma'bad bin Hilāl. In any event, it doesn't make sense to say as adh-Dhahabi said – '*ḥadith munkar*' after seeking to correct Bukhāri.

To add to the above, there is also the *Ṣaḥifa* of the Imām of guidance and leader of the believers, namely Ali bin Abi Ṭālib (may Allah be pleased with him). He guarded and preserved this, keeping it within the sheath of his sword. This particular pamphlet included a number of important rulings, covering issues of *zakāt*, constitutional rules as well as some of the famous constitutional principles which were extracted from the constitution of Medina. More has been detailed on this point in our specialist work – *Obedience to the Rulers: Its Principles and Limits*. Furthermore, it also had an important comprehensive corpus concerning charity as has been reported from Ibn Ḥanafiya, in other words, Muḥammad bin Ali bin Abi Ṭālib; he said: 'Take this book and go with it to 'Uthmān, for verily it contains the orders of the Prophet (peace be upon him) with regards to charity (*ṣadaqa*).' That point is also elaborated in our work, *Obedience to the Rulers* as is the matter of the Constitution of Medina, which is a matter of paramount importance.

When the famous scholar of Islam and its premier narrator Abu Hurayrah Abdur-Raḥman Sakhr (may Allah be pleased with him) returned from Baḥrain, where he had been appointed to take care of some works as an assistant to its governor, al-'Alā bin al-Ḥaḍrami, he had to provide a detailed account to the ruler of Medina and leader of all believers, Umar bin al-Khaṭṭāb. It was well known that Umar was meticulous in scrutinising the actions of all public officials and Abu Hurayrah was no exception to this. So meticulous was this process of accountability, it even resulted in Abu Hurayrah being subject to a beating and having his wealth confiscated. A separate section has been prepared solely to detail this incident.[6] Following this incident, Abu Hurayrah retired from public office altogether. He turned his attention to scholarship, learning to read and write till he was proficient in both. He memorised the glorious Qur'ān, wrote his memorised materials from the Prophet (peace be upon him), which were in the region of four-thousand *aḥādith.* Thereafter, he devoted a part of every night to revise and commit them well to his memory till the end of his life. On rare occasions, he would use these written manuscripts to refresh his memory. One can therefore see that the use of written materials was prominent, even in the earliest epoch of Islam, in this specific incidence, within ten-years following receipt from the Prophetic source.

There is also the *Ṣaḥifa* of Jābir ibn Abdullah al-Anṣāry, which is famous, containing almost five-hundred *aḥādith* of the Prophet (peace be upon him). Although, it has not been ascertained with any degree of certitude whether he wrote them in the same direct manner from the Prophet (peace be upon him) like Abdullah ibn 'Amr and Anas bin Mālik did, or whether this was composed from memory after the death of the Prophet (peace be upon him), which is similar to Abu Hurayrah. It has been reported that he also had another book regarding *Ḥajj*, which carried the name 'The Smaller Rites (or rituals)' (*al-manasik al-ṣagheer*) as supported by the famous long *ḥadith* which has been reported in the *Ṣaḥīḥ* of Imām Muslim.

Other than what has been detailed above, it is known that there

---

6 The section entitled 'The beating of Abu Hurayrah and confiscation of his wealth' is included in a separate appendix to the Arabic edition.

were other works in existence, other *Ṣaḥifa's* and books, by other companions such as Sa'd bin 'Ubāda al-Anṣāri who had a book or books of *ḥadith* taken from the Prophet (peace be upon him), as cited by Imām Bukhāri, which goes on to explain that this *Ṣaḥifa* was a copy of another *Ṣaḥifa* which was held by Abdullah bin Abi 'Aufa. Again he had written these *aḥādith* by his own hand.

There is also Abu Rāfi who was the *mawla* of the Prophet (peace be upon him). People gathered collectively to read upon him from his dictated collections. Within the book was recorded the supplication at the start of the prayer, as well as tribute paid to Abu Bakr bin Abdar-Raḥman al-Ḥārith, one of the seven-renowned jurists of Medina. Asmā' bint 'Umays had a book which contained within it a collection of some *aḥādith.* There was also the book found in the sheath of the sword which belonged to Muḥammad bin Maslama al-Anṣāry when he died; it began 'In the name of Allah ar-Raḥman ar-Raḥeem, I heard that the Prophet (peace be upon him) saying *Verily your Lord in the end of your epoch...'* And also there was what was written by Subaya' al-Aslamiya to Abdullah bin 'Utba reporting from the Prophet (peace be upon him) that he ordered her with *nikāḥ* shortly after her husband's death after he developed; and a lot other than this.

This is some of what has been written from the corpus of the noble Prophetic *aḥādith*, immediately during the time of the Prophet (peace be upon him) or within a short period after his passing from this world. These *aḥādith* being directly taken from the Prophet (peace be upon him) and as has been seen, read-back and confirmed with him. Taken in the round, it is arguable that more than half of the entire corpus of *aḥādith* which we currently posses today was recorded in this manner as detailed above. Memorisation and oral transmission was dominant at the time of the Companions, and this is the case for those who lived through paganism and Islam and those who missed the honour of companionship, but lived through both the Islamic and pre-Islamic epoch (*mukhaḍrameen*). It is the same for the first class of the reporters after the companions; i.e. the great successors (*Kibār at-*

Tābi'een). Many of this class used to deliver their narrations on special occasions as well as providing comment upon great events and delivering legal judgements. In addition to this, they would narrate both from memory and by way of dictation from written material in the many study circles and other gatherings of knowledge, designated to learning and disseminating the Prophet's *aḥādith*, much the same as was done at that earlier stage in the lifetime of the Prophet (peace be upon him).

As has been attested from the writing of Abdullah ibn 'Amr ibn al-'Aāṣ, the companions took turn in attendance at the Prophet's *ḥalaqa* where he would teach. We know of Umar bin al-Khaṭṭāb rotating his attendance with that of Abdullah ibn 'Amr. Some companions would be in attendance in the morning, others would be in attendance to learn later in the day or evening. Each taking it in turn to attend at the classes delivered by the Prophet (peace be upon him). The subsequent *ḥalaqa's* of the leading companions such as Abdullah ibn 'Amr ibn al-'Aāṣ, Ibn Mas'ud, Ibn 'Abbās and other then them continued also in the same vein. Moreover, teaching and delivering knowledge by way of designated *ḥalaqa*, special seminars, and assemblies dedicated to narrating / dictating *aḥādith*, where the teacher would dictate to the students and / or the students would read back to the teacher, was a common feature which the *Ṣaḥabah* bequeathed to subsequent generations. They in turn, continued in this manner. Indeed, every scholar and student of knowledge utilised written manuscripts for the dispensation of knowledge. Sessions were characterised by the dictation from the teacher (Shaykh) to his students; or the reading of a student (who would be an excellent orator and narrator) back to the teacher, while the teacher checks what is being read either by way of memory or against his own manuscript. Each of the other students in attendance would not be sitting idly, but rather also dictating what is being read. Transmission of *aḥādith* took this format and was a noted feature amongst the senior and junior *Tābi'een*.

An illustrative example of this is that of the great scholar of *ḥadith*, Imām Muḥammad ibn Shihāb az-Zuhri. He had a large personal library that was transported on camels for him. Az-Zuhri was one of the class of the junior *Tābi'een* (which is the class that learned from some of the companions, who lived longer and died latest). He always used to revise his books whenever he was alone, to the extent that his wife became bored with that, and made a statement to the effect that those books were harder on her than her co-wives!

Another example which can be gleaned is that of the major figure of *ḥadith*, Abdal-Aziz bin Marwān, as reported by Ibn Sa'd in *aṭ-Ṭabaqāt al-Kubra*:

> كَثِيرُ بْنُ مُرَّةَ الْحَضْرَمِيُّ، ويكنى أبا شجرة. وكان ثقة: قَالَ عَبْدُ اللَّهِ بْنُ صَالِحٍ عَنِ اللَّيْثِ بْنِ سعد قال: حدثني يزيد بن أبي حبيب أَنَّ عَبْدَ الْعَزِيزِ بْنَ مَرْوَانَ كَتَبَ إِلَى كَثِيرِ بْنِ مُرَّةَ الْحَضْرَمِيِّ. وَكَانَ قَدْ أَدْرَكَ بِحِمْصَ سَبْعِينَ بَدْرِيًّا مِنْ أَصْحَابِ رَسُولِ اللَّهِ، صلى الله عليه وسلم، (قَالَ لَيْثٌ: وَكَانَ يُسَمِّي الْجُنْدَ الْمُقَدَّمَ). قَالَ: فَكَتَبَ إِلَيْهِ أَنْ يَكْتُبَ إِلَيْهِ بِمَا سَمِعَ مِنْ أَصْحَابِ رَسُولِ اللَّهِ، صلى الله عليه وسلم، مِنْ أَحَادِيثِهِمْ، إلا حديث أبي هريرة فإنه عندنا
>
> Kathir bin Murra al-Ḥaḍarami and (his) *kunya* Abu Shajara. And he was trustworthy (*thiqa*). Abdullah bin Ṣāliḥ said from al-Layth bin Sa'd – Yazeed bin Abi Ḥabeeb narrated to me that Abdal-Aziz bin Marwān wrote to Kathir bin Murra al-Ḥaḍarami he had seen in Ḥimṣ seventy Badri companions of the Prophet (peace be upon him). Layth said – it was called the 'veteran soldiers.' He said: he wrote to him that - write what you hear from the companions of the Prophet (peace be upon him) from their *aḥādith*, except the *hadith* of Abu Hurayrah, since we have them.

The just and arguably *Rāshid Khaleefa,* Umar bin Abdal-Aziz ibn Marwān (may Allah be pleased with him) was also a prominent trustworthy narrator. He began the collection and writing of *aḥādith* in a comprehensive manner; this was formally done given his status as ruler of Islamic lands. Specifically, he reported the *ḥadith* of Amra' bin Abdal-Raḥman which was the channel of narration to the mother of the believers, 'Aisha (may Allah be pleased with her). He ordered the judge of Medina, Abu Bakr bin Muḥammad bin Amr bin Ḥazm (who was the grandson of the aforementioned Amr bin Ḥazm, governor of the Prophet for the region of Najrān) to undertake this mission. Abu Bakr was from amongst the prominent *Tābi'een*, being an Imām of jurisprudence (*fiqh*) as well as *ḥadith* and established as a *thiqa* (trustworthy) narrator himself. It is arguable he had inherited his father's collection and manuscripts. All of this took place roughly around the year 100 AH.

The following generations of major, middle and lower-order *Tābi'een,* continued with this method, progressing to the point where they made the narration of *aḥādith* into an actual academic subject or as some would say, a science. Gatherings dedicated to narrating and dictating *aḥādith* had their own particular etiquettes, procedures, and even records of attendance. These can still be accessed in the (former) great centres of Islamic learning. The notion of 'spontaneous narration' waned considerably. The idea that *ḥadith* were simply narrated by wise old men, story-tellers and preachers at Friday prayers are something of a misnomer; in fact the stringent protocols underpinning the science of *ḥadith*, made such instances incredibly rare.

Given what has been expounded on this topic thus far, one may credibly ask, what the actual meaning of the term – '*Aṣr at-Tadween* (Era of documentation of the *Sunnah*) – refers to? Discerning the meaning of this can be made easier by replacing this with its correct terminology, which is the 'the Era of Publication' or '*Aṣr an-Nashr wal-Warrāqeen.* To clarify the matter further, we would say that by the end of the first-Islamic century and at the beginning of the second, paper had become more widespread and available. The industry in paper in the Muslim world emanated from Samarkand in Central Asia, in turn, originating from China.

By the middle of the second Islamic century and the consolidation of 'Abbāsid rule, the paper industry grew considerably, spreading throughout the Muslim world. High quality paper was for the first time available at reasonably low prices. Publishing books became much easier and with this grew the sale of books, which the mass public began to consume. Books of poetry, literature and Arabic language spread widely, as did the writings of Ibn Al-Muqaffa', the translations of *Kaleela and Dimnah*, and many other literary works from Persia and as far afield as India. Therefore, the profession of publishing appeared. The publisher, *Al-Warrāq*, was a person who hired a large number of scribes, copyists, sub-editors and the like, to prepare books *en-masse* for publication and sale. Thus the *Warrāq* was not merely a publisher, but also a printer and a literary agent in the modern sense of the term. With this literary revolution engulfing the Islamic world, scholars of *ḥadith* did not, at least initially, give approval to the publication of such materials. Though the production of the *Warrāq* was of high quality with few mistakes, it was able to reach the level of authentication required by the growing *ḥadith* science. Scholars still preferred to obtain material in the 'traditional' manner, through attendance upon a Shaykh and recording by dictation and / or presentation. They feared that the strict principles of narration via transmission be lost and that the distorted or forged versions would spread as happened with the people of the previous two books; namely the Jews and Christians. Yet Abu Ja'far Al-Manṣur was not convinced and insisted that common Muslims, who were not dedicated to studying *ḥadith* sciences had the right to see the truth of Prophetic *ḥadith* themselves and have such books and libraries in their own houses.

As for students of knowledge, their Imām's, scholars of *ḥadith* placed a premium upon receipt of authentic reliable transmission in a direct manner. However, they were also able to continue with this while correct versions which were obtained from the *Warrāq* and utilising this material either by reading or by presenting them to their qualified teachers. I would submit that history has shown that the *Ameer al-Mu'mineen* Abu Ja'far was correct in his policy. The rigorous discipline of *ḥadith* narration and transmission, with its associated dedicated gatherings continued for several centuries and was not undermined by the widespread dissemination of books. Indeed, in actuality, it worked in tandem with it. In the first wave of publication, came the *Muwaṭṭā'* of Imām Mālik, the works of the two Sufyāns – Sufyān ath-Thawri and Sufyān ibn 'Uyayna. There was also the works of the two Ḥammāds, Ḥammād ibn Zayd and Ḥammād ibn Salamah and that of Sa'eed ibn Abi Aruba. All of these works were compiled and put into public circulation by around 145 AH. Following this, we may note a further three distinct 'waves' of publication:

- *Second wave* - saw the publication of the *Muṣṣanaf* of Abdar-Razzāq; *Sunan* Ḥumaydi, the *Musnad* of aṭ-Ṭayālisi, the works of al-Wāqidi and many others. We may posit a nominal date-marker for the second wave as being 190 AH.

- *Third wave* – included all the famous books carrying the titles of *Musnad* and *Al-Jāmi*, such as the *Musnad* of Aḥmad bin Ḥanbal; *Musnad* Isḥāq bin Rāhawayh; *Muṣṣanaf* Ibn Abi Shayba, *Sunan* Sa'eed bin Manṣur, the *Ṭabaqāt* of Ibn Sa'd, the *Sunan* of ad-Dārimi and many others. Again, the nominal date-marker for this wave is 220 AH.

- *Fourth wave* – the nominal date-marker for this wave is 250 AH. Within this phase came the blessed books of *Ṣaḥīḥ* by Imām Bukhāri and Muslim. With them, albeit slightly after, were the famous *Sunan* works from Abu Dāwud, Tirmidhi and Ibn Mājah. There was also the *Musnad* of Baqi bin Makhlad in Spain; the *Musnad* of Abu Ya'la and al-Bazzār as well as the *Sunan* of Imām Nasā'i. By this juncture, the collection and compilation of the Prophetic *ḥadith* was by and large assembled and disseminated.

- *Fifth wave* – what was left over from the preceding compilations became featured in later works. During this era, the large collections of Ṭabarāni appeared; there was also the *Ṣaḥīḥ* of Ibn Ḥibbān, *Sunan* Dāraquṭni, and the *Mustadrak* of al-Ḥākim. Another feature were books about narrators, which also contained full channels of narration and *isnād*, such as *Al-Kāmil fi aḍ-Ḍua'fā'* (compendium of weak narrators) and that of Ibn 'Ady as well as others. Most of these books and compilations became widespread. Any mistakes made by scribes and copyists which were contained therein were not of any major import, any attempts at deliberate falsification were thus detected. It would be absurd to suggest that widespread and deliberate forgeries could easily creep into this corpus.

Notwithstanding the above, a very small number of *aḥādith* and a minority of alternate channels for better known *ḥadith* could be identified in books of *fiqh* (jurisprudence), *uṣul* (foundational methodology and principles), as well as in books of history and works dedicated to profiling *ḥadith* narrators. Arguably some of the most important of these were *as-Sunan al-Kubra* by Imām Bayhaqy; *al-Iḥkām fi Uṣul al-Aḥkām* (Judgement on the Principles of Law) and *al-Muḥalla bil Athār* (The Adorned Treatise) by Imām Abu Muḥammad Ali Ibn Ḥazm, and *Tārikh Baghdād* (History of Baghdad) by the grand Imām al-Khaṭeeb Baghdādi. The nominal date-marker for these works where completed by is 450 AH.

Despite this, narrating and dictating *aḥādith* has remained within the Islamic world. Whether that be in the far west in Morocco or in the east in the Indian sub-continent, scholars and students of knowledge have continued to receive *ḥadith* in the 'traditional manner', namely by attendance in the audience of the Shaykh, dictating and reading back to him. With the advances made in modern technology and computers, valuable books are being digitised at an incredible rate. One could argue that this is a new method of preservation. Although admittedly, there are some texts that are not as reliable as first thought, since they are not based upon the best manuscripts. However, a large number of researchers, scholars and students of knowledge are seeking to correct this, by the grace and mercy of Allah.

What has been said thus far regarding *aḥādith* is also applicable to the Prophetic *Seerah* (life and biography), particularly for the period post-migration in Medina which also covers the great battles, contrary to those who are ignorant of this. Compilation within this field began many years earlier than that of the *Sunan* or *Musnad* collections and were prepared under the title of *al-Maghāzi* (the battles or conquests). Such works were published and well received amongst the Muslim masses. This is a historical fact and it is of no surprise it was well received, given that the vast majority of people can readily digest biographies, stories and history in general, as opposed to turgid rigorous style employed within the *Sunan* or *Musnad* collections. In fact, public sessions or recitals were held on the topic of *al-Maghāzi* during the time of the rightly-guided Caliphs. The recitals were employed as a means of inspiring soldiers and urging Muslims to fight in the cause of Allah. These sessions were called 'storytelling' and were delivered by a 'storyteller.'

Also there was the work of *al-Maghāzi* prepared by the *Tābi'* Imām 'Abbān bin Uthmān bin 'Affān (may Allah be pleased with him). He made a fatal error though when he presented this work to the tyrant Caliph al-Waleed bin Abdal-Malik bin Marwān, may the curse of Allah be upon him. Al-Waleed denounced the work ordering it to be destroyed because of the facts reported therein which exposed and detailed the crimes of Bani Umayah. Faced with this, 'Abbān bin Uthmān did not have the courage to recompose the book after its destruction and it was lost to posterity; there is no power or might save in Allah! Without doubt many other writers compiled works of *al-Maghāzi*, such as Imām Muḥammad ibn Shihāb az-Zuhri. Directly following such works were that produced by the Imām *Maghāzi* and *Seerah* - Muḥammad ibn Isḥāq ibn Yasār who died in the year 150 AH. He produced a huge comprehensive biography but a lot of doubtful information was enclosed. Much of it was re-worked and edited by Imām Ibn Hishām and thereafter became known as the *Seerah* of Ibn Hishām – which became a landmark work, some would say the standard for biographical works about the Prophet (peace be upon him). Work has continued upon the *Seerah* even up to the present, Shaykh Ṣafi-ur-Raḥman al-Mubārakpuri, with his monumental work *ar-Raḥeeq al-Makhtum* (the Sealed Nectar); may Allah reward him abundantly for his effort. Mubārakpuri's work has received international acclaim, being translated into numerous languages.

People have queried why such biographical works are not used in determining matters of general legislation and rulings, or *aqeedah*, given that they generally are taken from the historical background. The reason for this is that the authors of such historical works have tended to drop the channels of transmission in general as well as putting narratives together to make a coherent readily accessible narrative. Whilst this does provide an accurate picture of historical events overall, it does not produce legal certainty to the requisite standard which can be used as proof in matters of *Deen*. It shouldn't therefore be of great surprise that scholars of *ḥadith*, applying strict principles have regarded such works in general as having no substantive basis to them. That is not to say that they are works of fabrication, but that they do not meet the required legal standards to be utilised for matters of creed and legislation. One could liken this form of reporting to be akin to that found in contemporary journalism as found in newspapers, the radio and television. Although a generic picture is provided of actual events, such manner of reporting is not generally viewed as being admissible evidence in a judicial capacity.

There has to be physical evidence, witness statements, official documentation and the like which can withstand rigorous and detailed cross-examination. Matters related to *Deen*, be they creedal or legislative, without doubt rank highly thus requiring the rigorous methodologies which have accompanied them to date.

The work as detailed here is but a brief overview. To do real justice to the subject as a whole would inevitably require a separate volume altogether. Such works are being produced and are dealing a death-blow to the claims of the Orientalists. One notable work in this regard, is that submitted originally as a PhD thesis at Cambridge University by the renowned Shaykh Dr Muḥammad Muṣṭafa al-'Azami;[7] may Allah reward him abundantly for his noble distinguished work. His work has fundamentally deconstructed the theories which the Orientalists have held sacrosanct for over a century and he has, by the grace of Allah, demonstrated that they are utterly false. Given the ground-breaking nature of the Shaykh's work, all those who had a semblance of intellectual honesty from amongst the Orientalists have thus abandoned the bizarre opinions of the likes of Goldzieher and Schacht. Work is ongoing within this field and many are being published which have only further entrenched the strength of the Prophetic *Sunnah*, providing even further substantiation to its truthfulness, underpinned with a sound rigorous academic approach.[8] Taken in the round, all such works provide yet further evidence to the truthfulness which Allah himself attests will be established, step-by-step, in the glorious Qur'ān:

سَنُرِيهِمْ آيَاتِنَا فِي الْآفَاقِ وَفِي أَنفُسِهِمْ حَتَّىٰ يَتَبَيَّنَ لَهُمْ أَنَّهُ الْحَقُّ أَوَلَمْ يَكْفِ بِرَبِّكَ أَنَّهُ عَلَىٰ كُلِّ
شَيْءٍ شَهِيدٌ، أَلَا إِنَّهُمْ فِي مِرْيَةٍ مِّن لِّقَاءِ رَبِّهِمْ أَلَا إِنَّهُ بِكُلِّ شَيْءٍ مُّحِيطٌ

[7] M. M. 'Azami (2000), *Studies in Early Ḥadith Literature* (Kuala Lumpur: Islamic Book Trust)

[8] For example Dr Muḥammad Hamidullah (2003), *An Introduction to the Conservation of Ḥadith: in light of the Ṣaḥifa of Hammām ibn Munabbih* (Kuala Lumpur: Islamic Book Trust)

We will soon show them our signs in the universe and in their own souls, until it will become quite clear to them that it is the truth. Is it not sufficient as regards your Lord that He is a witness over all things? Now surely they are in doubt as to the meeting of their Lord; surely He encompasses all things.[9]

Just as this occurred at the very dawn of Islam and was witnessed by the Quraysh, it is constantly recurring throughout the ages, including our present time and indeed, will continue until the day of judgement.

أَوَلَمْ يَكْفِ بِرَبِّكَ أَنَّهُ عَلَىٰ كُلِّ شَيْءٍ شَهِيدٌ

Is it not sufficient as regards your Lord that He is a witness over all things?

[9] *Qur'ān* 41: 53/54

Part III.

Fundamental Issues of *Uṣul* and *'Aqeedah*

1 The Seal of Prophethood

The principle that Muḥammad (peace be upon him) is the 'Seal of the Prophets' is confirmed in the Qur'ānic verse by which it is established as a central tenet of the Islamic faith:

مَّا كَانَ مُحَمَّدٌ أَبَا أَحَدٍ مِّن رِّجَالِكُمْ وَلَٰكِن رَّسُولَ اللَّهِ وَخَاتَمَ النَّبِيِّينَ وَكَانَ اللَّهُ بِكُلِّ شَيْءٍ عَلِيمًا

Muḥammad is not the father of any of your men, but he is the Messenger of Allah and the Seal of the Prophets; and Allah is cognisant of all things.[1]

The verse is unequivocal in meaning, beaming as clear as the brightest sun. In the *Tafsir* of this verse, the grand Imām aṭ-Ṭabari has written the following:

> Concerning the interpretation of the verse - *Muḥammad is not the father of any of your men, but he is the Messenger of Allah and the Last of the Prophets; and Allah is cognisant of all things* - Allah mentions that O mankind! Muḥammad is not the father of Zayd

[1] *Qur'ān* 33: 40

ibn Ḥāritha nor is he the father of anyone of your men, (none of whom gave birth to Muḥammad), which would prohibit him from marrying his wife if he separated from her. However, he is the Messenger of Allah and the Seal of the Prophets by which Prophethood has ended. Consequently, he has been made the stamp of Prophethood, which no one will reopen after him until the establishment of the final hour. And Allah knows all things pertaining to your actions; your words and other than these. He is the possessor of omnipotent knowledge and nothing is hidden from Him. It is in the manner in which we have cited here that the people of interpretation have (sought to expound) the meaning of this verse. Among those who narrated Prophetic traditions regarding the meaning of the above verse (we have) the following:

Bishr narrated to us he said Yazeed narrated to us he said Sa'eed narrated to us from Qatādah regarding his words: *Muḥammad is not the father of any of your men* was revealed regarding Zayd, that he was not his son. I swear by my age that he did give birth to male children for he was the father of Abu'l-Qāsim, Ibrāhim, aṭ-Ṭayyib and al-Muṭṭahir. The meaning of His words: '*However, he is the Messenger of Allah and the Seal of the Prophets*,' means that he is the last of them: '*And Allah knows all things.*'

Muḥammad ibn 'Ammāra narrated to me he said Ali bin Qādim narrated to us he said Sufyān narrated to us from Nasser bin Dhu'luuq from Ali bin al-Ḥussain regarding His words: '*Muḥammad is not the father of anyone of your men*'; this verse was revealed regarding Zayd ibn Ḥāritha. The phrase: '*the Messenger of Allah*, may Allah bless him and grant him peace, is placed in the accusative case, which gives it the meaning of reiteration of the phrase.

However, it did not occur to the mind of Imām aṭ-Ṭabari, nor indeed the mind of any other classical scholar that there would emerge a controversy surrounding the meaning of the expression *khātim* - 'seal', or *Khātam an-Nabi'een* 'Seal of the Prophets' because during that time there was only one meaning of the phrase, which included: 'stamping; closure; shutting; completion;' and the like of what can be advanced to embrace the affairs in their finality or in their end. The Arabs had no other explanation of the meaning of this phrase other than that. The stipulation of the expression '*seal*' has three distinct connotations, which is utilised in seven other places within the Qur'ān; which I will narrate consecutively as they appear in the noble book:

خَتَمَ اللَّهُ عَلَىٰ قُلُوبِهِمْ وَعَلَىٰ سَمْعِهِمْ وَعَلَىٰ أَبْصَارِهِمْ غِشَاوَةٌ وَلَهُمْ عَذَابٌ عَظِيمٌ

Allah has set a seal upon their hearts and their hearing; there is a covering over their eyes, and there's great punishment for them. [2]

قُلْ أَرَأَيْتُمْ إِنْ أَخَذَ اللَّهُ سَمْعَكُمْ وَأَبْصَارَكُمْ وَخَتَمَ عَلَىٰ قُلُوبِكُم مَّنْ إِلَٰهٌ غَيْرُ اللَّهِ يَأْتِيكُم بِهِ انظُرْ كَيْفَ نُصَرِّفُ الْآيَاتِ ثُمَّ هُمْ يَصْدِفُونَ

Say: Have you considered that if Allah takes away your hearing and your sight and sets a seal on your hearts, who is the god besides Allah that can bring it to you? See how we repeat the communications, yet they turn away. [3]

الْيَوْمَ نَخْتِمُ عَلَىٰ أَفْوَاهِهِمْ وَتُكَلِّمُنَا أَيْدِيهِمْ وَتَشْهَدُ أَرْجُلُهُم بِمَا كَانُوا يَكْسِبُونَ

On that day, We will set a seal upon their mouths, and their hands shall speak to Us, and their feet shall bear witness of what they earned. [4]

أَمْ يَقُولُونَ افْتَرَىٰ عَلَى اللَّهِ كَذِبًا فَإِن يَشَإِ اللَّهُ يَخْتِمْ عَلَىٰ قَلْبِكَ وَيَمْحُ اللَّهُ الْبَاطِلَ وَيُحِقُّ الْحَقَّ بِكَلِمَاتِهِ إِنَّهُ عَلِيمٌ بِذَاتِ الصُّدُورِ

Or do they say: He has forged a lie against Allah? But if Allah pleased, He would seal your heart; and Allah will blot out the falsehood and confirm the

[2] *Qur'ān* 2: 7
[3] *Qur'ān* 6: 46
[4] *Qur'ān* 36: 65

truth with His words; surely, He is cognisant of what is in the breasts.[5]

أَفَرَأَيْتَ مَنِ اتَّخَذَ إِلَٰهَهُ هَوَاهُ وَأَضَلَّهُ اللَّهُ عَلَىٰ عِلْمٍ وَخَتَمَ عَلَىٰ سَمْعِهِ وَقَلْبِهِ وَجَعَلَ عَلَىٰ بَصَرِهِ
غِشَاوَةً فَمَن يَهْدِيهِ مِن بَعْدِ اللَّهِ أَفَلَا تَذَكَّرُونَ

Have you then considered him who takes his low desire for his god, and Allah has made him err having knowledge and has set a seal upon his ear and his heart and put a covering upon his eye. Who can then guide him after Allah? Will you not then be mindful?[6]

يُسْقَوْنَ مِن رَّحِيقٍ مَّخْتُومٍ ، خِتَامُهُ مِسْكٌ وَفِي ذَٰلِكَ فَلْيَتَنَافَسِ الْمُتَنَافِسُونَ

They will be served a sealed nectar, its seal [perfumed with] a fragrant musk, let those who strive, strive for this.[7]

Imām aṭ-Ṭabari is widely acknowledged as being an established proof concerning matters of Arabic language and linguistics. This is in tandem with the fact that he was a major Imām in a number of Islamic sciences such as the Qur'ān, *Tafsir* and *ḥadith*; regarded across the spectrum as being a *mujtahid muṭlaq*. He further elaborated on the controversies of the expression: 'seal', when he first presented its appearances in the consecutive order as they appear in the Qur'ān. He mentioned the unique linguistic meanings in an abridged manner, then proceeded to elaborate on its diverse issues covering the points of 'guidance and error'; 'the flooding of sins over the heart,' and others.

With reference to the first verse (*al-Baqara* verse 7) regarding the *Tafsir* of His words: '*Allah has placed a seal on their hearts and their hearing*', aṭ-Ṭabari writes:

---

[5] *Qur'ān* 42: 21
[6] *Qur'ān* 45: 23
[7] *Qur'ān* 83: 25/26

The etymological root of the word 'seal' is 'imprint'; for the 'signet' it is a 'stamp' which is usually utilised when one says: 'I have sealed the book' following an impression being made. For when someone says to us: 'How does He seal the hearts?' The expression 'seal' here means an impression which is made upon the containers, the receptacles or the encasements, because it is said that the hearts of the servants are the containers which comprise sciences; and the receptacles in which (they) are placed the realisation of matters. Thus the meaning of placing a seal upon their hearts and upon their hearing by which they comprehend what is heard, is that before them a barrier is placed which prevents the heart and hearing from attaining (the) realisation of the truths of news of the unseen. Thus, the analogous meaning of the expression 'seal' carries with it the same meaning of an imprint that is made upon any container or receptacle. If it is asked - is this an attribute from its attributes by which we can better comprehend it? Is it the same as the seal which is known and is apparent to sight, or is it something different? It is said that the people of Qur'ānic *Tafsir* differ (regarding) the descriptions of this seal. We will discuss the description of the seal after discussing some of the words of the interpreters:

Esa bin Uthmān bin Esa ar-Ramli narrated to me he said Yaḥya bin Esa narrated to us from al-'Amash he said: Mujāhid showed us his hand, and said: 'They used to show me that the heart was no larger than this, (meaning by that the palm). When a servant commits a sin, it encloses upon like this, (and he then closed his small finger upon his palm). When he commits another sin, it encloses upon it like this, (he then closed the next finger upon his palm). When he commits another sin, it encloses upon it like this, (he then closed his middle finger upon his palm).' He did this until all of his fingers had closed upon his palm and said: 'Then the heart is imprinted upon with an impression'. Mujāhid said: 'They used to show me that this closing on the heart was doubt which overcomes it.'

Abu Kareeb narrated to us he said Waki' narrated to us from al-'Amash from Mujāhid, he said: 'The heart is like the palm of the hand; and when a sin is committed the fingers grasp down upon it until all the fingers enclose upon it. Our companions used to show us that this encompassment is a kind of doubt that overwhelms the heart.'

Al-Qāsim ibn al-Ḥasan narrated to us he said al-Ḥussain bin Dāwud narrated to us he said Ḥajjaj narrated to me he said Ibn Jurayj narrated to us he said that Mujāhid said: 'I was informed that sins encircle the heart with what it has been forbidden it until eventually the heart becomes accustomed to it and thus, sins become firmly imprinted upon it. This impression is the seal.' Ibn Jurayj said: 'This seal is the sealing of the heart and the hearing.'

Al-Qāsim narrated to us he said al-Ḥussain narrated to us Ḥajjaj narrated to me from Ibn Jurayj, he said Abdullah bin Kathir narrated to me that he heard Mujāhid say: 'This encompassing doubt is easier than, the impression upon the heart. The impressions made upon the heart are easier than the heart being completely locked. The heart being completely locked is the severest of them all.'

Concerning the second, verse 46 of *Surah al-An'ām*, aṭ-Ṭabari comments as follows:

Here Allah the exalted says to His Prophet Muḥammad may Allah bless him and grant him peace: 'Say O Muḥammad to those who turn away from Me deviating with the idols and false deities and who deny you: 'Have you who associate deities besides Allah not seen, that if Allah desired to make you deaf by seizing your hearing; your actions; seizes your sight and places a seal over your hearts; stamping it so that you are unable to comprehend words, or have insight into clear evidence, or have clear understanding of anything; is there a deity besides Allah that you can bring that is worshipped by all those who worship; who can return what Allah has seized of your hearing, sight and understanding?' In this verse, you can see that the expression 'seal' was only utilised in the middle of the sentence which suffices as a proof in its interpretation that it is a synonym of the expression 'to make an imprint.'

In relation to verse 65 of *Surah Ya Seen*, aṭ-Ṭabari writes:

(Regarding the) interpretation of His words: '*This day have We placed a seal over their mouths and their hands will speak out,*' what Allah the exalted means when He states as such, is that 'this day have We stamped over the mouths of those who associate deities besides Allah.' The expression 'this day' refers to the day of judgement. The meaning of His words: '*and their hands will speak out,*' means that they will speak out regarding what they did in this life from disobedience of Allah. The meaning of His words: '*...and their feet will testify against them,*' in summation has the same meaning as what preceded.

Concerning verse 42 of *Surah ash-Shoora*, aṭ-Ṭabari writes:

(Regarding the) interpretation of His words, here Allah the exalted mentions that do those who associate deities besides Allah say that Muḥammad has invented a lie against Allah, while he brings revelation which is in opposition to anything which can be construed to come from his own whims. If Allah willed O Muḥammad, He could imprint over your heart causing you to forget this Qur'ān which has been revealed to you.

Regarding the fifth verse mentioned, which is verse 23 of *Surah Jāthiya* aṭ-Ṭabari writes:

The meaning of His words: '*places a seal on his hearing and his*

> *heart*'; means that He imprints over their hearing where they are unable to hear the admonitions of Allah and the verses of His Book, where they can reflect, be attentive, consider or apprehend what is in it of light, clarity and guidance. The meaning of His words: '*his heart*' is that it too is imprinted upon where it is unable to conceive or grasp anything of the truth.

With regard to the remaining sixth and seventh verses quote above, verses 25/26 in *Surah Al-Muṭaffifin*, Imām aṭ-Ṭabari comments at length regarding them, in particular, noting the differing opinions that have been held amongst the scholars regarding their precise meaning:

> The meaning of His words: '*They will be given to drink from exquisite sealed nectar*,' is that these righteous people will be given to drink a pure wine which is not diluted by anything. Based upon what we have received from the people of Qur'ānic interpretation from chains of authorities which amount to almost ten, all of which agree that the '*sealed nectar*' is wine. The meaning of His words: '*Its seal will be musk*,' is that the people of Qur'ānic interpretation differ regarding its meaning. Some of them say that it means that it will be blended, mixed or intermixed with musk. Those who interpret it in that fashion base their opinions on the following narrations:
>
> Ibn Ḥumayd narrated to us he said Mihrān narrated to us from Sufyān from Ash'ath bin Abi ash-Sha'shā' from Yazeed bin Mu'āwiya and 'Alqama from Abdullah ibn Mas'ud that the meaning of His words: '*Its seal will be musk*,' does not mean that it is sealed literally, but that it is intermixed with musk.
>
> Ibn Bishār narrated to us he said Yaḥya bin Sa'eed and Abdar-Raḥman narrated to us, they said, Sufyān narrated to us from Ash'ath bin Sulaym from Yazeed bin Mu'āwiya from 'Alqama from Abdullah ibn Mas'ud who said regarding the meaning of His words: '*Its seal will be musk*,' the expression 'seal' does not mean the kind of seal that closes a thing. Have you not heard one of your

women say: 'So-and-so perfume was intermixed with musk'?'

Muḥammad bin 'Ubaid al-Maḥārabi narrated to us he said Ayub narrated to us from Ash'ath bin Abi ash-Sha'shā' what he narrated on the authority of 'Alqama regarding His words: '*Its seal will be musk*,' means that it will be intermixed with musk.

Abu Kareeb narrated to us he said Waki' narrated to us from al-'Amash from Abdullah bin Murra from Masrooq from Abdullah that the meaning of: '*Its seal*' is that its seal will be intermixed with musk; which means that its taste and fragrance will be mixed with it.

Waki` narrated to us from his father from ibn Abi ash-Sha'shā' from Yazeed bin Mu'āwiya from 'Alqama that the meaning of: '*Its seal will be musk*,' is that its taste and fragrance will be that of musk. Others said that its meaning is that the last of their drink will be sealed with musk which will be placed in it. Those who hold this opinion base their evidence on the following traditions:

Ali narrated to me he said Abu Ṣāliḥ narrated to us he said Mu'āwiya narrated to me from Ali from Ibn 'Abbās who said regarding His words: '*Its seal will be musk*,' means that it will be wine whose seal will be made with musk.

Muḥammad bin Sa'd narrated to me he said my father narrated to me, my uncle narrated to me, he said my father narrated to me from his father from Ibn 'Abbās that the meaning of His words: '*Its seal will be musk*,' means that Allah will indulge them with wine and it will be the last thing until it will be sealed with musk.

Bishr narrated to us he said Yazeed narrated to us he said Sa'eed narrated to us from Qatādah that the meaning of: '*Its seal will be musk*,' is that its final consequence will be that of musk, in that their wine will be first intermixed with camphor and then sealed with musk.

Ibn Abdal' al-'Alā narrated to us he said Ibn Thawr narrated to us from Ma'mar from Qatādah that the meaning of: '*Its seal will be musk*' is that its final outco

me will be with musk.

I narrated from al-Ḥussain he said I heard Abu Mu'ādh say: 'Ubaid narrated to us, he said I heard aḍ-Ḍaḥḥāk say regarding His words: '*Is seal will be musk*'; means that Allah will indulge them with wine; and they will find that in the last of it will be the fragrance of musk.'

Abdal' al-'Alā narrated to us he said Ḥātim bin Wardān narrated to us he said Abu Ḥamza narrated to us from Ibrāhim and al-Ḥasan regarding the meaning of this verse: '*Its seal will be musk*' is that its result or final outcome will be musk.

Ibn Ḥumayd narrated to us he said Yaḥya bin Wāḍiḥ' narrated to us he said Abu Ḥamza narrated to us from Jābir from Abdar-Raḥman bin Sābiṭ from Abu Dardā' that the meaning of His words: '*Its seal will be musk*' is that it is a beverage which is as bright as silver with which those who will be given it to drink will seal their drinking. Even if a man from this life were to enter one of his fingers in it and then take it out, the fragrance of it would remain with him even after his spirit has been taken.

Other scholars said that the meaning of His words: '*Its seal will be musk*' is that it will be sealed with a clay covering made from musk. Those who hold to this opinion take their evidence from the following traditions:

Muḥammad ibn 'Amr narrated to me he said Abu 'Aāṣim narrated to us he said Esa narrated to us and al-Ḥarith narrated to me he said al-Ḥasan narrated to us he said Waraqā' (narrating to) all of us from Ibn Abi Najeeḥ from Mujāhid, he said: 'The meaning of His words: *Its seal will be musk* means that its seal will be sealed with a clay covering made from musk.'

Yunus narrated to us he said Ibn Wahb reported to us he said that Ibn Zayd said regarding His words: '*Its seal will be musk*' means that the wine will be sealed musk.

Therefore with Allah its seal will be musk, while today in this life wine is sealed with clay. The foremost of the opinions which is most correct with us in what we related above is the opinion of those who said its meaning is: 'Its last or final outcome will be musk.' That is to say that it will be the fragrance of its perfume, in that the fragrance at the end of its drinking will give off the fragrance of musk. We say that this opinion is foremost in soundness of the preceding opinions because in the language of the Arabs there is no other linguistic meaning to the expression 'seal' other than 'an imprint' and 'completion' like their saying: 'So and-so sealed the Qur'ān, when they mean that he came to its ending.

Since the meaning of 'stamp' when referring to the drink of the people of paradise has a finite meaning, it is understood that their drink flows like the flowing of the water in a river and does not ripen or age like the wine of this world's life which would require it to be closed and sealed. Thus the concept of 'sealing' here is specific and the soundest opinion would mean that it applies to the final outcome of the drink by which it is sealed. As for the expression of 'seal' with the meaning of 'intermixing', we do not know this to be heard from the language of the Arabs.

One can see how Imām aṭ-Ṭabari likes to digress and elaborate when given the chance and in spite of that he only discovered in the expression of 'seal' the meanings of 'to imprint upon', 'to close', 'to end' or 'to complete'. And he discovered no other meaning in the language of the Arabs beside these. The preponderate meaning of the final verse: '*Its seal will be musk*' is that its final outcome and completion will become like the perfumed fragrance of musk. Unlike the fragrance of the wine of this world's like which diffuses a foul odour from the mouth of its drinker. This is the meaning that al-Yatim gave and it is exclusively mentioned by the author of the *Mukhtār aṣ-Ṣiḥāḥ'*. In this work under the section of the letter arrangement (خ ت م) it is stated:

> The expression 'to seal a thing' is to be taken as illustration for something that is 'closed' (*makhtoom*) and 'shut' (*mukhattam*) when it is intensified to express amplification; like the expressions: 'Allah sealed it with good'; and 'He sealed the Qur'ān' meaning that he reached its ending. Thus, the conclusion of a thing is the opposite of its beginning. The expressions [الخَاتَمُ] (with the letter *ta* inflexed with the *fat'ha*); (with the letter *ta* inflexed with the *kasra*); [الخَيْتَامُ]; and [الخَاتَامُ] all have one meaning. And its plural form is [الخَوَاتِيمُ]. The expression [تَخَتَّمَ] means to wear a ring while the expression: [خاتِمةُ الشيء] ('to seal a thing') means its ending. Thus, Muḥammad, may Allah bless him and grant him peace is the Seal of the Prophets, upon them be blessings and peace. The expression [الخِتَامُ] (sealing wax) is clay used to seal a thing, thus the meaning in Allah ta`ala's words: '*Its seal will be musk*'; i.e. it's ending will be with musk, since the last fragrance which will exude from the wine or its drinker will be the fragrance of musk.

Indeed, here the expression '*takhatm*' which means to wear a ring, but the original meaning of the word 'ring' (*khātim*) is so named because initially the ring was used to seal envelopes and letters which were officially sent by kingdoms, where the messages were secured with red wax and then stamped with the ring. Thus the envelopes or messages could not be opened except by breaking the seal. Consequently, it was impossible to tamper or interfere with the letter and its contents without it being apparent and obvious. Thereafter rings became a sought of adornment which were worn upon the fingers and in some cases, were still utilised in many regions for its original purpose of sealing messages and closing envelopes, such as in the Arabian Peninsula.

In addition to this, there is the interpretation of the 'Ruḥ-Allah and His word', the Messiah, Esa ibn Maryam, peace be upon him and his mother, when he will say on the Day of Judgement: '*Have you not seen how when a container which has goods inside of it has a seal upon it that it is impossible to access what is in it until the seal is broken?*' It will be said: 'No' He will say: '*Likewise, Muḥammad, may Allah bless him and grant him peace is the Seal of the Prophets.*' This was as the Messenger of Allah Muḥammad, the Seal of the Prophets, informed us, upon him and his family blessings and peace. This has reached us with the soundest chain of authority in the *Musnad* of Imām Aḥmad bin Ḥanbal:[8]

> 'Affān narrated to us Ḥammād bin Salama narrated to us Thābit narrated to us from Anas that the Prophet (peace be upon him) said: *The day of judgement will be elongated for its people to the extent that some of the people will say to others: 'Let's go to Adam the father of mankind so that he can intercede for us with our Lord; and he can inform us of what will happen with us.' They will then go to Adam and say: 'O Adam you are the one whom Allah created with His Hand and caused to live in His Paradise, so intercede for us with your Lord, and inform us what will become of us.' He will say: 'I am unable to bring you relief, however go to Nuḥ who is the head of the Prophets.' They will then proceed to him and say: 'O Nuḥ intercede for us with your Lord, and inform us what will befall us.' He will say: 'I am unable to bring relief for you, however go to Ibrāhim, the intimate friend of Allah azza wa jalla'. They will then proceed to him and say: 'O Ibrāhim intercede for us with your Lord and inform us what will become of us.' He will say: 'I am unable to bring you relief, however go to Musa, whom Allah azza wa jalla chose for His Message and Speech'. They will then proceed to him and say: 'O Musa intercede for us with your Lord azza wa jalla, and inform us what will become of us.' He will say: 'I am unable to bring you relief, however go to Esa, the Spirit belonging to Allah and His Word'.*
>
> *They will then proceed to Esa and say: 'O Esa intercede for us with your Lord and inform us what will become of us.' He will say: 'I am unable to bring relief to you, however go to Muhammad, may*

[8] *Musnad* Aḥmad Vol. 3 sec. 247, no. 13,615

Allah bless him and grant him peace, for he is the Seal of the Prophets. This Day he is present and his sins of the past and the future have been forgiven.' He (Esa) will then say: 'Have you not seen how when a container which has goods inside of it has a seal upon it that it is impossible to access what is in it until the seal is broken? It will be said: 'No' He will say: 'Likewise, Muhammad, may Allah bless him and grant him peace is the Seal of the Prophets'.

The Messenger of Allah (peace be upon him) then said: '*They will then come to me and say: 'O Muḥammad intercede for us with your Lord and inform us of what will befall us.' I will say: 'Yes'. I will then go to the door of Paradise and take hold of door handle in order to open It. Then a voice will be heard: 'Who are you?' I will say: 'Muḥammad'. Then the door will be opened for me, and I will then fall into prostration and give praises to my Lord, azza wa jalla, with a praise that no being before or after me will ever praise Him with. He will then say to me: 'Lift your head! Speak and I will listen! Ask and I will give you! Intercede and I will accept your intercession!' I will say: 'Indeed O Lord, my Ummah! My Ummah!' He, Allah will then say: 'Go and take out those in whose hearts is the weight of a barley seed of faith'. I will then take them out and then go and fall into prostration and give praises to my Lord, azza wa jalla, with a praise that no being before or after me will ever praise Him with. He, Allah will then say: 'Lift your head! Ask and I will give you! Intercede and I will accept your intercession!'*

I will say: 'Indeed O Lord, my Ummah! My Ummah!' Allah will then say: 'Go and take out those in whose hearts is the weight of a fruit seed of faith'. I will then take them out and then go and fall into prostration and say what I said before. He, Allah will then say what He said before and then say: 'Go and take out those in whose hearts is the weight of an atom of faith'. I will then take them out.

This tradition is also found in the *Musnad* of al-Ḥārith as it is in al-

Haythami's *az-Zawā'id,*[9] via a second channel which has nothing untoward about it:

> حدثنا العباس بن الفضل حدثنا حماد بن سلمة حدثني علي بن زيد عن أبي نضرة عن بن عباس قال: خطب رسول الله، صلى الله عليه وسلم، قال: إذا كان يوم القيامة طال على الناس الحساب] فساق الحديث بنحوه إلى أن قال: [ولكن ائتوا عيسى فإنه يشفع لكم إلى ربكم فيأتونه فيقولون: أنت روح الله وكلمته فاشفع لنا إلى ربك فليحاسبنا فقد طال علينا الحساب، فيقول: (إني لست هناك: إني عُبدت من دون الله؛ ولكن أرأيتم لو كان متاع في وعاء عليه خاتم ثم كان يوصل الى ذلك المتاع حتى يفك الخاتم، فأتوا محمدا، صلى الله عليه وسلم، فإنه خاتم النبيين)؛.. إلخ]
>
> Al-'Abbās bin al-Faḍl narrated to us Ḥammād bin Salama narrated to us Ali bin Zayd narrated to me from Abu Naḍra from Ibn 'Abbās who said: The Prophet (peace be upon him) addressed us and he said: *On the day of judgement when the standing for accounting becomes long for the people* (sic. Thereafter continuing with the wording of the previous chain) *Go to Esa for he will intercede with your lord. They will go to him and say you are but the Spirit of Allah and his word, so intercede with your lord on our behalf; so that he may account us for indeed we have waited a long time. He* (Esa) *will say: 'This is not my station. Verily I was worshipped* (by people) *do you not see that if there was a drinking vessel / goblet that was sealed who can access it until the seal is removed? Go to Muhammad peace be upon him because he is the seal of the Prophets.*

Likewise, we say indeed that Allah and His Messengers spoke the truth, and we bear witness that there is no deity except Allah and that Muḥammad is His Messenger, the seal of the Prophets and Messengers. That Esa is the servant of Allah, His Messenger, a Word and Spirit belonging to Him which He cast into the chaste virgin Maryam, the champion of truth; that the Paradise is true; the Fire is

[9] Vol. 2 sec. 1012 no. 1135

true; the Hour is true there is no doubt about it; and that Allah will resurrect those who are in the graves. We deny and are completely free of Musaylama, the al-Aswad al-'Ansi, the Bahai; the Qadiāni's and others among the lying impostors. Allah says:

وَمَنْ أَظْلَمُ مِمَّنِ افْتَرَىٰ عَلَى اللَّهِ كَذِبًا أَوْ قَالَ أُوحِيَ إِلَيَّ وَلَمْ يُوحَ إِلَيْهِ شَيْءٌ وَمَن قَالَ سَأُنزِلُ
مِثْلَ مَا أَنزَلَ اللَّهُ وَلَوْ تَرَىٰ إِذِ الظَّالِمُونَ فِي غَمَرَاتِ الْمَوْتِ وَالْمَلَائِكَةُ بَاسِطُو أَيْدِيهِمْ أَخْرِجُوا
أَنفُسَكُمُ الْيَوْمَ تُجْزَوْنَ عَذَابَ الْهُونِ بِمَا كُنتُمْ تَقُولُونَ عَلَى اللَّهِ غَيْرَ الْحَقِّ وَكُنتُمْ عَنْ آيَاتِهِ
تَسْتَكْبِرُونَ

And who is more unjust than he who forges a lie against Allah, or says: It has been revealed to me; while nothing has been revealed to him, and he who says: I can reveal the like of what Allah has revealed? And if you had seen when the unjust shall be in the agonies of death and the angels shall spread forth their hands: Give up your souls; today shall you be recompensed with an ignominious chastisement because you spoke against Allah other than the truth and you showed pride against His communications.[10]

From this it is clear without doubt that the expression 'the Seal of the Prophets' can only mean that he is the last of them. Yet its meaning is stronger than that, because Prophethood is like a container which is closed and has a stamp upon it, from which nothing can exit or enter until the great establishment of the hour. Thus, the Prophethood of the foregoing Prophets is well established and cannot be repealed. It is inconceivable for this description to be repealed and that Muḥammad is the last of them, and this description also can never be repealed from him. For there will be no new Prophet after him. This does not mean he is merely a witness for their Prophethood and a means to measure it only, although he is a witness for them. Nor does it mean that he is merely the certifier of them, although he does certify them. Nor does it mean that he is merely their nobility, although he does ennoble them. This is because the expression 'seal' does not comprise any of the

[10] *Qur'ān* 6: 93

above meanings in Arabic; although these meanings have been established for him, upon him and his family be blessings and peace as in other texts.

In the aforementioned verse its definition provides a definitive certain proof, which only a *kāfir* denies, that Muḥammad (peace be upon him) is the last of the Prophets and their seal. There will be no Prophet or Messenger after him. Whosoever claims that there is one after him is without doubt a liar. There is no difference between such liars whether past or present, be they: Musaylama al-Ḥanafi al-Arabi al-Adnāni the liar; or al-Aswad al-'Ansi al-Arabi al-Qaḥṭāni the liar; or al-Bahai the lying Persian; or Ghulam Aḥmad al-Qadiāni al-Hindi the liar; or anyone else. This includes the 'false messiah', namely *al-Masiḥ ad-Dajjāl*, who has been foretold to appear before the end of time. All of them have lied; or will invent lies against Allah. Each of them are the enemies of Allah and each of them have been cursed and have earned the anger of Allah.

As for a previous Prophet, namely Esa ibn Maryam (peace be upon him), he was commissioned as a Prophet *prior* to Prophethood being sealed and locked. He is a Prophet now and will be so when he returns to this world. Upon his return, his Prophethood will not be a new dispensation, since all of the laws that were previously brought have been abrogated and their communities as they have been described in the previous scriptures have ceased. Therefore upon his return, Esa ibn Maryam (peace be upon him) will be considered as part of the final *Ummah* of Muḥammad, adhering to his message and following the final law that he brought. It is not permissible to deny this essential truth for those who truly believe in Allah and the last day. Whoever denies this then Allah is independent of the entire world. Allah, may His omnipotence be majestic, knows that there are those who dispute and deny the finality of the Prophethood of Muḥammad ibn Abdullah al-Hāshimi al-'Arabi (peace be upon him). Thus He makes clear in undisputed, unambiguous expressions on the tongue of His Prophet, evidence which further proves the above.

Among them are his words:

- *There is to be no Prophet after me*
- *Verily I am the seal of the Prophets and there will be no prophet after me*
- *There will be no Prophet after me and there will be no religious community after you*
- *I am the seal of the Prophets and you are the last of the religious communities*
- *I am the subsequent one (which is the one after whom there will be no prophet)*
- *I am the last of the Prophets and my masjid is the last of masjid's*
- *I have been sent and the hour is at hand*

The Prophetic traditions narrated regarding the 'great intercession' establish this. The words of the Messiah on the day of judgement were previously mentioned where mankind will say: 'O Muḥammad you are the Messenger of Allah and the Seal of the Prophets whom Allah has forgiven for what has passed and what is to come; so intercede on our behalf to your Lord! Do you not see our condition? Do you not see what has befallen us?'[11] As well as in the Prophetic tradition narrated regarding the house whose construction was complete with the exception of one brick; about which the people asked him and he said: '*I am that brick and I am the seal of the Prophets.*'[12] All the Prophetic traditions verify that Prophethood has ceased and that there only remains 'glad tidings' which are true dreams as he, upon him be blessings and peace said: '*Nothing remains of Prophethood except*

[11] The *ḥadith* is also collected by Bukhāri and Muslim

[12] Muslim recorded these *aḥādith* this in the book of virtues (chapter on the seal of the Prophets) narrated by Abu Hurayrah and Jābir. Bukhāri similarly, in the book of virtues and merits of the companions (chapter the last of all the Prophets)

glad tidings.'[13]

Additionally there are a very large number of Prophetic traditions other than these with established sound chains of authorities from narrators such as Abu Hurayrah, Sa`d ibn Abi Waqqās, Asmā bint 'Umaysh, the mother of the believers Umm Salama, Abdullah ibn Umar ibn al-Khaṭṭāb, Ali ibn Abi Ṭālib, Thawbān, Ḥudhayfah ibn al-Yaman, Fāṭima bint Qays, Abi Umāma al-Bahili, Abdullah ibn 'Amr ibn al-'Aāṣ, Jubayr ibn Maṭ`am, Anas ibn Mālik, Ibn 'Abbās, Abu'Ṭufayl, the mother of the believers 'Aisha, Umm Karaz al-Ka`biya, Abdullah ibn Abi Awfa, Abdullah ibn Mas`ud, al-'Irbāḍ ibn Sariya as-Salami, 'Uqba ibn 'Aāmir, and Jābir ibn Abdullah - may the pleasure and peace of Allah be upon all of them. All of these narrations have been transmitted with the soundest chains of authorities, where each chain stands as a legal proof by itself, not to speak of when they are joined together. The veracity of this principle has also been established by others such as Sahl ibn Sa`d, Muḥammad ibn 'Adi ibn Ka`b and an-Nu`mān ibn Bashir. Each of these Prophetic traditions and narratives are congruent, unambiguous and diverse, which makes it impossible for an intelligent person to entertain misgivings about their veracity. These narrations are the strongest unbroken and clear transmission in the world. No one doubts this except the one upon whom the pen has been lifted and he is unfortunately included among the idiotic madmen.

The consensus of the companions (*Ijmā' aṣ-Ṣaḥabah*) confers upon the finality of Prophethood, that Muḥammad (peace be upon him) is the last of the Prophets and Messengers; no Prophet or messenger will come after him. The companions fought anyone who would claim Prophethood after he (peace be upon him) departed this world. History has also attested to this fact and known by Muslims and non-Muslims alike. Every imposter claiming Prophethood has failed to establish that claim and been exposed as a liar. In fact, the

---

[13] Bukhāri book 91, no. 9 and others

consensus upon this issue is greater even than the *Ijmā' aṣ-Ṣaḥabah*, because it has been recurrently transmitted from the time of the Prophet (peace be upon him) until now, every Muslim carrying that message and being part of this consensus; all safe in the knowledge of the certainty of this point without having the need to consult the book or examine chains of transmission.

Each of these Prophetic traditions and narratives are congruent, unambiguous and diverse, which makes it impossible for an intelligent person to entertain misgivings about their veracity. These narrations are the strongest unbroken and clearest recurrent transmission in the world (*tawātur*). No one doubts this except the one upon whom the pen has been lifted and he is unfortunately included among the idiotic madmen. In the following chapters, I will discuss the details of the occasions of the above narrated traditions.

2 An excellence that exceeds all others

Allah the exalted conferred enormous favour upon his unlettered messenger, Muḥammad the last and the seal of Prophets, over all previous Prophets. Allah favoured him with unique qualities that were not granted to any predecessor. These are numerous with each one containing special significance:

- Allah ended Prophethood with him; no Prophet or messenger will be sent after him until the day of judgement.

- The entire earth was made a means of purification and a place of prayer for him. Whenever the time of prayer becomes due on any of his servants, he can purify himself and pray. The previous nations used to offer their prayers only in temples, hermitages, churches or synagogues built for that purpose.

- He (peace be upon him) was made victorious over his enemies by means of awe and fear, despite presiding at great distance and a whole months travelling.

- His nation still enjoys the fruits of this advantage, even during its weakest eras; fear and terror still fill the hearts of heavily-armed armies who possess nuclear weapons, when they meet some of the so-called 'terrorists' on the battlefield, although Muslims may possess nothing but light weapons.

- Allah made the spoils of war lawful to him and to his *Ummah* with which they may supply and strengthen themselves, while previous nations used to offer them as sacrifices and burn them.

- Allah distinguished his last Prophet (peace be upon him) with intercession for all human beings and raised him to a station praised by earlier generations.

- The banner of *Al-Ḥamd* (praising Allah) will be given to him on the day of judgement under which all the Prophets since the time of Adam (peace be upon him) will be.

- He (peace be upon him) was granted the gift of the answered supplication, which he chose to make as intercession for his *Ummah* on the day of judgement, while all the previous Prophets (peace be upon them all) chose to have their supplication answered during their earthly lives.

- He (peace be upon him) was also granted *'Jawāmi' al-Kalim'* the shortest expression with the widest meaning, being able to utilise single sentences that bore wide meanings and contain deep wisdom. Although his speech was concise, it conveyed the exact meaning, which prevented irrelevancy and idle talk.

- He (peace be upon him) was sent to all human beings, or rather to all mankind as well as the *jinn*, while the Prophets before him were sent to their own nations or specific locales.

Prophet Muḥammad (peace be upon him) had many other great privileges, lofty positions and the most honourable of status, which has made him the Imām of all Prophets and the best of all Messengers; may the peace and blessings of Allah be upon him and his family. As for the fact that the Prophet (peace be upon him) was sent from Allah to all mankind, it is an acknowledged undoubted truth, supported by many conclusive evidences. Allah has said:

قُلْ يَا أَيُّهَا النَّاسُ إِنِّي رَسُولُ اللَّهِ إِلَيْكُمْ جَمِيعًا الَّذِي لَهُ مُلْكُ السَّمَاوَاتِ وَالْأَرْضِ لَا إِلَٰهَ إِلَّا هُوَ يُحْيِي وَيُمِيتُ فَآمِنُوا بِاللَّهِ وَرَسُولِهِ النَّبِيِّ الْأُمِّيِّ الَّذِي يُؤْمِنُ بِاللَّهِ وَكَلِمَاتِهِ وَاتَّبِعُوهُ لَعَلَّكُمْ تَهْتَدُونَ

Say: O people! Surely I am the Messenger of Allah to you all - of Him whose is the kingdom of the heavens and the earth, there is no god but He; He brings to life and causes to die therefore believe in Allah and His Messenger, the unlettered Prophet who believes in Allah and His words, and follow him so that you may walk in the right way. [1]

وَمَا أَرْسَلْنَاكَ إِلَّا كَافَّةً لِّلنَّاسِ بَشِيرًا وَنَذِيرًا وَلَٰكِنَّ أَكْثَرَ النَّاسِ لَا يَعْلَمُونَ

And We have not sent you but to all mankind as a bearer of good news and as a warner, but most men do not know. [2]

Regarding this subject, Imām Bukhāri records the following *ḥadith* in *al-Jāmi aṣ-Ṣaḥīḥ al-Mukhtaṣr* with one of the strongest channels of narration:

حدثنا عبد الله حدثنا سليمان بن عبد الرحمن وموسى بن هارون قالا: حدثنا الوليد بن مسلم حدثنا عبد الله بن العلاء بن زبر حدثني بسر بن عبيد الله

[1] *Qur'ān* 7: 158
[2] *Qur'ān* 34: 28

حدثني أبو إدريس الخولاني قال: سمعت أبا الدرداء رضي الله عنه يقول: كانت بين أبي بكر وعمر رضي الله عنهما محاورة، فأغضب أبو بكر عمر، فانصرف عنه عمر مغضبا فأتبعه أبو بكر يسأله أن يستغفر له فلم يفعل حتى أغلق بابه في وجهه، فأقبل أبو بكر إلى رسول الله، صلى الله عليه وسلم، فقال أبو الدرداء: ونحن عنده، فقال رسول الله، صلى الله عليه وسلم: أما صاحبكم هذا فقد غامر- أي غاضب- وحاقد. قال: وندم عمر على ما كان منه فأقبل حتى سلم وجلس إلى النبي، صلى الله عليه وسلم، وقص على رسول الله، صلى الله عليه وسلم، الخبر قال أبو الدرداء، فغضب رسول الله، صلى الله عليه وسلم، وجعل أبو بكر يقول: والله يا رسول الله لأنا كنت أظلم، فقال رسول الله، صلى الله عليه وسلم: هل أنتم تاركو لي صاحبي؟ إني قلت: يا أيها الناس إني رسول الله إليكم جميعا، فقلتم: كذبت، وقال أبو بكر: صدقت

Abdullah narrated to us Sulaymān bin Abdar-Raḥman and Musa bin Hārun narrated to us, they said, Al-Waleed bin Muslim narrated to us Abdullah bin al-'Ala bin Zubr narrated to us Bisr bin 'Ubaidallah narrated to me Abu Idrees al-Khawlāni narrated to me, he said I heard Abu Dardā' say: There was a dispute between Abu Bakr and Umar, and Abu Bakr made Umar angry, so he left angrily. Abu Bakr followed him, requesting him to ask forgiveness for him, but Umar refused to do so and closed his door in Abu Bakr's face. So Abu Bakr went to Allah's Messenger (peace be upon him) while we were with him. Allah's Messenger (peace be upon him) said: *This friend of yours must have quarrelled (with somebody).* In the meantime Umar repented and felt sorry for what he had done so he came and greeted (those who were present) and sat with the Prophet (peace be upon him) and related the story to him. Allah's Messenger (peace be upon him) became angry and Abu Bakr started saying – 'O Allah's Messenger (peace be upon him)! By Allah, I was more at fault (than Umar).' Allah's Messenger (peace be upon him) said: *Are you (people) leaving for me my companion? (Abu Bakr), are you (people) leaving for me my companion? When I said: O people I am sent to you all as the Messenger of Allah you said I told a lie, while Abu Bakr said you have spoken the truth*.

The *ḥadith* is reported widely; Bukhāri has it in another part of his *Ṣaḥīḥ;*[3] Abdullah ibn Aḥmad bin Ḥanbal records it in *Faḍā'il aṣ-Ṣaḥābah* (virtues of the companions);[4] Ṭabarāni in the *Musnad ash-Shāmiayn* as well as in the *Mu'jam al-Kabir,*[5] and Bayhaqy has this in the *Sunan al-Kubra.*[6] Without question the matter is known from amongst the certainties of religion. Even most of the non-Muslims attest to the fact that he (peace be upon him) acted according to the message he bore. He (peace be upon him) sent messages to kings and tyrants inviting them to follow and obey him. This is a clear truth or rather an established historical fact beyond all doubt and if we attempt to elucidate every proof for this, volumes could be written.

Some may argue that *perhaps* there were Prophets sent in the pre-historic age of whom we do not know and who might have been sent to all mankind. In reply, we would submit that this is highly unlikely. Not least because nothing of the sort has reached us or been confirmed by the revelation we have now or of the revelation sent previously. Besides which, it would contradict history and the natural occurrence of events. Although we would concede that it is not an outright impossibility, since it still falls within the remit of Allah's decree. Adam (peace be upon him) was sent to his family which represented humankind at that time, but they are not humanity as a whole, which lives until the extinction of the human race and the establishment of the final hour. Thus it would not be right to say that he was sent to all humanity, but that he was sent to his family who were the only human beings at that specific time. Furthermore, it has been recorded by many successive reports that the Prophet (peace be upon him) was the only Prophet favoured above all others to be sent to all of humanity. By necessity therefore none before him had this privilege. The sheer

---

[3] Bukhāri Vol. 3 sec. 1,339, no. 3,461

[4] Abdullah ibn Aḥmad ibn Ḥanbal (virtues) Vol. 1 sec. 241, no. 297 and sec. 349, no. 502

[5] *Musnad ash-Shāmiayn* Vol. 2 sec. 208, no. 1,199 and Vol. 1 sec. 448, no. 789; in the *Mu'jam* Vol. 12 sec. 372, no. 13,383

[6] *Sunan al-Kubra* Vol. 10 sec. 236, no. 20,884

number of evidences which establish this point is staggering. Aside from that which will be presented as quotations from the famous Qur'ān interpreters (aṭ-Ṭabari and Ibn Kathir), a selection of the various *aḥādith* (which is over twenty) will be cited to demonstrate this, together with comments in relation to the transmission and narrators where applicable.

Imām aṭ-Ṭabari writes in his *Tafsir* regarding the interpretation of the following verse:

تِلْكَ الرُّسُلُ فَضَّلْنَا بَعْضَهُمْ عَلَىٰ بَعْضٍ مِّنْهُم مَّن كَلَّمَ اللَّهُ وَرَفَعَ بَعْضَهُمْ دَرَجَاتٍ وَآتَيْنَا عِيسَى ابْنَ مَرْيَمَ الْبَيِّنَاتِ وَأَيَّدْنَاهُ بِرُوحِ الْقُدُسِ وَلَوْ شَاءَ اللَّهُ مَا اقْتَتَلَ الَّذِينَ مِن بَعْدِهِم مِّن بَعْدِ مَا جَاءَتْهُمُ الْبَيِّنَاتُ وَلَٰكِنِ اخْتَلَفُوا فَمِنْهُم مَّنْ آمَنَ وَمِنْهُم مَّن كَفَرَ وَلَوْ شَاءَ اللَّهُ مَا اقْتَتَلُوا وَلَٰكِنَّ اللَّهَ يَفْعَلُ مَا يُرِيدُ

We have made some of these Messengers to excel the others among them are they to whom Allah spoke, and some of them He exalted by rank; and We gave clear miracles to Jesus son of Mary and strengthened him with the holy spirit. And if Allah had pleased, those after them would not have fought one with another after clear arguments had come to them, but they disagreed; so there were some of them who believed and others who denied; and if Allah had pleased they would not have fought one with another, but Allah brings about what He intends. [7]

> By saying '*these messengers*,' Allah means all of them whose stories were mentioned in this Chapter. Among them are Musa bin 'Imrān, Ibrāhim, Ismā'il, Isḥāq, Ya'qub, Samuel, Dāwud and all other Prophets mentioned in this chapter. The meaning of Allah's words is, they are My Messengers and I preferred some of them over the others. I spoke to some of them like Musa and I raised the ranks of some of them over the others with high and honourable positions.

---

[7] *Qur'ān* 2: 253

> Muḥammad bin ‘Amr narrated to me he said Abu ‘Aāṣim narrated to us he said Esa narrated to us from Ibn Abi Najeeḥ from Mujāhid regarding the words of the exalted: 'Allah spoke to some of them and raised others in ranks' He spoke to Musa and sent Muḥammad to all of mankind.
>
> Al-Muthanna narrated to me he said Abu Ḥudhayfah narrated to us he said Shubal narrated to us from Ibn Abi Najeeḥ from Mujāhid about this (and he reports) among that which proves the validity of what we are saying is the *ḥadith* of the Prophet (peace be upon him) in which he said: *I have been granted five (things) which were not granted to anyone before me (and these are): I have been sent to all the red and the black (i.e., to the different races of humanity). I have been made victorious by awe, for the enemy gets frightened of me from a distance of a one-month journey. The earth has been made a place of prayer and a means of purification (i.e., through dry ablution) for me. The spoils of war have been made lawful for me, while they were never made lawful to anyone before me. It was said to me, 'Ask (for anything) and you will be granted it.' So, I made it an intercession for my nation, which will be granted to my nation for he who does not associate anything with Allah.*

Commenting on the previous verse, aṭ-Ṭabari says:

> In relation to the interpretation of the verse: ‘Say: O people! Surely I am the Messenger of Allah to you all - of Him whose is the kingdom of the heavens and the earth, there is no god but He; He brings to life and causes to die therefore believe in Allah and His Messenger, the unlettered Prophet who believes in Allah and His words, and follow him so that you may walk in the right way.’ [8] Allah is saying to His Prophet (peace be upon him) to say to all of mankind that he is the Messenger of

[8] *Qur’ān* 7: 158

> Allah to all of them, not to some of them and not the other, as it was the case with the previous Messengers before him. They used to be sent to some people and not all. If they were sent like that, my message is not concerned with some among you and not the others; it is for all of you.

And in relation to the verse that he (peace be upon him) is sent to all mankind as a bearer of glad tidings and with a warning, aṭ-Ṭabari says:

> In relation to the interpretation of the verse: 'And We have not sent you but to all mankind as a bearer of good news and as a Warner, but most men do not know.'[9] Allah says that He did not send Muḥammad, especially to those who disbelieved among his nation, but He sent him to all people whether they were Arab or foreigners, whether they have red or black skin. You were sent in order to preach with good omen those who obeyed you and to threaten those who disobeyed, but the majority of people do not know that Allah sent you to all mankind. People who interpreted this verse said the same as we have mentioned.
>
> Bishr narrated to us he said Yazeed narrated to us he said Sa'eed narrated to us from Qatādah who said [sic. regarding the verse] Allah sent Muḥammad to Arabs and foreigners. The most beloved among them is the one who obeys Allah most. It was mentioned that the Prophet (peace be upon him) said: '*I am the one who will precede Arabs (i.e. first to enter Paradise). Ṣuhayb will precede Byzantium. Bilāl will precede the Ethiopians. And Salmān will precede Persians*.'

Imām Bukhāri records the following *ḥadith* in *al-Jāmi aṣ-Ṣaḥīḥ al-Mukhtaṣr*:

---

[9] *Qur'ān* 34: 28

حدثنا محمد بن سنان قال: حدثنا هشيم (ح) قال: وحدثني سعيد بن النضر قال: أخبرنا هشيم قال: أخبرنا سيار قال: حدثنا يزيد هو بن صهيب الفقير قال: أخبرنا جابر بن عبد الله أن النبي، صلى الله عليه وسلم، قال: أعطيت خمسا، لم يعطهن أحد قبلي: نصرت بالرعب مسيرة شهر، وجعلت لي الأرض مسجدا وطهورا فأيما رجل من أمتي أدركته الصلاة فليصل، وأحلت لي المغانم ولم تحل لأحد قبلي، وأعطيت الشفاعة، وكان النبي يبعث إلى قومه خاصة وبعثت إلى الناس عامة

Muḥammad bin Sinān narrated to us he said Hushaym narrated to us (*ḥawala*) he said and Sa'eed bin an-Naḍr narrated to me he said Hushaym reported to us he said Sayār reported to us he said Yazeed, who is ibn Ṣuhayb al-Faqeer, narrated to us he said Jābir ibn Abdullah reported to us that the Prophet (peace be upon him) said: *I have been given five things which were not given to anyone else before me: Allah made me victorious by awe, for a distance of one month's journey; the earth has been made for me* (and for my followers) *a masjid and ritually pure therefore anyone of my followers can pray wherever the time of a prayer is due. The booty has been made lawful for me yet it was not lawful for anyone else before me. I have been given the right of intercession. Every Prophet used to be sent to his nation only, but I have been sent to all mankind.*

Muslim has the same narration albeit with slightly variant wording:

حدثنا يحيى بن يحيى أخبرنا هشيم عن سيار عن يزيد الفقير عن جابر بن عبد الله الأنصاري قال قال رسول الله صلى الله عليه وسلم أعطيت خمسا لم يعطهن أحد قبلي كان كل نبي يبعث إلى قومه خاصة وبعثت إلى كل أحمر وأسود وأحلت لي الغنائم ولم تحل لأحد قبلي وجعلت لي الأرض طيبة طهورا ومسجدا فأيما رجل أدركته الصلاة صلى حيث كان ونصرت بالرعب بين يدي مسيرة شهر وأعطيت الشفاعة حدثنا أبو بكر بن أبي شيبة حدثنا هشيم أخبرنا سيار حدثنا يزيد الفقير أخبرنا جابر بن عبد الله أن رسول الله صلى الله عليه وسلم قال فذكر نحوه

> Yaḥya bin Yaḥya narrated to us Hushaym reported to us from Sayār from Yazeed al-Faqeer from Jābir ibn Abdullah al-Anṣāri who said that the Prophet (peace be upon him) said: *I have been conferred upon five* (things) *which were not granted to anyone before me* (these are): *Every Messenger was sent particularly to his own people, whereas I have been sent to all the red and the black, the spoils of war have been made lawful for me and these were never made lawful to anyone before me; the earth has been made sacred and pure and a mosque for me, so whenever the time of prayer comes for any one of you he should pray wherever he is, and I have been supported by awe from the distance (which one takes) one month to cover and I have been granted intercession.*

The narration of Jābir (may Allah be pleased with him) is recorded in most *ḥadith* collections, be they *Ṣaḥīḥ*, *Musnad*, *Sunan* or otherwise. It has one of the most authentic channels of transmission. Similarly, Imām Muslim records another *ḥadith* this time on the authority of Abu Hurayrah:

> حدثنا يحيى بن أيوب وقتيبة بن سعيد وعلي بن حجر قالوا: حدثنا إسماعيل وهو بن جعفر عن العلاء عن أبيه عن أبي هريرة أن رسول الله، صلى الله عليه وسلم، قال: فضلت على الأنبياء بست: أعطيت جوامع الكلم، ونصرت بالرعب، وأحلت لي الغنائم، وجعلت لي الأرض طهورا ومسجدا، وأرسلت إلى الخلق كافة، وختم بي النبيون

> Yaḥya ibn Ayub, Qutayba ibn Sa'eed and Ali ibn Ḥujr narrated to us, they said Ismā'il, and he is ibn Ja'far narrated to us from al-'Alā' from his father from Abu Hurayrah that the Messenger of Allah (peace be upon him) said: *I have been given superiority over the other Prophets in six respects: I have been given words which are concise but comprehensive in meaning; I have been helped by terror* (in the hearts of enemies): *spoils have been made lawful to me: the earth has been made for me clean and a place of worship; I have been sent to all mankind*

and the line of prophets is closed with me.

Again, this narration has one of the most authentic channels of transmission and is found in most *ḥadith* collections, be they *Ṣaḥīḥ*, *Musnad*, *Sunan* or otherwise. There is another narrative that is recorded in *Musnad* al-Bazzār with some additions:

> كَتَبَ إِلَيَّ حَمْزَة بن مالك يخبر أن عمه سفيان بن حمزة حدثه عن كثير بن زيد، عَن الوليد بن رباح، عَن أَبِي هُرَيرة، عَن النَّبِيّ، صلى الله عليه وسلم، قال: فضلت بخصال ست لم يعطهن أحد قبلي: غفر لي ما تقدم من ذنبي وما تأخر، وَأُحِلَّتْ لِيَ الْغَنَائِمُ وَلَمْ تُحَلَّ لأَحَدٍ قَبْلِي، وجعلت أمتي خير الأمم، وجعلت لي الأرض مسجدًا وطهوراً، وأعطيت الكوثر، ونصرت بالرعب، والذي نفسي بيده إن صاحبكم لصاحب لواء الحمد يوم القيامة تحته آدم فمن دونه
>
> (It was) written upon Ḥamza bin Mālik, (being) reported that his uncle, Sufyān bin Ḥamza narrated to him from Kathir bin Ziad from al-Waleed bin Rabāḥ from Abu Hurayrah from the Prophet (peace be upon him) who said: *I have been given superiority over the other prophets in six respects which were not given to anyone else before me: my past and present sins were forgiven, the spoils of war have been made lawful for me, and these were never made lawful to anyone before me, my nation was made the best among other nations, the earth has been made sacred and pure and a mosque for me, I was given Al-Kawthar and I have been supported by awe. By He in whose hands my soul is! Your Companion* (the Prophet*) is the one who will hold the flag of praise during the day of judgement, followed by Adam (peace be upon him) and whoever came after him.*

Writing in *Mu'jama' az-Zawā'id*, al-Haythamy cited the narration as being from al-Bazzār and said that the *isnād* was good. I would submit that when searched it can also be found within the wording of

Musnad Sirāj, with the channel as: Muḥammad ibn Ismā'il al-Bukhāri narrated to us Ismā'il bin Abi Awais narrated to us my brother narrated to me from Sulaymān from Kathir bin Ziad from al-Waleed bin Rabāḥ from Abu Hurayrah. It is also in the *Explanation of the Principles of Aqeedah of Ahl-as-Sunnah wal-Jamā'h* by Abu Qasim al-Lilalukā'i with an intersected channel - Esa bin Ali reported to us Abdullah bin Muḥammad al-Baghawi reported to us he said Ḥazma bin Mālik al-Aslami narrated to us he said my uncle Esa bin Sufyān bin Ḥazma narrated to us from (*ḥawala*) and 'Ubaidallah bin Aḥmad and Muḥammad bin al-Ḥussein al-Fārisi reported to us they said: al-Ḥussein bin Ismā'il reported to us he said Ḥazma bin Mālik narrated to us he said my uncle narrated to us he said Kathir, that is to say, Ibn Zayd narrated to us from al-Waleed, he is Ibn Rabāḥ from Abu Hurayrah. I would submit that this is a very good *isnād* and authentic by the standards of Imām Bukhāri, as per the narration from the Prophet (peace be upon him) that says: *'Indeed a woman grants (assurances of protection) to the Muslims.'* Concerning this Imām Tirmidhi said: 'I asked Muḥammad and he said: 'This *ḥadith* is *Ṣaḥīḥ*. Kathir bin Ziad heard from Al-Walid bin Rabah, and Al-Walid bin Rabah heard from Abu Hurayrah, and he is *muqārib* (average) in *ḥadith*.'[10] In the *Ṣaḥīḥ* of Ibn Ḥibbān he records as follows:

أخبرنا إسحاق بن إبراهيم ببست حدثنا حماد بن يحيى بن حماد بالبصرة حدثنا أبي حدثنا أبو عوانة عن سليمان عن مجاهد عن عبيد بن عمير عن أبي ذر قال: قال رسول الله، صلى الله عليه وسلم: أعطيت خمسا لم يعطهن أحد قبلي: بعثت إلى الأحمر والأسود، وأحلت لي الغنائم ولم تحل لأحد قبلي، ونصرت بالرعب فيرعب العدو من مسيرة شهر، وجعلت لي الأرض طهورا ومسجدا، وقيل لي سل تعطه واختبأت دعوتي شفاعة لأمتي في القيامة وهي نائلة إن شاء الله لمن لم يشرك بالله شيئا

Isḥāq ibn Ibrāhim reported to us in Bust; Ḥammād bin Yaḥya bin Ḥammād narrated to us in Baṣra, his father narrated to us

[10] See *Sunan* Tirmidhi, book of military expeditions, chapter entitled: '*what has been related about the assurance of protection granted by a woman and a slave*.'

> Abu ‘Awāna narrated to us from Sulaymān from Mujāhid from ‘Ubaidallah bin ‘Umair from Abu Dharr who said the Messenger of Allah (peace be upon him) said: *I have been given five things which were not given to anyone else before me. I have been sent to the red and the black, the spoils of war have been made lawful for me and these were never made lawful to anyone before me, Allah made me victorious by awe, for a distance of one month's journey, the earth has been made ritually pure for me and a masjid and it was said to me ask and you will be answered. I saved my (supplication) as an intercession* (on the day of judgement) *for my Ummah. It is guaranteed to whoever does not associate anything with Allah.*

Shaykh Shu’ayb al-Arnā’uṭ said the *ḥadith* is *Ṣaḥīḥ*. In a slightly longer narrative Al-Ḥākim has the following in the *Mustadrak*:

> حدثنا أبو بكر أحمد بن كامل بن خلف القاضي حدثنا محمد بن جرير الفقيه حدثنا أبو كريب سمعت أبا أسامة وسئل عن قول الله عز وجل: {وَمَا أَرْسَلْنَاكَ إِلَّا كَافَّةً لِلنَّاسِ بَشِيرًا وَنَذِيرًا}، فقال حدثنا الأعمش عن مجاهد عن عبيد بن عمير عن أبي ذر رضي الله عنه قال: طلبت رسول الله، صلى الله عليه وسلم، ليلة فوجدته قائما يصلي فأطال الصلاة ثم قال: أوتيت الليلة خمسا، لم يؤتها نبي قبلي: أرسلت إلى الأحمر والأسود (قال مجاهد: الإنس والجن)، ونصرت بالرعب فيرعب العدو وهو على مسيرة شهر، وجعلت لي الأرض مسجدا وطهورا، وأحلت لي الغنائم ولم تحل لأحد قبلي، وقيل لي سل تعطه فاختبأتها شفاعة لأمتي فهي نائلة من لم يشرك بالله شيئا

> Abu Bakr Aḥmad bin Kāmil bin Khalf al-Qāḍi narrated to us Muḥammad bin Jarir al-Faqihi narrated to us Abu Kareeb narrated to us – he heard Abu Salama and asked his (view) regarding what Allah the exalted said (in the verse): ‘*And We have not sent you but to all mankind as a bearer of good news and as a Warner, but most men do not know*’, so he said al-‘Amash narrated to us from Mujāhid from ‘Ubaid bin ‘Umair from Abu Dharr who said: I sought the Messenger of Allah (peace be upon him) one night and he found him standing

> performing prayer. He (peace be upon him) prolonged the prayer and then said: *I had been given this night five matters which were not given to any Prophet before me. I have been sent to the red and the black* (Mujāhid said: that is mankind and jinn), *I have been supported by awe (by which the enemy is overwhelmed) from the distance (which one takes) one month to cover, the earth has been made ritually pure for me and a masjid, the booty has been made lawful to me and these were never made lawful to anyone before me, and it was said to me ask and you will be answered. I saved my (supplication) as an intercession (on the day of judgment) for my Ummah. It is guaranteed to whoever does not associate anything with Allah.*

Al-Ḥākim said: 'This is an authentic *ḥadith* according to the conditions of al-Bukhāri and Muslim, but they did not record it with these wordings, but they recorded some separate wordings to it.' I would submit that it is from amongst the most authentic *ḥadith's* to be found as it is transmitted through al-'Amash according to the conditions of al-Bukhāri and Muslim, but it is even above them in that. The narration is also reported in a number of collections such as in *Musnad* Aḥmad,[11] the *Muṣṣanaf* of Imām Abu Bakr ibn Abi Shayba;[12] the *Musnad* of Dārimi,[13] and al-Ḥārith in his *Musnad* as it is in al-Haythami (*az-Zawā'id*)[14] as well as many others.

Imām Aḥmad records in his *Musnad* the next *ḥadith* on the authority of Abu Musa al-Ash'ari:

> حدثنا حسين بن محمد حدثنا إسرائيل عن أبي إسحاق عن أبي بردة عن أبي موسى قال: قال رسول الله، صلى الله عليه وسلم: أعطيت خمسا: بعثت إلى الأحمر والأسود، وجعلت لي الأرض طهورا ومسجدا وأحلت لي الغنائم ولم

---

[11] *Musnad* Aḥmad Vol. 5 sec. 145, 148, 162, no. 21,337, 21,352 and 21,472
[12] *Muṣṣanaf* Ibn Abi Shayba, Vol. 6 sec. 304, no. 31,650
[13] *Musnad* Dārimi Vol. 2 sec. 295, no. 2,467
[14] Vol. 2 sec. 877, no. 942

تحل لمن كان قبلي، ونصرت بالرعب شهرا، وأعطيت الشفاعة وليس من نبى الا وقد سأل شفاعة وإني أخبأت شفاعتي ثم جعلتها لمن مات من أمتي لم يشرك بالله شيئا

Ḥussein bin Muḥammad narrated to us Isrā'il narrated to us from Abu Isḥāq from Abi Burda from Abu Musa who said that the Messenger of Allah (peace be upon him) said: *I have been given five things. I have been sent to the red and the black, the earth has been made ritually pure for me and a masjid, the spoils of war have been made lawful for me and these were never made lawful to anyone before me, Allah made me victorious by awe, (by His frightening my enemies) for a distance of one month's journey, and I have been given the right of intercession. Every Prophet asked Allah for an intercession and I saved my intercession (on the day of judgement) for whoever died from among my nation that does not associate anything with Allah.*

Regarding this, a-Haythami said: 'Aḥmad recorded it *mutaṣṣil* (connected / uninterrupted) and *mursal* (loose); Ṭabarāni (said) its men are the men of *Ṣaḥīḥ.*' In relation to the *isnād* it is an authentic channel of transmission. Imām Abu Bakr ibn Abi Shayba records the same in his *Muṣṣanaf.*[15] Imām Aḥmad records another tradition in his *Musnad* on the authority of Abu Umāmah:

حدثنا محمد بن أبي عدى عن سليمان يعنى التيمي عن سيار عن أبي أمامة ان رسول الله، صلى الله عليه وسلم، قال: فضلني ربي على الأنبياء عليهم الصلاة والسلام (أو قال على الأمم) بأربع، قال: أرسلت إلى الناس كافة، وجعلت الأرض كلها لي ولأمتي مسجدا وطهورا فأينما أدركت رجلا من أمتي الصلاة فعنده مسجده وعنده طهوره، ونصرت بالرعب مسيرة شهر يقذفه في قلوب أعدائي، وأحل لنا الغنائم

Muḥammad bin Abi 'Adi narrated to us from Sulaymān – that

[15] *Muṣṣanaf* Ibn Abi Shayba, Vol. 6 sec. 304, no. 31,645

is to say – at-Taymi from Sayār from Abu Umāmah that the Messenger of Allah (peace be upon him) said: *Allah distinguished me above the Prophets (peace be upon them)* [the narrator had doubted that he said on the nations] *with four matters. I have been sent to all mankind, the earth has been made all for me (and for my nation) the earth has been made ritually pure for me and a masjid, therefore anyone of my nation can pray wherever the time of a prayer is due; he has his place of prayer and what he will use in ablution, I have been helped by terror (in the hearts of enemies) for a distance of one month's journey and the booty has been made lawful for me.*

The narration is also reported by Bayhaqy in the *Sunan al-Kubra,*[16] and Ṭabarāni in his *Mu'jam al-Kabir,*[17] in more than one place. Imām Aḥmad again records similarly but this is via Ibn 'Abbās:

حدثنا عبد الصمد حدثنا عبد العزيز بن مسلم حدثنا يزيد عن مقسم عن بن عباس ان رسول الله، صلى الله عليه وسلم، قال: أعطيت خمسا لم يعطهن نبي قبلي، ولا أقولهن فخراً: بعثت إلى الناس كافة الأحمر والأسود، ونصرت بالرعب مسيرة شهر، وأحلت لي الغنائم ولم تحل لأحد قبلي، وجعلت لي الأرض مسجدا وطهورا، وأعطيت الشفاعة فأخّرتها لأمتي فهي لمن لا يشرك بالله شيئا

Abdus-Ṣamad narrated to us Abdal-Aziz bin Muslim narrated to us Yazeed narrated to us from Miqsam from Ibn 'Abbās that the Messenger of Allah (peace be upon him) said: *I have been given five things which were not given to anyone else before me and I did not say that out of pride. I have been sent to all of mankind – the red and the black; Allah made me victorious by awe, (by His frightening my enemies) for a distance of one month's journey. The booty has been made lawful for me yet it*

---

[16] *Sunan al-Kubra* Vol. 1 sec. 222, no. 999
[17] *Mu'jam al-Kabir* Vol. 8 sec. 239, 257 no. 7,931 and 8,001

was not lawful for anyone else before me. The earth has been made ritually pure for me and a masjid. I have been given intercession and I saved it for my Ummah (on the day of judgement). It is guaranteed to whoever does not associate anything with Allah.

Imām Aḥmad also has the following:

حدثنا على بن عاصم عن يزيد بن أبي زياد عن مقسم ومجاهد عن بن عباس قال: قال رسول الله، صلى الله عليه وسلم: أعطيت خمسا لم يعطهن أحد قبلي ولا أقوله فخرا: بعثت إلى كل أحمر وأسود فليس من أحمر ولا أسود يدخل في أمتي الا كان منهم، وجعلت لي الأرض مسجدا

Ali bin 'Aāṣim narrated to us from Yazeed bin Abi Ziyād from Miqsam and Mujāhid from Ibn 'Abbās that the Prophet (peace be upon him) said: *I have been given five things which were not given to anyone else before me and I did not say that out of pride. I have been sent to everyone red and black; it is not red nor black that enters in my Ummah except that they are a part of it. And the earth is made a masjid for me.*

Again this particular narration is reported in other places, such as being cited by Imām Abu Bakr ibn Abi Shayba in his *Muṣṣanaf,*[18] and by 'Abd bin Ḥameed in his *Musnad.*[19] Contained within this chain is Yazeed bin Abi Ziyād who is considered as having slight weakness. Imām Aḥmad records many *aḥādith* from him. Various other authorities and Imām's regarded him as tolerable, such as al-Haythamy. In *Mu'jama' az-Zawā'id* he said: 'The men Aḥmad (narrated from) are men of *Ṣaḥīḥ* except for Yazeed ibn Abi Ziyād, he has *ḥasan ḥadith.*' Ibn Kathir regarded this chain of transmission as a good chain in his *Tafsir;* the rest of his narrators are strong so it may

[18] *Muṣṣanaf* Ibn Abi Shayba, Vol. 6 sec. 303, no. 31,643
[19] *Musnad* Vol. 1 sec. 216, no. 643

be reach the level of the *ḥasan Ṣaḥīḥ,* which can be regarded as relied upon proofs, particularly when considered against other narrations as provided from Ibn 'Abbās. Imām aṭ-Ṭabarāni has the next two narrations contained within his *Mu'jam al-Kabir*:

حدثنا عبدان بن أحمد حدثنا عبد الله بن حماد بن نمير حدثنا حصين بن نمير حدثنا بن أبي ليلى عن الحكم عن مجاهد عن بن عباس عن النبي، صلى الله عليه وسلم، قال: أعطيت خمسا لم يعطهن نبي قبلي: أرسلت إلى الأحمر والأسود وكان النبي يرسل إلى خاصة، ونصرت بالرعب حتى إن العدو ليخافوني من مسيرة شهر أو شهرين، وأحلت لي الغنائم ولم تحل لمن قبلي، وجعلت لي الأرض مسجدا وطهورا، وقيل لي سل تعطه فادخرت دعوتي شفاعة لأمتي فهي نائلة إن شاء الله لمن مات لا يشرك بالله شيئا

'Abdān bin Aḥmad narrated to us Abdullah bin Ḥammād bin Numayr narrated to us Huṣṣein bin Numayr narrated to us Ibn Abi Layla narrated to us from al-Ḥakam from Mujāhid from Ibn 'Abbās that the Prophet (peace be upon him) said: *I have been sent to the red and the black; previous Prophet's were sent to specific (people); I have been helped by terror (in the hearts of enemies) by a journey's distance of one or two months. The booty has been made lawful for me yet it was not lawful for anyone else before me. The earth has been made ritually pure for me and a masjid. I have been given intercession and I saved it for my Ummah* (on the day of judgement). *It is guaranteed to whoever does not associate anything with Allah.*

حدثنا سلمة بن إبراهيم بن يحيى بن سلمة بن كهيل حدثني أبي عن أبيه عن جده عن سلمة بن كهيل عن مجاهد عن بن عباس قال: قال رسول الله، صلى الله عليه وسلم: أعطيت خمسا لم يعطها نبي قبلي: بعثت إلى الناس كافة الأحمر والأسود وإنما كان النبي، صلى الله عليه وسلم، يبعث إلى قومه، ونصرت بالرعب يرعب مني عدوي على مسيرة شهر، وأعطيت المغنم، وجعلت لي الأرض مسجدا وطهورا، وأعطيت الشفاعة فأخرتها لأمتي يوم القيامة

Salama bin Ibrāhim bin Yaḥya bin Salama bin Kuhayl narrated to us my father narrated to me from his father from his grandfather from Salama bin Kuhayl from Mujāhid from Ibn 'Abbās that the Prophet (peace be upon him) said: *I have been given five things that no Prophet before me had: I am sent to all people, to the red and the black, previous Prophets peace be upon them were sent to their own nation; I have been helped by terror (in the hearts of enemies) by a journey's distance of one month. I have been permitted the booty; I have been given the earth as a masjid and of ritual purity and the last being intercession for my Ummah on the day of judgement.*

Bayhaqy has recorded similarly in his *Sunan al-Kubra*:

أنبأ أبو بكر أحمد بن الحسن القاضي حدثنا أبو العباس محمد بن يعقوب حدثنا الحسن بن علي بن عفان حدثنا عبيد الله بن موسى حدثنا سالم أبو حماد عن السدي عن عكرمة عن بن عباس قال: قال رسول الله، صلى الله عليه وسلم: أعطيت خمسا لم يعطهن أحد قبلي من الأنبياء: جعلت لي الأرض طهورا ومسجدا ولم يكن نبي من الأنبياء يصلي حتى يبلغ محرابه، وأعطيت الرعب مسيرة شهر يكون بيني وبين المشركين مسيرة شهر فيقذف الله الرعب في قلوبهم، وكان النبي يبعث إلى خاصة قومه وبعثت أنا إلى الجن والإنس، وكانت الأنبياء يعزلون الخمس فتجئ النار فتأكله وأمرت أنا أن أقسمها في فقراء أمتي، ولم يبق نبي إلا أعطى سؤله وأخرت شفاعتي لأمتي

Abu Bakr Aḥmad bin al-Ḥasan al-Qāḍi reports: Abul' 'Abbās Muḥammad bin Ya'qub narrated to us al-Ḥasan bin Ali bin 'Afān narrated to us 'Ubaidallah bin Musa narrated to us Sālim Abu Ḥammād narrated to us from as-Suddi from 'Ikrima from Ibn 'Abbās that the Prophet (peace be upon him) said: *I have been given five things which were not given to any Prophet before me. The earth has been made for ritually pure and a masjid, while there is no one among the Prophets was allowed to perform prayer till he reaches his sanctuary (miḥrāb). I have been supported by awe, for a distance of one month's journey between me and the disbelievers, Allah throws awe in their hearts, all Prophets were sent to their own nations and I was sent to jinn and mankind, the Prophets used to separate one fifth (of the booty) and set it on fire, I was ordered to divide it and give it to the poor ones of my Ummah, and every Prophet was answered for his request, while I saved my (supplication) as an intercession (on the day of judgement) for my Ummah.*

Imām aṭ-Ṭabarāni has the next narration in *Mu'jam al-Kabir*:

حدثنا محمد بن عبد الله الحضرمي حدثنا عبد الرحمن بن الفضل بن موفق حدثنا أبي حدثنا إسماعيل بن إبراهيم عن مجاهد عن بن عباس قال: نصر رسول الله، صلى الله عليه وسلم، بالرعب مسيرة شهرين على عدوه

Muḥammad bin Abdullah al-Ḥaḍrami narrated to us Abdar-Raḥman bin al-Faḍil bin Muwafiq narrated to us my father narrated to us Ismā'il bin Ibrāhim narrated to us from Mujāhid from Ibn 'Abbās who said that the Prophet (peace be upon him) was supported by awe for a distance of one month's journey.

In the *Mustadrak*, al-Ḥākim has the following *athar* (narrative) again from Ibn 'Abbās:

أخبرنا أبو زكريا يحيى بن محمد العنبري حدثنا محمد بن عبد السلام حدثنا إسحاق بن إبراهيم أنبأ يزيد بن أبي حكيم حدثنا الحكم بن أبان قال: سمعت عكرمة يقول: قال بن عباس رضي الله عنهما: إن الله فضّل محمدا، صلى الله عليه وسلم، على أهل السماء وفضّله على أهل الأرض، قالوا: يا بن عباس فبما فضّله الله على أهل السماء؟ قال: قال الله عز وجل: {وَمَنْ يَقُلْ مِنْهُمْ إِنِّي إِلَهٌ مِنْ دُونِهِ فَذَلِكَ نَجْزِيهِ جَهَنَّمَ كَذَلِكَ نَجْزِي الظَّالِمِينَ}، وقال لمحمد، صلى الله عليه وسلم: {إِنَّا فَتَحْنَا لَكَ فَتْحًا مُبِينًا * لِيَغْفِرَ لَكَ اللَّهُ مَا تَقَدَّمَ مِنْ ذَنْبِكَ وَمَا تَأَخَّرَ}، الآية؛ قالوا: فبما فضّله الله على أهل الأرض؟ قال: إن الله عز وجل يقول: {وَمَا أَرْسَلْنَا مِنْ رَسُولٍ إِلَّا بِلِسَانِ قَوْمِهِ}، الآية، وقال لمحمد، صلى الله عليه وسلم: {وَمَا أَرْسَلْنَاكَ إِلَّا كَافَّةً لِلنَّاسِ بَشِيرًا وَنَذِيرًا}، فأرسله إلى

الجن والإنس

Abu Zakariyā Yaḥya bin Muḥammad al-Anbari reported to us Muḥammad bin Abd as-Salām narrated to us Isḥāq bin Ibrāhim narrated to us Yazeed bin Abi Ḥakeem reports: al-Ḥakam bin 'Abān narrated to us he said: I heard 'Ikrima who said – Ibn 'Abbās said – 'Verily Allah favoured Muḥammad (peace be upon him) above the inhabitants of heaven and those of earth.' They said: O Ibn 'Abbās, Allah favoured him above the inhabitants of heaven? He said 'Allah has declared: *And whoever of them should say – Surely I am a god besides him, such a one do we recompense with hell; thus do we recompense the unjust.*[20] And in relation to Muḥammad (peace be upon him): *Surely we have given to you a clear victory. That Allah may forgive your community their past faults and those to follow and complete his favour to you and keep you on a right way.*[21] The verse, they said (showing) Allah's favour above the inhabitants of the earth? (Ibn 'Abbās said) 'Allah the exalted has said: *And we did not send any Prophet but with the language of his people.*[22] And the verse for Muḥammad (peace be upon him): *And we have not sent you but to all mankind as a bearer of good news and as a Warner;*[23] He was sent to mankind and the *jinn*.'

Thereafter al-Ḥākim commented saying: 'This *ḥadith* is *Ṣaḥīḥ*; regarding the *isnād* al-Ḥakam bin Abān is accepted by the majority of the scholars of Islam, but not recorded by the two Shaykh's.' This particular narration is also reported by Abu Ya'la in his *Musnad,*[24] as well as in the *Musnad* of Dārimi.[25] Imām Aḥmad records the next *ḥadith* on the authority of Abdullah ibn 'Amr ibn al-'Aāṣ; Bayhaqy

---

[20] *Qur'ān* 21: 29
[21] *Qur'ān* 48: 1/2
[22] *Qur'ān* 14: 4
[23] *Qur'ān* 34: 28
[24] *Musnad* Abu Ya'la Vol. 1 sec. 96, no. 2,705
[25] *Musnad* Dārimi Vol. 1 sec. 39, no. 46

also records in *Sunan al-Kubra*[26]:

حدثنا قتيبة بن سعيد حدثنا بكر بن مضر عن بن الهاد عن عمرو بن شعيب عن أبيه عن جده ان رسول الله، صلى الله عليه وسلم، عام غزوة تبوك قام من الليل يصلي فاجتمع وراءه رجال من أصحابه يحرسونه حتى إذا صلى وانصرف إليهم فقال لهم: لقد أعطيت الليلة خمسا ما أعطيهن أحد قبلي: أما أنا فأرسلت إلى الناس كلهم عامة، وكان من قبلي إنما يرسل إلى قومه، ونصرت على العدو بالرعب ولو كان بيني وبينهم مسيرة شهر لمُلِئَ مني رعبا، وأحلت لي الغنائم آكلها وكان من قبلي يعظمون أكلها كانوا يحرقونها، وجعلت لي الأرض مساجد وطهورا أينما أدركتني الصلاة تمسحت وصليت وكان من قبلي يعظمون ذلك إنما كانوا يصلون في كنائسهم وبيعهم، والخامسة هي ما هي؟! قيل لي سل فإن كل نبي قد سأل! فاخرت مسألتي إلى يوم القيامة فهي لكم، ولمن شهد أن لا إله إلا الله

Qutayba bin Sa'eed narrated to us Bakr bin Muḍar narrated to us from ibn al-Hād from 'Amr bin Shuayb from his father from his grandfather that the Prophet (peace be upon him) during the year of the battle of Tabuk was standing performing prayer during the night. Some of his Companions gathered behind him in order to guard him till he finished his prayer and said to them: *I had been given this night five matters which were not given to any one before me. I have been sent to all mankind while whoever was before me used to be sent to his nation, Allah made me victorious by awe, (by His frightening my enemies) for a distance of one month's journey, the booty has been made lawful to me to consume while those who were before me used to burn it, the earth has been made a masjid for me and ritually pure whenever it is a time of prayer I wipe and pray while those who were before me were forbade to do so, they used to pray in their churches and the fifth is what it is. It was said to me ask as every Prophet asked (for something). I saved my supplication (as an intercession) on the day of judgement. It is guaranteed to you and to whoever believes that there is no god but Allah.*

---

[26] *Sunan al-Kubra* Vol. 1 sec. 223, no. 1,000

In *az-Zawā'id* another similar *ḥadith* is recorded, this time on the authority of Abu Sa'eed al-Khudri:

> عن أبي سعيد قال: قال رسول الله، صلى الله عليه وسلم: أعطيت خمسا لم يعطها نبي قبلي: بعثت إلى الأحمر والأسود وإنما كان النبي يبعث إلى قومه، ونصرت بالرعب مسيرة شهر، وأطعمت المغنم ولم يطعمه أحد كان قبلي، وجعلت لي الأرض طهورا ومسجدا، وليس من نبي إلا وقد أعطي دعوة فتعجلها وإني أخرت دعوتي شفاعة لأمتي وهي بالغة إن شاء الله من مات لا يشرك بالله شيئا

> From Abu Sa'eed who said that the Messenger of Allah (peace be upon him) said: *I have been given five things which were not given to any prophet before me. I have been sent to the red and the black while every messenger was sent particularly to his own people. Allah made me victorious by awe, (by His frightening my enemies) for a distance of one month's journey. The booty has been made lawful for me yet it was not lawful for anyone else before me. The earth has been made for me a thing to perform Ṭayammum and a place for praying, and every prophet was guaranteed the answer of a supplication and they asked for it. I saved my supplication as an intercession (on the day of judgement) for my Ummah. It is guaranteed to whoever dies and does not associate anything with Allah.*

Al-Haythamy said that Ṭabarāni reports this in *al-Awsaṭ* and the *isnād* is *ḥasan*. The complete *isnād* as it is in Ṭabarāni's *Mu'jam al-Awsaṭ* is: Muḥammad bin 'Abān narrated to us Ibrāhim bin Suwayd al-Jadthou'ee reported to us 'Aāmir bin Mudrak narrated to us Fuḍeel bin Marzooq narrated to us from 'Aṭiya from Abu Sa'eed.[27] In *Ṣaḥīḥ* Ibn Ḥibbān we have the following narrated by 'Auf ibn Mālik:

[27] *Mu'jam al-Awsaṭ* Vol. 7 sec. 257, no. 7,439

أخبرنا أبو يعلى حدثنا هارون بن عبد الله الحمال حدثنا بن أبي فديك عن عبيد الله بن عبد الرحمن بن موهب عن عباس بن عبد الرحمن بن ميناء الأشجعي عن عوف بن مالك عن النبي، صلى الله عليه وسلم، قال: أعطيت أربعا لم يعطهن أحد كان قبلنا وسألت ربي الخامسة فأعطانيها: كان النبي يبعث إلى قريته ولا يعدوها وبعثت كافة إلى الناس، وأرهب منا عدونا مسيرة شهر، وجعلت لي الأرض طهورا ومساجد، وأحل لنا الخمس ولم يحل لأحد كان قبلنا، وسألت ربي الخامسة فسألته أن لا يلقاه عبد من أمتي يوحده إلا أدخله الجنة فأعطانيها

Abu Ya'la reported to us Hārun bin Abdullah al-Ḥimāl narrated to us Ibn Abi Fudeek narrated to us from 'Ubaidallah bin Abdar-Raḥman bin Mawhib from 'Abbās bin Abdar-Raḥman bin Maynā' al-Ashshaji from 'Auf bin Mālik that the Prophet (peace be upon him) said: *I have been given four things which were not given to any other else before me, and I asked my Lord for the fifth and He answered it for me: any messenger used to be sent to his own people and didn't beyond it while I was sent to all people. Our enemy was frightened from us for a distance of one month's journey, the earth has been made for me a thing to perform Ṭayammum and a place for praying, the one fifth of the booty was made lawful for me while it was not lawful for anyone else before me, and I asked Allah for the fifth. I asked Him that there will be no one among my nation that meets Him, while he believes in His unity, except he will enter him in paradise, and Allah answered it for me.*

'Ubaidallah bin Abdar-Raḥman bin Mawhib who narrates on the authority 'Abbās bin Abdar-Raḥman bin Maynā' al-Ashshaji is not a strong narrator. Al-Ḥāfiz (ibn Ḥajar) said of him '*maqbool*' (acceptable) only! It is also narrated from Sā'ib ibn Yazeed in *Mu'jam al-Kabir:*

حدثنا الحسين بن إسحاق التستري حدثنا هشام بن عمار حدثنا يحيى بن حمزة حدثنا إسحاق بن عبد الله بن أبي فروة عن يزيد بن خصيفة أنه أخبره عن السائب بن يزيد قال: قال رسول الله، صلى الله عليه وسلم: فضلت على

> الأنبياء بخمس: بعثت إلى الناس كافة، وادخرت شفاعتي لأمتي، ونصرت بالرعب شهرا أمامي وشهرا خلفي، وجعلت لي الأرض مسجدا وطهورا، وأحلت لي الغنائم ولم تحل لأحد قبلي
>
> Al-Ḥasan bin Isḥāq at-Tastari narrated to us Hishām bin 'Aāmar narrated to us Yaḥya bin Ḥamza narrated to us Isḥāq bin Abdullah bin Abi Farwa narrated to us from Yazeed bin Khaṣeefa that he narrated from Sā'ib bin Yazeed who said that the Messenger of Allah (peace be upon him) said*: I have been preferred to all Prophets by five matters: I have been sent to all people, I saved my (supplication as) an intercession (on the day of judgement) for my Ummah, I was supported by awe for a distance of one month's journey forward and backward, the earth was made a masjid for me and ritually pure, and the booty was made lawful to me while it was not lawful for anyone else before me.*

Although the reported text is not at great variance with what has been reported thus far, I would submit that Isḥāq bin Abdullah bin Abi Farwa is *matrook* (rejected) and accused. Amongst the authorities in *Tafsir*, this matter did not go unnoticed or unreported. For example, in the *Tafsir* of Ibn Kathir he writes:

> It was recorded in *Ṣaḥīḥ* Bukhāri and Muslim that Jābir ibn Abdullah (may Allah be pleased with him) narrated that the Messenger of Allah (peace be upon him) said: *I have been given five things which were not given to any prophet else before me. Allah made me victorious by awe, (by His frightening my enemies) for a distance of one month's journey, the earth has been made for me a masjid and ritually pure, the booty has been made lawful for me, I was given the right to intercede, every messenger was sent particularly to his own people while I have been sent to all people.*
>
> Imām Aḥmad said: Muḥammad bin Abi 'Adi narrated to us from Sulaymān at-Taymi from Sayār from Abu Umāmah the

Messenger of Allah (peace be upon him) said: *Allah distinguished me above the Prophets (peace be upon them)* [the narrator had doubted that he said on the nations] *with four matters. I have been sent to all mankind, the earth has been made all for me* (and for my nation) *the earth has been made ritually pure for me and a masjid, therefore anyone of my nation can pray wherever the time of a prayer is due; he has his place of prayer and what he will use in ablution, I have been helped by terror (in the hearts of enemies) for a distance of one month's journey and the booty has been made lawful for me.*

At-Tirmidhi recorded the *ḥadith* from Sulaymān at-Taymi from Sayār al-Quraishi al-Amwa'i their *mawla* of Damascus resident in Baṣra from Abu Umāmah the Messenger of Allah (peace be upon him). Regarding this he said it was *ḥasan Ṣāḥīḥ*. Sa'eed bin Manṣur said: Ibn Wahb reported (that) Amr bin al-Ḥārith reported to us that Abu Yunus narrated to him from Abu Hurayrah that the Messenger of Allah (peace be upon him) said: '*I have been helped by terror (placed in the heart of the enemy),*' as reported by Muslim from the *ḥadith of* Ibn Wahb.

Imām Aḥmad said: Ḥussein bin Muḥammad narrated to us Isrā'il narrated to us from Abu Isḥāq from Abu Burda from his father from Abu Musa who said that the Messenger of Allah (peace be upon him) said: '*I have been given five things. I have been sent to the red and the black, the earth has been made a masjid – a place for praying and ritually pure; the booty has been made lawful for me yet it was not lawful for anyone else before me, Allah made me victorious by awe, (by His frightening my enemies) for a distance of one month's journey, and I was given the right to intercede. Every Prophet asked for intercession and I saved my right to intercede* (on the day of judgement) *for whoever died and did not associate anything with Allah.*' This was narrated by Aḥmad alone.

Al-'Aufi reports from Ibn 'Abbās that he said regarding the

> verse: *Soon We shall cast terror into the hearts of those who have disbelieved*[28], Allah threw fright in the heart of Abu Sufyān, so he returned to Mecca. The Prophet (peace be upon him) said – '*Verily! Abu Sufyān had attacked some among you and Allah throws terror in his heart.*' Ibn Abi Ḥātim recorded it.

In addition to the above, Ibn Kathir also writes in his *Tafsir*:

> Concerning the statement of Allah where he says: *And say to those who have been given the scripture and to the unlettered: Do you submit yourselves? Then if they submit, they are then certainly guided; but if they turn back, then upon you is only the delivery.*[29] There are several verses mentioned in relation to this subject as well as numerous *aḥādith*. It is known as an acknowledged fact that the Prophet (peace be upon him) was sent to all mankind.
>
> Al-Bukhāri recorded concerning the interpretation of this verse: Abdullah narrated to us Sulaymān bin Abdar-Raḥman and Musa bin Hārun narrated to us, they said Al-Waleed bin Muslim narrated to us Abdullah bin al-'Ala' bin Zubr narrated to me Bisr bin 'Ubaidallah narrated to me from Abu Idrees al-Khawlāni who said I heard Abu Dardā' say: There was a dispute between Abu Bakr and Umar, and Abu Bakr made Umar angry, so he left angrily. Abu Bakr followed him, requesting him to ask forgiveness for him, but Umar refused to do so and closed his door in Abu Bakr's face. So Abu Bakr went to Allah's Messenger (peace be upon him) while we were with him. Allah's Messenger (peace be upon him) said: *This friend of yours must have quarrelled (with somebody).* In the meantime Umar repented and felt sorry for what he had done so he came and greeted (those who were present) and sat with the Prophet (peace be upon him) and related the story to him.

[28] *Qur'ān* 3: 151
[29] *Qur'ān* 3: 20

Allah's Messenger (peace be upon him) became angry and Abu Bakr started saying – 'O Allah's Messenger (peace be upon him)! By Allah, I was more at fault (than Umar).' Allah's Messenger (peace be upon him) said: *Are you (people) leaving for me my companion? (Abu Bakr), are you (people) leaving for me my companion? When I said O people I am sent to you all as the Messenger of Allah you said I told a lie, while Abu Bakr said you have spoken the truth.*

This was recorded only by Al-Bukhāri. Imām Aḥmad records: Abduṣ-Ṣamad narrated to us Abdal-Aziz bin Muslim narrated to us Yazeed narrated to us from Miqsam from Ibn 'Abbās that the Prophet (peace be upon him) said: *I have been given five things which were not given to anyone else before me and I did not say that out of pride. I have been sent to all of mankind – the red and the black; Allah made me victorious by awe, (by His frightening my enemies) for a distance of one month's journey. The booty has been made lawful for me yet it was not lawful for anyone else before me. The earth has been made ritually pure for me and a masjid. I have been given intercession and I saved it for my Ummah (on the day of judgement). It is guaranteed to whoever does not associate anything with Allah.*

Additionally Imām Aḥmad also records: Qutayba ibn Sa'eed narrated to us Bakr bin Muḍar narrated to us from Ibn al-Hād from 'Amr bin Shu'ayb from his father from his grandfather that the Prophet (peace be upon him) during the year of the battle of Tabuk was standing performing prayer during the night. Some of his Companions gathered behind him in order to guard him till he finished his prayer and said to them: *I had been given this night five matters which were not given to any one before me. I have been sent to all mankind while whoever was before me used to be sent to his nation, Allah made me victorious by awe, (by His frightening my enemies) for a distance of one month's journey, the booty has been made lawful to me to consume while those who were before me used to burn it, the earth has been made a masjid for me and ritually pure whenever it is a time of prayer I wipe and pray while those who were before me were forbade to do so, they used to pray in their churches and the fifth is what it is. It was said to me ask as every prophet asked (for something). I saved my supplication (as an intercession) on the day of judgement. It is guaranteed to you and to whoever believes that there is no god but Allah.*

Its *isnād* is good and it is a strong channel of transmission. Imām Aḥmad also cites: Muḥammad bin Ja'far narrated to us Shu'ba narrated to us from Abi Bishr from Sa'eed bin Jubayr from Abu Musa al-Ash'ari from the Messenger of Allah (peace be upon him) that he said: '*Whoever hears about me from among my nation or the Jews and Christians and did not believe in me he will not enter Paradise.*' This *ḥadith* is also in Muslim albeit with slightly different wording: *'By him in whose hand my life is! He who amongst the community of Jews or Christians hears about me, and does not believe in me, he will be in the fire.'*

Imām Aḥmad records: Ḥasan narrated to us Ibn Lahia' narrated to us Abu Yunus narrated to us and he is Sulaym bin Jubayr from Abu Hurayrah from the Messenger of Allah (peace be upon him) that he said: '*By him in whose hand my life is! He who amongst the community of Jews or Christians hears about me and does not believe in that with which I have been sent with and dies in this state* (of disbelief), *he shall be but one of the denizens of the fire.*' This was recorded by Aḥmad only. Imām Aḥmad also has: Ḥussein bin Muḥammad narrated to us Isrā'il narrated to us from Abu Isḥāq from Abi Burda from Abu Musa who said that the Messenger of Allah (peace be upon him) said: '*I have been given five things. I have been sent to the red and the black, the earth has been made ritually pure for me and a masjid, the spoils of war have been made lawful for me and these were never made lawful to anyone before me, Allah made me victorious by awe, (by His frightening my enemies) for a distance of one month's journey, and I have been given the right of intercession. Every Prophet asked Allah for an intercession and I saved my intercession (on the day of judgement) for whoever died from among my nation that does not associate anything with Allah.*'

> The *ḥadith* has an authentic chain of transmission, but they did not record it. Imām Aḥmad also recorded similarly from Ibn Umar with a good *isnād* and it is also recorded in the two *Ṣāḥīḥ's*. He further recorded another narrative from Jābir bin Abdullah who narrated that the Messenger of Allah (peace be upon him) said: *I have been given five things which were not given to any prophet else before me. Allah made me victorious by awe, (by His frightening my enemies) for a distance of one month's journey, the earth has been made for me a masjid and ritually pure, the booty has been made lawful for me, I was given the right to intercede, every messenger was sent particularly to his own people while I have been sent to all people.*

Ibn Kathir also writes in his *Tafsir*:

> From 'Ikrima from Ibn 'Abbās who said that Allah preferred Muḥammad (peace be upon him) to the people of the heaven and to the Prophets. It was said: ' Ibn 'Abbās! In what did Allah prefer him to the Prophets?' He said: 'Allah the exalted says - '*And We did not send any messenger but in the language of his people, that he may make clear to them.*'[30] And He says to His Prophet (peace be upon him): '*And We have not sent you....except to all mankind.*' [31] Allah had sent him to the *jinn* and mankind.'
>
> The saying of Ibn 'Abbās was recorded in Bukhāri and Muslim on the authority of Jābir (may Allah be pleased with him) who narrated that the Messenger of Allah (peace be upon him) said: *'I have been given five things which were not given to anyone else among Prophets before me. Allah made me victorious by awe, (by His frightening my enemies) for a distance of one month's journey. The earth has been made for me (and for my followers) a masjid and ritually pure, therefore*

[30] *Qur'ān* 14: 4
[31] *Qur'ān* 34: 28

anyone of my followers can pray wherever the time of a prayer is due. The booty has been made lawful for me yet it was not lawful for anyone else before me. I have been given the right of intercession (on the Day of Resurrection). Every Prophet used to be sent to his nation only but I have been sent to all mankind.'

And it was recorded in the *Ṣaḥīḥ* that the Messenger of Allah (peace be upon him) said: '*I have been sent to the red and the black.*' Mujāhid said that he meant *jinn* and mankind while others said that he meant the Arabs and the non-Arabs - and both of them are right.

Indeed all of these are authentic chains of transmission narrated on the authority of a large number of companions: Jābir bin Abdullah, Abu Hurayrah, Abu Dharr Al-Ghifāri the most truthful from among creation, the trustworthy Abdullah ibn 'Abbās; Abdullah ibn 'Amr ibn al-'Aāṣ who wrote the honourable words of the Messenger (peace be upon him), Abu Musa al-Ash'ari and Abu Umāmah - may Allah be pleased with all of them. These *aḥādith* were recorded in books of *Ṣaḥīḥ*, *Sunan*, *Musnad*, *Muṣṣanaf* and *Mu'jam* and even in books of *Tafsir*, literature and Arabic language. As a collective they are taken as definite evidence, whosoever denies this collective body is a *kāfir*. There are also other a large amount of other narrations from other companions that prove that the Messenger of Allah (peace be upon him) was sent to all mankind and that he was preferred and distinguished by that; every Prophet and Messenger was just sent to his own nation or locale. However this would require a separate volume to list all of them.

Undoubtedly Allah has bestowed great virtue upon Muḥammad (peace be upon him). Notwithstanding this though, the fundamental point which is to be taken forward is that the aforementioned matters are established principles of the Islamic doctrine and creed; it is mandatory to believe in them and denial would take one outside the fold of Islam.

3 All previous Prophetic laws are abrogated

It was proved by overwhelming evidence, the denial of which is *kufr* (disbelief), that the previous Prophets and Messengers were just sent to their own specific tribes, peoples, locales or nations. Similarly, it was also proved that unlike previous Prophets and Messengers the Prophet Muḥammad (peace be upon him) was sent to all of mankind. To argue that the previous nations or peoples still exist presently seems incredulous. By the passage of time they have perished; long ceasing to be considered as distinct nations addressed by a particular Prophet or Messenger. In fact, they are now considered as a part of Muḥammad's (peace be upon him) nation. That is to say, each previous nation lost its description as a specific nation as well as its independent identity and became just individuals, groups, tribes, or peoples included in the nation of Muḥammad (peace be upon him).

The call of previous Prophets now has no legal significance, because the law they were sent with would address those who are no longer existent. Nobody in the present world is ordered to follow the law which was brought by Musa (Moses, peace be upon him), although there are existing individuals and tribes descended from Bani Israel. However, the nation of Musa (peace be upon him), described once as a nation of divine message, is gone, it has vanished through the passage of time. In a similar manner, nobody is required to follow the specific laws which were brought by Esa (Jesus, peace be upon him).

One can reasonably ask, so what has happened to those previous messages? Have the commands and prohibitions that Allah gave to those previous peoples evaporated entirely? Allah forbid! What has happened is that these specific laws and injunctions were *abrogated* in totality by him, exalted be his names. The precise moment of abrogation was the moment revelation descended upon the final messenger sent to all of mankind, namely Muḥammad (peace be upon him). By Allah saying that he has sent Muḥammad (peace be upon him) as a Prophet and Messenger to *all* of mankind, by necessity, he has thereby abrogated all the previous messages, since the people they specifically addressed no longer exist. All the laws and detailed rulings that were applicable to the previous nations via their Prophets and Messengers have been abrogated totally. Every injunction that applied previously whether that be an obligation or prohibition, no longer applies anymore. Yet it is more than this – it is not merely the fact that they no longer apply, but it is prohibited to seek to apply them now following the advent of Muḥammad (peace be upon him).

Each of the previous Prophets and Messengers were not sent to us, nor have they addressed us in any manner, thus it is inconceivable that the specific laws that they brought could in some manner now apply to us. Following an abrogated religion and leaving the abrogating one is a major crime, it constitutes an annulment of the commands of Allah and rebellion against his sovereignty. Those that would purport to argue for the dictum of 'the law of the previous Prophets is our law too'[1] are presiding over an absurdity. Whatever may appear to be similar in our present divine law brought by Muḥammad (peace be upon him) to that brought by previous Prophets or Messengers should not be construed as being in any way an

---

[1] The original Arabic for the term in the book as well as that found in the books of jurisprudence (*fiqh*) is: *Shara' min qablina shara' lanā*. We have chosen this phraseology above as opposed to a literal translation for the sake of clarify in English.

affirmation or continuance of that legislation. How could it be the case that Allah abrogated all of the previous divine laws and at the same time re-legislated them as being 'Islamic laws' now?

The incredulity of the saying 'the law of the previous Prophets is our law too' should be evident by the fact that Muḥammad (peace be upon him) was sent to all mankind and even the *jinn*. His followers from amongst mankind are considered as being one *Ummah* subsuming all different races, tribes and nations on earth. As it is described as one nation, it therefore has only one creed and one law. While each one of the previous Prophets used to be sent to specific peoples, locales or nations, each of whom had a law and a method that differed from the others, even if they were under the same rule. Whoever claims that these laws are ours, he must do the following:

- Implement all of these laws at the same time from the same view and consideration; that is, to gather between opposing contrasts; which is an impossible matter to occur from both the reasonable and legal point of view.

- Make every law connected with a specific nation that would be followed by this *Ummah* only and not by any other nation from among mankind. If applied, by rights, anyone from the Far East – for example Japan, would be able to argue that this is the law sent to Israel – it cannot be obligatory now since I was not addressed with it originally. Even if present at the time of Musa (peace be upon him) it wouldn't have been obligatory to follow as he wasn't sent to the Japanese! Consequently, how could it ever apply now after the advent of Muḥammad (peace be upon him)?

From the Islamic legal point of view, this is impossible, as it contradicts the universality of the Muḥammad's message (peace be upon him) and the unity of his *Ummah*, whereas both matters were proved through definite and absolute proofs. Common people and scholars, Muslims and *mushrikeen* (polytheists) know these two matters in Islam as an acknowledged fact, as we mentioned earlier; this is but an additional proof put forward here. Some have tried to escape from this quandary by arguing with the following: 'The law of the previous Prophets becomes ours too, but only if it is mentioned in the Qur'ān or the *Sunnah.*' In reply we would posit that this line of argument is of no use. If it is mentioned in the present revelation it is by way of a report. If it is mentioned in the form of an address to the believers now, then it becomes a new law, however similar it may appear to that which has gone previously. The newly enacted law becomes mandatory to follow not because of anything that has gone previously, but because we are commanded with it now in the present revelation. It is prohibited to say now 'the law of the previous Prophets is our law too' or that it somehow 'becomes part of our laws'. One could say though that this is a new law for us, which appears similar to that previously revealed; legally that is tenable.

Writing in '*Issues from al-Uṣul*'[2], the second book of *al-Muḥalla bil athār*, the grand Imām of Andalusia, Ibn Ḥazm argued as follows:

> *Mas'ala* 102: *Sharī'ah* of Previous Prophets.
>
> It is not permissible to follow any *Sharī'ah* of a Prophet (that came) before our Prophet (Muḥammad), as Allah has said:
>
> لِكُلٍّ جَعَلْنَا مِنكُمْ شِرْعَةً وَمِنْهَاجًا

---

[2] This appears in the *Muḥalla* after the book of *Tawḥeed.* Although *al-Muḥalla* is primarily a work of *fiqh* (jurisprudence) the section provides a good introduction to the doctrinal principles that Ibn Ḥazm held and utilises throughout the book. His major work on *Uṣul* is entitled: *al-Iḥkām fi Uṣul al-Aḥkām* (Judgement on the Principles of Law).

> *....for every one of you did We appoint a law and a way....*[3]

> Aḥmad ibn Muḥammad ibn al-Jasour narrated to us Wahb ibn Massara narrated to us Muḥammad ibn Waḍḍāḥ[4] narrated to us Abu Bakr ibn Abi Shayba narrated to us Hushaym reported to us from Sayyār from Yazid al-Faqir he reported to us from Jābir ibn Abdullah that the Messenger of Allah (peace be upon him) said: *I have been given five (things) that have not been given to anybody before me: I have been supported with horror for a distance of one month; the whole earth has been made a masjid and ṭahur (purified / clean) for me anyone from my Ummah, man or woman, can pray wherever they are; the spoils of war have been permitted to me whereas they were not for previous nations; I have been given the intercession, and every previous Prophet has been sent to his own people whereas I have been sent to all of mankind.*

> Since these messengers have been sent to their own specific people they are not addressing us – so how can their *Sharī'ah* apply or even be obligatory upon us? What makes our current *Sharī'ah* applicable is that we have been addressed with it. Whoever denies this, would therefore deny this *ḥadith* and the special *faḍeelah* (virtues) that has been given to Muḥammad (peace be upon him). Whoever says that the laws of the previous Prophets apply to us now given the advent of the Prophet Muḥammad (peace be upon him) who is sent to all of mankind is lying. And with Allah is all success.

Hats off to Ibn Ḥazm for furnishing us with this deep, thoughtful analysis! We also formally adopt this viewpoint and to it add the following dictum:

---

[3] *Qur'an* 5: 48

[4] Up to that point is Ibn Ḥazm's *isnād* to Imām Abu Bakr ibn Abi Shayba

- *All previous divine laws were abrogated with the advent of the last Prophet, who was sent to all of mankind, namely Muḥammad ibn Abdullah (peace be upon him). The abrogation was absolute. Hence that is why is it unlawful to try and implement or follow a previous Sharī'ah to begin with.*

All rulings sent to us after the revelation of the first word of the Qur'ān word - *Iqra'* (read!) [5] is a new law even if it appears to be similar to that previously issued or even if it is identical. Without doubt the reality of the matter is that it is new, so is absolutely unlawful to say that it is an acknowledgment of a previous law, as that which is abrogated becomes necessarily void and non-existent. Its return is the establishment of a new law not a confirmation of a previous one that still exists and applies. The glorious Qur'ān and the honourable *Sunnah* are full of proofs which confirm this reasoning, for the words of Allah and that revealed to his Messenger (peace be upon him) are never in contradiction to one another.

أَفَلَا يَتَدَبَّرُونَ الْقُرْآنَ وَلَوْ كَانَ مِنْ عِندِ غَيْرِ اللَّهِ لَوَجَدُوا فِيهِ اخْتِلَافًا كَثِيرًا

Do they not then contemplate over the Qur'ān? If it were from any other than Allah, they would have found in it much discrepancy / contradiction.[6]

Allah the exalted and majestic says:

وَأَنزَلْنَا إِلَيْكَ الْكِتَابَ بِالْحَقِّ مُصَدِّقًا لِّمَا بَيْنَ يَدَيْهِ مِنَ الْكِتَابِ وَمُهَيْمِنًا عَلَيْهِ فَاحْكُم بَيْنَهُم بِمَا أَنزَلَ اللَّهُ وَلَا تَتَّبِعْ أَهْوَاءَهُمْ عَمَّا جَاءَكَ مِنَ الْحَقِّ لِكُلٍّ جَعَلْنَا مِنكُمْ شِرْعَةً وَمِنْهَاجًا وَلَوْ شَاءَ اللَّهُ لَجَعَلَكُمْ أُمَّةً وَاحِدَةً وَلَٰكِن لِّيَبْلُوَكُمْ فِي مَا آتَاكُمْ فَاسْتَبِقُوا الْخَيْرَاتِ إِلَى اللَّهِ مَرْجِعُكُمْ جَمِيعًا فَيُنَبِّئُكُم بِمَا كُنتُمْ فِيهِ تَخْتَلِفُونَ

[5] *Qur'an* 96: 1
[6] *Qur'an* 4: 82

And We have revealed to you the Book with the truth, verifying what is before it of the Book and a guardian over it, therefore judge between them by what Allah has revealed, and do not follow their low desires (to turn away) from the truth that has come to you; for every one of you did We appoint a law and a way, and if Allah had pleased He would have made you (all) a single people, but that He might try you in what He gave you, therefore strive with one another to hasten to virtuous deeds; to Allah is your return, of all (of you), so He will let you know that in which you differed.[7]

Contained within the aforementioned verse is the Arabic word '*muhaymin*' [المهيمن] which is one of the ninety-nine names of Allah and is often translated as 'The Protector'. Many interpretations have been given to this word including: 'the witness and trustworthy, the faithful, the vigilant guardian'. But the foremost interpretation seems to be on two distinct levels, firstly, meaning the dominated controller who has the power over everything and whose commands are decisively accomplished; secondly this word refers to one who undertakes the responsibility of ruler and disposes all affairs. In *Fatḥ al-Bāri* Al-Ḥāfiz (Ibn Ḥajar) tried to summarise these interpretations and said the following:

> They said regarding the word '*muhaymin*' that the Qur'ān is trusted over all the books that preceded it. As cited by Abu Ḥātim from the channel of Ali bin Abi Ṭalḥa from Ibn 'Abbās in relation to the statement of Allah 'and *muhaymin* over it' he said the Qur'ān is trusted over all the books that preceded it. Furthermore as reported by Abd' bin Ḥumayd from the channel of Arbada at-Tamimi from Ibn 'Abbās in relation to the statement of Allah 'and *muhaymin* over it' he said 'entrusted over it'. Ibn Qutayba and others followed by the majority said: knowing it is trusted.
>
> Some postulate it as being *mu'aymin*, the *ha* (ه) being read

---

[7] *Qur'an* 5: 48

> as a *hamza* (ء); *mu'aymin* means the one who offers peace and security. That is rejected because that is not the preponderant meaning, given that it is from amongst the names of Allah the exalted and not simply reduced to that. The truth is that its root has the meaning that he is superseded by something. *Al-Haymana* to protect and watch over, that is why it is said when a man watches over something and protects it he has '*haymana*' over it. (Or) a man dominates a man if he becomes his watcher, hence he is *muhaymin*. Abu 'Ubaida said: it didn't come in the speech of the Arabs on this construction except four words: *mubayṭar*, *musayṭir, muhaymin* and *mubayqar*.

On the same subject in *Fatḥ al-Bāri,* Al-Ḥāfiz (Ibn Ḥajar) continues:

> Al-Bayhaqy mentioned, 'This explanation of the scholars of *Tafsir* with regard to the term '*al-mahaymin*' is that it means 'supervisor'. He then cites a narration from at-Taymi on the authority of Ibn 'Abbās in reference to the verse, '*(he is) muhaymin* over it.' Ibn 'Abbās states that it means 'protector'; in another narration from Ali bin 'Abi Ṭalhah, Ibn 'Abbās is reported to say that '*al-Muhaymin*' means 'supervisor'. In yet another narration from Mujāhid, Ibn 'Abbās is reported to say, '*al-Muhaymin*' means the witness. It is said that '*al-Muhaymin*' means the observer over an object and guardian of it. It is also said that *al-haymanah* is to be in authority over something as a poet once said:
>
> 'Is it not that the best of the people after their Prophet is their next *muhaymin* guiding them towards the good and the bad? The one in authority over the people wants to protect them even after his time has passed.'
>
> It is therefore correct that this poetry implies that he wants security for them and what has been mentioned is in accordance with this.'

I would submit that Bayhaqy struck the point in his interpretation of the word '*al-muhaymin*' with it being based upon the 'people care for them.' Not taken advantage of the poetic lines which is mentioned, the understanding of the sense of '*al-ḥākim*' the ruler and '*al-musayṭir*' the dominant. While the meanings of witness and trustee are there they are not derived from the word itself. From the requirements of the *Shari'* meaning it can be discerned to encompass that the trusted ruler watching over affairs, or else failing in that would be considered treacherous or even criminal. This is similar to what has come in *Lisān al-Arab*: 'In the *ḥadith* of 'Ikrima – I know Ali peace be upon him was from amongst the '*muhayminăt'*; any issues of dominance, which is the thing to do, to make her act is headed to matters such custodians.' As for Imām aṭ-Ṭabari although he provides a lengthy and beautiful comment, he doesn't necessarily approach the intended meaning with his interpretation.

Imām Ibn Kathir was closer to the mark in seeking to flesh out the meaning of the word *muhaymin* in his *Tafsir*. He writes:

> The statement of Allah '*muhaymin* over it': Sufyān ath-Thawri and other than him said: from Ibn Isḥāq from at-Tamimi from Ibn 'Abbās (who said) entrusted over it. And it's said from Ali bin Abi Ṭalḥa from Ibn 'Abbās – *al-muhaymin* is the trustworthy, the Qur'ān is trusted over all the books that preceded it. As well it has been reported from 'Ikrima, Sa'eed bin Jubayr, Mujāhid, Muḥammad bin Ka'b, 'Aṭiya, al-Ḥasan, Qatādah, 'Aṭā al-Khurasāni, as-Suddi and Ibn Zayd about this. Ibn Jarir (Imām aṭ-Ṭabari) said: the Qur'ān is trustworthy over the books that preceded it. Therefore, whatever disagrees with the Qur'ān is false. Al-Wālabi said that Ibn 'Abbās said that *muhayminan* means 'witness.' Similar was said by Mujāhid, Qatāda and as-Suddi. Al-'Awfi said that Ibn 'Abbās said that *muhayminan* means dominant over the previous scriptures. These meanings are similar, as the word *muhaymin* includes them all. Consequently, the Qur'ān is trustworthy, a witness

> and dominant over every scripture / book that preceded it. This glorious book which Allah revealed as the last and final book of all times. The Qur'ān includes all the good aspects of previous scriptures and even more, which no previous scripture ever contained. This is why Allah made it trustworthy, a witness and dominant over them. Allah promised that he will protect the Qur'ān and swore by his most honourable self when doing so. Verily Allah the exalted says: *Surely we have revealed the Dhikr and we will most surely be its guardian.*[8]

The comments from Ibn Kathir are good indeed. But it's unfortunate that the majority of exegetes simply regurgitated the interpretation of Ibn 'Abbās regarding word *al-muhaymin* as being a witness, then a trustee or entrusted which only slightly fits into the overall context unlike the ruling concerning it. Ultimately this is due to *taqleed* (imitation), laziness about being diligent and having independent thought. We have found in the book of history written by Imām aṭ-Ṭabari,[9] regarding the death of Abu Shurayḥ, some lines of poetry which serve to provide some elaboration upon the linguistic meaning of this word:

> [Al-Walīd] wrote to wrote to Uthmān about [these young men] and he wrote back to put them to death. Thus, [Al-Walīd] executed them at the gate of the Official Palace [*al-qaṣr*] in the square [*al-raḥabah*]. Concerning this [event] 'Amr b. 'Āsim al-Tamīmī said:
>
> *Never feed on your neighbours immoderately, O dissolute men, in the reign [mulk] of Ibn 'Affān*
>
> *For Ibn 'Affān, whom you have put to the test, has cut off thieves by the well-established law of [our] salvation*

---

[8] *Qur'ān* 15: 9

[9] Ṭabari *History of Prophets and Kings*, Vol. 2 p. 439 (Arabic); the English is taken from the translation and is at Vol. 15, *The Crisis of the Early Caliphate*, p. 46

> *Without fail he acts in accordance with the Book, keeping close watch over every neck and fingertip among them.*

It would appear from these verses that the meaning relates to control. But control and dominance appears in the word of '*muhaymin*', as stated in *al-Iṣāba fi Tamiyiz aṣ-Ṣaḥāba* by al-Ḥāfiz Ibn Ḥajar; during the biography of al-Fāria' bin Abi aṣ-Ṣalt may Allah be pleased with her, sister of Umayyah bin Abi aṣ-Ṣalt, the famous poet. The following stanzas are from his *qaṣīdah*:

> To you is all praise, all blessings, all favours, our Lord. There is nothing higher than you at all, neither is there a more absolute *muhaymin* or majestic king upon the throne of the heavens. Your power humbles masses and causes them to prostrate.

In my opinion, there is no meaning for *muhaymin* here except that it means the one who decrees and controls, who possesses absolute authority, and who is in ultimate disposal of all affairs. And this is what circulated among the tongues of the people from all levels in the later centuries. Therefore, if it is said *al-Haymanah al-'Ajnabiyyah*[10] then all listeners understand this term as 'dominance, control, or foreign occupation' and nothing else – this is the correct opinion *alḥamdulillah*. This is what Allah has meant by the term - that *muhaymin* means the one who decrees and controls, who possesses absolute authority, and who is in ultimate disposal of all affairs - nothing else is meant by it.

It is not that the Qur'ān is *muhaymin*, *ḥākim*, controlling or dominating the previous books except if it is abrogating them, it cannot imitate them rationally or legally in terms of what Allah has

---

[10] *Haymanah* is the root word of the term '*muhaymin*'.

commanded or prohibited. This is because essentially they are of one rank, originating ultimately from the same source, namely Allah the exalted. Thus it is not an issue of the last revelation dominating or controlling those previous to it. It is *nāsikh* (abrogating) and that is *mansookh* (abrogated) by necessity. This will not be its condition or place. It cannot be imagined except as this. Yet it is another proof concerning the matter of the previous laws being abrogated in totality and that we are not originally addressed by them. To reiterate again, the argument that the 'law of the previous Prophet's is our law too' is invalid and a great lie. Should one realize the ramifications of such a statement and still adhere to it, one would fall into *kufr* (disbelief).

ثُمَّ جَعَلْنَاكَ عَلَىٰ شَرِيعَةٍ مِّنَ الْأَمْرِ فَاتَّبِعْهَا وَلَا تَتَّبِعْ أَهْوَاءَ الَّذِينَ لَا يَعْلَمُونَ

Then we have made you follow a course in the affair, therefore follow it, and do not follow the low desires of those who do not know. [11]

The Prophet (peace be upon him) had his own independent specific law that differs from other previous ones. This law was revealed to him from the very beginning of his call, when he was at Mecca, as attested by the aforementioned verse, which is Meccan in origin according to the majority of scholars. That was why he did not ask any of the people of the book about any of their rules or judgments. In fact, this was forbidden, as it will be mentioned soon. Perhaps some people hated that, in particular the Jews, but Allah let them know after a while when they were at Medina that his steady, stable tradition was to make a specific law for every nation. Every such law is a law of Allah, in its time and for its nation among which it was legislated; applying it at its time is considered an act of obedience to Allah. The important point is to rush headlong toward good deeds and strive like in a race towards all virtues, rather than becoming bogged down in the

[11] *Qur'ān* 45: 18

technicalities of the specific law. If a certain divine law is abrogated, the new one will also be a law of Allah; obeying it is an obligation, while disobeying it is prohibited. Allah the exalted and glorious outlines this meaning when he says:

وَأَنزَلْنَا إِلَيْكَ الْكِتَابَ بِالْحَقِّ مُصَدِّقًا لِّمَا بَيْنَ يَدَيْهِ مِنَ الْكِتَابِ وَمُهَيْمِنًا عَلَيْهِ فَاحْكُم بَيْنَهُم بِمَا أَنزَلَ اللَّهُ وَلَا تَتَّبِعْ أَهْوَاءَهُمْ عَمَّا جَاءَكَ مِنَ الْحَقِّ لِكُلٍّ جَعَلْنَا مِنكُمْ شِرْعَةً وَمِنْهَاجًا وَلَوْ شَاءَ اللَّهُ لَجَعَلَكُمْ أُمَّةً وَاحِدَةً وَلَٰكِن لِّيَبْلُوَكُمْ فِي مَا آتَاكُمْ فَاسْتَبِقُوا الْخَيْرَاتِ إِلَى اللَّهِ مَرْجِعُكُمْ جَمِيعًا فَيُنَبِّئُكُم بِمَا كُنتُمْ فِيهِ تَخْتَلِفُونَ

And We have revealed to you the Book with the truth, verifying what is before it of the Book and a guardian over it, therefore judge between them by what Allah has revealed, and do not follow their low desires (to turn away) from the truth that has come to you; for every one of you did We appoint a law and a way, and if Allah had pleased He would have made you (all) a single people, but that He might try you in what He gave you, therefore strive with one another to hasten to virtuous deeds; to Allah is your return, of all (of you), so He will let you know that in which you differed.[12]

According to the majority this *Surah, al-Mā'ida,* was revealed in Medina. A large number of *ḥadith* exist also to corroborate the points that we have made thus far, that the argument of the law of the previous Prophets being part of our present law is totally invalid. The Prophet (peace be upon him) said: '*If Musa were alive among you today and you followed him, leaving me, you would have gone astray.*' Musa (peace be upon him) was a Prophet and an infallible Messenger who did not disobey Allah's orders. If alive today, he would have no other choice than to follow Muḥammad (peace be upon him), otherwise he would be acting in disobedience to Allah. It is known by necessity that the law of Musa has now been totally abrogated, so if he was to be resurrected now it would be impermissible for him to follow any other than Muḥammad (peace be upon him); to do so would make

[12] *Qur'an* 5: 48

him sinful, Allah forbid! This *ḥadith* is yet another evidence that proves all the previous religions and laws have been totally abrogated; we are not addressed by them at all. Hence the statement, 'the law of the previous Prophets is our law too' is not simply false or an absurdity, it stands in open opposition to the express statement of Muḥammad (peace be upon him).

One individual tried belatedly to conclusively address this problem. He was the Imām Abul'Farj Nur-ad-Deen ibn Burhān ad-Deen Ali bin Ibrāhim Aḥmad al-Ḥalabi (died 1044 AH). His solution though, wasn't much of a solution. Writing in the *Seerah of Ḥalab fi Seerah al-Ameen al-Mā'moon* he said:

> You should know that he (peace be upon him) sender of all Prophet's and their nations to appreciate his presence in their time. Because Allah the exalted took along them and upon their nations confirmed on faith with him and supported him to be on the messengership and message to the nations. Prophethood and his message are more inclusive, and to be his law in those times for those nations that came by their Prophets, because the provisions and laws vary according to the people and the times. As-Subki said: all the Prophets and their nations from among his nation, peace be upon him, He (peace be upon him) said to Umar bin al-Khaṭṭāb – '*By him in whose hand my soul rests, if Musa peace be upon him were alive he would follow me.*'

Another demonstrable proof is the fact that the Prophet Muḥammad (peace be upon him) led in prayer all the other Prophets in his night journey to *Bait al-Maqdis*. The previous Prophets were resurrected for him, they moved one another to lead the prayer, then they made him at the front or Jibreel (Gabriel, peace be upon him) did so. Thus, Muḥammad (peace be upon him) led them in the prayer, which proved that their manner of prayer was abrogated, as they prayed according to his prayer. Prayer is considered the main pillar of religion; other previous acts of worship were abrogated *a fortiori*. This is the fifth piece of evidence, which proves that all previous laws and religions have been abrogated, and that we are not addressed by them at all. Yet again it shows the absurdity of the statement 'the law of the previous Prophets is our law too'; it is false statement and its use is forbidden. The primacy of the Prophet (peace be upon him) and his law can also be ascertained from a number of narratives that have reached us. As recorded by Imām Muslim:

وحدثني زهير بن حرب حدثنا حجين بن المثنى حدثنا عبد العزيز وهو بن أبي سلمة عن عبد الله بن الفضل عن أبي سلمة بن عبد الرحمن عن أبي هريرة قال: قال رسول الله، صلى الله عليه وسلم: لقد رأيتني في الحجر وقريش تسألني عن مسراي فسألتني عن أشياء من بيت المقدس لم أثبتها، فكربت كربة ما كربت مثله قط»، قال: «فرفعه الله لي أنظر إليه ما يسألوني عن شيء إلا أنبأتهم به، وقد رأيتني في جماعة من الأنبياء فإذا موسى قائم يصلي فإذا رجل ضَرْب جعد كأنه من رجال شنوءة، وإذا عيسى بن مريم عليه السلام قائم يصلي أقرب الناس به شبها عروة بن مسعود الثقفي، وإذا إبراهيم عليه السلام قائم يصلي أشبه الناس به صاحبكم يعني نفسه، فحانت الصلاة فأممتهم، فلما فرغت من الصلاة قال قائل: (يا مُحَمَّد هذا مالك صاحب النار فسلم عليه، فالتفت إليه فبدأني بالسلام

And Zuhayr bin Ḥarb narrated to me Ḥujeen bin al-Muthanna narrated to us Abdal-Aziz and he is ibn Abi Salama narrated to us from Abdullah bin al-Faḍl from Abu Salama bin Abdar-Raḥman from Abu Hurayrah who said that the Messenger of Allah (peace be upon him) said: *I found myself in Ḥijr and the Quraysh were asking me about my night journey. I was asked about things pertaining to Bait-ul-Maqdis which I could not preserve (in my mind). I was very much vexed, so vexed as I had never been before. Then Allah raised it (Bait al-Maqdis) before my eyes. I looked towards it, and I gave them the information about whatever they questioned me I also saw myself among the group of Messengers. I saw Moses saying prayer and found him to be a well-built man as if he was a man of the tribe of Shanu'a. I saw Jesus son of Mary (peace be upon him) offering prayer, of all men he had the closest resemblance with 'Urwa bin Mas'ud ath-Thaqafi. I saw Ibrāhim (peace be upon him) offering prayer; he had the closest resemblance with your companion* (the Prophet) *amongst people. When the time of prayer came I led them. When I completed the prayer, someone said: Here is Mālik, the keeper of the Hell; pay him salutations. I turned to him, but he preceded me in salutation.*

The narration is also in *Sunan al-Kubra* of Imām Nasā'i, the chain though is slightly different, reported as: Muḥammad ibn Rāfi' reported to us he said Ḥubayn bin al-Muthanna narrated to us Abdul-Aziz ibn Abi Salama narrated to us the specific channel and text to its end. In the *Sunan* of an-Nasā'i there is the following as part of a long *ḥadith*:

أخبرنا عمرو بن هشام قال: حدثنا مخلد عن سعيد بن عبد العزيز قال: حدثنا يزيد بن أبي مالك قال: حدثنا أنس بن مالك أن رسول الله، صلى الله عليه وسلم، قال: أتيت بدابة فوق الحمار ودون البغل، خطوها عند منتهى طرفها، فركبت ومعي جبريل عليه السلام فسرت إلى أن قال: ثم دخلت بيت المقدس فجمع لي الأنبياء عليهم السلام فقدمني جبريل حتى أممتهم، ثم صعد بي إلى السماء الدنيا،...

'Amr bin Hishām reported to us he said Makhlad narrated to us from Sa'eed bin Abdal-Aziz he said Yazeed bin Abi Mālik narrated to us he said Anas bin Mālik narrated to us that the Prophet (peace be upon him) said: *I was brought an animal that was larger than a donkey and smaller than a mule, whose stride could reach as far as it could see. I mounted it, and Jibreel was with me, and I set off* [until when he said]. *Then I entered Bait Al-Maqdis* (Jerusalem) *where the Prophets peace be upon them were assembled for me, and Jibreel brought me forward to lead them in prayer. Then I was taken up to the first heaven*....(etc).

The narration is also recorded by many other collectors, such as aṭ-Ṭabarāni in *Mu'jam al-Kabir,*[13] as well as in *Musnad ash-Shāmiayn;*[14] Abu Ya'la recorded it in his *Musnad*[15] as did al-Ḥārith / al-Haythami.[16] In *Mu'jam al-Awsaṭ* Ṭabarāni records a long narration:

حدثنا علي بن سعيد الرازي قال: حدثنا الحسين بن عيسى بن ميسرة الرازي قال: حدثنا هارون بن المغيرة قال: حدثنا عنبسة بن سعيد عن ابن ابي ليلى عن اخيه عيسى عن ابيه عبد الرحمن بن ابي ليلى أن جبريل أتى النبي، صلى الله عليه وسلم، بالبراق فحمله بين يديه وجعل يسير به]؛ فساق الحديث حتى قال: [حتى أتينا بيت المقدس فإذا هو بنفر جلوس فقالوا حين أبصروه مرحبا بمُحَمَّد النبي الأمي وإذا في النفر الجلوس شيخ فقال محمد، صلى الله عليه وسلم: من هذا؟ قال: أبوك ابراهيم، ثم سأله فقال: من هذا؟ قال: موسى، ثم سأله من هذا قال: هذا عيسى ابن مريم، ثم اقيمت الصلاة فتدافعوا حتى قدّموا مُحَمَّدا، صلى الله عليه وسلم،...إلخ]؛

Ali bin Sa'eed ar-Rāzi narrated to us he said al-Ḥussein bin Esa bin Maysara ar-Rāzi narrated to us he said Hārun bin Mughira narrated to us he said 'Anbasa ibn Sa'eed narrated to us from Ibn Abi Layla from his brother Esa from his brother Abdar-Raḥman ibn Abi Layla that Jibreel came to the Prophet (peace be upon him) with *al-Burāq* carrying him along making him walk [quoting the *ḥadith* until he said] Until he came to *Bait al-Maqdis* where there happened to be a gathering and they said welcome Muḥammad the unlettered. So he greeted the gathering and a man said: Muḥammad peace be upon him, who is this? Your father Ibrāhim; then he asked and said who is this? He said Musa. Then he asked and said who is this? He replied: Jesus son of Mary. Then the time of prayer came, so they moved one another until they let Muḥammad (peace be upon him) lead the prayer, etc.

[13] Ṭabarāni, *Mu'jam al-Kabir*, Vol. 10 sec. 70, no. 9,976
[14] Ṭabarāni, *Musnad ash-Shāmiayn*, Vol. 1 sec. 196, no. 341
[15] *Musnad* Abu Ya'la Vol. 8 sec. 451, no. 5,036
[16] *Musnad* Vol. 1 sec. 267, no. 22

I would submit that Ibn Abi Layla is Muḥammad bin Abdar-Raḥman bin Abi Layla has weakness of memory; it is with this, *mursal*. In *az-Zawā'id* 'the report of aṭ-Ṭabarāni in *al-Awsaṭ* is *mursal.* We don't know of this report except from this *isnād* by Ibn Abi Layla with *irsāl* in it; Muḥammad bin Abdar-Raḥman bin Abi Layla and he is *ḍaef* (weak).' However, as it appears in *Fatḥ al-Bāri Sharḥ Ṣaḥīḥ al-Bukhāri*, an alternate channel is mentioned: 'and in the *ḥadith* of Abi Amāma when in aṭ-Ṭabarāni in *al-Awsaṭ* then he mentioned prayer until the coming of Muḥammad.' It also appears in *ad-Dar al-Manshoor* of Imām Suyuṭi, he writes: 'And as reported by aṭ-Ṭabarāni in *al-Awsaṭ*, Ibn Mardawayh from the channel of Muḥammad bin Abdar-Raḥman bin Abi Layla from his brother Esa from his father Abdar-Raḥman from his father Abi Layla that Jibreel...' Perhaps it is connected (*mawṣul*) via Ibn Mardawayh and Allah knows best.

On a final note to conclude this matter, the Arabs of Najd and Ḥijāz, who were mostly Adnāni, they were upon the law of Ismā'il albeit with many distortions prior to the advent of the Prophet (peace be upon him). With the advent of the new law which he (peace be upon him) brought, that which was being followed by the Arabs was repealed one by one. For example, a girl being owned by her father and married off, this was repealed; the idea that women were not allowed to inherit, was repealed and many more like this. It is noteworthy that many of the great Imām's of *fiqh* missed these points.

4 'If my companion Moses was alive, he would be following me'

The Prophet (peace be upon him) said: '*If Musa were alive among you today, then if you followed him and left me, you would have gone astray.*' Several narrations have been reported to establish this. Abdullah ibn Thābit and others have narrated that Umar once came to the Prophet (peace be upon him) and said:

يا رسول الله إني مررت بأخ لي من قريظة فكتب لي جوامع من التوراة بالعربية، لنزداد به علما الى علمنا، أحب أن أعرضها عليك، فتغير وجه رسول الله، صلى الله عليه وسلم، وغضب حتى احمرت عيناه، قال: فقلت لعمر: مسخ الله عقلك! أما ترى ما بوجه رسول الله، صلى الله عليه وسلم؟!، وقال أبو بكر: ثكلتك الثواكل! ما ترى بوجه رسول الله، صلى الله عليه وسلم،؟!، وقالت الأنصار: يا معشر الأنصار السلاح السلاح، غضب نبيكم، صلى الله عليه وسلم)، فجاءوا حتى أحدقوا بمنبر رسول الله، صلى الله عليه وسلم، فقال عمر: رضيت بالله ربا وبالإسلام دينا وبمُحَمَّد، صلى الله عليه وسلم، [رسولاً] نبيا، قال: فسري عنه، ثم قال: أمتهوّكون فيها يا بن الخطاب، والذي نفسي بيده، إني أوتيت جوامع الكلم وخواتمه، واختصر لي الحديث اختصارا، ولقد جئتكم بها بيضاء نقية، فلا تهوّكوا، ولا يغرنكم المتهوّكون! لا تسألوا أهل الكتاب عن شيء فإنهم لن يهدوكم وقد ضلوا،

فإنكم إما أن تُصدقوا بباطل، أو تُكذبوا بحق، والذي نفسي بيده لو أصبح موسى فيكم حيا اليوم فاتبعتموه وتركتموني لضللتم عن سواء السبيل ضلالاً بعيداً، والذي نفسي بيده لو أن موسى، صلى الله عليه وسلم، كان حيا ما وسعه إلا أن يتبعني، إني حظكم من النبيين، وأنتم حظي من الأمم، ثم نزل عن المنبر

O Messenger of Allah, I have passed by a fellow brother of mine from the people of Quraytha. He wrote short rich expressions for me from the Torah in Arabic, so that we can learn more knowledge to ours. I would like to show them to you. Thereupon, the Messenger's face changed and he became so angry that his eyes were red. He (the narrator) said I then said to 'Umar: 'may Allah distort your mind! Cannot you see what has occurred to the face of the Messenger of Allah?' and Abu Bakr said: 'May the bereft be bereaved of you! Can't you see what has occurred to the face of the Messenger of Allah? And the Al-Anṣār said: 'O people of the Anṣār, you must get ready with your weapons at once, for your Prophet (peace be upon him) is angry.' Thereupon, they came all over until they surrounded the pulpit of the Messenger of Allah (peace be upon him). Then Umar said: I am pleased with Allah as My Lord, with Islam as my religion and with Muḥammad (peace be upon him) as a Messenger and a Prophet.

He (the narrator) said he then cheered up, and then he said: *O the son of al-Khaṭṭāb are you confused about it? By the one in whose hand is my life, I have been given pithy expressions and their seals, speech has been abbreviated for me and I have brought it to you pure and sound. Therefore, do not be confused, and do not be deceived by the confused! Do not ask people of the book about anything, for they will never guide you while they have gone astray. Thus, either you would believe in falsehood or belie a truth. By the one in whom my soul rests, if Musa (peace be upon him) was alive, he could not do anything but follow me. I am your share of the Prophets, and you are my share of the nations.*' Then he got down from the pulpit.

The authenticity of this long *ḥadith* is established.[1] Statements like '*Do not ask the people of the book about anything*' and '*Neither believe nor belie what the people of the book report to you,*' have been established from other transmissions on the authority of Ibn Mas'ud and other companions.[2] One of these versions was reported on the authority of Abu Namla al-Anṣāri, as collected in *Ṣaḥīḥ* Ibn Ḥibbān:

أخبرنا بن قتيبة قال: حدثنا حرملة قال: حدثنا بن وهب قال: أخبرنا يونس عن بن شهاب أن نملة بن أبي نملة الأنصاري حدثه أن أبا نملة أخبره أنه بينما هو جالس عند رسول الله، صلى الله عليه وسلم، جاء رجل من اليهود فقال: هل تكلم هذه الجنازة؟ فقال رسول الله، صلى الله عليه وسلم: الله أعلم، فقال اليهودي: أنا أشهد أنها تتكلم، فقال رسول الله صلى الله عليه وسلم: ما حدثكم أهل الكتاب فلا تصدقوهم ولا تكذبوهم وقولوا آمنا بالله وملائكته وكتبه ورسله: فإن كان حقا لم تكذّبوهم، وإن كان باطلا لم تصدّقوهم، وقال: قاتل الله اليهود، لقد أوتوا علماً

Ibn Qutayba reported to us he said Ḥarmala narrated to us he said Ibn Wahb narrated to us he said Yunus reportd to us from Ibn Shihāb that Namla bin Abi Namla al-Anṣāri narrated to him that his father Abu Namla narrated to him that when he was sitting with the Messenger of Allah (peace be upon him) and a Jew was also with him, a funeral passed by him. He asked - Muḥammad, does this funeral speak? The Prophet (peace be upon him) said: *Allah knows best.* The Jew said: I bear witness it speaks. The Messenger of Allah (peace be upon him) said: *Whatever the people of the book tell you, do not verify them, nor falsify them, but say: We believe in Allah and His Messenger. If it is false, do not confirm it and if it is right, do not falsify it.*

[1] The Arabic edition contains an appendix with the full discussion of the channels of reporting for this *ḥadith*. For the sake of brevity here, it is reported in *Musnad's* of Aḥmad, al-Bazzār, Abu Ya'la and others.

[2] Ibid.

Shaykh Shu'ayb al-Arnā'uṭ said the *isnād* is strong. It is also reported quite widely such as by Abu Dāwud in his *Sunan,*[3] *Musnad* Aḥmad,[4] Ibn Abi 'Aāsim 'Amr ash-Shaybāni in *al-Aḥād wal Mathāni,*[5] by Abdar-Razzāq in his *Muṣṣanaf;*[6] aṭ-Ṭabarāni has it in *Mu'jam al-Kabir,*[7] Bayhaqy in his *Sunan al-Kubra*[8] and in other places with several chains of transmission. In the *Mustadrak a'la Ṣaḥīḥayn* of Al-Ḥākim we also have:

> أخبرناه أبو الفضل الفقيه حدثنا عثمان بن سعيد الدارمي أخبرنا عبد الله بن عبد الجبار بحمص حدثنا الحارث بن عبيدة حدثنا الزهري عن سالم عن أبيه عن عامر بن ربيعة قال: كنا مع رسول الله، صلى الله عليه وسلم، فمر بجنازة فقال رجل من اليهود: (يا مُحَمَّد تكلم هذه الجنازة؟!)، فسكت رسول الله، صلى الله عليه وسلم، فقال اليهودي: (أنا أشهد أنها تكلم)، فقال رسول الله، صلى الله عليه وسلم: إذا حدثكم أهل الكتاب حديثا فقولوا آمنا بالله وملائكته وكتبه ورسله

> Abu Faḍl al-Faqihi he reported it to us Uthmān bin Sa'eed ad-Dārimi narrated to us Abdullah bin Abdal-Jabbār reported to us in Himṣ, al-Ḥārith bin 'Ubaida narrated to us az-Zuhri narrated to us from Sālim from his father from 'Aāmir bin Rabi'a who said: We were once with the Messenger of Allah (peace be upon him) and then he passed by a funeral. Thereupon a Jew said - O Muhammad, can this funeral (i.e., deceased) speak? The Messenger of Allah (peace be upon him) was silent. Then the Jew said: I bear witness that it can speak. Thereupon the Messenger of Allah (peace be upon him) said: *When people of the book convey any report to you, you should say - we believe in Allah, His Angels, His Books and His Messengers.*

---

[3] *Sunan* Abu Dāwud Vol. 3 sec. 318, no. 3,644
[4] *Musnad* Aḥmad Vol. 4 sec. 136, no. 17,264
[5] *al-Aḥād wal Mathāni* Vol. 4 sec. 142, no. 2,121
[6] *Muṣannaf* Abdar-Razzāq Vol. 6 sec. 111, no. 10,160
[7] Ṭabarāni, *Mu'jam al-Kabir*, Vol. 22 sec. 350, no. 874 / 879
[8] Bayhaqy, *Sunan al-Kubra*, Vol. 2 sec. 10, no. 2,071

After narrating this Al-Ḥākim said: 'This *ḥadith* known from al-Ḥārith bin 'Ubaida ar-Rahāwi from az-Zuhri, we wrote it also in the copy of Yunus from Yazeed from az-Zuhri: Abul'-Qāsim Abdullah bin Mahdi narrated to us my uncle narrated to us a man narrated to us (whose name is Abul'-Qāsim bin Mabroor) Zayd bin Yunus narrated to us from Yazeed from az-Zuhri, he said: Sālim said – verily Abdullah ibn Umar said: 'when at the funeral of Rāfi' bin Khadeej…' then he mentioned the rest of the *ḥadith.* Despite this, I would say that al-Ḥārith bin 'Ubaida ar-Rahāwi is not strong in this narration and is most probably fallen as a narrator. Aṭ-Ṭabarāni records an *isnād* for this in the *Musnad ash-Shāmiayn*: 'Uthmān bin Khālid bin Umar as-Salafi narrated to us Abdal-Jabbār al-Khabā'iri narrated to us al-Ḥārith bin 'Ubaida narrated to us Baqia bin al-Waleed narrated to us from Zubaydi from az-Zuhri from Sālim bin Umar from 'Aāmir bin Rabi'a about it.

The *isnād* contained within *Ma'rifa aṣ-Ṣaḥābah* of Abu Nu'aym al-Aṣbahāni states: Abu Isḥāq bin Ḥamza narrated to us Aḥmad bin Khālid Umar as-Salafi narrated to us his father narrated to us Ḥārith bin 'Ubaida narrated to me az-Zubaydi narrated to us from az-Zuhri from Sālim ibn Abdullah from his father from 'Aāmir bin Rabi'a, about it. As for the wording: '*report from Bani Israel and there is no harm / objection'* which has often been misunderstood, it has been reported on the authority of many companions with the best chain of transmissions. One of them is what has been reported on the authority of Abdullah ibn 'Amr ibn al-'Aāṣ in the following authentic channel as recorded by Imām Aḥmad in his *Musnad*:

حدثنا أبو المغيرة حدثنا الأوزاعي حدثني حسان بن عطية قال: أقبل أبو كبشة السلولي ونحن في المسجد فقام إليه مكحول وابن أبي زكريا وأبو بحرية فقال: سمعت عبد الله بن عمرو يقول: سمعت رسول الله، صلى الله عليه وسلم، يقول: بلّغوا عني ولو آية، وحدّثوا عن بني إسرائيل ولا حرج، ومن كذب على متعمدا فليتبوأ مقعده من النار

Abul-Mughira al-Awzā'i narrated to us Ḥassān bin 'Aṭiya narrated to me he said Abu Kabsha as-Saluli accepted and we were in the *masjid* and stood to him. Makḥoul and Ibn Abi Zakariyā and Abu Baḥriya (were there) so he said: I heard Abdullah ibn 'Amr say – I heard the Messenger of Allah (peace be upon him) say: *Convey (my teachings) from me to the people even if it were a verse and tell others the stories of Bani Israel, for it is not sinful to do so. And whoever tells a lie about me intentionally, will surely take his place in the (Hell) Fire.*

Without question the *ḥadith* is authentic and has a consecutive succession of transmitters concurring upon its report, from one another (*musalsal*). Imām Aḥmad records it also from other authentic channels, as have many other collectors amongst them Bukhāri, Ibn Ḥibbān, ad-Dārimi, aṭ-Ṭabarāni, Ḥumaydi and others. We also have similar from Abu Sa'eed al-Khudri as it appears in *Sunan al-Kubra*:

أنبأ الفضل بن العباس بن إبراهيم قال: حدثنا عفان قال: حدثنا همام قال: حدثنا زيد بن أسلم عن عطاء بن يسار عن أبي سعيد الخدري عن النبي، صلى الله عليه وسلم، قال: حدّثوا عن بني إسرائيل ولا حرج، وحدّثوا عني ولا تكذبوا عليّ

al-Faḍl al-'Abbās bin Ibrāhim reports, he said 'Affān narrated to us he said Hammām narrated to us he said Zayd bin Aslam narrated to us from 'Aṭā bin Yassār from Abu Sa'eed al-Khudri from the Prophet (peace be upon him) who said: *Report about Bani Israel and there is no objection and report from me but never attribute lies to me.*

The *ḥadith* is very authentic, it is also found in the *Musnad* of Imām Aḥmad from other authentic channels. Abu Dāwud has collected similarly in his *Sunan* with a good *isnād* according to the conditions of Imām Muslim:

> حدثنا أبو بكر بن أبي شيبة حدثنا علي بن مسهر عن محمد بن عمرو عن أبي سلمة عن أبي هريرة قال: قال رسول الله، صلى الله عليه وسلم: حدثوا عن بني إسرائيل ولا حرج
>
> Abu Bakr ibn Abi Shayba narrated to us Ali bin Mushir narrated to us from Muḥammad bin Umar from Abi Salama from Abu Hurayrah who said: the Messenger of Allah (peace be upon him) said: *Relate traditions from Bani Israel there is no harm in it.*

The same is also reported by Imām Aḥmad in his *Musnad,*[9] in the *Musnad* of Ḥumaydi,[10] in the *Muṣṣannaf* of Abu Bakr ibn Abi Shayba,[11] and many others. In addition to this, similar has been reported from Jābir ibn Abdullah, as it appears in the *Musnad* of 'Abd ibn Ḥameed:

> حدثني بن أبي شيبة حدثنا وكيع عن الربيع بن سعد عن بن سابط عن جابر قال: قال رسول الله، صلى الله عليه وسلم: تحدثوا عن بني إسرائيل فإنه كانت فيهم الأعاجيب، ثم أنشأ يحدث قال: «خرجت طائفة منهم فأتوا مقبرة من مقابرهم فقالوا: لو صلينا ركعتين فدعونا الله عز وجل يخرج لنا بعض الأموات يخبرنا عن الموت، قال: ففعلوا، فبينا هم كذلك إذ طلع رجل رأسه من قبر، بين عينيه أثر السجود فقال: يا هؤلاء ما أردتم إلي؟! فوالله لقد مت منذ مائة سنة فما سكنت عني حرارة الموت حتى كان الآن فادعوا الله أن يعيدني كما كنت
>
> Ibn Abi Shayba narrated to me Waki' narrated to us from ar-Rabia' bin Sa'eed from ibn Sābiṭ from Jābir who said that the Messenger of Allah (peace be upon him) said: *Narrate about Bani Israel for there used to be wonders about them.* Thereafter he narrated the following: *A group of them went out to one of their cemeteries. Then they said - Let us perform two*

[9] *Musnad* Aḥmad Vol. 2 sec. 474, no. 10,134 & Vol. 2 sec. 502, no. 10,536
[10] *Musnad* Ḥumaydi Vol. 2 sec. 292, no. 1,165
[11] *Muṣṣannaf* ibn Abi Shayba Vol. 5 sec. 318, no. 26,485

> *rak'ahs and then supplicate to Allah the exalted to resurrect some of the dead people to tell us about death. They did so, and during their performance, the head of a man rose out of a grave. Between his eyes there was the trace of prostration. Thereupon he said - O you people, what do you want from me? For by Allah, I have died a hundred years ago and the heat (pain) of death has not cooled down upon me until now. So please supplicate Allah to return me to my previous state.*

The same also appears in the *Muṣṣanaf* of Abu Bakr ibn Abi Shayba, albeit abridged without the mention of this additional story.[12] The longer version is also found in *Fawā'id Tamām* from an alternate channel to that of Ibn Abi Shayba,[13] and also at the end of *Tārikh Baghdād* from different channels to both of these.[14] Concerning the *isnād* from the *Musnad* of 'Abd ibn Ḥumayd it is authentic and its narrators are the men of *Ṣaḥīḥ* except for what has been said in relation to ar-Rabia' bin Sa'eed al-Jufi; the majority view is that he is not, however he is *thiqa* for those who have known him, such as Yaḥya ibn Ma'een (in *Tārikh ibn Ma'een Riwaya ad-Douri*), Ya'qub bin Sufyān (*Marifa wa-Tārikh*) and Ibn Ḥibbān. Abu Ḥātim said that there is nothing wrong with him (*lā bā'sa bihi)*. As for the *mutā'akhireen* al-Haythami was candid and Ibn Kathir inclusively. As for adh-Dhahabi and al-Ḥāfiz saying he was unknown (*majhoul*) this is detailed elsewhere.[15]

Much confusion surrounds the issue of how these *aḥādith* are to be understood as well as that about the precise status of the reports which come from Bani Israel. Many of the previous Imām's provided very useful comments on this subject, which we will consider in detail. On this subject al-Ḥāfiz's comments are instructive. Writing in *Fatḥ al-Bāri* he said:

---

[12] *Muṣṣannaf* ibn Abi Shayba Vol. 5 sec. 318, no. 26,486
[13] *Fawā'id Tamām* of Tamām bin Muḥammad ad-Dimishqi Vol. 1 pp. 217/218
[14] *Tārikh Baghdād* Vol. 1 sec. 129
[15] The appendix to the Arabic edition discusses this in further detail

It is clear that the undesirability of this deed is one of disapproval not prohibition. It is better in this matter to differentiate between the person who has not become well grounded in knowledge and firm in belief, as it is not allowed for such person to study anything of the knowledge of the people of the book. On the other hand, the one who possesses firm knowledge and belief is allowed, especially in terms of responding to opposing ideas. This has been proved by the reference of previous and modern Imām's to the Torah in order to make the Jews believe in Muḥammad (peace be upon him). If they had not been convinced of the permissibility to study previous creeds and laws they would not have done so.

As for the inferred prohibition, due to the signs of anger appearing and the allegation that if it had not been a sin, he would not have been angry about it, we say that he could be angry about an undesirable deed or by committing the less worthier, if it has occurred from someone for whom it was not proper to do so. For example, he (peace be upon him) was angry with Mu'ādh for making the dawn prayer longer by reading (a longer chapter of Qur'ān). He could also be angry with someone who failed to understand clear matters, just like the one who asked about finding stray camels. This has been mentioned in the book of knowledge, concerning anger in exhortation and also in the book of good manners, concerning what is permissible while being angry.

Additionally in another place and concerning the same subject he writes:

The Prophet's statement '*and report about Bani Israel and there is no objection*', i.e. there is no trouble at all for you in reporting from them, for he (peace be upon him) had previously prevented Muslims from learning from them and studying their books. After that the matter became more flexible, as if the prohibition occurred before the stability of Islamic Judgments and religious principles for fear of the occurrence of affliction. Therefore, when this danger disappeared permission was given concerning listening to stories from Jews and Christians, so that Muslims may learn lessons. It has also been said that the meaning of the Arabic word *'Lā Ḥaraj'* is that there should not be any trace of anger in your heart due to what you hear from them as wonders, for that used to happen to them many times. Another interpretation is that there is no objection in not reporting from them, for the first statement *'Report'* is an imperative, which entails an obligation. Therefore, he meant to convey something other than an obligation and that it is the permission by saying that there is no objection; i.e. there is no objection in leaving reporting from them. Another interpretation of the statement is that the narrator of such reports should not feel annoyed due to what is often found in their stories as offensive words, like their statement – 'Go you and your Lord and fight you two,' and their statement – 'Make a god for us.' Another interpretation of the statement is that it concerns Bani Israel itself and the (personage) of Ya'qub (peace be upon him). Therefore what is meant is report from them, concerning their story with their brother Yusuf (Joseph), but this is the most unlikely view.

According to Mālik, it is permissible to report from them what is known to be good. As for what is known to be false, it is impermissible to be reported. Another interpretation is, 'Report from them concerning what came in the Glorious Qur'ān and the authentic *ḥadith*.' A third one is the permission to report from them in any way of reporting whether through continuance or discontinuance of narrators, due to the impossibility of continuity in reporting from them. On the contrary, the basis of reporting Islamic Judgments is continuity, but that is possible due to recentness of time.

According to ash-Shāfi'i, it is a well-known fact that the Prophet (peace be upon him) did not allow telling lies. Therefore the statement means report from Bani Israel

> concerning what you do not know to be falsehood. As for what you permit, you have no objection to report it of them. This is equivalent to his statement, '*When people of the book report to you, do not believe or belie them.*' However, no permission or prohibition has been stated about reporting what is absolutely true.

May Allah have mercy upon al-Ḥāfiz. He has mixed this matter up. The judgment of the three different issues has been confusing for him and for many other scholars, but he made them one matter. In actuality, the matter can be explained as follows:

First issue: asking people of the Book

Asking the people of the book or other disbelievers about something concerning 'religion' in order to seek knowledge and guidance (note Umar's statement – 'So that we can learn more knowledge to ours.') this is an absolutely prohibited matter, without any doubt. He (peace be upon him) became so angry that his eyes became red due to Umar's act, until Abdullah bin Thābit said: 'May Allah distort your mind! Can't you see what has occurred to the face of the Messenger of Allah?' and Abu Bakr shouted 'May the bereft be bereaved of you! Can't you see what has occurred to the face of the Messenger of Allah?' The Anṣār even summoned each other to prepare their weapons. This cannot happen except if it is considered a great matter. The Prophet (peace be upon him) justified asking the people of the book or disbelievers about matters in their religion in several things different in rank according to their importance.

The reason is that whatever the people of the book possess as books and stories have been distorted. Many words have been changed or even added. Therefore truth and falsehood are mixed in them to the extent that it is impossible to differentiate assuredly between its parts at all. These books are even incomplete due to the deliberate deletion or loss of some sections. So what they have in their hands is dark and impure. It cannot be considered as an authority or source of evidence. On the other hand, that which Muḥammad (peace be upon him) brought is forever luminous, pure, conclusive and adequate. One should take note of his statement – *'I have been given pithy expressions and their seals, speech has been abbreviated for me and I have brought it to you pure and sound.'* Allah the exalted has guaranteed its preservation, in the sense that it will remain pure until the day of judgement. It is definitely an authority, which can be used as evidence. Therefore how can an intelligent person who is seeking the truth leave the pure source and turn to what is mixed with impurity? It is true that the person who has not found except the impure, can be excused if he drinks from it being obliged to do so, like the state of the believers in the previous books before Muḥammad's mission (peace be upon him), but never after his mission.

Secondly, we have previously mentioned that the previous divine books have been distorted by people of the book and parts of them have been lost. Transgression and hypocrisy spread among their rabbis, clergymen and monks who displaced true right words from their places and they 'interpreted' their books in astounding ways. They also make the books into paper sheets, disclosing some of it and concealing much. They kept it in dead languages, which the majority of people do not know, in order to monopolise its interpretation and have a dominant influence over the common people with its knowledge; it was used to flatter rulers and devour people's property with falsehood. Due to all these reasons, they are far astray from the true guidance. Whoever is misguided, it will not be wise to expect from him to guide others and it is impermissible to trust his legal opinions or even consider his suggestions. As for the knowledge of 'religion' it must be learned only from guided righteous people and not from those who have gone astray, as the Prophet (peace be upon him) explained '*For they will never guide you while they have gone astray.*'

Thirdly, there is another serious point to be considered: if we assume that the previous books were preserved word-by-word and sound-by-sound, like the preservation of the Qur'ān and if we assume that those who knew them like clergymen, rabbis and monks were trustworthy and did not displace words from its correct places and did not conceal anything that Allah has revealed, and that they convey about Allah, without fearing anyone but Allah, that they are really the heirs of the Prophets, they would not still be considered as a source of guidance any longer. This is because *all* of these books have been abrogated from beginning to end, whether they were big or small. If Musa (peace be upon him), who is one of the greatest of the previous Messengers of Allah and the one with much legislation, was revived today, he would be obliged to follow Prophet Muḥammad (peace be upon him) unreservedly. Musa (peace be upon him) is the Messenger of Allah. He was an infallible Prophet who is not allowed to disobey Allah in any of his previous revealed orders and prohibitions. It is known by necessity that all that which is revealed to him is abrogated the moment Muḥammad (peace be upon him) was sent. If the people followed Musa and left Muḥammad, they would have been misguided; they will be disbelievers. The moment these verses were revealed, all previous creeds were abrogated:

اقْرَأْ بِاسْمِ رَبِّكَ الَّذِي خَلَقَ ، خَلَقَ الْإِنسَانَ مِنْ عَلَقٍ

Read in the name of your Lord who created; created man from a clot.[16]

قُلْ يَا أَيُّهَا النَّاسُ إِنِّي رَسُولُ اللَّهِ إِلَيْكُمْ جَمِيعًا

Say: O people! Surely I am the Messenger of Allah to you all.[17]

Things thus revert back to the state when Allah said to Adam and his wife:

[16] *Qur'an* 96: 1/2
[17] *Qur'ān* 7: 158

وَلَا تَقْرَبَا هَذِهِ الشَّجَرَةَ

Do not go near this tree.[18]

Things went back to there state even before this order came to them. Neither were there any prescribed prayers, charity or fasting. There were no orders till this one came, this means that the law of previous nations and Prophets is not our law, as we have previously proven with supporting evidences. Some scholars contradicted this saying but this is a grievous error on their behalf. We ask Allah to forgive them and we seek refuge with Allah from such erring.

When al-Ḥāfiz Ibn Ḥajar considered the strong anger of the Prophet (peace be upon him) as just dislike (of a matter), it was strange. It is one of the faults of scholars. We seek refuge with Allah from such evils. What is stranger than that is Ibn Ḥajar's comparison drawn from the incident of the Prophet's reproaching Mu'ādh for prolonging the prayer. It would have been better if he considered prolonging the prayer by the Imām as a prohibited act - which is the truth - instead of making the case an easy one. Verily, when the Prophet (peace be upon him) was angry with the man asking about the lost camels, the preferable opinion is that he felt in the man's question an attempt to make lawful talking or riding them. It is very clear in the wordings of the *ḥadith*. He was not very angry because of the question, but he was angry with the evil intentions of the man. It was an evil forbidden intention whose owner deserved dispraise, reproach and scolding.

Second issue: People of the book reporting about 'religion'

The second issue is different from the first case and is its opposite. It

---

[18] *Qur'ān* 2: 35

is related to the people of the Book telling us about some matters of 'religion' like those of the unseen, of the day of judgement and of the attributes and names of Allah. It is when they tell us voluntarily without our asking them, for asking them about such matters is prohibited as we said before. In such cases proper rationality dictates to reject any statement that is not supported by requisite proof. Even if these statements were based on their books and deduced from their texts, nothing could be done but examine them carefully because their texts were not certain and their truthfulness were not proven from the outset. This is what we call the 'reasonable cognitive approach'. Judging any matter rightfully while it has not been proven yet is to abstain from accepting or rejecting it. Then the Islamic law came imposing this same sound 'cognitive' approach on all Muslims and became the binding law. Otherwise this would mean believing in falsehood, which is prohibited. It can lead to foolishness, disbelief, going astray and even belying what is true. The same approach is applied with those who have already disobeyed Allah and His Messenger and dared to ask them. The sin of asking them at the beginning, does not justify sinning again, by belying or believing them without proof. This is our proper response to their telling us about any matters of 'religion', whether they said it voluntarily or were answering one of our questions.

Third issue: Narrating stories about the people of the book

Lastly we turn the issue of narrating about the people of the book or relating stories from their own long history, be that of wars, afflictions, their rise and fall; the good and evil rulers which presided over them as well the stark contrast between their truthful and perverted scholars. All of this is to draw wisdom, learn lessons, study the history of nations and society, particularly as it relates to the people of Israel as they were at one juncture, carriers of a divine message. From this vantage point it is worthwhile to study their books so as to filter contradictions and to clarify ambiguities. It would be even better if this examination was supported by studying their monuments and ruins and what other historians have said about them and all the other methodologies of research. It is known for sure – as we have said before - that it is not permissible to accept their narrations and take them for granted. They must be subjected to careful scrutiny. If anything is proven from this, it would be permissible to discuss it, so as to learn important lesson about the pitfalls which they fell into.

There have been some inaccurate interpretations over the ages in relation to the aforementioned *aḥādith.* When great scholarly figures like Ibn Ḥajar err, it can cause the matter to become confused in many other minds. We cannot now find a Muslim who asks the people of the book, seeking guidance but everyone now seeks it from the books of philosophers. Those are worse than the people of the book and they are the farthest from guidance and inspiration. People think that such books are but the product of reasonable research, neglecting the Qur'ān and *Sunnah.* These books are not better than those of the people of Israel because they are full of imaginary, hypothetical assertions and fantastical points. Believing in stories relayed from the people of the book and taking them for granted has become widespread, particularly in the field of *Tafsir.* Some people even tried to interpret the verses of the Qur'ān in a way that agrees with these fables. Praise be to Allah for that is a great injustice done to Islam.

On the other hand, objective research aimed at refuting their books substantively decreased across Islamic history. Imām Abu Muḥammad Ali ibn Ḥazm from Andalusia arguably made the first research study in the history of humanity, dealing with the books of Christians and Jews with the groundbreaking work of *al-Fiṣal bayn al-Milal wa'an-Niḥal.*[19] Unfortunately the majority of Muslim scholarship did not follow his lead but neglected the subject altogether, except that is for Imām Ibn Taymiyya who provided a useful contribution with the work entitled *al-Jawāb aṣ-Ṣaḥīḥ li man Baddala*

[19] The work is usually rendered (loosely) into English as: *'The Separator Concerning Religions, Heresies and Sects.'*

Deen al-Masiḥ.[20] Other efforts in this field regretfully fall too far short of even these works. There is neither might nor power, save in Allah.

What has been mentioned thus far is established as truth with evidences. It is not correct to argue that it is a new matter that has been introduced without legal precedent (*bidāh'*). Notable personalities have held the same position. In *al-Jāmi aṣ-Ṣaḥīḥ al-Mukhtaṣr* Imām Bukhāri recorded the following on the authority of Ibn 'Abbās

حدثنا علي بن عبد الله حدثنا حاتم بن وردان حدثنا أيوب عن عكرمة عن بن عباس رضي الله عنهما قال: كيف تسألون أهل الكتاب عن كتبهم وعندكم كتاب الله أقرب الكتب عهدا بالله، تقرؤونه محضا لم يُشَبْ؟

Ali bin Abdullah narrated to us Ḥātim bin Wardān narrated to us Ayub narrated to us from 'Ikrima from Ibn 'Abbās, he said: How can you ask the people of the scriptures about their books while you have Allah's book (the Qur'ān) which is the most recent of the books revealed by Allah and you read it in its pure undistorted form?

Bukhāri also recorded another tradition again from Ibn 'Abbās with slightly different wording and reported via 'Ubaidallah bin Abdullah:

حدثنا موسى بن إسماعيل حدثنا إبراهيم أخبرنا بن شهاب عن عبيد الله بن عبد الله أن بن عباس قال: كيف تسألون أهل الكتاب عن شيء، وكتابكم الذي أنزل على رسول الله أحدث وفي رواية: أحدث الأخبار بالله؛ تقرؤونه محضا لم يُشَبْ؛ وقد حدّثكم أن أهل الكتاب بدّلوا كتاب الله وغيّروه، وكتبوا بأيديهم الكتاب وقالوا: هو من عند الله ليشتروا به ثمنا قليلا؛ ألا ينهاكم ما جاءكم من العلم عن مسألتهم؟! لا والله ما رأينا منهم رجلا يسألكم عن الذي أنزل عليكم!

---

[20] Again, the work is usually rendered, however loosely, into English as - '*The correct response to those who have corrupted the religion of the Messiah.*'

> Musa bin Ismā'il narrated to us Ibrāhim narrated to us Ibn Shihāb reported to us from 'Ubaidallah that Ibn 'Abbās said: Why do you ask the people of the scripture about anything while your book (Qur'ān) which has been revealed to Allah's Messenger (peace be upon him) is newer and the latest? You read it pure, undistorted and unchanged, and Allah has told you that the people of the scripture (Jews and Christians) changed their scripture and distorted it and wrote the scripture with their own hands and said, 'It is from Allah,' to sell it for a little gain. Does not the knowledge which has come to you prevent you from asking them about anything? No, by Allah, we have never seen any man from them asking you regarding what has been revealed to you!

Imām Bukhāri has similar reports also collected within his *Ṣaḥīḥ* on this.[21] Others have reported similarly, such as al-Ḥākim in the *Mustadrak*[22] and Bayhaqy in *Sunan al-Kubra.*[23] Overall these traditions provide some additional clarity to this matter of querying matters of religion with the people of the book.

---

[21] Bukhāri Vol. 2 sec. 954, no. 2,539 & Vol. 6 sec. 2,736 no. 7,085
[22] *Mustadrak* Vol. 2 sec. 289, no. 3,041
[23] *Sunan al-Kubra* Vol. 8 sec. 249, no. 16,904 & Vol. 10 sec. 163, no. 20,400

5 Prohibition relating to excessive questioning

There is a misconception which is held in many quarters, that during the time of revelation the Prophet (peace be upon him) was being inundated with questions regarding matters of law by his companions. Rather the opposite is the case. It is noteworthy to consider this point in substantive detail as it forms a prelude to a wider and far-reaching principle of law that is very often overlooked. Allah and His Messenger (peace be upon him) stressed the prohibition of asking too many questions. There is no difference here between the question posed by the man - 'Who is my father?' and the question of the foolish Bedouin about *Ḥajj*, asking whether it should be performed annually. This matter has been established by way of absolute proof as demonstrated by the following verse and accompanying *aḥādith* which we will examine in detail in this section. Allah unequivocally stated:

يَا أَيُّهَا الَّذِينَ آمَنُوا لَا تَسْأَلُوا عَنْ أَشْيَاءَ إِن تُبْدَ لَكُمْ تَسُؤْكُمْ وَإِن تَسْأَلُوا عَنْهَا حِينَ يُنَزَّلُ
الْقُرْآنُ تُبْدَ لَكُمْ عَفَا اللَّهُ عَنْهَا وَاللَّهُ غَفُورٌ حَلِيمٌ

O you who believe! Do not ask questions about things which if declared to you may trouble you, and if you ask about them when the Qur'ān is being revealed, they shall be declared to you; Allah pardons this, and Allah is forgiving, forbearing.[1]

To further clarify the status of this verse, it is important to consider the various points raised by the classical scholars of *Tafsir*. Writing in his *Tafsir* Imām aṭ-Ṭabari said:

> Concerning the interpretation of the verse, it means, O you who believe! Do not ask about matters which if disclosed to you may distress you. And if you ask about them during the revelation of the Qur'ān, they will be disclosed to you. Allah passes over this, for Allah is most forgiving, most forbearing. It was revealed to the Messenger of Allah (peace be upon him) because of the questions that were asked to him by some people, sometimes (seeking to) examine him and sometimes to mock him. One said to him: 'Who is my father?' Another said when his camel was lost, 'Where is my camel?' and Abdullah bin Ḥudhayfah asked him about his father. That was why Allah addressed people commanding them not to ask about such matters. Allah is saying to them do not ask about things which if made plain to you, may cause you trouble. Many Companions of the Messenger of Allah (peace be upon him) interpreted the verse as such.

Following on from this, Imām aṭ-Ṭabari mentions ten narratives, most of which are authentic bearing the above meaning. Thereafter he states: 'Others said that this verse was revealed to the Messenger of Allah (peace be upon him) because of a question he was asked about *Ḥajj*.' Yet again he mentions several narrations which further establish this point, most of which are authentic. He then provides two narratives in relation to those who have said as much to support the following view: '....it was revealed because they asked the Messenger of Allah (peace be upon him) about *al-Baḥira*, *as-Sā'iba*, *al-Waṣeela*

[1] *Qur'ān* 5: 101

and *al-Ḥāmi.*'[2] Thereafter he says:

> The most correct amongst the sayings concerning this subject is the saying of those who said that it was revealed because of the many questioners who used to ask the Messenger of Allah (peace be upon him) about various matters, like the one (asked by) ibn Ḥudhayfah about his father; the one about *Ḥajj* and the like. All these narrations are reported by companions, successors and the majority of exegetes. The saying of Mujāhid on the authority of Ibn 'Abbās is not far from rightness; what was reported by the companions and successors disagreed with it and that is only why we do not prefer it. Still, this question about *al-Baḥira, as-Sā'iba, al-Waṣeela* and *al-Ḥāmi* could be among the questions the Prophet (peace be upon him) was asked and Allah hated; like for example, when He hated the question about *Ḥajj*; is it annually or just once and as He hated the question about the father of Abdullah ibn Ḥudhayfah.
>
> That was why the verse was revealed, placing a prohibition on people posing such questions. Each one of these questioners was as part of the reasoning for the revelation of this verse, including what concerned him and what concerned others. I think that this saying is the most valid one about the verse, as the sources of these different accounts mentioned are authentic, and it is more proper to know the most correct from these existing accounts than just to be existent while they are not correct.

Ibn Kathir argued along the same lines in his *Tafsir*, although he does provide some additional comments that are noteworthy:

> Allah the exalted forbade believers in this glorious verse to ask

[2] See *Qur'ān* chapter 5, verse 103

the Prophet (peace be upon him) too many questions about matters not yet revealed. That is to say, if you ask about details after its revelation, it will be revealed to you, but do not ask about the matter before its revelation, as it may become forbidden just because of this question. It was recorded in the *Ṣaḥīḥ* that Sa'd ibn Abi Waqqās (may Allah be pleased with him) narrated that the Prophet (peace be upon him) said: '*The most sinful person among the Muslims is the one who asked about something which had not been prohibited, but was prohibited because of his asking*.' When the Messenger of Allah (peace be upon him) was asked about the case of a man who found another man with his wife: if this man (i.e., the husband) talks, he will talk with a great matter, and if he keeps silent he will keep silent with the same.

The Messenger of Allah (peace be upon him) hated such questions and criticised them. After that, Allah revealed the ruling of *Li'ān*. In *Ṣaḥīḥ* Bukhāri and Muslim it is recorded that al-Mughira bin Shu'bah (may Allah be pleased with him) narrated that the Messenger of Allah (peace be upon him) used to forbid *Qeel* and *Qāl* (idle useless talk or talking too much about others), asking too many questions and wasting one's wealth extravagantly.

It was also recorded in *Ṣaḥīḥ* Muslim that Abu Hurayrah (may Allah be pleased with him) narrated that the Messenger of Allah (peace be upon him) said: *'Leave me what I have left to you. Verily, the people before you went to their doom because of putting too many questions to their Prophets and disagreeing with them. So avoid that which I forbid you to do and do that which I command you to do, to the best of your capacity*.' This was said by the Prophet (peace be upon him) after saying: *'O people! Allah has made Ḥajj obligatory for you; so perform Ḥajj*. Thereupon, a person said - O Messenger of Allah, (is it to be performed) every year? He (the Prophet) kept quiet, and he repeated this three-times thereafter the Messenger of Allah (peace be upon him) said: *'If I were to say yes it would have become obligatory (for you to perform it every year) and you would not be able to do it.'* Then he said, *'Leave me as I leave you.'* That was why Anas bin Mālik (may Allah be pleased with him) narrated: 'We were forbidden to ask anything (without the genuine need) from the Prophet (peace be upon him). It therefore pleased us that an intelligent person from the dwellers of the desert should come and ask him while we listen to it.' Regarding the same, al-Ḥāfiz Abu Ya'la al-Mawṣily mentioned in his *Musnad*: Abu Kareeb reported to us Isḥāq bin Sulaymān reported to us from Abi Sinān from Abi Isḥāq from al-Barā' bin Aā'zib who said: 'A whole year would pass while I want to ask the Messenger of Allah (peace be upon him) about a matter. But I was afraid from him and we used to wish that some Bedouin will come and ask him.'

Al-Bazzār said: Muḥammad bin al-Muthanna reported to us Ibn Fuḍeel reported to us from 'Aṭā bin as-Sā'ib from Sa'eed bin Jubayr from Ibn 'Abbās who said: I did not see a nation better than the Companions of Muḥammad (peace be upon him); they only asked him about twelve issues all of which are in the *Qur'ān: They ask you about the intoxicants and games of chance;*[3] *They ask you concerning the Sacred Month and fighting in it,*[4] *They ask you about the orphans.*[5] And others like them. Allah says: *Do you desire to question your Messenger as Musa was questioned previously?*[6] *'Do you'* here means that they really wanted to ask him, but it is a reproving interrogation for all: believers and *mushrikeen* (polytheists). Muḥammad (peace be upon him) is the Messenger of Allah to all. Allah also says: *The People of the Scripture ask of you that you should bring down to them a scripture from above; but they have indeed asked of Musa a bigger thing than that, when they said: show us Allah openly. Then rumbling overtook them for their wrongdoing.*[7]

---

[3] *Qur'ān* 2: 219
[4] *Qur'ān* 2: 217
[5] *Qur'ān* 2: 220
[6] *Qur'ān* 2: 108
[7] *Qur'ān* 4: 153

Explaining the occasion of the revelation - Muḥammad ibn Isḥāq said: Muḥammad bin Abi Muḥammad narrated to me from 'Ikrima or Sa'eed from Ibn 'Abbās who said: Rāfih' bin Ḥuraymila or Wahb bin Zayd said – (this means) O Muhammad! Bring a book to us from heaven that we can read. Gush forth to us rivers in order so that we would follow and believe you. Hence Allah revealed this verse. Abu Ja'far ar-Rāzi said from ar-Rabih' bin Anas from Abul'Aāliya concerning this verse (*Do you desire to question your Messenger as was questioned Musa in the past?*[8]), that a man said to the Prophet (peace be upon him), O Messenger of Allah! (I wish that) our expiations are like the expiations of Bani Israel! The Prophet (peace be upon him) said three-times: '*O Allah! We do not want to.*' Then he said '*What Allah gave you is better than what He had given Bani Israel. Whoever did a sin from among them found it written on his door with its expiation. If he expiated, it used to be disgrace during his lifetime and if he did not, it would be disgrace in his hereafter. Whatever Allah gave you is better than what He had given Bani Israel.*' Then he recited the following verse: *But whoever does evil or does injustice to his soul, then asks forgiveness of Allah, he will find Allah most forgiving, most rewarding.*[9]

The Prophet (peace be upon him) said: '*The five prayers and from one Friday prayer to the next, is an expiation (of the sins committed in between their intervals).*' Additionally ibn 'Abbās (may Allah be pleased with him) narrated that the Prophet (peace be upon him) said: '*If someone intends to do a bad deed and he does not do it, Allah will not write it (in his account) with Him. And if he does it (the bad deed), Allah will write one bad deed (in his account). And if he intends to do a good deed and he does not do it, Allah will write for him a full good deed (in his account with Him); and if he does it, Allah will write for him (in his account) with Him (a reward equal) from ten to seven hundred times, to many more times. Verily,*

---

[8] *Qur'ān* 2: 108
[9] *Qur'ān* 4: 110

> *Allah does not put to destruction anyone except he who is doomed to destruction.*' Then Allah revealed the verse (2:108).
>
> Mujāhid said that the occasion of revelation of this verse is that the Quraysh asked Muḥammad (peace be upon him) to turn the mountain of *Ṣāfa* into gold. He said: '*Yes, and it would be to you like the table to Bani Israel.*' They refused and retracted. As-Suddi and Qatādah said the same occasion. What is meant here is that Allah blamed whoever asked the Messenger (peace be upon him) about any matter while meaning obstinacy and suggestion. Exactly like Bani Israel, when they asked Musa (Moses, peace be upon him) out of their obstinacy and disbelief. Allah says: *Do you desire to question your Messenger as was questioned Musa in the past*? Whoever prefers disbelief and abandons faith has left the right path and is heading toward ignorance and deception. This was the case of those who refused to believe, follow and obey prophets, preferring instead to disobey, accuse their prophets of lying, and ask them questions without real need out of their obstinacy and disbelief. As Allah says: *Do you not see those who have exchanged Allah's favour with kufr and have made their people alight in the abode of perdition? (Into hell) they shall enter it and an evil place it is to reside in.*[10]

From what has been presented thus far by the exegete's aṭ-Ṭabari and Ibn Kathir, we can reasonably conclude that the meaning of the verse is general and concerned all questions. In this regard there is essentially no difference here between the obdurate question 'who is my father' or 'where is my father – in paradise or hell' and the question from the ignorant Bedouin who asked whether *Ḥajj* had to be performed annually. In order to complete the definite evidence concerning the meaning of the verse and to explain the subject from all its aspects, we will mention the most important and authentic accounts regarding this with their chains of transmission, beginning with *ḥadith*

---

[10] *Qur'ān* 14: 28/29

narrated by Abu Hurayrah (may Allah be pleased with him) as recorded by Imām Muslim in his *Ṣaḥīḥ*:

حدثني حرملة بن يحيى التجيبي أخبرنا ابن وهب أخبرني يونس عن ابن شهاب أخبرني أبو سلمة بن عبد الرحمن وسعيد بن المسيب قالا كان أبو هريرة يحدث أنه سمع رسول الله صلى الله عليه وسلم يقول ما نهيتكم عنه فاجتنبوه وما أمرتكم به فافعلوا منه ما استطعتم فإنما أهلك الذين من قبلكم كثرة مسائلهم واختلافهم على أنبيائهم

Ḥarmala ibn Yaḥya at-Tajeebe narrated to me Ibn Wahb reported to us Yunus reported to me from Ibn Shihāb, Abu Salamah ibn Abdar-Raḥman and Sa'eed ibn Musayib reported to me, they said Abu Hurayrah narrated that he heard the Messenger of Allah (peace be upon him) say: *Avoid that which I forbid you to do and do that which I command you to do to the best of your capacity. Verily the people before you went to their doom because they had put too many questions to their Prophets and then disagreed with their teachings.*

The narration is well known and can be found in almost all the major *ḥadith* collections via authentic chains of transmission. In *al-Jāmi aṣ-Ṣaḥīḥ al-Mukhtaṣr* Imām Bukhāri recorded:

حدثنا إسماعيل حدثني مالك عن أبي الزناد عن الأعرج عن أبي هريرة عن النبي صلى الله عليه وسلم قال دعوني ما تركتكم إنما هلك من كان قبلكم بسؤالهم واختلافهم على أنبيائهم فإذا نهيتكم عن شئ فاجتنبوه وإذا أمرتكم بأمر فأتوا منه ما استطعتم

Ismā'il narrated to us Mālik narrated to me from Abi Zinād from al-'Araj from Abu Hurayrah from the Prophet (peace be upon him) who said: *Leave me as I leave you for the people who were before you were ruined because of their questions and their differences over their Prophets. So, if I forbid you to do something, then keep away from it. And if I order you to do something, then do of it as much as you can.*

Without doubt this *isnād* is authentic as the brightest sun; it is considered the 'golden chain' from Abu Hurayrah as is commonly said, although we believe that Ibn Shihāb az-Zuhri from Abu Salamah ibn Abdar-Raḥman and Sa'eed ibn Musayib from Abu Hurayrah is just as authentic and indeed stronger. Again, Muslim has another version of this albeit with the additional contextual backdrop:

وحدثني زهير بن حرب حدثنا يزيد بن هارون أخبرنا الربيع بن مسلم القرشي عن محمد بن زياد عن أبي هريرة قال خطبنا رسول الله صلى الله عليه وسلم فقال أيها الناس قد فرض الله عليكم الحج فحجوا فقال رجل أكل عام يا رسول الله فسكت حتى قالها ثلاثا فقال رسول الله صلى الله عليه وسلم لو قلت نعم لوجبت ولما استطعتم ثم قال ذروني ما تركتكم فإنما هلك من كان قبلكم بكثرة سؤالهم واختلافهم على أنبيائهم فإذا أمرتكم بشيئ فأتوا منه ما استطعتم وإذا نهيتكم عن شيئ فدعوه

And Zuhayr bin Ḥarb narrated to me Yazeed bin Ḥārun narrated to us ar-Rabih' bin Muslim al-Qurayshi reported to us from Muḥammad bin Ziyād from Abu Hurayrah who said: Allah's Messenger (peace be upon him) addressed us and said: *O people, Allah has made Ḥajj obligatory for you; so perform Ḥajj.* Thereupon a person said: Messenger of Allah, (is it to be performed) every year? He (the Prophet) kept quiet, and he repeated (these words) thrice, whereupon Allah's Messenger (peace be upon him) said: *If I were to say yes, it would become obligatory (for you to perform it every year) and you would not be able to do it.* Then he said: *Leave me with what I have left to you, for those who were before you were destroyed because of excessive questioning, and their opposition to their apostles. So when I command you to do anything, do it as much as it lies in your power and when I forbid you to do anything, then abandon it.*

There is a good useful addition which is mentioned in *Ṣaḥīḥ* Ibn Ḥibbān with a strong chain of transmission accompanied with a useful comment made by Imām Abu Ḥātim Ibn Ḥibbān al-Bus'ty:

> أخبرنا عمر بن محمد الهمداني قال: حدثنا عبد الملك بن شعيب الليث بن سعد قال: حدثني أبي عن جدي عن محمد بن عجلان: حدثني زيد بن أسلم عن أبي صالح عن أبي هريرة عن رسول الله صلى الله عليه وسلم وذاد فيه : وما أخبرتكم أنه من عند الله فهو الذي لا شك فيه
>
> Umar bin Muḥammad al-Hamdāni reported to us he said Abdal-Malik bin Shu'ayb al-Layth bin Sa'd narrated to us he said my father narrated to me from my grandfather from Muḥammad bin 'Ajlān: Zayd bin Aslam narrated to me from Abi Ṣāliḥ from Abu Hurayrah from the Messenger of Allah (peace be upon him): *Whatever matter I informed you of, undoubtedly it is from Allah.*

Abu Ḥātim ibn Ḥibbān may Allah be pleased with him said:

> This *ḥadith* includes a clear statement: the prohibited matters forbade by the Messenger of Allah (peace be upon him) are all definite and obligatory until evidence proves it is not. In addition, the Prophet's orders are obligatory, depending on one's capacity, until evidence proves it is not. Allah the exalted says '*and whatever the Messenger gives you, take it and whatever he forbids you then abstain*'[11] and '*But no, by your Lord they do not believe until they appoint you a judge in all what is in dispute between them, then they do not find in their souls any objection on what you have decided, and they submit with an entire submission.*'[12]

[11] *Qur'ān* 59: 7
[12] *Qur'ān* 4: 65

Shaykh Shu'ayb al-Arnā'uṭ said the *isnād* is strong according to the conditions of Muslim. Abu Hurayrah (may Allah be pleased with him) was not the only one who narrated that meaning, as Sa'd bin Abi Waqqās (may Allah be pleased with him) narrated similarly in the same subject but from a different view. In *al-Jāmi aṣ-Ṣaḥīḥ al-Mukhtaṣr*, Imām Bukhāri recorded the following:

حدثنا عبد الله بن يزيد المقرئ حدثنا سعيد حدثني عقيل عن ابن شهاب عن عامر بن سعد بن أبي وقاص عن أبيه أن النبي صلى الله عليه وسلم قال إن أعظم المسلمين جرما من سأل عن شيئ لم يحرم فحرم من أجل مسألته

Abdullah bin Yazeed al-Muqra' narrated to us Sa'eed narrated to us 'Uqayl narrated to me from Ibn Shihāb from 'Aāmir bin Sa'd bin Abi Waqqās from his father that the Prophet (peace be upon him) said: *The most sinful person among the Muslims is the one who asked about something which had not been prohibited, but was prohibited because of his asking.*

Imām Muslim also records this narration with a slight variant wording:

و حدثناه أبو بكر بن أبي شيبة وابن أبي عمر قالا حدثنا سفيان بن عيينة عن الزهري و حدثنا محمد بن عباد حدثنا سفيان قال أحفظه كما أحفظ بسم الله الرحمن الرحيم الزهري عن عامر بن سعد عن أبيه قال قال رسول الله صلى الله عليه وسلم أعظم المسلمين في المسلمين جرما من سأل عن أمر لم يحرم فحرم على الناس من أجل مسألته و حدثنيه حرملة بن يحيى أخبرنا ابن وهب أخبرني يونس ح و حدثنا عبد بن حميد أخبرنا عبد الرزاق أخبرنا معمر كلاهما عن الزهري بهذا الإسناد وزاد في حديث معمر رجل سأل عن شيئ ونقر عنه وقال في حديث يونس عامر بن سعد أنه سمع سعدا

And Abu Bakr ibn Abi Shayba and Ibn Abi Umar narrated it to us, they said Sufyān bin Uyayna narrated to us from az-Zuhri and Muḥammad bin 'Abād narrated to us Sufyān narrated to us he said: I saved and memorised in the name of Allah *ar-*

> *Raḥman, ar-Raḥeem* az-Zuhri from 'Aāmir bin Sa'd from his father who said that the Messenger of Allah (peace be upon him) said: *The greatest sinner of the Muslims amongst Muslims is one who asked about a certain thing which had not been prohibited and it was prohibited because of his asking about it*

Further to the above, the next *ḥadith* which is also authentic and is recorded on the authority of an-Nawwās ibn Samān provides even greater clarity upon the issue at hand; as collected by Muslim:

> حدثني هارون بن سعيد الأيلي حدثنا عبد الله بن وهب حدثني معاوية يعني ابن صالح عن عبد الرحمن بن جبير بن نفير عن أبيه عن نواس بن سمعان قال أقمت مع رسول الله صلى الله عليه وسلم بالمدينة سنة ما يمنعني من الهجرة إلا المسألة كان أحدنا إذا هاجر لم يسأل رسول الله صلى الله عليه وسلم عن شيء قال فسألته عن البر والإثم فقال رسول الله صلى الله عليه وسلم البر حسن الخلق والإثم ما حاك في نفسك وكرهت أن يطلع عليه الناس
>
> Hārun bin Sa'eed al-Ayli narrated to me Abdullah bin Wahb narrated to us Muā'wiya – that is to say - Ibn Ṣāliḥ narrated to us from Abdar-Raḥman bin Jubayr bin Nufayr from his father from Nawwās ibn Samān who said: I stayed with Allah's Messenger (peace be upon him) for one year. What obstructed me to migrate was (nothing) but (persistent) inquiries from him (about Islam). It was a common observation that when anyone of us migrated (to Medina) he ceased to ask (questions) from Allah's Messenger (peace be upon him). So I asked him about virtue and vice. Thereupon Allah's Messenger (peace be upon him) said: *Virtue is a kind disposition and vice is what rankles in your mind and that you disapprove of its being known to the people.*

Moreover, there is also the *ḥadith* that has been narrated upon the authority of Abu Thalabah al-Khushani. The narration is authentic and relates to the same subject; this has been cited by Ibn Ḥazm, who also judged it as authentic in his seminal work *al-Iḥkām fi Uṣul al-Aḥkām* (Judgement on the Principles of Law):

> حدثنا أحمد بن قاسم حدثنا أبي قاسم بن محمد بن قاسم حدثنا جدي قاسم بن أصبغ أخبرنا بكر بن حماد أخبرنا حفص بن غياث عن داود بن أبي هند عن مكحول عن أبي ثعلبة الخشني قال: قال رسول الله، صلى الله عليه وسلم: إن الله فرض فرائض فلا تضيعوها، وحد حدودا فلا تعتدوها، ونهى عن أشياء فلا تنتهكوها، وسكت عن أشياء، من غير نسيان لها: رحمة لكم، فلا تبحثوا عنها!
>
> Aḥmad ibn Qāsim narrated to us Abu Qāsim ibn Muḥammad ibn Qāsim narrated to us my grandfather Qāsim ibn Aṣbagh narrated to us Bakr ibn Ḥammād reported to us Ḥafṣ ibn Ghayāth reported to us from Dāwud ibn Abi Hind from Makḥoul from Abu Thalabah al-Khushani who said: the Messenger of Allah (peace be upon him) said: *Allah, the Exalted, has laid down certain duties which you should not neglect, and has put certain limits which you should not transgress, and has kept silent about other matters out of forgiveness for you and not out of forgetfulness, so do not seek to investigate them.*

Imām Bayhaqy recorded similarly in his *Sunan al-Kubra,*[13] via Ḥafṣ bin Ghayāth albeit in *mawquf* (halted) form which is admittedly weak. The correct reporting for this narration should not be halted at Ḥafṣ bin Ghayāth; that is mistaken. Al-Ḥākim also collected this narration and authenticated it in *al-Mustadrak a'la Ṣaḥīḥayn* with a slight variation in wording:

> حدثني علي بن عيسى حدثنا محمد بن عمرو الحرشي حدثنا القعنبي حدثنا

[13] Bayhaqy, *Sunan al-Kubra*, Vol. 10 sec. 12, no. 19,509

علي بن مسهر عن داود بن أبي هند عن مكحول عن أبي ثعلبة الخشني رضي الله عنه قال: قال رسول الله، صلى الله عليه وسلم: إن الله حد حدوداً فلا تعتدوها، وفرض لكم فرائض فلا تضيعوها، وحرم أشياء فلا تنتهكوها، وترك أشياء، من غير نسيان من ربكم ولكن رحمة منه لكم، فاقبلوها ولا تبحثوا فيها!

Ali bin Esa narrated to me Muḥammad ibn 'Amr al-Ḥarshi narrated to us al-Qa'nabi narrated to us Ali bin Mashour narrated to us from Dāwud ibn Abi Hind from Makḥoul from Abu Thalabah al-Khushani who said: the Messenger of Allah (peace be upon him) said: *Verily, Allah has set some limits, so do not trespass them and He has ordained some obligations, so do not neglect them; He has sanctified some things so do not violate them; and He has refrained from mentioning other matters not* (out of) *forgetfulness, but as a way of being merciful to you, so accept* (that) *and do not look for them!*

The narration is also recorded by Dāraquṭni in his *Sunan,*[14] in a *marfu'* (elevated) form via the channel of Isḥāq al-Azraq; aṭ-Ṭabarāni has this in *Mu'jam al-Kabir,*[15] Ibn 'Asākir has this in his collection[16] via the channel of Yazeed bin Hārun; Ibn Ḥazm has it in the *Iḥkām*[17] in another place in *marfu'* (elevated) form via the channel of Muḥammad bin Faḍeel. It is also in *Faqih al-Mutafaqih*[18] of al-Khaṭib al-Baghdādi via the channel of Zuhayr bin Isḥāq, again *marfu'*. It is arguable that Imām Dāraquṭni fell prey to this as a result of *irsāl* when recording his tradition. As for those who would argue that Imām Makḥoul did not hear from Abu Thalabah al-Khushani, we categorically assert that this is invalid. We have conducted an in-depth study of this matter, which is not available elsewhere, which proves beyond reasonable doubt that

---

[14] Dāraquṭni, *Sunan*, Vol. 4 sec. 183, no. 42
[15] Ṭabarāni, *Mu'jam al-Kabir*, Vol. 22 sec. 223, no. 589
[16] Ibn 'Asākir, *Mu'jam*, Vol. 2 sec. 965, no. 1,232
[17] Ibn Ḥazm, *al-Iḥkām fi Uṣul al-Aḥkām*, Vol. 8 sec. 24
[18] Al-Khaṭib Baghdādi, *Faqih al-Mutafaqih*, Vol. 2 sec. 16

Makḥoul was a great successor, may Allah be pleased with him.[19] The next narration to be taken into account is that which is found in Al-Ḥākim's *al-Mustadrak a'la Ṣaḥīḥayn*, recorded on the authority of Abu Dardā':

أخبرنا أبو جعفر محمد بن علي الشيباني حدثنا أحمد بن حازم الغفاري حدثنا أبو نعيم حدثنا عاصم بن رجاء بن حيوة عن أبيه عن أبي الدرداء رضي الله عنه رفع الحديث قال: ما أحل الله في كتابه فهو حلال، وما حرم فهو حرام، وما سكت عنه فهو عافية، فاقبلوا من الله العافية: فإن الله لم يكن نسيا، ثم تلا هذه الآية: وَمَا نَتَنَزَّلُ إِلَّا بِأَمْرِ رَبِّكَ لَهُ مَا بَيْنَ أَيْدِينَا وَمَا خَلْفَنَا وَمَا بَيْنَ ذَٰلِكَ وَمَا كَانَ رَبُّكَ نَسِيّاً

Abu Ja'far Muḥammad bin Ali ash-Shaybāni reported to us Aḥmad bin Ḥāzim al-Ghafāri narrated to us Abu Nu'aym narrated to us 'Aāṣim bin Rajā bin Ḥaywa narrated to us from his father from Abu Dardā' who raised the *ḥadith* and said: *Whatever was considered lawful by Allah in His Book is lawful and whatever was considered unlawful is unlawful and He has refrained from mentioning other matters so it is forgiveness from Him. Accept from Allah His Forgiveness, as Allah never forgets anything*, (then he mentioned this verse): *And we do not descend but by the command of your Lord; to Him belongs whatever is before us and behind us and whatever in between, and your Lord is not forgetful.*[20]

Al-Ḥākim said that the narration is authentic, but they (Bukhāri and Muslim) did not record it; ath-Dhahabi concurred with him in this. It has also been reported in a number of other places, such as in the *Sunan* of Dāraquṭni;[21] the *Sunan al-Kubra* of Bayhaqy,[22] by Ṭabarāni

[19] The Arabic edition contains the full appendix which discusses Makḥoul as a narrator and dispels several criticisms levelled against his reporting from previous scholars, which as it transpires, were based upon a mistaken understanding of his life chronology.
[20] *Qur'ān* 19: 64
[21] Dāraquṭni, *Sunan*, Vol. 2 sec. 217, no. 12

in the *Musnad ash-Shāmiayn*[23] and in a number of other places. Al-Ḥāfiz (Ibn Ḥajar) attributed it to al-Bazzār and al-Ḥākim in *Fatḥ al-Bāri* with different wording and some additions. He said al-Bazzār recorded the following *ḥadith* with a valid chain of transmission and al-Ḥākim regarded it as authentic. I would submit that it is *ḥasan* (good) and reasonable on the basis of 'Aāṣim bin Rajā bin Ḥaywa; hence the narration is *ḥasan Ṣaḥīḥ*.[24] A similar version of this *ḥadith* was narrated by 'Umair bin Qatāda al-Janda'y al-Laythi through a reasonable chain of transmission which doesn't have serious objections raised about it; it is recorded in Al-Ḥākim's *al-Mustadrak a'la Ṣaḥīḥayn*:

حدثنا يحيى بن عثمان بن صالح حدثنا عمرو بن خالد الحراني حدثنا محمد بن سلمة الحراني عن بكر بن خنيس عن أبي بدر عن عبد الله بن عبيد بن عمير عن أبيه عن جده قال: كانت في نفسي مسألة قد احزنتني لم اسأل رسول الله، صلى الله عليه وسلم، عنها ولم اسمع أحدا يسأله عنها فكنت أتحيّنه، فدخلت ذات يوم وهو يتوضأ، فوافقته على حالين كنت أحب أن أوافقه عليهما: وجدته فارغاً، طيب النفس، فقلت: يا رسول الله ائذن لي فأسألك؛ قال: نعم: سل عما بدا لك؛ قلت: يا رسول الله: ما الإيمان؟!، قال: السماحة والصبر؛ قلت: وأي المؤمنين افضلهم إيماناً، قال: احسنهم خلقاً؛ قلت: فأي المسلمين أفضل إسلاماً، قال: من سلم المسلمون من يده ولسانه؛ قلت: أي الجهاد أفضل؟!، فطأطأ رأسه فصمت طويلا حتى خفت أن اكون قد شققت عليه، وتمنيت أن لم أكن سألته، وقد سمعته بالأمس يقول: إن أعظم الناس في المسلمين جرما لمن سأل عن شيء لم يحرم عليهم فحرم من أجل مسألته؛ فقلت: أعوذ بالله من غضب الله، وغضب رسوله؛ فرفع رأسه فقال: كيف قلت؟!، قلت: أي الجهاد أفضل؟!، قال: كلمة عدل عند امام جائر

Yaḥya ibn Uthmān ibn Ṣāliḥ narrated to us 'Amr bin Khālid al-Ḥirāni narrated to us Muḥammad bin Salama al-Ḥirāni narrated to us from Bakr ibn Khanees from Abi Badr from Abdullah ihn

---

[22] Bayhaqy, *Sunan al-Kubra*, Vol. 10 sec. 12, no. 19,508

[23] Ṭabarāni, *Musnad ash-Shāmiayn*, Vol. 3 sec. 209, no. 2,102

[24] The appendix to the Arabic edition has greater detail concerning this and the narrators contained within this tradition.

> 'Ubaid bin 'Umair from his father from his grandfather who said: There was a question inside me and I was sad that I had not asked the Messenger of Allah (peace be upon him) about it nor heard anyone asking him about it. I was waiting for the proper time for it. Then I entered upon him once while he was performing ablution. I found him in the two moods I loved to find him; I found him unoccupied and at peace. So I said - O Messenger of Allah! Can I have your permission to ask you? He said: *Yes, ask about whatever concerns you.* I said: O Messenger of Allah! What is faith? He said: *leniency and patience.* I said: Who has the best faith among believers? He said: *Whoever has the best manners.* I said: Who is the best Muslim among Muslims? He said: *The one who avoids harming Muslims with his tongue and hands.* I said: What (kind) of fighting in the cause of Allah is the best? He bowed his head and kept silent for a long time, such that I feared I troubled him and wished that I did not ask him, as I heard him saying the day before - *The most sinful person among the Muslims is the one who asked about something which had not been prohibited, but was prohibited to people because of his asking.* So I said: I seek refuge with Allah from the anger of Allah and the anger of His Messenger (peace be upon him). He raised his head and said: *What did you say (ask)?* I said - what is the best among *Jihād*?' He said: *The best Jihād is (to speak) a word of justice to an oppressive ruler.*

Hats off to 'Umair bin Qatādah for these great and productive questions! How fortunate was he to have enjoyed hearing the perfect statements directly from the Messenger of Allah (peace be upon him) directly without recourse to an intermediary. Similarly, this also has reached us from Salmān al-Fārsi as recorded by Imām Tirmidhi in his *Sunan*:

> حدثنا إسماعيل بن موسى الفزاري حدثنا سيف بن هارون البرجمي عن سليمان التيمي عن أبي عثمان عن سلمان قال: سئل رسول الله، صلى الله

> عليه وسلم، عن السمن والجبن والفراء فقال: الحلال ما أحل الله في كتابه، والحرام ما حرم الله في كتابه، وما سكت عنه فهو مما عفا عنه
>
> Ismā'il bin Musa al-Fuzāri narrated to us Sayf bin Hārun al-Burjumi narrated to us from Sulaymān at-Taymi from Abi 'Uthmān from Salmān who said: The Messenger of Allah was asked about fat, cheese, and furs, so he said: *The lawful is what Allah made lawful in His Book, the unlawful is what Allah made unlawful in his Book, and what He was silent about; then it is among that for which He has pardoned.*

After citing this narration Tirmidhi comments as follows:

> There is something on this topic from Al-Mughirah, and this *ḥadith* is *ghareeb* (strange), we do not know of it being *marfu'* (raised / elevated) except from this route. Sufyān and others reported it from Sulaymān at-Taymi from Abu Uthmān from Salmān as his own saying. It is as if the *mawquf'* (halted) narration is more correct. I asked Al-Bukhāri about this *ḥadith* and he said: 'I do not think it is preserved. Sufyān reported it *from* Sulaymān at-Taymi from Abu Uthmān from Salmān in *mawquf'* form.' Al-Bukhāri (also) said: 'Sayf bin Hārun is *muqārib* (average) in *ḥadith* and as for Sayf bin Muḥammad from 'Aāṣim his narrations are left.'

The narration is also found in several places, such as in *Sunan* Ibn *Mājah,*[25] al-Ḥākim's *Mustadrak,*[26] Ṭabarāni's *Mu'jam al-Kabir*[27] and in the *Sunan al-Kubra* of Bayhaqy.[28] I would argue that Sayf bin Hārun is *thiqa aā'bid.* Mistaking him for being weak is a quite grave. The Imām and established authority, Sufyān ibn 'Uyayna raised his

---

25 Ibn Mājah, *Sunan,* Vol. 2 sec. 1,117, no. 3,367

26 Al-Ḥākim, *Mustadrak,* Vol. 4 sec. 129, no. 7,115

27 Ṭabarāni, *Mu'jam al-Kabir,* Vol. 6 sec. 250, no. 6,124

28 Bayhaqy, *Sunan al-Kubra*, Vol. 10 sec. 12, no. 19,507

ḥadith. These *ḥadith* have come through several different ways, such as via Abu Abdullah al-Jundly from Salmān *marfu'* and the *ḥadith* in this form are authentic.[29]

أخبرني علي بن محمد بن دحيم الشيباني بالكوفة حدثنا أحمد بن حازم الغفاري حدثنا أبو نعيم حدثنا مُحَمَّد بن شريك المكي عن عمرو بن دينار عن أبي الشعثاء عن بن عباس رضي الله عنهما قال: كان أهل الجاهلية يأكلون أشياء ويتركون أشياء تقذرا فبعث الله تعالى نبيه، صلى الله عليه وسلم، وأنزل كتابه وأحل حلاله، وحرم حرامه: فما أحل فهو حلال، وما حرم فهو حرام، وما سكت عنه فهو عفو وتلا هذه الآية: {قُلْ لا أَجِدُ فِي مَا أُوحِيَ إِلَيَّ مُحَرَّماً عَلَى طَاعِمٍ يَطْعَمُهُ إِلَّا أَنْ يَكُونَ مَيْتَةً أَوْ دَماً مَسْفُوحاً أَوْ لَحْمَ خِنْزِيرٍ فَإِنَّهُ رِجْسٌ أَوْ فِسْقاً أُهِلَّ لِغَيْرِ اللَّهِ بِهِ فَمَنِ اضْطُرَّ غَيْرَ بَاغٍ وَلا عَادٍ فَإِنَّ رَبَّكَ غَفُورٌ رَحِيمٌ}

Ali bin Muḥammad bin Duḥaym ash-Shaybāni reported to me in Kufa, Aḥmad bin Ḥāzim al-Ghafāri narrated to us Abu Nu'aym narrated to us Muḥammad bin Shareek al-Makki narrated to us from Amr bin Dinār from Abu ash-Sha'shā from Ibn 'Abbās who said: The people of pre-Islamic times used to eat some things and leave others alone, considering them unclean. Then Allah sent His Prophet (peace be upon him) and sent down His Book, marking some things lawful and others unlawful; so what He made lawful is lawful, what he made unlawful is unlawful, and what he said nothing about is pardoned. And he recited: *Say: I do not find in that which has been revealed to me anything forbidden for an eater to eat of except that it be what has died of itself, or blood poured forth, or flesh of swine-- for that surely is unclean-- or that which is a transgression, other than (the name of) Allah having been invoked on it; but whoever is driven to necessity, not desiring nor exceeding the limit, then surely your Lord is forgiving, merciful.*[30]

[29] The appendix to the Arabic edition has greater detail concerning this and the narrator in question
[30] *Qur'ān* 6: 145

It is also reported by Abu Dāwud in his *Sunan,*[31] al-Ḥākim said that the *isnād* is authentic, but they (Bukhāri and Muslim) did not record it; I would submit that it is well established and authentic. Moreover, this also comes to us via a major successor, namely 'Ubaid bin 'Umair, as cited by Abdar-Razzāq in his *Muṣṣanaf* with an authentic *isnād*:

عبد الرزاق عن ابن عيينة عن عمرو بن دينار أنه سمع عبيد بن عمير يقول: أحل الله حلاله وحرم حرامه فما أحل فهو حلال وما حرم فهو حرام وما سكت عنه فهو عفو

Abdar-Razzāq from ibn 'Uyayna from Amr bin Dinār that he heard 'Ubaid bin 'Umair say: Allah has outlined the *ḥalāl* and the *ḥaram*, other than the *ḥalāl* and the *ḥaram* that upon which there is silence it is regarded as forgiven.

It is also recorded in the *Tafsir* of Imām aṭ-Ṭabari in two places with an authentic *isnād's*:

حدثنا هناد قال، حدثنا ابن أبي زائدة قال، أخبرنا ابن جريج، عن عطاء قال: كان عبيد بن عمير يقول: إن الله تعالى أحلّ وحرَّم، فما أحلّ فاستحلُّوه، وما حرَّم فاجتنبوه، وترك من ذلك أشياء لم يحلها ولم يحرمها، فذلك عفو من الله عفاه. ثم يتلو: {يَا أَيُّهَا الَّذِينَ آمَنُوا لَا تَسْأَلُوا عَنْ أَشْيَاءَ إِنْ تُبْدَ لَكُمْ تَسُؤْكُمْ}

Ḥannād narrated to us he said Ibn Abi Zāida narrated to us Ibn Jurayj reported to us from 'Aṭā who said 'Ubaid bin 'Umair he said: Verily Allah the exalted (clarified) the *ḥalāl* and the *ḥarām*; as for the *ḥalāl* he has legislated as such and refrain from what is *ḥaram*. Leave the matters which have not been detailed as *ḥalāl* and *ḥarām* - that has been pardoned from the mercy of Allah. (Then he recited): *O you who believe! Do not ask questions about things which if declared to you may trouble*

[31] *Sunan* Abu Dāwud Vol. 3 sec. 355, no. 3,800

you. [32]

حدثنا ابن المثنى قال: حدثنا الضحاك قال: أخبرنا ابن جريج قال: أخبرني عطاء، عن عبيد بن عمير أنه كان يقول: إنّ الله حرّم وأحلّ؛ ثم ذكر نحوه

Ibn Muthanna narrated to us he said ad-Ḍaḥḥāk narrated to us he said Ibn Jurayj reported to us he said 'Aṭā reporeeted to me from 'Ubaid bin 'Umair that he was saying Allah has forbidden and permitted, therefore he mentioned about it.

The last of the Prophets sent to mankind, Muḥammad (peace be upon him) used to become very angry with whoever asked him such questions, as is demonstrated in the *ḥadith* which is narrated upon the authority of Abu Qatādah al-Anṣāri (may Allah be pleased him) as collected by Imām Muslim:

حدثنا محمد بن المثنى ومحمد بن بشار واللفظ لابن المثنى قالا حدثنا محمد بن جعفر حدثنا شعبة عن غيلان بن جرير سمع عبد الله بن معبد الزماني عن أبي قتادة الأنصاري رضي الله عنه أن رسول الله صلى الله عليه وسلم سئل عن صومه قال فغضب رسول الله صلى الله عليه وسلم فقال عمر رضي الله عنه رضينا بالله ربا وبالإسلام دينا وبمحمد رسولا وببيعتنا بيعة قال فسئل عن صيام الدهر فقال لا صام ولا أفطر أو ما صام وما أفطر قال فسئل عن صوم يومين وإفطار يوم قال ومن يطيق ذلك قال وسئل عن صوم يوم وإفطار يومين قال ليت أن الله قوانا لذلك قال وسئل عن صوم يوم وإفطار يوم قال ذاك صوم أخي داود عليه السلام قال وسئل عن صوم يوم الاثنين قال ذاك يوم ولدت فيه ويوم بعثت أو أنزل علي فيه قال فقال صوم ثلاثة من كل شهر ورمضان إلى رمضان صوم الدهر قال وسئل عن صوم يوم عرفة فقال يكفر السنة الماضية والباقية قال وسئل عن صوم يوم عاشوراء فقال يكفر السنة الماضية

Muḥammad ibn Muthanna and Muḥammad bin Bashār narrated

[32] *Qur'ān* 5: 101

> to us – and this is the wording of ibn Muthanna – they said Muḥammad bin Ja'far narrated to us Shu'ba narrated to us from Ghaylān bin Jarir who heard Abdullah bin Ma'bad az-Zamāni from Abu Qatādah al-Anṣāri that the Messenger of Allah (peace be upon him) was asked about his fasting. The Messenger of Allah (peace be upon him) felt annoyed. Thereupon 'Umar (Allah be pleased with him) said: We are pleased with Allah as the Lord, with Islam as our Code of Life, with Muḥammad as the Messenger and with our pledge (to you for willing and cheerful submission) as a (sacred) commitment! He was then asked about perpetual fasting, whereupon he said: He neither fasted nor did he break it, or he did not fast and he did not break it. He was then asked about fasting for two days and breaking one day. He (the Prophet) said: *And who has strength enough to do it?* He was asked about fasting for a day and breaking for two days, whereupon he said: *May Allah bestow upon us strength to do it*. He was then asked about fasting for a day and breaking on the other, whereupon he said: *That is the fasting of my brother Dāwud (David, peace be upon him)*. He was then asked about fasting on Monday, whereupon he said: *It was the day on which I was born, on which I was commissioned with Prophethood or revelation was sent to me,* (and he further) said: *Three days' fasting every month and of the whole of Ramadan every year is a perpetual fast*. He was asked about fasting on the day of '*Arafa* whereupon he said: *It expiates the sins of the preceding year and the coming year*. He was asked about fasting on the day of *'Ashura* whereupon be said: *It expiates the sins of the preceding year.*

Muslim records this through various authentic channels of transmission in his *Ṣaḥīḥ*. It is also recorded widely by many authorities of *ḥadith* in their collections: *Mujtabi min as-Sunan* and *Sunan al-Kubra* of Imām an-Nasā'i; *Musnad* Aḥmad, *Ṣaḥīḥ* Ibn Khuzayma, Al-Ḥākim's *al-Mustadrak a'la Ṣaḥīḥayn* and many others. The *isānd's* for this *ḥadith* are authentic and well established. Bayhaqy has this in *Sunan al-Kubra* via the following *isnād* which doesn’t contain Shu’ba:

أخبرنا أبو بكر مُحَمَّد بن الحسن بن فورك أنبأ عبد الله بن جعفر حدثنا يونس بن حبيب حدثنا أبو داود حدثنا حماد بن زيد وهشام ومهدي قال حماد ومهدي عن غيلان بن جرير وقال هشام عن قتادة عن غيلان بن جرير عن عبد الله بن معبد الزماني عن أبي قتادة رضي الله تعالى عنه، أن أعرابيا سأل رسول الله، صلى الله عليه وسلم، عن صومه: فغضب حتى عرف ذلك في وجهه، فقام عمر بن الخطاب رضي الله تعالى عنه فقال: رضينا بالله ربا وبالإسلام دينا وبك نبيا، أعوذ بالله من غضب الله وغضب رسوله، فلم يزل عمر رضي الله تعالى عنه يردد ذلك حتى سكن، ثم ساق الحديث بطوله إلى منتهاه بنحو حديث الإمام مسلم

Abu Bakr bin Muḥammad bin al-Ḥasan bin Fawrak reported to us Abdullah ibn Ja’far reports, Yunus bin Ḥabeeb narrated to us Abu Dāwud narrated to us Ḥammād bin Zayd, Hishām and Mahdi narrated to us he said Ḥammād and Mahdi from Ghaylān bin Jarir and he said Hishām from Qatādah from Ghaylān bin Jarir from Abdullah Ma’bad az-Zamāni from Abu Qatādah al-Anṣāri, from him that he narrated that a Bedouin asked the Messenger of Allah (peace be upon him) about his fast. The Messenger of Allah (peace be upon him) became angry until it was shown in his face. Thereupon, 'Umar (may Allah be pleased with him) stood up and said - We are satisfied with Allah as our Lord, with Islam as our religion, and with you as our Prophet. We seek refuge with Allah from the anger of Allah and that of His Messenger! 'Umar kept on repeating these words until his (the Prophet's) anger calmed down. The rest of the *ḥadith* is recorded similar to the *ḥadith* of Imām Muslim.

Regarding this, Bayhaqy said: ‘Muslim recorded it in his *Ṣaḥīḥ* from Yaḥya bin Yaḥya and other than him from Ḥammād bin Zayd and from other channels from Mahdi bin Maymoon.’ The same is also reported by Abu Dāwud in his *Sunan*.[33] Ibn Ḥibbān records this

[33] Abu Dāwud, *Sunan*, Vol. 2 sec. 322, no. 2,425

narration in his *Ṣaḥīḥ* with the following *isnād* with an additional insightful comment:

أخبرنا أبو يعلى حدثنا خلف بن هشام البزار حدثنا حماد بن زيد عن غيلان بن جرير عن عبد الله بن معبد عن أبي قتادة به بطوله إلى قوله: وددت انى طوقت ذاك

Abu Ya'la reported to us Khalf bin Hishām al-Bazzār narrated to us Ḥammād bin Zayd narrated to us from Ghaylān bin Jarir from Abdullah ibn Ma'bad from Abu Qatādah al-Anṣāri in a long narrative (as above) till he said: I wished that I could bear that.

Abu Ḥātim said: The Prophet (peace be upon him) was not angry because of this question asking about the fast but he (peace be upon him) was angry because the person asked him – 'O Messenger of Allah! How do you fast?' The Prophet (peace be upon him) hated this question about his own way of fasting because he feared that if he tells the questioner he will not bare such kind of fasting or he feared for the questioner and all of his *Ummah* that if he tells them it may be imposed upon them and they will fail to perform it.

Regarding this, Shaykh Shu'ayb al-Arnā'uṭ said: 'It has a good chain of transmission according to the conditions of Muslim.' As already mentioned earlier as part of the long quote from Ibn Kathir, al-Ḥāfiz Abu Ya'la al-Mawṣily mentioned in his *Musnad*:

أخبرنا أبو كريب أخبرنا إسحاق بن سليمان عن أبي سنان عن أبي إسحاق عن البراء ابن عازب قال: إن كان ليأتي علي السنة أريد أن أسأل رسول الله، صلى الله عليه وسلم، عن الشيء فأتهيب منه، وإن كنا لنتمنى الأعراب

Abu Kareeb reported to us Isḥāq bin Sulaymān reported to us from Abi Sinān from Abi Isḥāq from al-Barā' bin Aā'zib who said: A whole year would pass while I wanted to ask the Messenger of Allah (peace be upon him) about a matter. But I was afraid from him and we used to wish that some Bedouin will come and ask him.

حدثنا قتيبة قال: حدثنا الليث عن جعفر بن ربيعة عن بكر بن سوادة عن مسلم بن مخشي عن ابن الفراسي أن الفراسي قال لرسول الله، صلى الله عليه وسلم: أسألُ يا رسول الله؟!، قال: لا، وإن كنت سائلا، لا بد، فاسأل الصالحين

Qutayba narrated to us he said al-Layth narrated to us from Ja'far bin Rabih' from Bakr bin Sawāda from Muslim bin Makhshi from Ibn al-Firāsi that al-Firāsi said to the Messenger of Allah (peace be upon him): May I ask, Messenger of Allah?[34] The Prophet (peace be upon him) said: *No, but if there is no escape from it, ask the righteous (aṣ-Ṣāliḥeen).*

Imām an-Nasā'i has this in both his *Sunan* and *Sunan al-Kubra*[35] with the only difference in terms of narration being 'Qutayba reported to us' instead of 'Qutayba narrated to us' as above. Imām Abdullah bin Aḥmad bin Ḥanbal has this narration albeit with slight variation regarding the channel of transmission and how it was reported.[36] Ṭabarāni has this in *Mu'jam al-Kabir* and he narrates as follows:

حَدَّثَنَا مُطَّلِبُ بْنُ شُعَيْبٍ الْأَزْدِيُّ، حَدَّثَنَا عَبْدُ اللهِ بْنُ صَالِحٍ، حَدَّثَنِي اللَّيْثُ، عَنْ جَعْفَرِ بْنِ رَبِيعَةَ، عَنْ بَكْرِ بْنِ سَوَادَةَ، عَنْ مُسْلِمِ بْنِ مَخْشِيٍّ، عَنِ ابْنِ الْفِرَاسِيِّ، أَنَّ أَبَاهُ الْفِرَاسِيَّ، أَتَى النَّبِيَّ، صلى الله عليه وسلم، فَقَالَ: يَا رَسُولَ اللهِ، أَسْأَلُ؟ قَالَ: لَا، وَإِنْ كُنْتَ لَا بُدَّ سَائِلًا، فَسَلِ الصَّالِحِينَ

Muṭṭalib ibn Shu'ayb al-Azdi narrated to us Abdullah bin Ṣāliḥ

[34] In the standard English translation of this *ḥadith* this is rendered as 'May I beg?', which doesn't give the reader the full context and is slightly misleading
[35] Nasā'i, *Sunan*, Vol. 5 sec. 95, no. 2,587; *Sunan al-Kubra*, Vol. 2 sec. 50, no. 2,368
[36] Vol. 4 sec. 334, no. 18,965

narrated to us al-Layth narrated to me from Ja'far bin Rabih' from Bakr bin Sawāda from Muslim bin Makhshi from Ibn al-Firāsi that his father al-Firāsi said: O Messenger of Allah, can I ask? He replied: *No, but if there is no escape from it, ask the righteous.*

The same is also in *Taḥzeeb al-Kāmil* with the addition in transmission being clarification of Muslim bin Makhshi as being Muslim bin Makhshi al-Mudalja, Abu Mu'āwiya al-Maṣri from the channel of Ṭabarāni. Bayhaqy has this in *Sunan al-Kubra* from an alternate way:

وأخبرنا أبو طاهر الفقيه أنبأ علي بن إبراهيم بن معاوية النيسابوري حدثنا مُحَمَّد بن مسلم بن وارة حدثني مُحَمَّد بن موسى بن أعين قال: وجدت في كتاب أبي عن عمرو بن الحارث عن بكر عن مسلم بن مخشى أن الفراسي حدثه عن أبيه بنحوه

And Abu Ṭāhir al-Faqihi reported to us Ali bin Ibrāhim bin Mu'āwiya an-Nisāburi reports, Muḥammad bin Muslim bin Wāra narrated to us Muḥammad bin Musa bin 'Ayn narrated to me he said: I found in the book of my father from Amr bin al-Ḥārith from Bakr from Muslim bin Makhshi that al-Firāsi's father told him about it.

Al-Ḥāfiz (Ibn Ḥajar) summarised most of the accounts mentioned about this subject *Fatḥ al-Bāri,* he writes:

The chapter of the disapproval of asking too many questions, interfering in what is not our concern and the saying of Allah – '*O you who believe! Do not ask questions about things which if declared to you may trouble you'*. As if he mentioned this verse to be evidence that establishes the disapproval, which indicates that he approved some of what was mentioned in explaining this verse. We had mentioned the difference in opinion concerning the occasions of its revelation within the *Tafsir of Surah al-Mā'ida.* Ibn al-Muneer felt that it is about asking too many questions both in the past and at the present. And the saying of al-Bukhāri showed his approval and the *ḥadith's* which he mentioned in the chapter, supported his view. While a group among the jurists including the judge - Abu Bakr bin al-'Araby denied it. He said that some ignorant people believed that this verse prohibited asking about matters concerned with disasters till it really happened, while it is not; the verse cleared that what is prohibited is asking questions that may cause hardship and difficulty to the Muslims while questions about disasters are not like that. The matter is exactly as he said, because this verse suggests that it is concerned with the time of revelation. Included in the *ḥadith* of Sa'd which he mentioned at the beginning of *al-Muṣṣanaf* in the chapter of whoever asks about something which had not been prohibited, but was prohibited to people because of his asking - approved that.

Like that could happen and was included in the meaning of the *ḥadith* of Sa'd. Al-Bazzār recorded the following *ḥadith* with a valid chain of transmission and Al-Ḥākim regarded it as an authentic *ḥadith* that Abu Dardā' (may Allah be pleased with him) narrated that the Messenger of Allah (peace be upon him) said: '*Whatever was considered lawful by Allah in His Book is lawful and whatever was considered unlawful is unlawful and He has refrained from mentioning other matters so it is forgiveness from Him. Accept from Allah His forgiveness, as Allah never forgets anything.*' Dāraquṭni recorded that Abu Thalabah narrated that the Messenger of Allah (peace be upon him) said: '*Verily, Allah has ordained some obligations, so do not neglect them; He has set some limits, so do not cross them; He has refrained from mentioning other matters not (out of) forgetfulness, do not look for them.*' It has a support narrated by Salmān as recorded by Tirmidhi and another narrated by Ibn 'Abbās and recorded by Abu Dāwud. Muslim also recorded what was mentioned originally by al-Bukhāri as it was mentioned above in the book of knowledge on the authority of Anas (may Allah be pleased with him) that he narrated: '*We were forbidden to ask anything (without the genuine need) from the Messenger of Allah (peace be upon him). It, therefore, pleased us that an intelligent person from the dwellers of the desert should come and asked him (the Prophet) while we listen to it.*'

He went on mentioning the story of the oath of condemnation in *ḥadith* narrated by 'Umar and how the Messenger of Allah (peace be upon him) hated the questions and criticised them. Muslim recorded that Nawwās ibn Samān (may Allah be pleased with him) narrated that he stayed with the Messenger of Allah (peace be upon him) for one year at Medina. Nothing obstructed me to migrate but inquiries to him (about Islam). It was a common observation) that when anyone of us migrated (to Medina) he ceased to ask (too many questions) the Messenger of Allah (peace be upon him). He meant here that he came to Medina as a newcomer but did not emigrate to it and he remained in that state for one year in order not to lose his right to ask questions. This *ḥadith* indicates that the prohibition of asking too many questions is addressing those people other than Bedouins whether they are newcomers or others. Aḥmad recorded that Abu Umāma (may Allah be pleased with him) narrated: 'When this verse was revealed in which Allah says *Do not ask about matters*….. we used not to ask him (peace be upon him). So we went to a Bedouin and gave him a garment as a bribe and said to him - ask the Prophet (peace be upon him). Furthermore, Abu Ya'la recorded that al-Barā' (may Allah be pleased with him) narrated: 'A whole year would pass while I want to ask the Messenger of Allah (peace be upon him) about a matter. But I was afraid from him and we used to wish that some Bedouin (will come and ask him).' They wished that a Bedouin may come and ask him while they are listening and benefit from such questions.

The *aḥādith* that are mentioned in this section are all proven and definite containing no doubts. By combining them with the verse (5:

101) and with the narrations that have been reported via Ibn 'Abbās and others in explaining this verse, clarity can be brought to the subject. The primary point is that Allah and His Messenger (peace be upon him) severely prohibited asking too many questions; arguing and disagreeing with the Prophet (peace be upon him); indulging in too many details, hair-splitting and dialectics. Even asking about matters that had not yet been raised or addressed by the revelation was also covered by this, notwithstanding the type of matters which people did ask the Prophet (peace be upon him), as noted earlier on. All of this has been demonstrated beyond any doubt by definite evidence, which has the effect of reaching certitude. For anyone to deny this would be clear *kufr* (disbelief). Thus, it is well established as a basic rule that other secondary issues can be built upon. All praise is to Allah for protecting the *Dhikr* – the Qur'ān and *Sunnah*.

One issue though remains, namely how do we interpret the narrations which we find in the reliable books of *ḥadith,* such as in Bukhāri, that indicate some of companions in fact did ask the Messenger of Allah (peace be upon him) direct questions? Would the existence of these questions contradict what we have previously mentioned above concerning the prohibition of asking too many questions? In short, it is not a disaster that this in fact did occur. Nobody claims that the companions – may Allah be pleased with them all - were infallible or that they were above committing mistakes. If we go through Bukhāri we will find also several narrations that includes the punishment of adulterers, thieves, slanderers, and the Prophet (peace be upon him) scolding whoever indulged in backbiting. And we mentioned previously that the Prophet (peace be upon him) became angry concerning some questions and he reproved them and that the above verse was revealed concerning one of those incidents.

Secondly, most direct questions were in fact asked by Bedouins, people who were not living in Medina, those living outside the sacred precincts and by people from among delegations which were given a clear legal right to ask, as the Prophet (peace be upon him) used to ask them when they were about to leave - *Do you have anything left (want to ask about it)*? or words to that effect. This of course includes asking about whatever is not known by them or obscure in their minds. Thirdly, the severe prohibition is concerned with asking about matters that were not prohibited; that there is no text which was revealed talking about a particular matter. Pursuing the aforementioned line of argumentation seems to indicate that whoever takes issue with this is in fact displaying an underlying mistrust of Allah or having some kind of doubt that maybe Allah forgets some matters, misses things or that his Prophet (peace be upon him) hid something or neglected some matter. All of this is impossible and constitutes clear *kufr* (disbelief). Such mistrust may lead to the revelation of a judgment that prohibits a matter that was not prohibited before as a punishment for the whole nation. Asking about details of any judgment that was already revealed, seeking explanation of some small matters that were already legislated, details of any act of worship, or about rites that were legislated previously, this is not considered as being part of the prohibited questioning.

One can therefore discern that taken in the round, the cumulative legal effect of all these evidences establishes clearly that the basic ruling was one of permissibility. Put another way, the companions did not hesitate in carrying on with their normal lives and actions; when a commandment was revealed they put it into effect, when a matter was declared prohibited, they avoided the prohibition. Where the text was silent upon a matter, they implicitly understood that this was by default falling within the realm of permissibility.

6 Permissibility is the original or default ruling

Thus far we have exhaustively shown with compelling evidence, reaching the level of certitude, the following key principles:

- We are not originally addressed with the laws of the previous Prophets (peace and blessings upon all of them). These laws have been totally abrogated from beginning to end, an immediate and total abrogation, once the revelation descended to Muḥammad (peace be upon him), the last of the Prophets.

- We are certain that the Prophet (peace be upon him) received revelation and laws throughout his tenure as a Prophet over twenty-three years. No complete book was sent to him from the outset; the Qur'ān and *Sunnah* being revealed in stages.

- A severe prohibition was placed upon seeking to question the Prophet (peace be upon him); from arguing and disputing with him and indulging in all manner of disputation.

- The companions did not hesitate in carrying on with their normal lives and actions during the period of revelation. They did this without asking or waiting for a revelation to be sent.

What was the original ruling concerning acts, speech and objects / things, was it prohibition or permissibility (*ibāḥa*)? What did the Muslims do during the period of revelation regarding these matters that had no text yet to classify them? There are two fundamental phases which must be considered. Firstly, prior to the advent of the Prophetic mission - there is no specific judgment before laws were sent down. The ruling in relation to acts, speech and objects / things is not permissibility as some might think. Permissibility (*ibāḥa*) is a legal judgment only specified by a statement from the law-maker. How can there be a judgment before there was such a statement - this is impossible. People did what they wished according to their own whims and interests till the message of Allah comes to them. This is a case of applying non-divine laws and not a divine permissibility. There is a great and fundamental difference between the two states. They are as far from each other as heaven and earth and it is an obvious matter to any reasonable person.

The second phase is what occurs during the period of revelation. Once the message has been sent *everyone* is obliged to believe in it and then follow it, for people were only created to worship Allah. They are ordered to listen to and obey all commandments and orders, to abstain from all matters prohibited. Submission to Allah means: surrendering, obeying and yielding to Him with love and respect. It is not just a mere collection of acts and rituals, be that bowing, prostrating or otherwise. The question that is raised now, is there a general ruling to which we refer in all things and actions till it is abrogated or altered? Or does such a ruling even exist?

The answer to this can be deduced from the plethora of evidence mentioned in the previous chapter on the prohibition relating to excessive questioning. These evidences establish the prohibition of asking too many questions. Further to this, the Prophet (peace be upon him) clearly stated: '*Leave me as I leave you.*' Such a statement is not ambiguous and can have only one meaning. It meant - do whatever you wish and say whatever you wish, and believe whatever you choose to believe, for it is lawful for you; make use of all things, for they were created pure, lawful and blessed for you to use it in every possible way; fulfil your contracts, meet your promises, keep on doing your customs and continue on following your prevailing systems regarding marriage and inheritance etc. All of this can be carried out till the specifications regarding what is obligatory, recommended, disliked and prohibited has been detailed by revelation. This must be the meaning and implication of the phrase - '*Leave me as I leave you*'. To argue otherwise would be tantamount to saying that the Prophet (peace be upon him) would be allowing people to do prohibited acts, to leave obligations and to go on with their evil contracting system. He would no longer be a Messenger of Allah, commanding the good and forbidding the evil; this would be the qualities of a false imposter not a true prophet. Allah forbid that Abul'-Qāsim (Muḥammad, peace be upon him) the last of the Prophets should be thought of in that manner. Arguably this principle ought to be known by the necessity of perception and reason, as well as by the necessities of the *Sharī'ah*, as it has been made explicit by several texts, in brief:

- Abu Dardā' (may Allah be pleased with him) who narrated that the Prophet (peace be upon him) said: *Whatever was considered lawful by Allah in His Book is lawful and whatever was considered unlawful is unlawful and He has refrained from mentioning other matters so it is forgiveness from Him. Accept from Allah His Forgiveness, as Allah never forgets anything*, (then he mentioned this verse): '*....and your Lord is not forgetful.*'[1]

[1] *Qur'ān* 19: 64

- There is also the *ḥadith* of Abu Thalabah al-Khushani who said, the Messenger of Allah (peace be upon him) said: '*....and has kept silent about other matters out of forgiveness for you and not out of forgetfulness, so do not seek to investigate them.*' The word 'forgiveness' mentioned here is the forgiveness granted after the revelation of the laws; it is called absolute permissibility and not 'forgiveness' before the revelation of a law, which is called 'absence of divine law'; no account or punishment follows it for they are only applied *after* laws are established and proven.

- The Prophet (peace be upon him) said: '*The most sinful Muslim is the one who asked about something which had not been prohibited, but was prohibited because of his asking.*' This means that the thing asked about was *originally lawful before* the question posed resulted in its prohibition. This necessitates in the absence of a legal text denoting a prohibition (or an obligation) the matter is lawful and within the realm of permissibility. For it to be otherwise is impossible. There is no more 'absence of divine law' after the revelation of the verse of the Qur'ān: '*Read! In the name of your Lord...*'[2] It is almost as if Allah said to people then: 'Do whatever you wish, for I have forgiven you all things and have gave you my permission in all actions until I specify for you what is prohibited, what is obligatory and till I show you what is desirable and what is disliked. Until that time everything is lawful and is forgiven, out of my gentleness and mercy not out of negligence or forgetfulness. So, do not ask your Prophet frequently, do not ask too many questions and argue or you will taste the calamity of your affairs.' Put another way – continue, as what you are doing is considered lawful until further notice and clarification.

---

[2] *Qur'ān* 96: 1

- Lastly, what has been transmitted to us from history and biographies has established that the Prophet (peace be upon him) and his companions undertook transactions, various professions, marriages, travel, underwent medical treatment and practiced all of life's affairs without asking or waiting for a revelation to be sent except in very limited instances. Necessity dictates that they implicitly knew that permissibility was the original ruling regarding all things and actions and that it is the general default position.

Some may deny this, postulating an extreme example, such as what if an owner of a brothel continued in this iniquitous practice, living off its profits; surely this would invalidate this principle? In response, we would argue, so what if that was the case! Such practices would be considered lawful *until* revelation comes to specify that it is prohibited. Shocking as it may seem that is how it is. Some may even argue that this goes against the thinking of 'sound minds' and reason. In response, we would argue that the matter cannot be judged by a reasoning that is flawed. He that created the mind and reason is more knowledgeable of them; such matters should be left to him. If he wishes he shall put this into consideration out of his leniency and mercy and if he wishes, he shall neglect it out of being from matters of worship. What you should do is to accept the reason for which you were created, that is exclusively to worship Allah making your devotion sincere and turning to him in repentance; not to argue with the orders of the Lord or put yourself forward before his Messenger (peace be upon him). In any event the jurists of Islam have concurred that lawfulness is the default ruling regarding things / objects, as Allah says:

هُوَ الَّذِي خَلَقَ لَكُم مَّا فِي الْأَرْضِ جَمِيعًا ثُمَّ اسْتَوَىٰ إِلَى السَّمَاءِ فَسَوَّاهُنَّ سَبْعَ سَمَاوَاتٍ وَهُوَ بِكُلِّ شَيْءٍ عَلِيمٌ

It is He who created all that is on the earth for you, then turned to the sky and made the seven heavens; it is He who has knowledge of all things.[3]

There are many verses mentioning the gifts which Allah conferred upon mankind. Such gifts out of his bounty would not be true gifts unless all these things and utilities were lawful except that which was prohibited. All things must have been pure in origin except that which was ordained impure. This is an admissible and decisive proof and here are some additional proofs - everything that was created in this universe from among things, entities in themselves, and their utilities are:

-Permissible for humans
-Pure from the religious ritual point of view

There is no difference between gases (like air and vapour), liquids (like water, juice and milk), and solid entities (like iron, copper, dust and rocks). There is no difference between simple compounds like water and air and complex mixtures like clay and soil. There is no difference between inanimate objects (like rocks and mountains) and living beings (like cattle and birds). All of these things are among the items which Allah has placed in this universe and they are pure and permissible for a human being to utilise. The utilisation can mean terminating them like slaughtering a sheep, eating a loaf of bread, and making use of one of its utilities such as riding animals, smelling roses, and looking at the beautiful sights of mountains and plains. All of this is permissible except for that which is excluded by a legal text specifying its prohibition, its impurity or both. Permissibility and purity are two separate things. Being prohibited does not entail being impure and vice versa.

Indeed, a minority of Islamic scholars argued that the original

[3] *Qur'ān* 2: 29

principle concerning acts is different from that concerning things / objects. According to this view, man and his actions do not fall under the previous discussion, for Allah favoured man by granting him the right to utilise all other creatures. We know by the necessity of perception and reason that the one favoured (mankind) is different from the favoured thing itself which is the rest of things in the universe. Thus, the previous evidences supporting the permissibility and purity of things does not entail that permissibility is the original ruling regarding man's actions. Mankind was only created to worship Allah, to obey his orders and abstain from his prohibitions. Consequently, man cannot do or intend to do any action without the express permission of Allah. In response, we would submit that this is a good point that draws a clear distinction between actions - man's voluntary actions which is the only thing taken into account here - and all things created in the universe other than man. The one certain truth is that man is only created to worship Allah, as clearly established in the verse:

وَمَا خَلَقْتُ الْجِنَّ وَالْإِنسَ إِلَّا لِيَعْبُدُونِ

And I have only created man and jinn so that they should worship me. [4]

Submission to Allah means to yield, surrender and obey with love and honour. It is not a simple collection of rituals that involve bowing or prostrating. Worship is obedience, based on love and sanctification as will be discussed elsewhere. All of that has nothing to do with the fact that permissibility is the default ruling regarding neither all things nor all actions, for permissibility is a legal judgment. Obeying Allah in that which he has designated permissible is not different from obeying him in adhering to duties and abstaining from prohibitions. When Allah ordains that permissibility is the default ruling regarding things,

---

[4] *Qur'ān* 51: 56

this is his judgment that cannot be refused. This is the meaning of submission to Allah which is the reason behind the creation of mankind. If he ordained things to be prohibited, this is his judgment that cannot be neglected and that must be obeyed.

فَمَن يَعْمَلْ مِثْقَالَ ذَرَّةٍ خَيْرًا يَرَهُ ، وَمَن يَعْمَلْ مِثْقَالَ ذَرَّةٍ شَرًّا يَرَهُ

Hence he who has done an atom's weight of good shall see it and he who has done an atom's weight of evil shall see it. [5]

The aforementioned verse and those of similar import are not directly relevant to the present discussion; it is just an indication to the comprehensive account and reward or punishment for each deed no matter how minute it is. Good is what Allah has classified as good and evil is what Allah has dispraised and called evil and nothing else. What is the relationship between that and the original judgment regarding actions and things? There is no relationship whatsoever, for we only seek the judgment of Allah. We wish to submit to Allah surrendering to his judgment and nothing else, regardless of the nature of that judgment. It might be prohibiting drinking camel's milk in the same matter that it was prohibited to the people of Israel or making it lawful as ordained in our last and final law. Thus, there is no other choice than discussing this matter from such an angle.

The statement that permissibility is the original or default ruling on all things / objects unless a textual proof denotes otherwise, necessarily requires that all acts that are related to these things are permissible as well. Otherwise that notion of permissibility would lose its meaning and become absurd. To say that a ewe is lawful, means that it is permissible to slaughter it, skin it, tan its skin, sell it, buy it, bury it or dissolve its fat and benefit from that fat or manufacture soap from it. In this way from what cannot be counted concerning human

[5] *Qur'ān* 99: 7/8

actions that are related to the ewe itself or its utility. This is a big part of human behaviour that has necessarily been basically permissible, unless a textual proof denotes otherwise; an example of this being the textual proof that outlaws torturing animals or branding them with fire on their faces.

Allah has bestowed great favour upon mankind giving us the senses, the heart, the soul and the mind. Mankind has been created with the best stature. Together with the texts already cited, necessity dictates that all actions proceeding from this form are basically permissible, unless a textual proof denotes otherwise. To elaborate this point with a simple example, all manner of expression from the lips and tongue is permissible, including speaking, whistling, humming, mumbling, crying, weeping, lamentation, wailing, articulation and speech and various sounds etc. Allah has said:

مَّا يَلْفِظُ مِن قَوْلٍ إِلَّا لَدَيْهِ رَقِيبٌ عَتِيدٌ

He utters not a word but there is by him a watcher at hand.[6]

The stressed prohibition in the Qur'ānic verse of asking '*questions about things which if declared to you may trouble you*' requires the necessity of permitting all things and all actions, unless textual evidence denotes otherwise. A human being can never be void of activities in the course of life. Given that the verse says not to ask until the legislator provides detailed explanation, the meaning of the verse is evidently established: do as you will, for it is permissible unless the legislator specifies otherwise. As previously mentioned, the Prophet (peace be upon him) clearly said: '*Leave me as I leave you for the people who were before you were ruined because of their questions and their differences over their Prophets. So, if I forbid you to do something, then keep away from it. And if I order you to do something,*

[6] *Qur'ān* 50: 18

then do of it as much as you can.' Is it therefore conceivable that someone who has been made infallible by Allah and who conveys the most perfect conveyance about him, commands people to leave him until it is he who specifies otherwise; would he be leaving them to commit matters unlawful and not establish obligations? Allah forbid!

The Prophet (peace be upon him) also said: '*The most sinful Muslim is the one who asked about something which had not been prohibited, but was prohibited because of his asking.*' Yet again the *ḥadith* provides definite evidence that the thing asked wrongly, affectedly and unjustly, was permissible before the question, which then led to a prohibition. The word 'things' here in its lexical meaning includes everything: genus, qualities and actions. Furthermore, he (peace be upon him) clearly said: '*Verily, Allah has ordained some obligations, so do not neglect them; He has set some limits, so do not trespass them; He has refrained from mentioning other matters not (out of) forgetfulness, so do not look for them. It is mercy from Allah, so accept it.*' Can the matter be any clear than this? In a separate Qur'ānic verse Allah has said that he has explained to us in detail what has been forbidden:

وَمَا لَكُمْ أَلَّا تَأْكُلُوا مِمَّا ذُكِرَ اسْمُ اللَّهِ عَلَيْهِ وَقَدْ فَصَّلَ لَكُم مَّا حَرَّمَ عَلَيْكُمْ إِلَّا مَا اضْطُرِرْتُمْ إِلَيْهِ
وَإِنَّ كَثِيرًا لَّيُضِلُّونَ بِأَهْوَائِهِم بِغَيْرِ عِلْمٍ إِنَّ رَبَّكَ هُوَ أَعْلَمُ بِالْمُعْتَدِينَ

And what reason have you that you should not eat of that on which Allah's name has been mentioned, and He has already made plain to you what He has forbidden to you - excepting what you are compelled to; and most surely many would lead (people) astray by their low desires out of ignorance; surely your Lord-- He best knows those who exceed the limits. [7]

Matters prohibited have all been explained, declared and clarified in detail. The same thing has been applied to the religious obligations,

[7] *Qur'ān* 6: 119

for abandoning them is a sin and prohibited. Allah has blamed, scolded and condemned in this verse, whosoever abstained from some food, lest that he falls into a forbidden thing *which has not been detailed.* This has been a proof that all things, whether properties and actions, are lawful unless there is an explicit detailed statement to prohibit or make something an obligation. Jābir ibn Abdullah as well as many other companions (may Allah be pleased with them all) had this very same understanding. He referred to them in the collective by saying using the word 'we' when he said: 'We used to practice *al-A'zl* (*coitus interruptus*) during the lifetime of the Messenger of Allah (peace be upon him) while the Qur'ān was being revealed.'[8] In the version which Muslim records, Isḥāq added that Sufyān said: 'Had it been something to be prohibited from, the Qur'ān would have stated so.'[9] Writing in *Fatḥ al-Bāri* al-Ḥāfiz (Ibn Ḥajar) said:

> Ibn Daqiq al'Eid has explained it, concerning what is in al-'Umda. He said that Jābir's inference of the establishment from Allah is strange and it is possible that it is the establishment of the Messenger (peace be upon him) but it is conditioned by his knowing about that. And it is enough for him to know about the statement of the companion that he did it at his lifetime. Regardless, the issue is a well known issue in the study of *Uṣul* and in the study of *ḥadith* that if the companion adds it to during the lifetime of the Prophet (peace be upon him), it would have the judgment of traceability according to the majority because it is obvious that the Prophet (peace be upon him) saw that and approved it, due to the abundance of their causes about their asking him concerning judgments, though the judgment of traceability is not added to it according to some people. And this is from the beginning,

---

[8] The *ḥadith* is recorded by Bukhāri, Muslim and many others. The wording above is cited from Bukhāri - book of marriage, chapter on *al-'Azl* with the following *isnād*: Ali bin Abdullah narrated to us Sufyān narrated to us he said 'Amr reported to me from 'Aṭā who heard Jābir ibn Abdullah say (etc.)

[9] Muslim book of marriage chapter on the ruling of *al-'Azl*

for Jābir made it clear that it happened during the lifetime of the Prophet (peace be upon him). Several methods have been reported proving that he saw it. Now what is apparent to me is that the person who deduced that, be it Jābir or Sufyān, the person meant by the revelation of the Qur'ān, that what is read is more general than what worship is done by reciting it, or other than that, from that which is revealed to the Prophet (peace be upon him). It is as if he says, we have done it at the time of legislation. And had it been unlawful, we would not have been approved to it. In relation to this, the statement of Ibn 'Umar (may Allah be pleased with him) provides for the following: 'During the lifetime of the Prophet we used to avoid chatting leisurely and freely with our wives lest some divine inspiration might be revealed concerning us. But when the Prophet had died, we started chatting leisurely and freely (with them).' Recorded by al-Bukhāri]

I would argue that the statement of those who said: '*Jābir's inference of the establishment from Allah is strange*,' means nothing. But what is truly astonishing is how al-Ḥāfiz (may Allah have mercy upon him) commented. *That* is what is truly strange. Does Allah not surround all things by his knowledge? And was the statement of the Prophet (peace be upon him) from himself and not revelation? Allah forbid! This is not what happened but it is from Allah and it is Allah who guarantees both the protection and explanation of the *Dhikr* - as he has already confirmed to us: *Therefore it is upon us (rests) its explanation.*[10]

As for the *ḥadith* of Ibn 'Umar (may Allah be pleased with him), it is in conformity with that reported from Jābir and confirms the notion of permissibility being the underlying or default ruling. The full narration as recorded in Bukhāri is as follows:

---

[10] *Qur'ān* 75: 19

حدثنا أبو نعيم حدثنا سفيان عن عبد الله بن دينار عن ابن عمر، رضي الله عنهما، قال: كنا نتقي الكلام والانبساط إلى نسائنا، هيبة أن ينزل فينا شيء على عهد النبي، صلى الله عليه وسلم، فلما مات النبي، صلى الله عليه وسلم، تكلمنا وانبسطنا

> Abu Nu'aym narrated to us Sufyān narrated to us from Abdullah bin Dinār from Ibn Umar who said: During the lifetime of the Prophet (peace be upon him) we used to avoid chatting leisurely and freely with our wives lest some divine inspiration might be revealed concerning us. But when the Prophet (peace be upon him) had died, we started chatting leisurely and freely (with them).[11]

Arguably this is from amongst the most authentic chains of transmission. Ibn Mājah recorded this but with the following channel to Sufyān: 'Muḥammad bin Bashār narrated to us Abdar-Raḥman bin Mahdi reported to us Sufyān narrated to us'. Imām Aḥmad also reports this in *Musnad* with the channel: Abdar-Raḥman narrated to us Sufyān narrated to us (et al).

In addition to the above we may add to these points the various narratives where the Prophet (peace be upon him) used to inform his companions about matters that they were completely unaware of; he (peace be upon him) only knew them via revelation. An example of this is the advice given to the delegation of 'Abdul-Qais not to make *nabeeth* in certain containers which were like 'hollowed stumps,' vessels smeared with pitch, pumpkins, and green jars. They were astonished that he knew some of them, though they are unknown to the people of Mecca and Medina; only the people of Al-Yamāma knew about them. As recorded and authenticated by Imām Muslim:

حدثني مُحَمَّد بن بكار البصري حدثنا أبو عاصم عن بن جريج (ح) وحدثني

---

[11] The standard rendering of this narration into English is that wording. What Ibn Umar is referring to by this 'leisurely talk' is intimate sexual talk between spouses.

مُحَمَّد بن رافع، واللفظ له، حدثنا عبد الرزاق أخبرنا بن جريح قال: أخبرني أبو قزعة أن أبا نضرة أخبره وحسنا أخبرهما أن أبا سعيد الخدري أخبره: أن وفد عبد القيس لما أتوا نبي الله، صلى الله عليه وسلم، قالوا: يا نبي الله جعلنا الله فداءك، ماذا يصلح لنا من الأشربة؟، فقال: لا تشربوا في النقير! ، قالوا: يا نبي الله، جعلنا الله فداءك، أو تدري ما النقير؟، قال: نعم، الجذع ينقر وسطه؛ ولا في الدباء، ولا في الحنتمة، وعليكم بالموكى

> Muḥammad bin Bakkār al-Baṣri narrated to me Abu 'Aāṣim narrated to us from ibn Jurayj (*ḥawala*) and Muḥammad bin Rāfi'h narrated to me and it's his wording – Abdar-Razzāq narrated to us Ibn Jurayj reported to us he said Abu Qaza'ah reported to me that Abu Naḍra reported and told him that Abu Sa'eed al-Khudri informed him that when the delegation of the tribe of Abdul-Qais came to the Prophet of Allah (peace be upon him) (its members) said: Messenger of Allah, may God enable us to lay down our lives for you, which beverage is good for us? He (the Prophet) said: *Not to speak of beverages, I would lay stress) that you should not drink in the wine jars*. They said: Apostle of Allah, may God enable us to lay down our lives for you, do you know what *al-naqir* is? He (the Prophet) replied: *Yes, it is a stump which you hollow out in the middle, and added: Do not use gourd or receptacle (for drink). Use water-skin the mouth of which is tied with a thong* (for this purpose).

It is also recorded in the *Musnad* of Imām Aḥmad[12] with essentially the same *isnād*: 'Abdar-Razzāq narrated to us and he reports, they said Ibn Jurayj narrated to us Abu Qaza'ah reported to me with it, before my presence.' I would submit that this is very authentic and well established particularly given the wording from Ibn Jurayj. The words, 'and good, told them' it is inverse wording and authentic; and he reported well. In any event, it is a good report from Abu Qaza'ah as is evident from the channel. In *Sharḥ al-Ma'āni al-Athār* its reported as: Ali narrated to us he said Ḥajjāj narrated to us from Ibn

[12] *Musnad* Aḥmad Vol. 3 sec. 57, no. 11,561

Jurayj he said Abu Qaza'ah reported to me that Abu Naḍra reported to him that Abu Sa'eed al-Khudri narrated to them, as follows. In a lengthy *ḥadith* recorded and authenticated by Imām Muslim we have the following:

حدثنا يحيى بن أيوب حدثنا ابن علية حدثنا سعيد بن أبي عروبة عن قتادة قال: حدثنا من لقي الوفد الذين قدموا على رسول الله، صلى الله عليه وسلم، من عبد القيس قال سعيد: وذكر قتادة أبا نضرة عن أبي سعيد الخدري في حديثه هذا أن أناسا من عبد القيس قدموا على رسول الله، صلى الله عليه وسلم، فقالوا: يا نبي الله: إنا حي من ربيعة، وبيننا وبينك كفّار مضر، ولا نقدر عليك إلا في أشهر الحرم فمرنا بأمر نأمر به من وراءنا وندخل به الجنة إذا نحن أخذنا به! ، فقال رسول الله، صلى الله عليه وسلم: «آمركم بأربع وأنهاكم عن أربع: اعبدوا الله ولا تشركوا به شيئا، وأقيموا الصلاة وآتوا الزكاة وصوموا رمضان وأعطوا الخمس من الغنائم؛ وأنهاكم عن أربع: عن الدباء والحنتم والمزفت والنقير، قالوا: (يا نبي الله ما علمك بالنقير؟!، قال: بلى، جذع تنقرونه فتقذفون فيه من القطيعاء (قال سعيد: أو قال من التمر) ثم تصبون فيه من الماء حتى إذا سكن غليانه شربتموه حتى إن أحدكم، أو إن أحدهم، ليضرب ابن عمه بالسيف»، قال: (وفي القوم رجل أصابته جراحة كذلك، قال: وكنت أخبؤها حياء من رسول الله، صلى الله عليه وسلم، فقلت: (ففيم نشرب يا رسول الله؟!، قال: «في أسقية الأدم التي يلاث على أفواهها، قالوا: يا رسول الله إن أرضنا كثيرة الجرذان، ولا تبقى بها أسقية الأدم؟!، فقال نبي الله، صلى الله عليه وسلم: وإن أكلتها الجرذان، وإن أكلتها الجرذان، وإن أكلتها الجرذان، قال: وقال نبي الله، صلى الله عليه وسلم، لأشج عبد القيس: إن فيك لخصلتين يحبهما الله، الحلم والأناة

Yaḥya bin Ayub narrated to us ibn 'Aliya narrated to us Sa'eed bin Abi Aruba narrated to us from Qatādah who said: (It was) narrated to us from among the delegates of the 'Abd al-Qais tribe narrated this tradition to him. Sa'id said that Qatādah had mentioned the name of Abu Naḍra on the authority of Abu Sa'eed al-Khudri who narrated this tradition: That people from the- tribe of 'Abd al-Qais came to the Messenger of Allah (peace be upon him) and said: Messenger of Allah, we belong to the tribe of Rabi'a and there live between you and us the unbelievers of the Mudar tribe and we find it impossible to come to you except in the sacred months; direct us to a deed which we must communicate to those who have been left behind us and by doing which we may enter heaven. Upon this the Messenger of Allah (peace be upon him) said: *I enjoin upon you four (things) and forbid you to do four (things): worship Allah and associate none with Him, establish prayer, pay zakāt, and observe the fast of Ramaḍān, and pay the fifth part out of the booty. And I prohibit you from four (things): dry gourds, green-coloured jars, hollowed stumps of palm-trees, and receptacles.*

They (the members of the delegation) said: Do you know what *al-naqir* is? He replied: *Yes, it is a stump which you hollow out and in which you throw small dates*. Sa'eed said: He (the Prophet) used the word *tamar* (dates). (The Prophet then added): *Then you sprinkle water over it and when its ebullition subsides, you drink it (and you are so intoxicated) that one amongst you, or one amongst them strikes his cousin with the sword.* He (the narrator) said: There was a man amongst us who had sustained injury on this very account due to (intoxication), and he said that he tried to conceal it out of shame before the Messenger of Allah (peace be upon him). I, however, inquired from the Messenger of Allah (it we discard those utensils which you have forbidden us to use), then what type of vessels should be used for drink? He replied: *In the waterskin the mouths of which are tied (with a string)*. They (again) said: Prophet of Allah, our land abounds in rats and water-skins cannot remain preserved. The Prophet of Allah (peace be upon him) said: *(Drink in water-skins) even if these are nibbled by rats.* And then (addressing) al-Ashajj of 'Abd al-Qais he said: *Verily, you possess two such qualities which Allah loves: insight and deliberateness.*

After this Imām Muslim said: 'Muḥammad bin al-Muthanna and Ibn Bishār narrated to us, they said Ibn Abi 'Adi narrated to us from Sa'eed from Qatādah who said: it was narrated to me from among the delegates of the 'Abd al-Qais tribe, that they came to the Prophet (peace be upon him) with the likeness of this *ḥadith* of ibn 'Aliya, that in it he referred to hollowed stumps of palm-trees and receptacles or dates and water, but didn't say Sa'eed said or he said from dates.' This narration is also found in the *Musnad* of Imām Aḥmad[13] with the channel – Yaḥya ibn Sa'eed narrated to us from Ibn Abi 'Aruba, Qatādah narrated to us, who met with the delegation and he mentioned Abu Naḍra from Abu Sa'eed about it. The reference to '*al-naqeer'* was known in Al-Yamāma only and unknown to the people of Ḥijāz as outlined by al-Bayhaqy in *Sunan* al-Kubra:

حدثنا أبو بكر بن فورك أنبأ عبد الله بن جعفر حدثنا يونس بن حبيب حدثنا أبو داود حدثنا عيينة بن عبد الرحمن بن جوشن حدثني أبي قال: كان أبو بكرة ينتبذ له في جرة فقدم أبو برزة من غيبة كان غابها فنزل بمنزل أبي بكرة قبل أن يأتي منزله فذكر الحديث في إنكار ما نبذ له في جرة، وقوله لامرأته: وددت إنك جعلتيه في سقاء، وأن أبا بكرة حين جاء قال: قد عرفنا الذي نهينا عنه، نهينا عن الدباء والنقير والحنتم والمزفت، فإما الدباء فإنا معشر ثقيف بالطائف كنا نأخذ الدباء فنخرط فيها عناقيد العنب ثم ندفنها ثم نتركها حتى تهدر ثم تموت. وأما النقير فإن أهل اليمامة كانوا ينقرون أصل النخلة فيشدخون فيه الرطب والبسر ثم يدعونه حتى يهدر ثم يموت. وأما الحنتم فجرار كان يحمل إلينا فيها الخمر، وأما المزفت فهي هذه الأوعية التي فيها هذا الزفت

Abu Bakr bin Fawrak narrated to us Adallah bin Ja'far reports, Yunus bin Ḥabeeb narrated to us Abu Dāwud narrated to us 'Uyayna bin Abdar-Raḥman bin Jawshan narrated to us my father narrated to me he said: Wine used to be made for Abu Bakrah in a jar. And then one day, Abu Barzah came from a long absence. He stayed at Abu Bakrah's house before he went to his own house. He mentioned the *ḥadith* regarding the prohibited of wine for him, and his statement to his wife - I would like you to put it in water skin. When Abu Bakrah came, he said: we have known what we have been forbidden from. We have been forbidden from dry gourds, receptacles,

[13] *Musnad* Aḥmad Vol. 3 sec. 23, no. 11,191

> hollowed stumps of palm-trees and green-coloured jars. As for the dry gourds, we the people from the tribe of Thaqeef in Ṭā'if, used to take dry gourds, and mix clusters of grapes in them, and then bury them till they simmer and die. As for hollowed stumps of palm-trees, they are jars that wine used to be transported to us in them. As for green-coloured jars, they are these vessels that contain this pitch.

Abu Dāwud aṭ-Ṭayālisi also reported similarly in his *Musnad*.[14] Regarding this al-Bayhaqy commented as follows:

> This is the way it has been reported about Abu Bakrah. According to a group of scholars, what is meant by prohibition from making wine in these vessels is that when malmsey is put in them, it quickly becomes so strong that it becomes intoxicating, whereas in water skins, it is unlikely to become so. And then, permission was granted regarding all sorts of vessels, as long as they do not drink intoxicants. And only Allah knows best.

The Prophet (peace be upon him) once surprised the companions on another occasion and without prior notice, when an embarrassing matter arose. Imām Aḥmad records this incident in the *Musnad:*

> حدثنا عبد الصمد قال: حدثنا حفص السراج قال: سمعت شهرا يقول: حدثتني أسماء بنت يزيد أنها كانت عند رسول الله، صلى الله عليه وسلم، والرجال والنساء قعود عنده فقال: لعل رجلا يقول ما يفعل بأهله، ولعل امرأة تخبر بما فعلت مع زوجها؟!، فأرم القوم فقلت: إي والله يا رسول الله إنهن ليقلن وإنهم ليفعلون! ، قال: «فلا تفعلوا، فإنما ذلك مثل الشيطان لقي شيطانة في طريق فغشيها والناس ينظرون

[14] *Musnad* Abu Dāwud aṭ-Ṭayālisi Vol. 1 sec. 120, no. 882

> Abd aṣ-Ṣammad narrated to us he said Ḥafṣ as-Sirāj narrated to us he said I heard Shahr saying Asmā bint Yazeed narrated to me - she was once at the mosque of the Messenger of Allah (peace be upon him), and men and women were sitting there. All of a sudden, he said: *It may be that some men of you talk about what they do with their wives, and it may be that some women talk about what they have done with their husbands?* Thereupon, people became shocked, and then I said – Yes! By Allah, O Messenger of Allah, they (women) do say such things regarding what they do! He said: *You should not do that, for that is like the he-devil who met a she-devil in a street, and slept with her while people were looking (at them)!*

The narration is also recorded by aṭ-Ṭabarāni in *Mu'jam al-Kabir*.[15] The report is authentic; I would submit that Shahr ibn Ḥawshab is *thiqa* and *ṣadooq* (trustworthy and truthful). Though at times some reports appear incomplete with some illusionary points; al-Ḥāfiz (Ibn Ḥajar) said regarding him in *at-Taqreeb*: '*ṣadooq* (trustworthy) but he has a lot of *irsāl* and illusions.' Yet the narration he has reported here has been delivered well and he is known for narrating from Asmā bint Yazeed. Therefore, this chain of transmission is good on its own virtue, without doubt. It is witnessed, for he has memorised here the following *ḥadith* from a completely independent chain away from Abu Hurayrah. It is inconceivable that there is a connivance of falsehood or the occurrence of error by chance.

> حدثنا إسماعيل بن إبراهيم عن سعيد الجريري عن أبي نضرة عن رجل من الطفاوة قال: نزلت على أبي هريرة، قال: ولم أدرك من صحابة رسول الله، صلى الله عليه وسلم، رجلا أشد تشميرا ولا أقوم على ضيف منه؛ فبينما أنا عنده وهو على سرير له وأسفل منه جارية له سوداء ومعه كيس فيه حصى ونوى، يقول: سبحان الله سبحان الله، حتى إذا أنفذ ما في الكيس ألقاه إليها فجمعته فجعلته في الكيس ثم دفعته إليه فقال لي: ألا أحدثك عني وعن رسول

[15] Ṭabarāni, *Mu'jam al-Kabir*, Vol. 24 sec. 163, no. 414

الله، صلى الله عليه وسلم! قلت: بلى، قال: فإني بينما أنا أوعك في مسجد المدينة إذ دخل رسول الله، صلى الله عليه وسلم، المسجد فقال: «من أحس الفتى الدوسي، من أحس الفتى الدوسي»، فقال له قائل: هو ذاك يوعك في جانب المسجد حيث ترى يا رسول الله، فجاء فوضع يده علي وقال لي معروفا فقمت، فانطلق حتى قام في مقامه الذي يصلي فيه ومعه يومئذ صفان من رجال وصف من نساء، أو صفان من نساء وصف من رجال، فأقبل عليهم فقال: إن أنساني الشيطان شيئا من صلاتي فليسبح القوم وليصفق النساء، فصلى رسول الله، صلى الله عليه وسلم، ولم ينس من صلاته شيئا. فلما سلم أقبل عليهم بوجهه فقال: «مجالسكم: هل منكم إذا أتى أهله أغلق بابه وأرخى ستره ثم يخرج فيحدث فيقول: فعلت بأهلي كذا وفعلت بأهلي كذا؟!»، فسكتوا، فأقبل على النساء فقال: «هل منكن من تحدّث؟!»، فجثت فتاة كعاب على إحدى ركبتيها وتطاولت ليراها رسول الله، صلى الله عليه وسلم، ويسمع كلامها فقالت: (إي والله: إنهم ليحدّثون، وإنهن ليحدّثن!)، فقال: «هل تدرون ما مثل من فعل ذلك؟! إن مثل من فعل ذلك مثل شيطان وشيطانة لقي أحدهما صاحبه بالسكّة قضى حاجته منها والناس ينظرون إليه»، ثم قال: ألا لا يفضينّ رجل إلى رجل، ولا امرأة إلى امرأة إلا إلى ولد أو والد- قال: وذكر ثالثة فنسيتها- ألا إن طيب الرجل ما وجد ريحه ولم يظهر لونه، ألا إن طيب النساء ما ظهر لونه ولم يوجد ريحه

Ismā'il bin Ibrāhim narrated to us from Sa'eed al-Juriri from Abi Naḍra from a man from al-Ṭufāwa who said: I once happened to be a guest of Abu Hurayrah (may Allah be pleased with him). I did not find any one among the companions of the Prophet (peace be upon him) more devoted to worship and more hospitable than him. One day I was with him when he was sitting on his bed. He had a bag which contained pebbles or kernels. A black slave girl of his was sitting below. He was saying: Glory be to Allah, Glory be to Allah) (with the pebbles or kernels). When the pebbles or the kernels in the bag came to the end, he would make her collect them and put them back into the bag, and then she would give them to him. After a while, he said to me 'Should I tell you about the Messenger of Allah and me? I said, Yes. He said, Once while I was suffering from fever in the mosque of Medina, the Messenger of Allah (peace be upon him) suddenly came and entered the mosque, and then asked: *Who saw the youth of Ad-Daus? Who saw the youth of Ad-Daus?* A man replied to him, O Messenger of Allah, there he is, suffering from fever in the corner of the mosque as you can see. He came over, put his hand on me and had a kind talk with me, and I rose. He then began to walk till he reached the place where he used to perform his prayer. On that day, there were two rows of men and one row of women, or two rows of women and one row of men (the narrator is doubtful). He turned to them and then said: *If Satan makes me forget anything during the prayer, the men should say - Glory be to Allah, and the women should clap their hands*. The Messenger of Allah (peace be upon him) then performed the prayer and he did not forget anything during the prayer.

When he ended the prayer by pronouncing the final salutation he turned immediately to them with his face and then said: *(please) stay at your places: Is there any man among you who approaches his wife, closes the door, covers himself with a curtain, and then come out and says, I have done such and such with my wife?* They all kept silent. He then turned to the women and said (to them): *Is there any woman among you who narrates it?* Thereupon, a young busty girl knelt on one of her knees and raised her head so that the Messenger of Allah (peace be upon him) could see her and hear her talk. She said - Yes, by Allah! They talk (about secrets of intercourse), they really talk about it! He then said: *Do you know the likeness of the one who does that? Certainly, the likeness of this act is the likeness of a male devil and a female devil who met each other in the street, and he fulfilled his desire with her while people are looking at him.* Then he said: *Beware! No man should sleep in the same bed under the same cover while another man is sleeping therein, and no woman should sleep in the same bed under the same cover while another woman is sleeping therein, unless the other party, man or woman, is either an offspring or a parent.* He (the narrator) said, he mentioned a third one but I have forgotten. *Certainly, the perfume of men is that whose scent can be scented and its colour does not appear (like rose water), and the perfume of women is that whose colour can be seen, but its scent cannot be scented (like henna).*

The narrative is reported quite widely, such as in the *Sunan* of Abu Dāwud,[16] in Bayhaqy's *Sunan al-Kubra,*[17] in the *Muṣṣanaf* of Ibn Abi Shayba[18] as well as in other places. Albāni said that the narration was weak in his commentary on the *Sunan* of Abu Dāwud. I would concur to a degree given the presence of an unknown man from Ṭufāwa. Indeed, it is not from a companion but there is no fear of *ikhtilāṭ* (confusion/mixing up) regarding al-Juriri; yet there are a multiplicity of the narrations from him – Ismā'il bin Ibrāhim (Ibn 'Ulaya), Bishr and Ḥammād bin Zayd as well as Yazeed bin Zureeh'. Besides, Bayhaqy said: 'All of them are established Imām's and from them he heard from al-Juriri before his *ikhtilāṭ.*' To reiterate, admittedly the chain of transmission contains an unknown man from al-Ṭufāwa, but the rest are well known and trustworthy; the girl is certainly Asmā bint Yazeed bin as-Sakan (may Allah be pleased with her), the narrator of the previous *ḥadith*. That *ḥadith* of hers has certainly established the sincerity and accuracy of the man of Ṭufāwa (may Allah have mercy upon him) is made evident. Therefore, all praise and thanks is only to Allah, the lord of all the worlds.

We have no doubt that anyone who examines the collections of *Sunan,* the person would find a greater number of narratives are like this; i.e. where the Prophet (peace be upon him) explained things which were happening even though none of the companions had formally raised it. It may be without an occasion that requires that or without the Prophet (peace be upon him) being previously informed about anything concerning them; just by a revelation that might suddenly be revealed to him by Allah. This is what we really mean by the following statement: *'the approval of the Qur'ān concerning what happened at the time of the revelation, is like the approval of the Prophet (peace be upon him) regarding what he saw and heard and*

[16] *Sunan* Abu Dāwud Vol. 2 sec. 254, no. 2,174
[17] Bayhaqy, *Sunan al-Kubra,* Vol. 7 sec. 194, no. 13,876
[18] Ibn Abi Shayba, *Muṣṣanaf,* Vol. 2 sec. 161, no. 7,661 & Vol. 4 sec. 39, no. 17,560

there is no difference.' What is more, the first one is stronger and higher in rank, which is the origin and it is more general and more numerous. Nonetheless, we do not mind the statement where it was said: 'Had it been something to be prohibited, the Qur'ān would have stated so', because in actuality, it is the truth with its previously cited proofs. But as for his statement: 'while the Qur'ān was being revealed', it means the importance of the time of the revelation, without any difference between the Qur'ān and the *Sunnah,* as previously mentioned and as it is evident like the way the sun is evident to us, regarding our previous evidences concerning the authenticity of *Sunnah,* and that it is a revelation and part of the protected *Dhikr.*

The point is also clearly established by the tradition reported from Ibn Umar regarding the 'leisurely talk'. We know for a fact that the Prophet (peace be upon him) did not discuss this with their wives, nor did he used to spy on private matters that occurred in their bedrooms to see what they did or hear what they talk about. With the death of the Prophet (peace be upon him) we know with certitude that revelation came to an end, the *Deen* was completed; prior to that all commands and prohibitions which Allah decided upon were outlined completely with detail where necessary. As the Prophet (peace be upon him) said: *'I have left you on a straight forward path as clear as the day and night and no one would go astray therefore except he who is doomed to be a looser.'* Allah protected the *Dhikr* in its totality – the Qur'ān and the *Sunnah*; he protected the Arabic language as it is necessary for the *Dhikr* and will not be understood except by this medium until the day of judgement, because the Prophet (peace be upon him) is the seal and last of all the Prophets and Messengers. There is neither a Prophet nor any message after him. There can be neither abrogation nor a new creed after him except for those who changed his creed, exchanging his favour with unbelief and thereby going astray.

Now that the Prophet (peace be upon him) is no longer with us it becomes the responsibility and duty of people in general, including the scholars, to exert themselves in returning to the divine legal texts only in order to extract guidance from them; to maintain diligence in following the authentic *aḥādith* and form true conclusive judgments. In other words, in our era questioning does become necessary in the sense that we must acquaint ourselves with the ruling of Allah in every matter. The *Deen* in totality contains no gaps, nor is there a matter which exists that is not covered by the revelation. But those who seek to clarify matters pertaining to religion *now* should be asking the right question, namely asking about the evidence that proves a matter to be obligatory, prohibited, desired or undesired. Questions should not be framed in the manner of 'is this matter permissible (*mubāḥ*)?' since it is the general default position, as established by the exhaustive evidence already cited. Stated differently questions that are framed as - 'what is the evidence for the permissibility of so and so?' become an absurdity given that permissibility is the default ruling. It is legal texts which raise a matter to being an obligation or a prohibition.

We said that the right question is the one which is asking about the evidence that proves a matter to be obligatory or prohibited; desired or undesired in itself. The use of 'in itself' is but precautionary, because man can be rewarded for doing matters that are permissible if he intends to do it in order to help him in doing some obligations and desirable matters or in order to accustom himself to keep away from doing undesirable and prohibited matters. People can be undertaking matters with a consciousness, while intending to do a particular deed assured that Allah permitted it as such, thereby rendering to the judgement of Allah, content in the knowledge that he has allowed the matter. Reward is not given according to the naked deed in and of itself as such, but rather according to the intention whether it is to help him in doing other obligatory or desirable acts or because of consciousness and remembrance of Allah or any other considerations than that which are more than doing the deed in itself as a mere deed. It is inaccurate to say then that the permissible was turned into desirable because it is not desirable in itself, and reward is to be given according to other aspects and matters that accompanied it.

It is not appropriate to mix them, otherwise measures of *Sharī'ah* will be disturbed and truth will mix with falsehood. That is why, both the matter which is desirable in itself, that whoever did it will be rewarded and whoever did not will not be punished and the matter which is undesirable in itself, that whoever did not do it will be rewarded and whoever did it will not be punished, need an independent evidence because they are not like the original absolute permissibility. Whatever was not like it needs evidence, otherwise it would be a saying about Allah without knowledge and a judgment that Allah did not permit. That is to say, it would be innovation in the religion and this is exactly the way that leads to misguidance and ultimately to disbelief.

The subject of intention and its influence on both reward and punishment is considered in a separate section entitled 'the reward of deeds rests upon intention and everybody will be rewarded according to what he/she has intended.' All of the forgoing discussion is not an aberration, nor is it a matter that has just been introduced. As already referred to, many famous Imām's adopted the same view, from the classical period of Islam up to the present, although, some of them did not always apply this diligently when it came to matters of *fiqh* (jurisprudence). To take just one example, we provide a long quote here from *al-Iḥkām fi Uṣul al-Aḥkām* (Judgement on the Principles of Law) by Imām Abu Muḥammad Ali Ibn Ḥazm (may Allah be merciful to him):

> If they said that they want to see evidence for all incidents we should say that if we failed to do such a thing, our failure is not evidence to be taken, neither against Allah nor His Messenger (peace be upon him). We did not claim that we are Allah; Allah alone knows about all these incidents. It is enough that we are sure that Allah, the exalted explained to us whatever happened or will happen from among the judgments of the religion till the day of judgement. We present to you one text that included every incident that happened or will happen till the day of judgement; it is the same *ḥadith* which we

mentioned above. The Messenger of Allah (peace be upon him) said: '*Leave me with what I have left to you. Verily the people before you went to their doom because they had put too many questions to their Prophets and then disagreed with their teachings. So do that which I command you to do to the best of your capacity and avoid that which I forbid you to do*.'

According to this text it is legal that whatever was not mentioned by the Prophet (peace be upon him) is neither an obligation as he did not command us with that, nor forbidden as he did not forbade us to do it. What is left from that is therefore permissible. Whoever claimed that it is forbidden must bring the evidence that the Prophet (peace be upon him) forbade us from doing it and when he brings it, we will listen and obey, otherwise his claim is null and void. Whoever claimed that it is obligatory must bring the evidence that the Prophet (peace be upon him) commanded us with and when he brings it we will listen and obey, but if he did not, his saying will be null and void. It was proved by this text that whatever the Prophet (peace be upon him) commanded us with is an obligation except that what we were not able to do and whatever he forbade us from doing is a forbidden matter except what he explained to be undesirable or desirable. There is no judgment in religion that was left without being mentioned here.'

What then has been left after all of this? Was there any incident in the world that would not be included in the saying of whoever claims something to be obligatory and we say to him that if you bring a text from the Qur'ān or an authentic text narrated by the Messenger of Allah (peace be upon him) or consensus that proves what you said, we will listen and obey and it will be obligatory and whosoever then denies its obligation, will be a *kāfir* (disbeliever). However, if he did not bring a text or a consensus, he is a liar and this matter is not an obligation. Whoever claims that something is forbidden, we should answer that, if you bring a text or a consensus that proves its illegality, it will be forbidden and we will listen and obey and whoever wants to violate it then will be sinner but if he did not bring a text or consensus, he is liar and this thing is not forbidden. Is there any judgment in the whole world that is not included in this? Then it is true that the text includes every judgment that has happened or will happen till the day of judgement and there is no way that any incident is not included in these three judgments.

Ḥadith's of the Messenger of Allah (peace be upon him) showed the same that were indicated in these verses. Abu Hurayrah (may Allah be pleased with him) narrated that the Prophet (peace be upon him) said: '*Leave me with what I have left to you, Verily the people before you went to their doom because they had put too many questions to their Prophets and then disagreed with their teachings. So avoid that which I forbid you to do and do that which I command you to do to the best of your capacity.*' Abu Muḥammad (Ibn Ḥazm) said: This *ḥadith* includes all what we have mentioned. The Prophet (peace be upon him) explained that if he forbade us to do anything, it is our duty to avoid it and if he commanded us with something it is also our duty to do it according to our capacity. Whatever he forbade or commanded us, it is our duty not to search for it during his lifetime and if the matter is like that, so it was imposed that every Muslim should neither forbid nor obligate it. If it is neither forbidden nor obligatory, it is then permissible as there is no other branch other than these three divisions. If two of them are null, then the third is obligatory. This is the case according to this text, to listening and to mind not to understand other than it except an unacceptable induction conducted by way of that *Qiyās* (analogy), they see that the expiation for intentionally having food during a day of Ramaḍān is the same expiation for intentionally having intercourse with one's spouse. Likewise, they have defined the minimum value of stolen properties incurring the amputation of the thief's hand to be like that of the conventional minimum value of a dowry.

Then we should ask the same question of them. If you

claimed that there are some incidents that have neither judgment in the Qur'ān nor in the *Sunnah*, so say to us what do you use to do with them? As it is according to you obligatory but not to us as it is null and not existing. So tell us if you really found these incidents, do you neglect its judgment while this is not your opinion or you will judge them while there is no other branch but these three divisions. If you judge them, tell us about your judgment; did you judge them according to Allah and His Messenger (peace be upon him) and if you said yes, so you have contradicted yourselves as you already said that there is no text that proves them either from Allah or from His Messenger (peace be upon him). Your next saying proves the untruth of your previous saying. And if you said that you judged not according to judgment of Allah or His Messenger (peace be upon him), we seek refuge with Allah from every judgment in religion that is not legislated by Allah, the exalted. This is enough for whoever has a mind. All matters are clear and others are null. Praise be to Allah!

(Numerous) *aḥādith* prove this matter. Sa'd bin Abi Waqqās (may Allah be pleased with him) narrated that the Prophet (peace be upon him) said: '*The most sinful person among the Muslims is the one who asked about something which had not been prohibited, but was prohibited because of his asking.*' The Prophet (peace be upon him) is saying that whatever was not prohibited by Allah is not prohibited. And the Prophet (peace be upon him) also said the same about the obligatory matters. Abu Hurayrah (may Allah be pleased with him) narrated that the Messenger of Allah (peace be upon him) gave them a sermon and said – *'O people! Allah has made Ḥajj obligatory for you; so perform Ḥajj.'* Thereupon a person said: O Messenger of Allah, (is it to be performed) every year? He (the Prophet) kept quiet and he repeated (these words) thrice, whereupon Messenger of Allah (peace be upon him) said: *'If I were to say yes, it would become obligatory (for you to perform it every year) and you would not be able to do it.*' Then he said: '*Leave me with what I have left to you. Verily the people before you went to their doom because they had put too many questions to their Prophets and then disagreed with their teachings. So do that which I command you to do to the best of your capacity and avoid that which I forbid you to do*.' Abu Muḥammad said that the Messenger of Allah (peace be upon him) said that whatever he did not set as obligatory is not obligatory and whatever he said to be obligatory is obligatory according to one's capability and that which he did not forbid is lawful and that which he forbade is unlawful. So *Qiyās* (analogy) has nothing to do with it. Texts (have) covered everything people disagreed about and every incident that will happen till the day of judgement. Allah says:

أَمْ لَهُمْ شُرَكَاءُ شَرَعُوا لَهُم مِّنَ الدِّينِ مَا لَمْ يَأْذَن بِهِ اللَّهُ وَلَوْلَا كَلِمَةُ الْفَصْلِ لَقُضِيَ بَيْنَهُمْ وَإِنَّ الظَّالِمِينَ لَهُمْ عَذَابٌ أَلِيمٌ

Or have they associates who have prescribed for them any religion that Allah does not sanction? And were it not for the word of judgment, decision would have certainly been given between them; and surely the unjust shall have a painful punishment.[19]

One should seriously ponder over the comments that Imām Abu Muḥammad Ali Ibn Ḥazm (may Allah be merciful to him) has furnished us with. Our viewpoint regarding the original / default ruling being one of permissibility can be summed up as the following dictum:

- *The original ruling of all things (or objects), acts / actions and sayings is permissibility. The original ruling in contracts and conditions is permissibility and correctness. Thus fulfilling contracts, which were correctly concluded, is an obligation*

[19] *Qur'ān* 42: 21

and conditions that were agreed about are also obligatory as they were correctly agreed upon.

We would also stress that this rule entails by necessity, that the original ruling of all things and entities in the universe is (ritual) purity. By way of greater clarity, our statement concerning the original ruling of permissibility required that such things are clear in their origin from any 'positive' rules (*aḥkām waḍiya*). Nothing among them should be: cause, condition, license etc. to other thing, or other among 'positive' rules except through some piece of evidence. The same is to be applied to incidents that happened in the universe such as the rising of the sun, rain, eclipses etc., until text establishes other than that.

7 What is the original ruling concerning worship?

Many hold the view that while the original ruling concerning matters is permissibility, this does not hold true for matters that directly pertain to worship (*'ibādah*). Hence the saying – *'the original ruling concerning all 'acts of worship' is prohibition until evidence stipulates otherwise'* which is almost common parlance. Given what we have presented in the previous chapters, we argue that this statement is futile. The sentence '*the original ruling concerning all "acts of worship" is prohibition until evidence stipulates otherwise*' is meaningless. Whoever said as much has *presumed* that there are acts that deserve to be called 'worship' in-and-of-itself. Holding a view like this is a terrible mistake which leads to many other greater mistakes. Such matters will be considered in greater detail in the other sections of the present work.

Historically, the idea of a collection of rituals or rites being termed as 'worship' relates to acts that are done with the express purpose of gaining closeness to a divinity or divine entity. Worship is thus understood in this manner. Essentially it is the performance of certain actions and / or rituals as a means of approach or sanctification towards a divine or God-like entity. The 'worshipper' therefore utilises these rituals to get closer to that divine being; seeking its contentment and love; avoiding its wrath or punishment and seeking to obtain mercy and benefits, worldly or otherwise. Consequently, the performer of these rituals undertakes them in the belief that the particular divine being loves them to be performed and / or has obligated them.

After the message of Muḥammad (peace be upon him) any judgment that was proved to be desirable or obligatory means that this judgment is different from the definite and original permissibility, a matter that is not established except by way of evidence. In actuality, the truth concerning this matter is that Allah is only 'worshipped' by what he himself has judged as obligatory or desirable. Put another way – Allah is only to be worshipped in the manner through which he has legislated. This maxim is not altogether new, rather it is a consequence of our previous statement – 'the original ruling of all things (or objects), acts / actions and sayings is permissibility.' The original ruling in contracts and conditions is permissibility and correctness. Fulfilling contracts, which were correctly concluded, is an obligation and conditions that were agreed about are also obligatory as they were correctly agreed upon. The original ruling of all things and entities in the universe is (ritual) purity. All definite evidence is based upon this, so whoever believes in Allah and the final day is not allowed to believe in other than this or to act according to other than it and whomsoever disbelieves, Allah is self-sufficient and free of all needs.

8 A '*Sunnah Tarkiyah*'?

Previously we detailed the authentic statements that have reached us from the Prophet (peace be upon him) where he was reported to have said:[1]

- *Leave me as I leave you for the people who were before you were ruined because of their questions and their differences over their Prophets. So, if I forbid you to do something, then keep away from it. And if I order you to do something, then do of it as much as you can.*

- *Leave me with what I have left to you, for those who were before you were destroyed because of excessive questioning, and their opposition to their Prophets. So when I command you to do anything, do it as much as it lies in your power and when I forbid you to do anything, then abandon it.*

[1] See chapter five entitled for the full *isnād* and wording for each of the six *aḥādith* that are listed here.

- *Whatever matter I informed you of, undoubtedly it is from Allah.*

- *Verily, Allah has set some limits, so do not trespass them and He has ordained some obligations, so do not neglect them; He has sanctified some things so do not violate them; and He has refrained from mentioning other matters not (out of) forgetfulness, but as a way of being merciful to you, so accept (that) and do not look for them!*

- *The most sinful person among the Muslims is the one who asked about something which had not been prohibited, but was prohibited because of his asking.*

- *Whatever was considered lawful by Allah in His Book is lawful and whatever was considered unlawful is unlawful and He has refrained from mentioning other matters so it is forgiveness from Him.*

Undoubtedly the Prophetic words (peace and blessings be upon him) are invaluable as are the following points which we may take directly from these *aḥādith*:

1. That he, may the peace and blessings of Allah be upon him, was indeed an eloquent Arab; protected with infallibility by Allah in delivering the message and gifted with *'Jawāmi' al-Kalim'*, the shortest expression with the widest meaning, being able to utilise single-sentences that bore wide meanings and contain deep wisdom. Given this, there was nothing preventing him from saying or expressing – 'whatever I have left, you all must leave.' On the contrary though he said: '*…and*

He has refrained from mentioning other matters not (out of) *forgetfulness, but as a way of being merciful to you, so accept* (that) *and do not look for them!'* Some though have insisted upon not accepting the express wording that has been authentically reported. Instead, they have devoted copious pages and volumes trying to resist it.

2. That the notion of '*Tark*'[2] is a purely abstract matter which doesn't fit into the argument for something. Also, the notion of '*tark*' doesn't denote any connotation as it is not relating to a specific act or action. Literally, it is nothingness, thus not an evidence for anything. Therefore, there is nothing in the world that can be titled as '*Sunnah Tarkiyah*', in other words, the *Sunnah* of leaving, abandonment and non-performance, originally.

3. The notion of '*Tark*' as an abstraction can be considered the opposite to an abstraction regarding acts. Previously we noted that of the certain indicators relating to the acts of the Prophet (peace be upon him), such as the indicators which provide definitive conclusive proof that whatever he undertook is not prohibited for the rest of his *Ummah*, unless that is, he has specified that what he is undertaking is specific to him. Therefore, there must be independent indicators or connotations to demonstrate that the act is to be considered as obligatory (*wājib*), recommended (*mustaḥab*) or disliked (*makruh*). So this must by necessity show according to the dictates of reason and implications, that '*tark*' (non-performance) as an abstract proof can only demonstrate that what he (peace be upon him) forsakes

[2] Literally leaving but also understood as being non-performance or abandonment

is not to be considered as obligatory (*wājib*), unless he has outlined that it relates to his own specialities. Consequently, there must be indicators or connotations which demonstrate that to forsake a matter as it is prohibited (*ḥarām*), disliked (*makruh*), recommended (*mustaḥab*) or falls within the general ambit of permissibility (*mubāh*). As was mentioned in the previous chapter,[3] which related to the study of the requirements relating to the textual designation of the Prophet (peace be upon him) as '*Uswatun Ḥasana'* – the best example or exemplar, he will never perform a matter prohibited for his *Ummah* and neither will he leave that which has been made obligatory either.

4. The notion of '*Tark*' as an abstraction, in essence relates to the non-performance of an act. It is closer and more like that of the abstraction of '*iqrār'* (approval, endorsement), which is a left-speech. And recognising the consequent judgment of absolute permissibility likened to that speech, as given by the necessity of reason. This is what the *Sharī'ah* evidences indicate as mentioned above. Although some may claim that they are the people of consideration, insight, measurement and balance; deriding those who would reject *Qiyās* (analogy). But they might fall headlong towards innovation in seeking how to justify the notion of *Tark* as an abstraction constituting some form of undesirability of prohibition.

5. That the Prophet (peace be upon him) might leave some deliberately recommend actions intentionally, for some other considerations, which can be outlined in considerable detail.

---

[3] See Part II, chapter 7

First Consideration

One of the first considerations is that the Prophet (peace be upon him) may leave some of the devotional recommended rites in order not to impose a burden upon people. As has been referred to by Imām Ibn Khuzaymah in his *Ṣaḥīḥ* under the chapter heading of:

> 'What has been mentioned regarding the Prophet (peace be upon him) abandoning some devotional and supererogatory practices, even though he urged people to perform them, lest they become obligatory or recommended upon them desirably; although the Prophet (peace be upon him) never ceased to undertake matters obligatory.'

This point is borne out by some of the most authentic *aḥādith*. For example, as is narrated in *al-Jāmi aṣ-Ṣaḥīḥ al-Mukhtaṣr* by Imām Bukhāri:

> حدثنا يحيى بن بكير حدثنا الليث عن عقيل عن بن شهاب أخبرني عروة أن عائشة، رضي الله تعالى عنها، أخبرته أن رسول الله، صلى الله عليه وسلم، خرج ليلة من جوف الليل فصلى في المسجد وصلى رجال بصلاته، فأصبح الناس فتحدثوا فاجتمع أكثر منهم فصلوا معه، فأصبح الناس فتحدثوا فكثر أهل المسجد من الليلة الثالثة، فخرج رسول الله، صلى الله عليه وسلم، فصلى فصلوا بصلاته فلما كانت الليلة الرابعة عجز المسجد عن أهله حتى خرج لصلاة الصبح، فلما قضى الفجر أقبل على الناس فتشهد ثم قال: أما بعد فإنه لم يخْفَ عليّ مكانكم ولكني خشيت أن تفرض عليكم فتعجزوا عنها، فتوفي رسول الله، صلى الله عليه وسلم، والأمر على ذلك
>
> Yaḥya bin Bukeer narrated to us al-Layth narrated to us from 'Uqayl from Ibn Shihāb, 'Urwa reported to me that Aisha may Allah the exalted be pleased with her, reported to him that once in the middle of the night the Messenger of Allah (peace be

> upon him) went out and prayed in the *masjid* and some men prayed with him. The next morning the people spoke about it and so more people gathered and prayed with him (in the second night). They circulated the news in the morning, and so, on the third night the number of people increased greatly. Allah's Messenger (peace be upon him) came out and they prayed behind him. On the fourth night, the mosque was overwhelmed by the people till it could not accommodate them. Allah's Messenger (peace be upon him) came out only for the *Fajr* prayer and when he finished the prayer, he faced the people and recited '*Tashah-hud*' and then said: *To proceed - verily your presence was not hidden from me, but I was afraid that this prayer might be made compulsory and you might not be able to carry it out.*

Bukhāri said 'Yunus succeeded / followed it'; Imām Muslim also recorded this in his *Ṣaḥīḥ,*[4] the follow up of Yunus which is the reference as made by Bukhāri. Several Imām's also cite this in their collections, such as *Ṣaḥīḥ* Ibn Ḥibbān,[5] in the *Musnad* of Aḥmad;[6] the *Sunan al-Kubra* of Nasā'i,[7] *Musnad* Isḥāq ibn Rāhaway,[8] *Muṣṣanaf* Abdar-Razzāq,[9] as well as in *Mu'jam al-Awsaṭ* of Ṭabarāni[10] as well as others. Bayhaqy recorded similarly via a long channel in *as-Sunan al-Kubra* in the same manner as Bukhāri but with some important additions after the Prophetic statement of '*...you might not be able to carry it out*' from what happened at the time of Umar bin al-Khaṭṭāb.

> The Prophet (peace be upon him) encouraged people to perform the optional night prayers during *Ramaḍān* without any

---

[4] Muslim Vol. 1 sec. 525, no. 761
[5] Ibn Ḥibbān Vol. 6 sec. 286, no. 2,544 & sec. 285, no. 2,543
[6] *Musnad* Aḥmad Vol. 6 sec. 169, no. 25,401
[7] *Sunan al-Kubra* Nasā'i Vol. 2 sec. 86, no. 2,503
[8] *Musnad* Ibn Rāhaway Vol. 2 sec. 305, no. 827
[9] *Muṣṣanaf* Abdar-Razzāq Vol. 4 sec. 265, no. 7,747
[10] *Mu'jam al-Awsaṭ* Vol. 2 sec. 6, 1,043

> obligation, saying, '*Whoever performs the prayer of night during Ramaḍān hoping for faith and gaining reward from Allah, his all previous sins will be forgiven*.' Then the Prophet (peace be upon him) died. The matter was left unchanged during the time of Abu Bakr (may Allah be pleased with him). But during the *Khilafah* of Umar (may Allah be pleased with him), the situation was changed. 'Urwa said Abdar-Raḥman bin Abd al-Qāri informed me, (he was) one of workers of 'Amr (may Allah be pleased with him), as he worked with Abdullah bin al-Arqam in the treasury of the Muslims. He said that Umar bin al-Khaṭṭāb (may Allah be pleased with him) got out during one night of *Ramaḍān*, then Abdar-Raḥman got out with him, who showed around the *masjid* while all people were in the *masjid* as separated groups or individuals; a man might pray alone and others might pray the same prayer also. Umar said: By Allah, I think it will be more suitable to gather all those people under one Imām in order to all pray congregationally. So he commanded Ubay bin Ka'b (may Allah be pleased with him) to lead the people during the month of *Ramaḍān* for the optional night prayers. Once Umar (may Allah be pleased with him) got out and Abdar-Raḥman bin Abd al-Qāri was with him, while people performed the optional night prayer congregationally, then he said to Abdar-Raḥman – 'What a delightful innovation! The optional prayer at the end of night, during the time where people sleep is the best one.' He referred to the optional prayers at the end of night because people performed these prayers in the first part of the night.[11]

After this, al-Bayhaqy said 'It was narrated by Bukhāri in the *Ṣaḥīḥ* about Ibn Bakir and not the *ḥadith* of Abdar-Raḥman bin Abd al-Qāri; but he documented this in relation to the *ḥadith* of Mālik from az-Zuhri.' Also, the *ḥadith* of 'Aisha, mother of the believers, may Allah be pleased with her, is one of the soundest authentic traditions on record. Similar has been reported from Anas ibn Mālik, as set out in

[11] Given the length of the narrative, the Arabic text has been omitted.

the *Musnad* of Aḥmad via an authentic channel of transmission:

> حدثنا يزيد (هو ابن هارون) أخبرنا حميد (هو الطويل) عن أنس أن رسول الله، صلى الله عليه وسلم، كان ذات ليلة يصلي في حجرته، فجاء أناس من أصحابه فصلوا بصلاته، فخفف ثم دخل البيت ثم خرج، ففعل ذلك مرارا كل ذلك يصلي وينصرف، فلما أصبح قالوا: (يا رسول الله: صلينا معك البارحة ونحن نحب ان تمدّ في صلاتك! ، فقال: قد علمت بمكانكم، وعمدا فعلت ذلك
>
> Yazeed (he is Ibn Hārun) narrated to us Ḥumayd (he is aṭ-Ṭaweel) reported to us from Anas that the Messenger of Allah (peace be upon him) was praying one evening just outside the apartment. Some people came and prayed behind him so he made the prayer brief and then entered back into his house. Then he came out and did the same thing several times and each time people would pray behind him. The next morning people asked – O Messenger of Allah, you prayed and we prayed behind you, we would like you to make your prayer a bit longer. He said: *I knew you were there so I deliberately made it brief.*

Imām Aḥmad also has this in another place in the *Musnad*;[12] it is also reported in the *Musnad* of Ibn Ḥumayd,[13] *Musnad* Abu Ya'la in several places,[14] as well as in the *Sunan al-Kubra* of Bayhaqy[15] and in other collections as well. In his *Ṣaḥīḥ*, Imām Bukhāri records the following from 'Amra from 'Aisha which is similar to the narration of Anas bin Mālik:

> حدثنا محمد قال: أخبرنا عبدة عن يحيى بن سعيد الأنصاري عن عمرة عن عائشة قالت: كان رسول الله، صلى الله عليه وسلم، يصلي من الليل في

---

[12] *Musnad* Aḥmad Vol. 3 sec. 103, no. 12,024
[13] *Musnad* Ibn Ḥumayd Vol. 1 sec. 413, no. 1,409
[14] *Musnad* Abu Ya'la Vol. 6 sec. 401, no. 3,755; Vol. 6 sec. 461, no. 3,859 & Vol. 8 sec. 223, no. 4,788
[15] *Sunan al-Kubra* Bayhaqy Vol. 3 sec. 110, no. 5,021 & Vol. 3 sec. 110, no. 5,023

حجرته وجدار الحجرة قصير فرأى الناس شخص النبي، صلى الله عليه وسلم، فقام أناس يصلون بصلاته فأصبحوا فتحدثوا بذلك، فقام ليلة الثانية فقام معه أناس يصلون بصلاته صنعوا ذلك ليلتين أو ثلاثا، حتى إذا كان بعد ذلك جلس رسول الله، صلى الله عليه وسلم، فلم يخرج فلما أصبح ذكر ذلك الناس، فقال: إني خشيت أن تكتب عليكم صلاة الليل

Muḥammad narrated to us he said 'Abda reported to us from Yaḥya bin Sa'eed al-Anṣāri from 'Amra from Aisha, she said: Allah's Messenger (peace be upon him) used to pray in his room at night. As the wall of the room was low, the people saw him and some of them stood up to follow him in the prayer. In the morning, they spread the news. The following night the Prophet (peace be upon him) stood for the prayer and the people followed him. This went on for two or three nights. Thereupon Allah's Messenger (peace be upon him) did not stand for the prayer the following night, and did not come out. In the morning, the people asked him about it. He replied that he was afraid that the night prayer might become compulsory.

The *ḥadith* from 'Aisha, mother of the believers (may Allah be pleased with her) is from amongst the most authentic reported. It provides an unequivocal religious proof in relation to the points being raised herein. Bayhaqy also recorded this in *Sunan al-Kubra*[16] and it appears in several other collections. A similar meaning is also reported from the narration of Zayd ibn Thābit, which again, is strong and authentic. As cited by Bukhāri in his *Ṣaḥīḥ*:

حدثنا إسحاق أخبرنا عفان حدثنا وهيب حدثنا موسى بن عقبة سمعت أبا النضر يحدث عن بسر بن سعيد عن زيد بن ثابت أن النبي، صلى الله عليه وسلم، اتخذ حجرة في المسجد من حصير، فصلى رسول الله، صلى الله عليه وسلم، فيها ليالي حتى اجتمع إليه ناس؛ ثم فقدوا صوته ليلة، فظنوا أنه قد نام، فجعل بعضهم يتنحنح ليخرج إليهم فقال: ما زال بكم الذي رأيت من

[16] *Sunan al-Kubra* Bayhaqy Vol. 3 sec. 110, no. 5,021

صنيعكم حتى خشيت أن يكتب عليكم، ولو كتب عليكم ما قمتم به، فصلوا أيها الناس في بيوتكم فإن أفضل صلاة المرء في بيته إلا الصلاة المكتوبة

> Isḥāq narrated to us 'Affān reported to us Uhayb narrated to us Musa bin 'Uqba narrated to us: I heard Abu Naḍra report from Busr bin Sa'eed from Zayd bin Thābit that the Prophet (peace be upon him) took a room made of date palm leaves mats in the *masjid.* Allah's Messenger (peace be upon him) prayed in it for a few nights till the people gathered (to pray the night prayer behind him). Then on the fourth night the people did not hear his voice and they thought he had slept, so some of them started humming in order that he might come out. The Prophet (peace be upon him) then said: *You continued doing what I saw you doing till I was afraid that this might be enjoined on you, and if it were enjoined on you, you would not continue performing it. Therefore, O people! Perform your prayers at your homes, for the best prayer of a person is what is performed at his home except the compulsory congregational prayer.*

This *ḥadith* is widely reported, appearing in several collections. Bukhāri and Muslim cite this in their respective books.[17] Imām Nasā'i has this in his *Sunan*[18] as does Ibn Ḥibbān in his *Ṣaḥīḥ;*[19] Abu Dāwud records this in his *Sunan* in several places[20] as does Aḥmad in the *Musnad.*[21] Imām aṭ-Ṭaḥāwi records this in *Sharḥ al-Ma'āni al-Athār*[22] in *Mu'jam al-Kabir* Ṭabarāni has this in several places,[23] reporting it with some additional wording, like 'they would cough, raise their voices and throw pebbles and sand on his door. The Messenger of Allah (peace be upon him) came out angry because of this.' Ṭabarāni

---

[17] Bukhāri Vol. 1 sec. 256, no. 698 & Muslim Vol. 1 sec. 540, no. 781
[18] *Sunan* Nasā'i Vol. 3 sec. 198, no. 1,599
[19] Ibn Ḥibbān Vol. 6 sec. 239, no. 2,491
[20] *Sunan* Abu Dāwud Vol. 1 sec. 274, no. 1,044 & Vol. 2 sec. 69, no. 1,447
[21] *Musnad* Aḥmad Vol. 5 sec. 182, no. 21,622 & Vol. 5 sec. 187, no. 21,675
[22] *Sharḥ al-Ma'āni al-Athār* Vol. 1 sec. 350
[23] *Mu'jam al-Kabir* Vol. 5 sec. 144, no. 4,892/3/5 & Vol. 5 sec. 145, no. 4,896

also records this in *Mu'jam aṣ-Ṣagheer*,[24] as does Bayhaqy in *Sunan al-Kubra*[25] and it appears in other collections as well. In summary, we can discern from these narrations that it has been authentically reported that some of the companions cleared their throats, some had thrown pebbles at his (peace be upon him) door to alert him to their presence. He (peace be upon him) left them till morning and scolded them for these actions. It may be the case that 'Aisha mistook the throwing of pebbles to be knocks at the door.

Second Consideration

The second matter to consider in relation to this subject is that the Prophet (peace be upon him) might abandon some devotional deeds and voluntary acts, whose virtues have been established to treat the Muslims with kindness and not overburden them with hardships. Indeed he (peace be upon him) the best exemplar with the most beautiful pattern of conduct abandoned the *Jihād* at times, though this was from amongst the most beloved acts in the world for him. He (peace be upon him) did this in order to not place hardship upon his *Ummah*. Abu Hurayrah reported that the Prophet (peace be upon him) said:

> *Allah has undertaken to look after the affairs of one who goes out to fight in His way believing in Him and affirming the truth of His Prophets. He is committed to His care that he will either admit him to Paradise or bring him back to his home from where he set out with a reward or (his share of) booty. By the one in whose hand rests the life of Muḥammad - if a person gets wounded in the way of Allah, he will come on the day of judgment with his wound in the same condition as it was when it was first inflicted; its colour being the colour of blood but its*

[24] *Mu'jam aṣ-Ṣagheer* Vol. 1 sec. 329, no. 544
[25] *Sunan al-Kubra* Bayhaqy Vol. 2 sec. 494, no. 4,382

smell will be the smell of musk. By the one in whose hand rests the life of Muḥammad - if it were not to be too hard upon the Muslims, I would not lag behind any expedition which is going to fight in the cause of Allah. But I do not have abundant means to provide them with riding beasts, nor have they abundant means so that they could be left behind. By the one in whose hand rests the life of Muḥammad - I love to fight in the way of Allah and be killed, to fight and again be killed and to fight again and be killed.

I would submit that this is one of the most authentic *ḥadith's* in existence. Imām Muslim has this in his *Ṣaḥīḥ* with the following *isnād*: Zuhayr ibn Ḥarb narrated to me Jarir narrated to us from 'Umāra - and he is Ibn al-Qa'qā'a - from Abu Zur'a from Abu Hurayrah, as well as through other channels.[26] It is also found in the collections of Bukhāri,[27] Ibn Ḥibbān,[28] Ibn Mājah,[29] Aḥmad,[30] Isḥāq ibn Rāhaway,[31] Bayhaqy,[32] Ibn Abi Shayba[33] and other than them. Thus the Prophet (peace be upon him) abandoned some expeditions, although getting to every expedition was the most beloved thing for him more than anything in this world as he reported to us.

<u>*Third Consideration*</u>

The Prophet (peace be upon him) declared that the best fasting was what the Prophet Dāwud (peace be upon him) undertook. The format of this fast was that he used to fast on alternate days. However, it has not been reported to us that the Prophet Muḥammad (peace be upon

---

26 Muslim Vol. 3 sec. 1,495, no. 1,876; sec. 1,497, no. 1,876 & sec. 1,498, no. 1,876
27 Bukhāri Vol. 1 sec. 22, no. 36
28 Ibn Ḥibbān Vol. 11 sec. 39, no. 4,736
29 *Sunan* Ibn Mājah Vol. 2 sec. 920, no. 2,753
30 *Musnad* Aḥmad Vol. 2 sec. 231, no. 7,157 & Vol. 2 sec. 384, no. 8,970
31 *Musnad* Ibn Rāhaway Vol. 1 sec. 226, no. 182
32 *Sunan al-Kubra* Bayhaqy Vol. 9 sec. 39, no. 17,669 & Vol. 9 sec. 157, no. 18,265
33 *Muṣṣanaf* Ibn Abi Shayba Vol. 4 sec. 202, no. 19,316

him) ever fasted in this manner. So why did he abandon the best and practice otherwise? We do not know, because he (peace be upon him) did not clarify it for us. Moreover, it is known that this manner of fasting is not part of our religion, which Allah has promised to preserve and informing us that it is complete in every manner. If there was any specific merit now he (peace be upon him) would have clarified it for us. Although the Prophet (peace be upon him) is the best of all Prophets and Messengers and the most perfect example, the following should not always be assumed:

1. That every act including those of *ibādah* undertaken by the Prophet (peace be upon him) is represented in the best form. Generally, the precedence and the perfection do not mean the completing in every imagined part except for Allah, the Exalted.
2. That other Prophets had preference or primacy in certain other areas. It is not doubted that Musa (peace be upon him) had been chosen among the people, and all other Prophets as he was spoken to directly by Allah; that Esa ibn Maryam (peace be upon him and his mother) is termed the word of Allah and a spirit preceding him; his birth being miraculous as is his life.

The superiority of Bilāl and Abu Dharr over Mu'ādth ibn Jabal may Allah be pleased with them all, shouldn't attract conflict or suspicion, this is despite the fact that clearly Mu'ādth was known to be very well versed in what is considered *ḥalāl* and *ḥarām* more than most companions. Most of companions came before Abdullah ibn 'Abbās, having a status not achieved by him, for example being from amongst the companions who fought at *Badr*, *Uhud* or who took the pledge of allegiance with the Prophet (peace be upon him) under the tree. Yet despite this, he had a greater knowledge than most being the interpreter of the Qur'ān and a great scholar of Islam. Indeed, some of the earlier companions such as Abdar-Raḥman ibn 'Awf read Qur'ān under the tutelage of Ibn 'Abbās, correcting their understanding and recitation with him. Further to this, the primacy of the companions of Muḥammad (peace be upon him) within this *Ummah* is acknowledged. However, this does not mean that every virtue and good deed rests with them until the day of judgement. Every point advanced in relation to this is but a misconception, being argued from an emotional or reactionary basis, that which doesn't stand scrutiny.

Fourth Consideration

As has been established previously with decisive evidences, the original rule concerning things / objects, acts and sayings is one of permissibility. The Prophet (peace be upon him) placed great emphasis upon the forbiddance of asking too many questions lest this lead to destruction; he also declared that he would elucidate all the commands and prohibitions that Allah revealed. Allah has told us '*....and your Lord is not forgetful.*'[34] Following on from this, we have established that his non-performance or lack of comment upon an act by necessity denotes its permissibility. It is not the case that this non-performance constitutes a matter of prohibition, since the Prophet (peace be upon him) clearly said:

دعوني ما تركتكم، إنما أهلك من كان قبلكم سؤالهم واختلافهم على أنبيائهم؛ فإذا نهيتكم عن شيء فاجتنبوه، وإذا أمرتكم بأمر فأتوا منه ما استطعتم

> *Leave me as I leave you for the people who were before you were ruined because of their questions and their differences over their Prophets. So, if I forbid you to do something, then keep away from it. And if I order you to do something, then do of it as much as you can.*

---

[34] *Qur'ān* 19: 64

The Prophet (peace be upon him) might abandon or not perform some deeds for other considerations that we do not know. In any event, the abandonment or non-performance relates to *not doing something*; hence it is not a proof of anything as we have outlined thus far. Some people may hurriedly respond to what has been said by saying, that what has been presented is a disservice to their arguments and what they claim to hold. They would claim that they have never asserted that an abstract '*Tark*' is such a thing or a proof. Rather, in their eyes, the argument is thus: that the proof relating to the '*Tark*' of the Prophet (peace be upon him) is of an act that is not surmountable, together with the requirement and absence of an impediment, and other points of control.

In response, we would assert that despite the hatred, arrogance and the vicious reaction that often accompanies proponents of this viewpoint, there are very important fundamental principles that need to be elucidated. For the sake of completeness and intellectual honesty, the following quote is presented in full, from the work of Dr. Muḥammad ibn Ḥussein ibn Ḥasan al-Jizāni, entitled: *Ma'ālim Uṣul al-Fiqh inda' Ahl-as-Sunnah wal-Jamā'ah*,[35]

> The origin of this book: stems from a doctoral thesis that was submitted at the University of Medina al-Munawara. The committee (to which this was presented) was comprised of the virtuous Dr. 'Amr ibn Abdul-Aziz, professor and supervisor of *Uṣul al-Fiqh* in the Department of Graduate Studies at Umm Al-Qura University, Makkah al-Mukarama; Dr. Ali ibn 'Abbās al-Hikmi, Head of Graduate Studies Department at Umm Al Qura University, Makkah. Dr Ahmad Muhammad Abdal-Wahhāb, Professor of *Uṣul al-Fiqh*, from the department of graduate studies at the Islamic University of Medina
>
> (The thesis) was approved with first-honours on 25-1-1415

[35] As it appears in the electronic version of *Shāmila* website, fifth edition, 1427hijri, Vol. 1 sec. 2

(AH), conferring the title of 'Shaykh' which in Latin has the designation of doctorate (PhD). The author is expected to be able to adduce new material (sic. a contribution to knowledge), or so is the accepted universal custom these days. It is also accepted by contemporary modern standards, that the author must have written (the thesis) themselves and built upon the works of the previous contribution to scholarship. (*From between the bowels and blood*) his butter (*pure milk, easy and agreeable to swallow for those who drink*). And now (to proceed) to the text itself:

Beginning of the text transcript (Vol. 1 sec. 123/130)

Fifth:

A binding proof (relating) to his *Tark* (non-performance, abandonment) peace be upon him: to do one act from amongst others; it is purported (to be) by way of two types from the companions, may Allah be pleased with them all, namely:

1. That he peace be upon him gave an authorisation for such and such not to be performed, like his companions saying in relation to the *Eid* prayer: (that The Messenger of Allah peace be upon him offered the *Eid* prayer without the *adthān* and the *iqamāh*).
2. There is a reason why the companions did not narrate what the Messenger of Allah peace be upon him might not have done, they or at least one of them would have exhausted themselves to make this available to the *Ummah*. Therefore, none of them has indulged in this and it has never been narrated in a book. As an example, is that he peace be upon him abandoned / did not perform the (verbal) pronouncement of the intention when entering the prayer; and he left/abandoned the supplication after the prayer; for the future of the faithful who believe in his supplication, after *fajr* and *aṣr* or in the congregational prayer.

And his *Tark* (non-performance/abandonment) peace be upon him concerning an act from amongst the acts, is a

proof, thus it is obliged to act as he acted, to leave whatever he left. Accordingly, that requirement must fulfil two conditions:

a. *First condition*: that there is a reason present for this action during his time, peace be upon him, and that there is a need for him to perform the act. If this is the case and he peace be upon him did not do it, thereby not performing the act, then it is a *Sunnah,* that should be taken, to leave that act also. If the necessary obligation was not present as a condition, then for this reason, his (peace be upon him) non-performance does not constitute a *Sunnah,* because his abandonment/non-performance is due to the absence of a requisite condition. (Such as) fighting those withholding the *zakāt* only, as this was because of the absence of reason but when Abu Bakr, may Allah be please with him, fought only the withholders of the *zakāt* he was not acting contrary to the *Sunnah* of the Messenger of Allah peace be upon him.

As for what some rulers did in introducing the *adthān* for the two 'Eids, that is an innovation (*bidā'*), because the Messenger of Allah peace be upon him left that act given it wasn't necessary. He peace be upon him commanded (performance) of the *adthān* on Friday, and prayed the two 'Eids without either an *adthān* or *iqama*; not performing/leaving that was the *Sunnah.* No one may (place) an addition to that, (similar to the fact that) no one may increase the requisite number of prayers or units of prayer.

That was similar to what happened, such as making the sermon prior to the prayer of the two 'Eids, by the needs of the people, which was done by some rulers and they obliged it. People had become despondent before listening to the sermon, which was during the era of the Messenger of Allah peace be upon him. That wasn't stopped until it was heard by the majority of them. Nor was it sufficient to leave, peace be upon him, the act (present) with its requirements.

b. *Second condition:* The absence of symptoms and restrictions, because he peace be upon him, may actually leave one of the acts with the presence of the existence of the necessary reason because of another reason not allowing him to do that. That is like when he peace be upon him left the *qiyām* in *Ramaḍān* with his companions after a few nights and explained that he feared that it would be obligated upon them. During the time of Umar, may Allah be pleased with him, he (organised this) gathering under one reciter. By doing so, it wasn't against the *Sunnah* of the Messenger of Allah peace be upon him. (Also), that is how the Qur'ān was compiled, (given that) there was a prohibition on doing this during the lifetime of the Messenger of Allah peace be upon him, as the revelation was still ongoing. Allah (is at liberty) to change what he wants and decide what he wants. If it had been collected into one compendium it wouldn't have been possible or very difficult to change it, (though) it was settled by the death of the Messenger peace be upon him; the people being assured (then) that there would be no increase or decrease to it. As for his peace be upon him leaving the *adthān* for the two 'Eids, there were no objections, so that was a Prophetic *Sunnah* that must be followed. To summarise this matter, that his *Tark,* peace be upon him, is not without the following submissions:

The First Submission: Completeness of this *Sharī'ah* and the complete disregard for any additions to it by innovators and those inclined to that. Allah has completed this *Deen* and nothing is ever lacking therein. From amongst the proofs for this introduction is the words of the almighty: *This day have I perfected for you your religion and completed My favor on you and chosen for you Islam as a religion* [al-Mā'ida, 3]. And he peace be upon him said: '*By Allah, I am leaving you upon something like Bayḍā* (white, bright, clear path) *the night and day of which are the same.*'[36]

The Second Submission: His statement peace be upon him, for this *Deen* and his duty to convey it completely, so that nothing

---

[36] Although not cited in as part of the lengthy quotation, the narration is to be found in *Sunan* Ibn Mājah, the book of *Sunnah*, narrated upon the authority of Abu Dardā', may Allah be pleased with him.

small or large was neglected, it all reached his *Ummah*. Amongst the proofs that (establish) that, he the exalted said: O Messenger! Deliver what has been revealed to you from your Lord; and if you do it not, then you have not delivered His message [al-Mā'ida, 67]. The Prophet (peace and blessings of Allah be upon him) complied with this and adhered to the command to deliver the message. His nation bore witness to the conveyance of this message and that he delivered it in full, as set out in the sermon of the farewell pilgrimage.

The Third Submission: Allah has preserved this *Deen* and guaranteed to maintain it from being lost. Allah outlined all the factors and facilitated the transference (of this message), ensuring it would survive and continue, up to this day and forever, God-willing. The evidence for this is the verse - *Verily, We have revealed the Dhikr and We will most surely be its guardian* [al-Ḥijr, 9]. For indeed, one witnesses the truth of that; Allah has preserved his book and the *Sunnah* of his Prophet peace be upon him. And the jurisprudence of the Muslim scholars in relation to the (fundamental) principles, terminology of *ḥadith* and *Uṣul al-fiqh*, as well as the fundamentals of Arabic language.

Ibn Qayyim said: "Indeed, his '*Tark*', peace be upon him, is a *Sunnah* and it is the same as his acts, (that are) *Sunnah*. If we would like to act upon that which he has left/abandoned, then it is exactly like leaving what he has undertaken, and there is no difference.

If it is said: from where did it reach you that he did not undertake the action, that is non-textual and doesn't require non-textual nothingness? But this question seems quite far-fetched, about the understanding of the matter and his *Sunnah*. If the question were correct, then it would be considered recommended and acceptable to us (then) to pronounce the *adthān* for *Tarāweeḥ*. And he said: from where did it reach you? And there is another desirable matter also, to wash for every prayer. And he said: from where (was that) that it wasn't

> reported?...And (that) opens the door of *bidā'*. And he said: everyone who calls unto *bidā'* said: from where (was that) that it wasn't reported?
>
> It should be noted that the matter of the *Sunnah* of abandonment/non-performance – *Tark*, is based upon firm well established premises.

Turning now to the required comment upon all of this:

Firstly - What is mentioned in the first eight lines (or so) about how the Companions reported the matter of '*Tark*' and/or its importance has nothing to do with the subject-matter of whether it is an actual legal proof. It must be placed within the study of the *Dhikr* and its preservation. Since Allah has declared the undertaking for the protection of the *Dhikr*, there cannot be any remaining doubt concerning anything that has been left or abandoned for the *Deen*. If that is, there can be anything of this type to be spoken of originally. Allah the exalted has given the guarantee concerning the preservation of the *Deen*. It shouldn't be a concern as to the precise method for that, or even seeking to try and enumerate subdivisions and categorisations. Every form of '*Tark*' is thus not a legal proof in matters of *Deen*, as it is not from the protected preserved *Dhikr*; attention shouldn't be given to whether it has been conveyed to us or not. Indeed, the main point of research should in fact be: is the issue of '*Tark*', either some or all of it, even a legal proof? If it is the former or even the latter, then what would be its substantive conditions? Do some take formal precedence over others and upon what basis?

Secondly - Without justification the author then fell into exaggeration by claiming: 'And his *Tark* (non-performance, abandonment) peace be upon him concerning an act from amongst the acts, is a proof, thus it is obliged to act as he acted, to leave whatever he left. Accordingly, that requirement must fulfil two conditions…' In reply, there is nothing untoward at first. Perhaps it was the case that he wanted to formulate a general rule first, then proceed to the evidences relating to it. There appears to be some hesitancy in the phrasing 'it is obliged to act as he acted'. Perhaps he meant to elucidate, doing what he peace be upon him did is obligatory. Or to argue that what he has not done is obligatory not to do also. If the latter is the intended meaning, then it is without doubt the height of falsehood.

Thirdly - Dr. Muḥammad ibn Ḥussein ibn Ḥasan al-Jizāni tried to set out the justification in the first condition by arguing 'The existence of the reason for this and to need to do this action', but it wasn't dependent upon any necessity, reasoning, nor for that matter upon the texts of the revealed sent-down revelation, which is the book and the Prophetic *Sunnah.* Rather, his line of argumentation sought to dispense with the burden of proof by the following examples:

First example: his abandonment of fighting those who didn't render the obligatory charity (*zakāt*). I would state in reply, this is complete ignorance. The Prophet peace be upon him prepared to fight the *Khuzā'ah* when the *fāsiq* fabricated lies against them, that much is well known. But Allah the almighty explicated the lying *fāsiq* until the Day of Judgement. It may be said: did Abu Bakr not stand as witness to this when in heated debate with Umar? We would say, why was this so? Did they forget or did they not then marshal it during this argument? On the other hand, the incidents of accidents and calamities will never cease until the end of the world. So it is necessary to bring forth the ruling of Allah by the most diligent *ijtihād*, suitable to the case. It is therefore not of the matter from *Sunnah* or even innovation (*bidā'*) but rather under the chapter of *ijtihād.*

Second example: The Prophet peace be upon him left performing the call to prayer for the two 'Eid prayers. What some of the rulers who performed the call to prayer for the two 'Eid prayers, undoubtedly, it is an innovation (*bidāh'*). In reply, strictly speaking, that isn't correct. Firstly, the city of Medina was a small entity and the time was generally well known to all, particularly given that many were keen to attend prayer in congregation as well as circles of knowledge held by the Prophet peace be upon him. If all the individuals of a given household couldn't attend, they would rotate attendance, as was the known practice that Umar did with his brother from the Ansār. Hence there wasn't a pressing need to announce the call to prayer for that of 'Eid. Secondly, the *adthān* is the notice to people that the time of prayer has entered and to invite them to it. The Muslims were consulting one another and the Seal of the Prophets was amongst them. He would no doubt be involved in deliberations such as the call to prayer as a matter of course. One such striking example is the narrative of how the call to prayer came about, as it was being discussed; the bell was touted as a method and then the blessed vision came. He peace be upon him would often command a man to call for the congregational prayer, but also for emergency meetings other than that. However, we don't know whether this was made in the same formulation as the present wording of the *adthān*. But with the expansion of the city and the absence of the Prophet's blessed personality, this created a new situation with its own particular needs and requirements. Our question to Dr. Jizāni is why did he depart so noticeably from any discussion concerning the first Friday congregational prayer held by the leader of the believers, Uthmān ibn 'Affān? No doubt, Uthmān is trustworthy in matters of *Deen* and it is not that he intended to innovate or introduce something new in matters of *Deen*, in stark contrast to the tyrants of Bani Umayyah. Yet the *Deen* was completed prior to the death of the Prophet peace be upon him. Innovation in *Deen* is the same: there is no difference between it being with good intent and requisite evidence, as well as the good faith of the leader of the believers, Uthmān ibn 'Affān, may Allah be pleased with him, or being with a bad intention, the misguided argument of a hypocrite.

The claim of Dr. Jizāni that the Prophet peace be upon him left the *adthān* of the two 'Eids because there was no need for it, is to cast stones into the unseen. It is to say something about Allah without having any knowledge. Given that we are prevented from exaggeration and asking unnecessary questions, the matter is best left there, instead of delving into speculation and departing from what is clearly established (*muḥkam*). That which is clearly established, the *muḥkam*, and it is indeed the truth with certitude: it is impossible for the infallible Seal of the Prophets, the Prophet Muḥammad peace be upon him, to leave that which has been made obligatory (*wājib*) upon his *Ummah*. The exception being that is, where it relates to his specialism as a Prophet and there is a decisive proof to establish that. Every legal ruling (*ḥukm*) by necessity, like disapproval, recommendation, prohibition and the like, is established by independent evidence (*dalil*) and not recourse to *'Tark'*. Moreover, it is known with certitude: it is impossible for the infallible Seal of the Prophets, the Prophet Muḥammad peace be upon him, to undertake any matter that is prohibited for his *Ummah*. Again, the exception being where this relates to his own specialism as a Prophet, for which we have a decisive evidence to establish that. All that is necessary, recommended, permissible, disliked etc. needs to be established by requisite evidence, not merely reference to an act.

Fourth comment

When Dr. Jizāni spoke in relation to the second condition, namely the 'absence of impediments', he mixed this together with the first condition. There are other impediments that could have been mentioned, some of which we have elucidated previously. There are matters that the Prophet peace be upon him did not do, even though they are praiseworthy, such as the intermittent fasting, and he did not clarify why he did not undertake it. As for the example concerning the collection of the Qur'ān, that is a clear mistake. The Prophet peace be upon him had his own specific *muṣḥaf,* which was attributed to Uthmān ibn Abi al-'Aāṣ ath-Thaqafi, when he was appointed as the ruler of Ṭā'if. It is not clear whether a new copy was re-written for him. Each of the most important Qur'ān memorisers had their own *muṣḥaf,* such as Ali ibn Abi Ṭālib, 'Ubay ibn Ka'b, Abdullah ibn Mas'ud and Zayd ibn Thābit and Umm Waraqa ash-Shaheeda, may Allah be pleased with them all. Allah has confirmed that the collection and preservation of the book rests with him, the exalted and majestic: '*Surely upon us (devolves) the collection and its recitation.*'[37]

What was suggested by Umar during the period of apostasy, was to transcribe the *muṣḥaf,* acting in the capacity of Imām. That text was to be according to the final recitation and would be devoid of the commentaries and explanatory notes that scribes had made. It would also contain none of the abrogated verses that were originally recited. In short, it would be a uniform copy for the *Ummah*.

Fifth comment

Following this admixtures and general mischievous whisperings, Dr. Jizāni marshals a cited quote from Imām Ibn al-Qayyim. In a way, the use of this quote seems to be what he has premised his argument upon, particularly given the inability to provide any textual evidence to substantiate his view. The first quoted sentence from Ibn al-Qayyim is: "Indeed, his '*Tark*', peace be upon him, is a *Sunnah* and it is the same as his acts, (that are) *Sunnah*. If we would like to act upon that which he has left/abandoned, then it is exactly like leaving what he has undertaken, and there is no difference." Although there are different editions, at the time of writing, the edition present here, is the study and commentary by Ṭaha Abdur-Ra'ouf Sa'd.[38] Despite perusal of this publication, no substantive evidence is present to substantiate his position. There isn't any evidence for this statement which is *mursal,* but only sporadic examples of some of what the Prophet peace be upon him left. Nothing further. The saying attributed to Imām Ibn al-Qayyim is *mursal*, it is a mere claim, or assertion that has no

[37] *Qur'ān* 75: 17

[38] Published by Al-Azhar Library, Cairo, Egypt [1388/1968]; electronic comprehensive library [sec. 2 / p. 460]

substantive proof within it. Even if Imām Ibn al-Qayyim was considered as an infallible Imām following the *Rāfiḍah* school of thought, the attributed statement wouldn't become a valid argument. Emphasis is placed that it isn't incumbent to do what the Prophet peace be upon him left/abandoned, nothing else. From the necessity of perception and reason we know that what is not recommended, may fall into another categorisation: either obligated, disliked or prohibited outright. So what are the parameters of what is being claimed ultimately?

Following on from that, the next comment attributed to Imām Ibn al-Qayyim is: "If it is said: from where did it reach you that he did not undertake the action, that is non-textual and doesn't require non-textual…" etc. Foremost, as we have mentioned previously, this doesn't fall within the subject matter of 'the proof of *Tark*', but rather within the chapter about the protection and preservation of the *Dhikr*. There does seem to be some subconscious recognition that this statement and its underlying reasoning is inherently flawed, hence the need to return to it and attempt to strengthen it somehow.

Imām Ibn al-Qayyim wanted to round-off the chapter that he had called 'innovation' (*bidāh'*). His comment is noteworthy: "And there is another desirable matter also, to wash for every prayer. And he said: from where (was that) that it wasn't reported?...And (that) opens the door of *bidāh'*. And he said: everyone who calls unto *bidāh'* said: from where (was that) that it wasn't reported?" To respond we would say, to claim that it is necessary to wash at every prayer requires an independent proof, because it relates to the matter of taking this point of washing and making it desirable. It cannot be established as being an obligation without a requisite proof. Hence there is no substance to placing this within a research concerning what the 'Prophet left,' for it is inconceivable that evidence has been 'lost'as the *Dhikr* is preserved and protected.

Sixth Comment

Dr. Jizāani appears to sense that all which he has marshalled is but sentiments, incomplete examples. Vague references devoid of substantive proof cannot be construed as being 'well-established, firm introductions,' as he alludes to. In fact, the textual evidences which do exist are in stark contrast to what Dr. Jizāani purports to claim:

a. Allah perfected the elucidation of the Qur'ān, and his Prophet (peace be upon him) had the complete perfect message that was delivered. He peace be upon him was granted '*Jawāmi' al-Kalim'*, the shortest expression with the widest meaning. Given this, such words make us wonder at how he expressed the following:

   Avoid that which I forbid you to do and do that which I command you to do to the best of your capacity. Verily the people before you went to their doom because they had put too many questions to their Prophets and then disagreed with their teachings.

   The most sinful person among the Muslims is the one who asked about something which had not been prohibited, but was prohibited because of his asking.

   Whatever was considered lawful by Allah in His Book is lawful and whatever was considered unlawful is unlawful and He has refrained from mentioning other matters so it is forgiveness from Him. Accept from Allah His Forgiveness, as Allah never forgets anything.

   Leave me with what I have left to you, for those who were before you were destroyed because of excessive questioning, and their opposition to their apostles. So when I command you to do anything, do it as much as it lies in your power and when I forbid you to do anything, then abandon it.

Whatever matter I informed you of, undoubtedly it is from Allah.

Verily, Allah has set some limits, so do not trespass them and He has ordained some obligations, so do not neglect them; He has sanctified some things so do not violate them; and He has refrained from mentioning other matters not (out of) forgetfulness, but as a way of being merciful to you, so accept (that) and do not look for them! [39]

b. He peace be upon him, said all of that. Moreover, he did not say: do what I do, but leave or abandon what I leave. That undoubtedly is the phantasm of some minds. Allah is fully cognisant of all matters and his knowledge encompasses all knowledge. Do such individuals really have the audacity to claim that Allah would have forgotten to instruct his Prophet to say this?

The perfection and preservation of this *Deen* by necessity, prevents the need to develop a rule or principle that has not been subjected to the decisive proofs of the *Deen* itself. But rather the innovation in the development of such a 'rule of law' is, in general, worse and more difficult to invent by creating a partial case with no tangible basis or reality.

Yet this is exactly what the proponents of those who claim that there is a '*Tark an-Nabi*' which is a 'proof.' The same individuals level accusations of heresy and innovation at others, yet they

[39] See chapter five for the references and Arabic text for the *aḥādith* that are listed here.

themselves are guilty of this with a principle that has no basis in *Deen*. The *Deen* which includes its legal system has been established as complete. Secondly, that the Prophet (peace be upon him) discharged his duty to convey the message to in totality, without leaving any matter be it great or small, he has informed his *Ummah* of this.

The decisive truth, concerning that which the Prophet (peace be upon him) left, was silent about and tacitly approved: all of that at root, falls within the realm of original permissibility, absolutely. Hence there is no truth in someone claiming that whatever the Prophet left, we must leave also. To claim as such, is but a heinous innovation of the Wahābi's. But what the Prophet has left, we have analysed, if we want to leave as such or do as such, may Allah forbid that we should say that it is reprehensible or that it is prohibited, in the absence of any evidence or substantive proof to the contrary.

However, it is clear that extremist elements, be they from the sect of Wahābism or others, seek to practice a form of intellectual terrorism. That much is clear from when they express loudly and arrogantly express the statement: how can you do what the Prophet (peace be upon him) or his companions didn't do? No doubt it is designed to level any opposition into surrender and submission, whether that be from amongst the minor students of knowledge or amongst the general masses.

To deliver the knockout blow to all the imposters, those within the boundaries of extremes and outright liars, one may ask them forthrightly: is it not that the original ruling concerning acts, contracts, conditions is but one of absolute general permissibility, as demonstrated by the exhaustive evidences? So how is it now that you have made this matter now one of impermissibility or that which is disliked? Did not the Prophet (peace be upon him and his family) expressly state the following:

- *Leave me as I leave you for the people who were before you were ruined because of their questions and their differences over their Prophets. So, if I forbid you to do something, then keep away from it. And if I order you to do something, then do of it as much as you can.*
- *Indeed, Allah has laid down certain duties which you should not neglect, and has put certain limits which you should not transgress, and has kept silent about other matters out of mercy for you and not out of forgetfulness, so do not seek to investigate them*
- *The greatest sinner amongst the Muslims is one who asked about a thing which had not been forbidden for the Muslims and it was forbidden for them because of his persistently asking about it.*

Clearly, he stated: '*leave me as I leave you…*' and he is never reported to have said: 'whatever I have left, so you should leave it.' Furthermore, this is not considered a *bidāh'* – innovation or heresy, but is in fact similar to the argument put forward by the grand Imām Abu Muḥammad Ali Ibn Ḥazm in his seminal work *al-Iḥkām fi Uṣul al-Aḥkām* (Judgement on the Principles of Law) [Vol. 4 sec. 56]. He writes:

> (From) what we have mentioned previously concerning *al-'Istisā'* (taking the Prophet as an exemplar in matters which are obligatory) in relation to his actions; and as for the one who says, 'We demand evidence - therefore if we find something which substantiates that an action is obligatory we adopt the position. Similarly, if we do not find it then we consider those actions as a part of '*Istisā* only.' Then this statement is the same as our opinion except that we always consider an action to be from '*Istisā* when we do not find evidence indicating its obligatory status. However, if there is such evidence, we adopt the position that it is obligatory and with Allah, the most High,

is success.

Abu Muḥammad said: and as for the thing that reached him (peace be upon him), or he saw them, or he heard, which he did not explicitly reject neither did he command to enjoin in, then it is considered permissible because Allah the exalted described him (peace be upon him) and has said: *Those who follow the Apostle-Prophet, the Ummi, whom they find written down with them in the Torah and the Bible (who) enjoins them good and forbids them evil, and makes lawful to them the good things and makes unlawful to them impure things, and removes from them their burden and the shackles which were upon them; so those who believe in him and honour him and help him, and follow the light which has been sent down with him, these it is that are the successful.* [40]

Therefore if a thing is supposedly *munkar*, then without a doubt the Prophet (peace be upon him) would have prohibited it. If he did not designate it has *munkar* (or prohibited) then it is considered as being permissible (*mubāh*). The *mubāh* is that which is 'known' and whatever the Prophet (peace be upon him) knew, then it is from the 'known'. There is no 'known' except that which the Prophet knew and, likewise, there is nothing declared as *munkar* except what the Prophet has declared it as such. An example of this is the singing of the two young girls in the house of the Prophet (peace be upon him). He heard their singing and did not rebuke them for it. Rather when Abu Bakr rebuked them, the Prophet rebuked him for doing that. Therefore, this text that we have mentioned demonstrates the duty of one to rebuke those who prohibit actions that the Prophet (peace be upon him) himself knew of and gave tacit approval to. Another example is when Umar prohibited the dancing of two black slave girls to which the Prophet (peace be upon him) rebuked Umar due to his decree preventing those girls from doing that.

Another example is the games that the Prophet (peace be

[40] *Qur'ān* 7: 157

upon him) saw ‘Aisha play; where (she had) a doll (that was) a horse with wings. (This) was used despite his (peace be upon him) prohibition on images. This circumstance is an exception to what he (peace be upon him) had prohibited. It is like the prohibition of having images on one’s garments despite the fact that he permitted such a garment if it had a small image on it. It is an exception from him on a general ruling of what he has prohibited with regard to images. So when ‘Aisha cut out the images from a garment and two pillows which he (peace be upon him) would recline upon it was not because he prohibited the use of them. It is therefore correct to state that whatever is on a garment, which has an image on it, is *makrūh* and not *ḥarām* nor *mustaḥab*; rather the one who leaves it is rewarded and the one who uses it does not incur sin. In this instance, the Prophet (peace be upon him) chose the better of the two options as well as ‘Aisha and Fāṭima. Therefore, it is correct to state that garments that have images, even pillows, are permissible and okay to have and are not *mustaḥab*. We do not dislike it initially rather we love it.

Likewise, if he (peace be upon him) left something and did not prohibit it or command for it to be done it is considered permissible to do according to us but *makrūh*. The one who leaves it is rewarded and the one who does it incurs neither sin nor reward. An example is like the one who lies down and eats or the one who listens to the musical instrument of the shepherd – if these acts were *ḥarām* then they would not have been made permissible by the Prophet (peace be upon him) for others to do. Consequently, if they were recommended acts then the Prophet (peace be upon him) would have done them and he would not have left them in dislike. Hence we consider such actions as *makrūh* and we do not consider them to be *ḥarām*.

And if one says, ‘A group had slept in the presence of the Messenger of Allah (peace be upon him) then woke and prayed without being ordered to perform ablution, do you not see that as evidence against your position?’ It should be said to that person, and with Allah is success, that not one person has narrated that the Messenger of Allah (peace be upon him) saw them sleeping and neither do I know whether they were sleeping as the *ḥadith* reports that he (peace be upon him) delayed the *'Ishā'* prayer to the later part of the night when the people fell asleep to the point that one could hear them snore and Umar shouted 'The women and young boys are asleep!' Thus the *ḥadith* is clear in that it shows that they were sleeping whilst the Prophet (peace be upon him) was absent and not among them. Rather, I know from this *ḥadith* that it was only Umar who knew that the women and children were sleeping. Furthermore, these two groups of people are not obligated to attend prayers in congregation. Also it should be asked, how does one argue using this *ḥadith* to hold the opinion that they slept a short sleep whilst sitting? Of course it cannot be argued as this *ḥadith* does not intend that, so perhaps there were those among them who slept leaning on his companion or on the wall or lying down or in deep sleep. It is unknown to those who did not attend their presence how they had slept.

These types of arguments are not acceptable for the one who has a slight ounce of honesty in their faith. Therefore, when it is authentically reported that he (peace be upon him) was absent and textual evidence has not reached us that he knew of them sleeping then his command (peace be upon him) to perform ablution after sleep, as reported from Ṣafwān bin 'Assāl al-Marādī, is applied generally and we adhere to that. We do not remove that which we have been ordered due to a matter in which we do not know whether the Prophet (peace be upon him) was aware of the circumstances or not. If it were authentically established that he (peace be upon him) knew that they were asleep and that he allowed them to pray without performing ablution, then we would hold the opinion that ablution is not needed for the one who has slept under any circumstances. And if it were authentically narrated in that report that Umar said 'the people slept', then he would not have commented on them as his words 'the people slept' mean those who were waiting for the Prophet (peace be upon him).

And how can this be when every group amongst them differs in this narration because they claim that it refers to certain types of sleep over others, despite the fact that there is no basis amongst any of us to do this. Therefore, if one were to say, 'Is it permissible to state that the Messenger of Allah did not know of this?' It should be responded that it is permissible to hold this opinion just as it is permissible according to you, the people of the Shāfi'i, Māliki, and Ḥanafi schools, when Jābir said, 'We used to sell the mothers of our children during the time of the Messenger of Allah (peace be upon him)' despite the fact that this issue is more known than that of the people sleeping during the night. Those people were in need of light when they were in the corner of the mosque and, as it is stated among the Māliki's, he (peace be upon him) was unaware when the family of Abu Bakr slaughtered a horse and they gave it to them and him (peace be upon him) in Medina. This is more known than the issue of a group sleeping in the corner of the mosque. They did this due to the lack of housing that they had in Medina during the time of the Prophet (peace be upon him), the difficulty in living, the lack of stability, the closeness of Abu Bakr's family with the Prophet (peace be upon him), and their proximity to him.

Therefore, how can it be said that he was unaware of them slaughtering a horse that they would then feed to him and he was not unaware of a group of people sleeping in the corner of the mosque whilst he was in their absence? If it were true that he (peace be upon him) was present in the mosque then it may have been possible to state that he was aware of them sleeping in the corner of the mosque. Yet how can that be the case when it is authentically reported that he (peace be upon him) was absent from them despite the fact that some have specified what type of sleep they were in; namely that they were sitting, neither leaning, nor lying down, nor reclining and who ever brings this argument he is lying and with Allah is his success.

We would disagree only slightly with the above as it relates to the *fiqh* issue of whether sleep necessitates ablution (*wuḍu*) and a couple of other items. Yet the basic purport of the argument that Ibn Ḥazm advanced remains correct. His reasoning presented, invalidates all the arguments relating to the repealed act, or the allegation that it is an innovation (*bidāh'*), merely on the basis that the Prophet (peace be upon him) did not do it. More grotesque and insidious is the additional argument accompanying this, that a ruling is invalid because the Prophet's companions (may Allah be pleased with them) did not do it. How is this valid? Their explicit words, the apparent of their actions as well as their approvals are not a proof, so how can what they leave – an argument based upon nothingness - be regarded as a legal proof? It is an argument that has no substantive basis either in law or reason. By Allah, those marshalling it are misguided innovators; they are the ignorant and the perverse and are incredibly shallow minded. Or even perhaps, Allah forbid, incredibly stubborn disbelievers.

9 Actions are by intentions

Deserving reward and praise from Allah for any action performed depends upon the underlying intention. The same exists with regards to punishment and dispraise from Allah. For example, if one were to hunt using a weapon and accidently kill someone that would be considered as manslaughter. But despite the individual causing the death of another life unintentionally, he would not be classed as being a murderer and sinful for that as such. It is not comparable to someone who kills with the intention of taking another life, even if the end result appears the same in both scenarios. The distinction is that of the underlying intention. Perception and reason confirm this, as does the *Sharī'ah*. Scholars of Islam are also in unanimous agreement over this principle. Allah the exalted and majestic states:

مَّن كَانَ يُرِيدُ الْعَاجِلَةَ عَجَّلْنَا لَهُ فِيهَا مَا نَشَاءُ لِمَن نُّرِيدُ ثُمَّ جَعَلْنَا لَهُ جَهَنَّمَ يَصْلَاهَا مَذْمُومًا مَّدْحُورًا، وَمَنْ أَرَادَ الْآخِرَةَ وَسَعَىٰ لَهَا سَعْيَهَا وَهُوَ مُؤْمِنٌ فَأُولَٰئِكَ كَانَ سَعْيُهُم مَّشْكُورًا

Whoever desires this present life, We hasten to him therein what We please for whomsoever We desire, then We assign to him the hell; he shall enter it despised, driven away. And whoever desires the hereafter and strives for it as he ought to strive and he is a believer; (as for) these, their striving shall surely be accepted.[1]

قُلْ أَمَرَ رَبِّي بِالْقِسْطِ وَأَقِيمُوا وُجُوهَكُمْ عِندَ كُلِّ مَسْجِدٍ وَادْعُوهُ مُخْلِصِينَ لَهُ الدِّينَ كَمَا بَدَأَكُمْ تَعُودُونَ

Say: My Lord has enjoined justice, and set upright your faces at every time of prayer and call on Him, being sincere to Him in obedience; as He brought you forth in the beginning, so shall you also return.[2]

فَادْعُوا اللَّهَ مُخْلِصِينَ لَهُ الدِّينَ وَلَوْ كَرِهَ الْكَافِرُونَ

Therefore call upon Allah, being sincere to Him in obedience, though the unbelievers are averse.[3]

هُوَ الْحَيُّ لَا إِلَٰهَ إِلَّا هُوَ فَادْعُوهُ مُخْلِصِينَ لَهُ الدِّينَ الْحَمْدُ لِلَّهِ رَبِّ الْعَالَمِينَ

He is the Living, there is no god but He, therefore call on Him, being sincere to Him in obedience; (all) praise is due to Allah, the Lord of the worlds.[4]

وَمَا أُمِرُوا إِلَّا لِيَعْبُدُوا اللَّهَ مُخْلِصِينَ لَهُ الدِّينَ حُنَفَاءَ وَيُقِيمُوا الصَّلَاةَ وَيُؤْتُوا الزَّكَاةَ وَذَٰلِكَ دِينُ الْقَيِّمَةِ

And they were not enjoined anything except that they should serve Allah, being sincere to Him in obedience, upright, and keep up prayer and pay the poor-rate, and that is the right religion.[5]

وَلَوْ أَرَادُوا الْخُرُوجَ لَأَعَدُّوا لَهُ عُدَّةً وَلَٰكِن كَرِهَ اللَّهُ انبِعَاثَهُمْ فَثَبَّطَهُمْ وَقِيلَ اقْعُدُوا مَعَ الْقَاعِدِينَ

---

[1] *Qur'ān* 17: 18/19
[2] *Qur'ān* 7: 29
[3] *Qur'ān* 40: 14
[4] *Qur'ān* 40: 65
[5] *Qur'ān* 98: 5

And if they had intended to go forth, they would certainly have provided equipment for it, but Allah did not like their going forth, so He withheld them, and it was said (to them): Hold back with those who hold back.[6]

Arguably one of the most famous statements of the Prophet (peace be upon him) is:

إنما الأعمال بالنيات وإنما لكل امرئ ما نوى، فمن كانت هجرته إلى الله ورسوله فهجرته إلى الله ورسوله، ومن كانت هجرته إلى دنيا يصيبها أو إلى امرأة ينكحها فهجرته إلى ما هاجر إليه

Actions are to be judged by intentions and a man will have only what he intended. So whoever emigrated for Allah and His Messenger, his emigration will be for Allah and His Messenger; and whoever emigrated for worldly benefits or for a woman to marry, his emigration would be for what he emigrated for.

Without doubt this is one of the most authentic *ḥadith's* in the world. All Imām's of *ḥadith* have agreed upon its authenticity as has the *Ummah* as a whole. Almost every Imām of *ḥadith* has cited this in their respective collections such as: Bukhāri, Muslim, Tirmidhi, Abu Dāwud, Aḥmad bin Ḥanbal, an-Nasā'i, Ṭabarāni, Ibn Ḥibbān, Abu Dāwud aṭ-Ṭayālisi, Ḥumaydi, Ibn Khuzayma and many others. It is substantiated by literally dozens of authentic channels of transmission from Yaḥya bin Sa'eed al-Anṣāri from Muḥammad bin Ibrāhim al-Taymi from 'Alqama bin Waqqāṣ from Umar bin al-Khaṭṭāb. It was mentioned in *Talkheeṣ al-Ḥabeer fi aḥādith ar-Rāf'i al-Kabir*: 'Al-Ḥāfiz Abu Sa'eed Muḥammad bin Ali al-Khashāb said it was narrated by Yaḥya bin Sa'eed from about two-hundred and fifty people.' Al-Ḥāfiz Abu Musa said: 'I heard Abdal-Jalil bin Aḥmad say in *al-*

[6] *Qur'ān* 9: 46

Mudthākara, that Abu Ismā'il al-Harawy Abdullah bin Muḥammad al-Anṣāri said: 'I wrote this *ḥadith* from seven-hundred people from amongst the companions of Yaḥya bin Sa'eed. I searched for it in the different books and volumes until I went through more than three-thousand volumes, but did not reach seventy chains for it.' Imām Mālik recorded it but not in the *Muwaṭṭā'* and it was recorded in all other reliable books.

The meaning of this narration has been narrated through various different channels of transmission on the authority of a large number of companions such as: Ali ibn Abi Ṭālib, Sa'd ibn Abi Waqqās, Abu Sa'eed al-Khudri, Ibn Umar, Ibn Mas'ud, Ibn 'Abbās, Abu Hurayrah, 'Utba bin Abdus-Salamy, Hilāl bin Suwayd, 'Ubāda bin aṣ-Ṣāmit, Jābir ibn Abdullah, 'Uqba bin 'Aāmir, Abu Dharr, 'Utba bin Muslim and Mu'āwiya bin Abu Sufyān. Its meaning is *mutawātir* given the multiplicity of concurrent narrations, which we will consider in greater detail. Reason also supports its meaning as does numerous Qur'ānic verses. In his *Ṣaḥīḥ* Imām Muslim records from the channel of al-'Araj from Abu Hurayrah:

> حدثنا أبو بكر بن أبي شيبة وزهير بن حرب وإسحاق بن إبراهيم واللفظ لأبي بكر قال إسحاق: أخبرنا سفيان وقال الآخران: حدثنا بن عيينة عن أبي الزناد عن الأعرج عن أبي هريرة قال: قال رسول الله، صلى الله عليه وسلم: «قال الله عز وجل: إذا هم عبدي بسيئة فلا تكتبوها عليه، فإن عملها فاكتبوها سيئة، وإذا هم بحسنة فلم يعملها فاكتبوها حسنة، فإن عملها فاكتبوها عشراً
>
> Abu Bakr ibn Abi Shayba, Zuhayr bin Ḥarb and Isḥāq bin Ibrāhim narrated to us - and this is the wording of Abu Bakr; Isḥāq said: Sufyān reported to us and he said (from) the other two - Ibn 'Uyayna narrated to us from Abi Zinād from al-'Araj from Abu Hurayrah who said that the Messenger of Allah said: *Allah the exalted and majestic said: Whenever My bondsman intends to commit an evil, do not record it against him, but if he actually commits it, then write it as one evil. And when he*

> *intends to do good but does not do it, then take it down as one act of goodness, but if he does it, then write down ten good deeds* (in his record).

Similar is recorded in the *Ṣaḥīḥ* Bukhāri,[7] *Ṣaḥīḥ* Ibn Ḥibbān,[8] the *Musnad* of Aḥmad,[9] in the *Sunan* of Tirmidhi[10] and others. Shaykh Shu'ayb al-Arnā'uṭ said the *isnād* is authentic. In the *Ṣaḥīḥ* of Ibn Ḥibbān the following is recorded from the channel of Muḥammad ibn Sireen from Abu Hurayrah:

> أخبرنا عبد الله بن مُحَمَّد الأزدي قال: حدثنا إسحاق بن إبراهيم قال: حدثنا النضر بن شميل قال: حدثنا هشام عن محمد عن أبي هريرة عن رسول الله، صلى الله عليه وسلم، عن الله، جل وعلا، قال: من هم بحسنة فلم يعملها كتبت له حسنة، فإن عملها كتبتها بعشر أمثالها إلى سبع مائة؛ وإن هم بسيئة فلم يعملها لم أكتب عليه، فإن عملها كتبتها عليه سيئة واحدة
>
> Abdullah bin Muḥammad al-'Azdi reported to us he said Isḥāq ibn Ibrāhim narrated to us he said an-Naḍr bin Shameel narrated to us he said Hishām narrated to us rom Muḥammad from Abu Hurayrah from the Messenger of Allah (peace be upon him) from Allah the exalted and majestic who said: *Whoever intends to do good deed but does not do it, it will be written down as one deed of goodness, but if he does it, I will write it down as ten good deeds till seven hundred (in his record) and if he intends to commit an evil, but does not do it, I will not write it. If he actually commits it, I will record it against him as one evil deed.*

Shaykh Shu'ayb al-Arnā'uṭ said 'It has an authentic chain of transmission according to the conditions of Bukhāri and Muslim.' It

[7] Bukhāri Vol. 6 sec. 2,725, no. 7,062
[8] Ibn Ḥibbān Vol. 2 sec. 105, no. 380
[9] *Musnad* Aḥmad Vol. 2 sec. 242, no. 7,294
[10] *Sunan* Tirmidhi Vol. 5 sec. 265, no. 3,073

really is as he has said; it has also been cited in Muslim, in *Musnad* Aḥmad and in the *Musnad ash-Shāmiayn.* From the channel of al-'Alā' from his father from Abu Hurayrah we have the next narration, again in *Ṣaḥīḥ* Ibn Ḥibbān:

> أخبرنا الفضل بن الحباب قال: حدثنا القعنبي قال: حدثنا عبد العزيز بن محمد عن العلاء عن أبيه عن أبي هريرة أن رسول الله، صلى الله عليه وسلم، قال: قال الله تبارك وتعالى: إذا هم عبدي بالحسنة فلم يعملها كتبتها له حسنة، فإن عملها كتبتها له عشر حسنات، وإن هم عبدي بسيئة ولم يعملها لم أكتبها عليه، فإن عملها كتبتها واحدة،
>
> Al-Faḍl bin al-Ḥubāb reported to us he said al-Qa'nabi narrated to us he said Abdal Aziz bin Muḥammad narrated to us from al-'Alā' from his father from Abu Hurayrah that the Messenger of Allah (peace be upon him) said: *Allah the almighty said - whenever My servant intends to do good, but does not do it, I write one good act for him, but if he does it, I write from him ten good deeds. When he intends to commit an evil, but does not actually do it, I do not record it. But if he does it, I write only one evil.*

After mentioning this, Abu Ḥātim provides a useful additional comment, he writes:

> When Allah said - whenever My servant intends - He meant If my servant determines. He called determination intention because determination is the end of the intention. The Arabs in their language give the name of the start to the end and the name of the end to the start, as intention is not to be written down for the servant as it is just an idea that has no judgment. Allah records one good deed for whoever intends to do one, even if he does not determine to do it, and does not do it for the favour of Islam. It is the favour of Allah that He grants His servants with Islam. It is among His favour also, that He writes

> for His servant what he intends to do from good deeds, and does not do as good deeds, and what he intends to do from evil deeds, and does not do as good deed also. If He writes it down as an evil deed it would be justice. But his favour precedes His justice as His mercy precedes His anger. It is from His favour and mercy that He does not write all the evil deeds of Muslim children, who do not attain age of puberty, while He writes what they do from among good deeds.

Shaykh Shu'ayb al-Arnā'uṭ rightly observed that this *ḥadith* '…has an authentic chain of transmission according to the conditions of Muslim.' Contained with the *Ṣaḥifa* of Hammām ibn Munabih, is the next narration by way of Hammām ibn Munabih reporting from Abu Hurayrah from the Messenger of Allah (peace be upon him) who said:

> وقال رسول الله، صلى الله عليه وسلم: قال الله تعالى: إذا تحدث عبدي بأن يعمل حسنة فأنا أكتبها له حسنة ما لم يعملها فإذا عملها فأنا أكتبها له بعشر أمثالها؛ وإذا تحدث بأن يعمل سيئة فأنا أغفرها ما لم يعملها فإذا عملها فأنا أكتبها له بمثلها
>
> *Allah the exalted has said - If My servant talked about doing a good deed, I will write it for him as a good deed if he did not do it, if he really did it, I will write it as ten double good deeds. If he talked about doing evil deed, I will forgive it for him as long as he did not do it, but if he did it I will write it for him as it is.*

The next narration is from the *Sunan* of Imām Tirmidhi via the channel of Sa'eed bin al-Musayib from Abu Hurayrah:

> حدثنا عمران بن موسى القزاز حدثنا عبد الوارث بن سعيد حدثنا علي بن زيد عن سعيد بن المسيب عن أبي هريرة قال: قال رسول الله، صلى الله عليه وسلم: إن ربكم يقول: {كل حسنة بعشرة أمثالها إلى سبعمائة ضعف،

والصوم لي وأنا أجزي به، الصوم جنة من النار، ولخلوف فم الصائم أطيب عند الله من ريح المسك، وإن جهل على أحدكم جاهل وهو صائم فليقل إني صائم

'Imrān bin Musa al-Fazāz narrated to us Abdal-Wārith bin Sa'eed narrated to us Ali bin Zayd narrated to us from Sa'eed bin Musayib from Abu Hurayrah who said - the Messenger of Allah said: *Indeed your Lord said: 'Every good deed is rewarded with ten of the same up to seven hundred times over. Fasting is for Me, and I shall reward for it.' Fasting is a shield from the Fire. The smell coming from the mouth of the one fasting is more pleasant to Allah than the scent of musk. If one of you is abused by an ignorant person while fasting, then let him say: 'Indeed I am fasting.'*

After citing this, Imām Abu Esa at-Tirmidhi says: 'In this chapter from Mu'ādth bin Jabal, Sahl bin Sa'd, Ka'b bin 'Ajra, Salāma bin Qayṣr and Basheer bin al-Khaṣāṣiya. His name is Basheer Zaḥm bin Ma'bad and al-Khaṣāṣiya is his mother.' He also says: 'The *ḥadith* of Abu Hurayrah is *ḥasan* and *ghareeb* (strange) from this channel.' Al-Albāni said it is authentic; it is also reported by Aḥmad from this channel. I would submit that Ali bin Zayd bin Jud'ān is not strong but this *ḥadith* is authentic according to its evidences, it was followed by some summarised wordings, as it is mentioned in *Mu'jam al-Awsaṭ*:

حدثنا أحمد بن محمد بن نافع قال: حدثنا أحمد بن صالح قال: حدثنا عبد الله بن وهب قال: أخبرني عمرو عن بكير عن بن المسيب عن أبي هريرة عن رسول الله، صلى الله عليه وسلم، قال: كل حسنة يعملها بن آدم بعشر أمثالها إلى سبعمائة ضعف إلا الصيام هو لي وأنا أجزي به

Aḥmad bin Muḥammad bin Nāfi' narrated to us he said Aḥmad bin Ṣāliḥ narrated to us he said Abdullah bin Wahb narrated to us he said 'Amr reported to me from Bakeer from ibn al-Musayib from Abu Hurayrah from the Messenger of Allah (peace be upon him) who said: *Every good deed that is done by*

> *the son of Adam is to be doubled from ten to seven hundred doubles except for fasting, it is for Me, and I will give reward for it.*

This is also reported by an-Nasā'i in his *Sunan,*[11] as have others. In relation to this Imām Ṭabarāni said: 'Amr is the only one to narrate this on the authority of Bakeer.' I would submit: why is this problematic? I say this because all of the narrators are firm, reliable and trustworthy. A further narration is found in the *Musnad* of Isḥāq ibn Rāhaway:

> أخبرنا جرير عن عطاء بن السائب عن أبي عبد الرحمن السلمي عن أبي هريرة عن رسول الله، صلى الله عليه وسلم، قال: من همّ بحسنة فلم يعملها كتبت له حسنة، فإن عملها كتبت عشرا؛ ومن همّ بسيئة فلم يعملها لم تكتب عليه، فإن عملها كتبت سيئة

> Jarir reported to us from 'Aṭā bin as-Sā'ib from Abu Abdar-Raḥman as-Salami from Abu Hurayrah from the Prophet (peace be upon him) who said: *Whoever intends to do a good deed but does not do it, it will be written down as one deed of goodness, but if he does it, it will be written down as ten good deeds (in his record) and if he intends to commit an evil, but does not do it, it will not be written. If he actually commits it, it will be recorded against him as one evil deed.*

There is no fear from this except that of the *ikhtilāṭ* (mixing up) of 'Aṭā bin as-Sā'ib who appears within the *isnād*, if this was before or prior to his *ikhtilāṭ* then the channel would be considered authentic. In the *Mu'jam al-Awsaṭ* it comes via the channel of al-Faḍl from Abu Hurayrah:

---

[11] *Sunan* Nasā'i Vol. 4 sec. 165, no. 2,219

حدثنا عبد الله بن مُحَمَّد بن عزيز الموصلي حدثنا غسان بن الربيع حدثنا بن ثوبان عن عبد الله بن الفضل عن أبي هريرة عن النبي، صلى الله عليه وسلم، قال: إن الله، تبارك وتعالى، يقول: إذا همّ عبدي بسيئة فلم يعملها فلا تكتبوها، وإن عملها فاكتبوها واحدة، وإن تركها من أجلي فاكتبوها حسنة؛ وإذا هم بحسنة فلم يعملها فاكتبوها حسنة، وإن عمَلها فاكتبوها بعشر أمثاها إلى سبع مائة ضعف

Abdullah bin Muḥammad bin 'Azeez al-Mawṣili narrated to us Ghassān bin ar-Rabih' narrated to us Ibn Thawbān narrated to us from Abdullah bin al-Faḍl from Abu Hurayrah from the Messenger (peace be upon him) who said: *Verily Allah the almighty has said – Whenever my servant intends to commit an evil and does not do it,* (angels) *do not record it against him, but if he actually commits it, then write it as one evil deed. And if he abandons it for my sake, write it as one good deed. And when he intends to do good deed but does not do it, then write it down as one deed of goodness, but if he did it, then write down as ten good deeds till seven hundred doubles (in his record).*

The narration is also contained within the *Musnad ash-Shāmiayn.*[12] I would submit that in the round, we can say that this is *tawātur* (recurrent reports) *maqṭu* (cut-off) and it is authentic from Abu Hurayrah. This is due to the various channels of transmission – from Al-'Araj, Muḥammad ibn Sireen, al-'Alā, Hammām ibn Munabih, Sa'eed bin al-Musayib, Abu Abdar-Raḥman as-Salami and Abdullah Abdullah bin al-Faḍl – all through Abu Hurayrah as mentioned above. Each of these narrators is '*thiqa thabt*' - firm, reliable and trustworthy.

Other than this there are other transmissions of note. The following is in Muslim and via the channel of Thābit al-Bunāni from Anas bin Mālik:

[12] *Musnad ash-Shāmiayn*, Vol. 1 sec. 88, no. 123

حدثنا شيبان بن فروخ حدثنا حماد بن سلمة حدثنا ثابت البناني عن أنس بن مالك أن رسول الله، صلى الله عليه وسلم، قال: أتيت بالبراق، وهو دابة أبيض طويل فوق الحمار ودون البغل يضع حافره عند منتهى طرفه، فساق حديث الإسراء والمعراج بطوله، ونصح موسى صلوات الله وسلامه عليه لنبينا مُحَمَّد، عليه وعلى آله الصلاة والسلام، بمراجعة ربه في عدد الصلوات، حتى قال: فلم أزل ارجع بين ربي تبارك وتعالى وبين موسى عليه السلام حتى قال: يا مُحَمَّد: إنهن خمس صلوات كل يوم وليلة لكل صلاة عشر فذلك خمسون صلاة؛ ومن همّ بحسنة فلم يعملها كتبت له حسنة، فإن عملها كتبت له عشرا؛ ومن همّ بسيئة فلم يعملها لم تكتب شيئا، فإن عملها كتبت سيئة واحدة قال: فنزلت حتى انتهيت إلى موسى، صلى الله عليه وسلم، فأخبرته فقال: ارجع إلى ربك فاسأله التخفيف! ، فقال رسول الله، صلى الله عليه وسلم، فقلت: قد رجعت إلى ربي حتى استحييت منه

Shaybān bin Farrouk narrated to us Ḥammād ibn Salama narrated to us Thābit al-Bunāni narrated to us from Anas bin Mālik that the Messenger of Allah (peace be upon him) said: *Al-Burāq was brought to me. It is an animal white and long, larger than a donkey and smaller than a mule; it would place its hoof a distance equal to the range of its sight.* He narrated the whole *ḥadith* of the night journey and ascension and how Musa (peace be upon him) advised the Prophet (peace be upon him) to talk to His Lord about the number of the prayers, until the Prophet (peace be upon him) said*: I then kept on going back and forth between my Lord and Musa, 'til He said to me, 'There are five prayers every day and night. O Muḥammad, each being counted as ten, so that makes fifty prayers. He who intends to do a good deed and does not do it, will have a good deed recorded for him; and if he does it, it will be recorded for him as ten; whereas he who intends to do an evil deed and does not do, it will not be recorded for him; and if he does it, only one evil deed will be recorded. I then came down and when I came to Musa and informed him. He said - Go back to your Lord and ask Him to make it lighter!* Upon this, the Messenger of Allah (peace be upon him) said: *I returned (so often) to my Lord until I felt ashamed.*

The same *ḥadith* was also recorded both in a summarised and long version in *Musnad* Abu Ya'la,[13] the wording being:

حدثنا شيبان حدثنا حماد عن ثابت عن أنس أن رسول الله، صلى الله عليه وسلم، قال: من همّ بحسنة فلم يعملها كتبت له حسنة، فإن عملها كتبت له عشرا، ومن همّ بسيئة فلم يعملها لم يكتب عليه شيء، فإن عملها كتبت له سيئة واحدة

Shaybān narrated to us Ḥammād from Thābit narrated to us from Anas that the Messenger (peace be upon him) said: *He who intended to do good, but did not do it, one good was recorded for him. He who intended to do good and also did it, ten good deeds were recorded for him. And he who intended evil, but did not commit it, no entry was made against his name, but if he committed that, it was recorded.*

Shaykh Ḥussein Asad said: '*isnād Ṣaḥīḥ*'; it is really as he said and it is according to the conditions of Muslim as you see. Another follow-up channel to this is in *Musnad* al-Ḥārith – *Zawā'id al-Haythami* we find:

حدثنا يعلى حدثني عبد الحكم عن أنس أن رسول الله، صلى الله عليه وسلم، قال: من همّ بحسنة فعملها كتبت له عشر حسنات، فان لم يعملها كتبت له حسنة واحدة، ومن همّ بسيئة فعملها كتبت عليه سيئة واحدة فان لم يعملها لم يكتب عليه شيء

Ya'la narrated to us Abdal-Ḥakam narrated to me from Anas that the Messenger of Allah (peace be upon him) said: *Whoever intends to do a good deed and does it, it will be written down for him as ten good deeds, but if he does not it will be written one good deed. If he intends to commit an evil, and does it will be written one evil deed for him (in the record). If he does not*

[13] *Musnad* Abu Ya'la Vol. 6 sec. 171, no. 3,451

do it, it will be not be written against him.

In the *Musnad* of Aḥmad the next narration from Abu Dharr al-Ghifāri is judged to be authentic:

حدثنا عفان حدثنا أبو عوانة عن عاصم عن المعرور بن سويد عن أبي ذر قال: سمعت رسول الله، صلى الله عليه وسلم، الصادق المصدوق يقول: قال الله عز وجل: الحسنة عشر أو أزيد والسيئة واحدة أو اغفرها؛ فمن لقيني لا يشرك بي شيئا بقراب الأرض خطيئة جعلت له مثلها مغفرة

'Affān narrated to us Abu 'Awāna narrated to us from 'Aāsim from al-Ma'roor bin Suwayd from Abu Dharr who said, I heard the Messenger of Allah (peace be upon him) the truthful say: *Allah the exalted said – ten rewards or more and for bad* (deeds) *one* (record) *or pardoning. If he meets me without associating any partner yet with sins as great as the earth, repenting, he would be granted forgiveness.*

From the *Mu'jam Ṣagheer* we have the next narration:

حدثنا صدقة بن مُحَمَّد بن خروف المصري حدثنا هشام بن مُحَمَّد السدوسي حدثنا مُحَمَّد بن أبي عدي حدثنا أشعث بن عبد الملك عن الحسن عن صعصعة بن معاوية عن أبي ذر رضي الله تعالى عنه، قال: قال رسول الله، صلى الله عليه وسلم: من همّ بحسنة فلم يعملها كتبت له حسنة، فإن عملها كتبت له عشر أمثالها إلى سبع مائة وسبع أمثالها، ومن همّ بسيئة فلم يعملها لم تكتب عليه، فإن عملها كتبت عليه سيئة أو يمحها الله عز وجل

Ṣadaqa bin Muḥammad bin Kharouf al-Maṣri narrated to us Hishām bin Muḥammad al-Sadousi narrated to us Muḥammad bin Abi 'Adi narrated to us Ash'ath bin Abdal' Malik narrated to us from al-Ḥasan from Ṣa'ṣa'ah' bin Mu'āwiya from Abu Dharr who said that the Messenger of Allah (peace be upon him) said: *Whoever intends to do good deed but does not do it, it will be written down as one deed of goodness, but if he does it, it will be written down as ten good deeds till seven hundred doubles and the seven double of that (in his record) and if he intends to commit an evil, but does not do it, it will not be written. If he actually commits it, it will be recorded against him as one evil deed or may Allah forgive it for him.*

Imām aṭ-Ṭabarāni said: 'Ash'ath is the only narrator that recorded this *ḥadith* on the authority of al-Ḥasan.' I would submit that there is no harm in that; Ash'ath bin Abdal' Malik is *thiqa* being amongst the men found as narrators in Bukhāri and he is an accepted narrator by the majority.

The next narration is found in the *Musnad* of Abu Dāwud aṭ-Ṭayālisi with an authentic *isnād* and good wording:

حدثنا شعبة عن واصل عن المعرور بن سويد عن أبي ذر قال: قال رسول الله، صلى الله عليه وسلم: قال ربكم عز وجل: الحسنة بعشر والسيئة بواحدة وأغفرها، ومن لقيني بقراب الأرض خطيئة لا يشرك بي لقيته بقراب الأرض مغفرة؛ ومن همّ بحسنة ولم يعملها كتبت له حسنة، ومن همّ بسيئة فلم يعملها لم يكتب عليه شيء، ومن تقرب مني شبرا تقربت منه ذراعا، ومن تقرب مني ذراعا تقربت منه باع

Shu'ba narrated to us from Wāṣil from al-Ma'roor bin Suwayd from Abu Dharr who said that the Messenger of Allah (peace be upon him) said: *Your lord the exalted has said: A good deed (ḥasanat) is* (multiplied) *by ten and a bad deed (sayyi'at) accredited as one. Whosoever meets me with sins as great as the earth, by does not associate a partner with me, I will grant forgiveness as great as the earth. Whoever intends a good deed (ḥasanat) and doesn't act upon it, I will record a good deed to him. And whoever intends an evil deed but doesn't act upon it, nothing is recorded. And whoever draws close to me by a span, I draw close by a span. And whoever draws close to me by an arm's length, I draw close to him by an arm's length.*

Thereafter Imām Abu Dāwud aṭ-Ṭayālisi said: 'It is not regarded as being 'raised' Shu'ba narrating from Wāṣil but the people consider it raised from al-'Amash from al-Ma'roor'. I would submit that from the scholars it isn't raised from al-'Amash albeit partly.

In the round all of the previously cited narrations not only prove that the rewards of deeds, which includes sayings or statements and the notion of punishment are according to intention, but they establish the proof that intention alone without deed is deserving of reward. If Allah, the exalted grants us favour by not punishing us, it is from amongst his infinite mercy and justice. If he really punishes us for our sins, it would still be considered justice. There is no god but Allah, in Allah we put our trust and only by him are we supported. Further to this, it has also reached us that: 'If somebody intended to do a bad deed and he does not do it, then Allah will write a full good deed (in his account) with Him.' Indeed Allah removes sins out of his grace just as he promises to forgive those seeking true repentance. It is also established that none goes astray except he that is doomed as a loser. The following narrations establish these points. In *al-Jāmi aṣ-Ṣaḥīḥ al-Mukhtaṣr* Imām Bukhāri records:

حدثنا أبو معمر حدثنا عبد الوارث حدثنا جعد أبو عثمان حدثنا أبو رجاء العطاردي عن بن عباس، رضي الله تعالى عنهما، عن النبي، صلى الله عليه وسلم، فيما يروي عن ربه، عز وجل، قال: قال: إن الله كتب الحسنات والسيئات، ثم بيّن ذلك: فمن همّ بحسنة فلم يعملها كتبها الله له عنده حسنة كاملة، فإن هو همّ بها وعملها كتبها الله له عنده عشر حسنات، إلى سبعمائة ضعف إلى أضعاف كثيرة؛ ومن همّ بسيئة فلم يعملها كتبها الله له عنده حسنة كاملة، فإن هو همّ بها فعملها كتبها الله له سيئة واحدة

Abu Ma'mar narrated to us Abdal-Wārith narrated to us Ja'd Abu Uthmān narrated to us Abu Rajā' al-'Aṭāridi narrated to us from ibn 'Abbās from the Prophet (peace be upon him) who when narrating about his Lord said: *Allah ordered that the good and the bad deeds be written, and He then showed (the way) how (to write). If somebody intends to do a good deed and he does not do it, then Allah will write for him a full good deed (in his account with Him); and if he intends to do a good deed and actually did it, then Allah will write for him* (in his account) *with Him* (its reward equal) *from ten to seven hundred times to many more times: and if somebody intended to do a bad deed and he does not do it, then Allah will write a full good deed (in his account) with Him, and if he intended to do it (a bad deed) and actually did it, then Allah will write one bad deed.*

The narration is also found in the *Sunan al-Kubra* of Imām an-Nasā'i:

أخبرنا قتيبة بن سعيد قال: حدثنا جعفر عن الجعد أبي عثمان قال: حدثنا أبو رجاء العطاردي عن بن عباس عن رسول الله، صلى الله عليه وسلم، فيما يرويه عن ربه تبارك وتعالى: إن ربكم رحيم: من همّ بحسنة فلم يعملها كتبت له حسنة، فإن عملها كتبت له عشرا إلى سبعمائة إلى أضعاف كثيرة، ومن همّ بسيئة ولم يعملها كتبت له حسنة، فإن عملها كتبت واحدة أو يمحاها الله، ولا يهلك على الله إلا هالك

Qutayba ibn Sa'eed reported to us he said Ja'far narrated to us from al-Ja'd Abu Uthmān he said Abu Rajā' al-'Aṭāridi narrated to us from Ibn 'Abbās from the Messenger of Allah (peace be upon him) reporting from his Lord, blessed most high: *Verily your Lord is merciful. Whoever intends to do a good deed and he does not do it, it will be written for him a full good deed (in his account with Allah). And if he actually did it, it will be written (equal) from ten to seven hundred times to many more times, and whoever intended to do a bad deed and he does not do it, it will be written a full good deed, and if he actually did it, it will be written one bad deed (in his account) or Allah will remove it (forgive) and no one would go astray therefore except he who is doomed to be a loser*.

Another amazing *ḥadith* concerning the same subject is reported in Ibn Ḥibbān with the channel from Khuraym bin Fātik:

أخبرنا الحسن بن سفيان قال: حدثنا مُحَمَّد بن بشار قال: حدثنا أبو داود قال: حدثنا شيبان النحوي قال: حدثنا الركين بن الربيع عن أبيه عن عمه (وهو يسير بن عميلة عن خريم بن فاتك الأسدي قال: قال رسول الله، صلى الله عليه وسلم: الناس أربعة، والأعمال ستة: موجبتان، ومثل بمثل، وحسنة بعشر أمثالها، وحسنة بسبع مائة ضعف؛ والناس موسع عليه في الدنيا والآخرة، وموسع عليه في الدنيا مقتور عليه في الآخرة، ومقتور عليه في الدنيا موسع عليه في الآخرة، ومقتور عليه في الدنيا والآخرة، وشقي في الدنيا وشقي في الآخرة؛ والموجبتان: من قال: لا إله إلا الله أو قال: مؤمنا بالله دخل الجنة، ومن مات وهو يشرك بالله دخل النار، ومن همّ بحسنة فعملها كتبت له عشرة أمثالها، ومن همّ بحسنة فلم يعملها كتبت له حسنة، ومن همّ بسيئة فلم يعملها كتبت له حسنة، ومن همّ بسيئة فعملها كتبت له سيئة واحدة، غير مضاعفة، ومن أنفق نفقة فاضلة في سبيل الله فبسبع مائة ضعف

Al-Ḥasan bin Sufyān reported to us he said Muḥammad bin Bashār narrated to us Abu Dāwud narrated to us he said Shaybān an-Naḥwe narrated to us he said ar-Rakeen bin Rabih' narrated to us from his father from his uncle (and he is Yuseer bin 'Ameela) from Khuraym bin Fātik al-Asadi who said that the Messenger of Allah (peace be upon him) said: *People are four* (kinds) *and deeds are six* (types). *Two unavoidable, like for like, one good deed that equals (in reward) ten of its double and one good deed that equals (in reward) seven hundred of its double. People will either be relieved in both this life and the hereafter, others will be relieved in this life and restricted in the hereafter, who will be restricted in this life and relieved in the hereafter, and who will be restricted in both this life and the hereafter; miserable during both this life and the hereafter. The two unavoidable means: paradise and hellfire; whoever said there is no god but Allah* (the sub-narrator doubted. Is it these words or whoever believes in Allah) *will enter paradise and whoever died while he is disbelieving in Allah, will enter*

> *hellfire. Whoever intends to do a good deed and actually did it, it will be written for him as ten-fold, whoever intends to do a good deed but did not do it will be written for him as one good deed; whoever intends to do evil and did not do, it will be written for him as one good deed, and whoever intends to do evil and actually did it, it will be written for him as one evil deed without doubling. Whoever spent his extra* (money) *seeking Allah alone, it equals* (in reward) *seven hundred fold.*

Shaykh Shu'ayb al-Arnā'uṭ said the *isnād* is *Ṣaḥīḥ*. Similar was recorded with a few differences in the order of wording in the *Mustadrak*, in *Mu'jam al-Kabir* and via several channels in *al-Aḥād wal Mathāni*. In the *Musnad* Shihāb the next narration is reported on the authority of Abdullah ibn 'Amr ibn al-'Aāṣ:

> أخبرنا عبد الرحمن بن عمر المعدل أنبأنا أبو الفضل يحيى بن الربيع حدثنا عبد السلام بن مُحَمَّد الأموي حدثنا سعيد بن كثير بن عفير حدثنا بن لهيعة عن عمرو بن شعيب عن أبيه عن عبد الله بن عمرو أن رسول الله، صلى الله عليه وسلم، قال: من همّ بذنب ثم تركه كانت له حسنة، ومن همّ بذنب ثم عمله ثم استغفر الله منه غفر له
>
> Abdar-Raḥman bin 'Amr al-Mu'dal reported to us Abu Faḍl Yaḥya bin ar-Rabih' reports, Abdas-Salām bin Muḥammad al-Amwi narrated to us Sa'eed bin Kathir bin 'Ufeer narrated to us Ibn Lahiya narrated to us from Amr bin Shu'ayb from his father from Abdullah ibn 'Amr that the Messenger of Allah (peace be upon him) said: *Whoever intends to do sin and then did not, it will be (written) for him as a good deed and whoever intends to do sin and actually did it and then he asked Allah for forgiveness for that sin, Allah will forgive him.*

The aforementioned *ḥadith* is not *Ṣaḥīḥ* in and of itself, but can be considered as *ḥasan Ṣaḥīḥ* according to the weight of evidence. In addition to this, there are several texts which confirm the statement or even maxim, 'intention alone without accompanying deed is deserving of reward' which are worthy of consideration. Imām Muslim has the following two *ḥadith* in his *Ṣaḥīḥ* in the book of government (*Kitāb al-Imāra*):

حدثني أبو الطاهر وحرملة بن يحيى واللفظ لحرملة قال أبو الطاهر أخبرنا و قال حرملة حدثنا عبد الله بن وهب حدثني أبو شريح أن سهل بن أبي أمامة بن سهل بن حنيف حدثه عن أبيه عن جده أن النبي صلى الله عليه وسلم قال من سأل الله الشهادة بصدق بلغه الله منازل الشهداء وإن مات على فراشه ولم يذكر أبو الطاهر في حديثه بصدق

Abu Ṭāhir and Ḥarmala bin Yaḥya narrated to me and (this is) the wording of Ḥarmala - Abu Ṭāhir said reported to us and he said Ḥarmala, Abdullah bin Wahb narrated to us Abu Shurayḥ narrated to me that Sahl bin Abi Umāma bin Sahl bin Ḥunaif who learned the tradition from his father who (in turn) learned it from his grandfather-that the Messenger of Allah (peace be upon him) said: *Who sought martyrdom with sincerity will be ranked by Allah among the martyrs even if he died on his bed.* [In his version of the tradition by Abu Ṭāhir, the words 'with sincerity' aren't mentioned.]

حدثنا محمد بن عبد الرحمن بن سهم الأنطاكي أخبرنا عبد الله بن المبارك عن وهيب المكي عن عمر بن محمد بن المنكدر عن سمي عن أبي صالح عن أبي هريرة قال قال رسول الله صلى الله عليه وسلم من مات ولم يغز ولم يحدث به نفسه مات على شعبة من نفاق

Muḥammad ibn Abdar-Raḥman ibn Sahm al-Anṭāki narrated to us Abdullah ibn Mubārak reported to us from Uhayb al-Makki from Umar bin Muḥammad al-Munkadr from Sami from Abu Ṣāliḥ from Abu Hurayrah who said that the Messenger of Allah (peace be upon him) said: *One who died but did not fight in the way of Allah nor did he express any desire (or determination) for Jihād died the death of a hypocrite.*

Despite this, there have been some amongst those who are unqualified and did not acquire the requisite knowledge of *fiqh* who were of the view that these narrations contradicted others, such as that found in *al-Jāmi aṣ-Ṣaḥīḥ al-Mukhtaṣr* of Imām Bukhāri:

حدثنا عبد الرحمن بن المبارك حدثنا حماد بن زيد حدثنا أيوب ويونس عن الحسن عن الأحنف بن قيس قال: ذهبت لأنصر هذا الرجل، فلقيني أبو بكرة فقال: أين تريد؟!، قلت: أنصر هذا الرجل! ، قال: ارجع فإني سمعت رسول الله، صلى الله عليه وسلم، يقول: إذا التقى المسلمان بسيفيهما فالقاتل والمقتول في النار! ، فقلت: يا رسول الله: هذا القاتل، فما بال المقتول؟!، قال: إنه كان حريصا على قتل صاحبه

Abdar-Raḥman bin Mubārak narrated to us Ḥammād bin Zayd narrated to us Ayub and Yunus narrated to us from al-Ḥasan from al-Aḥnaf bin Qays who said: While I was going to help this man, Abu Bakra met me and asked where are you going? I replied - I am going to help that person. He said, go back for I have heard Allah's Messenger (peace be upon him) saying, *'When two Muslims fight (meet) each other with their swords, both the murderer as well as the murdered will go to the Hell-fire.'* I said: O Allah's Messenger (peace be upon him)! It is all right for the murderer but what about the murdered one? Allah's Messenger (peace be upon him) replied: '*He surely had the intention to kill his companion.*'

This is also narrated by Hishām ibn Ḥassān, Mu'alla ibn Ziyād and al-Mubārak ibn Faḍala from al-Ḥasan from al-Aḥnaf from Abu Bakra from the Prophet (peace be upon him). Moreover this *isnād* is of the utmost connectivity, authenticity and good wording. Imām Bukhāri records this from alternate channels elsewhere in his *Ṣaḥīḥ*.[14] He said following some of them: 'Its reported (by) Ma'mar from Ayub and reported by Bakkār bin Abdal-Aziz from his father from Abi Bakra;

---

[14] Bukhāri Vol. 6 sec. 2,520, no. 6,481 & Vol. 6 sec. 2,595, no. 6,672

Ghundar said – Shu'ba narrated to us from Manṣur from Rabi' bin Ḥirāsh from Abi Bakra from the Prophet (peace be upon him) and there was no raising or lifting in relation to Sufyān (reporting) from Manṣur.'

The *ḥadith* is reported very widely and has been recorded by a large number of Imām's: Muslim records this in his *Ṣaḥīḥ;*[15] Nasā'i has this in several places in his *Sunan* as well as in *Sunan al-Kubra,*[16] as does Abu Dāwud in his.[17] It is in *Ṣaḥīḥ* Ibn Ḥibbān[18] as well as in several places in the *Musnad* of Aḥmad;[19] Ibn Abu 'Aāṣim 'Amr ash-Shaybāni records this in *al-Aḥād wal-Mathāni,*[20] Bayhaqy records this in several places in his *Sunan al-Kubra*[21] and other than them. In his *Musnad* Imām Aḥmad has the following narration with an authentic channel of narration:

حدثنا مُحَمَّد بن جعفر حدثنا شعبة عن منصور عن ربعي بن حراش عن أبي بكرة عن النبي، صلى الله عليه وسلم، إنه قال: إذا المسلمان حمل أحدهما على صاحبه السلاح فهما على طرف جهنم، فإذا قتل أحدهما صاحبه دخلاها جميعا

Muḥammad bin Ja'far narrated to us Shu'ba narrated to us from Manṣur from Rabi' bin Ḥirāsh from Abu Bakra from the Prophet (peace be upon him) who said: *When one Muslim wields his weapon against his brother, both of them are at the edge of Hell, and if one of them kills the other, they will both enter it.*

[15] Muslim Vol. 4 sec. 2,214, no. 2,888
[16] *Sunan* Nasā'i Vol. 7 sec. 125, no. 4,120/3 & sec. 126, no. 4,124; *Sunan al-Kubra* Vol. 2 sec. 316, no. 3,585/3,588
[17] *Sunan* Abu Dāwud Vol. 4 sec. 103, no. 4,268
[18] Ibn Ḥibbān Vol. 13 sec. 275, no. 5,981 & sec. 320, no. 5,981
[19] *Musnad* Aḥmad Vol. 5 sec. 51, no. 20,456; 20,537/8
[20] Shaybāni *al-Aḥād wal-Mathāni* Vol. 3 sec. 208, no. 1,563/4
[21] Bayhaqy *Sunan al-Kubra* Vol. 8 sec. 190, no. 16,569/71

Ibn Mājah also records this narration in his *Sunan* and it is also found in other collections.[22] I would submit that there is no doubt that al-Aḥnaf ibn Qays (may Allah be pleased with him) was right, when he was carrying arms in support of the Imām of truth, Ali ibn Abi Ṭālib (may the grace of Allah be upon him) against those who were transgressing beyond all bounds (*fi' al-Bāghiya*) and he fought them in line with the command of Allah. Abu Bakra misjudged the matter here by linking it to the specific incident to the Prophetic *ḥadith*. However Allah has not obliged us to accept the opinion of Abu Bakra, nor are we obliged to follow him in this. As in the indistinguishable, preserved and firm following words - Imām Aḥmad records in his *Musnad* on the authority of Abu Musa al-Ash'ari:

> حدثنا يزيد قال أخبرنا سعيد عن قتادة عن الحسن عن أبي موسى عن النبي، صلى الله عليه وسلم، قال: إذا المسلمان توجها بسيفهما فقتل أحدهما صاحبه فهما في النار، قيل: يا رسول الله هذا القاتل فما بال المقتول؟ قال: إنه أراد قتل صاحبه
>
> Yazeed narrated to us he said Sa'eed reported to us from Qatādah from al-Ḥasan from Abu Musa from the Messenger (peace be upon him) who said: *If two Muslims meet (and fight) with their weapons and one of them kills the other, the killer and the slain will both be in Hell.* It was said: O Messenger of Allah, (we understand about) the killer, but what about the one who is killed? He said: *He wanted to kill his companion*

Elsewhere in the *Musnad* Imām Aḥmad records the same but from a different authentic channel – Abdar-Razzāq narrated to us Ma'mar reported to us from Qatādah from al-Ḥasan from Abu Bakra. Similar narrations are found in *the Sunan* and *Sunan al-Kubra* of Nasā'i,[23] in

---

[22] *Sunan* Ibn Mājah Vol. 2 sec. 1,312, no. 3,965

[23] *Sunan* Nasā'i Vol. 7 sec. 125, no. 4,119/21; *Sunan al-Kubra* Vol. 2 sec. 315, no. 3,584/6

the *Sunan* of Ibn Mājah[24] as well as in other collections. Imām Aḥmad has the next narration in the *Musnad* with an authentic *isnād*:

حدثنا يزيد بن هارون أخبرنا سليمان عن الحسن عن أبي موسى عن النبي، صلى الله عليه وسلم، قال: إذا تواجه المسلمان بسيفيهما فقتل أحدهما صاحبه فهما في النار، قيل: يا رسول الله هذا القاتل فما بال المقتول؟ قال: إنه أراد قتل صاحبه

Yazeed bin Hārun narrated to us Sulaymān reported to us from al-Ḥasan from Abu Musa al-Ashari from the Prophet (peace be upon him) who said: *If two Muslims meet (and fight) with their weapons and one of them kills the other, the killer and the slain will both be in Hell.* It was said: O Messenger of Allah, (we understand about) the killer, but what about the one who is killed? He said: *He wanted to kill his companion*

The narration is also found in the *Sunan* and the *Sunan al-Kubra* of Nasā'i,[25] in the *Musnad* of 'Abd bin Ḥameed,[26] in the *Sunan* of Ibn Mājah[27] as well as in other collections. Imām Nasā'i also has this with an authentic *isnād* in the *Sunan al-Kubra*:

أخبرنا مجاهد بن موسى قال: حدثنا إسماعيل وهو بن علية عن يونس عن الحسن عن أبي موسى الأشعري أن رسول الله، صلى الله عليه وسلم، قال: إذا تواجه المسلمان بسيفيهما فقتل أحدهما صاحبه فالقاتل والمقتول في النار، قال رجل: يا رسول الله هذا القاتل فما بال المقتول؟!، قال: (إنه أراد قتل صاحبه

Mujāhid bin Musa reported to us he said Ismā'il narrated to us - and he is Ibn 'Ulaya - from Yunus from al-Ḥasan from Abu

---

[24] *Sunan* Ibn Mājah Vol. 2 sec. 1,311, no. 3,964
[25] *Sunan* Nasā'i Vol. 7 sec. 124, no. 4,118 & *Sunan al-Kubra* Vol. 2 sec. 315, no. 3,583
[26] *Musnad* A'bd bin Ḥameed Vol. 1 sec. 192, no. 543
[27] *Sunan* Ibn Mājah Vol. 2 sec. 1,311, no. 3,964

Musa al-Ash'ari that the Prophet (peace be upon him) said: *If two Muslims confront each other with swords, and one kills the other, they will both be in Hell.* It was said: O Messenger of Allah, (we understand about) the killer, but what about the one who is killed? He said*: He wanted to kill his companion*

And this is also reported in the *Sunan* of Ibn Mājah on the authority of Anas ibn Mālik:

حدثنا سويد بن سعيد حدثنا مبارك بن سحيم عن عبد العزيز بن صهيب عن أنس بن مالك عن النبي، صلى الله عليه وسلم، قال: ما من مسلمين التقيا بأسيافهما إلا كان القاتل والمقتول في النار

Suwayd ibn Sa'eed narrated to us Mubārak bin Suḥaym narrated to us from Abdal-Aziz bin Ṣuhayb from Anas ibn Mālik from the Prophet (peace be upon him) who said: *There are no two Muslims who confront one another with their swords, but both the killer and the slain will be in Hell.*

The difficulty with the aforementioned narration is that Mubārak bin Suḥaym as a narrator is classified as *munkar al-ḥadith* and consequently rejected (*matrook*).

Regarding the subject under consideration there is no discrepancy here. The one who was killed did not intend to kill the other and then abandoned this determination, returning to his house, so that he may deserve the reward of the one good deed. He changed from just determination to action. He went out of his house, held his sword and hit the other with an intention to kill him except that he was killed first, otherwise he would have been the killer. Whoever lacked the required intellect, to the degree that he did not understand these obvious truths, he must leave *fiqh* (jurisprudence) and deducing *aḥkām* to those that are qualified to do this, or at the very least, find a new vocation. Allah has written beneficence for everything and he does not place a burden upon a soul greater than it can bear. If one cannot encompass such matters then one must devote oneself to what is viable.

Consequently it has been conclusively demonstrated that one may be rewarded for intention alone as the Qur'ān and the aforementioned *aḥādith* show. *A fortiori* one can be rewarded for a purely permissible act if accompanied by a good intention (*niya*) of mind or intellect and a conscientious heart, seeking only the pleasure of Allah the exalted. An example would be if this was also done in order to help one achieve the obligatory and desirable matters, or in order to accustom oneself to keep away from doing undesirable and prohibited matters. Someone may be undertaking a matter with such 'consciousness' while intending to do such deeds, their heart aware that Allah permitted such a deed and that doing the matter is but submitting to the judgment of Allah, being happy with the permission provided by Allah or any other good considerations which were mentioned in the aforementioned evidences. Reward here is according to this intention and this remembrance of the heart and not limited according to the permissible deed, as it is a mere permissible deed in itself. The permissible deed in itself, for whoever does it is neither deserving reward nor punishment, it will never be turned into a desirable matter, otherwise measures of *Sharī'ah* will be disturbed and truth will mix with falsehood, Allah forbid.

The evidence which we have outlined above and others like it is the correct position and not like which was mentioned by other even famous scholars such as Imām an-Nawawi. In his commentary upon *Ṣaḥīḥ* Muslim he wrote: 'And this evidence is that the permissible matters (*mubāḥāt*) become matters of obedience accompanied with intentions and charities,' thereafter citing the *ḥadith* where the Prophet (peace be upon him) said: '*....and in man's sexual intercourse (with* *his wife) there is a Ṣadaqa…'*[28] Indeed the *ḥadith* is authentic, similar has been reported where he (peace be upon him) said: '*And you should do the same, as it is among the best of your deeds to perform what is lawful* (meaning: intercourse with your wives).'[29] Such narrations are definite and they establish that intercourse with one's spouse, as a mere naked act, is desirable in-itself; that whoever did it will be rewarded. So therefore it is not a mere permissible deed that whoever did it will neither be rewarded nor punished. How then did Imām an-Nawawi make it a mere permissible deed, as it is to be understood from his statement and then put the condition that there should be a certain intention behind this in order to gain reward? On the contrary, other Imām's like Ibn Ḥazm was sharper to the point, recognising this matter by citing the verse where Allah said:

....فَإِذَا تَطَهَّرْنَ فَأْتُوهُنَّ مِنْ حَيْثُ أَمَرَكُمُ اللَّهُ ...

....then when they have cleansed themselves, go in to them as Allah has commanded you... [30]

He understood it as to be obligatory, not just desirable or permissible; in other words having intercourse even if once after the wife had completed the rituals of purification following her menstrual cycle. A persuasive argument indeed!

One should note, where is the word 'intention' mentioned in the

[28] The *ḥadith* is recorded by Imām Muslim in the book of *zakāt*, chapter entitled: the word charity may apply to all good deeds. The wording is a short excerpt of a longer narration, the *isnād* for which is: Abdullah bin Muḥammad bin Asmā' aḍ-Ḍuba'ee narrated to us Mahdi bin Maymoon narrated to us Wāṣil *mawla* Abu U'yayna narrated to usfrom Yaḥya bin 'Uqayl from Yaḥya bin Ya'mar from Abul-Aswad ad-Diyali from Abu Dharr.

[29] *Musnad* Aḥmad. The *isnād* for this *ḥadith* is: Abdar-Raḥman bin Mahdi narrated to us from Mu'āwiya - that is to say - Ibn Ṣāliḥ from Azhar bin Sa'eed al-Ḥarāzi who said I heard Abu Kabsha al-Anmāri who said (etc).

[30] *Qur'ān* 2: 222

aḥādith that Imām an-Nawawi cited? Surely this would be needed to substantiate his argument, that a permissible deed can be *turned* into a desirable matter according to one's intention, thereby being a matter of obedience. The use of the phrase 'act of obedience' here is not good either. Perhaps an-Nawawi meant by this 'desirable matters' (*mustaḥabāt*) otherwise, performing something permissible is an act of obedience, abandoning forbidden matters is an act of obedience and performing the obligations is an act of obedience. In short, obedience is obeying the dictates of the *Sharī'ah.* Following the judgment of Allah and the creed he ordains is obedience; no difference in that between considering what was forbidden as forbidden, what was lawful as lawful, what was obligation as obligation, and so on.

Therefore to reiterate and stress this point again, it is not lawful to say that what is permissible is turned with a 'good intention' to something desirable, as it is not desirable in and of itself. Reward is due according to other matters that accompanied it. It is not then lawful to mix between them, otherwise measures of the *Sharī'ah* will be disturbed and truth will mix with falsehood. That is why, the matter which is desirable in itself, whoever does it deserves to be rewarded and praised by Allah and whoever did not do it, does not deserve to be punished or dispraised by Allah. Concerning the matter which is undesirable in itself, whoever did not do it, deserves to be rewarded and praised by Allah and whoever did it, does not deserve to be punished or dispraised by Allah. Both of these two matters need independent evidence because they are not like the absolute original state of permissibility. Whatever was not like it, needs evidence, otherwise it would be a saying without knowledge and a judgment that Allah did not permit. That is to say, it would be innovation (*bidāh'*) in the religion and this is exactly the way that leads to straying from the religion and ultimately in the extreme, *kufr* (disbelief).

10 Islam is the complete *Deen*

All actions and deeds that are voluntary in nature are judged according to the legal framework that Allah the exalted has revealed. Nothing is left out; there are no gaps. Allah the exalted himself says:

وَيَوْمَ نَبْعَثُ فِي كُلِّ أُمَّةٍ شَهِيدًا عَلَيْهِم مِّنْ أَنفُسِهِمْ وَجِئْنَا بِكَ شَهِيدًا عَلَىٰ هَٰؤُلَاءِ وَنَزَّلْنَا عَلَيْكَ الْكِتَابَ تِبْيَانًا لِّكُلِّ شَيْءٍ وَهُدًى وَرَحْمَةً وَبُشْرَىٰ لِلْمُسْلِمِينَ

And on the day when We will raise up in every people a witness against them from among themselves, and bring you as a witness against these and We have revealed the Book to you explaining clearly everything, and a guidance and mercy and good news for those who submit.[1]

يَا أَيُّهَا الَّذِينَ آمَنُوا أَطِيعُوا اللَّهَ وَأَطِيعُوا الرَّسُولَ وَأُولِي الْأَمْرِ مِنكُمْ فَإِن تَنَازَعْتُمْ فِي شَيْءٍ فَرُدُّوهُ إِلَى اللَّهِ وَالرَّسُولِ إِن كُنتُمْ تُؤْمِنُونَ بِاللَّهِ وَالْيَوْمِ الْآخِرِ ذَٰلِكَ خَيْرٌ وَأَحْسَنُ تَأْوِيلًا

O you who believe! Obey Allah and obey the Messenger and those in authority from among you; then if you differ about anything, refer it to Allah and the Messenger, if you believe in Allah and the last day; this is better and

[1] *Qur'ān* 16: 89

very good in the end.[2]

وَمَا اخْتَلَفْتُمْ فِيهِ مِن شَيْءٍ فَحُكْمُهُ إِلَى اللهِ ذَٰلِكُمُ اللهُ رَبِّي عَلَيْهِ تَوَكَّلْتُ وَإِلَيْهِ أُنِيبُ

And in whatever thing you disagree, the judgment thereof is (in) Allah's (hand); that is Allah, my Lord, on Him do I rely and to Him do I turn time after time.[3]

Reason, as well as continuous multiple reports from the annals of human history dictate that people have differed and quarrelled in all matters conceivable. Even the simplest points that one may think would be beyond matters of disputation were in fact by some, the Sophists being a case in point. In light of this, we are obliged to refer matters for judgement back to the judgement of Allah. The notion of reference must always return back to Allah and his Messenger (peace be upon him) as a matter of necessity. For it will provide the resolution to every matter in dispute. It is incredulous to believe that Allah would sanction reference to other than that. One must have absolute certitude that the book and the *Sunnah* contain all necessary judgements which can resolve disputes; only the ignorant and the stubborn disbelievers would have otherwise!

We see that Allah the exalted referred back in his revelation – Qur'ān and *Sunnah* – all matters as they pertain to this world to the people. We mean the characteristics of this tangible physical world and its nature (like pollinating palm trees), that is, *the world as it is.* He referred physics, chemistry, astronomy, geology, medicine, agriculture, industry, engineering and the like to people. He referred it to experience, to examining and reasoning, totally and fully with all its stages of inspection, examining, studying, formulating theories, utilising and applying them. He kept whatever is left, essentially, *the world as it ought to be*, which is 'religion' or general law and the

[2] *Qur'ān* 4: 59
[3] *Qur'ān* 42: 10

certain way of living to himself. He kept especially those aspects regarding his divine essence, his angels, the final day and the like. All the reckoning and calling people to account, ordaining things as lawful or unlawful and judging people's characters, whether they are good or evil. Our present *Sharī'ah*, that has been revealed to mankind has included all the deeds of people with their judgments in the most perfect manner. Allah says:

حُرِّمَتْ عَلَيْكُمُ الْمَيْتَةُ وَالدَّمُ وَلَحْمُ الْخِنزِيرِ وَمَا أُهِلَّ لِغَيْرِ اللَّهِ بِهِ وَالْمُنْخَنِقَةُ وَالْمَوْقُوذَةُ وَالْمُتَرَدِّيَةُ وَالنَّطِيحَةُ وَمَا أَكَلَ السَّبُعُ إِلَّا مَا ذَكَّيْتُمْ وَمَا ذُبِحَ عَلَى النُّصُبِ وَأَن تَسْتَقْسِمُوا بِالْأَزْلَامِ ذَٰلِكُمْ فِسْقٌ الْيَوْمَ يَئِسَ الَّذِينَ كَفَرُوا مِن دِينِكُمْ فَلَا تَخْشَوْهُمْ وَاخْشَوْنِ الْيَوْمَ أَكْمَلْتُ لَكُمْ دِينَكُمْ وَأَتْمَمْتُ عَلَيْكُمْ نِعْمَتِي وَرَضِيتُ لَكُمُ الْإِسْلَامَ دِينًا فَمَنِ اضْطُرَّ فِي مَخْمَصَةٍ غَيْرَ مُتَجَانِفٍ لِّإِثْمٍ فَإِنَّ اللَّهَ غَفُورٌ رَّحِيمٌ

Forbidden to you is that which dies of itself, and blood, and flesh of swine, and that on which any other name than that of Allah has been invoked, and the strangled (animal) and that beaten to death, and that killed by a fall and that killed by being smitten with the horn, and that which wild beasts have eaten, except what you slaughter, and what is sacrificed on stones set up (for idols) and that you divide by the arrows; that is a transgression. This day have those who disbelieve despaired of your Deen, so fear them not, and fear Me. This day have I perfected for you your Deen and completed My favour on you and chosen for you Islam as a Deen; but whoever is compelled by hunger, not inclining wilfully to sin, then surely Allah is Forgiving, Merciful. [4]

Stressing after this the bestowing of proportionality concerning the judgement where faced with being forced to eat prohibited kinds of food, which were previously revealed in an earlier Meccan revelation. Allah said at the end of the aforementioned verse '….*but whoever is compelled by hunger, not inclining wilfully to sin, then surely Allah is Forgiving, Merciful.' Deen* is perfect now, the *Deen* of Islam and no other. Anything else would be regression to at best, an earlier now

[4] *Qur'ān* 5: 3

superseded *Sharī'ah* and at worst ignorance and disbelief. Grace is complete now and any other thing would be defective and calamitous resulting from disobeying Allah, breaching his orders and neglecting his laws. The final abode would be hellfire and a permanent curse. Adhering to the legal judgments is the main reason behind creating man. It is the meaning of human existence. Allah says in the famous oft-quoted verse -

وَمَا خَلَقْتُ الْجِنَّ وَالْإِنسَ إِلَّا لِيَعْبُدُونِ

And I have not created the jinn and the men except that they should worship Me. [5]

To worship (*'Ibādah*) is to render the utmost obedience and submission, out of humility and choice to Allah the exalted; based upon the recognition of his prerogative of command (*ḥākimiyyah*) that he alone by his glorious self, determines what is to be commanded or prohibited. That right is absolute, without any precondition, except that which he has prescribed upon himself to undertake or forbidden himself from, or a condition that he will fulfil himself. Such cognisance is but the apex of the expression of firm belief (*'itiqād*) with decisive certainty; borne of absolute faith (*'Iman*) in Allah as he is the one true God. For verily, there is no other god/deity but him; the one and only, the necessarily existent; *al-Ḥayy al-Qayum* (the living, the self-subsisting); *al-Awwal* (the first); ageless and eternal, without beginning or end. For he is *al-Bāqi* (the ever-lasting), the eternal. He acts according to his will, creating what only he chooses and determines. He cannot be questioned over what he does, and he governs and according to his judgement and is swift in calling to account. What is not worship (*'Ibādah*), in and of itself, is the prostration and bowing; standing and sitting, pilgrimage and fasting, may Allah forbid. Such acts are ritual acts of devotion. Expressed

[5] *Qur'ān* 51: 56

differently, the worship of Allah is obeying every order and abstaining from every prohibition as we shall discuss elsewhere in this book God-willing.

This perfect complete *Sharī'ah* has made certain acts obligatory - termed '*farā'iḍ*' or '*wājibāt*' making them duty bound. Exceptions do exist like where an individual is unable to perform them or a specific legal exception is set out. For example, one is not obliged to fast while travelling, even if this travel is dubbed by some nowadays as being comfortable. At the same time it is obligatory on those who have tiresome physical jobs, whose burden might exceed that of travelling, as long as the person is capable. Other acts have been declared prohibited – termed as '*muḥaramāt*'. No one is given leave to undertake these acts without a specific legal injunction, such as being allowed to lie under certain circumstances. One can be exempted from the prohibited under necessity (i.e. pain of death or the like) and coercion. Even in these particular circumstances, there is no license given to take another life or harm another in their body, period. The one subject to such a form of coercion does not have a legal get out clause allowing such harm, because no one individual has a greater right of preservation than another.

Moreover, necessity and coercion even under pain of death does not provide licence for a Muslim to support enemy combatants who are engaged in war, or operations other than war, whether that involves killing or not. The majority of scholars agree that the one coerced to kill is not allowed to do so, for this person is not worthier of preservation than another. This point was eloquently expressed by the famous Imām and scholar of Islam: Abul-'Abbās Aḥmad ibn Abdal-Ḥaleem Ibn Taymiyyah in *Fatāwa al-Kubra*:

> There is no doubt that it is obligatory on him, if he was forced to be present not to fight, even if Muslims killed him. It is the same if disbelievers forced him to be on their side to fight against Muslims. If a man forced another to kill an innocent

> Muslim, Muslims agree that it is not permissible to do it. Even if he is forced under threat of death, saving himself by killing that Muslim is not worthier than the alternative. He has no right to do another person injustice by killing him in order not to be killed himself. If he did that, retaliation is on both the one forcing and the one forced to kill, according to the majority of scholars such as Aḥmad, Mālik and ash-Shāfi' in one of his opinions. His other opinion states that retaliation is on the one forcing alone. This agrees with the opinion of Abu Ḥanifah and Muḥammad. It was said that retaliation is on the direct forced person, as it was related from Zafar while Abu Yusuf obligates paying the blood money, instead of taking retaliation, which is not obligatory according to him.

Similar has been written in other areas of his works such as in *Majmu' al-Fatāwa.* The respected Imām also has another opinion that is worthy of consideration in which is to be found in *Kutub wa-Rasā'il wa Fatāwa Ibn Taymiyyah fi Fiqh* (books, letters and *Fatāwa* of Ibn Taymiyyah in *fiqh*):

> The Prophet (peace be upon him) ordered the one forced to fight in ordeals, to break his sword. He is not allowed to fight even if he may be killed. It was recorded in *Ṣaḥīḥ* Muslim that Abu Bakrah (may Allah be pleased with him) narrated that the Prophet (peace be upon him) said: *There would soon be turmoil (fitan). Behold! There would be turmoil in which the one who would be seated would be better than one who would stand and the one who would stand would be better than one who would run. Behold! When the turmoil comes or it appears, the one who has camel should stick to his camel and he who has sheep or goat should stick to his sheep and goat and he who has land should stick to the land.* A person said: Allah's Messenger, what is your opinion about one who has neither camel nor sheep nor land? Thereupon, he said: *He should take hold of his sword and beat its edge with the help of stone and then try to*

find a way of escape. O Allah, I have conveyed (thy Message); O Allah, I have conveyed (thy Message); O Allah, I have conveyed (thy Message). A person said: Allah's Messenger, what is your opinion if I am drawn to a rank in spite of myself, or in one of the groups and made to march and a man strikes with his sword or there comes an arrow and kills me? *Thereupon he said: He will bear the punishment of his sin and that of yours and he would be one amongst the denizens of Hell.*[6]

Each of these quotes from Ibn Taymiyyah are truly excellent, may Allah raise his rank. One should carefully examine them and ponder over their meanings. It is unfortunate that despite his sharp and insightful comments as we have seen, he made catastrophic mistakes in other branches of Islamic knowledge, none more so than in his categorisation of *Tawḥeed* and understanding of the reality of *Shirk* (polytheism). Although he may have thought that this was addressing some of the ignorant practices that he saw in his time, history has shown that his tripartite division of *Tawḥeed* has caused more problems in understanding than it sought to address. Moreover, it became a sword drenched in the blood of the people of Islam wielded by Shaykh Muḥammad ibn Abdal-Wahāb and his companions; the disastrous legacy of which we are still tirelessly working to reverse.

Returning to our main subject, there are actions, which praise be to Allah, are the majority of the deeds of people, they are left for the person to decide whether to do them or not. Doing some of them could be preferable. These are called 'desirable' (*mustaḥabāt*) actions. Leaving some actions might be more appropriate, and these are called 'undesirable' (*makroohāt*) actions. In cases, it might be on equal terms and then actions would be known as 'permissible' (*mubāḥāt*) actions. The person ordered of these actions might do the permissible one, or

---

[6] The *ḥadith* is found in *Ṣaḥīḥ* Muslim, the book of tribulations / portents of the last hour, ch. The onset of tribulations is like rainfall.

leave them, according to his choice. It also depends upon each case and interest. One can carry out a permissible deal and leave another permissible one, for one could be of the view that the first will make more profit than the second. One could even avoid a third permissible one for fear of loss. Considering the best interest and profits – or losses and harm – is only possible if the action is originally permissible. So one must make sure of the legality of any action and one must first seek what the judgment of Allah is regarding a matter. If it was proven that it is an optional deed, only then could one consider the best interest and profits - or the losses and harm. Consequently, it is not lawful for anyone who believes in Allah and the final day to leave an obligation without any legal permit (*rukhṣa*) or just for not being able to do it. One cannot simply commit that which has been deemed prohibited without any compulsion, under the pretext of 'warding off an evil' or consideration of wider interests / benefit (*maṣlaḥa*). There is definitely neither evil in what Allah has obligated nor benefit in what Allah has prohibited.

Whatever is said beyond this is from the whisperings of *Shayṭān*; defamation of the perfect *Sharī'ah* and neglect for what man has been created for, namely the worship of Allah – obedience to his commands, the *aḥkām Sharī'ah*, which is in contrast to what many are told, to only consider one's existence, subsistence and 'interest', material or otherwise. Moreover, we were not ordered to grant victory and power as they are among actions of Allah. We are ordered to perform *Jihād* and to rule according to what Allah has revealed. Allah has obliged us to call people to his *Deen*, if we have the required knowledge, to spread his call and to propagate the truth. Allah never ordered us with 'the spread of religion' or 'emergence of religion'; such acts are among his actions while others are among the voluntary actions of the servants of Allah, which are according to legal capacity.

The legal texts are the text of the revelation, namely the Qur'ān and the *Sunnah*. These revelatory sources are enough, praise be to Allah, for dealing with all incidents found in life, from the day of the death of the Prophet (peace be upon him) until the end of the world. It is never to be said that incidents and events are infinite while the texts are finite, because the infinite incidents are individual incidents and personal events, while types of incidents and kinds of events are finite and limited, that are included perfectly and completely in these texts. The prayer of Zayd is not like the prayer of 'Amr but the kind of prayer is one or a few of such limited kinds that are included in texts, and so on.

Imām Ibn Mājah recorded in his *Sunan* a narration upon the authority of Salmān al-Farsi with an extremely authentic chain of transmission:

حدثنا عليّ بن محمد حدثنا وكيع عن الأعمش، ح و حدثنا محمد بن بشّار حدثنا عبد الرّحمن حدثنا سفيان عن منصور والأعمش عن إبراهيم عن عبد الرّحمن بن يزيد عن سلمان الفارسي، رضي الله عنه، قال: قال له بعض المشركين، وهم يستهزؤون به: إني أرى صاحبكم يعلّمكم كل شيء حتى الخراءة؟!، قال: أجل: أمرنا أن لا نستقبل القبلة، ولا نستنجي بأيماننا، ولا نكتفي بدون ثلاثة أحجار، ليس فيها رجيع ولا عظم

Ali bin Muḥammad narrated to us Waki' narrated to us from al-'Amash (*ḥawala*) Muḥammad bin Bashār narrated to us Abdar-Raḥman narrated to us Sufyān narrated to us from Manṣur and al-'Amash from Ibrāhim from Abdar-Raḥman bin Yazeed from Salmān who said that one of the *mushrikeen* said to him, while they were making fun of him: I see that your companion (the Prophet) is teaching you everything, even how to relieve yourself? He said: Yes indeed. He has ordered us not to face the *Qiblah* or to clean ourselves with our right hands and not to be content with anything less than three stones, which are not to include any excrement or bones.

In the wording of Aḥmad,[7] who also records this with an authentic chain, it is as follows:

قال رجل: إني لأرى صاحبكم يعلمكم كيف تصنعون حتى إنه ليعلمكم إذا أتى أحدكم الغائط؟!، قال: قلت: نعم، أجل، ولو سخرت: إنه ليعلمنا كيف يأتي أحدنا الغائط، وإنه ينهانا أن يستقبل أحدنا القبلة، وأن يستدبرها، وأن يستنجي أحدنا بيمينه، وأن يتمسح أحدنا برجيع ولا عظم، وأن يستنجي بأقل من ثلاثة أحجار

....A man said: Verily I see that your companion (the Prophet) is teaching you, does he teach you how to defecate? He (Salmān) said: Yes, notwithstanding (this) ridicule. He has taught us how to defecate. He has ordered us not to face the *Qiblah* or to clean ourselves with our right hands and not to be content with anything less than three stones, which are not to include any excrement or bones.

Similar has been recorded, albeit without the element of ridiculing, with authentic channels of transmission by Imām Muslim, Tirmidhi, an-Nasā'i and others. One should seriously ponder over this incident. Note the question posed by this stubborn *mushrik* (polytheist) with his intellect no better than that of a donkey, contrasted by Salmān; determined in his response, speaking with an excellent manner, patience and paying attention to detail. If the statement of Salmān is true and by Allah we testify to its truthfulness; there is no god / deity but Allah, how then can anyone claim who believes in Allah and the last day, that the final *Sharī'ah* is somehow incomplete? That there are in some way 'gaps', 'loopholes' or that the texts cannot encompass the full range of human action and experience. Those that do hold this viewpoint proceed on the basis of desires, innovation and heresy. They seek to beguile others through beautiful names which hide an ugly and sinister agenda; they seek to aggrandise themselves and

---

[7] *Musnad* Aḥmad Vol. 5 sec. 437, no. 23,753 & 23,756

ultimately mislead people. From amongst the beautified terms that they marshal we find them saying that they have 'the understanding of the *Salaf aṣ-Ṣāliḥ* (righteous predecessors)'; that they are seeking to 'block the means (*Sadd al-Dhara'i*)'; they have the considerations of public interest and are preventing greater evil and the favoured hyperbole of the treasonous government scholars, that they are preventing *fitna*, sedition and tribulation. Meanwhile Allah the majestic states –

وَمِنْهُم مَّن يَقُولُ ائْذَن لِّي وَلَا تَفْتِنِّي أَلَا فِي الْفِتْنَةِ سَقَطُوا وَإِنَّ جَهَنَّمَ لَمُحِيطَةٌ بِالْكَافِرِينَ

And among them there is he who says: Allow me and do not try me. Surely into trial have they already tumbled down and most surely hell encompasses the disbelievers.[8]

In addition to this, Imām Ṭabarāni has recorded the following *ḥadith* on the authority of Abu Dharr:

حدثنا محمد بن عبد الله الحضرمي حدثنا محمد بن عبد الله بن يزيد المقري حدثنا سفيان بن عيينة عن فطر عن أبي الطفيل عن أبي ذر قال: تركنا رسول الله، صلى الله عليه وسلم، وما طائر يقلب جناحيه في الهواء إلا وهو يذكر لنا منه علماً؛ قال: فقال، صلوات الله وسلامه وتبريكاته عليه وعلى آله: ما بقي شيء يقرّب من الجنة، ويباعد من النار، إلا وقد بُيِّنَ لكم

Muḥammad ibn Abdullah al-Ḥaḍrami narrated to us Muḥammad bin Abdullah bin Yazeed al-Muqri narrated to us Sufyān ibn 'Uyayna narrated to us from Fiṭr from Abu Ṭufayl from Abu Dharr who said: the Messenger of Allah (peace be upon him) told us that there is no bird that flies in the air (sky), except that it has some knowledge from him. He said that the Messenger of Allah (peace be upon him) said: *There is nothing left that will further you to Paradise, and separate from the*

[8] *Qur'ān* 9: 49

hellfire, except that it was explained to you.

The *ḥadith* is authentic - *Ṣaḥīḥ* and supports the point of this subject here regarding the completeness of *Deen*.[9] In the *Musnad* of Aḥmad he records the following narration:

حدثنا بن نمير حدثنا الأعمش عن منذر حدثنا أشياخ من التيم قالوا قال أبو ذر لقد تركنا محمد، صلى الله عليه وسلم، وما يحرك طائر جناحيه في السماء إلا أذكرنا منه علما

Ibn Numayr narrated to us al-‘Amash narrated to us from Mundthir, a Shaykh from at-Taym narrated to us they said (that) Abu Dharr said: Verily Muḥammad (peace be upon him) left us with (this): *What drives the bird's wings in the sky, except that it remembers us and notes this knowledge.*

This narration is recorded elsewhere in the *Musnad,*[10] as well as in the *Musnad* of Abu Dāwud aṭ-Ṭayālisi,[11] and in other collections. In *al-Jāmi aṣ-Ṣaḥīḥ al-Mukhtaṣr* Imām Bukhāri records:

حدثنا موسى بن مسعود حدثنا سفيان عن الأعمش عن أبي وائل عن حذيفة رضي الله تعالى عنه قال: لقد خطبنا النبي، صلى الله عليه وسلم، خطبة: ما ترك فيها شيئا إلى قيام الساعة إلا ذكره؛ علمه من علمه وجهله من جهله. إن كنت لأرى الشيء قد نسيت فأعرفه كما يعرف الرجل إذا غاب عنه فرآه فعرفه!

Musa bin Mas’ud narrated to us Sufyān narrated to us from al-‘Amash from Abu Wā’il from Ḥudhayfah who said the Prophet (peace be upon him) once delivered a speech in front of us

[9] The Arabic edition has within the appendix a fuller discussion regarding the authenticity of this specific narration.
[10] *Musnad* Aḥmad Vol. 5 sec. 162, no. 21,477
[11] *Musnad* Ṭayālisi Vol. 1 sec. 65, no. 479

> wherein he left nothing but mentioned (about) everything that would happen till the (final) hour. Some of us stored that in our minds and some forgot it. (After that speech) I used to see events taking place (which had been referred to in that speech) but I had forgotten them (before their occurrence). Then I would recognise such events as a man recognises another man who has been absent and then sees and recognises him.

The *ḥadith* is also found in the *Ṣaḥīḥ* of Ibn Ḥibbān,[12] the *Sunan* of Abu Dāwud,[13] the *Musnad* of Aḥmad[14] and in other collections. Imām Muslim records the following again narrated on the authority of Ḥudhayfah:

> حدثني حرملة بن يحيى التجيبي أخبرنا بن وهب أخبرني يونس عن بن شهاب أن أبا إدريس الخولاني كان يقول قال حذيفة بن اليمان والله إني لأعلم الناس بكل فتنة هي كائنة فيما بيني وبين الساعة وما بي إلا أن يكون رسول الله، صلى الله عليه وسلم، أسر إلي في ذلك شيئا لم يحدثه غيري ولكن رسول الله، صلى الله عليه وسلم، قال وهو يحدث مجلسا أنا فيه عن الفتن فقال رسول الله، صلى الله عليه وسلم، وهو يعد الفتن منهن ثلاث لا يكدن يذرن شيئا ومنهن فتن كرياح الصيف ومنها صغار ومنها كبار قال حذيفة فذهب أولئك الرهط كلهم غيري

> Ḥarmala bin Yaḥya at-Tajeebe narrated to me Ibn Wahb reported to us Yunus reported to me from Ibn Shihāb that Abu Idris al-Khawlāni said that Ḥudhayfah bin al-Yamān said: By Allah, I have the best knowledge amongst people about every turmoil which is going to appear in the period intervening me and the last hour; and it is not for the fact that Allah's Messenger (peace be upon him) told me something confidentially pertaining to it and he did not tell anybody else about it, but it is because of the fact that I was present in the

---

[12] *Ṣaḥīḥ* Ibn Ḥibbān Vol. 15 sec. 6, no. 6,636
[13] *Sunan* Abu Dāwud Vol. 4 sec. 94, no. 4,240
[14] *Musnad* Aḥmad Vol. 5 sec. 389, no. 23,357

assembly in which he had been describing the turmoil. and he especially made a mention of three turmoil's which would not spare anything and amongst these there would be turmoil's like storms in the hot season. Some of them would be violent and some of them would be comparatively mild. Ḥudhayfah said: All (who were present) except I have gone (to the next world).

Similar is recorded in the *Musnad* of Aḥmad from a slightly different channel:

حدثنا يعقوب حدثنا أبي عن صالح يعنى بن كيسان عن بن شهاب قال: قال أبو إدريس عائذ الله بن عبد الله الخولاني سمعت حذيفة بن اليمان يقول والله إني لأعلم الناس بكل فتنة هي كائنة فيما بيني وبين الساعة وما ذلك أن يكون رسول الله، صلى الله عليه وسلم، حدثني من ذلك شيئا أسره إلى لم يكن حدث به غيري ولكن رسول الله، صلى الله عليه وسلم، قال وهو يحدث مجلسا أنا فيه سئل عن الفتن وهو يعد الفتن فيهن ثلاث لا يذرن شيئا منهن كرياح الصيف منها صغار ومنها كبار قال حذيفة فذهب أولئك الرهط كلهم غيري

Ya'qub narrated to us my father narrated to us from Ṣāliḥ - that is to say ibn Kaysān - from Ibn Shihāb he said: Abu Idris 'Aāidth-Allah bin Abdullah al-Khawlāni heard Ḥudhayfah bin al-Yamān say: By Allah, I have the best knowledge amongst people about every turmoil which is going to appear in the period intervening me and the last hour and it is not for the fact that Allah's Messenger (peace be upon him) told me something confidentially pertaining to it and he did not tell anybody else about it but it is because of the fact that I was present in the assembly in which he had been describing the turmoil. He (peace be upon him) especially made a mention of three turmoil's which would not spare anything and amongst these there would be turmoil's like storms in the hot season. Some of them would be violent and some of them would be comparatively mild. Ḥudhayfah said: All (who were present) except I have gone (to the next world).

Al-Ḥākim also has this recorded in the *Mustadrak*.[15] In his *Sunan,* Imām Tirmidhi has the following narrated on the authority of Abu Sa'eed al-Khudri:

حدثنا عمران بن موسى القزاز البصري حدثنا حماد بن زيد حدثنا علي بن زيد بن جدعان القرشي عن أبي نضرة عن أبي سعيد الخدري قال صلى بنا رسول الله، صلى الله عليه وسلم، يوما صلاة العصر بنهار ثم قام خطيبا فلم يدع شيئا يكون إلى قيام الساعة إلا أخبرنا به حفظه من حفظه ونسيه من نسيه وكان فيما قال إن الدنيا حلوة خضرة وإن الله مستخلفكم فيها فناظر كيف تعملون ألا فاتقوا الدنيا واتقوا النساء وكان فيما قال ألا لا يمنعن رجلا هيبة الناس أن يقول بحق إذا علمه قال فبكى أبو سعيد فقال قد والله رأينا أشياء فهبنا فكان فيما قال ألا إنه ينصب لكل غادر لواء يوم القيامة بقدر غدرته ولا غدرة أعظم من غدرة إمام عامة يركز لواؤه عند أسته فكان فيما حفظنا يومئذ ألا إن بني آدم خلقوا على طبقات شتى؛... إلخ

'Imrān bin Musa al-Fazzāz al-Baṣri narrated to us Ḥammād ibn Zayd narrated to us Ali bin Zayd ibn Juda'ān al-Qurashi narrated to us from Abu Naḍra from Abu Sa'eed al-Khudri who said: One day, the Messenger of Allah (peace be upon him) led us in prayer while it was still daytime. Then he stood to give us an address. He did not leave anything that would happen until the hour of judgement except that he informed us about it. Whoever remembered it remembered it, and whoever forgot it forgot it. Among what he said was: *Indeed the world is green and sweet, and indeed Allah has left you to remain to see how you behave. So beware of the world, and beware of the women.* And among what he said was: *The awe (status) of people should not prevent a man from saying the truth when he knows it.* He (one of the narrators) said: Abu Sa'eed wept, then he said: By Allah! We have seen things and we feared. And among what he said in it, was: *Indeed, for every treacherous person there shall be a banner erected on the day of resurrection in proportion to his treachery. And there is no treachery greater than the treachery of a leader to the masses'*

[15] Al-Ḥākim *Mustadrak* Vol. 4 sec. 518, no. 8,454

> *whose banner shall be positioned at his buttocks.* And among what we remember from that day is: *Behold! Indeed the children of Adam were created in various classes*...(etc).

Al-Ḥumaydi also has this in his *Musnad,*[16] as does Abu Ya'la[17] and other than them. In his *Mu'jam al-Kabir* Ṭabarāni records the next narration on the authority of Mughira:

> حدثنا الحسين بن إسحاق التستري حدثنا الحسن بن أبي السري العسقلاني حدثنا مكي بن إبراهيم حدثنا هاشم بن هاشم عن عمرو بن إبراهيم بن محمد عن محمد بن كعب القرظي عن المغيرة قال قام فينا رسول الله، صلى الله عليه وسلم، مقاما فأخبرنا بما يكون في أمته إلى يوم القيامة وعاه من وعاه ونسيه من نسيه

> Al-Ḥussein ibn Isḥāq at-Tastari narrated to us al-Ḥasan bin Abi as-Suri al-A'sqalāni narrated to us Makki bin Ibrāhim narrated to us Hishām bin Hishām narrated to us from 'Amr bin Ibrāhim bin Muḥammad from Muḥammad bin Ka'b al-Qurazi from al-Mughira who said the Prophet (peace be upon him) stood stationed before us and he informed us what will occur in his *Ummah* until the day of judgement. And he said to us a word; some of us have comprehended (it) whilst others of us have forgotten.

Abu Ya'la also records in his *Musnad*:

> حدثنا محمد بن أبي بكر حدثنا يحيى عن فطر بن خليفة عن عطاء قال: قال أبو الدرداء لقد تركنا رسول الله، صلى الله عليه وسلم، وما في السماء طير يطير بجناحه إلا ذكرنا منه علما

[16] *Musnad* Ḥumaydi Vol. 2 sec. 332, no. 752
[17] *Musnad* Abu Ya'la Vol. 2 sec. 354, no. 1,101

> Muḥammad bin Abu Bakr narrated to us Yaḥya narrated to us from Fiṭr bin Khalifa from 'Aṭā who said (that) Abu Dardā said: Verily the Messenger of Allah (peace be upon him) left us and the bird which flies in the sky with its wings, except that we mentioned it from its knowledge.

The claims of the Church of Najd, that is to say the sect of Wahābism and those adhering to their views who call themselves the '*Salafis'* are manifestly false. They implicitly argue that the *Deen* is imperfect until it has been explained by the *Salaf aṣ-Ṣāliḥ* (righteous predecessors) from the first three-centuries, inclusive of the companions and the rightly guided *Khulafa*. They say this without any recourse to serious thought or study, reflecting their own superficiality. Many of their statements are made without any sense of deep thought, as they are impervious to reason and blinded by their own vanities. Indeed their mantra about – 'the Qur'ān and *Sunnah* according to the understanding of the *Salaf aṣ-Ṣāliḥ*' refers without any doubt, to the notion that the *Deen* is in some way deficient and imperfect. It is a suggestion that the *Deen* was not completed before the death of the Prophet (peace be upon him), as if that the Prophet (peace be upon him) did not understand some matters, or that he did understand and failed to explain them - Allah preserve us from such banal nonsense! Their statements seek to undermine the seal of Prophethood and the universality of the Islamic message, yet they are blinded to how destructive their sect has truly become. The message of the Qur'ān and the *Sunnah* are accessible to whosoever wants to read and study them, for anyone who wants to engage their reason, pondering deeply over its meanings, as Allah orders us to in *Surah at-Tawba*. The honest truthful heart should ask, are they really the adherents of the *Salaf aṣ-Ṣāliḥ* - or should they properly be called, the *Khalaf Ṭāliḥ* (evil successors)!

These superficial zombies have abandoned seeking to understand the book of Allah and the *Sunnah*, preferring to retreat to the ivory tower of an imagined 'understanding of the *Salaf aṣ-Ṣāliḥ*' that all must bow to. Without seeking to understand what Allah has actually revealed they oscillate between various sayings, arguing we have Aḥmad bin Ḥanbal while you have Mālik bin Anas. They will remain lost in such endless circles, from contradicting sayings and different claims. Our discerned reader will become accustomed to their faulty understanding throughout this present work and will begin to see not only their heinous errors but how they have sought to entrench such erroneous views, all the while being impervious to what Allah has revealed. Most of those people claiming to be *Salafis* have arrived at an intellectual impasse. They have not examined the disastrous consequences of their *Salafi* assertions. They are just following other scholars, those that are not better in acquiring knowledge than them. Most of them do not know the sayings of the *Salaf* (predecessors) and their wide range of opinions that they took on matters of jurisprudence. To argue that they had a monolithic view on *all* issues is a flagrant lie. It is truly rare for any of them to have considered for example the *Muṣṣanaf* of Abu Bakr ibn Abi Shayba or the *Sunan* of Sa'eed bin Manṣur, even rarer that they have had anything more than a cursory look at the *Muṣṣanaf* of Abdar-Razzāq or even *al-Awsaṭ* by Ibn al-Mundhir. Yet they are proficient at levelling unsubstantiated allegations and fostering outright lies where it suits their agenda.

We mentioned in detail some of the points raised by the '*followers of Salafism*' because they claim to be the best among all the creation of Allah; that they are the *'ahl al-Aqeedah aṣ-Ṣāfiya aṣ-Ṣāḥīḥa'* – the people of the pure authentic creed, while all others are the people of innovation or even apostates and disbelievers. They claim that they are *'al-Firqa an-Nājiya'* or the *'Ṭā'ifa al-Manṣura'*, the saved victorious sect, yet they are more like the *Khawārij* in this regard. Without prejudice the adherents of '*Salafism*' must seriously revaluate their position, bearing in mind that the Prophet (peace be upon him) said: '*Whoever says that the people are ruined, he is himself more ruined than them.*'[18]

Amongst contemporary Islamic circles there still exists, unfortunately, those that cling to the false notion that there is somehow a 'legislative vacuum' or lacuna which people should fill. Exactly what to fill this imagined vacuum with prompts a number of differing viewpoints, be that according to one's own reason, according to the principles of equity (*Istiḥsān*); an ill-defined public interest (*maṣlaḥah mursalah*), making analogous comparisons (*Qiyās*), or even bizarrely acting within the 'spirit of the law'. Such notions are evidently false for the one who will take the time to seriously study them, since the revelation itself provides us with a succinct creed; a complete set of rituals for worship and the most complete set of transactions. The *ḥadith* of Salmān mentioned earlier which is concerned with purity and manners of relieving oneself should prove sufficient in counteracting these deadly tendencies which left unchecked, have the potential of leading to disbelief. Concerning transactions, it is enough to mention all kinds of sales that were proved by the text as unlawful, which are more than forty-types, some of them are very rare and even unknown nowadays. Even if it is only mentioned that one type of sale is prohibited, that in itself is sufficient evidence to establish that sales *other than this kind* are lawful, as we mentioned previously, especially when considering the verse in which Allah says: '*But Allah permitted trade and forbidden usury.*' [19]

Where then is the legislative vacuum or gaps within the *Sharī'ah*? These are but phantasms of the mind. Imām Muḥammad ibn Idris ash-Shāfi'i was correct when he said in *ar-Risāla*: 'There is nothing among the crises that happen to anyone among people of the religion of Allah except that there is an evidence in the Book of Allah that shows how to solve it.' Indeed he spoke the truth which is a definite and absolute

---

[18] The *ḥadith* is recorded widely and can be found in Muslim the book of virtue, enjoining good manners and joining of the ties of kinship, ch. the prohibition of saying 'the people are doomed'

[19] *Qur'ān* 2: 275

truth, regardless who knows and who does not know. Much the same was said by Imām Abu Muḥammad Ali Ibn Ḥazm, as cited earlier, in which he provides a lucid argument to those who would try and argue otherwise.

Such evil and accursed sayings generally stem from three sources. Firstly, from the disbelievers in general as well as the people who have hypocrisy (*nifāq*) in belief. They conceal disbelief (*kufr*) deep in their hearts while outwardly showing Islam, desiring to mix the *Sharī'ah* with *kufr*. Although they proceed in a cautious and gradual manner, this is ultimately their goal. It is as brazen as if they were to walk naked in the streets, exposing themselves to all and sundry. Unfortunately our present age, the late 14th Islamic century, is replete with these individuals who more often than not, occupy positions of power, influence and authority. Secondly, from the sinful people that are beset with laziness. They neither memorise the *Sunnah* nor revise it from its sources, failing to distinguish or differentiate what is authentic from what is not. Laziness has become all too easy for them, retreating to the comfort of *taqleed* (imitation) thereby missing the essential wisdom and guidance which the *Sunnah* affords. Finally, from those who are completely passive, content with their own ignorance and promoting obscurantism amongst the wider public. By relegating their own minds to the priests and rabbis they have set up rivals to Allah, obeyed lords whom they fervently follow, like braying animals.

We do not deny that some scholars have committed serious mistakes by comparing the *Sharī'ah* of Allah and man-made laws, which are full of gaps and loopholes that are required to be filled to patch up its shortcomings, be that with equity (*Istiḥsān*) considerations of an ill-defined public interest (*maṣlaḥah mursalah*), making analogous comparisons (*Qiyās*), or other intellectual acrobatics like acting within the 'spirit of the law'. The faithful, earnest, sincere scholar - whatever his rank - is not allowed to continue in such mistakes; we must take flight to the refuge of Allah, seeking his forgiveness. We ask Allah to forgive all those who committed such blunders from amongst scholars of this *Ummah*, who were sincere and made their best effort to find the truth. We ask Him to reward them for their effort. While the unqualified, faithless scholars who are sycophants as well as the unjust tyrannical rulers we pray to Allah to never forgive them, but to curse them, making their life here and in the life to come full of misery, despair and punishment.

11 Prophet Muḥammad permits all the good, outlaws all the evil

---

Allah the exalted, the majestic states the following in Qur'ān:

الَّذِينَ يَتَّبِعُونَ الرَّسُولَ النَّبِيَّ الأُمِّيَّ الَّذِي يَجِدُونَهُ مَكْتُوبًا عِندَهُمْ فِي التَّوْرَاةِ وَالإِنجِيلِ يَأْمُرُهُم بِالْمَعْرُوفِ وَيَنْهَاهُمْ عَنِ الْمُنكَرِ وَيُحِلُّ لَهُمُ الطَّيِّبَاتِ وَيُحَرِّمُ عَلَيْهِمُ الْخَبَائِثَ وَيَضَعُ عَنْهُمْ إِصْرَهُمْ وَالأَغْلاَلَ الَّتِي كَانَتْ عَلَيْهِمْ فَالَّذِينَ آمَنُوا بِهِ وَعَزَّرُوهُ وَنَصَرُوهُ وَاتَّبَعُوا النُّورَ الَّذِي أُنزِلَ مَعَهُ أُولَٰئِكَ هُمُ الْمُفْلِحُونَ

Those who follow the Messenger-Prophet, the Ummi, whom they find written down with them in the Torah and the Bible (who) enjoins them good and forbids them evil, and makes lawful to them the good things and makes unlawful to them impure things, and removes from them their burden and the shackles which were upon them; so (as for) those who believe in him and honour him and help him, and follow the light which has been sent down with him, these it is that are the successful. [1]

يَسْأَلُونَكَ مَاذَا أُحِلَّ لَهُمْ قُلْ أُحِلَّ لَكُمُ الطَّيِّبَاتُ وَمَا عَلَّمْتُم مِّنَ الْجَوَارِحِ مُكَلِّبِينَ تُعَلِّمُونَهُنَّ مِمَّا

---

[1] *Qur'ān* 7: 157

عَلَّمَكُمُ اللَّهُ فَكُلُوا مِمَّا أَمْسَكْنَ عَلَيْكُمْ وَاذْكُرُوا اسْمَ اللَّهِ عَلَيْهِ وَاتَّقُوا اللَّهَ إِنَّ اللَّهَ سَرِيعُ الْحِسَابِ

They ask you as to what is allowed to them. Say: The good things are allowed to you, and what you have taught the beasts and birds of prey, training them to hunt-- you teach them of what Allah has taught you-- so eat of that which they catch for you and mention the name of Allah over it; and be careful of (your duty to) Allah; surely Allah is swift in reckoning. [2]

الْيَوْمَ أُحِلَّ لَكُمُ الطَّيِّبَاتُ وَطَعَامُ الَّذِينَ أُوتُوا الْكِتَابَ حِلٌّ لَكُمْ وَطَعَامُكُمْ حِلٌّ لَهُمْ وَالْمُحْصَنَاتُ مِنَ
الْمُؤْمِنَاتِ وَالْمُحْصَنَاتُ مِنَ الَّذِينَ أُوتُوا الْكِتَابَ مِنْ قَبْلِكُمْ إِذَا آتَيْتُمُوهُنَّ أُجُورَهُنَّ مُحْصِنِينَ
غَيْرَ مُسَافِحِينَ وَلَا مُتَّخِذِي أَخْدَانٍ وَمَنْ يَكْفُرْ بِالْإِيمَانِ فَقَدْ حَبِطَ عَمَلُهُ وَهُوَ فِي الْآخِرَةِ مِنَ
الْخَاسِرِينَ

This day (all) the good things are allowed to you; and the food of those who have been given the Book is lawful for you and your food is lawful for them; and the chaste from among the believing women and the chaste from among those who have been given the Book before you (are lawful for you); when you have given them their dowries, taking (them) in marriage, not fornicating nor taking them for paramours in secret; and whoever denies faith, his work indeed is of no account, and in the hereafter he shall be one of the losers. [3]

فَبِظُلْمٍ مِنَ الَّذِينَ هَادُوا حَرَّمْنَا عَلَيْهِمْ طَيِّبَاتٍ أُحِلَّتْ لَهُمْ وَبِصَدِّهِمْ عَنْ سَبِيلِ اللَّهِ كَثِيرًا

Wherefore for the iniquity of those who are Jews did We disallow to them the good things which had been made lawful for them and for their hindering many (people) from Allah's way. [4]

We would hasten to add at this juncture that when we say that something is good (*tayib*) in itself or for considerations to do with that entity; or that something is deemed malignant / evil (*khabeeth*) in and of itself, for considerations related to that entity, this is said within the

[2] *Qur'ān* 5: 4
[3] *Qur'ān* 5: 5
[4] *Qur'ān* 4: 160

context of the present created world. It is but one of the possibilities of existence, but not necessity. It is like this because Allah the exalted *has made it that way* by virtue of his divine decree. Allah's omnipotent free will rules over everything and there is nothing whatsoever to place a limit or restriction upon it. There is no other authority beyond Allah or a higher right of appeal or audience. He is the most high, the wisest; the first – nothing existed before him – and he is the last – there is nothing after him. He is the all-knowing, the all powerful.

Therefore, a lawful (*ḥalāl*) thing is so because Allah made it so. He made it so within the framework of his own divine absolute will to objects with a specific design and attribute, rather than due to an internal necessity of the created object, or as an absolute necessary concept. Thus, there is an important distinction between the creative command of Allah and his own legislative will. In principle there is nothing to say that Allah cannot create something to be good (*ṭayib*) in and of itself, yet deem that as being prohibited as part of a *Sharī'ah* for whatever considerations as part of his legislative command. What constitutes the 'lawful', therefore, is what Allah the exalted decrees as lawful by his legislative command. Matters that are 'prohibited' are judged in the same way. Ultimately, Allah is the determining authority in the judgement of what constitutes the lawful and prohibited. Allah is the first and the last. He is the absolute authority and it is to him the eventual return ultimately is. There is no deity other than him. As cited previously the blessed verses from the Qur'ān provide us with unequivocal statements, establishing certain binding proofs. From these we may detail the following maxims:

- There is a fundamental distinction between what the concept of good (*ṭayib*) is and the concept of lawful (*ḥalāl*). The two concepts are independent of each other, with no necessity dictating that the two should coincide. What is deemed good (*ṭayib*) is as a result of Allah's divine will pertaining to its creation and destination (*qadr*) in that manner or fashion. Lawful (*ḥalāl*) relates to a matter being decided as such by the legislative command of Allah.

- Concerning the concept of what is malignant (*khabeeth*) and prohibited (*ḥarām*) they are also independent from each other in the same manner as described in relation to the good (*ṭayib*) and the lawful (*ḥalāl*).

- Nothing can dictate to Allah the exalted, ultimate lord, whose sovereignty is absolute. Hence if he wishes, he is fully able to prohibit some matters which are deemed to be good (*ṭayib*), just as he is fully able to keep the law (*Sharī'ah*) silent in relation to matters which are from amongst the *khabā'ith,* thereby not explicitly censuring them. Allah is fully conversant with what is good in and of itself and what is malignant or evil in and of itself. By way of ranks or degrees of consideration this in the grand scheme of things is secondary to Allah's overriding lordship and sovereignty. Allah judges as he wills, he legislates as he wills; Allah cannot be questioned as to what he does, though we will be questioned for what we do![5]

- Regardless of what Allah legislates, his judgement is absolute not being subject to revision or higher right of appeal. He, the exalted is accountable to none. Obedience to him is absolute without limit, being a binding rational necessity.

- For the final *Ummah* though, Allah has bestowed a number of distinct blessings. Not only have we been favoured with having Muḥammad (peace be upon him) as our Prophet and the seal of Prophethood itself, but Allah has synchronised the *Sharī'ah* revealed to him; thereby making lawful (*ḥalāl*)

---

[5] As expressed by the *Qur'ānic* verse found in 21: 23 and other places

> everything that is good (*ṭayib*) and prohibiting everything that is evil or malignant (*khabeeth*). The situation now is in contrast to some of the previous nations. They were burdened having shackles placed upon them. Yet now they have been given a reprieve. By accepting the final *Sharī'ah* and the Prophethood of Muḥammad (peace be upon him) they too can partake in the good (*ṭayib*) that was previously unlawful for them. Matters that are *khabeeth* have been made unlawful on this blessed *Ummah* by the mercy of Allah, whereas some were not in previous revealed legislation, like alcohol.

Without doubt Islam is the perfect complete *Deen*. Its revealed texts contain, by the grace of Allah, the judgment concerning all things, be they objects or actions until the day of judgement. This has obviated the need to dwell upon extensive studies into the reality or nature of an act or object in order to determine whether it is good or evil. Consequently we are assured that the reality as established by the revealed texts in the last blessed *Sharī'ah* as it relates to what is good (*ṭayib*) being lawful (*ḥalāl*) and what is *khabeeth* being prohibited (*ḥarām*). Allah the exalted has guaranteed this for us. Therefore we can assert with the fullest of knowledge, bearing witness by Allah, that all which he has made lawful in the last final *Sharī'ah* is good in and of itself. All which he has deemed unlawful is bad / evil in and of itself. Determining the precise nature via investigation of the nature of objects, utilities and perhaps even the ultimate value of some particular acts or statements – whether it is *ṭayib* or *khabeeth* becomes a secondary matter once the proper Islamic position has been established. Similar can be said of the philosophical speculation that has surrounded the notion of what is *ṭayib* or *khabeeth* in itself, whether that be on a microscopic level in terms of its basic constituents or in relation to its sociological effects via empirical evidence. Overall its relative importance or weight in terms of legislation becomes relegated. Man can only conduct investigation up to a given point and ultimately his knowledge is infinitesimally limited when compared to the creator and lord of the worlds, Allah the exalted, who is omniscient.

Even if we suppose the possibility in principle that man could have the ability to comprehend the nature of things from all necessary angles, the reality of human endeavours in legislation demonstrates otherwise. All nations, civilisations and people have witnessed laws being formulated, implemented and then either amended or repealed totally for one or more consideration that was not evident at the time when they were formulated. In the round, such factors buttress our belief that mankind will always come in second in relation to this, despite the onset of time and accumulation of successive generations of knowledge. Notwithstanding mankind's proclivity for placing other non-rational considerations at the forefront of mind, such as limited worldly benefit, even if the assumption is made that the human mind is in principle reaching a definitive judgement in relation to whether a matter is truly *ṭayib* or *khabeeth*; it would be only a theoretical intellectual endeavour. All the while we have the final *Sharī'ah* which Allah has given us providing the ultimate determiner of such things. The solution to human malaise in this area rests with the *ḥukm shari'*, as outlined previously; the legal texts provide the complete necessary guidance. Legal judgement is not permissible except by way of a legal text. Faith (*al-'Imān*) and Islam stipulate all matters to be referred back to Allah and his Messenger (peace be upon him). There is no valid alternate position.

Concerning what we have previously said about the Arabic word '*khabā'ith*' there is some conformity with the word '*al-fawāḥish*' – indecencies. Therefore, the fact that something is indecent is a matter of self; a reality that can be readily discernible. It has nothing to do with laws. Indecency is doing something beyond its proper limit. It is a concept that is often used in classifying the actions and statements, in addition to the relations and proportions, the abstract systems, and conventional positive matters. The notion of '*al-fawāḥish*' hasn't been used to describe an object or benefit; the word used in the legal texts for these is *khabeeth.* For the sake of clarity, for an object or action to be classified as *fāḥisha* - whether in itself or for some other consideration - it is because Allah the exalted has made it thus by way of his divine decree (*qadr*) and creative act. It has been given that nature, for want of a better word, by the absolute free will of Allah, which rules over everything. This is done within the framework of Allah's absolute will to create objects on specific moulds and attributes, rather than due to an internal necessity of the created object.

It is established by way of definite evidence that Allah has forbidden all manner of indecencies (*al-fawāḥish*), open or concealed, in this last *Sharī'ah*, just as he has forbidden the *khabā'ith* as detailed in the following Qur'ānic verses:

قُلْ إِنَّمَا حَرَّمَ رَبِّيَ الْفَوَاحِشَ مَا ظَهَرَ مِنْهَا وَمَا بَطَنَ وَالْإِثْمَ وَالْبَغْيَ بِغَيْرِ الْحَقِّ وَأَن تُشْرِكُوا
بِاللَّهِ مَا لَمْ يُنَزِّلْ بِهِ سُلْطَانًا وَأَن تَقُولُوا عَلَى اللَّهِ مَا لَا تَعْلَمُونَ

Say: My Lord has only prohibited indecencies (al-fawāḥish), those of them that are apparent as well as those that are concealed, and sin and rebellion without justice, and that you associate with Allah that for which He has not sent down any authority, and that you say against Allah what you do not know. [6]

قُلْ تَعَالَوْا أَتْلُ مَا حَرَّمَ رَبُّكُمْ عَلَيْكُمْ أَلَّا تُشْرِكُوا بِهِ شَيْئًا وَبِالْوَالِدَيْنِ إِحْسَانًا وَلَا تَقْتُلُوا أَوْلَادَكُم
مِّنْ إِمْلَاقٍ نَّحْنُ نَرْزُقُكُمْ وَإِيَّاهُمْ وَلَا تَقْرَبُوا الْفَوَاحِشَ مَا ظَهَرَ مِنْهَا وَمَا بَطَنَ وَلَا تَقْتُلُوا النَّفْسَ
الَّتِي حَرَّمَ اللَّهُ إِلَّا بِالْحَقِّ ذَٰلِكُمْ وَصَّاكُم بِهِ لَعَلَّكُمْ تَعْقِلُونَ

Say: Come I will recite what your Lord has forbidden to you-- (remember) that you do not associate anything with Him and show kindness to your parents, and do not slay your children for (fear of) poverty-- We provide for you and for them-- and do not draw nigh to indecencies, those of them which are apparent and those which are concealed, and do not kill the soul which

---

[6] *Qur'ān* 7: 33

Allah has forbidden except for the requirements of justice; this He has enjoined you with that you may understand. [7]

These Qur'ānic verses are unequivocal. Indeed Allah has forbidden all manner of sexual indecency in this last *Sharī'ah,* in fact any immorality whatsoever. Whether that be open or concealed or whether that be from statements, acts, relations, abstractions or systems. The same also applies to matters of convention and what concerns the *khabā'ith* as previously mentioned. What we had mentioned above about *khabā'ith* can also be said here about *al-fawāḥish* and with Allah is all success. Regarding previous nations, Allah permitted them to commit certain *khabā'ith* and *fāḥisha*, demonstrating how destructive they were to their societies. Examples of this are allowing alcohol to be drunk and the infamous grant of a monarchical ruling system which was requested from the people of Israel, despite Allah warning them of its long-term consequences. They persistently supplicated this to their Prophets and were warned that Allah would not answer their calls when it became burdensome. A fuller discussion of this point can be found in our work entitled *Ḥākimiyah wa Siyādat ash-Shar'.* Such incidents bolster the truthfulness of the Prophet's words (peace be upon him) as collected in *al-Jāmi aṣ-Ṣaḥīḥ al-Mukhtaṣr* by Imām Bukhāri where he is reported to have said:

حدثنا إسماعيل حدثني مالك عن أبي الزناد عن الأعرج عن أبي هريرة عن النبي، صلى الله عليه وسلم، قال: دعوني ما تركتكم: إنما أهلك من كان قبلكم سؤالهم، واختلافهم على أنبيائهم، فإذا نهيتكم عن شيء فاجتنبوه وإذا أمرتكم بأمر فأتوا منه ما استطعتم

Ismā'il narrated to us Mālik narrated to me from Abi Zinād from al-'Araj from Abu Hurayrah from the Prophet (peace be upon him) who said: *Leave me as I leave you for the people who were before you were ruined because of their questions*

[7] *Qur'ān* 6: 151

and their differences over their Prophets. So, if I forbid you to do something, then keep away from it. And if I order you to do something, then do of it as much as you can.

And also in the wording that has been reported by Imām Muslim in his *Ṣaḥīḥ*:

حدثني حرملة بن يحيى التجيبي أخبرنا ابن وهب أخبرني يونس عن ابن شهاب أخبرني أبو سلمة بن عبد الرحمن وسعيد بن المسيب قالا كان أبو هريرة يحدث أنه سمع رسول الله صلى الله عليه وسلم يقول ما نهيتكم عنه فاجتنبوه وما أمرتكم به فافعلوا منه ما استطعتم فإنما أهلك الذين من قبلكم كثرة مسائلهم واختلافهم على أنبيائهم

Ḥarmala ibn Yaḥya at-Tajeebe narrated to me Ibn Wahb reported to us Yunus reported to me from Ibn Shihāb - Abu Salamah ibn Abdar-Raḥman and Sa'eed ibn Musayib reported to me - they said Abu Hurayrah narrated to us that he heard the Messenger of Allah (peace be upon him) say: *Avoid that which I forbid you to do and do that which I command you to do to the best of your capacity. Verily the people before you went to their doom because they had put too many questions to their Prophets and then disagreed with their teachings.*

These *aḥādith* are truly *Ṣaḥīḥ*, being reported in almost all collections of *ḥadith.* At this juncture, we would hasten to emphasize the following points. Firstly, that Allah has taken upon his majestic-self in the final and complete *Sharī'ah* to prohibit the *khabā'ith* as well as the *fawāḥish.* Regarding previous revelations, that wasn't always the case. Sometimes they were left without a prohibition, thereby becoming permissible; Allah is the only absolute sovereign, able to legislate as he wills. Secondly, *fāḥisha* is something that is never commanded by Allah the exalted. It is neither commanded as being an obligation nor allowed to be desirable. He may not legislate against it, as in previous laws, but it is never commanded. That is above his sanctity and holiness, which is above any faults, just as he is above the notion of meanness and lowness. As stated previously, the verse is unequivocal, '*Allah does not enjoin / command fāḥisha.*' [8]

A number of simple examples can be given in order to further exemplify the general rules that we have elucidated thus far. The first example is that of pork which we are prohibited from eating by way of definite legal texts. The subject of 'pork meat' is no more than one of the following possibilities:

1. If someone believed that pork is prohibited because Allah has prohibited it, then he is a Muslim and a believer that has submitted the matter to Allah and His Messenger. No harm is done if he further believes that:

    a. Pork was prohibited because of its essential nature, i.e. that of being impure. Thus it is from the blessing, mercy and kindness of Allah that he has given his servants a straightforward rule which obviates the need to search out the true nature of this item. This is what people of Islam should believe in this last message as we mentioned above.

    b. The prohibition of eating pork is but a test, punishment, disciplining or for other reasons that are only known to Allah. It could be that Allah is exercising his legislative sovereignty in this regard. Pork could be good in itself from both sense perception and from a medical point of view; it may well be that it is the tastiest of all meats. This is a good opinion and a belief that could be accepted by those of the previous laws as well as by Muslims based

[8] *Qur'ān* 7: 28

upon the evidences outlined above. For example, the great philosopher of Alexandria, Philo who was a contemporary of Jesus (peace be upon him), articulated this point lucidly arguing to the Romans that pork may very well be the best of all meat, however God wishes to test who we love most – the meat or him?

2. If someone believed that eating pork is prohibited because of its nature, that of inner impurity, that it is *khabeeth,* then that mind would force any rational person to avoid impurity and harmful matters. This is what is expected from rational people before the coming of the message and evidence, while after the message and the establishment of evidence this opinion is an invalid belief that will cause its owner to renounce faith. He accepts the law of reason; he makes reason his lord and god and not Allah or he accepts the judgment of the mind without taking express permission of Allah. In any case this viewpoint is not what is considered as submission to Allah. Rather it is disbelief which contradicts Islam and leads one to exit the religion. Whoever believes in such a matter is a polytheist and disbeliever, except he who has an excuse of ignorance, had a wrong interpretation, was under compulsion, or similar from among reasons that would prevent the accusation of disbelief being levelled. This opinion would be more indecent and a greater disbelief if this person makes this prohibition obligatory on himself and others, according to the opinion of reason, which sees that this pork is *khabeeth* for reasons such as:

    a. This means that he obligates and forbids what Allah did not obligate or forbid, which rationally contradicts the *Tawḥeed* of Allah's divinity that among its characteristics is him being the ultimate sovereign.

b. It is an obvious accusation of lying, when confronted with the definite verse among the Qur'ān that indicates that some good matters were forbidden in the previous creeds. They were sent down as revelation and they were the true religion before being abrogated. This is an accusation aimed at Allah, contradicting the right which was obligated to him according to their invalid claim. Allah accordingly oppressed and transgressed which is more offensive than the previous accusation, as it is absolute disbelief, or it is a doubt that the Qur'ān is not revealed by Allah, which again is disbelief causing one to exit the fold of Islam.

The whole subject will differ completely if a legal text from this last honourable *Sharī'ah* was revealed describing a certain matter, entity or act as being *khabeeth.* Then we can conclude that it is definitely prohibited in this *Sharī'ah* of Muḥammad (peace be upon him). Unless that is, it acts as an explanation that was revealed with a certain specification in mind, as is the case with regard to the foodstuffs of garlic, onions and others, which have strong pungent smells. Turning to the evidences from the *Sunnah,* we will note that there are a large body of *aḥādith* that exist concerning the Prophet's (peace be upon him) comment on these foods being *khabeeth* or *khabā'ith.* However the clarification is also apparent in these evidences, which we will now consider, that it was limited to that of its odour and people attending the *masjid* after consuming them. To begin, Imām Muslim records in his *Ṣaḥīḥ* the following on the authority of Abu Sa'eed al-Khudri:

وحدثني عمرو الناقد حدثنا إسماعيل بن علية عن الجريري عن أبي نضرة عن أبي سعيد قال: لم نعد أن فتحت خيبر فوقعنا أصحاب رسول الله، صلى الله عليه وسلم، في تلك البقلة: الثوم، والناس جياع فأكلنا منها أكلا شديدا ثم رحنا إلى المسجد فوجد رسول الله، صلى الله عليه وسلم، الريح، فقال: من أكل من هذه الشجرة الخبيثة شيئا فلا يقربنا في المسجد، فقال الناس:

> (حَرُمَتْ، حَرُمَتْ)، فبلغ ذاك النبي، صلى الله عليه وسلم، فقال: أيها الناس: إنه ليس بي تحريم ما أحل الله لي، ولكنها شجرة أكره ريحها!
>
> And 'Amr al-Nāqid narrated to me Ismā'il bin 'Ulaya narrated to us from al-Jariri from Abu Naḍra from Abu Sa'eed who said: We made no transgression but Khaybar was conquered. We, the Companions of the Messenger of Allah (peace be upon), fell upon this plant. i e. garlic. Because the people were hungry, we ate it to our heart's content and then made our way towards the *masjid.* The Messenger of Allah (peace be upon him) sensed its odour and he said: *He who takes anything of this offensive plant (shajara khabeetha) must not approach us in the masjid.* The people said: Its (use) has been forbidden; its (use) has been forbidden. This reached the Messenger of Allah (peace be upon him) and he said: *O people, I cannot forbid (the use of a thing) which Allah has made lawful, but (this garlic) is a plant the odour of which is repugnant to me.*

The narration is also found in the *Musnad* of Aḥmad bin Ḥanbal as well as in the *Sunan al-Kubra* of Bayhaqy. It is also found in *Ṣaḥīḥ* Ibn Khuzayma as follows:

> أخبرنا أبو طاهر حدثنا أبو بكر حدثنا أبو موسى محمد بن المثنى حدثنا عبد الأعلى حدثنا سعيد الجريري (ح) وحدثنا أبو هاشم زياد بن أيوب حدثنا إسماعيل حدثنا سعيد الجريري عن أبي نضرة عن أبي سعيد قاله بمثل حديث مسلم، ثم قال ابن خزيمة: هذا حديث أبي هاشم، وزاد أبو موسى في آخر حديثه: وإنه يأتينني من الملائكة فأكره أن يشموا ريحها
>
> Abu Ṭāhir reported to us Abu Bakr narrated to us Abu Musa Muḥammad bin al-Muthanna narrated to us Abdal-'Ala narrated to us Sa'eed al-Jariri narrated to us (*ḥawala*) and Abu Hāshim Ziyād bin Ayub narrated to us Ismā'il narrated to us Sa'eed al-Jariri Abu Naḍra narrated to us from Abu Sa'eed, he said similarly to the *ḥadith* of Muslim, then Ibn Khuzayma said: 'This *ḥadith* has come from Abu Hāshim who increased

the *ḥadith* of Abu Musa at the end saying, *....and indeed the angels have come to me and I dislike that they go in this foul odour.*'

In the *Musnad* of Aḥmad bin Ḥanbal we find the following reported:

حدثنا عبد الملك بن عمرو قال: حدثنا خالد بن ميسرة حدثنا معاوية بن قرة عن أبيه قال: نهى رسول الله، صلى الله عليه وسلم، عن هاتين الشجرتين الخبيثتين وقال: من أكلهما فلا يقربن مسجدنا! ، وقال: ان كنتم لا بد آكليهما فأميتموهما طبخاً، قال يعنى البصل والثوم

Abdal-Malik bin 'Amr narrated to us he said Khālid bin Maysara narrated to us Mu'āwiya bin Qurra narrated to us from his father he said: The Prophet (peace be upon him) prohibited (us) from these two filthy trees / plants. And he said: *Whoever eats from them let him not approach our masjid*! And he said: *If it is necessary to eat them, deaden them by cooking*. He said *– that is to say – onion and garlic.*

The narration is also reported by Imām an-Nasā'i in the *Sunan al-Kubra* as well as in *Sharḥ Ma'āni al-Athār*. Furthermore in *Ṣaḥīḥ* Muslim we find:

حدثنا أبو بكر بن أبي شيبة حدثنا كثير بن هشام عن هشام الدستوائي عن أبي الزبير عن جابر قال: نهى رسول الله، صلى الله عليه وسلم، عن أكل البصل والكراث فغلبتنا الحاجة فأكلنا منها فقال: من أكل من هذه الشجرة المنتنة فلا يقربن مسجدنا، فإن الملائكة تأذى مما يتأذى منه الإنس

Abu Bakr ibn Abi Shayba narrated to us Kathir bin Hishām narrated to us from Hishām ad-Distuwā'ee from Abu Zubayr from Jābir who said: The Prophet (peace be upon him) forbade eating of onions and leek. When we were overpowered by a desire (to eat) we ate them. Upon this he said: *He who eats of*

> *this offensive plant must not approach our mosque, for the angels are harmed by the same things as men.*

The narration is reported in other collections, such as in *Ṣaḥīḥ* Ibn Ḥibban, *Musnad* Aḥmad, the *Sunan al-Kubra* of Bayhaqy and in *Musnad* Abu Ya'la. Shaykh Ḥussein Asad said: 'Its men (i.e. its narrators) are the men of *Ṣaḥīḥ*'. Also reported in Muslim is the following narration providing an additional clarification in regarding eating these items in private:

> وحدثني أبو الطاهر وحرملة قالا: أخبرنا بن وهب أخبرني يونس عن بن شهاب قال: حدثني عطاء بن أبي رباح أن جابر بن عبد الله قال، (وفي رواية حرملة وزعم) أن رسول الله، صلى الله عليه وسلم، قال: من أكل ثوما أو بصلا فليعتزلنا أو ليعتزل مسجدنا وليقعد في بيته، وإنه أتي بقدر فيه خضروات من بقول فوجد لها ريحا فسأل فأخبر بما فيها من البقول فقال: قربوها إلى بعض أصحابه فلما رآه كره أكلها قال: «كل: فإني أناجي من لا تناجي
>
> And Abu Ṭāhir and Ḥarmala narrated to me, they said Ibn Wahb reported to us Yunus reported to me from Ibn Shihāb he said 'Aṭā bin Abi Rabāḥ narrated to me that Jābir ibn Abdullah said (and in the channel of Ḥarmala he claimed) that the Messenger of Allah (peace be upon him) said: *He who eats garlic or onion should remain away from us or from our masjid and stay in his house.* A kettle was brought to him which had (cooked) vegetables in it. He smelled an (offensive) odour in it. On asking he was informed of the vegetables (cooked in it). He said: *Take it to such and such Companion.* When he saw it, he also disliked eating it. (Upon this) he (the Prophet) said: *You may eat it, for I converse with the one with whom you do not converse.*

This narration is also in the *Musnad* of Aḥmad although at the beginning it has the wording – '*to sit in his house*.' It is also in the *Ṣaḥīḥ* of Ibn Khuzayma similar to that of Aḥmad as well as being reported in *Mu'jam al-Ṣagheer* of Ṭabarāni. In the *Ṣaḥīḥ* of Ibn Khuzayma the following is reported:

أخبرنا أبو طاهر حدثنا أبو بكر حدثنا يونس بن عبد الأعلى حدثنا بن وهب أخبرني عمرو بن الحارث عن بكر بن سوادة ان أبا النجيب مولى عبد الله بن سعد حدثه ان أبا سعيد الخدري حدثه انه ذكر عند رسول الله، صلى الله عليه وسلم، الثوم والبصل والكراث وقيل: يا رسول الله وأشد ذلك كله الثوم أفتحرّمه؟ فقال رسول الله، صلى الله عليه وسلم: كلوه، ومن أكله منكم فلا يقرب هذا المسجد حتى يذهب ريحه منه

Abu Ṭāhir reported to us Abu Bakr narrated to us Yunus ibn Abdal-'Ala narrated to us Ibn Wahb narrated to us 'Amr ibn al-Ḥārith reported to me from Bakr bin Sawāda that Abu an-Najeed, *mawla* to Abdullah bin Sa'eed narrated to him that Abu Sa'eed al-Khudri narrated to him that he mentioned when the Prophet (peace be upon him) (mentioned about) onion, garlic and leeks. They said: Oh Messenger of Allah, the most severe of them is garlic - would you make it unlawful? So the Prophet (peace be upon him) said: *Eat it and he who eats it should not come near this masjid until its odour goes away.*

The narration is also reported in the *Sunan al-Kubra* of Bayhaqy. Imām an-Nasā'i in the *Sunan al-Kubra* there is the following:

أنبأ مُحَمَّد بن المثنى قال: حدثنا يحيى بن سعيد قال: حدثنا هشام قال: حدثنا قتادة عن سالم بن أبي الجعد عن معدان بن أبي طلحة أن عمر بن الخطاب قال: إنكم أيها الناس تأكلون من شجرتين ما أراهما إلا خبيثتين هذا البصل والثوم، لقد رأيت نبي الله، صلى الله عليه وسلم، إذا وجد ريحهما من الرجل أمر به فأخرج إلى البقيع، فمن أكلهما فليمتهما طبخا

Muḥammad bin al-Muthanna reports, he said Yaḥya bin Sa'eed

> narrated to us he said Hishām narrated to us he said Qatāda narrated to us from Sālim bin Abul'Ja'd from Ma'dān bin Abi Ṭalḥa that Umar bin al-Khaṭṭāb said: O people, you eat of two plants which I do not think are anything but bad, this onion and garlic. I have seen the Prophet of Allah (peace be upon him), if he noticed their smell coming from a man, ordering that he be taken out to Al-Baqi'. Whoever eats them let him cook them to death!

Imām an-Nasā'i also has the following channel concerning the same matter in the *Sunan al-Kubra* –Muḥammad ibn Abdullah ibn Mubārak reported to us he said Shabāba ibn Sawār narrated to us he said Shu'ba narrated to us from Qatādah, except to its limit. It is also reported in the *Musnad* of Ḥumaydi regarding this. In *Sharḥ Ma'āni al-Athār* there is:

> حدثنا فهد قال: حدثنا أبو غسان قال: حدثنا قيس عن أبي إسحاق عن شريك بن حنبل عن علي عن النبي، صلى الله عليه وسلم، قال: من أكل هذه البقلة فلا يقربنا، أو يؤذينا في مساجدنا
>
> Fahd narrated to us he said Abu Ghassān narrated to us he Qays narrated to us from Abu Isḥāq from Shareek bin Ḥanbal from Ali from the Prophet (peace be upon him) who said: *Whomsoever eats from this offensive plant shouldn't come close with this harmful (odour) in our masjid.*

After this Imām aṭ-Ṭaḥāwi said: 'The people disliked to eat onions because of the smell it would give and they would be insistent upon this because of these narrations. Latter on people differed with them in this and stressed that the Prophet only prohibited eating it when coming to the *masjid*. Not because it was *ḥarām* but because people were disturbed in the *masjid* by the smell.' Unlike the subject of consuming garlic and onions we find the opposite end of the scale so to speak, that concerning the prohibition of homosexuality. This prohibition though is categorical as from the various meanings which are extracted from the book of Allah. He the exalted says:

وَلُوطًا آتَيْنَاهُ حُكْمًا وَعِلْمًا وَنَجَّيْنَاهُ مِنَ الْقَرْيَةِ الَّتِي كَانَت تَّعْمَلُ الْخَبَائِثَ إِنَّهُمْ كَانُوا قَوْمَ سَوْءٍ فَاسِقِينَ

And (as for) Luṭ, We gave him wisdom and knowledge, and We delivered him from the town which wrought abominations; surely they were an evil people, transgressors.[9]

Allah clarifies in the following verses the ultimate form of *khabā'ith,* namely that of approaching men instead of women and committing acts of abomination. Allah blessed be his names says:

وَلُوطًا إِذْ قَالَ لِقَوْمِهِ أَتَأْتُونَ الْفَاحِشَةَ مَا سَبَقَكُم بِهَا مِنْ أَحَدٍ مِّنَ الْعَالَمِينَ

And (We sent) Luṭ when he said to his people: What! Do you commit an indecency which anyone in the world has not done before you? [10]

وَلُوطًا إِذْ قَالَ لِقَوْمِهِ أَتَأْتُونَ الْفَاحِشَةَ وَأَنتُمْ تُبْصِرُونَ ، أَئِنَّكُمْ لَتَأْتُونَ الرِّجَالَ شَهْوَةً مِّن دُونِ النِّسَاءِ بَلْ أَنتُمْ قَوْمٌ تَجْهَلُونَ

And (We sent) Luṭ, when he said to his people: What! Do you commit indecency while you see? What! Do you indeed approach men lustfully rather than women? Nay, you are a people who act ignorantly. [11]

أَئِنَّكُمْ لَتَأْتُونَ الرِّجَالَ وَتَقْطَعُونَ السَّبِيلَ وَتَأْتُونَ فِي نَادِيكُمُ الْمُنكَرَ فَمَا كَانَ جَوَابَ قَوْمِهِ إِلَّا أَن قَالُوا ائْتِنَا بِعَذَابِ اللَّهِ إِن كُنتَ مِنَ الصَّادِقِينَ

---

[9] *Qur'ān* 21: 74
[10] *Qur'ān* 7: 80
[11] *Qur'ān* 27: 54/55

What! Do you come to the males and commit robbery on the highway, and you commit evil deeds in your assemblies? But nothing was the answer of his people except that they said: Bring on us Allah's punishment, if you are one of the truthful. [12]

أَتَأْتُونَ الذُّكْرَانَ مِنَ الْعَالَمِينَ ، وَتَذَرُونَ مَا خَلَقَ لَكُمْ رَبُّكُم مِّنْ أَزْوَاجِكُم بَلْ أَنتُمْ قَوْمٌ عَادُونَ

What! Do you come to the males from among the creatures and leave what your Lord has created for you of your wives? Nay, you are a people exceeding limits. [13]

If the last two verses mentioned were the only ones revealed in relation to this subject, that would not suffice for a demonstrative prohibition in the last and final *Sharī'ah*. Given that the previous abrogated laws are not to be followed, additional evidence would be required substantiating this point. The acts undertaken by the people at the time of Luṭ (peace be upon him) were described as being *fāḥisha*. Consequently it is deemed to be *fāḥisha* in and of itself. According to what we mentioned above from amongst the definite rules, this action is definitely prohibited in this final *Sharī'ah* until the day of resurrection. The point becomes somewhat clearer when the verses in chapters seven and sixteen are also placed within view. Allah himself described these acts of homosexuality as being *fāḥisha*, thereby demonstrating its prohibition. All the companions of the Prophet Muḥammad (peace be upon him) understood similarly, as did those who followed them. In fact, all Muslims since that time have concurred upon the illegality of acts which are the same or similar to that which the people of Luṭ (peace be upon him) undertook.

To emphasise the point again, the fact that some matter, objects / entities, sayings and acts deserve to be call *khabeeth* or *fāḥisha* because of reasons bound with it in itself or for other considerations, is

[12] *Qur'ān* 29: 29
[13] *Qur'ān* 26: 165/166

only because Allah has made it like that through his determination of the universe in which we reside. They are not according to reasonable necessity or absolute concepts which cannot be violated. The whole universe with its fundamental system and initial conditions is a *possibility*, a contingent being, a creation and existing because Allah made it like that according to his destined formative and creative order. There are some possible universes that may have neither *khabeeth* nor *fāḥisha* in it – the most obvious being paradise. While there are other existing universes, that are not suitable for any legally competent to live in, or, they are even not suitable for any form of life. All that is possible and what is possible will never turn actually to the form of existing, except that if Allah makes, creates and permits it to be like that. Allah says: '*Certainly his command when he desires anything is to say to it 'be' and it is.*' [14]

There are indeed but a few categories of the obscene (*fāḥisha*) in all existing universes as they contradict absolute reasonable necessities. The idea that Allah has partners or offspring or that his knowledge is limited; that he transgresses or acts unjustly is false in all realities and considered obscene (*fāḥisha*). Allah is far above such notions. Truly, Allah is the one and only, the living, self-subsisting, his existence being the manifest truth. It is from among the impossibilities that any of such obscene matters could be regarded as obliged in any possible assumed creed in any existing universe. Various *aḥādith* serve to exemplify the point further, as recorded in *Ṣaḥīḥ* Bukhāri on the authority of Abu Hurayrah:

حدثنا إسحاق بن منصور قال وحدثنا عبد الرزاق أخبرنا معمر عن همام عن أبي هريرة قال: قال رسول الله، صلى الله عليه وسلم: كذبني بن آدم ولم يكن له ذلك وشتمني ولم يكن له ذلك أما تكذيبه إياي أن يقول إني لن أعيده كما بدأته وأما شتمه إياي أن يقول اتخذ الله ولدا وأنا الصمد الذي لم ألد ولم أولد ولم يكن لي كفؤا أحد لم يلد ولم يولد ولم يكن له كفوا أحد: كفؤا وكفيئا وكفاء

[14] *Qur'ān* 36: 82

واحد

Isḥāq bin Manṣur narrated to us he said Abdar-Razzāq narrated to us Ma'mar reported to us from Hammām from Abu Hurayrah who said, the Messenger of Allah (peace be upon him) said: (Allah says) *The son of Adam tells a lie against me and he hasn't the right to do so; and he curses me and he hasn't the right to do so. His telling a lie against me is his saying that I will not recreate him as I created him for the first time; and his cursing me is his saying that Allah has begotten children, while I am the self-sufficient master, whom all creatures need, who begets not nor was he begotten, and there is none like unto me.*

The same authentic narration can be found in the *Ṣaḥifa* of Hammām ibn Munabih;[15] it is also found in the *Ṣaḥīḥ* of Ibn Ḥibbān,[16] the *Musnad* of Aḥmad,[17] and in other collections. Bukhāri also has this narration as found in his *Ṣāḥīḥ:*

حدثني عبد الله بن أبي شيبة عن أبي أحمد عن سفيان عن أبي الزناد عن الأعرج عن أبي هريرة قال: قال النبي أراه قال يشتمني بن آدم وما ينبغي له أن يشتمني ويكذبني وما ينبغي له أما شتمه فقوله إن لي ولدا وأما تكذيبه فقوله ليس يعيدني كما بدأني

Abdullah bin Abi Shayba narrated to me from Abu Aḥmad from Sufyān from Abi Zinād from al-'Araj from Abu Hurayrah who said, the Messenger of Allah (peace be upon him) said: *I see that the son of Adam slights me, and he should not, he disbelieves in me and he ought not to do so. As for his slighting me, it is that he says that I have a son; and his disbelief in me is his statement that I shall not recreate him as I have created (him) before.*

---

[15] *Ṣaḥifa* Hammām ibn Munabih Vol. 1 sec. 56, no. 106
[16] *Ṣaḥīḥ* Ibn Ḥibbān Vol. 3 sec. 129, no. 848
[17] *Musnad* Aḥmad Vol. 2 sec. 318, no. 8,204

Bukhāri also records this in another place in the *Ṣaḥīḥ*.[18] A large number of collectors narrated this *ḥadith* in their respective works, such as in the *Musnad* of Aḥmad,[19] the *Sunan* and *Sunan al-Kubra* of Nasā'i[20] and in the *Ṣaḥīḥ* of Ibn Ḥibbān.[21] Then someone followed up the statement of the Prophet (peace be upon him), *and the initial creation [of him] is no easier for Me than remaking him.* In this statement is an explicit clarification that attributes, which are used to describe individuals and imply deficiency, are not permissible to ascribe to Allah, mighty and majestic is he. This is because logic necessitates that one should use the phrase 'difficult for me' instead of the phrase 'easier for me'. However, using a phrase implying difficulty was avoided as it is infers deficiency. Therefore it was replaced with a phrase implying ease which does not have the same ramifications.

Imām Aḥmad has the next narration in the *Musnad* with a good *isnād*:

> حدثنا حسن حدثنا بن لهيعة حدثنا أبو يونس عن أبي هريرة عن النبي، صلى الله عليه وسلم، قال ان الله عز وجل قال كذبني عبدي ولم يكن له ليكذبني وشتمني عبدي ولم يكن له شتمي فأما تكذيبه إياي فيقول لن يعيدني كالذي بدأني وليس آخر الخلق أهون على ان أعيده من أوله فقد كذبني ان قالها واما شتمه إياي فيقول اتخذ الله ولدا انا الله أحد الصمد لم ألد
>
> Ḥasan narrated to us Ibn Lahia narrated to us Abu Yunus narrated to us from Abu Hurayrah from the Prophet (peace be upon him) that - *Allah the exalted and majestic said: My slave denies me and curses me and he had no right to do so. As for his lie, it is (the claim) that he cannot be brought back as he was originally created. And as for his reviling me, it is his*

[18] *Ṣaḥīḥ* Bukhāri Vol. 4 sec. 1,903, no. 4,690
[19] *Musnad* Aḥmad Vol. 2 sec. 394, no. 9,103
[20] *Sunan* Nasā'i Vol. 4 sec. 112, no. 2,078; *Sunan al-Kubra* Vol. 1 sec. 666, no. 2,205; Vol. 6 sec. 409, no. 11,338 and Vol. 4 sec. 395, no. 7,667
[21] *Ṣaḥīḥ* Ibn Ḥibbān Vol. 1 sec. 501, no. 267

saying that Allah has taken a son, but I am Allah aṣ-Ṣamad, and not bitter.

Next Bukhāri records in his *Ṣaḥīḥ* on the authority of Ibn 'Abbās; Ṭabarāni also records this in *Mu'jam al-Kabir* and *Musnad ash-Shāmiayn,*[22] it also appears in other collections as well:

حدثنا أبو اليمان أخبرنا شعيب عن عبد الله بن أبي حسين حدثنا نافع بن جبير عن بن عباس عن النبي قال: قال الله كذبني بن آدم ولم يكن له ذلك وشتمني ولم يكن له ذلك فأما تكذيبه إياي فزعم أني لا أقدر أن أعيده كما كان وأما شتمه إياي فقوله لي ولد فسبحاني أن أتخذ صاحبة أو ولدا

Abul-Yamān narrated to us Shu'ayb reported to us from Abdullah bin Abi Ḥussein, Nāfi bin Jubayr narrated to us from Ibn 'Abbās from the Prophet (peace be upon him) who said: *Allah said: The son of Adam tells a lie against me, though he hasn't the right to do so. He abuses me though he hasn't the right to do so. As for his telling a lie against me, it is his saying that I will not recreate him as I created him for the first time. In fact, the first creation was not easier for me than a new creation. As for his abusing me, it is his saying that Allah has begotten children, while I am the one, the self-sufficient master whom all creatures need, I beget not, nor was I begotten, and there is none like unto me.*

As we can see from the aforementioned evidences taken from the Prophetic Sunnah, such statements are regarded as being false and obscene (*fāḥisha*) in all universes. They contradict the fact that Allah is the one and only manifest truth. It is among the impossibilities that any, of such matters, are obligations in any possible assumed creed, in any existing universe. In this universe in which we live now, during

[22] Ṭabarāni, *Mu'jam al-Kabir* Vol. 10 sec. 309, no. 10,751 and in *Musnad ash-Shāmiayn*, Vol. 4 sec. 139, no. 2,914

this present worldly life on this earth after the advent of Abul'-Qāsim, Muḥammad ibn Abdullah – the servant of Allah and his final Messenger the obligation is to turn only to the revelation. In other words, to only refer for all matters of judgement to the legal texts - the Qur'ān and the *Sunnah* – and nothing else, in order to search and locate the judgment of Allah in every issue. These legal texts are in effect like the 'ark of Noah' (*Safeena Nuḥ*). Whoever boards the ark is saved from danger and survives; whoever misses it, will drown and perish, no matter how he deceives himself, imagining that he can fight waves and escape from the flood by resorting to the mountains. To Allah and his Messenger is the return of all judgement to the revealed *Sharī'ah* legal texts. That is Islam and faith (*al-'Imān*), which is the core of what is considered being subservient to Allah, worshipping him, which is the vocation of all mankind and *jinn*. Even if the reasonable search concerning the essence of matters be they entities, actions or sayings were just in order to know if a matter is good (*ṭayib*), vile / evil (*khabeeth*) or indecent / obscene (*fāḥisha*), it is not lawful to be used in order to reach a legal judgment. As in this case, it is not turning to Allah and his Messenger. Even if it was lawful in objective study or a philosophical search in order to know the nature of matters and their essences, or to other than that from among the permissible, desirable and obligatory aims and targets, it is definitely not lawful if it was to know the judgment of Allah in such matters.

Thus there is no need for useless arguments such as - is the judgment of matters according to reason only, to *Sharī'ah* only, or to both of them through certain order or certain arrangement. We may say that this issue could be a subject for philosophical, intellectual or legal research, but it is purely theoretical, with no resultant action and it is not among the field of *Sunnah* or innovation (*bidāh'*) as some claimed from ancient times from amongst the *Mu'tazilah* or among those who claim to follow the '*Salafi*' Islam in modern times, who are proud of themselves and their sect. They claim that they are *'al-Firqa an-Nājiya'* or the *'Ṭā'ifa al-Manṣura'*, the saved victorious sect, brazenly asserting that only their followers would be admitted to paradise. We may say to them in response that Allah says:

وَقَالُوا لَن يَدْخُلَ الْجَنَّةَ إِلَّا مَن كَانَ هُودًا أَوْ نَصَارَىٰ تِلْكَ أَمَانِيُّهُمْ قُلْ هَاتُوا بُرْهَانَكُمْ إِن كُنتُمْ صَادِقِينَ ، بَلَىٰ مَنْ أَسْلَمَ وَجْهَهُ لِلَّهِ وَهُوَ مُحْسِنٌ فَلَهُ أَجْرُهُ عِندَ رَبِّهِ وَلَا خَوْفٌ عَلَيْهِمْ وَلَا هُمْ يَحْزَنُونَ

And they say: None shall enter paradise except he who is a Jew or a Christian. These are their vain desires. Say: Bring your proof if you are truthful. Yes! Whoever submits himself entirely to Allah and he is the doer of good (to others) he has his reward from his Lord, and there is no fear for him nor shall he grieve. [23]

Moreover we are only ordered but to the following:

اتَّبِعُوا مَا أُنزِلَ إِلَيْكُم مِّن رَّبِّكُمْ وَلَا تَتَّبِعُوا مِن دُونِهِ أَوْلِيَاءَ قَلِيلًا مَّا تَذَكَّرُونَ

Follow what has been revealed to you from your Lord and do not follow Awliyā' besides Him, how little do you mind. [24]

The *Deen* has been established as complete, as Allah says:

الْيَوْمَ أَكْمَلْتُ لَكُمْ دِينَكُمْ وَأَتْمَمْتُ عَلَيْكُمْ نِعْمَتِي وَرَضِيتُ لَكُمُ الْإِسْلَامَ دِينًا

This day have I perfected for you your Deen and completed My favour on you and chosen for you Islam as a Deen. [25]

Definitely this shows that every judgment, among all judgments till the day of resurrection is in this verse. We do not care if, what was made

---

[23] *Qur'ān* 2: 111/112
[24] *Qur'ān* 7: 3
[25] *Qur'ān* 5: 3

good by the text, is reasonable, unreasonable, can be realised by the mind; or not, can be realised reason then by *Sharī'ah*; by *Sharī'ah* and then by reason, or similar. This is the truth which must be believed upon as part of one's creed (*aqeedah*). It cannot be otherwise for those who believe in Allah and the last day. Whosoever disbelieves in this, Allah is rich, without need or partner, lord of all the worlds.

12 Verily, Allah does not command indecency

Previously we mentioned that it may be the case that Allah does not explicitly legislate (thereby permitting) against matters considered *fawāḥish* and *khabā'ith*, as well as prohibiting some from what is considered the *ṭayibāt* (good things), such as for Israel in previous *Sharī'ah's*. As an absolute dictum, Allah *does not command* towards *fāḥisha*, in other words, making it a religious duty that is ordered, recommended or considered desirable. This neither occurs in the previous *Sharī'ah's* nor in the present blessed final one. By greater reasoning, Allah did not permit - not in this universe or in other possible universes, something that deserves to be called *fāḥisha* originally. The conclusive proof which establishes this point unequivocally is the Qur'ānic verse where Allah the exalted, blessed be his names says:

وَإِذَا فَعَلُوا فَاحِشَةً قَالُوا وَجَدْنَا عَلَيْهَا آبَاءَنَا وَاللَّهُ أَمَرَنَا بِهَا قُلْ إِنَّ اللَّهَ لَا يَأْمُرُ بِالْفَحْشَاءِ أَتَقُولُونَ عَلَى اللَّهِ مَا لَا تَعْلَمُونَ

And when they commit an indecency (fāḥisha) they say: We found our fathers doing this, and Allah has enjoined it on us. Say: <u>Surely Allah does not enjoin</u>

<u>indecency</u>; do you say against Allah what you do not know? [1]

Contained therein is a report of certain truth; an eternal maxim which cannot be contradicted neither can it be abrogated, for reports cannot be subject to abrogation - that Allah the exalted does not command *fāḥisha*. He never commanded it previously, nor presently in any possible universe. Blessed are his names he says:

يَا أَيُّهَا الَّذِينَ آمَنُوا لَا تَتَّبِعُوا خُطُوَاتِ الشَّيْطَانِ وَمَن يَتَّبِعْ خُطُوَاتِ الشَّيْطَانِ فَإِنَّهُ يَأْمُرُ
بِالْفَحْشَاءِ وَالْمُنكَرِ وَلَوْلَا فَضْلُ اللَّهِ عَلَيْكُمْ وَرَحْمَتُهُ مَا زَكَىٰ مِنكُم مِّنْ أَحَدٍ أَبَدًا وَلَٰكِنَّ اللَّهَ يُزَكِّي
مَن يَشَاءُ وَاللَّهُ سَمِيعٌ عَلِيمٌ

O you who believe! Do not follow the footsteps of the devil and whoever follows the footsteps of the devil, then surely he bids the doing of indecency and evil (faḥshā' wa munkar); and were it not for Allah's grace upon you and His mercy, not one of you would have ever been pure, but Allah purifies whom He pleases; and Allah is Hearing, Knowing. [2]

It is inconceivable that Allah the exalted commands that which the devil, known as the enemy of Allah, commands! As mentioned previously, the purely rational judgement concerning a deed to be *khabeeth* or *ṭayib* would prove an extremely tall order. We have previously mentioned that the mental judgment on deeds to be evil or good may be very difficult. It is the same thing here regarding that which deserves to be called *fāḥisha*. That conceded, it may be even more difficult to make a judgment on an action or statement, in addition to a judgment on relations, proportions, abstract systems, positive and conventional matters as being *fāḥisha* on the basis of reason alone. If we suppose that it is possible in principle, it would be more difficult than judging something to be *khabeeth*, because it

[1] *Qur'ān* 7: 28
[2] *Qur'ān* 24: 21

requires us to consider the reasons of the action, the nature of the action itself, what it is composed of and what it is related to. And then considering what may result from it as things, actions and occurrences, which are almost not limited in this vast universe. It is definitely impossible therefore, to be established by the text of the *Sharīʼah* (or by the necessity of reason, though we regard it as unlikely that it can be perceived with sense or perception of mind separately), that an action be *fāḥisha* in itself and then Allah commands its performance as a religious duty or even as a desirable matter. The judgement concerning desirable matters is that it is a command to be done, though it is not an absolute binding command and the person who leaves it is not considered sinful. Furthermore, it is impossible that Allah commands that something should be done, and then it appears as an act which is *fāḥisha.*

We would hasten to clarify at this juncture that the juxtaposition between *khabeeth* and *ṭayib* regarding objects and benefits that are related to judgments of lawful (*ḥalāl*) and prohibited (*ḥarām*) in this last blessed *Sharīʼah*, still fit within the overarching binding principle concerning permissibility being the default ruling on all matters unless a textual proof indicates otherwise. What necessarily results from that is that a certain 'thing' must definitely be *ṭayib* or *khabeeth.* Invariably the juxtaposition has nothing to be compared with the concept of absolute *fāḥisha.* It is true that the Allah has guaranteed the prohibition of all *fāḥisha* in this last blessed *Sharīʼah.* But what is not *fāḥisha* regarding statements and actions, relations, proportions and abstract systems and conventional man-made matters, may be religious duties (*wājib*), desirable (*mustaḥab*), or undesirable (*makruh*), or even unlawful (*ḥarām*). It may be a 'positive / declaratory' (*al-waḍʼiya*) matter that falls under the concepts of: condition (*sharṭ*), cause (*sabab*), deterrent, concession (*rukhsa*) or intention etc as 'positive / declaratory' judgments. Therefore, when something (especially, statements and actions) is not considered as *fāḥisha* and as a result, it is not void and unlawful, no certain judgment is obligatory for it. There is no difference between the judgment being a commandment, such as an obligation, desirability, permissibility, undesirability or even prohibition, or a man-made judgment, such as making it a condition or deterrent, permission, intention or judging it as authentic, corrupt or void, etc. Concerning all of these matters Allah judges according to the divine wisdom which is the exclusive possession of sovereignty, lordship and dominion.

In order that our words do not appear to be general and too abstract, making it difficult to understand, it is better that we consider the following example. The most lucid being the matter of unveiling the private parts of an adult woman for other than her husband. This is one of the unlawful acts, which is known by necessity in Islam. It is one of the absolute recurrent proofs in the glorious Qur'ān, the *Sunnah* and the consensus of the people of Islam. Hence for a woman to unveil her private parts is absolutely prohibited, regardless of the specific rank of prohibition whether it is a major or minor prohibition. Additionally, it is considered *fāḥisha* by the necessity of legislation as it is prohibited. The evidence concerning this issue is illustrated in the following verse:

قُلْ إِنَّمَا حَرَّمَ رَبِّيَ الْفَوَاحِشَ مَا ظَهَرَ مِنْهَا وَمَا بَطَنَ وَالْإِثْمَ وَالْبَغْيَ بِغَيْرِ الْحَقِّ وَأَن تُشْرِكُوا
بِاللَّهِ مَا لَمْ يُنَزِّلْ بِهِ سُلْطَانًا وَأَن تَقُولُوا عَلَى اللَّهِ مَا لَا تَعْلَمُونَ

Say: My Lord has only prohibited indecencies, those of them that are apparent as well concealed, and sin and rebellion without justice, and that you associate with Allah that for which He has not sent down any authority, and that you say against Allah what you do not know.[3]

The division is comprehensive, showing that prohibited things are of four main categories:

[3] *Qur'ān* 7: 33

- Making statements about Allah without knowledge, this is the worst of them. It occurs only in statements and beliefs. However, unveiling the private parts is not part of the genus of statements and beliefs; therefore it does not belong to this category at all.

- *Shirk* with Allah. That is, ascribing partners to Allah. *Shirk* in creed or *aqeedah* is disbelief – *kufr,* such as ascribing another god alongside Allah. There is also *Shirk* of action, such as *Shirk Khafi'* such as showing off and being ostentatious. Unveiling the private parts does not belong to *Shirk* of belief or deed.

- It is not an aggressive sin in the sense of an infringement upon other people's rights. Indeed a woman unveiling her private parts may be disturbing for some, whereas it is exciting or delightful for others. But no one in the world would say that it would constitute aggression upon other people, such as shedding blood, taking people's wealth and consuming it unjustly; beating people on their backs and faces, violating the honour by levelling false accusations against a spouse or a breach of covenants and so on and so forth.

- Necessity dictates that this action must squarely fall within the fourth and last category, which is that of obscenities, *al-fawāḥish*. In reality, it is intuitively one of the most obvious of obscenities. We say, narrowly speaking, regarding the indecencies, injustice, oppression and aggression are also excesses beyond the proper limit. Therefore, it is *fāḥisha* and excess in the broad sense.

In the same manner, ascribing a partner with Allah is an aggression upon Allah's right, that of being worshipped alone without the association of any partner. It is also an assault upon reason and truth to claim the existence of another deity with Allah. In fact, it is actually a claim assuming the existence of that which is an absolute impossibility. *Shirk* - polytheism, therefore is an obscenity, *fāḥisha* and is excessiveness in the broadest sense. Making statements about Allah without knowledge, is deeper in *fāḥisha*, excessiveness, aggression upon Allah's due, and upon the mind, which is the cause of responsibility. If someone were to say that all prohibitions are *fawāḥish* according to this broad sense, the person would be right to say so. With regard to this, the addition of the other three categories in the Qur'ānic verse adds particular to the general. One will notice that the order of the main four categories in the Qur'ānic verse is in an ascending order to the general categorisation. This means that the worst sort of *fawāḥish*, in the narrow sense, such the acts committed by the people at the time of Luṭ, does not reach in terms of sin the highest rank, that of aggression - killing, rape or levelling false accusations against chaste married women. Yet again these are not in the same rank as ascribing a partner with Allah. Although they are falsehood and saying something about Allah without knowledge, yet they are less in rank, compared to someone who accuses Allah of wrong, foolishness and deviating from the truth, as the devil did, may Allah curse him. The topic is in itself vast however this short study here is but an introduction rather than a comprehensive analysis. What we have previously said is evident and confirmed by the word of Allah the exalted:

قُلْ تَعَالَوْا أَتْلُ مَا حَرَّمَ رَبُّكُمْ عَلَيْكُمْ أَلَّا تُشْرِكُوا بِهِ شَيْئًا وَبِالْوَالِدَيْنِ إِحْسَانًا وَلَا تَقْتُلُوا أَوْلَادَكُم مِّنْ إِمْلَاقٍ نَّحْنُ نَرْزُقُكُمْ وَإِيَّاهُمْ <u>وَلَا تَقْرَبُوا الْفَوَاحِشَ</u> مَا ظَهَرَ مِنْهَا وَمَا بَطَنَ وَلَا تَقْتُلُوا النَّفْسَ الَّتِي حَرَّمَ اللَّهُ إِلَّا بِالْحَقِّ ذَٰلِكُمْ وَصَّاكُم بِهِ لَعَلَّكُمْ تَعْقِلُونَ

Say: Come I will recite what your Lord has forbidden to you-- (remember) that you do not associate anything with Him and show kindness to your parents, and do not slay your children for (fear of) poverty-- We provide for you and for them-- and <u>do not draw nigh to indecencies</u>, those of them which *are apparent and those which are concealed, and do not kill the soul which Allah has forbidden except for the requirements of justice; this He has enjoined you with that you may understand.* [4]

Some may misunderstand this topic by putting forth an objection that at an earlier juncture, Allah commanded Ibrāhim (peace be upon him) to sacrifice his son. Taking another human life is a heinous crime, unless it is by way of due process of law or done in a legitimate war, or by defending oneself against an aggressor. According to this line of argumentation, Allah the exalted would appear to have commanded at least one *fāḥisha* which some, who do not understand the holistic nature of the ownership of the creator over his creation, would see as being a refutation of all what we have written thus far!

But this objection is invalid, built upon a corrupt foundational reasoning. All souls, including the souls of the children of Adam belong to Allah. He has sovereignty over them and he has the absolute sovereignty to do whatever he wants. Other than restrictions he has placed upon himself, which he has informed us of via revelation; he is not bound by our limitations. Placing oneself in harms way as an act of devout adherence to Allah's commandments or killing another person for the same purpose, within the prescribed limits of revelation, is not considered absolute *fāḥisha*. Such acts are however, challenged by the worldly-minded people, secularists who claim that man is not slave to his lord and creator. They would have us believe that man is the master of himself, being both lord and god in miniature. Such line of argumentation is at complete odds with *Tawḥeed*, which the Prophet of Islam, Muḥammad ibn Abdullah the last of the Prophets and the Messengers (peace be upon them) brought to us all. It is thus *kufr* (disbelief), which definitely contradicts Islam. Not only that, it also contradicts reason and logic.

On the other hand, placing oneself in harms way outside of

[4] *Qur'ān* 6: 151

prescribed limits is an act designated as being prohibited, unless it is done as an act of martyrdom. In the same way, killing another person is also prohibited, except by way of a legitimate *Jihād* such as defending oneself against a hostile aggressor or as part of a legitimate judicial process in a *Sharī'ah* court. Other types of killing apart from this would be considered, firstly as *fāḥisha* and *munkar*. It is transgression of prescribed limits and what is more, as wrongdoing and aggression on people's property and the possession of the creator. Therefore, it is unlawful in this context, as it is obvious from the Qur'ānic verse.

Secondly, making statements about Allah without knowledge; in the case of the one who kills himself or kills another purely as a sacrifice to be devout to Allah, just like sacrificial animals. This is because Allah abrogated that commandment, which He commanded Ibrāhim (peace be upon him) to perform and he ransomed Ismā'il with a great sacrifice. After that he did not command such a commandment in successive religions. It is not that he is not worthy, that human sacrifice should be made for him, as an act of devotion, but it is just that he has abrogated this kind of sacrifice, in order to bestow his favour, kindness and mercy upon us. Therefore, whoever does that, he would have committed a prohibited act by saying something about Allah without knowledge, which is an innovation in the religion, for he has made his action a devout act to Allah, while Allah did not make it a legal act of devotion and this is one of the main causes of prohibition as it is clear in the Qur'ānic verse.

About the author

Born in Mecca (Friday 8 November 1946), Professor Muḥammad ibn Abdullah al-Mas'ari (may Allah preserve him) is from the Dawāsir tribe, which is the modern name for the famous tribe of Hamdān and hails from a distinguished and scholarly family. His father, Sheikh Abdullah ibn Sulaymān ibn Abdur-Raḥman ibn Muḥammad al-Mas'ari, may Allah have mercy upon him (b. 1918 / d. 2005) was a learned scholar and one of the distinguished students of Sheikh Muḥammad ibn Ibrāhim al-Sheikh, may Allah have mercy upon him. He also held several distinguished posts from early on, from being an assistant judge to Sheikh Abdal-Aziz ibn Abdullah ibn Bāz, to becoming vice-President and later President of the Board of Grievances (*Diwān al-Mathālim;* the Supreme Administrative and Constitutional Court), and a Professor of Islamic studies at *Dar at-Tawḥeed,* in Ṭā'if.

His maternal grandfather was the distinguished Sheikh Muḥammad ibn Abdur-Razzāq (d. 1973), the founder of *Dar al-Ḥadith* Academy in Mecca and al-Imām al-Ḥaramayn, of Medina and Mecca.

Naturally growing up in this distinguished scholarly environment Professor Muḥammad al-Mas'ari was an outstanding student from a young age, benefiting enormously from study circles with his father and his associates. He has always had an insatiable desire for knowledge, leading him to peruse the rich collection of works from his father's library, covering both the Islamic sciences, philosophy and literature. A very early example of this, is the study he undertook of *Majmu' al-Fatāwa*, which is Ibn Taymiyyah's acclaimed work consisting of some 40 Volumes, following its publication in 1963. That study included a complete critical reading of the text accompanied with detailed comments, observations and criticisms.

In tandem with his studies in various branches of Islamic sciences, Muḥammad al-Mas'ari is also Professor Emeritus of Theoretical and Mathematical Physics. Published widely in the field of solar energy conversion, solid-state devices and QCD (quantum chromodynamics), some of his key achievements have been designing the first prototype electric car and the calculation of the Top-Quark mass within the framework of the renormalisation group equations.

However, it is his Islamic works that have made a quantum leap in contemporary Islamic thought, notable works include:

- The Seal of Prophethood
- Prohibition of building Mosques on Graves
- Najd and the Horn of the Devil
- The Constitution of Medina
- *Ḥākimiyyah* and the Sovereignty of *Sharī'ah*
- The Awaited Promised Mahdi

Professor Muḥammad al-Mas'ari lives in exile in London since 1994, where he currently continues his research and writing.

Index

A

abrogation, 179, 180, 193, 423, 427, 488, 510, 629
al-Dhikr al-Munazil, 221, 318, 319, 324, 326, 328
al-'Imān, 44, 84, 95, 98, 99, 101, 108, 124, 125, 126, 134, 312
al-Bahai
  liar, 387
al-Iḥkām fi Uṣul al-Aḥkām
  (Judgement on the Principles of Law), 23, 332, 365, 425, 470, 471, 512, 548
al-Iḥsān, 84, 87, 88, 91, 95, 96, 98
al-Lāt, 308, 309
al-Lawḥ al-Maḥfouz, 224
allegiance, 6, 46, 136, 167, 181, 261, 532
al-Masiḥ ad-Dajjāl
  Dajjāl antichrist, 387
al-Muḥalla bil Athār
  The Adorned Treatise, 365, 425
al-Qadr, 84, 87, 90, 91, 95, 96, 129, 130, 134
Andalusia, 425, 455
Arabic language, 18, 39, 144, 147, 243, 339, 345, 363, 374, 421, 510, 538
Arabs, 4, 9, 39, 97, 101, 108, 129, 144, 284, 294, 308, 313, 346, 373, 381, 398, 421, 429, 439, 559
archaeology, 330
ark of Noah, 625
as-Salaf aṣ-Ṣāliḥ, 310, 591, 597
aṭ-Ṭahāra, 93

B

Badr, vi, 96, 198, 276, 277, 473, 532
Baghdad, 92, 123, 188, 349, 365
Bani Israel, 422, 444, 445, 446, 447, 448, 449, 463, 464
banner, 6, 392, 595
Baṣra, 86, 260, 265, 267, 402, 416
battles, 366
bayān, 319, 321, 324, 328, 331, 340, 345
Bedouins, 267, 485, 486
Bible, 326, 549, 602

bidā', 456, 536, 539, 540, 544
blessings, 382, 383, 386, 388
brick, 388

C

Caliph, 366
Caliphate, 5, 431
Children of Israel, 109
Christianity, 17, 18
Church, 7, 59, 597
churches, 391, 412, 419
citizenship, 46, 49, 136
Civilisation, 15, 17
coitus interruptus, 498
colonialism, 60
commands, 22, 37, 56, 57, 109, 159, 161, 279, 354, 423, 428, 497, 510, 533, 588, 629
Constitution of Medina, 357
Consultation, 133
culture, 15, 16, 17, 18, 60

D

ḍaef, 117, 191, 439
Dajjāl, 312, 313
Damascus, 299, 416
dawah, 277
Deuteronomy, 185, 186
Dhimma, 242
dialectics, 486
divine will, 74, 604

E

Egypt, 42, 96, 106, 142, 350, 543
eight-shares, 115, 116, 117, 118
engineering, 14, 60, 330, 582
Enlightenment, 12
exegetes, 431, 460

F

fāḥisha, 608, 609, 610, 620, 621, 624, 628, 629, 630, 631, 632, 633, 634, 635
false deities, 376
fasting, 95, 103, 109, 115, 116, 117, 118, 164, 217, 453, 479, 481, 531, 542, 561, 562, 584
Fatwa, 45
fiqh, 252, 345, 362, 365, 423, 425, 439, 512, 538, 552, 573, 577, 586
forgetfulness, 79, 143, 158, 179, 180, 183, 217, 311, 470, 471, 484, 491, 497, 521, 522, 546, 548
fragrance, 379, 380, 381, 382
Friday prayers, 194, 362
fuqahā, 49

G

Ghulam Aḥmad al-Qadiāni al-Hindi liar, 387
ghusl, 88, 90, 91, 93, 95
globalisation, 18
golden chain, 466
grave, 203, 275, 447, 475
graves, 8, 385
Greek, 17
guidepost, 120, 121, 123, 124, 125

H

Ḥajj, 90, 101, 103, 111, 112, 116, 117, 119, 130, 131, 135, 143, 201, 265, 358, 458, 459, 460, 461, 464, 466, 515
Ḥakeem, 48, 202, 225, 231, 326, 350, 352, 356, 357, 411
Ḥākimiyah, 5, 6, 44, 72, 76, 609
heresy, 9, 309, 546, 548, 590
ḥifz, 339

ḥijāb, 208
Ḥikmah, 44, 204, 206, 207, 208, 209, 210, 211, 212, 219, 248, 286, 291, 293, 318, 327, 341
Himṣ, 443
house, 388
House of Saud, 6, 7
hypocrisy, 232, 281, 288, 300, 451, 600

I

Ibn Ḥazm, 9, 23, 240, 301, 332, 336, 365, 425, 426, 455, 470, 471, 512, 514, 516, 548, 553, 579, 600
Ibn Kathir, 396, 407, 415, 417, 420, 430, 431, 447, 460, 464, 481
Ibn Taymiyyah, 3, 455, 585, 586, 587, 638
ideology, 57, 58, 59
idolaters, 286
idolatry, 9, 49
idols, 70, 376, 583
Ijmā' aṣ-Ṣaḥābah, 345, 389
ijtihād, 80, 107, 142, 276, 280, 350, 540
  independent legal juristic reasoning, 80
ikhtilāṭ, 90, 509, 562
Imām aṭ-Ṭabari, 188, 189, 282, 294, 295, 299, 348, 371, 372, 374, 376, 378, 377, 378, 381, 396, 397, 398, 430, 431, 459, 464, 477
imperialism, 60
industry, 13, 16, 38, 362, 363, 582
infallibility, 140, 279, 280, 295, 306, 311, 521
innovation, 2, 66, 237, 248, 260, 512, 523, 526, 536, 540, 544, 546, 547, 548, 553, 580, 590, 598, 625, 635
intercede, 383, 384, 385, 388
intercession, 202, 211, 252, 384, 388, 392, 397, 399, 400, 403, 404, 405, 407, 408, 409, 410, 412, 413, 415, 416, 418, 419, 421, 426
Iraq, 7, 9, 64, 265, 266
irsāl, 439, 471, 506

J

Jāhiliyyah, 65, 110, 111, 284, 286
Jawāmi' al-Kalim, 392, 521, 545
Jerusalem, 109, 179, 181, 193, 267, 269, 437
justice, 202, 246, 249, 368, 474, 555, 560, 568, 608, 609, 631, 634

K

khabā'ith, 605, 607, 608, 609, 610, 613, 619, 628
khabar al-wāhid, 332, 341
khabeeth, 143, 263, 603, 605, 606, 607, 608, 612, 613, 620, 625, 629, 630
Khaleefa, 361
Khawārij, 9, 40, 49, 65, 253, 278, 598
Khilafah, 131, 355, 526
Khulafā, 131, 261, 262
khums, 136
Kufa, 129, 260, 267, 476

L

legislation, 13, 17, 46, 58, 66, 161, 280, 307, 367, 424, 452, 499, 606, 607, 631
lighthouse, 120, 121, 123, 124, 125, 126, 127, 128
Lisān al-Arab, 430
litigants, 31, 274, 275, 303, 304, 306, 308, 309
litterateur, 352

M

madhākara, 218
madthab, 310
Maḥdi, 61
maḥfouz, 345
major sins, 126, 136, 313
mansukh
abrogated, 344
marāseel, 248, 294
marfu', 117, 189, 471, 476
materialism, 58
mawḍu, 116, 336, 344
mawquf, 102, 104, 106, 470, 475
Mecca, 26, 172, 195, 198, 199, 260, 265, 267, 288, 289, 291, 294, 297, 417, 433, 500, 637
Medina, 24, 26, 31, 41, 65, 89, 90, 95, 133, 172, 189, 190, 199, 260, 267, 284, 290, 291, 299, 300, 305, 313, 357, 358, 359, 362, 366, 433, 434, 469, 485, 486, 500, 507, 534, 540, 552, 637, 638
miracles, 56, 305, 396
Mongols, 305
mubāḥāt, 275, 578, 587
mubiqāt, 135, 294
muḥadditheen, 347
muhaymin, 428, 429, 430, 431, 432
mujmal
ambivalent, 134, 334, 344
mukhaḍrameen, 359
mukhaṣiṣ, 344
munāfiqeen, 300
munkar, 119, 280, 345, 357, 549, 577, 629, 635
muqārib, 402, 475
muqqayad, 344
mursal, 23, 24, 36, 189, 190, 259, 405, 439, 543
Musaylama, 386, 387
mushrikeen, 288, 289, 294, 425, 462, 589
musk, 378, 379, 380, 381, 382
mustaḥabāt, 276, 580, 587
mutaṣṣil, 189, 345, 405
mutawātir, 98, 104, 301, 310, 341, 344, 345, 557
muṭlaq
absolute, 344, 374

N

Nabataeans, 296
Najd, 7, 439, 597, 638
Najrān, 225, 354, 362
nationalism, 339
nawāqiḍ, 135
New Testament, 139

O

obedience, 9, 20, 30, 40, 42, 49, 68, 81, 119, 120, 153, 154, 155, 160, 253, 257, 258, 433, 494, 555, 578, 580, 584, 588
Orientalists, 305, 337, 346, 347, 348, 368

P

Paradise, 383, 384, 385
perfume, 379, 381, 508
Persia, 129, 363
Persians, 61, 64, 398
philosophers, 59, 144, 455
pilgrimage, 86, 88, 90, 91, 93, 95, 103, 104, 105, 106, 111, 115, 116, 118, 120, 122, 123, 124, 125, 538, 584
pollinating, 23, 24, 26, 27, 38, 582
pollination, 26, 30, 38, 39, 41, 275
polytheism, 3, 4, 8, 135, 309, 587, 633

pre-Islamic, 4, 65, 80, 359, 476
prohibitions, 56, 57, 99, 141, 160, 161, 279, 423, 452, 494, 510, 533, 633
Prophethood, 372, 386, 387, 388, 389

Q

Qadr, 85, 88, 89, 91, 92, 94, 96, 238
qarā'in
  indicators, 342
Qiblah, 3, 589, 590
Qiyās, 514, 516, 523, 599, 600

R

racism, 18, 339
Ramaḍān, 84, 86, 88, 90, 91, 93, 95, 101, 103, 104, 105, 106, 107, 112, 116, 117, 120, 121, 122, 123, 124, 125, 130, 131, 135, 503, 514, 525, 537
receptacle, 375
Reformation, 59
representative democracy, 54, 59
revelation, 377
ribā, 136
ring, 382

S

saqṭ, 316
Saweeq, 308
sealed nectar, 378
Secularism, 54
sedition, 591
ṣeeghat-ḥaṣr, 147, 164, 320
Seerah
  biography, 139, 227, 341, 344, 346, 366, 367, 435
shadth, 342, 345
shares, 118, 119, 121, 122, 126
Shirk, 3, 7, 309, 587, 632, 633
socialism, 54, 58
Sophists, 582
sovereignty, 68, 76, 261, 423, 605, 611, 631, 634
spirituality, 20, 58
submission, 68, 72, 81, 160, 243, 261, 467, 479, 495, 547, 584, 612
Syria, 284

T

Ṭā'if, 298, 351, 353, 505, 542, 637
Tabuk, 114, 115, 253, 412, 418
Tafsir, 173, 188, 189, 257, 270, 282, 294, 295, 325, 371, 374, 375, 396, 407, 415, 417, 420, 421, 430, 455, 459, 460, 477, 484
Takfeer, 5
Tanzeel, 320
tawātur, 4, 139, 178, 239, 249, 305, 310, 337, 339, 341, 342, 343, 390, 563
Torah, 18, 71, 185, 211, 224, 326, 441, 448, 549, 602
treachery, 283, 289, 294, 295, 595
tribulation, 254, 591

U

Uḥud, 195, 196, 273
Ulemā, 7, 222
Urbanisation, 15, 16, 60
Uṣul, 181, 276, 345, 365, 370, 425, 498, 534, 538
Uṣul al-Fiqh, 345, 534, 538
usury, 599

V

vice, 99, 469, 493, 637
virtue, 7, 80, 160, 169, 187, 193, 194,

198, 276, 421, 469, 506, 533, 599, 604

W

Wahābi, 3, 9, 304, 308, 309, 310, 547
Wahābism, 5, 547, 597
wājib, 20, 259, 278, 522, 542, 630
wine, 378, 379, 380, 381, 382
world, 381, 387, 389, 390
worship, 3, 12, 19, 20, 39, 41, 43, 57, 76, 77, 87, 88, 95, 109, 120, 121, 122, 124, 125, 130, 134, 139, 141, 158, 172, 200, 202, 376, 400, 436, 487, 489, 492, 494, 499, 503, 507, 518, 584, 588, 599

Z

Zakāt, 84, 86, 90, 91, 93, 95, 101, 103, 105, 106, 130, 131, 196, 250, 251, 302